LEAGUE
Publications Ltd

RUGBY LEAGUE 2000-01
Flooded with memories

League Publications Ltd

First published in Great Britain in 2000 by
League Publications Ltd
Wellington House
Briggate
Brighouse
West Yorkshire HD6 1DN

Copyright © League Publications Ltd

A CIP catalogue record for this book is available from the British Library
ISBN 1-901347-07-9

Designed and Typeset by League Publications Limited
Printed by ColourBooks Ltd, Dublin, Eire

Contributing Editor	Tim Butcher
Contributors	Martyn Sadler
	Mike Latham
	Malcolm Andrews
	John Drake
Statistics, production and design	Daniel Spencer
Picture Editor	Victoria Matthers
Pictures	Andy Howard
	Andy Varley
	Gareth Copley
	Charles Knight
	Col Whelan

CONTENTS

ACKNOWLEDGEMENTS

Rugby League 2000/2001 is the fifth in League Publications Ltd's annual series of Rugby League Yearbooks and again would not have been possible without the hard work and inspiration of a number of individuals.

As ever we are indebted to the enthusiasm, hard work and dedication of all the contributors to Rugby League Express, Total Rugby League and Rugby League World who provide such a tremendous service to the game of Rugby League week-in, week-out.

So too to those hardy souls who plough the touchlines of playing fields throughout the land to bring us some exceptional action photography all year round.

In particular we would like to thank Malcolm Andrews, the karaoke king, and Mike Latham, who have contributed so much to the writing of this book, along with League Express editor Martyn Sadler.

The statistical review was once again put together with loving care by Daniel Spencer, with a little help from Tim Hanson. Daniel also designed the book this year, along with our chief photographer Vicky Matthers.

Thanks also to Super League Europe and the Rugby Football League for their help throughout the season. And to the great players and coaches of the great game that have given us all another fantastic year.

Tim Butcher, Contributing Editor

FOREWORD

The Northern Union was an organisation born out of controversy in 1895, and some people would no doubt claim, with some justification, that it has been dogged by controversy ever since.

That certainly seemed true as we saw the Lincoln Financial Group World Cup unfold in October and November, when every sports journalist who ever wrote a feature column seemed to compete with each other to take the biggest possible swipe at the game. Perhaps the stock phrase was that Rugby League has "delusions of grandeur," whatever that is supposed to mean, for having the cheek to organise a World Cup with 16 nations in it. None of us who are involved with this great game should pay the slightest attention to such misguided rantings.

When we first launched League Publications Limited in 1990, to produce our weekly newspaper League Express, which was intended to cover the whole gamut of Rugby League news, both in this country and abroad, we couldn't possibly have imagined that one day we would have a World Cup tournament comprising 16 nations.

That Rugby League managed to deliver a tournament with that number of teams ten years later, having gone through one of the most turbulent periods in the game's history, is a massive tribute to the sport itself, and is something that all Rugby League fans should be proud of.

League Publications first decided to publish a handbook charting the Rugby League year to mark the launch of Super League in 1996. This is now the fifth edition of the handbook, and once again we have charted the progress of a quite intriguing Rugby League season. Super League and the Northern Ford Premiership, the Challenge Cup, the World Club Challenge, the Australian NRL, the World Cup, and other international competitions are all covered in the pages of this book with the same degree of detail that readers have come to expect over the years.

The format is slightly different this year, however, at least in terms of our coverage of Super League. Instead of a chronological account of the Super League year, round by round, we have looked at Super League club by club, with an account of each club's season, and we have listed the key news headlines that affected each club throughout the season. It means that, whichever club you support, you can immediately find information of interest and relevance, while being able to check out on the news stories and the statistical information about your own club's rivals.

Whoever you support, the book tells a great story of a sport that is at the heart of its community. As always, we believe that it is a story worth telling, and we hope that you will agree with us that it is a story worth reading.

Martyn Sadler
Chairman, League Publications Limited

INTRODUCTION

When the Super League Champions St Helens took on the NRL Premiers Melbourne Storm back in January at the JJB Stadium in Wigan, most people realised the game had received a wake-up call.

The manner of Saints' 44-6 mauling by the Storm gave a very clear indication of the gap between the leading teams on opposite sides of the globe.

The World Club Challenge had hastily got itself a sponsor in Kelloggs, and the headline that accompanied the match report in the following Monday morning's League Express summed it all up: "Cereal killers!"

More poignantly, Malcolm Andrews, the paper's man in Sydney, reported that after watching the slaughter, he was worried about the game in Britain.

Interestingly enough, Super League Europe chairman Chris Caisley denied that the outcome of the first big match of 2000 reflected any lack of progress made in the domestic game.

"Melbourne played superbly, but to suggest that St Helens' defeat reflects the state of the game here isn't true," said Caisley.

Caisley seemed to be ignoring the fact that Melbourne appeared to be playing on a different level to St Helens, but by the end of the year that must have been obvious even to the SLE boss.

Australia had by that time won the Lincoln Financial Group World Cup, hardly in a canter. But a late scoring burst against the only serious challengers to their crown, New Zealand, in an astoundingly high-quality game at Old Trafford at the end of November, secured a 40-12 win - a record for a World Cup Final, and with it the Aussies' sixth straight World Cup.

The agonising worry for all British fans was that the week before the final the Kiwis had given John Kear's England a League lesson in a 49-6 mauling at the Reebok Stadium to end England's dreams of making a third consecutive final.

The strength, power and awareness of New Zealand, coached for the last time by Wigan mentor Frank Endacott, simply blew England away.

Wales' sterling display against the Aussies in the second semi-final in Huddersfield went some way to reassuring us all - a side written off as no-hopers by some before the tournament giving the Kangaroos one heck of a game and leading by 20-8 at one stage late in the first half, before succumbing to the Champions.

The failure of England, Ireland, Scotland or Wales to make it to the final gave the excuse to some people to call for the abandoning of the home nations policy, and the merger of the four nations back into Great Britain. The argument was that if Wales could push the Aussies, then Great Britain could beat them.

Introduction .

The theory overlooked the nationalistic pride of the players - many who qualified through the grandparent rule - who represented Scotland, Ireland and Wales. Ireland, as well as Wales, helped kindle interest in Rugby League once again in places where it had been allowed to lapse.

Sadly, as interest grew in those nations, and in the game itself, the tournament came to an end, but not before we witnessed the terrific development of some players who wouldn't even get the scent of a Great Britain call-up.

The home nations concept, and a greater emphasis on international Rugby League for its own sake, was supported by the evidence - with teams like Samoa, Fiji, PNG, France and Russia showing enough in the 2000 World Cup to prove that they could one day be major League playing nations.

But back to the World Club Challenge. Chris Anderson, the former Halifax player-coach, guided Melbourne through that game on the back of the Storm's 1999 Premiership.

He was also at the helm of the Kangaroos, who laid a claim to be the greatest ever Australian national side in that World Cup final. In a broadside, he laid the blame for the standards of the game in Britain on the safety-first game employed by - in the main - imported Aussie coaches employed by Super League clubs.

It was a theme that ran through the year 2000, with, at one time, after the sacking of John Kear by the Giants, no English coaches left at all in Super League. It was a state of affairs that worried some people - particularly English coaches - who feared that they were being frozen out.

From 2001, English clubs will only be allowed - under Department of Employment rules - to employ an overseas coach if he has two years experience in the NRL, or has coached a national side.

By the end of the year, Bradford Bulls - and Wakefield - had bucked the trend. The Bulls named assistant Brian Noble as the replacement for Matthew Elliott, who returned home to face the challenge at Canberra Raiders. The Wildcats, who had managed within the year to get themselves a heap of debt, appointed John Harbin - admittedly an Englishman brought up in Australia - as their new coach.

This was also a year when the game lost three chief executives - Neil Tunnicliffe calling it quits at the Rugby Football League; his replacement, Peter Howarth. a consultant brought in to sort out Red Hall, lasting a few weeks; and Super League (Europe) CEO Ian Robson also off to pastures new

By the time of the World Club Challenge, the Northern Ford Premiership was five rounds old, the Association of Premiership Clubs having decided that they would start their season on Boxing Day to accommodate two Bank Holidays.

It turned out the Christmas launch was a good idea, with some bumper crowds over the holiday period, sustained with the help of supporters from Super League clubs who took the chance to watch NFP football at their nearest clubs and thoroughly enjoyed the experience.

Once again the NFP threw up some tremendous football and benefited from an exciting end of season top-eight play-off that was covered in the 'raw' by Yorkshire TV.

It all ended with an excellent Grand Final won by the smallest of margins by

St Helens and Wigan enter the Old Trafford pitch before the 2000 Grand Final

Dewsbury Rams, who had also finished as league leaders.

The early finish tempted the APC bosses to start their 2001 season even earlier, at the start of December, the week after the culmination of the World Cup.

If the Grand Final concept was starting to appeal to the NFP fans, then supporters of Super League clubs were almost to a man sold on the idea. That is if the Super League Grand Final at Old Trafford in October was anything to go by.

St Helens' 29-16 victory over their most bitter enemy Wigan, in front of over 58,000 spectators, produced one of the most electric atmospheres ever experienced at Old Trafford, and was the greatest night of the year for Rugby League.

The game was certainly a candidate for the best match of the Super League season, but that was by no means clear cut, with two games involving the Bulls - who had looked unbeatable in the early stages of the season - probably edging it - both Wigan and St Helens beating them in the dying seconds of their match-ups.

When it came down to close finishes and exciting games, 2000 provided us with real riches.

So what should be the abiding memories of 2000 for Rugby League fans?

At the end of the year it would be hard to forget the pounding that Rugby League took from the media in 2000. Ironically, a tournament which should have advanced League a distance, ended up with the union mafia in the media sticking the boot in, even before the Cup started.

World Cup organisers had made the unforeseeable mistake of starting the tournament on a weekend when unprecedented flooding had blocked off many parts of the country, and the transport network was brought to a standstill.

That anyone turned out at all in the far flung places where League was taken, in the cold and wet, was in some ways surprising. But the fact is that thousands of people got the chance to see some high quality games for the very first time.

Clubs abandoned by Super League Europe in 1999 came back. Sheffield Eagles managed to get up and running for season 2000, and Gateshead Thunder are back a year later. Sadly Bramley were kept out by the Rugby Football League Council, who failed to support their plea for re-admission to the Northern Ford Premiership.

And then there was Murrayfield. With Wembley Stadium about to be knocked down, the RFL had decided to take the Challenge Cup Final north of the Border for the very first time.

They were slammed by some, and the game was almost flooded out (another League theme for 2000?), but a sell-out crowd turned up to see Bradford Bulls win their first Challenge Cup for 50 years, on one of the great Rugby League weekends of recent times.

A great weekend, and another great Rugby League year!

1
PERSONALITIES OF 2000

Sean Long

Sean Long bears perfect testimony to the adage that sometimes in life you have to take one step backwards in order to go forwards.

Long left hometown Wigan and dropped out of Super League to play for Widnes in 1997, looking to rebuild a career that had been disrupted by injury and which had yielded precious few first team opportunities at Central Park.

At Knowsley Road Long has developed into one of the true superstars of the modern game.

If Long's 1999 campaign had been outstanding, he surpassed that in 2000 and was again an integral figure in Saints' march to retaining their Super League title.

The season began with the successful halfback partnership of Long and Tommy Martyn threatened to be broken up by the arrival of Australian Darrell Trindall at the club.

At one time Martyn looked destined to be on his way out but the departure of coach Ellery Hanley and arrival of Ian Millward changed all that.

One of Millward's first tasks was to reinstate Long and Martyn's partnership and Saints just went from strength to strength after that.

Long and Martyn know each

other's game so well that each is the perfect foil for the other. Long is a brilliant, instinctive attacking player, light and quick with amazing vision and an eye for an opening, and his kicking skills in general play rank among the best.

But he is also creative and unselfish and plays Rugby League with an obvious joy that transmits to the spectators.

In addition Long is a nerveless goal-kicker, as shown by the way he handled the pressure conversion to Kevin Iro's try in the 1999 grand final. Long accumulated the points at a massive rate for Saints in 2000 and soon passed an individual milestone of 1000 points for the club as well as setting a new record for points in a Super League season.

Sean Long never regretted the day he took that one step backwards and should take even more steps forward in the years to come.

Terry O'Connor

The 2000 season began somewhat unpromisingly for Terry O'Connor as new Wigan coach Frank Endacott made it his early season policy to perm three props from four in his seventeen.

With Endacott adopting a rotation policy until he decided upon his top props, O'Connor was rested for the Cup defeat at Hull as Neil Cowie, Brady Malam and Tony Mestrov got their chance. He looked a disconsolate figure that day at The Boulevard.

But the determined O'Connor proved it was only a minor setback as he set about earning a starting place by right for the rest of the campaign, going from strength to strength as the Warriors adapted to life under the shrewd Kiwi coach.

O'Connor, burdened sometimes by having a reputation as one of the club's jokers off the field, is a deadly serious student of the game and a deep thinker about Rugby League.

He has adapted his game to cope with the new demands of the high-speed modern game, and produced a series of outstanding performances week-in, week-out.

Together with Cowie and hooker Terry Newton, O'Connor formed an outstanding Wigan front row with Mestrov and the under-rated Malam

making important contributions off the bench.

With crowd-pleasers outside him in the likes of Steve Renouf and Jason Robinson, and his great friend, Andrew Farrell, O'Connor uncomplainingly made the hard yards all season long for the Warriors, and helped bottle up the middle with his work-rate and tackling technique in defence.

Supremely fit and durable, O'Connor looked in his prime as Wigan took the minor premiers crown before suffering anguish in the grand final.

O'Connor's popularity and respect from his fellow professionals made him a natural choice to captain Ireland in the World Cup.

It was a job he took on with great relish and pride and, although the World Cup was tagged on to the end of a long and demanding season, O'Connor's performances confirmed him as the stand-out prop of 2000.

Jamie Peacock

For Jamie Peacock the year 2000 just kept getting better and better as the Bulls second row emerged as one of the biggest emerging stars of Super League, and capped that with some outstanding performances in the World Cup.

A Stanningley ARL product, Peacock began the season with just 22 first-grade appearances to his name, four of those in a loan spell at Featherstone Rovers in 1998.

In 1999 he had broken into the Bulls first team plans, making two starts and another 16 appearances from the bench. He made great strides in that year, seemingly deriving benefit from a spell with Wollongong University in Australia and was one of a clutch of promising Bulls youngsters of whom great things were expected in Super League VI.

The 22 year old Peacock already did enough in the early season games to cement a place in the Bulls' starting line-up for the Challenge Cup Final at Murrayfield. With Paul Deacon, Leon Pryce and Stuart Fielden, he took the step-up from being classed as a promising youngster to a fully-fledged first team player.

At 6ft 3 and a touch over 16 stones, Peacock's physique is ideal for the modern game.

Though the Bulls were to ultimately suffer disappointment in their quest for the grand final, Peacock's season did not end with the play-off defeat at Wigan that signalled the final game in charge for Matthew Elliott before his return to Australia.

Peacock was an integral member of England's World Cup squad and cemented his growing reputation with some mature performances.

In an otherwise bitterly disappointing team display as the Kiwis vanquished England 49-6 at Bolton, Peacock produced one of the individual highlights of the tournament, tracking back fully 80 metres to overhaul Nigel Vagana with a textbook try-saving tackle out of the top drawer.

Next season, with Noble elevated to head coach and the shrewd Karl Harrison joining him as assistant, Peacock will be in the ideal environment to further his career and cement his reputation as one of the rising stars of Super League.

Ian Millward

Two years after arriving in the English game as an unknown, Ian Millward established himself as one of the most recognisable and charismatic figures in Super League by leading Saints to their grand final success at Old Trafford.

Millward took over at Knowsley Road in difficult circumstances following Ellery Hanley's departure as head coach, but he soon stamped his authority on the club and, importantly, established an instant and enduring respect from his players.

Millward survived several tests of character along the way, notably in the shock defeat at Wakefield and the 42-4 hammering by Wigan in the minor premiership decider that the final game of the regular season became.

To recover from that defeat so quickly and beat Bradford in the play-offs in such exciting and emotionally draining circumstances, reflected enormous credit on Millward's coaching skills and his ability to summon a huge response from his players.

Not content with that, Saints then exacted revenge with a stunning reversal of form to march to the grand final on the back of a stunning victory at the JJB Stadium before defeating Wigan for the fourth time in five attempts in 2000 in the Grand Final.

Millward's coaching career is a triumph of ability and determination over adversity as he was forced to give up playing after suffering a broken neck as a 23 year old stand-off playing for Illawarra.

Millward helped out John Dorahy at Western Suburbs, and coached in the local competition before holding a reserve grade job for two years. He then became head coach at Wollongong University for three years before he took up a full-time coaching position with Illawarra.

Millward is only 40, and his fresh-faced enthusiasm for Rugby League hides the fact that he has been coaching for 15 years, and has the coaching experience of men much older.

Mick Higham

The Leigh Centurions hooker Mick Higham began the campaign having made just four senior starts, and with the talented Anthony Murray blocking his way to a regular place.

Murray, after all, had scored 20 tries for Leigh in 1999, and his effervescent attacking style had been one of the key components of the team's revival under coach Ian Millward.

In the early games of the season Millward adopted the policy of alternating both hookers, often bringing Murray off the bench after Higham had played 40-60 minutes.

But it was clear that Higham, whose early career bore much similarity to the former Leigh hooker, Paul Rowley, was a potential star in the making.

With searing pace off the mark and good hands, plus Murray's eye for a try, Higham soon looked thoroughly at home at senior level and displayed a maturity far beyond his years.

Higham had come up through the same youth set-up as Rowley, who had actually coached him for a while at Leigh East in the under-16s.

When Paul Terzis took over from Millward at Hilton Park he soon made a decision to play just one hooker, and the popular Murray was loaned out to Rochdale and will start the new campaign with Barrow.

Higham, meanwhile, went from strength to strength, and went on to surpass his great friend Murray's record for most tries in a season by a Leigh hooker.

When Leigh reached the NFP grand final at Gigg Lane, some of their more experienced players appeared slightly overawed by the tension and importance of the game.

But 20 year old Higham got on with the job and displayed the kind of form he had shown all season, scoring two tries in Leigh's heartbreaking one-point defeat.

Higham was a unanimous choice as man of the match by the press and lifted the Tom Bergin Trophy as some consolation for the desolation of a grand final defeat.

2
SUPER LEAGUE V

Joynt leads Saints to glory

SUPER LEAGUE V GRAND FINAL
ST HELENS 29 ....WIGAN WARRIORS 16

The 2000 Super League Grand Final was a magnificent sporting occasion, the third and best Grand Final since they were first introduced in 1998.

It was a triumph for Super League, with 58,132 noisy fans in the 'Theatre of Dreams' at Old Trafford, and a wonderful win for Saints - their fifth major trophy in the five years of Super League. No other club can match that achievement, and it tasted all the sweeter for Saints fans because it was achieved against their old enemy Wigan.

And there was something typically St Helens in this astonishing victory.

They led 11-4 at half-time, with tries by Sean Hoppe and Chris Joynt, one conversion by Sean Long and a field goal by Paul Sculthorpe, compared to Wigan's solitary try from Andy Farrell.

After the interval Saints extended their lead with another converted try by Joynt, and as the game approached three-quarter time, with Saints 17-4 ahead, there seemed little chance of a Wigan fightback.

But that was exactly what we got, as the Warriors struck with converted tries from youngster David Hodgson, who looks ready to step into the departed Jason Robinson's shoes in 2001, and Tony Smith, back in the side in his favoured stand-off position.

SAINTS: 17 Paul Wellens; 24 Steve Hall; 3 Kevin Iro; 15 Sean Hoppe; 5 Anthony Sullivan; 20 Tommy Martyn; 7 Sean Long; 8 Apollo Perelini; 9 Keiron Cunningham; 10 Julian O'Neill; 11 Chris Joynt (C); 22 Tim Jonkers; 13 Paul Sculthorpe. *Subs:* 14 Fereti Tuilagi for O'Neill (20); 12 Sonny Nickle for Perelini (28); 26 John Stankevitch for Jonkers (50); Perelini for Nickle (52); Jonkers for Stankevitch (66); Stankevitch for Perelini (67); O'Neill for Hall (74); 23 Scott Barrow not used.
Tries: Hoppe (7), Joynt (28, 50), Tuilagi (69), Jonkers (80);
Goals: Long 4; **Field-goal:** Sculthorpe

WARRIORS: 5 Jason Robinson; 2 Brett Dallas; 1 Kris Radlinski; 3 Steve Renouf; 26 David Hodgson; 6 Tony Smith; 7 Willie Peters; 8 Terry O'Connor; 9 Terry Newton; 10 Neil Cowie; 11 Mick Cassidy; 12 Denis Betts; 13 Andrew Farrell (C). *Subs:* 23 Brady Malam for Cowie (30); 17 Tony Mestrov for O'Connor (43); 19 Chris Chester for Cassidy (47BB, reversed 69); 14 Lee Gilmour for Betts (51); O'Connor for Mestrov (61); Cowie for Malam (67); Chester for Newton (75)
Tries: Farrell (13), Hodgson (58), Smith (61); **Goals:** Farrell 2

League Express Men of the Match:
Saints: Chris Joynt; **Warriors:** Andrew Farrell
Penalties: Sts 10-6; **HT:** 11-4; **Ref:** Russell Smith (Castleford); **Att:** 58,132

Suddenly there was one point in it, and Saints were playing their usual trick on their supporters of giving them heart attacks just when they thought they were coasting to victory.

But a match of many contrasts was pulled out of the fire by Saints, who were awarded two tough penalties in quick succession within virtually a minute of each other. First, Chris Chester interfered in the tackle, and then Lee Gilmour dragged Anthony Sullivan into touch when he was adjudged to have completed the tackle. The latter, in particular, seemed the harshest decision of the night, and Saints would score through Freddie Tuilagi, playing his last game for the club, in the next set of six, with Long keeping his cool to kick a magnificent conversion from the touchline.

Then, as Wigan fought back, they had a spell of five successive sets of six, with Steve Renouf reaching the line but being held up. To survive so many tackles so late in the game, with Andy Farrell firing on all cylinders, was a terrific defensive performance by St Helens. That they held on so well meant that they

Tommy Martyn and Ian Millward celebrate Saints' Grand Final win over Wigan

deserved to win the trophy. A late try by young forward Tim Jonkers virtually on the final whistle, converted by Long, was the icing on the cake for the Saints fans.

And if ever a captain had led by example it was their skipper Chris Joynt, with a punishing tackling effort, and a hand in the first four of Saints' five tries.

For their first, by Sean Hoppe, Joynt gave the final pass, magically keeping the ball alive when he should have been tackled.

He scored the second himself, breaking through the defence of Mick Cassidy, Andy Farrell and Kris Radlinski.

He added the third, supporting a break by Long in the trademark Joynt fashion.

And he even had a hand in Saints' fourth try by Tuilagi, when referee Russell Smith asked the video referee to check back a couple of tackles earlier in the game, when the ball had touched Joynt's hand in a passing movement, but had miraculously fallen backwards, avoiding the knock-on that would have scuppered the award of the try.

Joynt deservedly carried off the Harry Sunderland Trophy for a second time as man of the match in the Grand Final.

He first won the trophy back in 1993, in the old Premiership days, when Saints beat Wigan 10-4. Alongside Sonny Nickle, Joynt is one of the two surviving members of that Saints team, and he came into the game bidding for his second successive Super League triumph as Saints skipper.

He came into the Grand Final after having led his team in all 34 matches of an intense campaign, and he had led from the front in 61 successive Super League rounds and play-off matches over two Championship-winning seasons. It had been an outstanding run of consistency by the all-action Joynt, who has revelled in his leadership of the club since taking over the captaincy from Bobbie Goulding in 1997. His two tries in the Grand Final enabled him to finish as the season's top tryscoring forward in Super League with 18 touchdowns. After the game he was modest about his talents, as always.

"I'm a very fortunate person to do what I do," admitted Joynt.

"I'm glad I don't have to work on a building site or whatever, and I don't take anything for granted. And if I can instil that into younger kids coming through the club they are in for a great future."

Joynt was only the third player to win the Harry Sunderland Trophy twice, following Alan Tait of Widnes and Andy Farrell.

Despite a ten-year career bringing him many international calls and a succession of Final appearances, he continued to seek a higher standard and said: "I think I'm still improving. As long as you've got hunger for this game you can succeed. I have got hunger for it, and when you're well coached and well drilled I just love going to training. I loved it from the first day I started playing as a professional."

That attitude was not lost on Saints coach Ian Millward, who stressed the important part Joynt had played in his first season as the St Helens coach.

"He's been been great for me and is very good at carrying out instructions," he explained.

"He leads by example on the field. He's not one that says a lot, but what he does say is very specific and to the point. It was a great performance today, excellent."

It was an amazing match, too, for Andy Farrell, who also played a wonderful captain's role for Wigan.

Farrell charged on to Tony Smith's pass like a rhinoceros for Wigan's first try, bumping off Tim Jonkers and giving Saints fullback Paul Wellens little chance to halt him.

And he was involved in both Wigan's second and third tries, as well as giving out a variety of long and short passes throughout the game that would have earned a greater reward in almost any other match. But after the game Farrell was philosophical in defeat.

"When a team gets on a roll like that they are very dangerous. We were on a roll and then they got a penalty on their line, then another one and then another one straight away. But there are no excuses," said Farrell.

"I'm very proud of the way our players came back. We had a lot of spirit and fight in that second half. We played for the full 80 minutes, and you can't ask for more than that. I think it was a fantastic game, and I was very privileged to be a part of it. It's been a good season for us, just a sad way to finish, but we've all enjoyed this season."

The Saints players returned to Knowsley Road the following day to celebrate their success at a day dedicated to their fans, which represented another triumph for the club. The RFL had originally ordered their England and Wales squad players to fly out to Florida and South Africa respectively on Sunday morning for pre-World Cup warm-up games. Saints had protested vehemently, and the RFL backed down, but not before sacking Millward as assistant coach of Wales.

Joynt said after the game that his forced departure to Australia last season, the day after the Grand Final, had prevented him from celebrating that win properly. No man had earned the right to celebrate with his mates more than the Saints skipper, who put his mark on the 2000 Grand Final for his outstanding leadership throughout the game.

ST HELENS

Ecstasy from the depths of despair

On the morning of Saturday 11 March, if you had read your newspaper's sports section, you wouldn't have given a fig for Saints' chances of retaining their Super League title in 2000.

They had already been humiliated 44-6 by Melbourne Storm in the World Club Challenge at Wigan's JJB Stadium in January; they had been knocked out of the Challenge Cup 26-20 by Leeds Rhinos in February; and on the opening day of the Super League season on the first Friday in March they had been caned 32-10 in an embarrassing home defeat by Bradford Bulls.

But what seemed to be the biggest blow of all came the following Friday, when the Saints directors finally did the unthinkable and sacked their coach Ellery Hanley, claiming that Hanley had fundamentally breached his contract with them by failing to turn up for the official Super League launch in Bradford, making comments at a sponsors' launch that damaged the reputation of the club, and refusing to give an interview to the BBC prior to the Cup game at Leeds.

Reading the papers that Saturday you would have been forgiven for wondering about the future of the most successful club in the Super League era. Saints fans were up in arms, Hanley immediately signalled his intention to sue the club, and their rivals must have been licking their lips.

The following Monday Saints moved quickly to appoint Leigh coach Ian Millward to the now vacant coaching post, much to the alarm of Saints fans, who doubted whether the little known Aussie would come anywhere near to being able to fill Hanley's boots.

And the rest is now history.

Shown the door early - Ellery Hanley

25

Millward was in charge for Saints' second Super League game of the season at Hull - a game televised live by Sky Sports. Saints triumphed 28-20 at the Boulevard in the week after Hull had defeated their arch rivals Wigan in the Challenge Cup, with youngster Paul Wellens, in at fullback for the injured Paul Atcheson, putting down a marker for the future with two tries.

And one of the key decisions made by the new coach was to restore Tommy Martyn, who had been rejected by Hanley, back to a pivotal role in the side. How Martyn would repay Millward's faith!

"We all had a lot to prove tonight. It was a test of character for us and that was mentioned through the week," said Saints skipper Chris Joynt after the Hull game.

"I was sad to see Ellery Hanley go, but at the end of the day times change, and that's all in the past. I'm looking forward, and so are the rest of the team, to hopefully a great future with Ian as coach."

All of Joynt's hopes would come true.

The Hull game was the first of eleven straight wins for St Helens, including a 38-14 defeat of Wigan at Knowsley Road on Boxing Day, and a 42-14 revenge win over Leeds at Headingley.

By the time Saints fronted the Bulls at Odsal in early June, Millward had transformed the spirit of the club, as well as his own reputation. And, as if to emphasise the changes he had inspired, Saints battled mightily before going down just 17-16 at the home of the team that appeared to be the pretenders to their throne in the early part of the season.

As it turned out, Saints would finish second in the Super League table, beaten to the Minor Premiership by Wigan, who inflicted a massive 42-4 defeat on Saints at Knowsley Road in the last game of the regular season. The Saints fans, always subject to bouts of self-doubt, were convinced that their side wouldn't perform well in the play-offs, but Millward kept his cool.

"The scoreline says it was disappointing," he admitted.

"We tried very hard, but our thought processes were down, and it wasn't a good day at the office.

"But when I took on the job, if someone had told me we would finish second in the league I'd have been very happy. We start a new competition next week, and I know we can play a lot better and do a lot better. We've had 28 hard weeks and finished second in the competition. Now we'll see how we go in the play-offs.

"I'm upbeat and positive, and very proud of what the players have achieved. These are the same guys that won at Old Trafford, and we know we can handle the pressure."

Prophetic words!

A week later Saints showed what playing under pressure is all about, as Chris Joynt scored the winning try almost on the stroke of full-time to give Saints a last ditch 16-11 victory in their first play-off game against the Bulls.

Saints kept the ball alive amazingly for almost ten seconds after the full-time siren had sounded, with Long kicking the ball across the field to Kevin Iro, Dwayne West surging downfield to beat two despairing Bulls tacklers, and Joynt finishing off the movement in sheer ecstasy, with Sky TV viewers witnessing dramatic scenes of a despairing Bulls coach Matthew Elliott collapsing in his

Remarkable turnaround in fortunes - Tommy Martyn

Chris Joynt dives over to score in injury-time against Bradford in the play-offs

seat as Joynt streaked clear.

It was Wigan coach Frank Endacott's turn to experience the agony the following week, as Saints went to Wigan in the qualifying semi-final and spanked their erstwhile conquerors 16-54, scoring nine tries, with Anthony Sullivan's mesmerising length of the field effort just before the break being the pick of the bunch, and possibly the best try of the season in Super League.

That put Saints in the Grand Final, where they would again meet Wigan.

This time it would be much closer, but Saints triumphed again, 29-16, in front of a record Grand Final crowd of 58,132 fans.

It was a wonderful finale, earning Saints back-to-back Grand Final triumphs, to crown a season that had begun so badly. It was Saints' fifth major trophy success in the five-year Super League era.

2000 High - What else but that magnificent Grand Final win against the old enemy Wigan, as Saints triumphed 29-16 against their fiercest rivals.

2000 Low - the opening day 32-10 defeat by Bradford Bulls at Knowsley Road, as the Saints were out-muscled and out-thought by a team that was out to gain revenge for its 1999 Grand Final defeat. It was Ellery Hanley's last game in charge of Saints.

2000 Star - Tommy Martyn began the season not being wanted by coach Hanley, and ended it as the Super League Players' Player of the Year. What a transformation!

KEY DATES IN ST HELENS' SEASON

11 November 1999 - Super League (Europe) announces that the World Club Challenge between St Helens and Melbourne will be played at Wigan's JJB Stadium on 22 January, with Saints chief executive Mal Kay justifying the decision. "Our capacity at Knowsley Road is only 19,100 and insufficient to make the game financially viable. We also don't have undersoil heating, which is an important consideration at that time of year."

25 November - Saints announce that local company St Helens Glass will sponsor them in the new season, which will see a return to the traditional Saints home jersey of a red vee on a white background.

25 November - Saints confirm the signing of South Sydney's Darrell Trindall and extend Sean Hoppe's contract for another two years.

26 November - Keiron Cunningham faces a fitness battle after undergoing an elbow operation, he is left with an estimated six-week layoff.

22 December - St Helens shareholders agree to sell Knowsley Road and move to a new stadium in the town.

10 January 2000 - Saints reveal they are ready to listen to offers for Tommy Martyn, Vila Matautia, Andy Leathem, Paul Davidson and Andy Haigh.

17 January - Leigh coach Ian Millward urges his club to make a bid for Martyn.

22 January - Saints are hammered 44-6 by Melbourne Storm in the World Club Challenge.

31 January - Saints sign a new three-year deal with rising young star Paul Wellens.

4 February - Saints coach Ellery Hanley defends his overseas star Darrell Trindall at a sponsors' evening.

7 February - young winger Steve Hall signs a new two-year contract.

13 February - Darrell Trindall makes his debut for Saints in the Challenge Cup at Swinton, helping his side edge past the Lions 36-22.

27 February - coach Ellery Hanley refuses to be interviewed on the BBC Grandstand programme prior to the Challenge game against Leeds at Headingley.

29 February - Ellery Hanley is the only coach to miss the Super League launch, claiming that he had too much work to do in preparing his team to face Bradford Bulls in the Friday night game.

3 March - Saints are hammered 10-32 at home by Bradford Bulls in their opening Super League match of the season.

10 March - Saints sack Ellery Hanley, claiming "fundamental breaches of contract" by their coach, claiming that he made comments at a sponsors' launch

that damaged the reputation of the club, refused to give an interview to the BBC prior to a Challenge Cup game, and failed to attend the launch of Super League. Hanley commences legal action against the club.

13 March - the club appoints Leigh supremo Ian Millward as its new head coach, and Chairman Howard Morris withdraws his threat to resign.

17 March - Millward wins his first game in charge of Saints - a 28-20 victory against Hull at the Boulevard.

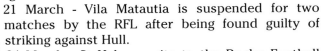

21 March - Vila Matautia is suspended for two matches by the RFL after being found guilty of striking against Hull.

24 March - St Helens write to the Rugby Football League claiming that their Samoan forward Vila Matautia has been the object of racial abuse, after being sin-binned at Hull and suspended for two matches.

4 April - Saints exchange contracts on the sale of their Knowsley Road ground to developers Wainhomes for £2.5 million, with Wainhomes agreeing to a two-year sponsorship deal with the club worth £540,000.

10 April - Saints part company with Darrell Trindall "on medical advice", claiming that Trindall's shoulder injury requires surgery, and that at no time had he been fit to fulfil his contractual obligations. Trindall commences legal action against the club.

16 April - Vila Matautia breaks his arm against the Halifax Blue Sox.

20 April - Paul Newlove tears his calf muscle in training, and expects a lengthy layoff.

21 April - Kevin Iro scores a hat-trick as Saints defeat Wigan 38-14 at Knowsley Road.

28 April - Saints football manager Eric Hughes claims to be ready to sign a new contract with Freddie Tuilagi "within the next week."

1 May - Kevin Iro equals the Super League record for tries in a game, with five against Huddersfield and Sheffield Giants in Saints' 50-30 win at Knowsley Road.

22 May - Saints hold an extraordinary general meeting of their shareholders, who agree to transfer their shares to a new company - Sporting Club St Helens Limited - which clears the way for the club's move to a new £12 million, 20,000 capacity stadium by the end of 2001.

9 June - Sale RUFC announces that it has signed Apollo Perelini on a contract to begin after the end of the Super League season.

14 June - Saints sign 19 year old centre Dwayne West from Wigan.

16 June - the club gives its Welsh internationals Chris Smith and Paul Atcheson

permission to talk to other clubs.

19 June - Saints sign 27 year old Newcastle Knights forward Peter Shiels on a three-year contract.

26 June - the club signs his fellow Newcastle forward David Fairleigh.

4 July - Saints announce that they lost £314,133 in the 1999 financial year, when they won the Super League title by beating Bradford Bulls at Old Trafford.

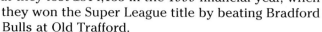

9 July - Tommy Martyn scores a hat-trick as Saints shock Wigan 30-28 at the JJB Stadium.

20 July - Paul Newlove agrees a new three-year contract.

21 July - coach Ian Millward agrees a new three-year contract with St Helens, committing him to the club until the end of 2003.

17 August - Saints centre Kevin Iro signs a new one-year deal.

23 August - Saints snap up Hull prop forward Wayne McDonald.

27 August - Sean Long scores 18 points against Salford City Reds, making his seasonal total 328 points, surpassing the previous Super League record of 326 points held by Leeds Rhinos star Iestyn Harris.

31 August - Saints part company with conditioner Nigel Ashley-Jones.

19 September - Saints have three players selected in the Super League 'dream team' - Tommy Martyn, Sean Long and Keiron Cunningham.

22 September - Losing 11-10 with just seconds remaining, Saints sensationally win their opening play-off game against Bradford Bulls, when Chris Joynt scores the decisive try almost on the stroke of full-time to give a last ditch 16-11 victory.

10 October - Sean Long is voted the Super League Man of Steel, with his colleague Tommy Martyn being voted the Super League Players' Player of the Year.

14 October - Saints overcome Wigan 29-16 at Old Trafford to win the Super League Grand Final for the second year in a row. Apollo Perelini and Fereti Tuilagi leave the club to go to rugby union.

23 October - St Helens insist that they should be able to play their World Club Challenge decider in January against Brisbane Broncos at Knowsley Road.

20 November - Saints chief executive Mal Kay blasts the decision to take the World Club Challenge game to Bolton's Reebok Stadium: "Our fans expressed their disgust at playing last season's World Club Challenge at Wigan by staying away, and there was a crowd of only 13,000. We wanted to learn from those mistakes by staging this match at Knowsley Road," said Kay.

25 November - Saints plans for a new stadium hit a snag, as a planning application is withdrawn.

Highs and lows - Kevin Iro takes on Wigan's Chris Chester in the Grand Final and
Anthony Sullivan tackled by Henry Paul during the Saints' opening day loss to the Bulls

WIGAN WARRIORS

Change in the air

It was all change for Wigan in Super League V.

And the changes began off the field, even before the end of the 1999 season, when Wigan moved out of their spiritual home Central Park and into the brand spanking new JJB Stadium, playing one play-off match there in the 1999 season, before playing a full season in Super League V.

The changes continued when former Super League (Europe) chief executive Maurice Lindsay returned to the club as Chairman following the 1999 Grand Final, after the expiration of his Super League contract.

Lindsay took a financial stake in the club, under the majority ownership of Wigan entrepreneur David Whelan, and immediately set about reshaping the club's coaching and playing roster.

He first parted company with coach Andy Goodway, before appointing Dean Bell from Leeds to shape up Wigan's youth policy, and then moving for New Zealand and former Auckland Warriors coach Frank Endacott, whose appointment was announced in early December.

"I have made no secret of the fact that I would love to coach in England, and I am delighted that the chance has come at a club as big as Wigan," said Endacott, who had told the media just a couple of days earlier that he hadn't been approached about the job.

"I went on national radio saying that, although Maurice had been in Australia, I hadn't heard anything, so I assumed I wasn't in line for the job," explained Endacott.

Frank Endacott arrives at the JJB Stadium

33

Big season - Terry O'Connor

"Then I had a phone call from Maurice at about 11.15pm the same night offering me the position. I'll tell you, I didn't get a wink of sleep that night after that call.

"We had to settle a few details over the next couple of days, but it wasn't a hard decision to make.

"It's a one-year deal, but I can live with that. It gives me a year's coaching up to the World Cup with the most famous club in the world. If we get the results there is a possibility it could be extended."

And indeed it was, when Endacott signed a two-year extension to his contract on the last day of July.

Players leaving Wigan under Lindsay's regime included Gavin Clinch (to the Giants), Brett Goldspink and Greg Florimo (Blue Sox), and Andy Johnson, Jon Clarke and Danny Moore (Broncos).

Inbound were Steve Renouf (Brisbane), Terry Newton (Leeds), both of whom had been signed by the pre-Lindsay regime, Brett Dallas (North Sydney), Willie Peters (Hull FC) and Brady Malam (Auckland Warriors).

And several Wigan players were to sign new contracts, including skipper Andy Farrell, who would sign a new six-year deal that would effectively tie him to Wigan for the rest of his career.

The news wasn't so good for the Wigan fans as far as their other superstar Jason Robinson was concerned. Throughout the year there was growing speculation that Robinson was ready to sign a contract to play rugby union when his Wigan contract expired at the end of the season. Robinson consistently refused to confirm the rumours, but at the end of the season he finally admitted that he had signed a deal to play union with the Manchester -based Sale club, and he would end his League career in the Grand Final at Old Trafford.

There was plenty of water to flow under the bridge before then, however.

After two Challenge Cup wins against outgunned NFP opponents the Warriors began their Super League season by overcoming a stern away challenge at Castleford Tigers, winning 30-24, and surviving a frantic Tigers late comeback from a 30-6 deficit.

"The most important thing was to come here and get the two points," said Endacott.

"We all know what happened last year, when Castleford beat Wigan three times."

The following week it was a different story, however, as Hull shocked Wigan in the quarter-final of the Challenge Cup, winning 14-4 and ending Endacott's dream of an appearance in the Cup final in his first season in charge of the club.

Endacott wouldn't lose again for ten weeks, although Wigan did go down 38-14 on Good Friday in the derby clash at St Helens, while their coach was in Auckland preparing the Kiwis for the Anzac Test.

The Warriors would go on to lose just three games all season - two of them against St Helens and one against Leeds. They had three particularly exciting encounters against the Bulls, drawing 12-12 at the JJB Stadium, registering a 30-18 victory at Odsal to end the Bulls' two-year unbeaten home record, and, with the help of a thrilling last second Kris Radlinski try, winning 20-19 at the JJB Stadium in August.

Super League V review

The win at Odsal was undoubtedly Wigan's greatest achievement of the season. It featured towering performances from hooker Terry Newton, who scored two tries, and veteran packman Denis Betts, who scored one in what was his best game since returning to Wigan from Auckland Warriors, as he helped the Warriors to fight back to win the game from being 18-8 down.

"I try to do my best every week, but it's the team's performance as a whole that concerns me, not that of individuals," said Betts.

"It's difficult to win here, because Bradford have so many fans, and they stage their gameday so well," he added.

Wigan finished first in the Super League table to take out the Minor Premiership, but they were unable to handle the threat from Saints from that point onwards. They went down 16-54 to a rampant Saints in the qualifying semi-final, and, after defeating the Bulls in the final eliminator they faced Saints again in the Grand Final at Old Trafford.

Down 17-4 at one point, they clawed their way back to 17-16, before their old rivals pulled away to grab the glory. Jason Robinson, Tony Smith, Willie Peters, Lee Gilmour, Tony Mestrov and Brady Malam all played their last game for Wigan in the Grand Final.

But with Matthew Johns, Adrian Lam and David Furner on board in 2001, as well as English international Francis Stephenson, Wigan will be confident that they will at last be able to turn the tables on their greatest foes.

The changes at the JJB Stadium are set to continue.

2000 High - Wigan's superb 30-18 victory at Bradford Bulls on the last day of June, which ended the Bulls' two-year unbeaten home record.
2000 Low - the 4-14 defeat by Hull in the Challenge Cup at The Boulevard.
2000 Star - Terry O'Connor had his best season for Wigan, giving them terrific drive in the middle of the field, and playing well enough to be appointed the Irish skipper in the World Cup.

On board for 2001 - Matthew Johns

KEY DATES IN WIGAN'S SEASON

11 October 1999 - Leeds hooker Terry Newton is linked with Wigan.

18 October - Maurice Lindsay becomes the new Wigan Chairman after resigning as chief executive of Super League (Europe).

25 October - Gavin Clinch leaves Wigan to join Huddersfield and Sheffield Giants.

26 October - A Rugby League tribunal decides that Wigan must pay Halifax Blue Sox £45,000 for youngster David Hodgson.

8 November - Wigan recruit a new marketing manager in Ian Riddoch from Super League (Europe).

11 November - Andy Goodway is sacked as Wigan coach.

11 November - Wigan prop Brett Goldspink signs for Halifax Blue Sox.

12 November - Wigan confirm the signing of Leeds hooker Terry Newton.

16 November - Wigan recruit Dean Bell from Leeds to oversee the club's youth development.

22 November - Greg Florimo leaves Wigan to join Halifax Blue Sox.

29 November - Wigan sign North Sydney winger Brett Dallas and Willie Peters from the newly merged Hull FC.

30 November - London Broncos sign Wigan stars Jon Clarke and Andy Johnson.

1 December - A Rugby League tribunal decides that Wigan must pay £90,000 for the signature of Leeds star Terry Newton.

2 December - Wigan appoint Frank Endacott to be their new coach for the 2000 season.

15 December - Wigan media manager Dave Swanton quits the club to move to Warrington Wolves.

16 December - Andy Farrell opens talks with Wigan for a new contract.

17 December - Australian centre Danny Moore leaves Wigan to join London Broncos.

19 December - Wigan media manager Dave Swanton leaves Wigan to join Warrington.

20 December - Wigan lose out in the chase for South Sydney's 20 year old superstar Craig Wing, with the Sydney Roosters securing his services.

20 December - London Broncos sign Wigan's Australian centre Danny Moore.

22 December - Wigan sign Auckland Warriors and New Zealand prop forward Brady Malam.

26 December - Wigan give debuts to new signings Steve Renouf, Willie Peters and Terry Newton in a 30-10 victory over St Helens in the traditional Boxing Day fixture.

4 January 2000 - Wigan Chairman Maurice Lindsay

issues a hands-off warning to Halifax Blue Sox over Chris Chester.

5 January - new coach Frank Endacott takes his first training session with his new club.

30 January - the Sunday Times reveals that Wigan star Jason Robinson is ready to listen to offers from rugby union.

7 February - Wigan skipper Andy Farrell denies a Sunday newspaper report that he is likely to join Australian club Canterbury Bulldogs.

13 February - rampant Wigan hammer Whitehaven 98-4 in the Challenge Cup, scoring 17 tries.

17 February - Andy Farrell signs a new six-year contract with the Warriors.

28 February - Wigan coach Frank Endacott denies a story that he is about to sign Kiwi star Quentin Pongia from Sydney Roosters.

5 March - Wigan survive a stirring Castleford fightback at The Jungle to win 30-24 in the opening game of the Super League season, after being ahead 30-6 at one stage.

11 March - Wigan go out of the Challenge Cup after a shock 14-4 defeat at Hull.

17 March - Wigan agree a new three-year deal with back row forward Simon Haughton.

3 April - Maurice Lindsay reports Wakefield Trinity to Super League Europe for making an illegal approach to Jason Robinson.

1 May - longserving Wigan star Mick Cassidy begins his testimonial with the club.

7 June - Wigan draw with the Bulls at the JJB Stadium in front of a new stadium record crowd of 17,365.

13 June - Wigan skipper Andy Farrell is suspended for one game, after being found guilty of headbutting Bradford hooker James Lowes in the 12-12 draw between the clubs.

13 June - Wigan announce that they have secured the services of Matthew Johns from Newcastle Knights for the 2001 season, and reports suggest that Sydney Roosters and PNG captain Adrian Lam will be joining him.

15 June - Wigan winger Liam Bretherton joins Leigh on loan until the end of the season.

19 June - Wigan sign Australian star David Furner from Canberra Raiders for next season.

30 June - Brett Dallas breaks his jaw in the game against Bradford at Odsal, and will be out until the play-offs. Wigan's 30-18 victory breaks a two-year unbeaten run by the Bulls at Odsal.

31 July - coach Frank Endacott signs a new deal with Wigan that will keep him at the club until the end of the 2002 season.

14 August - Wigan confirm, after weeks of speculation, that they have signed Papua New Guinea captain Adrian Lam from the Sydney Roosters.

27 August - Wigan break their JJB Stadium ground record attendance, registering 17,737 fans for their clash against Bradford Bulls.

28 August - 21 year old starlet Wes Davies signs a new three-year contract.

19 September - Wigan announce the capture of prop forward Francis Stephenson from the financially troubled Wakefield Trinity Wildcats.

19 September - Wigan have six players selected for the Super League 'dream team' - Kris Radlinski, Jason Robinson, Steve Renouf, Terry O'Connor, Denis Betts and Andy Farrell.

7 October - Andy Farrell kicks six goals against Bradford Bulls to become the second highest points scorer of all time at Wigan.

9 October - Wigan release second row forward Rob Ball.

14 October - Wigan go down 29-16 to St Helens in the Grand Final at Old Trafford. Jason Robinson plays his last game for Wigan before going into rugby union.

8 November - Wigan agree a one-year deal with former Warrington prop Mark Hilton.

Another big year from Andy Farrell

Kris Radlinski on the charge during Wigan's stunning win at Odsal in June

BRADFORD BULLS

So near and yet so far

After ending the 1999 season as Minor Premiers, but missing out on the Championship title after an agonising defeat by St Helens in the Grand Final, the Bulls entered the new millennium with the aim of completing what they called "unfinished business".

Coach Matthew Elliott kept his close season recruitment to a minimum, preferring instead to concentrate on securing the services of his existing squad on long term deals. He did, however, complete what many observers regarded as the most significant overseas transfer of the year, bringing former Aussie Test star Brad Mackay to Odsal to strengthen an already formidable pack.

A number of low-key friendly encounters against Leeds, Wakefield and Huddersfield and Sheffield Giants gave few clues as to what was to come. Indeed, they entered their first real test of the season with an away trip to Wakefield in the Challenge Cup with many expecting a close encounter against the much-strengthened Wildcats at Belle Vue, who included former Bulls Steve McNamara and Warren Jowitt in their side. The Bulls responded by racking up 46 points without reply, their intentions well and truly signalled.

The Challenge Cup was to prove the highlight of the season for the Odsal club. They went into the final at Murrayfield undefeated in Super League, to face local rivals Leeds Rhinos, who had just one victory to their name after a disastrous start. Despite allowing Leeds back into the game in the second half, which must have had many of their fans thinking "here we go again", harking back to that classic Wembley reversal against Saints in 1996, the Bulls finally edged the match 24-18 to secure their first Challenge Cup victory for 51 years, with Henry Paul collecting the Lance Todd Trophy.

Bulls coach Matthew Elliott holds aloft the Challenge Cup

Super League V review

In Super League the Bulls found themselves in a three-way battle for the top spot with St Helens and Wigan. Though they achieved two league successes against Saints, including a nail-biting 17-16 home win at a rain-sodden Odsal, and a rare away victory at Knowsley Road on the opening night, Wigan would yield them just a solitary point all season, coming in a midweek 12-all draw at the JJB Stadium, a match regarded by many as a classic played in front of a ground record crowd.

Later, Wigan became the first club to chalk up a victory over the Bulls at Odsal since August 1998 when they secured a 30-18 win; all the more disappointing for a Bradford side which had run up a club record score of 96-16 against Salford only the week before.

Against Wigan the Bulls uncharacteristically allowed an 18-8 lead to slip through their fingers.

"We just came up with a lot of dumb plays," said Bulls coach Matthew Elliott.

"They were isolated, but when you play against quality opposition like Wigan and come up with dumb plays you get punished.

"Collectively, from the coaching staff through to the players we weren't smart enough today. We prepared smart, but we just didn't do it on the day."

From that point on, the Bulls began to struggle to maintain their early season form. They slipped to third place in the table following a narrow 28-26 home defeat to Leeds in front of over 21,000 fans at Odsal, followed by a brutal 20-all draw at Halifax which saw skipper Robbie Paul stretchered off suffering from cracked ribs and a suspected punctured lung. Any chance of regaining top spot was finally blown in an amazing reversal at Wigan when, after leading the game 19-2 at one stage, two late sin-binnings allowed the Warriors to snatch a remarkable 20-19 win in the final seconds.

There was to be similar disappointment in the play-offs, when in equally dramatic style, the Bulls saw an 11-10 advantage turn into a 16-11 defeat against St Helens at Knowsley Road, as Chris Joynt scored the match-winning try on the stroke of full-time. But it would be Wigan who finally ended the Bulls' season, with a convincing 40-12 victory in the play-offs at the JJB Stadium.

That defeat marked the end of the reign of Super League's longest serving coach Matthew Elliott. Having brought both domestic prizes to Odsal in his four-year stint, Elliott had already confirmed the rumours which had been circulating all season that he was heading back to Australia to join Mal Meninga in the coaching set-up at Canberra Raiders. In appointing his successor, the Bulls broke with recent tradition by handing the job to an Englishman, Elliott's assistant Brian Noble. Noble has continued the trend by surrounding himself with an all British backroom team in Karl Harrison and Bernard Dwyer.

Although they did not join in the mid-season scramble for overseas signings, Bradford have made up for lost time since then, recently announcing the capture of NRL players Daniel Gartner and Shane Rigon, and adding even more power to their pack with Kiwi World Cup star Joe Vagana.

Whatever they go on to achieve next year, however, it will not be at Odsal Stadium. After 66 years at Rugby League's most famous 'hole in the ground' the Bulls will kick off Super League VI in the sumptuous surroundings of their footballing neighbours, Bradford City AFC's Valley Parade ground. The move is

Fantastic season for Henry Paul

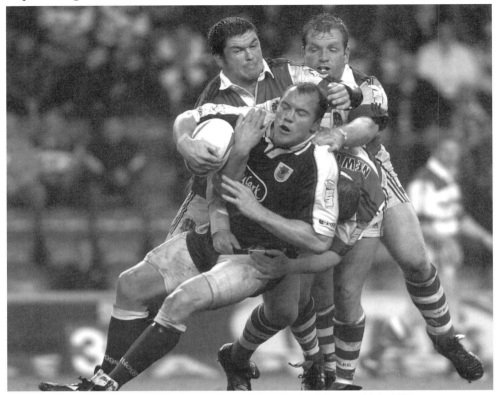

Brian McDermott in action against Wigan, the Bulls' bogey side in 2000

a temporary one, to allow for the redevelopment of Odsal, thus bringing to an end one of the game's longest running soap operas. But the move will not be without pain for the club's fans as prices rise to match the facilities on offer.

Despite play-off disappointment, the Bulls ended the year as the best supported club in the competition, crowds at Odsal the highest since 1964, with 203,278 spectators watching their 14 Super League games.

Their Community Programme achieved the distinction of delivering lifestyle messages to over 60,000 children – a record in British sport.

Henry Paul claimed the club's "goals in a match" and "points in a season" records for himself, while helping the club to become the Super League's top attacking force with 1,004 points on the board. And, with the Challenge Cup in the trophy cabinet, they ended 51 years of "unfinished business" for their supporters.

2000 High: The 24-18 Challenge Cup final victory against Leeds Rhinos at Murrayfield.
2000 Low: That last minute 20-19 defeat at Wigan, which cost the Bulls any chance of finishing the season as Minor Premiers.
2000 Star: Henry Paul. Just when you least expect it, just what you least expect – Paul is capable of turning any game on its head. Prolific points scorer for the club, and winner of the Lance Todd Trophy.

KEY DATES IN BRADFORD'S SEASON

14 October 1999 - the Bulls sign former Australian Test star Brad Mackay, while back-rower Jeremy Donougher is released.

15 October - Warren Jowitt leaves for Wakefield Trinity Wildcats.

18 October - Tongan back Phil Howlett, signed as a short term replacement when Danny Peacock retired through injury, is released.

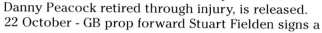

22 October - GB prop forward Stuart Fielden signs a contract extension to the end of the 2003 season.

3 November - Steve McNamara leaves after failing to agree terms.

30 November - the Bulls announce a new kit sponsorship deal with leisure suppliers Joe Bloggs.

8 December - the Bulls agree a £500,000 sponsorship deal with Shipley based Skylark Leisure.

8 December - New plans for the redevelopment of Odsal are unveiled.

16 December - Brian McDermott signs a new two-year contract. New Aussie recruit Justin Brooker arrives at Odsal.

20 December - Paul Deacon and Jamie Peacock sign 3-year contract extensions.

22 December - Gary Tasker, the Bradford Bulls chief executive, leaves to become community development director for Super League (Europe).

26 December - Bulls field a rookie line up against Leeds in the Boxing Day friendly at Headingley, going down 32-20.

10 January 2000 - Former Bulls winger Abi Ekoku is appointed as Chief Executive in succession to Gary Tasker.

13 January - Michael Withers extends his contract to the end of the 2002 season.

22 January - young stars Lee Radford and Alex Wilkinson agree contract extensions to the end of 2002.

8 February - fullback Stuart Spruce and back-rower Mike Forshaw sign extended contracts to the end of the 2001 season.

24 February - James Lowes extends his contract to the end of the 2001 season.

27 February - Michael Withers scores a hat-trick as the Bulls storm into the Challenge Cup quarter-finals with a 46-0 win over Wakefield at Belle Vue.

3 March - the Bulls open their Super League campaign with a 32-10 victory over reigning Champions St Helens in only their fifth league win on Saints soil since 1973.

19 March - the Bulls open their home Super League season with a 58-4 romp against Warrington Wolves in front of a 17,127 crowd.

24 March - Robbie Paul signs a three-year extension to his existing contract and will remain with the Bulls until the end of the 2003 season.

21 April - Henry and Robbie Paul are in the NZ team defeated 52-0 in the ANZAC

Test against Australia in Sydney.

29 April - the Bulls secure their first Challenge Cup win for 51 years with a tense 24-18 victory over local rivals Leeds Rhinos at Murrayfield. Henry Paul wins the Lance Todd Trophy as man of the match.

4 May - the Bulls drop their first league point of the season in a midweek 8-8 draw against Hull at the Boulevard. Matthew Elliott is named as the first winner of the Tetley's Bitter Super League Coach of the Month award.

19 May - the unbeaten run is extended to 15 matches with an emphatic 44-2 win over Leeds at Headingley.

26 May - Bernard Dwyer announces his retirement from the game due to injury.

28 May - their first defeat of the season sees Bulls go down 42-32 to Warrington at Wilderspool.

30 May - Prop forward Neil Harmon leaves the club by mutual consent.

7 June - Playing their third game in 11 days and with several key players injured, the Bulls return to the top of the Super League table after a thrilling 12-all draw against Wigan Warriors at the JJB Stadium, watched by a ground record crowd of 17,365.

25 June - the Bulls establish a new club record score with a 96-16 humiliation of Salford at Odsal.

28 June - Tevita Vaikona agrees a two-year extension to his contract to the end of the 2002 season.

30 June - Wigan become the first team to defeat the Bulls at Odsal since August 1998 with a 30-18 victory.

30 July - 21,237 fans pack Odsal to see the latest Bulls-Rhinos derby, which Leeds edge 28-26.

6 August - Matthew Elliott becomes the longest serving coach in Super League and the first to reach 100 games in charge. His team can only manage a 20-20 draw in a bad tempered game against Halifax at the Shay. Robbie Paul is stretchered from the field after suffering fractured ribs.

26 August - Robbie and Henry Paul launch their own band, Massey, with fellow Kiwi and former school friend Lazrus, releasing a double A-side CD single featuring the tracks 'Sin In The City' and 'Overkill'.

27 August - Reduced to 11 men in the final period of the game due to two controversial sinbinnings by referee Russell Smith, the Bulls are pipped 20-19 by Wigan in a crucial table-topping battle at the JJB Stadium, after leading the game 19-2.

5 September - Prop-forward Paul Anderson signs a one-year extension to his contract and will stay at the Bulls until the end of the 2002 season.

8 September - Billed as their final game at Odsal, the Bulls edge out Leeds 14-12 in front of 19,623 fans. The Bulls Millennium Masters team of all-time greats is revealed, and includes Keith Mumby; Eric Batten; Paul Newlove; Ernest Ward; Jack McLean; Willie Davies; Tommy Smales; Frank Whitcombe; James Lowes; Jimmy Thompson; Jeff Grayshon; Trevor Foster; Ellery Hanley; Henry Paul; Robbie Paul; Karl Fairbank; Ken Traill.

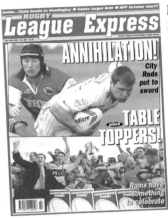

18 September - Nine Bulls players are selected in the England World Cup squad.

22 September - Leading 11-10 with just seconds remaining, the Bulls sensationally lose their opening play-off game to St Helens, when Chris Joynt scores the decisive try almost on the stroke of full-time to give Saints a last ditch 16-11 victory.

27 September - The Bulls pull out of the proposed redevelopment of Odsal Stadium.

28 September - Matthew Elliott announces he is to leave at the end of the season to take up an appointment in the NRL. It is later revealed that he will be joining Canberra Raiders.

30 September - the Bulls defeat Leeds 46-12 in the play-offs in Matthew Elliott's last match at Odsal.

5 October - Brian Noble is appointed to replace Matthew Elliott as Head Coach to become the only British coach in Super League.

7 October - the Bulls' season comes to an end with a disappointing 40-12 defeat against Wigan at the JJB Stadium.

12 October - Stuart Fielden is named as Super League's Young Player of the Year.

17 October - Karl Harrison is appointed as Assistant Coach to Brian Noble.

26 October - Scotland and Great Britain international Lee Gilmour signs from Wigan on a three-year contract.

8 November - the Bulls confirm that the redevelopment of Odsal Stadium is to go ahead after all. They will play at Valley Parade, home of FA Premiership club Bradford City, from next season until the work is completed in 2002.

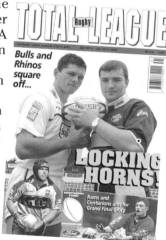

8 November - Justin Brooker leaves the Bulls to join Wakefield Trinity Wildcats.

10 November - Aussie back-rower Hudson Smith leaves the club by mutual consent. Prop Gareth Handford joins Castleford on six-month loan from January.

14 November - Northern Eagles second row forward Daniel Gartner signs a two-year contract.

16 November - 23 year old Shane Rigon, from NRL club Sydney Roosters, signs a two-year contract.

17 November - Bernard Dwyer is appointed as coach to the Bulls Academy side

20 November - New Zealand and Auckland Warriors prop Joe Vagana signs a three-year contract.

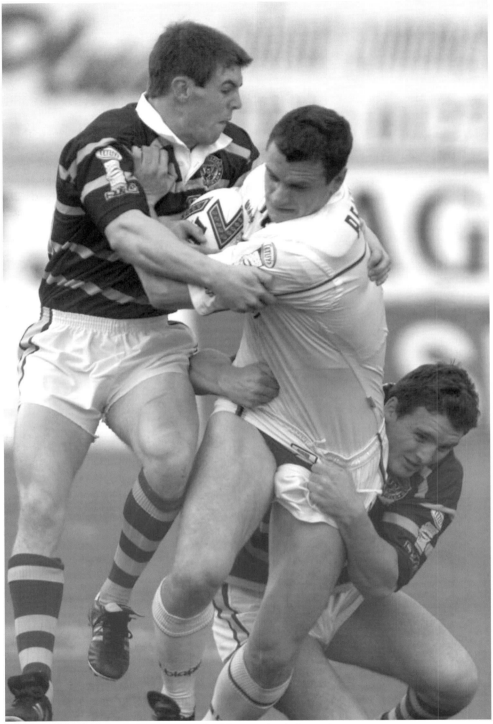

Bradford's rising star Jamie Peacock

LEEDS RHINOS

Contrasting fortunes

SUPER League V was a season of wildly contrasting fortunes for the Leeds Rhinos.

It began horribly, improved dramatically, but then ended once more on a low note.

After their disastrous start to Super League - five straight defeats - the Rhinos recovered superbly to seal a place in the top five. But they never quite managed to hit the high spots regularly enough to challenge the big three of Saints, Wigan and Bradford, despite ending up in fourth place in Super League.

In the Challenge Cup things were much better.

They defeated St Helens 26-20 at Headingley in a thriller, and comfortably held off the semi-final challenge of Hull at the McAlpine Stadium, in a game that would become infamous for a section of the Hull 'supporters' pulling down the posts at one end of the ground.

Against their arch rivals the Bradford Bulls they gave a creditable performance in a historic final at Murrayfield - the first time the Challenge Cup final had been played outside England - before going down 24-18, with winger Leroy Rivett, the Lance Todd winger at Wembley twelve months earlier, making some errors that would derail his career at Headingley. Rivett would eventually go on loan to Huddersfield and Sheffeld Giants, but ended the season unwanted by either club.

Found it difficult early on - Rhinos coach Dean Lance

Super League V review

The Rhinos' season would largely be characterised by the seemingly unending match-ups against their near neighbours from Odsal, who they would meet six times in total during the season, including the Boxing Day friendly encounter at Headingley. By the end of the season the two sets of supporters were sick of the sight of each other.

Leeds' Super League season began with those five successive defeats, starting with Wakefield and climaxing with a humiliating 44-10 reversal at Warrington on 16 April. It was hardly surprising that the Rhinos fans were calling for Lance's head, with chief executive Gary Hetherington giving public backing to his coach.

Hetherington made it plain that all the blame for the team's woes couldn't be placed at Lance's door, and Hetherington claimed that the slide had started towards the end of the 1999 season under previous coach Graham Murray. According to Hetherington, the Rhinos' power game had stopped working as well as it had in the early part of Murray's reign, and the team was going through a transition where it had to adjust its style of play.

It was the arrival of Graham Mackay, the Aussie who had been at Bradford a decade earlier, at the beginning of May that saw an upsurge in the Rhinos' fortunes, although not before the Bulls had come to Headingley and hammered their hosts 44-2 in another humiliating reveral for Lance in mid-May.

But from that point onwards things improved dramatically for Leeds, starting with Wigan at Headingley the following week, whom they beat 26-19 after trailing 19-6 on 55 minutes. But with the help of a superb two-try performance from their Kiwi star Richie Blackmore, the Rhinos fought back superbly, with lestyn Harris, playing his 100th game for Leeds, also making a massive contribution as the Rhinos' season suddenly came alive.

"That goes a long way to turning the club around," said Lance.

"It was important that we beat the best quality opposition, but even more important that we got the points."

And turn the club around it did. It was the first game of a 13-match winning run that stretched throughout June and July, taking the Rhinos into the top five, and putting them in pole position for a strike at the play-offs. Lance, who had survived numerous calls for his resignation earlier in the season, by now was looking a candidate for coach of the year.

Suddenly, however, the wheels came off again, with the Rhinos losing four out of their last five regular season matches, including an ignominious 18-6 reversal against London Broncos in their final game of the regular season.

Off the field, the Rhinos also experienced plenty of ups and downs, with perhaps the most negative publicity coming from winger Paul Sterling's allegation of racism against Lance for a decision he allegedly made earlier in the season not to select Sterling in the Leeds first team squad.

The case went to an industrial tribunal, which dismissed most of the substance of the allegation, while finding Lance guilty of "unconscious racism", and finding the club guilty of not investigating Sterling's allegations properly.

The best news for Rhinos fans came last December, when their superstar and captain lestyn Harris signed a new four-year contract in the face of a strong bid by the Welsh Rugby Union to lure him away to the other code.

Graham Mackay was selected in the Super League Dream Team

On the other hand, the Rhinos fans had to come to terms with the news that their other superstar Adrian Morley would be leaving the club at the end of the season to join former Rhinos coach Graham Murray at the Sydney Roosters club in the Australian NRL competition.

Other players to leave the club this year include the retiring Daryl Powell, who will stay on to coach the Rhinos' Academy team, Kiwi international Richie Blackmore, who will join the New Zealand Warriors in his homeland, Paul Sterling, the oldest player in Super League this year, who hasn't been offered a new contract, and David Barnhill, who will return home to Australia after fulfilling just one year of his two-year contract. Barnhill's compatriot Paul Bell returned home in March after suffering a serious shoulder and collar bone injury in the Rhinos' Challenge Cup win against Dewsbury Rams.

At the end of the season the Rhinos had an amazing 18 players representing the club in the Lincoln World Cup, comprising David Barnhill (Ireland), Richie Blackmore (New Zealand), Garreth Carvell (Scotland), Anthony Farrell (Wales), Darren Fleary (England), Iestyn Harris (Wales), Andy Hay (England), Graham Mackay (Scotland), Jamie Mathiou (Ireland), Barrie McDermott (Ireland), Adrian Morley (England), Hefin O'Hare (Wales), Scott Rhodes (Scotland), Keith Senior (England), Ryan Sheridan (Ireland), Kevin Sinfield (England), Paul Sterling (Wales), Chev Walker (England).

And next season the Rhinos supporters can look forward to an exciting Super League VI, with new overseas signings including World Cup finalist Tonie Carroll, together with former Kangaroo stars Brett Mullins and Bradley Clyde ready to spearhead next season's charge for honours.

2000 High - the Rhinos thrilling 28-26 win at Odsal against Bradford Bulls on 30 July - "the best win I've ever been involved with as a coach," according to Dean Lance

2000 Low - being hammered 44-2 at home by the rampant Bulls in May.

2000 Star - Graham Mackay came to Headingley unheralded and unnoticed, but by the end of the season he was the only Leeds player to gain selection in the Super League 'dream team'.

Ryan Sheridan in action against Bradford during the Rhinos' lowest point in 2000, a 2-44 home reverse

KEY DATES IN LEEDS' SEASON

12 October 1999 - the Rhinos re-sign Wembley hero and Lance Todd Trophy winner Leroy Rivett on a one-year contract.

17 November - Leeds' longest serving player Francis Cummins signs a new three-year contract, scotching rumours that he would be moving to Wakefield Trinity Wildcats.

17 November - Marvin Golden leaves Leeds to join Halifax Blue Sox on a one-year contract.

18 November - winger Paul Sterling, the oldest player in the club at 35 years of age, signs a new one-year contract.

24 November - Mick Cook takes over from Dean Bell as the Head of Youth Development at Headingley.

15 December - Iestyn Harris turns down overtures from the Welsh Rugby Union to sign a new four-year contract that will keep him at Headingley until the end of the 2003 season.

26 December - new coach Dean Lance takes charge of his first game as the club, gaining a 32-20 victory over the Bradford Bulls.

13 February 2000 - Leeds defeat Featherstone Rovers 48-12 at the Lionheart Stadium in the Challenge Cup, with Ryan Sheridan scoring three tries.

16 February - Leeds sign youngster Ewan Dowes to play both rugby codes at Headingley.

3 March - Leeds go down to a shock 18-22 Super League defeat to Wakefield Trinity Wildcats at Headingley on the opening day of the league season.

10 March - the Rhinos' Australian centre Paul Bell, 31, dislocates his shoulder and collar bone in his side's 42-10 Challenge Cup win against Dewsbury Rams.

20 March - Bell decides to return to Australia and terminates his contract after being told that his shoulder will need major surgery.

21 March - Adrian Morley receives a three-match ban from the RFL after being found guilty of a reckless high tackle on Wigan's Simon Haughton.

26 March - Leeds win their Challenge Cup semi-final against Hull 28-22, but some Hull fans run amok after the game, tearing down one set of posts at the McAlpine Stadium.

4 April - Barrie McDermott is suspended for two

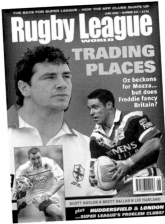

matches for making a reckless high tackle on Halifax Blue Sox scrum-half Andrew Dunemann.

11 April - after Leeds lose their opening four Super League games, chief executive Gary Hetherington issues an open letter to supporters giving reasons for the club's poor performances and defending coach Dean Lance.

11 April - Leeds managing director David Howes rules himself out of contention for the vacant post of chief executive of the RFL.

16 April - Leeds go down 44-10 at Warrington, their fifth successive Super League defeat since the start of the Super League season.

21 April - Leeds at last earn a Super League win, defeating Huddersfield and Sheffield Giants 20-10 at Headingley.

29 April - the Rhinos go down 24-18 against Bradford Bulls at Murrayfield in the Challenge Cup final.

2 May - the Rhinos give a debut to new signing Graham Mackay, in their 42-16 win over Salford City Reds.

14 May - Iestyn Harris scores his 1,000th point for Leeds in their 22-26 defeat by Hull at the Boulevard.

12 June - Leeds are strongly linked with Canberra Raiders star Brett Mullins.

26 June - the Rhinos announce that they have signed overseas stars Brett Mullins and Tonie Carroll from Canberra and Brisbane respectively, and are close to signing Bradley Clyde from the Canterbury Bulldogs.

8 July - Leeds confirm that they have completed the signing of Clyde.

21 July - Adrian Morley confirms that he will be leaving Leeds at the end of the season to join Australian club Sydney Roosters, coached by former Leeds boss Graham Murray.

2 August - Rhinos winger Leroy Rivett joins Huddersfield and Sheffield Giants on loan until the end of the season.

12 August - a joint team from the Rhinos and Leeds Tykes rugby union club takes part in the Middlesex Sevens rugby union tournament at Twickenham, but loses ignominiously.

25 August - Iestyn Harris scores the 100th try of his career as Leeds beat Wakefield Trinity 42-22.

19 September - Australian threequarter Graham

Alleged racism at Headingley - Paul Sterling

Mackay is the only Rhinos player to earn a place in the Super League 'dream team'.

26 September - winger Paul Sterling takes the Rhinos to an industrial tribunal alleging racism, after coach Dean Lance failed to select him for the first team squad earlier in the season.

30 September - Leeds go out of the play-offs 46-12 at Bradford, with Daryl Powell playing his last game for the club before taking over as its new Academy coach.

20 November - Rhinos' Kiwi centre Richie Blackmore signs for the New Zealand Warriors.

Leeds' Keith Senior takes on Henry Paul during the Rhinos' superb win at Odsal

CASTLEFORD TIGERS

Growing support

Castleford fans converge on London

CASTLEFORD TIGERS consolidated their 1999 achievement of finishing in fifth place in Super League, and contesting the play-offs for the second season in a row.

Unlike the previous year, however, they were unable to progress beyond the elimination play-off, going down 22-14 to Leeds Rhinos at Headingley, whereas the previous year they had posted great wins at Wigan and Leeds before bowing out at Knowsley Road against St Helens.

And they suffered disappointment in the Challenge Cup, going down unexpectedly by the odd point out of 21 against Halifax Blue Sox at home in the fifth round,

During the regular season the Tigers won 17 of their 28 games, but it was significant that, of their eleven defeats, nine came against top-four clubs. Despite going down narrowly 30-24 to Wigan in their opening game of the season, with Darren Rogers scoring an opening day hat-trick, in ten games against fellow top-five teams a solitary 20-16 home win against Leeds in August was the Tigers' only success.

The game against Wigan set the tone of the Tigers' season. They competed well throughout the game, but Wigan's flair, spearheaded by former Castleford star Tony Smith, allowed them to build up a 30-6 lead by the 64th minute, before the Tigers staged a stirring fightback, scoring four tries in the final 12 minutes. It just wasn't quite enough to win the game.

"Last year we beat Wigan by concentrating fully for the full 80 minutes, but tonight we took our foot off the pedal in two ten-minute spells," said Tigers coach Stuart Raper.

The Tigers' best and worst performances of the season both came against Warrington Wolves, who they will play four times in Super League VI.

At Wilderspool in May Castleford came back from an early 14-0 deficit to register a 37-26 win, with a sensational burst of second-half scoring, involving one try scored by Danny Orr that involved a multiple passing movement over 80 yards that must be a contender as Super League try of the season.

"We work hard on our skills, and we probably haven't produced that calibre of attacking rugby before this season, so those tries show just what we are capable of," said Raper.

But the boot was on the other foot two months later, when the Wolves came to The Jungle and registered a 32-18 win.

"We couldn't pass or catch the ball, and some of the players really have to look at themselves. I hope it is going to be a wake-up call," said a bemused Raper.

Throughout the season Raper was hamstrung by the Tigers' inability to compete with the other top clubs financially. They have signed Cronulla Sharks star Mitch Healey and former Warrington star Jon Roper for next season, but they are constantly outbid by other clubs for the biggest names in the game.

Players who departed The Jungle at the end of the season included Brad

Ian Tonks takes on Warrington's Jon Roper during the Tigers' win at Wilderspool

Davis, who has gone to Wakefield Trinity Wildcats, Logan Campbell, who has returned to Hull, and Andrew Purcell, whose knee injury has forced his retirement and his return to Australia.

Michael Eagar had a tremendous season for the Tigers, as did winger Darren Rogers, who finished joint top of the Super League tryscoring chart in the regular season, with 20 tries, and was unlucky to miss out on selection for the England World Cup squad, although he was later brought into the squad when Bradford star Nathan McAvoy was injured against the United States in Florida. Rogers was the only Tigers star to be selected for England, although they also had Eagar selected for Ireland, while Darren Shaw, Andrew Purcell and Adrian Vowles gained selection in the Scottish squad.

So Castleford may not have improved their league position, but they made great progress off the field in 2000.

They signed a high-profile new sponsor, in Internet retailer jungle.com, re-naming their Wheldon Road ground 'The Jungle', and they extended the sponsorship deal for a further two years later in the season.

And they increased their Super League home crowds by almost 15 percent, to an average 7,980. Many of those fans took part in one of the outstanding promotions of the season, when, supported by jungle.com, the Tigers took more than 5,000 supporters to The Valley for their league game in London on 11 June.

It was surely the most innovative marketing project of the whole Super League season.

The Tigers also increased their Super League record crowd at The Jungle during the 2000 season, when 11,702 fans turned out to see their home game against Leeds on the last day of May.

They also experimented with home games on Saturday evenings, playing Hull and Wakefield at home on that night, and drawing highly respectable crowds.

But the club will now have to survive without its Australian marketing manager Michael McDonald, who has done a fine job in drawing fans in to The Jungle with some innovative marketing ideas, and is now expected to return to Australia.

Whether the Tigers can ever generate enough income to be able to compete with the 'big four' is one of the biggest issues facing the club.

And the other point the Tigers will have to address in 2001 is the future of The Jungle itself. As other clubs either improve their stadium facilities or develop new grounds, the Tigers have to decide either to redevelop The Jungle, or to move to a new ground nearer the M62 motorway.

2000 High - In May the Tigers were outstanding at Wilderspool, winning 37-26 with some scintillating tries.

2000 Low - The Warrington result was reversed in July, when the Wolves came to The Jungle and earned a 32-18 victory, casting strong doubt on the Tigers ' Championship aspirations

2000 Star - Michael Eagar was the Tigers' outstanding player in Super League V, appearing in every Super League game and scoring 12 tries, second only to Darren Rogers' 20.

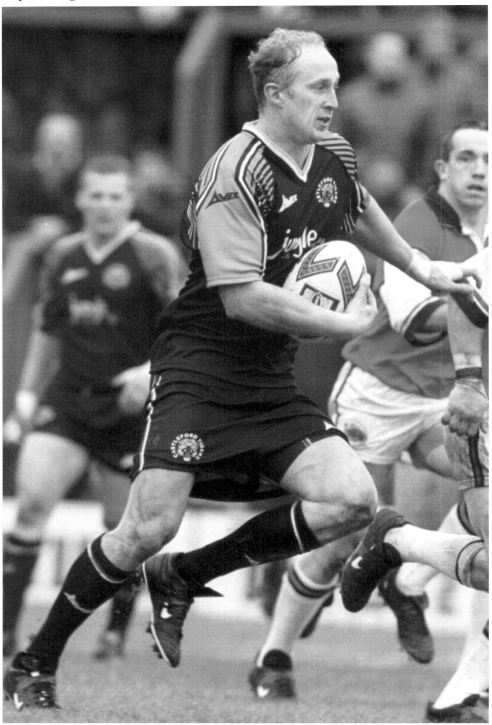

Darren Rogers received a late call-up to the England World Cup squad

KEY DATES IN CASTLEFORD'S SEASON

11th October 1999 - the Tigers sign Sheffield Eagles skipper Darren Shaw, the former London Broncos front-rower. And Tigers' fullback Jason Flowers commits himself to the club for two more years, although Francis Maloney leaves the club to join Wakefield Trinity Wildcats.

20 October - Barrie-Jon Mather signs for Castleford on a one-year contract, to run from the beginning of May, when his contract with Sale RUFC expires, until the end of August 2000. Veteran prop forward Dean Sampson extends his contract to the end of the 2001 season.

2 November - prop forward Nathan Sykes signs a new three-year contract.

10 November - the Tigers sign Hull Sharks centre Logan Campbell on a one-year contract.

12 November - Marketing duo Michael McDonald and Monique Baumann both sign new contracts with the club.

24 November - Tigers back row forward Lee Harland signs a new one-year contract.

6 December - Fijian forward James Pickering leaves the Tigers midway through a two year contract, whilst Barrie-Jon Mather denies that a permanent move to Rugby League is on the cards.

20th December - Castleford sign up Hull's Australian utility star Andrew Purcell on a one-year contract.

26th December - The Tigers play a scrappy 14-all Boxing Day draw with neighbours Wakefield.

1 January 2000 - the Tigers go down 26-14 at Headingley in a New Year's Day friendly.

15 January - former Sheffield Eagles director Terry Sharman joins the Tigers board of directors, alongside longstanding supporter Stephen Goodall.

19 January - the Tigers announce a new sponsorship deal with Internet retailer jungle.com, which will include renaming their Wheldon Road ground as 'The Jungle'.

21 January - the Tigers sign 26 year old forward Craig Wright on a one-year full-time contract, and 20 year old utility player Jamie Benn on a one-year part-time contract.

13 February - Dean Sampson scores three tries as the Tigers beat amateurs Oldham St Annes 64-8 in the Challenge Cup at The Jungle.

27 February - the Tigers go down to a shock 10-11 home Challenge Cup defeat against Halifax Blue Sox.

29 February - Jamie Benn is ruled to have no case to answer, after being put on report for a high tackle on Halifax star Daryl Cardiss.

5 March - the Tigers go down 24-30 at The Jungle in

their opening league game against Wigan with Darren Rogers scoring a hat-trick of tries.

9 April - Dean Sampson is dismissed for using an elbow as the Tigers go down 44-12 to Bradford Bulls at Odsal, but he is subsequently found not guilty by the RFL.

12 April - Australian forward Dale Fritz extends his contract with the Tigers until the end of the 2001 season.

15 April - the Tigers draw 8,358 fans to witness their Saturday night 22-12 defeat of Hull.

2 May - Dean Sampson is referred to the RFL Disciplinary Committee, after kicking Halifax star Jamie Bloem in the groin in the Tigers' televised 20-14 victory at Halifax. He was subsequently suspended for two matches.

11 May - the Tigers sign a one-year extension to skipper Adrian Vowles' contract, keeping him at The Jungle until the end of the 2001 season.

21 May - Barrie-Jon Mather makes his debut for the Tigers as they gain a stirring 37-26 win at Warrington.

31 May - the Tigers set a new Super League record crowd at The Jungle, when 11,702 spectators turn out for their 18-20 defeat by Leeds, who come back from an 18-6 half-time deficit.

11 June - the Tigers take more than 5,000 of their fans at a cost of £5 each to watch their 26-20 win at London Broncos, in a promotion financed by their sponsor jungle.com.

7 July - the Tigers announce an extension of their sponsorship deal with jungle.com for a further two years.

8 July - Dean Sampson is dismissed for punching Wakefield skipper Willie Poching, as the Tigers beat the Wildcats 16-12 at The Jungle. He is subsequently suspended for four matches.

27 July - Barrie-Jon Mather and Lee Harland sign extended contracts until the end of the 2002 season.

28 July - Richard Gay scores the 100th try of his career in the Tigers' 32-18 home defeat by Warrington Wolves.

4 August - the Tigers sign Dewsbury Rams scrum-half Barry Eaton on loan until the end of the season.

10 August - marketing manager Michael McDonald announces that he will quit the club at the end of the season.

16 August - winger Jon Wells signs a new contract until the end of the 2002 season.

23 August - the Tigers re-sign Australian hooker Aaron Raper to a new contract for the 2001 season.

1 September - the Tigers sign a new contract with Richard Gay until the end of the 2002 season.

Barrie-Jon Mather returned to the Tigers in 2000

7 September - the Tigers sign wing star Darren Rogers to a new two-year deal.

23 September - the Tigers' season ends when they are beaten 22-14 in the elimination play-off by Leeds at Headingley.

4 October - the Tigers confirm that they have signed Cronulla Sharks halfback Mitch Healey for the 2001 season.

15 November - the Tigers sign former Warrington star Jon Roper, Gareth Handford from Bradford Bulls, and 20 year old St George-Illawarra halfback Mark Lennon.

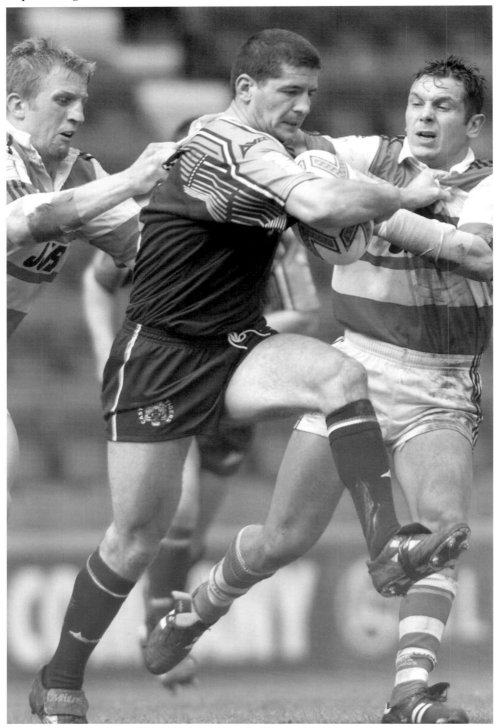

Michael Eagar - outstanding season for the Tigers

WARRINGTON WOLVES

Warrington Wolves finished in sixth place in Super League in 2000, just outside the play-off positions.

On the face of it, sixth place may look an entirely acceptable position in which to wrap up the season, and an uninformed observer may suspect that the Wolves had been unlucky in being squeezed out of the five.

But in reality Warrington's season could hardly be described as an unqualified success.

They never looked in with a serious chance of making the play-offs, despite having spent heavily on Brisbane Broncos superstars Allan Langer and Andrew Gee, and picking up Tawera Nikau from 1999 NRL Premiership winning Melbourne Storm.

Their fans had started the season buoyed with much optimism, with chief executive Peter Deakin whipping up enthusiasm in the town, and coach Darryl Van de Velde confident that the club would finally begin to realise its potential.

Succesful first season - Allan Langer

And it started brilliantly, when the Wolves hammered London Broncos 48-18 at home on the opening day of the season in front of 8,718 highly expectant fans, drawn to Wilderspool by the promotional flair of Wolves chief executive Peter Deakin.

The Wolves' Super League season as a whole, however, can be summed up by three hugely contrasting matches.

After that opening day win against the Broncos, and grabbing an exciting Challenge Cup win at Salford City Reds, the Wolves travelled to Odsal for the second round game against the Bulls, only to be steamrollered 58-4 by the power of a mighty Bradford side. It suddenly brought everyone connected with Warrington back to earth with a bump, and it seemed to shatter the club's confidence.

Down 42-0 at half-time, the Wolves just had no answer, as their defence was ripped to shreds.

But how things had changed by the last Sunday of May. By then the Wolves, with a 2-4 home record, were taking on the unbeaten Bulls at Wilderspool, and no one gave them a chance.

At 12-30 down at half-time, that view seemed to be confirmed - until the second half started. Warrington, inspired by the brilliant Langer, blitzed their opponents, scoring 30 second-half points and conceding just two. It was an amazing sight for the disbelieving Wolves supporters, and yet frustratingly they would lose their next home game to Wakefield Trinity Wildcats. Up one minute, down the next - it summed up Warrington's season.

Then, on 23 July, the visitors were the hapless Huddersfield and Sheffield Giants, marooned at the bottom of the league with only two Super League victories.

Leading 24-4 at half-time, everything looked good for Warrington - until the second half started. Wolves fans looked on in disbelief, as the Giants ran in 40 unanswered points.

"We lost the game on Friday afternoon," said Warrington coach Darryl Van de Velde after that game.

"The training session was poor, the players didn't respect the opposition, and the results are obvious."

That result left Warrington in eighth place, ten points behind the fifth placed club. Deakin apologised to the Wolves fans after the game, opening up a rift between him and Van de Velde that would never be properly healed.

Six wins out of their last eight matches would give their league position some respectability, but, for the fans, it remained one of those might-have-been seasons, hopefully building towards something better next year.

Players to depart from Wilderspool this year include 20-year veteran winger Mark Forster, hooker and former skipper Danny Farrar, French prop Jerome Guisset, after just one season at Wilderspool, prop forward Mark Hilton, whose career has been blighted with injury, and who deserves a change of luck with his new club Wigan, and Ian Knott and Jon Roper, neither of whom were retained by the Wolves.

And Alan Hunte has joined Pontypridd RUFC on a short term contract that could be extended, with the 30 year old former Great Britain star apparently ready to turn his back on Rugby League to follow in Jason Robinson's footsteps.

On the other hand, the Wolves have signed Tongan World Cup skipper Martin Masella from Wakefield Trinity Wildcats, Irish World Cup hero Kevin Campion from Brisbane Broncos, although there is some doubt about whether he might instead opt to join the New Zealand Warriors, London Broncos winger Rob Smyth, and New Zealand Maoris star David Kidwell from Parramatta.

The Wolves had plenty of representation in the World Cup, with seven players representing five nations.

Lee Briers and Dean Busby represented Wales, Tawera Nikau and Toa Kohe-Love represented the New Zealand Maoris, Lee Penny played for Scotland, Jerome Guisset played for France, and Mark Forster turned out for Ireland.

The Wolves also made plenty of news off the field in Super League V.

As the year comes to an end the club is waiting to see whether final planning permission will be granted for a new stadium, and how it will be financed, possibly by means of a ground share with another sports club. Former chief

Mark Forster is leaving Warrington after 20 years

Lee Penny in action against Huddersfield-Sheffield during the Wolves' shock home loss

executive Deakin had tried to bring Sale rugby union club on board, but would eventually leave to be the chief executive of that club without, as yet, having been able to tie up any firm groundshare deal between the two clubs.

Deakin himself stayed just long enough at Wilderspool to persuade the Warrington Borough Council planning committee to grant outline planning permission for the development, which was a shared scheme involving the construction of a Tesco supermarket.

The club is still awaiting news of whether the scheme will be called in for a decision by central government.

Meanwhile, the club is cooperating with Police in a fraud investigation into the activities of a former tax consultant to the club, with allegations that he withheld payments of tax to the Inland Revenue.

It was certainly a lively Super League V down Wilderspool way.

2000 High - the Wolves amazing 42-32 triumph against Bradford Bulls at Wilderspool on 28 May, the Bulls' first defeat in Super League V.
2000 Low - the abysmal 24-44 defeat by Huddersfield and Sheffield Giants on 23 July.
2000 Star - undoubtedly Allan Langer, who, at the age of 34, appeared in every Super League game of the season and always led from the front, showing that he had lost none of his great skills.

68

KEY DATES IN WARRINGTON'S SEASON

3 October 1999 - Warrington announce the signing of Melbourne Storm star Tawera Nikau for the 2000 season.

11 October - the Wolves release Mike Wainwright, who subsequently joins Salford City Reds.

13 October - Mark Hilton breaks his arm playing for England against France.

31 October - veteran winger Mark Forster breaks his arm playing for Ireland against Scotland.

17 November - the Wolves release long-serving utility back Chris Rudd.

24 November - Warrington sign Salford City Reds' stand-off half Steve Blakeley.

29 November - Mark Forster signs a new one-year deal with Warrington.

9 December - Cumbrian star Jon Roper signs a new deal at Wilderspool.

29 December - Wolves coach Darryl Van de Velde announces that Allan Langer will captain the side during the 2000 season.

7 January 2000 - Warrington announce the capture of French star Jerome Guisset, the first French player ever to play for the club.

27 February - Lee Briers sets a new club record with 40 points as the Wolves beat York Wasps 84-1 in the fifth round of the Silk Cut Challenge Cup.

5 March - the Wolves open their Super League season in great style, with a 48-18 win over London Broncos at Wilderspool.

16 March - the Wolves announce that local businesswoman Pauline Quayle is to become the club's first ever female director.

3 May - Steve Blakeley quits the Wolves to re-join Salford City Reds.

14 May - youngster Ian Sibbit suffers a shoulder injury against Salford that effectively ends his season, while Toa Kohe-Love is dismissed for a high tackle.

16 May - Toa Kohe-Love receives a two-match suspension from the RFL Disciplinary Committee.

26 May - the Wolves sign back-rower Mike Peters from Halifax Blue Sox.

31 May - Warrington announce that they will be moving into a new 12,000 capacity stadium in a joint scheme with Tesco.

8 June - the Wolves announce that Phones 4U will come on board at Wilderspool as an associate sponsor.

14 June - the Wolves launch a degree course in Rugby League in partnership with Manchester University and Warrington Collegiate Institute.

23 June - Lee Penny becomes the first Warrington player to score four tries in a Super League game, as he touches down four times against Leeds in the

Wolves' 24-28 defeat.

28 June - chief executive Peter Deakin asks Wolves fans to write to Warrington Borough Council in support of the Council granting planning permission for the club's new stadium.

18 July - Tawera Nikau is suspended for one game, after being found guilty of striking against Wigan.

23 July - Peter Deakin apologises to the Wolves fans for the club's performance in losing at home to Huddersfield and Sheffield Giants.

27 July - Brisbane Broncos second-rower Kevin Campion signs a contract that will bring him to Wilderspool in 2001.

15 August - Mark Forster launches his double testimonial season.

23 August - Warrington Borough Council planning committee approve the Wolves' joint planning application with Tesco for a new stadium.

30 August - the Wolves confirm that chief executive Peter Deakin has resigned in order to join Sale Sharks RUFC.

17 September - Danny Farrar makes his last appearance for Warrington in the final home game of the season against Salford at Wilderspool, as the Wolves celebrate a 34 percent increase in crowds over the previous Super League season.

19 September - the club confirms that assistant coach Paul Cullen is to move to Whitehaven as head coach.

28 September - the Wolves sign winger Rob Smyth from London Broncos on a three-year deal.

2 October - the club announces that it has released veteran winger Mark Forster, although Forster will have a testimonial to celebrate 20 years at Wilderspool.

3 October - French star Jerome Guisset returns to France to play for UTC.

4 October - the Wolves announce the signing of Wakefield Trinity Wildcats' Tongan star Martin Masella.

12 October - Lee Briers signs a new two-year deal with Warrington.

19 October - youngster Jamie Stenhouse signs a new one-year deal with the Wolves.

1 November - the Wolves are hit by news that the Police are investigating an income tax fraud possibly perpetrated by a third party against the club.

2 November - Gary Chambers agrees to coach the Wolves under-21 side for the new season.

6 November - the Wolves appoint Ian Gatcliffe as their new chief executive.

Super League V's top tackler Danny Farrar chaired off by Alan Hunte and
Allan Langer after his last game before retirement

8 November - Warrington announce that they have captured Parramatta and
New Zealand Maoris star David Kidwell for next season.

13 November - Warrington coach Darryl Van de Velde slams the Super League
fixture format agreed for the 2001 season, that puts his side into the tough half
of the draw.

16 November - Wolves star Alan Hunte joins Pontypridd RUFC for the winter.

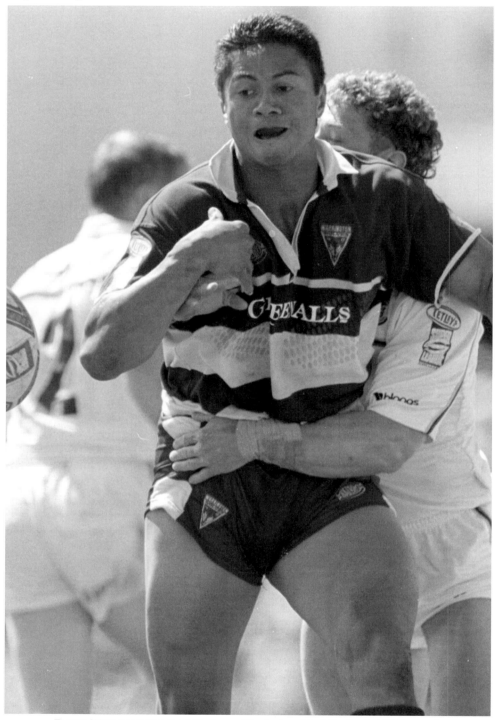

Tawera Nikau tackled by Brad Mackay as Warrington defeat Bradford at Wilderspool,
becoming the first side to beat the Bulls in 2000

HULL F.C.

Rising from the dead

As the 1999 season drew to a close Hull fans must have been in despair.

After a dismal 1999 season, which saw them finishing next to bottom of Super League, just above Huddersfield Giants, the Hull Sharks (as they then were) looked to be heading into the Northern Ford Premiership.

Owner David Lloyd had declared that he would make no further investment into the club, and a merger with Gateshead Thunder was on the cards. The prospect was for some of Hull's brightest young stars to head to the north-east, while the Humbersiders would drop down into the Northern Ford Premiership.

At least that was the initial plan.

The trouble is, the Northern Ford Premiership clubs, angry about not being consulted, wouldn't wear it, and were not prepared to vote for the deal at the RFL Special General Meeting on 15 November. Suddenly, in a dramatic announcement, it was revealed that the 'merger' would still happen, but that Hull would continue as a Super League club, while Gateshead would effectively be swallowed up in a move, lock, stock and barrel, to Humberside.

It was a highly controversial decision, particularly for the Gateshead fans, and appeared to contradict the fundamental principle of a merger, in that no games would be played in the north-east.

Gateshead chairman and Hull chairman David Kirkwood announce the merger

Super League V review

On the day after the Special General Meeting, Gateshead directors Shane Richardson and Kath Hetherington claimed that their club had lost £700,000 in its first season of operation, and they explained that the financial incentive - £1.25 million - to merge the two clubs had been too big to ignore.

A year later, with Gateshead re-emerging as an NFP club, the newly named Hull FC find themselves in a much stronger position. In the 2000 season they recorded the biggest percentage crowd increase in Super League, and they are now planning a move to a new 25,000 all-seater stadium for the 2003 season.

One player who was particularly affected by the decision to merge with Gateshead was former Great Britain prop forward Paul Broadbent, who had signed for Gateshead from Halifax a few weeks before the merger was announced.

"I signed for Gateshead, moved up there and got unpacked, and six weeks later they announced a merger," says Broadbent, who recognises the progress that has been made at Hull in the last twelve months.

"Shane Richardson and his colleagues have made great strides since they took over. Hull is a Rugby League area through and through, and they have turned the club into a very professional outfit which can only go forward."

During the 2000 season, however, Hull had plenty of ups and downs.

A superb Challenge Cup win against Wigan in early March was followed by a day of ignominy at the McAlpine Stadium, as a section of Hull fans tore down the posts after their team went out to Leeds in the semi-final of the Challenge Cup.

The RFL subsequently fined the club £50,000, suspending £30,000 of it because of the efforts made by the club to rid itself of the hooligan element that had blighted the Boulevard for many years.

"Beating Wigan in the Cup was a high point, because no one gave us a sniff," says Broadbent.

"Just the previous week we had lost in the last minute to a controversial try at Halifax in our opening league game.

"The semi-final was there to be won, and we didn't quite get the bounce of the ball. Most of us didn't see the trouble after the game, because we headed straight off to the changing rooms and heard about it in the bar afterwards.

"But the club officials were determined to get rid of the troublemakers, that element of the fans who had a tendency towards hooliganism. They wanted to get on top of it, and it gave them an opportunity to do that more quickly than they might have otherwise done. I haven't seen any real trouble since then."

The Hull directors made great efforts to clear the hooligans out of the Boulevard, and to make their ground a more welcoming place for away supporters. In striving to achieve that objective they became the first club to appoint an away supporters' liaison officer.

For Broadbent, the highlight of the season was the emergence of a new breed of young player at Hull last season.

"The young kids have come on no end," he contends.

"Having the experience of the Aussies in the team has helped them a lot. When we first went to Hull we found that the players there had had it easy for some time. They had got away with murder. Some of them found it hard to come to terms with the new discipline. But some of the guys who had been struggling

Had to pack his bags twice - Paul Broadbent

at the beginning of the season were regular first-teamers by the end. They took a leaf out of the Australians' books."

And there were other good things to recall about Hull's season.

"The other high point was against Bradford, although nobody gave us any credit for drawing with them four days after the Challenge Cup final," says Broadbent.

"But from that day Bradford didn't look as invincible as they had done. We were the first club to take a point off them, and it made other teams realise that they were beatable.

"On the other hand, the home game against Castleford was a four-pointer, and losing to them really destroyed our top-five chances. We would have been on a par with them if we'd won, but it was very difficult after that."

The problem Hull faced throughout the season was injuries, that affected so many key players.

"Tony Grimaldi had a neck injury early doors, and we lost so many more of our players as the season went on. Andrew Hick had a knee problem, I had a

Wigan-bound in 2001...
Brian Carney

twisted ankle, Will Robinson a broken hand, and Wayne McDonald, Stanley Gene and Dave Maiden also suffered serious injuries. We started with a 24-man squad, but by the end we were having to pull kids in from the Academy."

Broadbent is confident that Hull will have a successful 2001 season, despite the departure of several of the club's Australian stars, as it reduces its overseas quota to five players from 15 in 2000.

"They've made some good acquisitions of quality players, and if we can have an injury-free season I'm confident we can become a top five team," says Broadbent.

"The new stadium will be great for the club. There's a lot of history at the Boulevard, and the ground means a lot to the supporters. But the way the game is going, a modern new-look stadium represents a step into a more professional era.

"The supporters who have reservations about leaving the Boulevard will have their eyes opened wide when they see what is being planned for the club's future."

2000 High - that stunning Challenge Cup win against Wigan at the Boulevard in March.
2000 Low - Hull's 4-18 home defeat by Castleford Tigers on 25 June, which effectively ended their top-five challenge.
2000 Star - Richard Horne emerged onto the big stage, showing that he will be a major star of the future, while still only 18.

KEY DATES IN HULL'S SEASON

30 September 1999 - Gateshead Thunder announces that it is to 'merge' with Hull Sharks, with the Sharks to drop down to the Northern Ford Premiership and Super League matches to continue to be played at Gateshead. The new club would benefit by receiving twice as much News Limited funding as other Super League clubs.

1 October - the proposed merger is opposed by Bob McDermott, the Chairman of the Association of Premiership Clubs, who refuses to countenance the presence of Hull Sharks in the Northern Ford Premiership.

2 October - SLE Chairman Chris Caisley adds his concern to the proposal: "Anything that is less than a merger - a takeover, for instance - doesn't count. Super League would have to continue to be played in each of the two locations of the previously existing clubs," said Caisley.

15 November - At an RFL Special General Meeting it is announced that the Thunder will merge with the Sharks and, contrary to previous indications, will move to Hull, with the merged club playing in Super League and playing all its games at the Boulevard.

16 November - Gateshead directors Shane Richardson and Kath Hetherington reveal that their club lost £700,000 in its first season of operation.

25 November - coach Shaun McRae signs an extension to his contract that will keep him at the Boulevard until the end of the 2001 season.

1 December - Australian scrum-half Willie Peters is transferred to Wigan for £100,000.

14 December - Hull bring out a limited edition Millennium shirt, featuring 14 of the greatest stars to have played with the club.

24 January 2000 - JWE Telecom confirms that it will continue to sponsor Hull for the 2000 season.

18 February - David Topliss joins Hull as part-time football adviser.

3 March - after two easy Challenge Cup wins, Hull lose their opening Super League game of the season 27-30 at Halifax to a controversial late try.

11 March - Hull's season springs to life, as the club beats Wigan 14-4 in the Challenge Cup at the Boulevard in a televised game.

12 March - Hull release Andy Ireland and Michael Smith.

26 March - A group of Hull fans invades the pitch at the McAlpine Stadium, after their club loses an exciting Challenge Cup semi-final 22-28 to Leeds Rhinos. Some fans tear the posts down at one end of the ground, and 14 fans were arrested.

1 April - at a rally held at the Boulevard the club launches a fans' charter to counter the

troublemakers, and to improve the club's image in the light of the trouble at the McAlpine Stadium. It announces that any proven troublemakers will be banned for life from the Boulevard.

10 April - in a continuing effort to encourage new fans to come to the Boulevard,

the club becomes the first to appoint an away fans liaison officer, whose job is to advise and help visiting fans enjoy the Boulevard experience.

21 April - the club signs outstanding local youngsters Gary Peacham, Matty McGuire and Graeme Horne.

3 May - Hull draw 8-8 at home against Bradford Bulls, just four days after the Bulls won the Challenge Cup final at Murrayfield.

17 May - the Rugby Football League fines Hull £50,000, £30,000 of which is suspended for two years, for their supporters' part in the McAlpine Stadium Challenge Cup semi-final debacle.

4 July - Hull announce the signing of 28 year old Australian Test star Jason Smith from Parramatta for the 2001 season.

20 July - Richardson issues statement denying move to Cronulla.

30 July - the club beats Wakefield Trinity Wildcats 56-6, its highest winning margin in Super League V.

18 August - Hull announce the re-signing of Australian David Maiden for the new season.

29 August - the RFL decides that Hull centre Deon Bird can come off the overseas quota for next season, enabling him to sign a new contract with the club.

4 September - Hull halfback Will Robinson returns to Australia, where his mother-in-law is dangerously ill.

5 September - Hull announce that they will not be retaining Matt Schultz for the new season.

8 September - the club announces that it has signed St Helens winger Chris Smith and Wakefield Trinity Wildcats fullback Steve Prescott for the 2001 season.

12 September - Hull announce the signing of Tony Smith from Wigan

17 September - Hull end the regular season with a convincing win against a weakened Bradford Bulls.

5 October - The club announces a major sponsorship deal with Kingston Interactive Television.

26 October - Hull announce the signing of Logan Campbell, who will return to the Boulevard from Castleford Tigers.

30 October - the club confirms that agreement has been reached with Hull City Council to buy the Boulevard, with Hull moving into a new stadium for the 2002 season.

Injury problems affected Tony Grimaldi's season

Hull fans rallied to put right the damage caused by the Challenge Cup semi-final anarchy

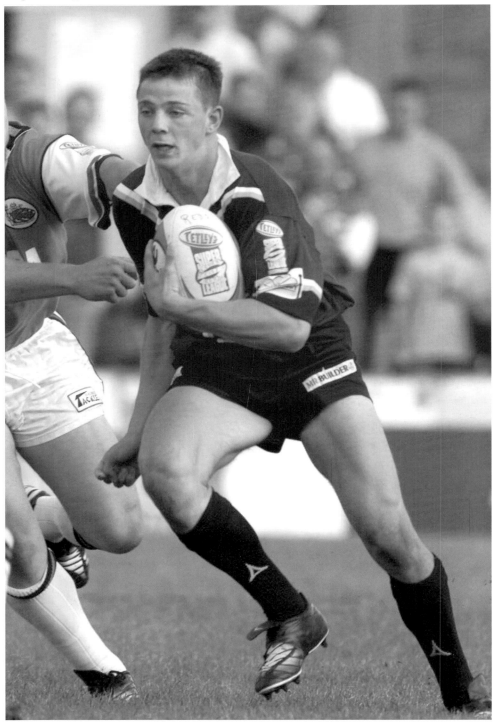

Leading the Hull new breed - Richard Horne

HALIFAX BLUE SOX

No blues

The Shay - developing into one of the best grounds in Super League

You could forgive Halifax Blue Sox fans if they were feeling quietly satisfied at the efforts of their club during the 2000 season, which had always been viewed by the club as a season of transition, in which the Blue Sox would bounce back from financial oblivion in 1999 to stand out as a club making progress both on and off the field.

A league position of eighth may look disappointing, especially when the Blue Sox started the season with three straight wins, but good housekeeping was the watchword at The Shay, with the club determined to keep its expenditure under control. A players' wage bill set at roughly £750,000 was more than £500,000 less than the average figure for a Super League club.

In their early season TV games the Blue Sox enjoyed particular successes. Grandstand screened their 11-10 Challenge Cup win against Castleford Tigers at The Jungle, and Sky Sports were on hand for their 24-18 win against Leeds, with Daryl Cardiss scoring a spectacular try, and former rugby union player Jim Naylor scorching in for a matchwinning interception try in front of a wildly enthusiastic crowd of Blue Sox fans gathered on the impressive new South Terrace.

Naylor, a native of Halifax, had signed for the Blue Sox on loan from the Newcastle rugby union club, and was making his debut for the Blue Sox.

"It was great to get clapped off at the end in front of my home town fans," he said.

The game star that night was young fullback Daryl Cardiss, however, who scored a 90-yard special in which he beat virtually the whole of the Leeds team for what must rank as possibly the individual try of the season in Super League.

The Blue Sox had some other good days in Super League V, but it was never quite as good again as it was that night against the Rhinos.

Despite suffering more than their fair share of defeats, however, they were well served in 2000 by their Australian contingent. Halfback Andrew Dunemann and veteran Aussie Test star Greg Florimo, playing out his last season before going into retirement, both had big seasons, while prop forward Brett Goldspink was the cornerstone of an aggressive Blue Sox pack.

But it wasn't just their overseas stars that gave Halifax cause for optimism.

Youngsters like Danny Tickle, Danny Halliwell, Lee Greenwood, Casey Mayberry, Matt Firth and Sean Penkywicz made their debuts this year, and all showed glimpses of their potential.

Next season they will be joined by Stuart Donlan from Leigh Centurions, and possibly Mick Higham from the same club, although that depends on whether the Blue Sox can win a tug of war for Higham against St Helens. Higham signed contracts with both clubs at the end of the season, but the Blue Sox signed one first, before Higham won a tribunal case at the RFL that declared him a free agent.

A downside for the Blue Sox was the dismissal and vilification of prop forward Andy Hobson, after an incident in which the Bulls' Robbie Paul was injured in a 20-20 draw at The Shay. That aside, Hobson was happy to reflect on a season that saw progress all round.

"I don't think too much was expected of us, but the management recruited well, and we didn't let ourselves or the competition down," says Hobson.

"We might not have won a trophy, but we were always competitive, and as a club we have a reputation for giving the young lads a go. If you took Flo and Ming (Mercer) out of our last side the average age was under 21."

Off the field, more than £3 million has been spent on the stadium in 2000, with the final results to be seen early in 2001, when the complete redevelopment of the main stand is finally completed, the Blue Sox claiming that their ground will then be the most atmospheric and scenic venue in Super League.

"Playing in such a great ground brings out the best in all the players," adds Hobson.

"Next season will be even better, and the new stand and facilities will inspire the team to even higher levels."

With the Blue Sox having recorded an encouraging rise in average attendances of 31.3 percent, from 4,352 in 1999 to 5,714 in 2000. The club is confident that in 2001, with its magnificent 'new' ground in place, it will be able to break the 6,000 barrier.

On the coaching front, player-coach Gary Mercer was joined by former Rochdale coach Steve Linnane in late June, and, with Mercer having signed a

There was an emotional farewell for Greg Florimo at the end of the season

Added direction to the Blue Sox attack - Andrew Dunemann

new one-year contract, the coaching team will take the Blue Sox to the end of 2001 and possibly beyond.

One departure from the Blue Sox who will be missed by many Halifax fans is hooker Paul Rowley, an England World Cup squad member, who will turn out for Huddersfield Giants during the 2001 season.

2000 High - The televised 24-16 home win against Leeds Rhinos was the Blue Sox's third win on the trot at the start of the season, and featured thrilling tries from Daryl Cardiss and Jim Naylor.

2000 Low - The 62-2 defeat by Bradford Bulls at Odsal was the heaviest defeat suffered during the season.

2000 Star - Andrew Dunemann had a massive influence on the side, giving the Blue Sox a sense of direction from halfback.

KEY DATES IN HALIFAX'S SEASON

21 October 1999 - a RFL tribunal decides that the Wigan Warriors must pay the Blue Sox £85,000 for the transfer of 18 year old winger David Hodgson.

10 November - Brett Goldspink signs from Wigan for the Blue Sox.

25 November - the Blue Sox capture Greg Florimo from Wigan, with the Warriors agreeing to fund part of Florimo's wages.

17 December - Martin Pearson returns to Halifax from Huddersfield and Sheffield Giants, in a swap deal that takes Richard Marshall to the Giants and includes a move for Lee Greenwood to The Shay.

2 February 2000 - the Blue Sox win 11-10 at Castleford in the Challenge Cup.

14 March - Player-coach Gary Mercer claims that his side was "cheated" by the referee after the 28-18 Challenge Cup defeat by Bradford Bulls at The Shay. He is subsequently fined £1,000 for the offence, and enraged Halifax fans organise collections to pay the fine.

1 April - Halifax defeat Leeds 24-16, after a length of the field try from Daryl Cardiss and a late interception try by Jim Naylor. The Blue Sox are at the top of Super League, undefeated after three rounds.

15 April - Blue Sox prop forward Andy Hobson agrees a new three-year deal to stay at The Shay.

1 May - the club transfer lists prop forward Lokeni Savelio after he fails to secure a first-team place.

1 May - the club's East Stand is used for the last time for the club's televised home game against Castleford Tigers, before being demolished for redevelopment.

11 May - Martin Hall quits as Gary Mercer's assistant coach, citing personal reasons, less than six months after joining the club.

12 May - the Blue Sox receive a 62-2 hammering at Odsal by the Bulls, as Bulls winger Justin Brooker scores a hat-trick.

19 May - the South Stand is closed for the London Broncos game for the start of roofing work.

31 May - Back rower Mike Peters leaves the Blue Sox to join Warrington, months after having been signed from Wigan.

9 June - Prop Jim Gannon is sent off, and then cleared, during the 36-22 defeat by Leeds Rhinos

at Headingley.

16 June - The South Stand re-opens, with the club claiming it is the most atmospheric and panoramic vantage point in Super League.

27 June - Rochdale Hornets' Australian coach Steve Linnane quits Spotland to join the Blue Sox as assistant coach.

30 June - Halifax record their biggest win of the season, a 66-2 hammering of the dispirited Giants at The Shay.

1 July - the bulldozers move into The Shay to re-locate the pitch, signalling a month on the road for the Blue Sox.

5 July - Gary Mercer announces that he will continue playing in 2001.

20 July - Jamie Bloes agrees a new three-year contract after outstanding performances against Wigan and St Helens.

22 July - Martin Pearson is sacked by the club after being banned for three months by the RFL for using recreational drug Ecstasy. The news came just a week after he was cleared of using a performance enhancing substance.

6 August - a torrid run of one win in nine games comes to an end with a sensational 20-20 draw with Bradford. Andy Hobson is sent off and Robbie Paul is carried off.

2 September - fullback Daryl Cardiss and winger Marvin Golden are dropped for the return match against Bradford after missing training.

3 September - All three completed stands at The Shay are open for the first time for the visit of the Bulls.

A youthful Halifax side eventually lose out 25-18.

17 September - the Blue Sox bring the curtain down on their season with a 54-18 win over Huddersfield and Sheffield Giants, with Greg Florimo, playing his last game for the club, leaving his boots on the centre spot after the game.

18 September - hooker Pual Rowley joins Huddersfield after seven seasons with Halifax.

22 September - the Blue Sox sign former St Helens and London star Paul Davidson.

21 October - coach Gary Mercer signs a new one-year contract.

15 November - the Blue Sox claim to be vindicated when a RFL tribunal decares Leigh stars Mick Higham and Stuart Donlan free agents.

Gary Mercer and Steve Linnane - joint coaching team worked well together

Halifax youngsters Jamie Thackray, Danny Tickle, Lee Greenwood, Matt Firth and David Foster

Jamie Bloem captained South Africa in the World Cup

SALFORD CITY REDS

Exceeding expectations

Martin Offiah was top tryscorer for the Reds following his arrival from London

Salford City Reds were the bookmakers favourites to finish at the bottom of the table before Super League V got under way.

So the Reds' achievement in finishing ninth in the table represents a highly creditable performance, and it could have been even better if key signing Graham Holroyd hadn't injured his shoulder in a pre-season friendly against Wigan.

Holroyd's injury kept him out of the side until June, by which time the Reds, lacking squad numbers, had fallen off the pace in Super League, and they would never be in with a realistic chance of making the top-five play-offs.

Sadly, with the absence of Holroyd, the Reds' speed merchants in their back division - Martin Offiah and Nick Pinkney - lost much of the service they would have wanted, although both players showed often enough that they had lost little of the potency that had characterised their play earlier in their careers.

Super League V review

With skipper Martin Crompton suffering a knee injury in May that would also end his season, the Reds were in serious trouble in the halfback department, having also lost Crompton's partner Steve Blakeley before the start of the season.

They signed a number of players on short-term deals, including Hull scrum-half Craig Murdock, Warrington stand-off John Duffy, and Brad Hepi, who had also played with Castleford Tigers, but things only began to improve when Holroyd returned, and when the Reds re-signed Blakeley in May.

The Reds began the season with a fine 22-21 Challenge Cup win against London Broncos at the Kingstonian soccer ground in West London, and, in the quarter-final of the same competition they featured in a thrilling televised tie against Warrington Wolves at The Willows. Sadly, the Reds went down 22-20 to a last-second try by Alan Hunte for the Wolves, setting the template for a season with more than its share of bad luck.

Salford had already begun the Super League season by securing a lively 18-10 opening day win at the newly-merged Huddersfield and Sheffield Giants, and throughout the season they would play well, and secure good results, against other teams occupying the lower positions in Super League.

Disaster struck in June, however, when the Reds went down to a appalling 96-16 defeat against Bradford Bulls at Odsal, a result that had some observers questioning their right to be in Super League.

"They were too big, too strong, too good, and there were too many of them," said Reds coach John Harvey after the game.

Later that week the Reds issued a public apology to their fans for their performance.

"Sunday was a nightmare, and I can only apologise to the Salford public for the display of incompetence and lack of commitment. It will not happen again," said Harvey.

The Reds were never candidates for the top five, but at least by the end of the season they were showing plenty of hope for the future, a 29-12 win at Halifax for the Colin Dixon Memorial Trophy perhaps being their best performance of the season, inspired by Blakeley, who had formed a fine halfback partnership with Holroyd.

"The players showed a lot of heart, as they have ever since the Bradford game," said Harvey, who signed a contract extension at the end of the season, and hopes to continue the Reds' climb up the league in 2001.

Reds owner John Wilkinson had put the club on the market earlier in the year, but as the season ended he had found no buyer, and appeared happy to retain his ownership of one of Super League's more unfashionable clubs.

And with Salford planning to move from the Willows during the 2003 season, the club is confident that it can retain and develop a strong Super League franchise in the Manchester conurbation over a lengthy period.

Kris Tassell joined the Reds from the North Queensland Cowboys at the beginning of the season. And, as the fullback or centre looks forward to representing Wales in the World Cup, he reflected on the Reds' year.

"It was a bit of a culture shock after the facilities we had back home, compared to the facilities here, but the Reds are dedicated to becoming more

Graham Holroyd's early season injury affected the Reds

Steve Blakeley - departed and then returned to the Willows from Warrington

professional in every aspect of what they are doing. You can see that this year, and it should be even better next year," says Tassell.

"I started off the season a little slow - it took me some time to get used to the footy over here. But the second half of the season wasn't too bad for me.

"The club started well in the Challenge Cup, but the wheels fell off a little as the season went on.

"The problem was that we didn't have any specialist halfback in the team, with the injury suffered by Graham Holroyd, and we didn't have a specialist kicker. At one point, for example, Paul Southern was having to kick goals for us.

"We had a couple of young blokes who filled in admirably, but it was good having Holly and Steve Blakeley together later in the season.

"The biggest blow to our season was that terrible defeat at Bradford.

"I just wish I hadn't played in that game; it was totally humiliating. At half-time it was something like fifty bloody nil, and what can the coach say in that situation?

92

"I've never been beaten by that much, even in the juniors. It was an absolute embarrassment. Leading up to the game we had a lot of injuries, and two blokes pulled out prior to the game, so we had a weak team. The Bulls were just too big and too strong.

"As it happened, though, that became the turning point of our season. After that we came back and strung together a couple of wins against Hull and Halifax, which was a really good, tough game.

"And with the new signings we have I'm very optimistic for next season. Mick Hancock and Francis Maloney will do great things for us, and Warren Jowitt is a great buy for the club. When we played Wakefield he cut us up, and he is a very good player.

"Next season we'll have a lot more depth, so that when we do get injuries we won't suffer like we did at Bradford.

"I've signed with the club for another year, and I hope to have a good season next year and then stay on even longer."

2000 High - The penultimate game of the season, when a 29-12 win at Halifax Blue Sox enabled the Reds to win the Colin Dixon Memorial Trophy, in honour of one of their great former players.
2000 Low - No doubt about it, that 96-16 drubbing at Bradford in June.
2000 Star - Martin Offiah struck a blow for older players last season, scoring 13 Super League tries and even landing a couple of field goals.

Bradford's Robbie Paul splits the Salford defence during the Reds' horror show at Odsal

KEY EVENTS IN SALFORD'S SEASON

18 November 1999 - the Reds sign former Warrington Wolves loose forward Mike Wainwright.

19 November - Australian fitness guru Rudi Meir arrives at the Willows to boost the Reds' pre-season conditioning programme.

19 November - the Reds sign Australian centre Jason Webber from Balmain

25 November - Salford announce a raft of signings for the new season, including former Great Britain superstar Martin Offiah, former Leeds and Halifax star Graham Holroyd, former Sheffield Eagles centre or winger Nick Pinkney, fullback Kris Tassell from North Queensland, and back-rower Jim Smith from South Sydney.

25 November - former England captain Steve Blakeley leaves Salford to join Warrington Wolves.

10 December - the Reds launch their new Millennium Shirt for Super League V.

14 December - Rudi Meir heads back to Australia confident that the Reds will have a successful new season.

1 January 2000 - David Hulme, the oldest player in Super League IV, quits Salford to join Widnes Vikings as player-coach.

19 January - Chairman John Wilkinson announces that he is putting the Reds up for sale.

26 January - Salford sign Warrington stand-off half John Duffy.

28 January - in a pre-season friendly against Wigan, new signing Graham Holroyd suffers a shoulder injury that will keep him out of the side until June.

13 February - the Reds open their season with a comfortable but unconvincing 34-18 Challenge Cup win at Barrow.

21 February - the Reds announce that they are to sign exciting South Sydney winger or centre Justin Loomans.

27 February - the Reds beat London Broncos in the Challenge Cup in the capital in a nailbiting finish.

3 March - the deal for Justin Loomans falls through.

5 March - the Reds gain a victory in their opening game of the season against Huddersfield and Sheffield Giants at the McAlpine Stadium, with youngster Simon Svabic scoring two tries and three goals.

7 March - the Reds announce the signing of 'The Skull' - Jason Nicol from South Sydney.

10 March - Salford sign Brad Hepi until the end of the season.

12 March - the Reds lose 20-22 at home to Warrington in the quarter-final of the Challenge Cup, with the Wolves grabbing the winner in injury time.

7 April - Salford sign former Hull scrum-half Craig Murdock.

16 April - Martin Offiah lands the first field goal of his career, but it doesn't stop the Reds being hammered 52-1 by Bradford at The Willows.

3 May - Salford controversially re-sign Steve Blakeley from Warrington Wolves.

Kris Tassell enjoyed a good season with Salford and Wales in the World Cup

New deal - John Harvey

7 May - Scrum-half Martin Crompton injures his knee ligaments against Halifax Blue Sox and is out for the season.

4 June - Graham Holroyd makes his return, and helps the Reds in their defeat of Huddersfield and Sheffield Giants.

15 June - Prop forward Neil Baynes signs a new deal with the Reds.

25 June - the Reds go down 96-16, their heaviest ever defeat, against Bradford Bulls at Odsal.

27 June - the Reds issue a public apology to their supporters for their abject performance at Odsal.

7 July - Graham Holroyd signs a new three-year deal to stay at The Willows.

23 July - Martin Offiah lands the second field goal of his career, and it secures a 23-22 win for Salford against Halifax Blue Sox.

17 September - Salford lose their last game of the season, 10-38 at Warrington, with Jim Smith and Jason Webber playing their last games for the club.

19 September - the Reds announce the capture of Francis Maloney and Warren Jowitt (both Wakefield) and Warren Stevens (Warrington).

19 September - Chairman John Wilkinson announces that the club will be applying for planning permission for a new stadium at Barton "by the end of October."

26 September - coach John Harvey agrees a one-year extension to his contract.

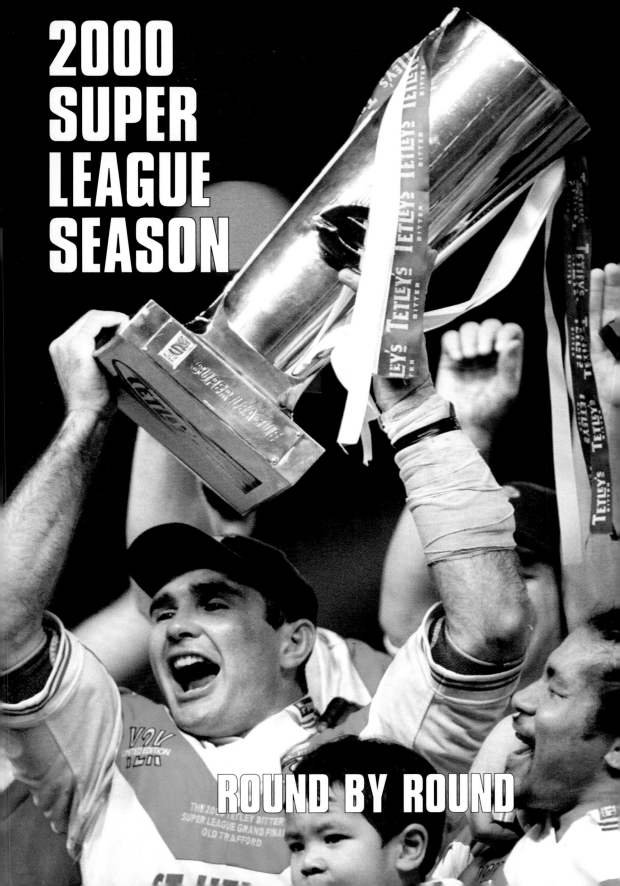

2000 SUPER LEAGUE SEASON

ROUND BY ROUND

CLOCKWISE FROM TOP LEFT: Bradford's Nathan McAvoy on the burst; Warrington Wolves' Danny Farrar is caught by Robbie Paul; Leeds Rhinos' Barrie McDermott fends off the challenge of the Hull defence; Hull's Matt Daylight is halted; Anthony Farrell dives over for a Leeds try; Bradford Bulls players James Lowes and Justin Brooker celebrate their passage through to the final.

CHALLENGE CUP SEMI FINALS

TOP: Michael Withers dives in to score the first try of the match for Bradford.
LEFT: Bradford Bulls celebrate their victory over Leeds Rhinos.
BOTTOM: Bradford's Mike Forshaw feels the force of Leeds' Daryl Powell and Anthony Farrell.
BOTTOM (INSET): Rhinos fans outside the ground at Murrayfield, the first time the Challenge Cup has been played away from Wembley since the war.

Silk Cut Challenge Cup
2000 WINNERS

TOBACCO SERIOUSLY DAMAGES HEALTH

CHALLENGE CUP FINAL

ROUND 1

ROUND 2

ROUND 3

TOP: Leeds Rhinos' Richie Blackmore looks to avoid the advancing Ryan Hudson. Wakefield Trinity Wildcats produced the first upset of Super League V by beating Leeds Rhinos at Headingley 18-22.
INSET: Bradford Bulls' Mike Forshaw is brought crashing down. The Bulls were in devastating form, crushing Warrington Wolves 58-4.

BELOW: Leeds Rhinos' Darren Fleary is dumped by Brett Goldspink (left) and Martin Moana in a memorable win for Halifax.

ROUND 5

LEFT: Dale Laughton in the thick of the action for Huddersfield-Sheffield Giants as they defeat Wakefield Trinity Wildcats to notch up their first Super League win of the season.
INSET: Warrington's Steve McCurrie tries to break through the tackle of Willie Poching.

ROUND 4

ROUND 6

ABOVE: St Helens' Kevin Iro scores a hat-trick in a game which sees Wigan crash to their first Super League defeat of 2000.

ROUND 9

ROUND 8

ABOVE: Halifax Blue Sox' Greg Florimo is brought crashing down during their victory at the Willows.
LEFT: London Broncos' Shane Millard looks for support against Wakefield at Belle Vue.

ROUND 7

RIGHT: Wigan's Kris Radlinski gets the ball away as Castleford's Aaron Raper closes in. The Tigers are defeated at the JJB Stadium 30-16.

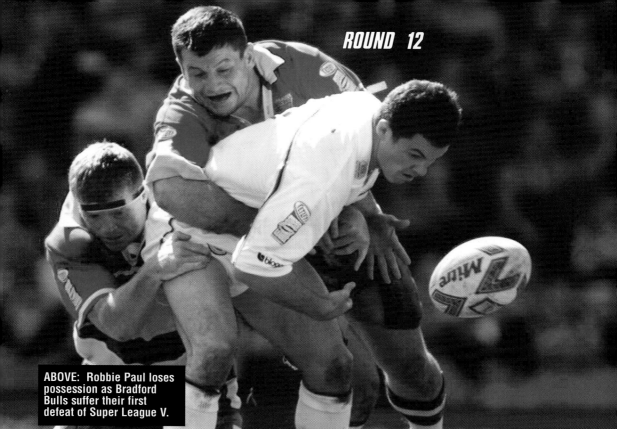

ROUND 12

ABOVE: Robbie Paul loses possession as Bradford Bulls suffer their first defeat of Super League V.

ROUND 10

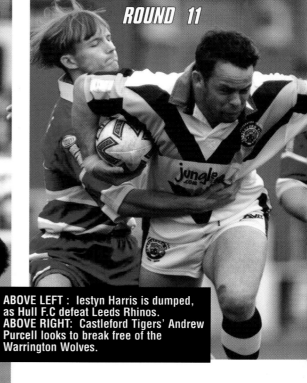

ROUND 11

ABOVE LEFT : Iestyn Harris is dumped, as Hull F.C defeat Leeds Rhinos.
ABOVE RIGHT: Castleford Tigers' Andrew Purcell looks to break free of the Warrington Wolves.

RIGHT: Salford City Reds' Jason Nicol busts a Broncos tackle.

ROUND 15

ROUND 13

ROUND 14

INSET: David Boyle touches down in Bradford's single point victory over St Helens.
RIGHT: Jon Roper take the full force of the Hull FC defence.

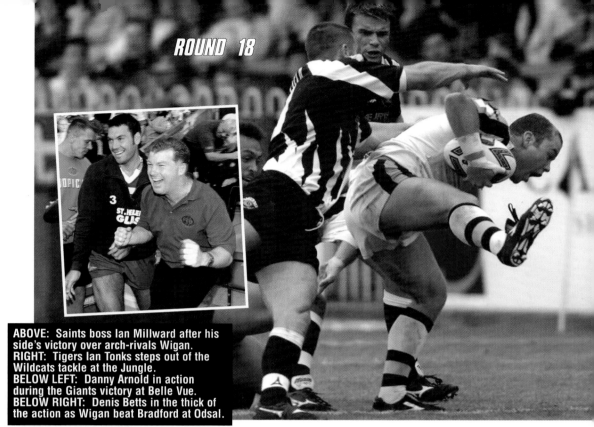

ROUND 18

ABOVE: Saints boss Ian Millward after his side's victory over arch-rivals Wigan.
RIGHT: Tigers Ian Tonks steps out of the Wildcats tackle at the Jungle.
BELOW LEFT: Danny Arnold in action during the Giants victory at Belle Vue.
BELOW RIGHT: Denis Betts in the thick of the action as Wigan beat Bradford at Odsal.

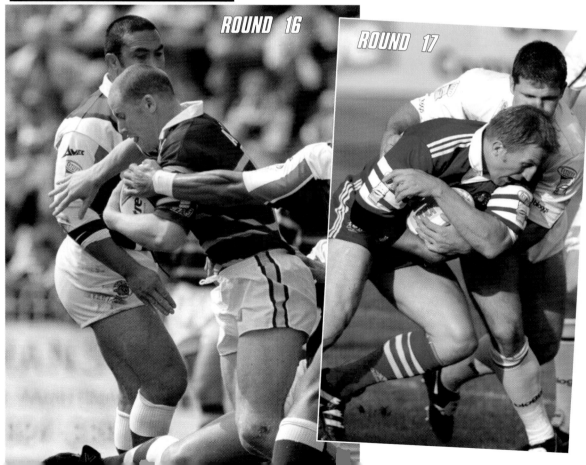

ROUND 16

ROUND 17

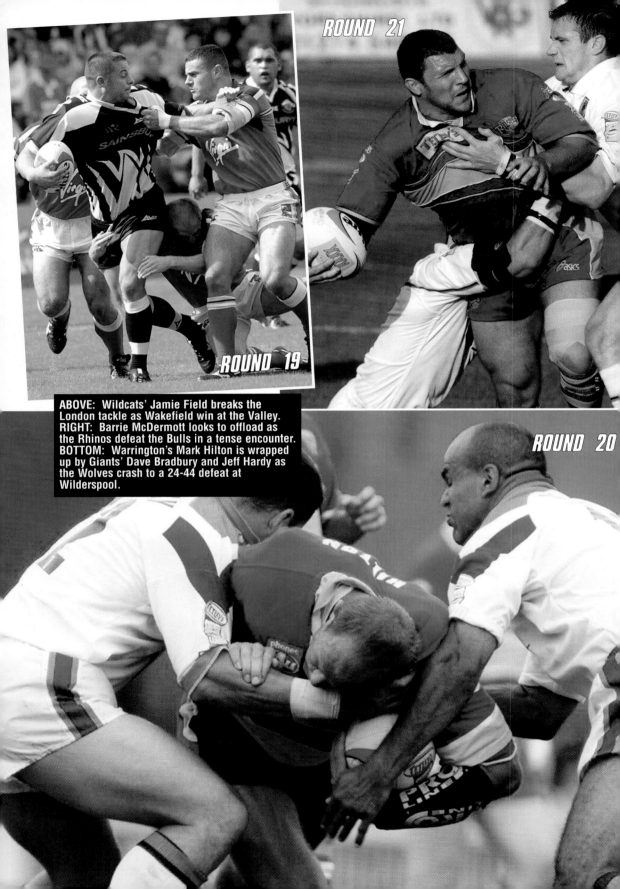

ROUND 21

ROUND 19

ROUND 20

ABOVE: Wildcats' Jamie Field breaks the London tackle as Wakefield win at the Valley.
RIGHT: Barrie McDermott looks to offload as the Rhinos defeat the Bulls in a tense encounter.
BOTTOM: Warrington's Mark Hilton is wrapped up by Giants' Dave Bradbury and Jeff Hardy as the Wolves crash to a 24-44 defeat at Wilderspool.

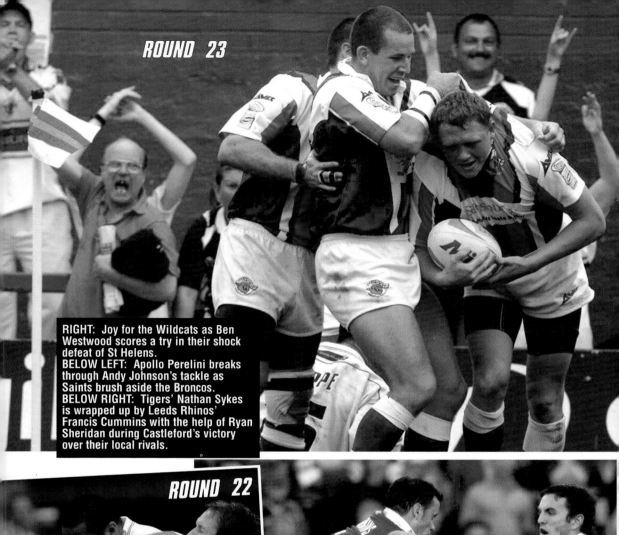

ROUND 23

RIGHT: Joy for the Wildcats as Ben Westwood scores a try in their shock defeat of St Helens.
BELOW LEFT: Apollo Perelini breaks through Andy Johnson's tackle as Saints brush aside the Broncos.
BELOW RIGHT: Tigers' Nathan Sykes is wrapped up by Leeds Rhinos' Francis Cummins with the help of Ryan Sheridan during Castleford's victory over their local rivals.

ROUND 22

ROUND 24

ROUND 25

LEFT: Bulls Paul Deacon brings Wigan Warriors prop Terry O'Connor to the ground during Wigan's last gasp victory over Bradford.

ROUND 26

LEFT & INSET: Salford's Graham Holroyd attempts to fend of the Hull tacklers in their point victory at the Willows; Luke Felsch looks for openings.

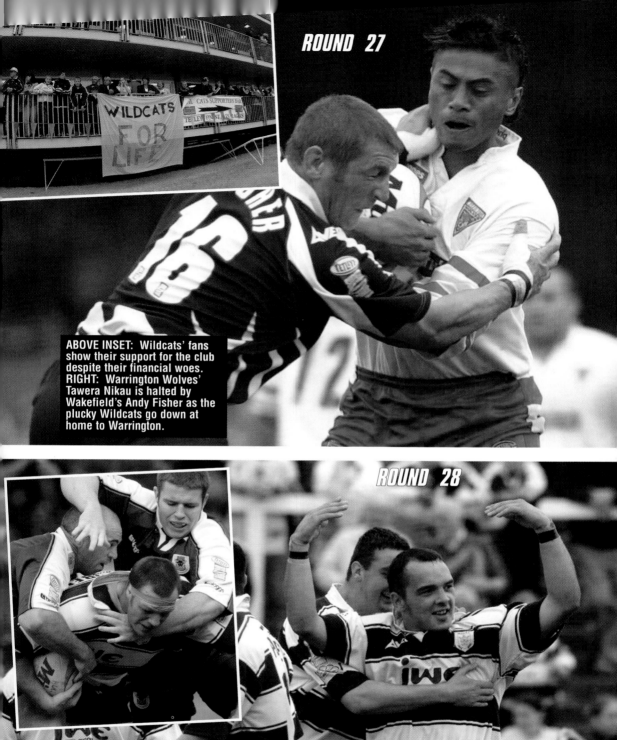

ROUND 27

ABOVE INSET: Wildcats' fans show their support for the club despite their financial woes.
RIGHT: Warrington Wolves' Tawera Nikau is halted by Wakefield's Andy Fisher as the plucky Wildcats go down at home to Warrington.

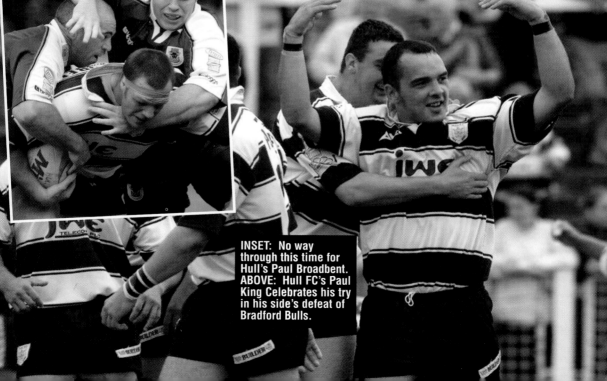

ROUND 28

INSET: No way through this time for Hull's Paul Broadbent.
ABOVE: Hull FC's Paul King Celebrates his try in his side's defeat of Bradford Bulls.

RIGHT: Sean Long and Chris Joynt celebrate victory over Bradford thanks to a last minute try by St Helens captain Joynt.

BOTTOM LEFT: Lee Jackson is dumped by Brad Davis, but Castleford are left heart broken as they are eliminated.
BOTTOM: Stuart Fielden on the burst as Bradford demolish Leeds.

ELIMINATION PLAY-OFF

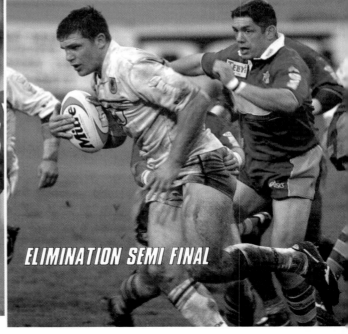

ELIMINATION SEMI FINAL

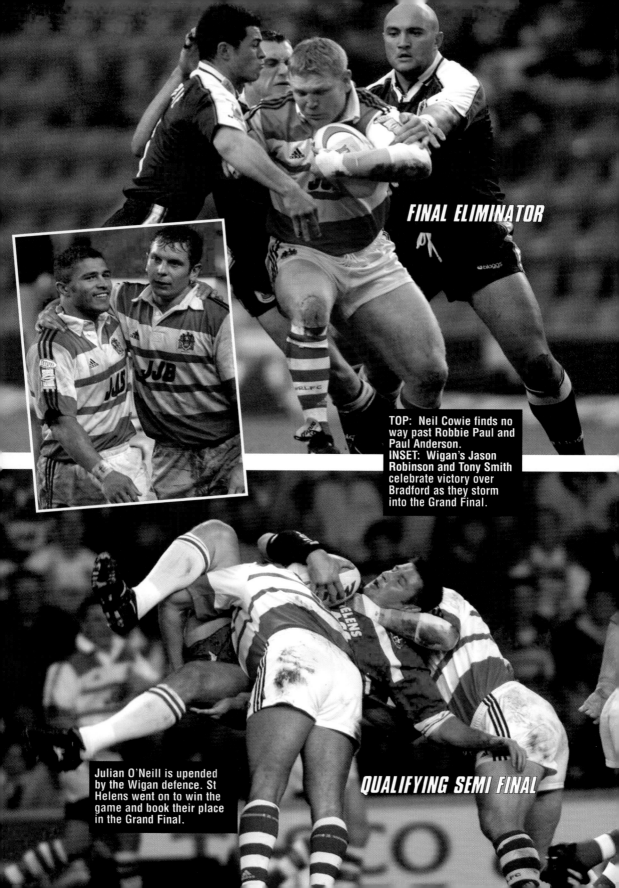

FINAL ELIMINATOR

TOP: Neil Cowie finds no way past Robbie Paul and Paul Anderson.

INSET: Wigan's Jason Robinson and Tony Smith celebrate victory over Bradford as they storm into the Grand Final.

Julian O'Neill is upended by the Wigan defence. St Helens went on to win the game and book their place in the Grand Final.

QUALIFYING SEMI FINAL

ST HELENS 29 .... WIGAN 16

CLOCKWISE FROM TOP: Sean Hoppe dives over to score the opening try for St Helens; a dejected Jason Robinson at the final whistle, his last game for Wigan; Lee Gilmour is halted by Apollo Perelini and Keiron Cunningham; Tim Jonkers celebrates his last minute try; St Helens players celebrate

WAKEFIELD T WILDCATS

Avoiding extinction

Wakefield Trinity Wildcats had a Super League V season that at times seemed more like fantasy than reality.

Impossible objectives, both financial and on the field, meant that initial optimism soon turned to despair, as cheques bounced, performances declined accordingly, and coach Andy Kelly was sacked.

And yet not much more than a year earlier things looked so bright for the Wildcats.

On 14 October last season the club proudly revealed its Mission Statement, and a raft of new signings, who were intended to build on the ten wins the club had achieved in Super League under Kelly in 1999.

"The Board of Wakefield Trinity Wildcats today announce radical changes within the organisation, which will pave the way to instil a new discipline, culture and ethos as they approach their second season in Super League," read the Mission Statement.

"The formation of a management company will facilitate resources and thus enable Andy Kelly, as Head Coach, to recruit, retain and strengthen the squad."

Sadly the reality, under new chief executive John Pearman, was to be very different.

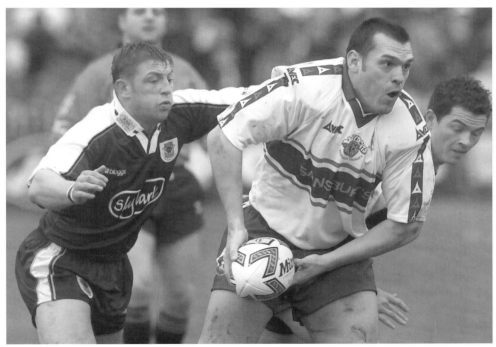

Selected for England - Wigan-bound Francis Stephenson

Super League V review

The Wildcats received an early jolt when they were drawn at home to Bradford Bulls in the fifth round of the Challenge Cup, going down 0-46 to an infinitely more powerful team.

The following week they were back on track, however, when they stunned Leeds Rhinos at Headingley 22-18.

But Trinity would only rarely rise to those heights again. They registered good away wins at Warrington, Salford and London, but failed badly all too often, particularly to bottom club Huddersfield and Sheffield Giants, to whom they lost three times.

Among rumours of player disaffection, Kelly was sacked at the end of May, after a run of five successive defeats.

The real high point of their season, and of Tony Kemp's brief coaching career, came when they defeated St Helens in August, 32-16 at Belle Vue.

"In the face of adversity it was a very good performance," said Kemp, who had managed his team in the face of acute financial uncertainty, with players having no idea whether they were ever going to receive another pay cheque. The coach himself had declared that he would not be staying with the club in 2001 because of the uncertainty.

Kemp had brought a raft of younger players into his side to face Saints, to replace some of his disillusioned older stars.

"A few young blokes out there today showed what could be done with enthusiasm. It was enthusiasm that won the game," he said.

It was the last win Trinity would have in 2000, and two games later the club terminated the contracts of its players over the age of 24.

One of the players whose contract was torn up was prop forward Francis Stephenson, for whom disaster would turn into opportunity, as Wigan Chairman Maurice Lindsay moved quickly to sign the England squad member.

Stephenson's initial hopes for the club in Super League V were not fulfilled.

"It was a fantastic place to be during the close season. Having stayed in Super League the previous season, we had new players, lots of promises and a new atmosphere of professionalism. Everything was very positive, and it was something I wanted to be part of. I thought the club would really go forward," says Stephenson, who admits that the Cup game against Bradford was a sobering experience.

"Going into the game I believed we could beat them, but I didn't really appreciate the preparation Bradford had done. That defeat didn't cause the problem, but it highlighted it, and the Leeds result the following week papered over the cracks.

"We thought we were going to be a top-five side, but as the season went on we were at the bottom end of the spectrum."

And Stephenson admits that the players had to accept their share of the blame.

"Some players were seriously lacking any real commitment at times. Individual players shone now and again, but there was no real cohesion in the team.

"We didn't have a balanced formula. Maybe it would have worked in a different environment, but if you are going to bring in such a large number of

Inspirational Wildcats Samoan skipper Willie Poching

players, you have to look more long term."

As the season went on players found their salary cheques bouncing, and Stephenson explains how that affected the team.

"It doesn't really enter your mind when you are playing the game. But if something goes against a team, it is hard to have the mental resolve to recover from it, if you believe you are playing for a club that doesn't really support what you are doing.

"It's like an army being led by generals who they don't respect. You can see the effect on team morale.

"We came back with a performance full of determination to beat St Helens, when some players were rested and others were dropped. That left a hard core of Wakefield players, and young players who had been asking for a chance. We were determined to show the public what we could do, and we succeeded once, at least."

Despite question marks over their survival, Trinity's creditors supported a creditors voluntary arrangement, giving the club a fair chance of survival, and with some recent signings, including Julian O'Neill of St Helens and Brad Davis of Castleford, Trinity are optimistic of another backs to the wall season under new coach John Harbin.

2000 High - Trinity's astonishing 32-16 win against St Helens on 13 August, as a young side battled with pride and hunger.

2000 Low - The 0-46 home defeat against Bradford in the Challenge Cup was hard to recover from, despite Trinity's win at Headingley the following week.

2000 Star - Willie Poching set a wonderful example for much of the season, and, despite the financial problems that afflicted the club, he never failed to give his best.

Paul Sampson returned to rugby union after cheques started bouncing

KEY EVENTS IN WAKEFIELD'S SEASON

28 September 1999 - chief executive Steve Ferres leaves the club, officially for health reasons after undergoing a major hip replacement operation, but with strong doubts about the direction the club was proposing to go in.

14 October - Trinity announce a new mission statement; a new chief executive, in former Wakefield Metropolitan Council leader John Pearman; and six new signings, in Martin Masella (Leeds), Warren Jowitt (Bradford), Francis Maloney (Castleford), Bright Sodje (Sheffield), and Tony Tatupu (Auckland).

3 November - the Wildcats announce the signing of Steve Prescott (Hull) and Ryan Hudson (Huddersfield).

4 November - Trinity confirm that they have agreed a three-year contract with Bradford Bulls loose forward Steve McNamara. And chief executive Pearman reveals that "we have authorised Andy Kelly to seek to secure the services of

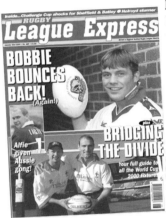

New Zealand international winger Jonah Lomu. We believe we can match any offers that may be on the table, and present this highly gifted and talented individual with the opportunity and incentive to build a new career in Rugby League in the company of the League's most ambitious club."

16 November - the Wildcats withdraw a contract offer to Leeds star Francis Cummins.

15 December - Wakefield sign Wasps rugby union winger Paul Sampson, the cousin of Castleford's Dean.

18 January - Trinity's annual general meeting reveals accrued debts of more than £1 million, but Chairman Ted Richardson assures shareholders that there is nothing to worry about. Meanwhile the club contracts with SGB Rovacabin to erect a new hospitality stand at the ground, estimated to cost £750,000.

24 January - Wakefield snap up former Saints and Huddersfield star Bobbie Goulding.

6 February - Trinity go down 24-12 in a pre-season friendly at Bradford.

7 February - Sir Brian Nicholson, the Chairman of BUPA, becomes the President of Trinity.

13 February - the Wildcats win 40-28 at Leigh in the fourth round of the Challenge Cup.

14 February - Trinity make an audacious bid to sign Australian Test star brothers Andrew and Matthew Johns.

27 February - Trinity are hammered 46-0 by Bradford Bulls in the fifth round of the Challenge Cup at Belle Vue, causing chief executive John Pearman to describe their performance as "pathetic", adding: "We have spent a million pounds in the off-season putting a team together, and we have to ask some fundamental questions

about value for money." Bobbie Goulding missed the game, having entered hospital for groin surgery.

3 March - Trinity, inspired by gamestar Steve McNamara, gain a late 22-18 win against Leeds Rhinos at Headingley in their opening Super League game.

31 March - Trinity confirm an interest in Wigan and Great Britain star Jason Robinson, as the club claims it would like to keep him in the game, rather than see him go to rugby union. "We have opened negotiations with Jason's agent David McKnight, and although we realise we will face tough competition, we will be doing our utmost to get Jason's signature," said Pearman.

3 April - Wigan Chairman Maurice Lindsay reports Trinity to Super League Europe for breaching the Super League Code of Conduct by making an illegal approach for Wigan star Jason Robinson.

9 April - Trinity unveil their new hospitality stand, while Bobbie Goulding makes his debut for Wakefield, as a last-gasp Willie Poching try earns a 28-24 home win against Warrington Wolves.

14 April - Trinity Chairman Ted Richardson denies claims that the club is under financial pressure as several players' salary cheques bounce. The problem is described as "a temporary blip".

3 May - Tony Kemp is promoted to assistant coach, while general manager John Harbin is given a more hands-on role to tighten up on discipline at the club. "Andy Kelly still remains as Head Coach, and these appointments are being made in order to provide him with more support," said Pearman. Meanwhile Kelly hits out at some of his players for Trinity's disappointing start to the season.

24 May - Trinity are fined £5,000 by Super League Europe for an illegal approach for Wigan's Jason Robinson.

26 May - Trinity announce a plan to merge with soccer club Emley.

30 May - the club sacks Andy Kelly and his assistant Jon Sharp after going down 36-10 at Halifax Blue Sox, leaving Tony Kemp and John Harbin in charge, while Kelly seeks legal advice.

31 May - Bobbie Goulding, who has missed four games through injury and family illness, injures his knee in training.

4 June - Tony Kemp is in charge for his first game, as Trinity go down 24-30 at home to Leeds, after a video decision disallowing a penalty try that RFL Referees' Controller Greg McCallum later admits was the wrong decision.

7 June - Trinity hold their AGM, with the club announcing a loss of £61,178 for the year ending 31 December 1999, and shareholders are told that chief executive John Pearman is to buy a majority stake in the club and invest

significant personal funds.

9 June - Trinity take Jason Critchley (Leicester RUFC) and Leeds hooker Andy Speak on loan.

9 June - the club reaches agreement with former coaches Andy Kelly and Jon Sharp on severance packages following their dismissals.

28 July - Trinity Chairman Ted Richardson reveals that the club has sacked its chief executive John Pearman for failing to inject promised funds into the club,

which now faces a liquidity crisis and debts claimed to be around £1.5 million. The club is unable to pay the contractor who erected its new hospitality stand earlier in the year.

1 August - Trinity sign halfback Dane Dorahy from Rochdale Hornets.

4 August - coach Tony Kemp announces that he will be leaving Trinity at the end of the season.

13 August - Trinity stun St Helens 32-16 at Belle Vue in the shock result of the season.

28 August - winger Paul Sampson returns to Wasps RUFC.

30 August - Wakefield make a presentation to their fellow Super League clubs, seeking their support for a proposed Creditors' Voluntary Arrangement.

3 September - Trinity lose for the third time in Super League to Huddersfield and Sheffield Giants.

6 September - Trinity enter a CVA and all existing player contracts for players over the age of 24 are terminated. Tony Kemp resigns, and the players are offered £120 per match to fulfil the club's final two fixtures under temporary coach John Harbin. Steve Prescott signs for Hull.

15 September - John Pearman writes to a local newspaper claiming to have been made a scapegoat for Trinity's problems.

20 - the Super League clubs approve BSkyB funding for Wakefield if they remain in Super League in the 2001 season, although they amend the CVA proposal.

27 September - Trinity's creditors adjourn a meeting to approve the club's proposed CVA, with their major creditor wanting more information.

4 October - Trinity finally gain approval from their creditors for a CVA, allowing the club to start afresh financially, but leaving former coach Andy Kelly with an outstanding claim for £10,000 that will not be paid.

4 October - Steve Ferres officially returns to the club as recruitment director.

11 October - Trinity recruit Brad Davis from Castleford Tigers, and re-sign Willie Poching and Gary Price.

20 October - Trinity sign Fijian star Waisale Sovatabua from Huddersfield Giants, and they re-

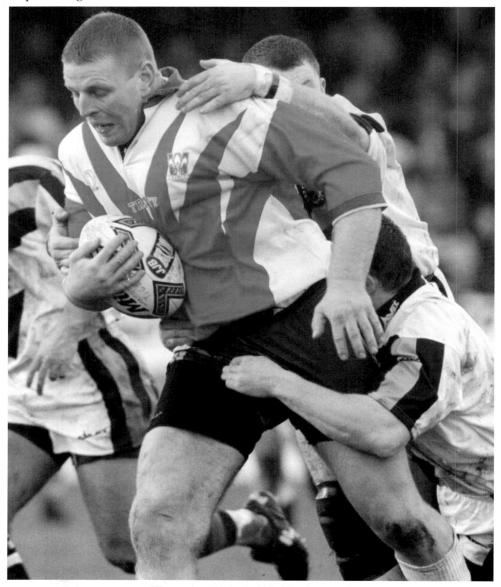

Warren Jowitt in typical blockbusting mood

sign their stars Frank Watene, Neil Law, Martyn Holland, Graham Law and Jamie Field.

27 October - Trinity director and acting chief executive Stuart Farrar resigns from the club.

8 November - the Wildcats confirm that John Harbin will be their coach in the 2001 season, and they sign St Helens prop Julian O'Neill and Bradford threequarter Justin Brooker.

17 November - Trinity announce the capture of former Halifax star Martin Pearson, when his suspension for drug abuse expires at the end of the year.

LONDON BRONCOS

Marking time

London Broncos had their most disappointing season since Super League began in 1996.

The club finished second from bottom, with coach John Monie paying the price, being sacked just three games before the end of the season.

The Broncos began the season full of optimism, with the decision to re-locate to The Valley, Charlton Athletic's superb stadium in south-east London, meaning that the club was returning to the Super League roots it had established there in the 1996 season, before its three-year stint in West London at The Stoop.

But things didn't go smoothly.

"Our preparation wasn't good, because we had too short a period to prepare after the switch," claims departing Broncos star and playmaker Karle Hammond, who will be playing with Widnes in 2001.

"The training facilities and atmosphere we created were a lot better in West London, and the club would have been better to allow us to continue training there, with a view to moving fully to Charlton at the end of the season."

And Hammond is anxious to deny rumours that one of the problems facing the Broncos in the 2000 season was that he and Monie didn't see eye to eye.

John Monie had a difficult season at London, and was sacked

"John wasn't used to running a struggling team, but there were no words between us, and I helped him out as much as I could. Everything went on smoothly, but we were decimated from the word go with injuries.

"That was particularly so for our young halfback Brendan Magnus, who was finished almost before he started, and quit at the same time as Shaun Edwards. In his short time with us he added speed and awareness to our attack, and looked very promising. It was difficult after that, with a different halfback every week, and with each player having different skills. It meant that I never settled into my role.

"And things never seemed to change. Our approach was trying out for a change in the game plan, but it didn't happen, and results didn't change.

"It was a real anti-climax, after we had reached Wembley last year."

And Hammond cites the departure of former coach Les Kiss as one key reason for the club's disappointment.

"I would have loved Les to have stayed, he was a brilliant coach," says Hammond.

"He was a genuine players' coach, dealing with players individually, and working on individual and group skills. We would try different things on the training park, and his results last year speak for themselves.

"He would have been a good replacement for John, or for any other club looking for a new coach."

And Hammond believes that, amid the gloom, there were some positive signs for London.

"Justin Dooley scooped all the club awards, and that was deserved for his wholehearted performances. He led by example, and was always on top of the hit-ups. Tulsen Tollett tried his best, as always, and Steele Retchless always gave everything.

"Dominic Peters made a name for himself last season, and with the right coaching he can go a long way in the game. Certain players are in the England squad because of the club they are at, but I would certainly have selected Dominic."

And Hammond believes the Broncos can turn the corner.

"There was no problem playing at Charlton. Even though they got low crowds, they were vocal and very enthusiastic.

"The speccies are very knowledgeable and loyal, and they deserve a winning team. And the players are a great bunch of lads, although I got unsettled, and I was not enjoying my football. I was determined to come back north, no matter what."

The Broncos' problems in 2000 were exemplified by their games against Salford City Reds. They played the Reds, who were the pre-season favourites to finish at the bottom of Super League, four times - once in the Challenge Cup, and three times in Super League, and they managed to lose each time. It was hard for Broncos fans to take.

The writing was on the wall as early as April, when the Broncos lost their second home Super League game of the season 24-33 to the Reds, with Brendan Magnus suffering the knee injury that aborted his career, leaving the club rudderless at halfback, after the retirement of veteran star Shaun Edwards.

League legend Shaun Edwards retired early on in 2000

Breaking new ground - London's Anthony Seibold on the charge against Warrington at Newport

Hammond was dismissed for showing dissent to the referee in that game, as coach John Monie realised that he was facing an uphill struggle for the rest of the season.

"The players were fresh, but we lacked finishing power," said Monie, who would repeat a similar mantra many times during the year.

In fact the Broncos would only win seven matches in the whole of the Super League season, although the encouraging thing was that their crowds rose slightly at The Valley, compared to those they attracted to The Stoop in West London, and their seventh win came in their last game of the season at Leeds Rhinos.

They did break new ground in the 2000 season, however, when they took a home game to Newport RUFC in Wales, going down 18-28 to Warrington Wolves.

Broncos chief executive Tony Rea had taken over the coaching reins for the Broncos' final three games of the season, and it was he who plotted their win against Leeds with one of the youngest Broncos sides of the season.

"I was very happy with the kids," said Rea.

"We were just patient, did the simple things and competed, there was nothing spectacular, just effort that was rewarded.

"The guys needed an 80-minute performance to prove to themselves just how good they are, and that showed in the outpouring of emotion. They can go away with a bit of faith for the off-season."

And Rea must have enjoyed the win himself. Less than a month later the club would be announcing that its chief executive would be changing roles to become the new coach, with former Leeds assistant coach Damien McGrath joining him at The Valley. And they will have plenty of material to work with.

With stars of the quality of Richie Barnett, Jim Dymock, Jason Hetherington and Tony Martin joining the club from Australia next season, the signs are that the Broncos could at last be back on the upward curve that their loyal supporters surely deserve.

2000 High - The final game of the season, when the Broncos went to Leeds and shocked the Rhinos 18-6.

2000 Low - The Broncos' second game at The Valley, when they went down 24-33 to Salford City Reds, and lost Brendan Magnus for the season with a cruciate ligament injury. They struggled at halfback from that point onwards.

2000 Star - No doubt about it, prop forward Justin Dooley had a great year, especially against the bigger clubs, and can look forward to another big year with better quality players around him.

Consistent performer - Greg Fleming

KEY DATES IN LONDON'S SEASON

12 October - the Broncos announce that coach Les Kiss will not be staying with the club in the 2000 season.

19 October - the club announces that former Wigan coach John Monie will be its coach for Super League V.

29 October - London sign 23 year old winger Frank Napoli from Australian club Burleigh Bears.

22 November - Danny Moore and Steve Barrow sign for London from Wigan Warriors.

24 November - the Broncos announce that they will play home games at The Valley, the home of Charlton Athletic FC, in Super League V.

29 November - the Broncos sign Wigan stars Jon Clarke and Andy Johnson on two-year contracts.

13 January- Abe Kerr joins the club as community development manager.

3 Febuary - London sign new scrum-half Brendan Magnus from Balmain Tigers.

13 February - the Broncos play their Challenge Cup 4th round tie at Kingstonian's Kingsmeadow Stadium, beating Cumbrian amateurs Wath Brow Hornets 44-18

16 Febuary - the Broncos sign former St. Helens front row forward Paul Davidon on a one year deal.

19 March - the Broncos play their first game at The Valley, and record a 34-18 win against Huddersfield and Sheffield Giants.

2 April - Tulsen Tollett makes his 100th appearance for the club against Castleford Tigers.

3 April - the Broncos sign former Bradford and Wakefield centre Kevin Crouthers.

9 April - Australian halfback Brendan Magnus tears his cruciate ligament against Salford City Reds, and is ruled out for the rest of the season. In the same game Karle Hammond is dismissed for arguing with the referee.

13 April - veteran halfback Shaun Edwards, the most successful player in the history of the game, announces his retirement, citing knee and head injuries as the reason for his decision.

20 April - the Broncos confirm that former Wigan centre Danny Moore is to leave the club to return to his homeland.

24 April - Danny Moore breaks his jaw in his last match for the club against Hull on Easter Monday.

25 April- the club re-signs Aussie scrum-half Glen Air to replace the injured Brendan Magnus.

27 April - Paul Davidson is confirmed to have broken his arm against Hull, although Kiwi star John Timu returns after being sidelined with an achilles injury for two months.

4 June - the Broncos play their 'home' game against Warrington Wolves at Newport, going down 18-28.

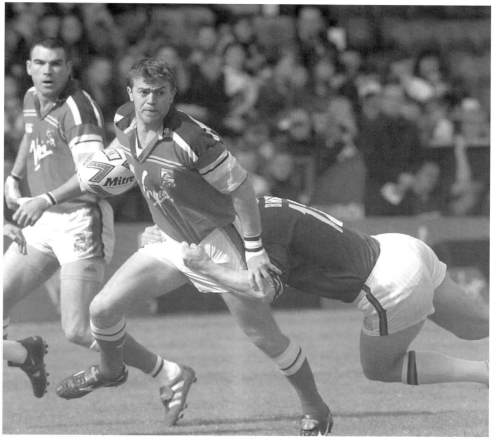

Karle Hammond will be turning out for Widnes in 2001

11 June - Castleford Tigers help the Broncos to register a crowd of more than 8,000 - easily their highest of the season - for the match between the two clubs, thanks to a travel and admission package heavily subsidised by Tigers sponsor jungle.com

25 June - the Broncos celebrate 20 years as a professional club at their home game against Wigan.

26 June - the club signs current Australian Test hooker Jason Hetherington and Melbourne Storm centre Tony Martin for Super League VI.

14 July- the Broncos re-sign front row forward Justin Dooley for a further two years.

31 July - the club announces the capture of New Zealand skipper and fullback Richie Barnett.

28 August - the Broncos sack John Monie with just three regular season games remaining.

11 October - chief executive Tony Rea moves over to become the Broncos' new coach.

8 November - former Leeds assistant Damian McGrath joins London as assistant coach.

Star turn for the Broncos - Justin Dooley

HUDDS-SHEFF GIANTS

Bottom again

Coaching casualty - John Kear

Huddersfield and Sheffield Giants could hardly have had a more disastrous season.

Formed from a merger of the former Huddersfield Giants and Sheffield Eagles on 1 October, the newly formed club fared no better than the old Giants, despite the influx of new players who came to it from the Eagles.

Finishing at the bottom of the league for the third season in a row, the Giants were almost everyone's easybeats except Wakefield Trinity Wildcats, who they managed to beat three times in Super League. Their only other win was away at Warrington Wolves on 23 July, when they shocked the whole of Super League with a 44-24 victory.

Outstanding young talent - Chris Thorman

Apart from those crumbs of comfort, however, the season was one of unrelenting misery for Giants fans, with injuries to key players causing massive disruption, and coach John Kear ultimately departing the club in July, although by then it was too late for stand-in coaches Phil Veivers and Jeff Hardy to turn the club around. Veivers himself would leave the club later in the year.

In retrospect, the decision to merge the two former clubs was a much harder task than anyone could have imagined when they set out.

For example, the club had to agree a total of 29 severance deals with players and staff who were previously employed by one or other of the previous clubs, and that was always going to be a massive drain on the new club's management and financial resources.

And with Kear citing the "culture clash" between the two former clubs - famously describing the Giants players as overpaid and under-achieving, in contrast to their Eagles colleagues as underpaid and over-achieving - as one important reason for its failure to fire on all cylinders, it was always going to be tough for the players themselves to put their hearts into the merger.

"It takes a while for a club to come together, and we found that players gelled in some positions, but not others," says former Eagles star Dale Laughton.

"We struggled, particularly at halfback, but nobody can claim they were consistent throughout the year.

"Sheffield hadn't been a classy side, but we had always fought for our victories. So I had been looking forward to a mid-table position in the competition this year.

"We started well in the friendlies, beating Leeds and St Helens, and we thought we were set fair. Maybe we should lose our friendlies next year.

"Of course it doesn't help to have injuries, but all clubs suffer them, and you have to cope with it, although we did lose key players at important times."

It wasn't until the third game of the season that Laughton realised what a tough season the Giants would be in for.

"We only just lost to Salford and London in the first two games of the season. If we could have won then it might have given us a bit more confidence. But the defeat (2-60) against Bradford in our third game knocked the stuffing out of us. From then on it went from bad to worse, and we just didn't have the players to pull us out of the mire.

"Our confidence drained away, and we were sticking the ball up our jumpers. John didn't know what to do himself. He tried to pick our mistakes out in video sessions, but there were just so many points to pick out, and the players just became confused and depressed. And John became very frustrated himself, but clearly couldn't pull us out of it."

And such was his despair that Laughton reveals that he would have been happy to leave the club.

"I didn't enjoy the season at all. I asked for a transfer midway through the season because, to be frank, I didn't learn anything under John this year, having already been with him for four years.

"But then Tony Smith came in as the new coach towards the end of the season, and since he arrived I've learned more than I learned in the whole of

Giants prop Dale Laughton in action against Wigan

my previous career.

"The little things he does are very important. And the way he comes across is very effective. He has also told me that if I think he is going wrong anywhere I can come and discuss it with him, and that shows he respects me.

"Our prospects for next season now depend on who he recruits. If he recruits decent players, and not second raters, then we can move up the table, although I am not going to make any rash predictions."

And Laughton will be staying at the Giants next season.

"If Tony knows he can coach you and improve you, then he will keep you. I am still desperate to learn, because, to be frank, I don't feel as though I've had a great deal of help to develop my game during the whole of my career. So I'm certainly looking forward to next season."

Giants chief executive Ralph Rimmer can also see light at the end of the tunnel.

"This year was always going to be a holding year, during which we would be putting building blocks in place, although I admit that we thought we would do better than we did," says Rimmer.

"We are completely changing the culture of the club, which is something we weren't able to do this year. We have a lot of young talent coming through, but we need the right type of professionals around them to nurture their abilitites.

"The success story is what we have done off the field. We want to develop a big club, and we do feel that we will be going in the right direction, both on and off the field."

The Giants have already made a raft of new signings for next year, as well as releasing a number of their established stars.

Now the pressure is on coach Smith to ensure that the club with the best ground in Super League has a team to match.

2000 High - That amazing 44-24 win at Warrington Wolves in July, as the Giants came back from a half-time deficit to blitz the Wolves with a second half super-show.

2000 Low - A shocking performane at Halifax Blue Sox just three weeks earlier, when the Giants were hammered 66-2. It was the straw the broke the camel's back for coach John Kear.

2000 Star - Throughout all the despair, young halfback Chris Thorman stood out as a natural talent and one to watch for the future.

New Giants coach Tony Smith

KEY DATES IN THE GIANTS' SEASON

30 September - the long-rumoured merger is finally confirmed, with Huddersfield Giants and Sheffield Eagles announcing that they are to formally combine, with the merged club coming into being the following day.

9 December - Gavin Clinch signs for the Giants from Wigan, and is seen by coach John Kear as a cornerstone signing.

4 February - Daio Powell breaks his arm for the third time in his career in a trial match against the Halifax Alliance team at Thrum Hall, and will play no further part in the Giants' season.

5 March - young prop forward Richard Marshall breaks his thumb in the Giants' opening league game against Salford City Reds, and will be out for 6 weeks.

19 March - prop forward Nick Fozzard breaks his arm against London Broncos, and is out for the season.

29 March - the Giants sign former Great Britain tourist David Bradbury, who had been on trial with Warrington, to replace Fozzard and Marshall.

16 April - the Giants earn their first win of the season, a narrow 35-34 victory

against Wakefield Trinity Wildcats at the McAlpine Stadium.

4 June - Australian fitness guru Rudi Meir joins the Giants for a three-week spell, during which time the club gains its second win of the

4 June - Karl Lovell suffers a knee ligaments injury against Salford City Reds, and will be out for virtually the rest of the season.

6 June - Football coordinator Barry Johnson leaves the club.

7 June - Steve Molloy is relieved of the club captaincy.

18 June - young French signing Sylvain Houles is injured against Hull, and returns to France after making just seven appearances for the club.

13 July - coach John Kear leaves the club.

6 August - the Giants record an attendance of just 2,102 fans for their 'home' game against Castleford Tigers at Sheffield's Bramall Lane ground. The club declares that it will take no more games to Sheffield, effectively ending the 'merger' between the Huddersfield Giants and Sheffield Eagles.

16 August - the club appoints Australian Tony Smith from Parramatta as its new coach, subject to him getting a work permit.

10 September - Gavin Clinch leaves the Giants to join Halifax Blue Sox.

7 September - the Giants declare that from now on they will revert to being called the Huddersfield Giants, dropping the 'Sheffield' part of their name.

12 - the club signs halfback Ben Kusto from Parramatta.

14 September - the Giants sign former Wakefield Trinity Wildcats star Steve McNamara.

18 September - they sign speedy Australian winger Andrew Frew from Australian club Northern Eagles.

Darren Turner congratulated on a try against Salford

20 September - the Giants continue their team strengthening for next season by signing Paul Rowley from Halifax Blue Sox.

20 September - the Giants announce that Johnny Lawless, Karl Lovell and Jimmy Carlton are to leave the club.

27 September - the Giants reveal a re-designed club badge for Super League VI.

29 September - the Giants release assistant coach Phil Veivers.

4 October - the Giants advise their New Zealand Maoris star Gene Ngamu to look for another club.

11 October - the Giants sign 19 year old Bradford centre Chris Langley.

13 October - the Giants sign winger Andrew Frew from the Northern Eagles.

18 October - David Atkins, 22, a second-rower from Canberra Raiders, joins the Giants on a two-year contract.

28 November - the Giants announce the signing of Australian utility back Graham Appo from North Queensland Cowboys on a one-year contract.

135

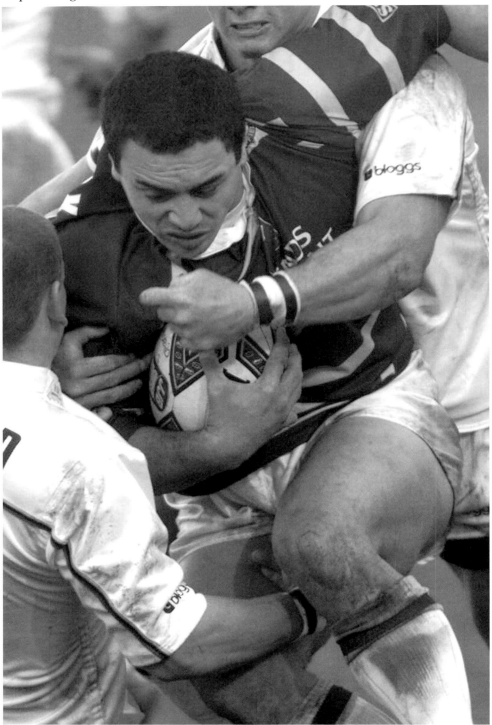

Solid season - David Lomax

3
THE CHALLENGE CUP

The High Road to Murrayfield

SILK CUT CHALLENGE CUP FINAL
BRADFORD BULLS 24 ....LEEDS RHINOS 18

THE BULLS won the Challenge Cup for the first time in 51 years but it was never the walkover that the pundits had predicted.

The Rhinos - who had won only one of their opening six Super League games - were never a 9/2 chance, and had the favourites on the ropes for much of the second half of a final that had looked unlikely to be played less than 48 hours before, with the Edinburgh ground under two feet of water.

Thankfully, the RFL pulled out all the stops to get the final played.

It was a tight game, with all of the six tries scored on the day involving kicks, reflecting the clinical organisation and total commitment of both sides' defences.

Henry Paul was the main architect of victory, with his three bombs that created two tries for Michael Withers in the first half, and one for Stuart Fielden in the 48th minute.

It was enough to earn Henry the Lance Todd Trophy, emulating little brother Robbie in 1996.

It was a close call, and he was pushed for the award by a tireless performance from Brian McDermott up front, and from Withers in the centre. As well as his two tries, the former Balmain star was always a danger with the ball, and he put the shackles on Richie Blackmore.

BULLS: 28 Stuart Spruce; 4 Nathan McAvoy; 20 Scott Naylor; 5 Michael Withers; 2 Tevita Vaikona; 6 Henry Paul; 1 Robbie Paul (C); 22 Brian McDermott; 9 James Lowes; 10 Paul Anderson; 19 Jamie Peacock; 12 Mike Forshaw; 13 Brad Mackay. *Subs:* 29 Stuart Fielden for Anderson (20); 11 David Boyle for Peacock (26); 3 Leon Pryce for McAvoy (31); 23 Bernard Dwyer for Mackay (70); Anderson for McDermott (71); McDermott for Fielden (75). **Tries:** Withers (9,16), McAvoy (28), Fielden (48); **Goals:** H Paul 4

RHINOS: 1 Iestyn Harris (C); 18 Leroy Rivett; 3 Richie Blackmore; 4 Keith Senior; 5 Francis Cummins; 6 Daryl Powell; 7 Ryan Sheridan; 8 Darren Fleary; 19 Dean Lawford; 10 Barrie McDermott; 11 Adrian Morley; 17 Anthony Farrell; 16 Andy Hay. *Subs:* 20 Jamie Mathiou for Lawford (28); 12 David Barnhill for Farrell (ht); 14 Marcus St Hilaire for Powell (50); McDermott for Fleary (54); Farrell for Morley (60BB, rev 65); Fleary for Mathiou (69); Farrell for Morley (70BB, rev 75). **Tries:** Hay (53), St Hilaire (74); **Goals:** Harris 5

League Express Men of the Match
Bulls: Michael Withers; **Rhinos:** Adrian Morley
Penalties: Bulls 7-6; **HT:** 14-2; **Ref:** Steve Presley (Castleford); **Att:** 67,247

If Leeds had gone on to complete an amazing comeback, Adrian Morley would surely have deserved the accolade, with a typical display featuring punishing defence, explosive running, and a couple of high shots, plus frequent visits to the blood bin.

For coach Matthew Elliott there was the tangible relief of snaring a trophy after the big game disappointments of Wembley in 1996 and 1997 and Old Trafford 1999.

"I'm just so proud of the players," he said in the aftermath.

"The first thing I thought of at full-time was the guys that missed out. As happy as I felt, I sunk a bit, because I would have liked them all to be involved.

"Everyone knows this was more than a 17-man trophy, and they will need to contribute to get us to the next one."

Henry Paul joined Elliott at the post-match press conference to reflect on his accolade, and a 25,000 mile round trip during the past fortnight with brother Robbie to play in the Anzac Test.

"It's a great honour," he said.

Bradford's Lance Todd Trophy winner Henry Paul chips through the Leeds defence as
Francis Cummins moves in

"I'm rapt you know but it is secondary to winning the game.

"As a half I didn't see much light. When I was throwing dummies all I could see were shoulders, heads and knees coming at me. I'm just rapt.

"Winning the Grand Final with Wigan was great but this is much better, way better. We've got a bunch of guys, like a family coming on.

"I was shattered after that game (Anzac Test). This was a chance to come back from that."

1999's Lance Todd winner Leroy Rivett might still be having nightmares about Murrayfield for a long time to come.

The winger was twice in no man's land as Henry Paul directed huge bombs to the Bulls left wing.

Paul hoisted the first skyer on nine minutes from the Rhinos 40.

Rivett never looked like getting into position to catch it, and Tevita Vaikona rose high to collect and managed to squeeze out a pass from the tackle for his centre Withers to sprint ten metres to dive over in the corner.

Seven minutes later the same kick went up, and Rivett and Blackmore between them were unable to defuse the danger. After the ball ricocheted back off Blackmore's leg, Withers was on hand to coolly scoop up the ball on the move and race over.

Fortunately, for the Rhinos, Henry was off target with both conversions, although he had opened the scoring with a seventh minute penalty goal from 30 metres after Barrie McDermott had decked him on the blindside as he ran a decoy.

But when, for once, the Rhinos defence failed to read a Bulls blindside ploy just before the half-hour mark, there looked to be no way back for Leeds.

Dean Lawford didn't number up, and Lowes and Boyle sent Nathan McAvoy striding down the right wing. The towering winger still had to put in one of the cheekiest chips, which he collected on the full, to round Iestyn Harris at fullback.

It was one of the finest pieces of individual skill seen in a Challenge Cup final, and though Henry's conversion attempt hit an upright and bounced out, the Bulls looked like kicking on and completing the predicted slaughter.

The slaughter never came, although Bradford went full tilt on attack right up to the half-time hooter.

Scott Naylor stepped Cummins down the right; Henry Paul bombed Rivett again and the winger was bundled dead; Rivett stripped the ball from Withers on the floor near the Leeds line but got away with it; Morley added to the pressure by offloading recklessly on his own ten metres. And Henry Paul missed an easy penalty goal just before half-time, when Darren Fleary was pulled for dropping the elbow on Fielden's face.

14-2 at the break, and it could well have been more, had the Rhinos defence not scrambled magnificently in the those last ten minutes of the half.

Curiously, Leeds had had marginally the better of the first half hour.

A Brian McDermott high tackle on Morley gave the Rhinos first go at the line, but Daryl Powell spilled the ball on the third tackle under pressure from Jamie Peacock.

At the other end Lowes put a kick into the Rhinos in-goal before Powell broke up the middle, and Ryan Sheridan's long kick saw Vaikona tackled on his own ten.

Withers gave away another penalty, dragging Rivett into touch after he was grounded, and Senior created space down the left and fed Francis Cummins on another promising attack.

Then, at the other side of the field, Blackmore took the ball within ten metres of the Bulls line before throwing a wild inside pass into the arms of the grateful Lowes.

After Withers' first try, some awesome Morley-McDermott defence forced the mistake, and a big run down the middle by Morley ended when a Harris stab to the line was cleaned up by Stuart Spruce.

But a Morley high tackle relieved the pressure on the Bulls, and the Rhinos' only first-half reward was a 30-metre Harris penalty goal after Steve Presley caught Bradford encroaching the ten metres at the play-the-ball.

A wild offload, this time by Barrie McDermott, was knocked on by Morley 15 metres out, and only a magnificent tackle by Harris and Farrell stopped Lowes grounding the ball.

The introduction of David Barnhill at the break helped the Rhinos step up a gear.

More fine work from Morley sent Fleary away up the middle, and when Harris kicked to the post on 45 minutes he was taken out by Fielden and the penalty was a formality.

14-4, and from being down and out the Rhinos were in sight.

They attacked down the left, but Senior's inside pass was a panic play, and the ball ended in the hands of Boyle.

Within three minutes Paul was putting up another kick to the left, this time from closer range and with less height.

But he couldn't have judged it better, as Fielden outjumped Harris to catch the ball and roll over the tryline, for a try okayed by the video ref, despite claims from Leeds that referee Steve Presley had indicated that the Bulls' chasers were offside, persuading Harris to leave the ball to bounce, waiting for an advantage that was never given. Instead Fielden was awarded the try and Henry kicked his second goal.

Then Withers broke down the left and fed Robbie Paul on the inside, but his kick was collected by Francis Cummins.

The direction of the game shot off at another tangent, however, as Sheridan put up a bomb a la Henry Paul. Cummins collected superbly, and fed Andy Hay, and the loose forward showed tremendous strength to get over in the corner, with the video ref being called to rule on a suspicion of obstruction by Hay on Leon Pryce.

Harris's conversion, and it was 20-10 and game on again.

A minute later, Harris's bomb to the Bulls posts, after Sheridan had made a fine break, was a peach, but Morley spoiled it by tackling Spruce in mid-air as he took the ball.

But a penalty against Brian McDermott for not playing the ball on the spot was advanced ten metres as Henry Paul threw the ball away - and received a push in the face from Lee Jackson - and Harris kicked the Rhinos two points nearer a stunning comeback.

An Anthony Farrell high tackle on Robbie Paul gave his brother another two-pointer just as the votes for the Lance Todd Trophy were being cast.

But another piece of Iestyn Harris magic set up a nailbiting finale. Harris's angled grubber in-goal had the Bulls wrongfooted, and substitute Marcus St Hilaire was the first to the ball, getting a fingertip to it and giving the video referee a difficult call.

It took a long time to decide, but the answer was positive, and Harris's conversion made it 22-18 with seven minutes remaining.

The Rhinos gave it their all, with Harris working like a man possessed. Rivett took another Henry Paul bomb, and broke clear from his own '20', but Stuart Spruce closed him down brilliantly. Then Andy Hay knocked on a tired pass from Harris.

Rivett's ball-stealing gave Henry Paul another simple two points, which left the draw the only escape route for the Rhinos.

As the clock reached 80 minutes Harris hoisted another desperate bomb which ricocheted into the arms of Lowes, who made the game safe.

GAMEBREAKER: The result wasn't decided until James Lowes ended up with the ball after Iestyn Harris's last-second bomb.

GAMESTAR: Henry Paul got no daylight from the Leeds mean-machine, but his attacking kicks effectively decided the destiny of the Challenge Cup.

TOP TACKLE: Iestyn Harris and Anthony Farrell's effort that kept James Lowes out on 22 minutes. Not only did the prevent him scoring, they carried him back into the field of play.

The Challenge Cup

The road to the historic Murrayfield final began on Saturday 4th December 1999, with teams from all parts of Great Britain and Ireland, and from all sectors of the game, playing for their own personal share of Challenge Cup glory.

Those clubs' share of the spotlight might not have been as big as the Rhinos' and the Bulls', but there was plenty of headline-grabbing along the way.

The highlight of the first two rounds was undoubtedly the fairytale progress of the Army Rugby League side.

They stunned Dewsbury Celtic - who had already reached the BARLA Yorkshire Cup Final by the time they travelled down to Aldershot - by 54-7; and then came through 24-10 against National Conference side Oulton Raiders to set up a third round tie against professional club Rochdale Hornets.

The Army finally met their match at Spotland but they made many friends in a 66-6 defeat.

All three Armed Services sides - in the Cup for the first time - were victorious in the first round - the Royal Air Force knocking out Conference second division side Normanton Knights 20-8 before Wigan St Judes knocked them out 40-6; and the Royal Navy shocking Hull Dockers with a 4-0 success, before finding Castleford Lock Lane too strong.

There was a little bit more history-making last December, when Widnes amateurs Farnworth beat Dublin Blues 54-2 in the first Challenge Cup tie to be played in Ireland.

Edinburgh Eagles were Scotland's representatives and they put up a fantastic display against Conference giants Woolston. After trailing 16-0 at the break the Scots staged a mighty comeback and the men from Warrington were hanging on for dear life, 17-12 ahead at the final whistle.

Cardiff Cougars went two better than the Eagles, winning through to the third round with wins at Durham and at home to Rochdale Mayfield before finding professional League experience too much when they were hammered 90-0 by Keighley Cougars.

The Army stunned Dewsbury Celtic in the first round of the Challrenge Cup

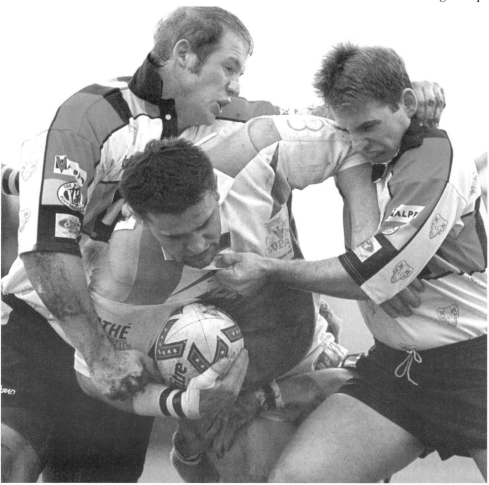

Villeneuve's Pierre Sabatie fallls to the challenge of Dewsbury duo Matthew Long and David Mycoe

There was also history-making in the third round when Villeneuve and St Gaudens became the first clubs from the French Federation to play in the Challenge Cup (Super League Paris Saint-Germain played in the 1997 competition).

St Gaudens found high-flying Doncaster Dragons in red-hot form at Belle Vue and went out 40-10.

French champions Villeneuve scraped through 26-16 against amateurs Lock Lane at the Jungle and then shocked NFP side Keighley Cougars with a 16-14 win at Cougar Park, finally meeting their match at Dewsbury Rams in round five, going out 36-10.

But we have got to remember the two big shocks of the third round.

Conference Premier Division side Oldham St Annes not only beat Batley Bulldogs on their own turf, they nilled them and Thornhill Trojans, struggling to get out of the Conference Premier Division relegation zone all season, pulled off a marvellous 16-14 win at Sheffield Eagles.

143

The Challenge Cup

The Bulls and the Rhinos - like all Super League clubs - entered the fray at the fourth round stage, Leeds Rhinos having too much class for Featherstone at Lionheart Stadium and the Bulls giving Huddersfield-Sheffield Giants the once-over at Odsal.

In round five, the Bulls overwhelmed Wakefield Trinity Wildcats too, 46-0, with Michael Withers scoring a hat-trick.

But the real crunch tie was set up by St Helens' visit to Headingley where the Rhinos won an almighty battle 26-20, Adrian Morley's injury-time try sealing the win.

The Cup-holders were rewarded with a home tie in the quarter-finals against the only NFP club left standing - Dewsbury Rams.

The Rams stunned the South Stand when they shot into a 6-0 lead but the class of returning skipper Iestyn Harris and prop Barrie McDermott took the Rhinos to a 42-10 win.

The Bulls, after mauling every thing in their path so far, didn't have it all their own way against Halifax Blue Sox at the Shay, but with Robbie Paul back to his vintage best, came through with a 28-18 win.

Which left two memorable semis for us to savour.

At Headingley another man-of-the-match performance from Henry Paul - some said it should have gone to little brother Robbie - guided the Bulls to a 44-20 win against the Wolves - who they had murdered 58-4 in the Super League the week before.

And skipper Iestyn Harris was at the heart of a battling Rhinos side as they overcame Hull 28-22 at the McAlpine Stadium, Huddersfield.

Leeds' Adrian Morley crashes past despairing St Helens fullback Paul Atcheson to score a match-winning try in Round Five

4 NORTHERN FORD PREMIERSHIP

DEWSBURY RAMS overcame the crushing disappointment of last year's Grand Final defeat to again emerge as the most consistent side in the Northern Ford Premiership.

Whichever side finished top of the table after the regular season had to prove themselves in a variety of conditions ranging from the depths of winter to some summer scorchers. It posed a challenge not only for coaches and players but also conditioners who had to prepare players for the stamina-sapping heavy months while bearing in mind the need to have players sharp and fast for the harder grounds.

But Dewsbury, again minor premiers, proved themselves the team of all seasons. "Rugby League is traditionally a game that rewards teams for finishing top of league tables, and to do so two years' running was a big achievement," says the Rams coach, Neil Kelly. "We lost only ten league games out of the last 56 so we have been consistent." The Rams also reached the quarter-final of the Challenge Cup and won the Trans Pennine Cup.

Captain and fullback Nathan Graham, goal-kicking halfback maestro Barry Eaton and loose forward Damian Ball were the Rams' stand-out players but it was essentially team-work that earned the Rams of respect of other teams and coaches.

Eaton scored 15 tries and kicked 169 goals during the season but was far more than a mere accumulator of points, steadily developing as a play-maker of the top quality. His halfback partner, Richard Agar, was troubled by injury but came up with the season's most decisive moment when it mattered most, kicking a late field-goal in the Rams' nerve-wracking 13-12 Grand Final win over Leigh.

Graham was the top try-scorer for the Rams but no less than seven other players also scored 10 tries or more, indicating what a team success it was. Among these, centre Dan Potter and winger Adrian Flynn were especially impressive while the strong running of second row Sean Richardson continually caught the eye.

Dewsbury won many plaudits for the manner in which they played. That reflected great credit on the coaching skills of Kelly, who has made a smooth transition from player to coach after a spell as player-coach and is regarded as the most promising of the up-and-coming breed of new English coaches. The former Great Britain prop Karl Harrison marked his first season in the coaching ranks with success at **KEIGHLEY COUGARS** who topped a thousand points in league action and provided some great entertainment for the Cougar Park faithful.

Harrison and his assistant Steve Deakin took over with just two contracted players but worked wonders to make the Cougars a feared attacking unit, especially suited to the harder grounds.

One of those players, loose forward Martin Wood, was consistently the NFP's outstanding talent with the ability to destroy defences at will and his starring role in the Cougars' early-season win over Dewsbury was one of the abiding memories of the campaign.

Harrison, who has left the club to become Brian Noble's assistant at Bradford, will be sorely missed but at least continuity will be assured by the

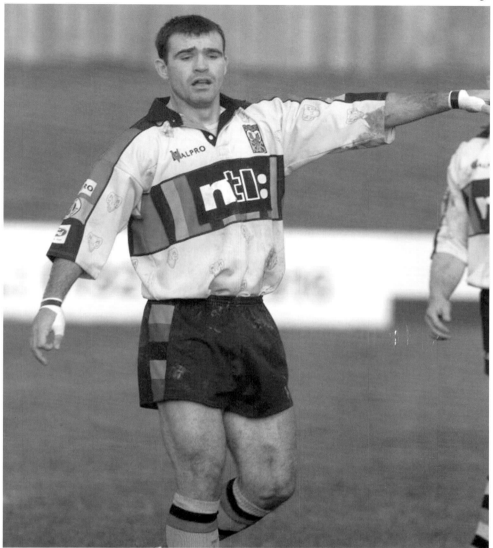

Top quality play-maker - Dewsbury's Barry Eaton

appointment of Deakin to the head-coaching job.

After a stunning play-off victory over Doncaster the Cougars' season ended in disappointment when they lost at Dewsbury but that could not detract from a marvellous campaign. Wood amassed nearly 400 points but it was far from a one-man effort with winger Jason Lee and scrum-half Nathan Antonik each scoring over 20 tries with other important contributions from forwards such as Steve Pickles, Jason Ramshaw, Danny Seal and Ian Hughes, who were all regular scorers.

Seal, who dropped out of Super League to re-build his career, was especially impressive and another unsung hero was second row Paul Harrison, the younger brother of the coach.

Keighley's top tryscorer Jason Lee

On the back of an aggressive player-recruitment drive, **DONCASTER DRAGONS** were transformed from last season's bottom club to a final position of third. St John Ellis's team of all the talents made Belle Vue a fortress and only some poor away form cost them an even higher placing. Craig Weston set a new club try-scoring record, while Latham Tawhai and Peter Edwards were other key players.

Weston scored 26 tries and looked a class apart while the New Zealander, Carl Hall, scored 21. With other important contributions from Lynton Stott, Steve Booth, Fata Sini, Tawhai and Neil Bennett, the Dragons were never short of firepower. They scored over 1,000 points in all games much to the delight of Ellis, who will be looking to improve further next season.

The Dragons' season ended in disappointment when they lost at Keighley in the play-offs but their revival in a town crying out for sporting success was one of the fairy tale stories of the season.

LEIGH CENTURIONS moved up one place to fourth despite the disruption caused by the mid-season departure of their coach, Ian Millward, to Saints. The new man, Paul Terzis, came from the same Illawarra background as Millward and quickly set his own mark on the side.

Nineteen year-old hooker Mick Higham was one of the NFP's outstanding talents while Paul Anderson and Simon Baldwin relished playing for their hometown club and Adam Bristow was an important acquisition.

Higham set a new record for tries by a Leigh hooker with 22 while former St Helens three-quarter Alan Cross made the most of the chance to play regular first team football and scored 19 tries.

Fullback Stuart Donlan, Anderson and captain Andy Fairclough also gave Leigh plenty of attacking options while prop forwards Tim Street and Dave Whittle were consistently outstanding in the pack. Terzis made the decision to retain the Australian Bristow as his overseas player for next year and reluctantly was forced to release Heath Cruckshank due to the reduction in quota players and the versatile forward has now joined Sheffield.

FEATHERSTONE ROVERS again finished fifth but this was a remarkable achievement for coach Peter Roe who lost half-a-dozen of his established players during the winter. "We over-achieved this year," Roe admitted. "The younger players, like Jamie Rooney, Stuart Dickens and Jamie Stokes, were our flag bearers this year."

Rooney displayed a maturity far above his years and was a superbly accurate goal-kicker and consistent try-scorer as well as taking on much of the play-making responsibilities from half-back.

Stokes, considered by many to be the best winger in the NFP, scored 23 tries while Dickens developed steadily as an outstanding prop forward prospect.

The Australian fullback, Michael Rhodes, enjoyed a successful first season with Rovers and the other overseas player, Maea David, who has subsequently come off the quota, was a tower of strength up front.

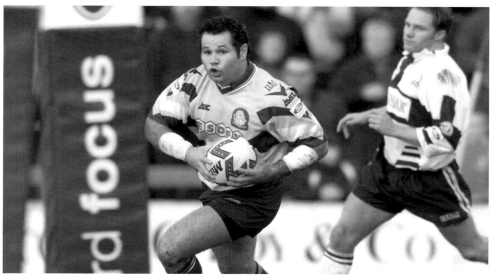

Chipped in with 21 tries - Doncaster's Carl Hall

149

Important acquisition for Leigh - Adam Bristow

OLDHAM matched the revival of Doncaster as player-coach Mike Ford shrewdly rebuilt the fortunes of the famous old club. After returning to Boundary Park, the Roughyeds ended the season in splendid form with Ford the inspiration.

It was pleasing to see the front row of Jason Clegg, Andy Procter, Leo Casey and hooker John Hough earn some reward in a winning side after their sterling efforts during the struggles while Oldham was a club in exile in Rochdale.

Ford still made an important contribution on the field and brought the best out of the many young players developing through the ranks. Of these the Gibbons twins, Anthony and David, were stalwarts and the former Wigan players, Neil Roden and Phil Farrell, made the most of their opportunities.

Fullback Mark Sibson, one of several players that Ford brought with him from Bramley, was an eye-catching attacking force and finished as the Roughyeds' top scorer with 23 tries though the former GB winger Joey Hayes and Hough were not far behind.

Pat Rich developed into a consistent points-scorer and passed the milestone of 100 goals late in the campaign. Ford's shrewdly kept an eye on the student ranks as a rich source of talent and many feel that he is serving a coaching apprenticeship that will end with him in Super League one day.

HULL KR came out of administration and promised a bright future as outstanding centre Whetu Taewa spearheaded a community programme aimed at ensuring the city's talented youngsters forged a career at Craven Park.

Already the seeds are being sown and under the watchful eye of the impressive Dave Harrison, Rovers hopefully laid the foundations for a dynasty in years to come.

With Harrison's departure just before the start of the new NFP season, that dynasty will now be under the watchful eye of former Academy coach Gary Wilkinson. It will be interesting to see quite how many of the promising young players emerge in the next few seasons.

Taewa, considered by many good judges to be the best centre outside Super League, scored 20 tries and the experienced halfback Mark Hewitt kicked over 100 goals. Club stalwarts such as Chris Charles, Mike Dixon and Paul Fletcher all made important contributions in the pack and the experienced Rob Nolan was an important acquisition in the backs. Rovers' fans stuck by the club impressively and were involved in a number of important fund raising ventures while giving their side one of the best away followings in the competition.

Rovers edged above **WIDNES VIKINGS** by virtue of a win in the penultimate game. The Vikings saw David Hulme succeed Colin Whitfield as coach during the campaign and Hulme responded by throwing in the youngsters who promise much for the future. Try-scoring hooker Phil Cantillon enjoyed a wonderful season for the Vikings.

Cantillon set a new record for most tries in a season by a hooker, with 30, and bore the brunt of much of the Vikings' attacking responsibilities. Damian Munro, Steve Gee and Paul Mansson were also regular scorers.

Hulme is determined to have a tilt at winning the NFP next year and has made several important acquisitions as he looks to build a Widnes side fit to grace probably the best stadium outside Super League and many people feel that the Vikings will be the team to beat.

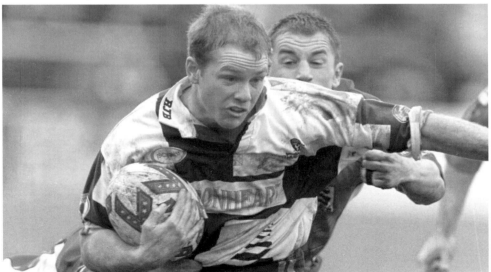

Succesful first season - Featherstone's Michael Rhodes

Northern Ford Premiership

An impressive early season win at Leigh marked **SWINTON** out as potential champions but the Lions slipped out of the picture and missed out on the top-eight as they never achieved any degree of consistency despite having a basis of players with Super League experience. Scrum-half Ian Watson again earned a bag full of man of the match awards, but subsequently left the club to join Widnes.

Phil Coussons was a top try-scorer with 18 with Andy Craig, Jason Roach and Paul Smith each accounted for 16.

Experienced professionals Ian Pickavance, Jon Neill and Paul Loughlin formed the backbone of the Lions side but, faced with the departure of several of his key players in the close season, coach Mike Gregory faces a daunting task to keep Swinton as a competitive force.

BARROW missed out on the play-offs for the simple reason that their away form was in direct contrast to that at home. At Craven Park the Border Raiders lost only two games but they won only two on their travels. The second row pairing of Stuart Rhodes and Geoff Luxon was explosive and halfbacks Darren Holt and Tane Manihera continued to shine.

Holt kicked over 100 goals and continued to develop as a play-maker while winger Glen Hutton finished top try-scorer with 17. The experienced Australian Rod Maybon, made an important contribution in the second half of the season and he will be back at Craven Park for another year when the coach, Paul Charlton, will be hoping that his side can banish their away-day blues.

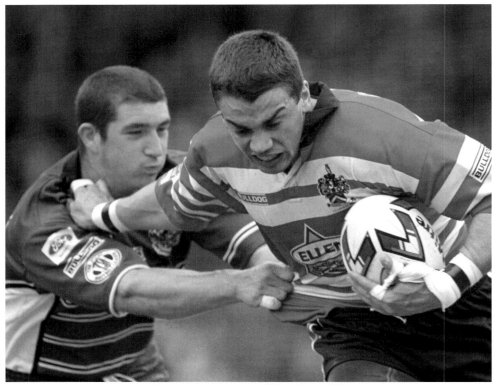

Consistent pointscorer - Oldham's Pat Rich

Top quality centre - Hull KR's Whetu Taewa

WHITEHAVEN WARRIORS edged above their great rivals, **WORKINGTON TOWN**, on points difference as former Kiwi warrior Kevin Tamati bowed out as coach. Tamati gave youth its fling and his successor, Paul Cullen, should derive the benefit, while Kiwi hooker Aaron Lester was again impressive.

The Purdham brothers, Garry and Rob, both looked to be accomplished players in the making and typified the depth of amateur talent on the West Cumbrian coast. Other youngsters such as Alan Bone, Dean Vaughan and Craig Walsh also made the most of their first team opportunities.

The experienced David Seeds finished as top scorer with 14 tries and halfback Lee Kiddie had a consistent season alongside the experienced Wayne Kitchin. Gary Murdock began to re-build Town's fortunes on his vast knowledge of local talent boosted by a handful of experienced players from outside. Centre Steve McGrady was a stand-out alongside Matt Sturm and Dave Watson.

Leigh Smith was top scorer for Town with 16 tries while the former England international, Paul Cook, took his accurate marksmanship to Derwent Park and finished just short of 100 goals. As with Whitehaven, Town's away form was often in direct contrast to that they displayed at home and this will be something that Murdock will be looking to address if they are to challenge for a play-off position.

Regular scorer - Widnes' Paul Mansson

ROCHDALE HORNETS suffered from a huge injury list but they had several outstanding players, notably young forwards Danny Sculthorpe and Darren Robinson and Australian halfbacks Dane Dorahy and Jason Demetriou.

Dorahy, who got a brief chance in Super League with Wakefield after the NFP season finished, threatened to be the outstanding player in the competition in the early weeks before his progress was hampered by injury. The developing Robinson was top scorer for Hornets with 15 tries and the centre-paring of Sean Cooper and Scott Martin each contributed 12. Danny Wood was the top points-scorer having taken over the goal-kicking role from Dorahy during the season. Sculthorpe looked to be one of the best prop forwards outside competition with an impressive array of creative skills.

When Hornets' Australian coach, Steve Linnane left the club to join Halifax as assistant to Gary Mercer, Hornets appointed Steve Deakin as his replacement. But Deakin left the club to take over from Karl Harrison at Keighley, without taking charge of a competitive game, and so the experienced hooker Martin Hall will now take up the senior coaching role at Spotland.

Hornets' ground sharing partnership with the Town's football side has resulted in them having a very impressive stadium that puts many Super League venues to shame.

154

Gained plenty of man of the match awards - Swinton's Ian Watson

SHEFFIELD EAGLES were revived under their passionate player-coach Mark Aston and earned a highly creditable 19 points after only getting the green light weeks before the season began. Chris Morley, Dave Larder and Gavin Brown prospered in a side that should be a top-eight hope next year.

Though Aston's appearances on the field were restricted by injury, his enthusiasm and willingness to surmount all obstacles placed in his way won him tremendous respect throughout the game. The Eagles suffered from a lack of fire-power and not one of their players reached the 10-try mark during the campaign with Neil Kite top scorer with 9. Though Morley and Larder have subsequently left the club, Aston will benefit from having a longer preparation time for the new NFP season. But he realises that the Eagles' revival will be a long haul after the lessons of the demise of Super League in the city have been fully absorbed. With a stalwart supporter base and some impressive community initiatives, the Eagles look to be on the way back.

Kicked over 100 goals - Barrow's Darren Holt

HUNSLET HAWKS felt the disappointment of missing out on a Super League place and most of their Grand Final-winning side departed in a cost-saving measure.

Player-coach David Plange threw in the youngsters and was rewarded with some promising displays, while older heads Shaun Irwin, Steve Pryce and Willie Swann held things together.

Swann, who played for Samoa in the World Cup, has subsequently joined Leigh and his departure will leave a huge gap for Plange to fill.

Chris Ross was a top scorer for the Hawks with 12 tries and 72 goals but impressive hooker Richard Pachniuk missed nearly half of the season through injury and was unable to repeat his try-scoring exploits of the previous campaign. Plange used 43 players during the season but will have learnt much from the campaign and he remains one of the best of the new breed of English coaches.

Whitehaven's experienced Wayne Kitchin pops over a goal

BATLEY BULLDOGS have appointed a new coach in Jon Sharp to succeed David Ward after a season in which the Bulldogs were competitive despite their lowly league placing. Fullback Craig Lingard and halfback Richard Price were the mainstays.

Lingard finished as top try-scorer with 19 while Price topped the points tally with 155 in all games. Winger Paul Gleadhill scored 16 tries and was consistent throughout while forward Paul Hicks produced some superb defensive stints in a pack in which John Clarke and Dave Luckwell were other stand-outs. The very existence of Rugby League was threatened in the Minster City of **YORK** but fortunately the Wasps lived to fight another day.

After coach Dean Robinson's departure, the long-serving Garry Atkins took over until the end of the year. Lee Crooks has subsequently taken on the head-coaching role. Kiwi forward Michael Smith, captain Alan Pallister and the on-loan Gareth Dobson provided some of the brighter moments. Craig Booth and Mark Cain each finished top of the Wasps' scoring ranks with nine apiece, though both had left the club before the season's end. The Hill brothers, Andy and Steve, Rich Hayes and Spencer Hargrave were stand-outs in a pack that competed with the best in the NFP despite the club's lowly position.

Accuarate kicking - Workington's Paul Cook

It was a season of despair for **LANCASHIRE LYNX** who managed only one win, ironically against former Lynx manager Tamati's Whitehaven. Former Great Britain coach Maurice Bamford succeeded Steve Hampson mid-season as coach but Lynx ended the year with a run of 24 straight defeats and used 72 players during the season.

Skipper David Jones and forward Paul Norton deserved medals for their loyalty and perseverance in a disappointing season for the Lynx. With the club cuttings its ties with Preston North End plc and re-forming as Chorley Lynx during the close season, the Kiwi legend, Graeme West, and Dennis Ramsdale will be hoping for better times ahead in the new season.

Outstanding young talent - Rochdale's Danny Sculthorpe

Prospered - Sheffield's Chris Morley

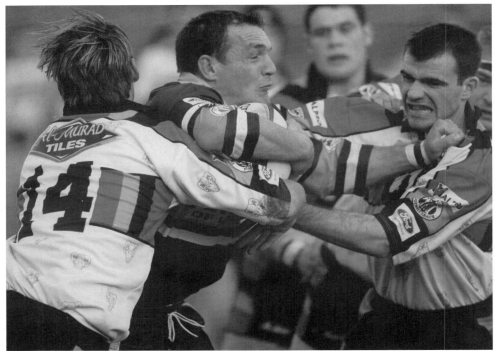

Held things together - Hunslet's Shaun Irwin

Consistent throughout - Batley's Paul Gleadhill

Provided brighter moments for York - Gareth Dobson

Jason Demetriou turned in impressive showings for Lancashire before departing to Rochdale

NFP Grand Final

DEWSBURY RAMS 13...LEIGH CENTURIONS 12
Played at Gigg Lane, Bury, Saturday 29 July 2000

RICHARD AGAR'S dramatic winning field-goal with just 134 seconds remaining on the clock made the sweetest music for the victorious Rams coach, Neil Kelly.

The NFP coach of the year was able to experience entirely different emotions after the despair of losing to Hunslet at Headingley in the grand final last year, when a field goal was again all that separated the sides.

"The field goal was like listening to a symphony, it was absolutely superb," said Kelly.

"We deserved it today and for our performances over the season."

Agar, one of ten survivors from last season's Grand Final side, kept the coolest head in the frenzied closing minutes with the scores locked at 12-12.

There was a certain inevitability about the winner after a costly knock-on by the Leigh scrum-half, Kieron Purtill, 40 metres out.

The Rams worked their way into a position for Barry Eaton to try his luck at a one-pointer only for the alert Liam Bretherton to charge down the effort.

But, as referee Robert Connolly waved 'play on', the Leigh second row forward, Simon Baldwin, was just unable to grasp a loose ball and conceded a scrum feed close to his own line.

On the fourth tackle, the 28 year old Agar received from Dan Potter at dummy-half and wrote himself into Dewsbury folklore with his angled twelve-metre clincher.

"I have struck the ball better, it was a bit of a sand iron," Agar grinned afterwards."

Ironically, Agar thought his season was over when he broke his hand in the penultimate game of the regular season.

But after missing three games, including Leigh's double success over the Rams in the final league game and first play-off game, he returned for the major semi-final against Keighley where his influence on the Rams side was immediately demonstrated.

The Centurions had only tears for souvenirs and the small consolation of their outstanding 19 year old hooker, Mick Higham, being a clear winner of the Tom Bergin Trophy as man of the match.

Higham's two tries spearheaded Leigh's revival from 10-0 down and helped him establish a new club record for tries in a season by a hooker, with 22.

As expected Leigh brought Simon Baldwin back into the side after his one-match suspension with the injured Phil Kendrick missing out.

The Rams were unchanged from the 17 that beat the Cougars so convincingly in the and looked far more assured in the opening stages as Leigh's ball control, so impressive in recent games, let them down.

Crucial mistakes cost Leigh dear as Purtill and Adam Bristow were left clutching at thin air as Daniel Frame exploded down the right channel from Eaton's pass.

The record-breaking Rams scrum-half was in support to take Frame's inside

Dewsbury's Adrian Flynn collared by Leigh's Paul Anderson

pass and complete a 60-metre move for a converted try after only 118 seconds.

The tendency of several Leigh forwards to tackle high was exposed when the Rams sub, Matthew Long, seconds after taking the field, scored with his first touch.

After the Leigh winger, Alan Cross, had fumbled a raking Agar kick to set up a ten-metre scrum, Long took Eaton's pass on the second tackle to plough his way over despite the attentions of three defenders.

But Higham, who was a constant menace around the ruck, pulled his side back into contention with his first try after Frame fumbled a Bristow grubber kick.

The Leigh prop, Tim Street, seized on the opportunity and twisted in a two-man tackle to send the supporting Higham scampering over with Bretherton converting.

Leigh could consider themselves fortunate to only trail by four points at the interval. But they fell six points behind when Eaton kicked a 64th minute penalty from 21 metres after Street, who had just returned to the field, was pulled up for ball stealing on Shayne Williams in a two-man tackle.

Opposing props Williams and Dave Whittle each received ten minutes in the sin bin after Whittle retaliated angrily to a raised elbow.

Earlier the Rams second row Sean Richardson was placed on report for a lunging high tackle on Stuart Donlan, the Leigh fullback.

But it took a double piece of magic by Higham to haul Leigh level and set up that tense final ten minutes.

It was Higham's shuddering tackle that dislodged the ball from Richard Baker's grasp as the Rams winger tried to clear his lines.

And in the subsequent Leigh attack, Higham showed his alertness from dummy-half to plunge between Eaton and Mark Haigh for his second try, that Bretherton again converted.

RAMS: 1 Nathan Graham (C); 2 Richard Baker; 4 Dan Potterl 3 Brendan O'Meara; 5 Adrian Flynn; 6 Richard Agar; 7 Barry Eaton; 8 Shayne Williams; 9 David Mycoe; 10 Mark Haigh; 11 Sean Richardson; 12 Daniel Frame; 13 Damian Ball *Subs:* 14 Gavin Wood not used; 15 Paul Delaney for Mycoe (53); 16 Ryan McDonald for Haigh (30); 17 Matthew Long for Williams (23); Haigh for McDonald (64)
Tries: Eaton (2), Long (23); **Goals:** Eaton 2; **Field goal:** Agar
Sin bin: Williams (66) - raised elbow in possession
On report: Richardson (20) - high tackle on Donlan

CENTURIONS: 1 Stuart Donlan; 5 David Ingram; 3 Paul Anderson; 4 Andy Fairclough (C); 2 Alan Cross; 6 Liam Bretherton; 7 Kieron Purtill; 8 Tim Street; 9 Mick Higham; 10 Andy Leathem; 11 Simon Baldwin; 12 Heath Cruckshank; 13 Adam Bristow. *Subs:* 14 James Arkwright for Cross (68); 15 Paul Norman for Street (36); 16 Radney Bowker not used; 17 Dave Whittle for Leathem (24); Street for Norman (62)
Tries: Higham (29, 69); **Goals:** Bretherton 2
Sin bin: Whittle (66) - retaliation

League Express Men of the Match
Rams: Richard Agar; **Centurions:** Mick Higham
Penalties: 4-4; **HT:** 10-6; **Referee:** Robert Connolly (Wigan)
Attendance: 8,487

THE PLAY-OFFS...

PRELIMINARY SEMI FINALS
Dewsbury 12 Leigh 29
Keighley 44 Doncaster 22

ELIMINATION SEMI FINALS
Featherstone 43 Widnes 24
Oldham 22 Hull KR 14

MINOR SEMI FINALS
Dewsbury 25 Featherstone 18
Doncaster 17 Oldham 24 (aet)

MAJOR SEMI FINALS
Dewsbury 38 Keighley 12
Leigh 18 Oldham 10

Gigg Lane was a splendid venue for a final that was perfectly staged with the colourful Leigh fans in the majority in the 8,487 crowd that created a real sense of occasion.

GAMEBREAKER: Richard Agar's late, winning field goal was a dramatic way to decide a grand final.

GAMESTAR: Mick Higham scored two tries and was Leigh's inspiration throughout.

TOP TACKLE: The tackle by Higham on Richard Baker that set up the position for Higham to score his second try.

5
INTERNATIONAL SCENE

SEASON DOWN UNDER

A Hollywood wordsmith couldn't have scripted the finish to the 2000 season Down Under better.

The game's popular little hero, Kevin Walters, was about to retire. The 2000 grand final would be his farewell appearance in Australia.

It would come after a couple of seasons in which he put aside the personal anguish that followed the death of his wife (and mother to their three young children) through cancer to become an inspiration for a Brisbane Broncos side that was rebuilding.

And four of his teammates would be playing their last match for Brisbane in the grand final, too.

Brad Thorn was going to try his luck in rugby union in his native land of New Zealand. The others were off to finish their careers in Britain - substitute winger-cum-back-rower Michael Hancock with Salford City, centre Tonie Carroll with Leeds and loose forward Kevin Campion with Warrington. Hancock was the last of those who played in the Broncos' debut game back in 1988.

Only a few can ever hope to finish with a grand final success. Among those who had were Ray Price and Mick Cronin, who managed it with Parramatta in 1986. Mal Meninga did likewise in 1994.

After the controversial eight-team playoffs, it was only fair that the two sides who topped the Premiership table after the 26 rounds of home-and-away matches should fight out the season's finale.

The Broncos were up against the Sydney Roosters, who were making their first grand final appearance since they were runners up to Canterbury in 1980.

That they had made it after two decades of disappointment had a lot to do with their recruitment of former Leeds Rhinos' coach Graham Murray, who provided a fresh outlook at Bondi Junction.

The Broncos lived up to their pre-match favouritism with a solid, if unspectacular, 14-6 victory. It was their third Premiership in four seasons and their fifth in the past nine years, confirming them as one of the great clubs of the modern era.

Walters wept openly as he hugged coach Wayne Bennett after the game.

"I don't normally believe in fairytales," he said. "But this is a fairytale ending. This was the ultimate finish."

After 14 seasons, 292 games for Brisbane and 11 Tests and two Kangaroo tours (1990 and 1994) it most certainly was the ultimate finish for Kevvie, only the fourth regular captain of Brisbane after Wally Lewis, Gene Miles and Allan Langer.

Brisbane's Lote Tuqiri touches down for a try against Sydney Roosters in the Grand Final

"There were a lot of tears at the end of the game knowing that five of the guys were leaving," said Bennett. "They have been a very special group and this has been a very special team.

"What a winner he (Walters) was. What an exceptional player he was. But I always knew that."

Bennett had warned his players before kick-off not to go out trying to win the grand final for the five who were departing.

"Do it for yourselves," he said. And they did.

The Broncos held a significant 10-2 lead at the break and held it all together in the second half.

Walters was inspirational.

But it was the two backs who were to be chosen in the World Cup squad, Darren Lockyer and Wendell Sailor, who stood out. Lockyer was to win the coveted Clive Churchill Medal as Man of the Match.

"What a dream come true," he said after becoming only the second fullback (after Newcastle's Robbie O'Davis in 1997) to be awarded the trophy named after the greatest fullback in Australian history. "Claiming the medal caps off a very special day."

Laurie Daley leaves the field with Brad Fittler following his last game

Had the Broncos not won, it is almost certain that the judges would have leaned to the Roosters' fullback Luke Phillips.

He had had no less than 21 pain-killing injections on injured ribs in the previous 10 days - just to ensure he made it onto the field. But everything Phillips did, either in attack or in defence (where he saved what looked like being two certain tries) had a stamp of class about it.

Englishman Harvey Howard capped a remarkable comeback from playing for Toowoomba, Brisbane's feeder club in the Queensland competition, to be one of the Broncos' best.

The disappointment of the season was the failure of any of the merged clubs to make it though to the playoffs.

Wests Tigers had looked good early in the season, losing only two of their first 10 matches. But then they plunged from second spot to finish 10th. And coach Wayne Pearce departed soon after the end of the season to be replaced by Terry Lamb, who still holds the record for the most number of senior games by any player in Australian history.

St George Illawarra, which the previous season had made the grand final, finished ninth. And, when overlooked as coach in 2001, David Waite, left early to accept a role in the English coaching leadership.

Northern Eagles (12th) was a real disappointment and ended the year with the Norths and Manly factions on the board bickering.

Kevin Walters was not the only player to wrap up his distinguished career in 2000.

Among the others, who could not boast the same fairytale finish as Walters, were:

● Laurie Daley (Canberra Raiders): The former Australian captain and stand-off (26 Tests between 1990 and 1999) bowed out in the 38-10 defeat by the Roosters in the elimination semi-finals. He had played 234 senior games for Canberra, scoring 445 points. He was in the Raiders' Premiership-winning sides of 1989, 1990 and 1994.

● Andrew Ettingshausen (Sharks): One of the select few in the '300 Club' with a club record of 328 senior appearances since debuting for Cronulla in 1983. He also finished with a club record of 165 tries. And twice he scored a club best of five tries in a match. He played 29 Tests from 1990 to 1997. ET wound up 2000 on a promotional swing through the country areas with Daley on what was dubbed the 'Good Guys Tour'.

● Tony Butterfield (Newcastle Knights): The last of the original Knights, having joined the fledgling side in the debut year of 1988 after two seasons with Penrith. He never played for Australia, but had a significant career with 233 senior appearances and was Newcastle captain for his last two seasons.

● Mark Geyer (Penrith Panthers): One of the most controversial players of the modern era. This firebrand appeared before the judiciary on no less than nine occasions during his 15-season career, resulting in a total of 34 weeks suspension. He played 176 first-grade games for the Panthers, Balmain Tigers and Western Reds and three Tests for Australia (1990-91).

● Daryl Halligan (Bulldogs): The former-Kiwi international retired after 10 seasons of Premiership battle, with North Sydney and the Bulldogs, taking with him a new pointscoring record. He passed Mick Cronin's old mark of 1,971 in the Round 20 match against Canberra and finished the season with a tally 2,034. In 1998 Halligan also beat Cronin's long-standing record of 28 consecutive successful attempts at goal. Halligan's Bulldogs' records - most points in career (1,490), most points in a season (270 in 1994), most in a match (28 twice) and most goals in a match (10 on three occasions). He also played 20 Tests for New Zealand (1992-98).

As the 2000 season ended, the Auckland Warriors were fighting for financial survival.

In their six seasons they had never matched the expectations of their fans. While the Kiwis offered a serious challenge to Australia in the Test arena, the Warriors rarely extended the top Australian clubs.

Their best effort was in their inaugural season when they finished 10th of the 20 teams, missing the playoffs only on points difference. In 1996 they were 11th (of 20), in the 1997 Super League 7th (of 10), in 1998 they finished 15th (out of 20), 1999 it was an 11th place finish (from 17) and in 2000 second last (of 14 teams).

Internal dissension didn't help as the majority shareholder, the Tainui Maori tribe, fought with fellow owners.

Eventually the club went broke.

And a consortium involving the NZRL and entrepreneur Eric Watson was given the licence for the new-look New Zealand Warriors to compete in the 2001 NRL Premiership.

But the players were left out of pocket for much of their 2000 season salaries.

The decision to allow a change of ownership angered the supporters of South Sydney which had taken the NRL to court in an effort to get reinstated to the elite competition.

In early November Souths lost their case. Justice Paul Finn of Australia's Federal Court refused to accept any of the Rabbitohs' arguments that they had been unfairly treated when axed from the competition at the end of the previous year.

Because of the intense public interest, Justice Finn took the unusual step of allowing live television coverage of his five-minute summary of the 180-page written judgement. It was unusual because Australian judges rarely allow cameras into their courts.

But Justice Finn realised the public concern about his decision.

He quoted from correspondence tabled by South Sydney in which the Rabbitohs argued: "In our view Rugby League is an icon to be preserved for the people who love and support it, not a product to be carved up to the media for their own financial gratification."

Justice Finn replied: "It usually is only fortuitous that some legal principle can be found that could provide such preservation as is sought...This is not one of the fortuitous cases."

The learned judge's decision would hardly be everyone's bedtime reading. The legal jargon - just like his brief summary to the television cameras - was virtually incomprehensible to the layman.

Suffice to say, Souths may have had the public sentiment behind their bid, but not one point of law was in their favour.

But while the Rabbitohs may have been skinned and ready for the cooking pot they refused to stop twitching. Outspoken club chairman George Piggins immediately called for a protest march through Sydney the following Sunday.

And 80,000 fans heeded his call. Not just South Sydney fans, but supporters of other clubs no longer in the big league - Western Suburbs, Balmain, North Sydney, Manly, Illawarra, St George and Newtown.

But still the NRL refused to budge on the South Sydney issue - as the Rabbitohs prepared to take the whole issue back to the Appeal Court.

It wasn't only South Sydney that had gone missing.

The end of the season saw a mass exodus of top players to Super League Europe for the 2001 season.

The strict enforcement of the salary cap meant that the NRL clubs could not match the big money being offered to veteran stars.

What money that was on offer had to be spent on current Test players and up-and-coming youngsters.

The result was the splitting - for the first time in their rugby career - of the Newcastle brothers, Matthew and Andrew Johns. The Knights did not even bother to make an offer to stand-off Matthew, who was snapped up by the Wigan

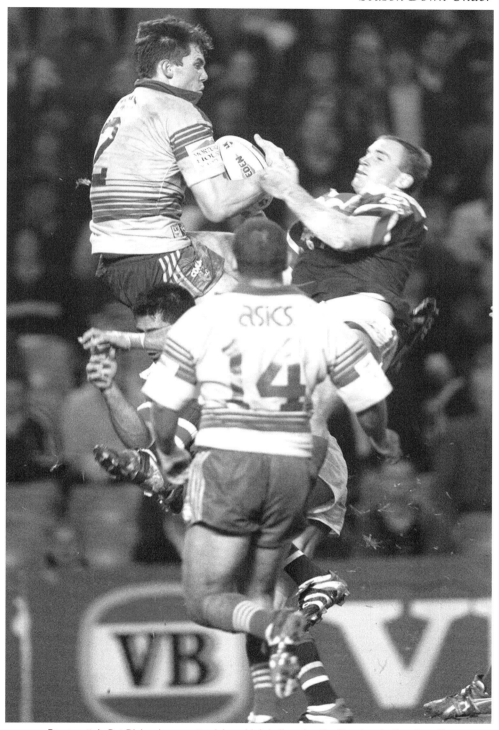

Parramatta's Pat Richards soars to claim a high ball agains the Roosters in the play-offs

Warriors. But Andrew turned his back on a massive offer from Wigan (and temptations from other British clubs and rugby union) to stay on with the Knights.

Matthew Johns was just one of 13 internationals to leave NRL clubs for greener pastures in the northern hemisphere. Between them they could boast a total of 134 Test appearances.

Many were near the end of their careers. But there were two of the World Cup captains - Richie Barnett (New Zealand) and Adrian Lam (Papua New Guinea).

Bulldog Jason Hetherington had played for Australia and Auckland Warrior Joe Vagana for the Kiwis in the Anzac Test and the World Cup. And Canberra's David Furner had been in Australia's World Cup 'train-on' squad.

The absence of every one of them would be sorely felt in the 2001 NRL Premiership.

THE 2001 BRITISH RECRUITS

BRADFORD BULLS: Joe Vagana (Auckland Warriors); Shane Rigon (Sydney Roosters); Daniel Gartner (Northern Eagles
CASTLEFORD TIGERS: Mitch Healey (Sharks)
HULL FC: Jason Smith (Parramatta Eels)
LEEDS RHINOS: Tonie Carroll (Brisbane Broncos); Bradley Clyde (Bulldogs); Brett Mullins (Canberra Raiders)
LONDON BRONCOS: Richie Barnett (Sydney Roosters); Jim Dymock (Parramatta Eels); Jason Hetherington (Bulldogs); Tony Martin (Melbourne Storm); Nigel Roy (Northern Eagles)
ST HELENS: David Fairleigh (Newcastle Knights)' Peter Shiels (Newcastle Knights)
SALFORD CITY REDS: Michael Hancock (Brisbane Broncos)
WARRINGTON WOLVES: Kevin Campion (Brisbane Broncos); David Kidwell (Parramatta Eels)
WIGAN WARRIORS: David Furner (Canberra Raiders); Matthew Johns (Newcastle Knights); Adrian Lam (Sydney Roosters)

Jubliant Wayne Bennett meets Brisbane fans after the Broncos' Grand Final win

NRL FINAL TABLE

	P	W	D	L	F	A	Pts
Brisbane Broncos	26	18	2	6	696	388	38
Sydney Roosters	26	16	0	10	601	520	32
Newcastle Knights	26	15	1	10	686	532	31
Canberra Raiders	26	15	0	11	506	479	30
Penrith Panthers	26	15	0	11	573	562	30
Melbourne Storm	26	14	1	11	672	529	29
Parramatta Eels	26	14	1	11	476	456	29
Sharks	26	13	0	13	570	463	26
St George-Illawarra Dragons	26	12	0	14	576	656	24
Wests Tigers	26	11	2	14	519	642	24
Bulldogs	26	10	1	15	469	553	21
Northern Eagles	26	9	0	17	476	628	18
Auckland Warriors	26	8	2	16	426	662	18
North Queensland Cowboys ●	26	7	0	19	436	612	12

● *two points deducted for interchange breach*

QUALIFYING FINALS

CANBERRA RAIDERS 34 ....**PENRITH PANTHERS 16**
Raiders: T - J Croker 2, J Lolesi, B Finch, T Payten, A McFadden; G - D Furner 5
Panthers: T - R Girdler, M Rodwell; G - R Girdler 4
Half-time: 12-16; **Referee:** Steve Clark
Attendance: 18,479 *at Bruce Stadium on August 4*

NEWCASTLE KNIGHTS 30 ....**MELBOURNE STORM 16**
Knights: T - A MacDougall, M Gidley, M Hughes, T Tahu, D Buderus; G - A Johns 5
Storm: T - T Martin, B Kimmorley; G - T Lavea 3, B Watts
Half-time: 8-10; **Referee:** Tim Mander
Attendance: 20,597 *at Marathon Stadium on August 5*

SYDNEY ROOSTERS 8 ....**PARRAMATTA EELS 32**
Roosters: T - R Cross; G - C Fitzgibbon 2
Eels: T - P Richards, D Vaealiki, PJ Marsh, D Moran; G - C Schifcofske 6
Half-time: 8-10; **Referee:** Bill Harrigan
Attendance: 21,377 *at SFS on August 5*

BRISBANE BRONCOS 34...**SHARKS 20**
Broncos: T - B Ikin 2, G Tallis 2, L Tuqiri, S Berrigan; G - D Lockyer 5
Sharks: T - A Dykes, S Donato, B Howland, P Mellor; G - M Rogers 2
Half-time: 6-20; **Referee:** Paul Simpkins
Attendance: 25,831 *at ANZ Stadium on August 6*

SEMI-FINALS

PARRAMATTA EELS 28 ....**PENRITH PANTHERS 10**
Eels: T - J Moodie, I Hindmarsh, D Moran, S Kelly; G - C Schifcofske 6
Panthers: T - R Beckett, J Cross; G - R Girdler
Half-time: 10-10; **Referee:** Bill Harrigan
Attendance: 25,746 *at SFS on August 12*

SYDNEY ROOSTERS 38 ....**CANBERRA RAIDERS 10**
Roosters: T - R Cross 2, A Minichiello 2, M Sing, C Wing; G - L Phillips 5, C Fitzgibbon 2
Raiders: T - M McLinden, L Vainikolo; G - D Furner
Hal-time: 12-0; **Referee:** Tim Mander
Attendance: 16,441 *at SFS on August 13*

PRELIMINARY FINALS

SYDNEY ROOSTERS 26 ....**NEWCASTLE KNIGHTS 20**
Roosters: T - L Phillips, R Cross, S Hegarty, B Fittler; G - C Fitzgibbon 5
Knights: T - D Albert, M Hughes, T Tahu, A Johns; G - A Johns 2
Half-time: 2-16; **Referee:** Bill Harrigan
Attendance: 33,727 *at SFS on August 19*

BRISBANE BRONCOS 16.....................................**PARRAMATTA EELS 10**
Broncos: T - D Lockyer, G Tallis, B Thorn; G - M De Vere 2
Eels: T - L Burt, J Moodie; G - C Schifcofske
Half time: 12-0; **Referee:** Tim Mander
Attendance: 31,087 *at Stadium Australia on August 20*

GRAND FINAL

BRISBANE BRONCOS 14 ....**SYDNEY ROOSTERS 6**

BRONCOS: 1 Darren Lockyer; 2 Lote Tuqiri; 3 Tonie Carroll; 4 Michael De Vere; 5 Wendell Sailor; 6 Ben Ikin; 7 Kevin Walters (C); 8 Shane Webcke; 9 Luke Priddis; 10 Dane Carlaw; 11 Gorden Tallis; 12 Brad Thorn; 13 Kevin Campion. *Subs:* 14 Harvey Howard; 16 Michael Hancock; 17 Shaun Berrigan; 18 Ashley Harrison
Tries: Tuqiri (17), Sailor (55); **Goals:** De Vere 3

ROOSTERS: 1 Luke Phillips; 2 Matt Sing; 3 Ryan Cross; 4 Shannon Hegarty; 5 Anthony Minichiello; 6 Brad Fittler (C); 7 Adrian Lam; 8 Ian Rubin; 9 Simon Bonetti; 10 Peter Cusack; 11 Bryan Fletcher; 12 Craig Fitzgibbon; 13 Luke Ricketson. *Subs:* 14 Dallas Hood; 15 David Solomona; 16 Shane Rigon; 17 Craig Wing
Try: Fitzgibbon (70); **Goal:** Phillips
Half-time: 10-2; **Referee:** Bill Harrigan; **Video referee:** John Gocher
Clive Churchill Medal (Man of the Match): Darren Lockyer *(Broncos)*
Attendance: 94,277 *at Stadium Australia on August 27*

THE 2000 SEASON'S RECORDS

LEADING POINTSCORERS

	T	G	FG	Pts
Joel Caine (Tigers)	15	82	0	224
Mat Rogers (Sharks)	18	70	0	212
Ryan Girdler (Panthers)	13	78	2	210
Daryl Halligan (Bulldogs)	7	88	0	204
Andrew Johns (Knights)	8	84	0	200
Michael De Vere (Broncos)	12	74	0	196
Tasesa Lavea (Storm)	7	81	0	190
Craig Fitzgibbon (Roosters)	5	77	0	174

LEADING TRYSCORERS

Nathan Blacklock (Dragons)	25
Timana Tahu (Knights)	20
Ryan Cross (Roosters)	18
Shannon Hegarty (Roosters)	18
Mat Rogers (Sharks)	18
Wendell Sailor (Broncos)	18
Lote Tuqiri (Broncos)	17

LARGEST CROWDS (Home & Away matches)

62,255	Roosters v Eels/Dragons v Sharks	Stadium Australia
29,849	Broncos v Storm	ANZ Stadium
27,643	Cowboys v Broncos	Dairy Farmers Stadium
27,505	Broncos v Raiders	ANZ Stadium
27,146	Broncos v Newcastle	ANZ Stadium

SMALLEST CROWDS

5,820	Roosters v Cowboys	SFS
6,000	Warriors v Raiders	Ericsson Stadium
6,024	Dragons v Cowboys	WIN Stadium
6,106	Eagles v Warriors	Brookvale Oval
6,572	Bulldogs v Cowboys	Stadium Australia

MOST POINTS IN A MATCH

26	Mat Rogers (Sharks) v Knights ●	Toyota Park
24	Tasesa Lavea (Storm) v Dragons	MCG
24	Michael De Vere (Broncos) v Panthers ●	ANZ Stadium
24	Michael De Vere (Broncos) v Dragons ●	WIN Stadium

● *equal club record*

MOST TRIES IN A MATCH

4	Darren Albert (Knights) v Tigers ●	Marathon Stadium
4	Matt Geyer (Storm) v Warriors	Olympic Park
4	Albert Torrens (Eagles) v Bulldogs ●	Brookvale Oval
4	Craig Gower (Panthers) v Eagles	Penrith Stadium

● *club record*

MOST GOALS IN A MATCH

9	Julian O'Neill (Cowboys) v Eagles	Dairy Farmers Stadium
9	Julian O'Neill (Cowboys) v Dragons	Dairy Farmers Stadium
9	Amos Roberts (Dragons) v Warriors ●	WIN Stadium

● *Premiership record for debut match*

BIGGEST WINS

60 pts	Storm 70 d Dragons 10	MCG
54 pts	Dragons 54 d Warriors 0	WIN Stadium
46 pts	Cowboys 50 d Dragons 4	Dairy Farmers Stadium
46 pts	Dragons 50 d Storm 4	WIN Stadium
46pts	Storm 56 d Warriors 10	Olympic Park

MOST TACKLES IN A MATCH

55	Logan Swann (Warriors) v Broncos	
52	Luke Priddis (Broncos) v Panthers	
51	Simon Bonetti (Roosters) v Knights	
49	Luke Priddis (Broncos) v Roosters	
48	Richard Swain (Storm) v Cowboys	

FASTEST TRIES

50sec	Chris McKenna (Sharks) v Dragons	Toyota Park
1min 19sec	Tasesa Lavea (Storm) v Broncos	ANZ Stadium
1min 19sec	Darren Smith (Bulldogs) v Storm	Olympic Park
1min 25sec	Brad Thorn (Broncos) v Tigers	ANZ Stadium
1min 29sec	Richard Villasanti (Tigers) v Knights	Campbelltown Stadium

DALLY M AWARDS

Player of the Year: Trent Barrett (Dragons)
Coach of the Year: Wayne Bennett (Broncos)
Rookie of the Year: Tasesa Lavea (Storm)
Captain of the Year: Kevin Walters (Broncos)
Representative Player of the Year: Ryan Girdler (Panthers)
Provan-Summons Medal (Fans' Choice): Andrew Johns (Knights)
Top votes in each position:
Fullback - David Peachey (Sharks); Winger - Nathan Blacklock (Dragons); Centre - Ryan Girdler (Panthers); Stand-off - Trent Barrett (Dragons); Scrum half - Brett Kimmorley (Storm); Prop - Shane Webcke (Broncos); Hooker - Craig Gower (Panthers); Second-rower - Nathan Hindmarsh (Eels); Loose-forward - Jason Croker (Raiders)

INDIVIDUAL CLUBS' PLAYERS OF THE YEAR

Auckland Warriors: Robert Mears; Brisbane Broncos: Wendell Sailor; Bulldogs: Hazem El Masri; Canberra Raiders: Jason Croker; Melbourne Storm: Rodney Howe; Newcastle Knights: David Fairleigh; Northern Eagles: Adam Muir; North Qld Cowboys: Julian O'Neill & Paul Bowman; Parramatta Eels: Nathan Hindmarsh; Penrith Panthers: Craig Gower; Sharks: David Peachey; St Geo Illawarra Dragons: Trent Barrett; Sydney Roosters: Brad Fittler; Wests Tigers: Tyran Smith

173

STATE OF ORIGIN

WHEN NSW ran up a record score in the third State of Origin clash of 2000 for a clean sweep in the series there were cries of anguish in the media.

Journalists and commentators alike expressed fears for the future of Rugby League's annual showpiece.

And Queensland reacted by going back to the future.

The QRL recalled Brisbane Broncos' coach Wayne Bennett (who had steered the Maroons to success in 1999) for the 2001 series - and turned to a new streamlined three-member selection panel.

Yet had a controversial refereeing decision gone Queensland's way in the opening encounter the whole Origin story could have unfolded in an entirely different way.

The Maroons had looked to have that match sewn up when they led with just over 10 minutes remaining.

Then Ryan Girdler levelled the scores at 16-all. But this was only after what seemed to have been a knock-on by NSW substitute Terry Hill early in the movement that led to the try.

Gorden Tallis blew up. He allegedly used four letter words to vent his spleen on referee Bill Harrigan, questioning his impartiality in no uncertain terms.

It was too much for the flamboyant whistle-blower who sent Tallis from the field - only the second player in the 20 years of the Origin to get his marching orders.

The fervent pleadings of Queensland captain Adrian Lam couldn't get Harrigan to change his mind. And one man down, the Queenslanders then saw Blues' fullback David Peachey score the winning try - also after an apparent knock-on.

While almost all of the media reckoned there had been knock-ons, Harrigan publicly stood by his decisions.

Lam noted: "Harrigan missed the knock on (that led to Girdler's try) and Gorden told him so, in no uncertain terms. That (send off) cost us the game."

But as Origin legend Wally Lewis pointed out: "When Bill's on the field, Bill's the boss. And the players have to understand that."

Lam was a real star.

However the player who stole the headlines was NSW winger Adam MacDougall.

ORIGIN 1

NEW SOUTH WALES 20..**QUEENSLAND 16**
Stadium Australia, May 10 2000

NSW: David Peachey (Sharks), Adam MacDougall (Newcastle Knights), Shaun Timmins (St Geo-Illawarra Dragons), Ryan Girdler (Penrith Panthers) Jamie Ainscough (St Geo-Illawarra Dragons), Brad Fittler (Sydney Roosters) (c), Brett Kimmorley (Melbourne Storm), Rodney Howe (Melbourne Storm), Geoff Toovey (Northern Eagles), Robbie Kearns (Melbourne Storm), Ben Kennedy (Newcastle Knights), Bryan Fletcher (Sydney Roosters) & Scott Hill (Melbourne Storm). *Subs:* Terry Hill (Wests Tigers), Michael Vella (Parramatta Eels), David Furner (Canberra Raiders) & Jason Stevens (Sharks).
Tries: MacDougall (22, 47), Girdler (70), Peachey (76); **Goals:** Girdler 2

QUEENSLAND: Darren Lockyer (Brisbane Broncos), Wendell Sailor (Brisbane Broncos), Paul Bowman (North Qld Cowboys), Darren Smith (Bulldogs), Mat Rogers (Sharks), Ben Ikin (Brisbane Broncos), Adrian Lam (Sydney Roosters) (c), Martin Lang (Sharks), Jason Hetherington (Bulldogs), Shane Webcke (Brisbane Broncos), Gorden Tallis (Brisbane Broncos), Brad Thorn (Brisbane Broncos) & Jason Smith (Parramatta Eels). *Subs:* Tonie Carroll (Brisbane Broncos), Paul Green (North Qld Cowboys), Russell Bawden (Melbourne Storm) & Steve Price (Bulldogs).
Tries: Rogers (16), Lam (32, 44); **Goals:** Rogers, Lockyer

League Express Men of the Match
NSW: Adam MacDougall; **Qld:** Adrian Lam
HT: 6-8; **Referee:** Bill Harrigan; **Attendance:** 61,511

Robbie Ross (Melbourne Storm) and Eric Grothe (Parramatta Eels) were originally chosen for NSW but withdrew through injury. They were replaced by Peachey and Ainscough.

The man they have dubbed 'Mad Dog' revealed after the game he had written his hopes for the match on his wristband. It showed 'M.O.M. 3 tries'.

M.O.M. stood for Man of the Match - and he was that. Three tries? Well, he scored two and was denied the hat-trick by a sensational covering tackle by Wendell Sailor.

The Blues wrapped up the Origin series with a 28-10 victory in the second encounter, at Brisbane's Suncorp Stadium (Lang Park).

But it was only after a fairy-tale return to the Origin fray by former Test fullback Tim Brasher, in his first interstate appearance in two years.

He made the side after the late withdrawal through injury of Peachey.

"I've missed four Origin matches…I don't intend missing any more," said the veteran of 19 Origin clashes. It's great to be back. It was hard to sit at home and watch the Origin games on television."

Brasher was brilliant in attack, especially in the second half, and his defence was rock-solid, saving at least two possible Queensland tries.

The Maroons had gone to the break ahead 4-0, thanks to two penalty goals by Mat Rogers. But the game came alive in the second half, with the Blues running in five tries for an easy victory.

The final Origin clash was one in which the Blues rewrote history.

The 56-16 victory by NSW was the biggest since the Origin was first played in 1980. And Ryan Girdler snared every conceivable individual Origin record.

● Most points in a match (32), beating the previous best of 18 by Michael O'Connor, in 1985.

● Most points in a series (52), topping O'Connor's 32 in 1987.

● Most goals in a match (10), beating Mal Meninga's seven in the first Origin game, at Lang Park 20 years earlier.

● Most goals in a series (16), passing Meninga's 13 in 1983.

● Most tries in a match (3), equalling the feats of Chris Anderson (1983) and Kerry Boustead (1984).

● Most tries in a series (5), beating the four by Boustead (1984), Allan Langer (1988) and Dale Shearer (1989).

But perhaps the most significant of all the big scoring feats of the Penrith Panther was his 32 points for the match. This equalled a long-standing record for all interstate matches, set by the man they called 'The Master', Dally Messenger,

ORIGIN 2

QUEENSLAND 10 ....NEW SOUTH WALES 28
Suncorp Stadium, May 24 2000

QUEENSLAND: Darren Lockyer (Brisbane Broncos), Matt Sing (Sydney Roosters), Paul Bowman (North Qld Cowboys), Darren Smith (Bulldogs), Mat Rogers (Sharks), Julian O'Neill (North Qld Cowboys), Adrian Lam (Sydney Roosters) (c), Martin Lang (Sharks), Jason Hetherington (Bulldogs), Shane Webcke (Brisbane Broncos), Gorden Tallis (Brisbane Broncos), Brad Thorn (Brisbane Broncos) & Jason Smith (Parramatta Eels). *Subs:* Tonie Carroll (Brisbane Broncos), Paul Green (North Qld Cowboys), Russell Bawden (Melbourne Storm) & Steve Price (Bulldogs).
Tries: Tallis (50); **Goals:** Rogers 3

NSW: Tim Brasher (North Qld Cowboys), Adam MacDougall (Newcastle Knights), Shaun Timmins (St Geo-Illawarra Dragons), Ryan Girdler (Penrith Panthers) Jamie Ainscough (St Geo-Illawarra Dragons), Brad Fittler (Sydney Roosters) (c), Brett Kimmorley (Melbourne Storm), Rodney Howe (Melbourne Storm), Geoff Toovey (Northern Eagles), Robbie Kearns (Melbourne Storm), Ben Kennedy (Newcastle Knights), Bryan Fletcher (Sydney Roosters) & Scott Hill (Melbourne Storm). *Subs:* Andrew Johns (Newcastle Knights), Adam Muir (Northern Eagles), David Furner (Canberra Raiders) & Jason Stevens (Sharks).
Tries: Fittler (44), Timmins (60), Hill (63), Furner (65), Girdler (78);
Goals: Girdler 4

League Express Men of the Match
Qld: Matt Sing; **NSW:** Tim Brasher
HT: 4-0; **Referee:** Bill Harrigan; **Attendance:** 38,796

Wendell Sailor (Brisbane Broncos) was chosen for Queensland but withdrew through injury and was replaced by Sing. Queensland stand-off Ben Ikin (Broncos) was unavailable for selection because of injury. David Peachey (Sharks) was chosen for NSW but withdrew through injury and was replaced by Brasher.

Scott Hill and Tim Brasher celebrate New South Wales' State of Origin success

when NSW beat Queensland 65-9 in Sydney way back in 1911.

A modest Girdler dismissed all the personal kudos.

"I think the 60-odd thousands fans appreciated the footy we played," was the way he described the evening's effort.

ORIGIN 3

NEW SOUTH WALES 56..**QUEENSLAND 16**
Stadium Australia, June 7 2000

NSW: Tim Brasher (North Qld Cowboys), Adam MacDougall (Newcastle Knights), Ryan Girdler (Penrith Panthers), Matthew Gidley, Jamie Ainscough (St Geo-Illawarra Dragons), Brad Fittler (Sydney Roosters) (c), Brett Kimmorley (Melbourne Storm), Jason Stevens (Sharks), Geoff Toovey (Northern Eagles), Robbie Kearns (Melbourne Storm), Ben Kennedy (Newcastle Knights), Bryan Fletcher (Sydney Roosters) & Scott Hill (Melbourne Storm). *Subs:* Andrew Johns (Newcastle Knights), Adam Muir (Northern Eagles), David Furner (Canberra Raiders) & Michael Vella (Parramatta Eels).
Tries: Girdler (16, 26, 52), Muir (18), Johns (43), Gidley (56, 80), Fletcher (65), MacDougall (71); **Goals:** Girdler 10

QUEENSLAND: Darren Lockyer (Brisbane Broncos), Wendell Sailor (Brisbane Broncos), Matt Sing (Sydney Roosters), Paul Bowman (North Qld Cowboys), Mat Rogers (Sharks), Ben Ikin (Brisbane Broncos), Adrian Lam (Sydney Roosters) (c), Martin Lang (Sharks), Jason Hetherington (Bulldogs), Shane Webcke (Brisbane Broncos), Gorden Tallis (Brisbane Broncos), Chris McKenna (Sharks) & Darren Smith (Bulldogs). *Subs:* Tonie Carroll (Brisbane Broncos), Julian O'Neill (North Qld Cowboys), Brad Thorn (Brisbane Broncos) & Craig Greenhill (Penrith Panthers).
Tries: Rogers (23), Smith (30), Tallis (77); **Goals:** Rogers 2

League Express Men of the Match
NSW: Ryan Girdler; **Qld:** Gorden Tallis
HT: 20-10; **Referee:** Bill Harrigan; **Attendance:** 58,767

NSW centre Shaun Timmins (St Geo-Illawarra Dragons) and prop Rodney Howe (Melbourne Storm) and Queensland loose-forward Jason Smith (Parramatta Eels) were unavailable for selection because of injury.

NSW WON THE SERIES 3-0
Man of the Series: Ryan Girdler *(NSW)*

Lam was shell-shocked by the size of the defeat.

"We gave them a head start with some silly mistakes and it just snowballed from there," he said. "Our performance was very un-Queensland-like. But I suppose there is always next year."

But not for Lam. He was going to Wigan.

And, of his fellow-Queenslanders, Jason Hetherington would be with the London Broncos, Tonie Carroll with Leeds, Jason Smith with Hull and Brad Thorn in New Zealand playing rugby union

It would be a real changing of the guard.

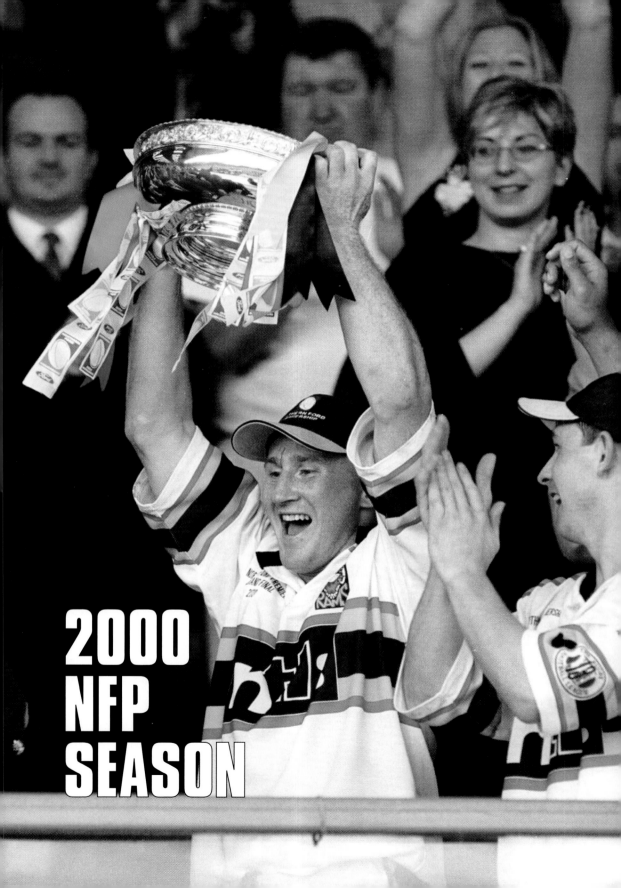

2000
NFP
SEASON

NFP SEASON

TOP LEFT: Leigh's Graeme Close is brought crashing down against Widnes.
TOP RIGHT: Cliff Eccles finds no way through as Leigh prove too strong.
LEFT: Keighley's Nathan Antonik gets the ball away as Dewsbury close in.

NFP SEASON

TRANS-PENNINE CUP FINAL

TOP: Oldham's Leo Casey barges through the Dewsbury defence.
LEFT: Dewsbury's Adrian Flynn is collared during a rain-soaked Trans Pennine Cup Final.
BELOW: Dewsbury celebrate victory over Leigh Centurions in the Trans-Pennine Cup Final at Ram Stadium.

NFP SEASON

TOP: Featherstone's Matt Bramald leaves Doncaster's Asa Amone in his wake.
LEFT: Doncaster's Craig Weston looks to offload as Keighley's Danny Seal moves in.
BELOW: Joey Hayes tries to skip past the tackle of Ian Kirke as Oldham see off Hull KR.

PRELIMINARY SEMI-FINALS

ABOVE: Leigh's Paul Anderson has his collar felt by Dewsbury's Billy Kershaw.
LEFT: Keighley's Nathan Antonik jumps over the tackle of Doncaster's Asa Amone.
BELOW: Shane McMenemy meets Rob Nolan as Oldham triumph over Hull Kingston Rovers.
BELOW LEFT: Eddie Kilgannon looks for a gap in the Featherstone defence as Widnes are outclassed.

ELIMINATIONS SEMI-FINALS

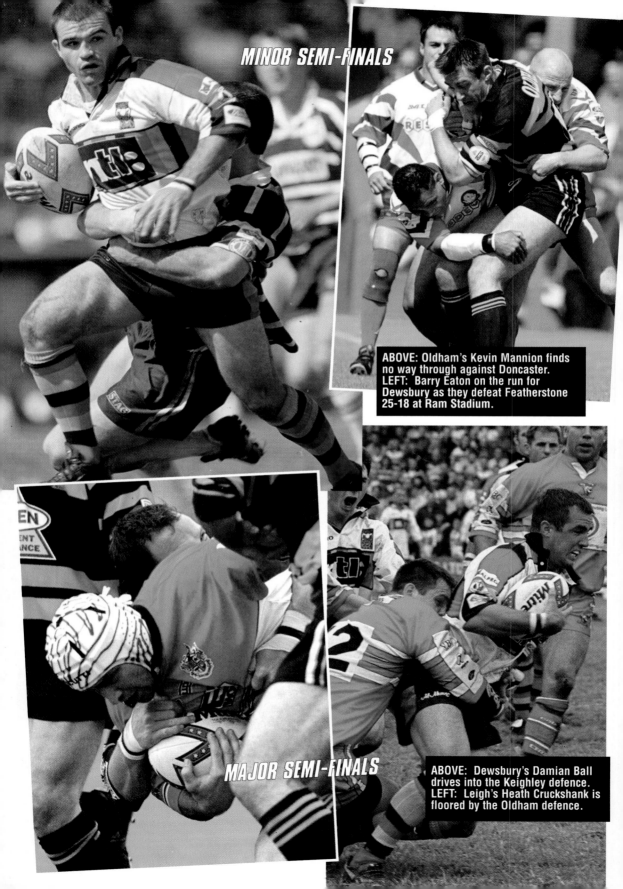

MINOR SEMI-FINALS

ABOVE: Oldham's Kevin Mannion finds no way through against Doncaster.
LEFT: Barry Eaton on the run for Dewsbury as they defeat Featherstone 25-18 at Ram Stadium.

MAJOR SEMI-FINALS

ABOVE: Dewsbury's Damian Ball drives into the Keighley defence.
LEFT: Leigh's Heath Cruckshank is floored by the Oldham defence.

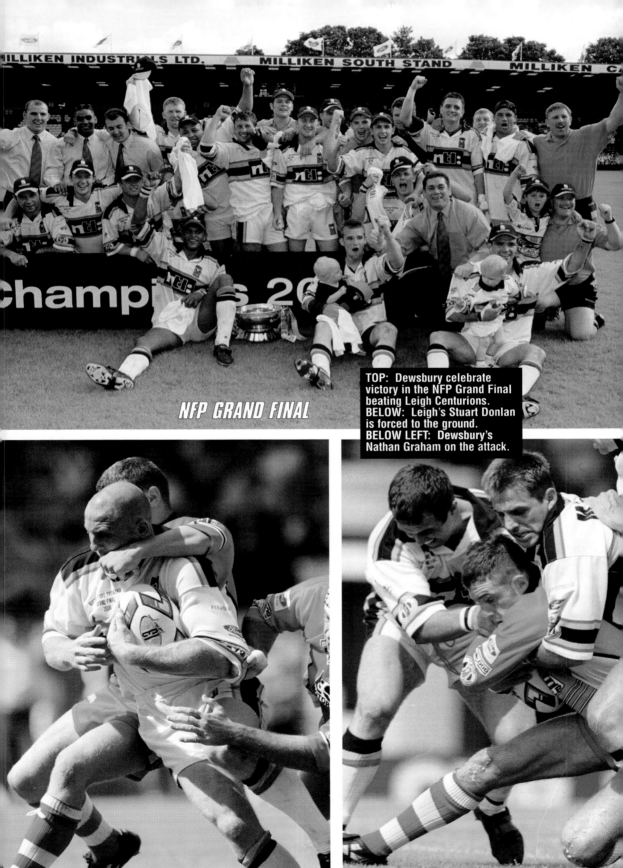

NFP GRAND FINAL

TOP: Dewsbury celebrate victory in the NFP Grand Final beating Leigh Centurions.
BELOW: Leigh's Stuart Donlan is forced to the ground.
BELOW LEFT: Dewsbury's Nathan Graham on the attack.

WOMENS WORLD SERIES

EMERGING NATIONS

TOP: GB & Ireland's Gemma Walsh is dumped by the New Zealand defence in the first game of the Womens World Series.
LEFT (INSET): New Zealand Ferns celebrate their win over GB &Ireland.
BELOW: BARLA GB & Ireland celebrate victory in the Emerging Nations final at Ram Stadium against Italy.
BELOW LEFT: USA's Tim Griffiths in action against Morocco.

CLOCKWISE FROM TOP: Australia's Wendell Sailor on the charge against Samoa. England's Andy Farrell is halted by David Barnhill. Henry Paul is grounded by France's Jerome Guisset. Keiron Cunningham leaves the PNG defence behind as Wales win 22-8.

RIGHT: New Zealand's Stacey Jones is brought down.
BELOW: Andy Farrell is collared by Craig Smith as England go out 6-49 to New Zealand.
BOTTOM: Wales' Ian Watson dives over for a try despite the attentions of Darren Lockyer. Despite an outstanding display in the first half, Australia overcome Wales 46-22.

WORLD CUP SEMI-FINALS

CLOCKWISE FROM TOP: Australia celebrate victory over New Zealand 40-12 at Old Trafford. Brad Fittler touches down for a try for Australia. New Zealand's Ruben Wiki on the charge.

WORLD CUP FINAL

WORLD CLUB CHALLENGE

Kellogg's WORLD CLUB CHAMPIONS 200

CLOCKWISE FROM TOP:
Melbourne Storm's Wayne Evans holds off the challenge of John Stankevitch. St Helens' Paul Sculthorpe breaks through. Melbourne Storm team celebrate victory over St Helens at the JJB Stadium, Wigan.

ANZAC TEST

CLOCKWISE FROM TOP: Australia's Darren Lockyer makes a break through the New Zealand defence. Joe Vagana is held up just short of the line in the opening minutes of the game, New Zealand fail to score as Australia win 52-0. Shaun Timmins takes the ball up for Australia.

STATE OF ORIGIN

CLOCKWISE FROM TOP: Brad Fittler and Bryan Fletcher celebrate Fletcher's try as NSW clinch the State of Origin. NSW's Michael Vella is lifted off the ground at the Suncorp Stadium, Brisbane. Queensland's Paul Bowman is held by the NSW defence. Scott Hill on the burst for NSW.

NRL SEASON

CLOCKWISE FROM TOP: Melbourne's Brett Kimmorley comes in for some close attention from Canberra's Brett Finch. Newcastle's David Fairleigh is slammed by the Parramatta defence. Cronulla's Martin Lang is caught by the Brisbane defence.

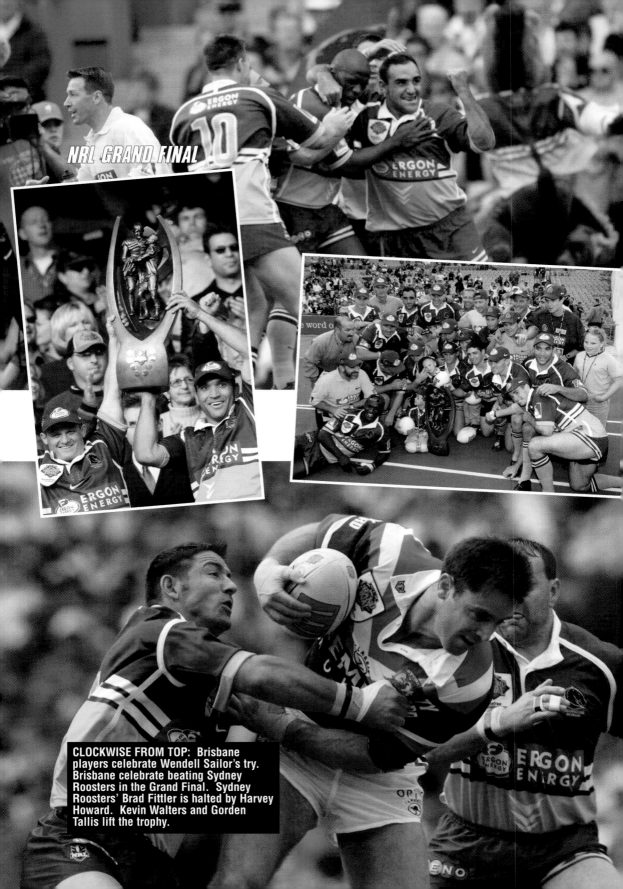

CLOCKWISE FROM TOP: Brisbane players celebrate Wendell Sailor's try. Brisbane celebrate beating Sydney Roosters in the Grand Final. Sydney Roosters' Brad Fittler is halted by Harvey Howard. Kevin Walters and Gorden Tallis lift the trophy.

WORLD CUP 2000

AUSTRALIA still ruled the world of Rugby League after their magnificent 40-12 World Cup Final win over New Zealand at Old Trafford.

The Kangaroos secured their sixth successive World title with a record-breaking seven-try victory over the Kiwis.

Man-of-the-match Wendell Sailor equalled the record for tries in a final with a decisive brace in four minutes, after the Kiwis had fought back to trail only 12-18 midway through the second half.

Mat Rogers, with six goals and twelve points, set new records for a final and Australia's winning margin surpassed their previous record 25-12 score-line against New Zealand in 1988, the Kiwis' only previous final appearance.

Sailor, with ten tries, and Rogers, with 27 goals and 70 points, also topped the World Cup 2000 scoring charts between them.

The Kangaroos have held the World Cup since 1975 and have won the trophy nine times out of a possible twelve since it was inaugurated in 1954.

The unstoppable Kangaroos - hot favourites at the start of the competition - dominated the final quarter, amassing 22 points in the last 14 minutes.

But it was the monster defensive effort demanded from the Kiwis in the first half that won the game for the Kangaroos.

Australian coach Chris Anderson dubbed the win: "as good a team performance as you could ask for under pressure."

Skipper Brad Fittler, Brett Kimmorley, Andrew Johns and Scott Hill all rivalled the magnificent Sailor for the man-of-the-match accolade.

Kimmorley's kicking game was superb and his ability to take the ball to the line and release his runners was never better demonstrated. Fittler, too, capped a memorable day with a fine try while Johns justified his switch to hooker with astute distribution. Hill's ability to join the line and combine with Fittler and Kimmorley was crucial.

Of the younger players, centre Matthew Gidley capped a magnificent personal tournament, while Trent Barrett looked another superstar in the making.

The world champions dominated right from the opening stages with Kimmorley dictating their attacks and soon demonstrating his vast repertoire of attacking kicks.

The Kiwis' first attack took eleven minutes to mount but Sailor calmly knocked away Jones' kick with a foot in the dead-ball area to set up a 20-metre tap.

The forward battle was as tough and unrelenting as forecast but the

Kangaroos looked to have made the breakthrough when Sailor blasted over in the right corner but the video referee ruled that Stephen Kearney's despairing tackle had succeeded in preventing Sailor from grounding the ball.

But the Kangaroos were not to be denied three minutes later when Sailor drilled the ball through and Gidley just got a hand to it before it went dead. The video referee gave his assent and Rogers converted from the touch-line.

It was the only score of the first half but Kimmorley began the second in the same dominant form and, after another testing kick, Nigel Vagana was trapped behind his own line by a magnificent Rogers tackle from dummy-half. From the resulting drop-out the Kangaroos engineered their second converted try as Johns and Fittler combined to send Nathan Hindmarsh stretching over on the left for a converted try.

But the crowd came to life as the Kiwis mounted their revival, Vainikolo grabbing his ninth try of the World Cup after Matt Rua had challenged Lockyer to Jones' high, angled kick to the left, Henry Paul adding the conversion after the video referee had again been called upon.

Within three minutes the Kangaroos restored their 12-point advantage when Kimmorley, dummied to the right before cutting through to unselfishly provide the supporting Darren Lockyer with a run-in on the inside.

THE 2000 RUGBY LEAGUE WORLD CUP FINAL

AUSTRALIA 40 ....**NEW ZEALAND 12**
Old Trafford, Manchester, Saturday 25 November, 2000

AUSTRALIA: 1 Darren Lockyer (Brisbane Broncos); 5 Wendell Sailor (Brisbane Broncos); 4 Matthew Gidley (Newcastle Knights); 3 Adam MacDougall (Newcastle Knights); 2 Mat Rogers (Cronulla Sharks); 6 Brad Fittler (C) (Sydney City Roosters); 7 Brett Kimmorley (Melbourne Storm); 8 Shane Webcke (Brisbane Broncos); 9 Andrew Johns (Newcastle Knights); 10 Robbie Kearns (Melbourne Storm); 11 Gorden Tallis (Brisbane Broncos); 12 Bryan Fletcher (Sydney City Roosters); 13 Scott Hill (Melbourne Storm). *Subs:* 17 Jason Stevens (Cronulla Sharks) for Webcke (13); 16 Darren Britt (Canterbury Bulldogs) for Kearns (20); 15 Nathan Hindmarsh (Parramatta Eels) for Fletcher (20); Fletcher for Tallis (27); Webcke for Stevens (57); Tallis for Fletcher (62); 14 Trent Barrett (St George-Illawarra) for MacDougall (64); Kearns for Hindmarsh (78).
Tries: Gidley (26), Hindmarsh (46), Lockyer (53), Sailor (66, 69), Fittler (74), Barrett (76); **Goals:** Rogers 6

NEW ZEALAND: 1 Richie Barnett (C) (Sydney City Roosters); 2 Nigel Vagana (Auckland Warriors); 3 Tonie Carroll (Brisbane Broncos); 4 Willie Talau (Canterbury Bulldogs); 5 Lesley Vainikolo (Canberra Raiders); 6 Henry Paul (Bradford Bulls); 7 Stacey Jones (Auckland Warriors); 8 Craig Smith (St George-Illawarra Dragons); 9 Richard Swain (Melbourne Storm); 10 Quentin Pongia (Sydney City Roosters); 11 Matt Rua (Melbourne Storm); 12 Stephen Kearney (Melbourne Storm); 13 Ruben Wiki (Canberra Raiders). *Subs:* 16 Nathan Cayless (Parramatta Eels) for Smith (14); 15 Joe Vagana (Auckland Warriors) for Pongia (14); 17 Logan Swann (Auckland Warriors) for Rua (20); Pongia for J Vagana (31); Smith for Cayless (31); Rua for Wiki (41); 14 Robbie Paul (Bradford Bulls) for Swain (58); J Vagana for Smith (58); Cayless for Pongia (58); Wiki for Kearney (70); Smith for J Vagana (75); Pongia for Cayless (75)
Tries: Vainikolo (50), Carroll (57); **Goals:** H Paul 2

League Express Men of the Match
Australia: Wendell Sailor; **New Zealand:** Stephen Kearney
Penalties: 3-3; **HT:** 6-0; **Ref:** Stuart Cummings (England); **Att:** 44,329

But the Kiwis were back in the game when centre Tonie Carroll received from Henry Paul and twice eluded Adam MacDougall - in for Ryan Girdler, injured the previous week - on a blockbusting 30-metre run for a try that Henry Paul converted.

With Bradford's Robbie Paul brought off the bench, the Kiwis spied their chance and Sailor, rescuing his side after Jones and Kearney combined to almost send Vainikolo in, knocked-on ten metres from his own line.

But the Kiwis were unable to take advantage of the opportunity and the Kangaroos took over after, first, Henry Paul had knocked on at dummy-half and then Carroll couldn't hold a pass, both in attacking positions.

The decisive try came in the 66th minute when Gidley took out three defenders with an exquisite inside pass and Sailor twisted over in Robbie Paul's last ditch tackle, Rogers again negotiating the tricky goal attempt.

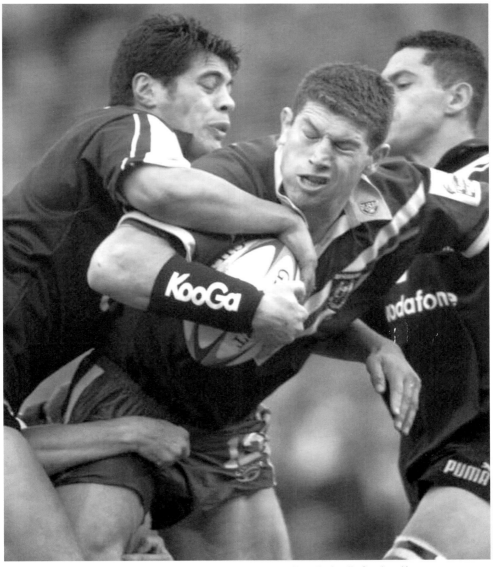

Australian forward Bryan Fletcher feels the force of New Zealand's Stephen Kearney

Henry Paul compounded the Kiwis' misery by kicking-off directly into touch and, three minutes later, the Australians were home and dry as Johns, Lockyer and Gidley laid on Sailor's second.

Fittler, stepping inside the cover from Lockyer's pass in his own inimitable way, and Barrett, with a magnificent 60-metre effort from Fittler's pass, added further converted tries in the dying minutes.

The weather gods had relented for the game but, after the presentations by Britain's Olympic legend Steve Redgrave had been completed, the rain returned.

The crowds were sent on their way home with a drenching to remind them of the horrific weather that had plagued the 2000 World Cup.

Quarter Finals

AUSTRALIA 66 ....**SAMOA 10**
Australia's 12-try romp over the brave but eventually outclassed Samoans at Watford brought the world champions' points-tally to 264 in four games.

Second row forward Bryan Fletcher led the way with his first senior hat-trick as Andrew Johns, the official man of the match, and Brett Kimmorley bossed the midfield, allowing Scott Hill and skipper Brad Fittler to make hay in the teeming rain.

The wet weather again followed the World Cup roadshow but the Australians adapted impressively to the conditions.

At 40-10, with ten minutes to go, Samoa coach Darrell Williams could have been well pleased with his side's efforts. But Australia ran in 26 points, including five tries, in the closing ten minutes as the mighty effort of the first half took its toll on the Samoan defence.

The Aussies had come through as group one winners with straight wins against England, 22-2; Fiji, 66-8 and Russia - a record 110-4 mauling at the Boulevard, Ryan Girdler smashing the World Cup points-in-a-match record with 46, from three tries and an amazing 17 goals.

Samoa had been a surprise in group four, going down to Ireland in Belfast by 30-16 before overcoming the Maori 21-16 in a superb match at Workington and then holding off Scotland by 20-12 in Edinburgh.

FRANCE 6 ....**NEW ZEALAND 54**
The Kiwis made smooth progress through to the semi-finals with a ten-try demolition of the French at Castleford.

They were too big, fast and powerful for a gallant France side with Robbie Paul - standing in for the rested Stacey Jones - leading the way with three tries and brother Henry adding seven goals.

History was against a French side that had improved steadily as the tournament had progressed as their last win over the Kiwis had been 20 years ago, by a 6-5 margin in Perpignan.

But the big defeat wasn't enough to disperse the new tide of optimism that had permeated French Rugby League on the back of a successful World Cup in 2000.

The French-based group three had been the most successful of the four groups, won by PNG thanks to an Adrian Lam-inspired 23-20 comeback win against the French in Paris, and then a 30-22 success over Tonga.

France had secured their place by beating Tonga in front of a packed house in Carcassonne and easily accounting for 12-man South Africa in Albi after Jamie Bloem had been sent off for dissent.

WALES 22 ....**PAPUA NEW GUINEA 8**
Wales progressed to the semi-finals with unexpected ease against a Papua New Guinea side that played with plenty of passion, courage and no little flair, but paid the price for a five-minute spell midway through the first half when they conceded two vital tries.

Having won more games than ever before on an overseas tour, the Kumuls returned home to bask in a heroes' welcome despite never really hitting their straps against a determined Welsh side.

A five-minute spell in the middle of the first half saw Wales score two vital tries.

First Adrian Lam, attempting to offload in a tackle, sent the ball straight into the hands of Jason Critchley who romped away from 40 metres for the game's opening try.

From the re-start, superb Welsh defence forced John Wilshere to concede a drop-out, and after Cunningham had gone close, the ball was spread wide to the left where Harris and Briers combined for the Warrington scrum-half to dummy through and stretch over near the corner.

Wales had finished their group in second place after comfortably beating the Cook Islands at Wrexham 38-6 and then surviving a real scare against the Lebanon, holding out for a 24-22 win in Llanelli. Defeat, by 58-18, to New Zealand in a match played under a closed roof in Cardiff, decided the group.

ENGLAND 26 ....**IRELAND 16**
The first meeting between the two home nations at Headingley was all that had been predicted with Ireland forcing England to battle all the way for their place in the semi-finals.

England needed to re-group when Ireland led 10-4 midway through the first half. Having fought back, they spread the ball wide to run in three excellent tries.

Stuart Fielden battered the Irish front line, and also stood out in defence, overhauling Kevin Campion to end the second-rower's 60-metre break just short of the England line. It was a crucial tackle as a try and goal would have pulled Ireland back to only 20-16 down with 15 minutes left.

England took full advantage of the try-saver to scramble possession from Ireland's next play and power back with a match-clinching try from Chev Walker.

Ireland had done their country proud throughout the World Cup, winning all their three group four matches on home soil, with captain Terry O'Connor leading from the front in tough wins against Samoa, 30-16, Scotland, 18-6, and the Maori, 30-16.

England had grown in stature since their opening day defeat at Twickenham with a 76-4 win over Russia and a 66-10 success over Fiji.

Semi Finals

ENGLAND 6 ....**NEW ZEALAND 49**
Red-hot New Zealand shattered England's World Cup dream at the Reebok Stadium with a near-perfect display.

Every Kiwi looked top class, none more so than Bradford Bulls' stand-off Henry Paul, who gave one of the outstanding performances of the tournament.

From the second minute, when he sent in Stephen Kearney for the first try to when he put Logan Swann through for the last, Paul was in total command. He was involved in five tries altogether and kicked nine goals including a field goal, with his first two-pointer giving him a century of points for New Zealand in Test and World Cup matches.

England raised faint hopes of a rally when they scored their only try early in the second half with Tony Smith touching down Sean Long's neat kick and Farrell adding the goal.

But New Zealand's response was to deliver another shattering blow as a typical hefty tackle caused Paul Sculthorpe to cough up the ball and a few swift passes brought Talau his first try.

It became a procession after that as Nigel Vagana, Vainikolo, Talau and Swann swept in for tries to rack up a record defeat for England, beating the 42-13 loss against France back in 1951.

AUSTRALIA 46 ....**WALES 22**
Australia made their predicted progress through to the World Cup Final but not before Clive Griffiths' gallant Welsh side had lifted the spirits of a nation.

The Welsh produced an outstanding display of enterprise and commitment to the cause, holding a 22-14 lead early in the second half before the Kangaroos dominated the latter stages of a truly memorable encounter.

Lee Briers, Keiron Cunningham, Paul Highton and skipper Iestyn Harris all played superbly in a wonderful team effort as the mighty Kangaroos were rocked by the sheer pride of a Wales side written off as no-hopers before the tournament.

But second-half tries by Bryan Fletcher, Darren Lockyer (two), Brad Fittler, Craig Gower and Ben Kennedy - the culmination of one of the most glorious passages of football ever seen in a World Cup - ended the impossible dream.

Dejected England trio Kris Radlinski, Andy Hay and Chev Walker leave the field after the semi-final loss to New Zealand

GROUP ONE

ENGLAND 2 ....**AUSTRALIA 22**
England: G - Farrell
Australia: T - Sailor 2, Gidley, MacDougall; G - Rogers 3

FIJI 38 ....**RUSSIA 12**
Fiji: T - Vunivalu 3, Tuqiri 2, Kuruduadua, Sovatabua; G - Tuqiri 5
Russia: T - Iliassov, Rullis; G - Jiltsov, Mitrofanov

AUSTRALIA 66 ....**FIJI 8**
Australia: T - Rogers 4, Kennedy 2, Girdler 2, Barrett, Hindmarsh, MacDougall, Gidley; G - Rogers 9
Fiji: T - Cakacaka, Tuqiri

ENGLAND 76 ....**RUSSIA 4**
England: T - Sinfield 3, Rowley 2, Peacock 2, Long 2, Hay, Walker, Pryce, Stephenson, Deacon; G - Farrell 5, Long 5
Russia: G - Mitrofanov 2

AUSTRALIA 110 ....**RUSSIA 4**
Australia: T - Sailor 4, Girdler 3, Barrett 2, Croker 2, Hindmarsh 2, MacDougall, Fletcher, Webcke, Tallis, Johns, Gidley; G - Girdler 17
Russia: T - Donovan

ENGLAND 66 ....**FIJI 10**
England: T - Peacock 3, Wellens 2, Rogers 2, Hay, Smith, Farrell, Naylor, Radlinski; G - Farrell 9
Fiji: T - Navale, Tuqiri; G - Vunivalu

Group One - Final Standings

	P	W	D	L	F	A	D	Pts
Australia	3	3	0	0	198	14	184	6
England	3	2	0	1	144	36	108	4
Fiji	3	1	0	2	56	144	-88	2
Russia	3	0	0	3	20	224	-204	0

GROUP TWO

LEBANON 0...**NEW ZEALAND 64**
New Zealand: T - Barnett 2, Carroll 2, Talau 2, Vainikolo 2, Jones 2, Jellick, Swann; G - Jones 6, H Paul 2

WALES 38 ....**COOK ISLANDS 6**
Wales: T - Tassell 3, Briers, Jenkins, Cunningham; G - Harris 7
Cook Islands: T - Temata; G - Piakura

COOK ISLANDS 10 ....**NEW ZEALAND 84**
Cook Islands: T - Noovao, Iro; G - Piakura
New Zealand: T - Barnett 2, Vaealiki 2, Lavea 2, R Paul 2, N Vagana, Vainikolo, Cayless, Lauiti'iti, Puletua, Wiki, Pongia; G - Lavea 12

WALES 24 ....**LEBANON 22**
Wales: T - Harris 2, Sterling, Cunningham, Davies; G - Harris 2
Lebanon: T - Saleh 2, Coorey, S El Masri; G - H El Masri 3

COOK ISLANDS 22 ....**LEBANON 22**
Cook Islands: T - Berryman 2, Joe, Toa; G - Berryman 2, Piakura
Lebanon: T - H El Masri 2, Touma, H Saleh; G - H El Masri 3

WALES 18...**NEW ZEALAND 58**
Wales: T - Briers, Atcheson, Farrell; G - Harris 3
New Zealand: T - Vainikolo 3, Barnett 2, Talau, H Paul, Wiki, Carroll, Lauiti'iti, N Vagana; G - H Paul 5, Lavea 2

Group Two - Final Standings

	P	W	D	L	F	A	D	Pts
New Zealand	3	3	0	0	206	28	178	6
Wales	3	2	0	1	80	86	-6	4
Lebanon	3	0	1	2	44	110	-66	1
Cook Islands	3	0	1	2	38	144	-106	1

GROUP THREE

FRANCE 20 ....**PAPUA NEW GUINEA 23**
France: T - Hechiche 2, Benausse, Dekkiche; G - Banquet 2
Papua New Guinea: T - Bai, Krewanty, Buko, Lam; G - Wilshere 2, Buko; FG - Lam

SOUTH AFRICA 18 ....**TONGA 66**
South Africa: T - Breytenbach, Barnard, Best; G - Bloem 2, O'Shea
Tonga: T - Vaikona 3, D Mann 2, W Wolfgramm, Liava'a, Masella, Moala, E Mann, Lomi, Kaufusi, Mason; G - Moala 6, D Mann

FRANCE 28 ....**TONGA 8**
France: T - Banquet, Sirvent, Dulac, Garcia, Jampy; G - Banquet 4
Tonga: T - D Fisi'iahi, P Fisi'iahi

PAPUA NEW GUINEA 16 ....**SOUTH AFRICA 0**
Papua New Guinea: T - Aila, Wilshere, Paiyo; G - Wilshere 2

FRANCE 56 ....**SOUTH AFRICA 6**
France: T - Jampy 3, Cassin 2, Banquet, Guisset, Sirvent, Tallec; G - Banquet 10
South Africa: T - de Villiers; G - Bloem

PAPUA NEW GUINEA 30 ....**TONGA 22**
Papua New Guinea: T - Gene 2, Mondo, Buko, Karl; G - Wilshere 5
Tonga: T - Moala 2, Vaikona, Mason; G - Moala 3

Group Three - Final Standings

	P	W	D	L	F	A	D	Pts
Papua New Guinea	3	3	0	0	69	42	27	6
France	3	2	0	1	104	37	67	4
Tonga	3	1	0	2	96	76	20	2
South Africa	3	0	0	3	24	138	-114	0

GROUP FOUR

IRELAND 30 ....**SAMOA 16**
Ireland: T - Joynt, Ricketson, Eagar, Carney, Prescott; G - Prescott 5
Samoa: T - Leauma, Milford, Betham; G - Geros 2

SCOTLAND 16 ....**AOTEAROA MAORI 17**
Scotland: T - Penny, Maiden, Bell; G - Mackay, Crowther
Aotearoa Maori: T - Toopi 2, Kidwell; G - Ngamu 2; FG - Ngamu

IRELAND 18 ....**SCOTLAND 6**
Ireland: T - Sheridan, Withers; G - Prescott 5
Scotland: T - Arnold; G - Crowther

AOTEAROA MAORI 16 ....**SAMOA 21**
Maori: T - Matthews, Nelson, Rauhihi; G - Goodwin 2
Samoa: T - Fa'afili 2, W Swann, Milford; G - Poching 2; FG - W Swann

IRELAND 30 ....**AOTEAROA MAORI 16**
Ireland: T - Forster, Carney, Barnhill, Withers, Sheridan; G - Prescott 5
Maori: T - Nelson, Te Rangi, Koopu; G - Perenara, Ngamu

SCOTLAND 12 ....**SAMOA 20**
Scotland: T - Vowles, Rhodes; G - Crowther 2
Samoa: T - Leauma 2, Solomona, Milford; G - Laloata 2

Group Four - Final Standings

	P	W	D	L	F	A	D	Pts
Ireland	3	3	0	0	78	38	40	6
Samoa	3	2	0	1	57	58	-1	4
Maori	3	1	0	2	49	67	-18	2
Scotland	3	0	0	3	34	55	-21	0

QUARTER FINALS

AUSTRALIA 66 ....**SAMOA 10**
Australia: T - Fletcher 3, Johns 2, Hill 2, MacDougall 2, Girdler, Fittler, Sailor; G - Rogers 9
Samoa: T - Solomona, Leauma; G - Laloata

ENGLAND 26 ....**IRELAND 16**
England: T - Senior, Peacock, Smith, Walker; G - Farrell 5
Ireland: T - Withers 2, Martyn; G - Prescott 2

NEW ZEALAND 54 ....**FRANCE 6**
New Zealand: T - R Paul 3, Rua, Pongia, Smith, Kearney, Jellick, Talau, Blackmore; G - H Paul 7
France: T - Sirvent; G - Banquet

WALES 22.......................................**PAPUA NEW GUINEA 8**
Wales: T - Critchley, Briers, Davies; G - Harris 5
Papua New Guinea: T - Wilshere; G - Wilshere 2

SEMI FINALS

AUSTRALIA 46 ....**WALES 22**
Australia: T - Fittler 2, Lockyer 2, Kimmorley, Sailor, Fletcher, Gower, Kennedy; G - Lockyer 4; Girdler
Wales: T - Watson, Tassell, Briers; G - Harris 4; FG - Briers 2

ENGLAND 6 ....**NEW ZEALAND 49**
England: T - Smith; G - Farrell
New Zealand: T - Vainikolo 2, Talau 2, Kearney, Wiki, N Vagana, Swann; G - H Paul 8; FG - H Paul

WORLD CUP FINAL 2000

AUSTRALIA 40 ....**NEW ZEALAND 12**
Australia: T - Sailor 2, Gidley, N Hindmarsh, Lockyer, Fittler, Barrett; G - Rogers 6
New Zealand: T - Vainikolo, Carroll; G - H Paul 2

TOP TRYSCORER: Wendell Sailor (Australia) 10

TOP GOALKICKER: Mat Rogers (Australia) 27

TOP POINTSCORER: Mat Rogers (Australia) 70 *(4 tries, 27 goals)*

199

INTERNATIONAL ROUND-UP

AUSTRALIA v NEW ZEALAND
(ANZAC TEST)

AUSTRALIA 52 ....**NEW ZEALAND 0**
AUSTRALIA: 1 Darren Lockyer (Brisbane Broncos), 2 Mat Rogers (Sharks), 3 Ryan Girdler (Penrith Panthers), 4 Shaun Timmins (St George Illawarra Dragons), 5 Wendell Sailor (Brisbane Broncos), 6 Brad Fittler (C) (Sydney Roosters), 7 Brett Kimmorley (Melbourne Storm), 8 Shane Webcke (Brisbane Broncos), 9 Jason Hetherington (Bulldogs), 10 Rodney Howe (Melbourne Storm), 11 Gorden Tallis (Brisbane Broncos), 12 Bryan Fletcher (Sydney Roosters), 13 Jason Smith (Parramatta Eels). *Subs:* 14 Jason Stevens (Sharks), 15 Robbie Kearns (Melbourne Storm), 16 Scott Hill (Melbourne Storm), 17 Chris McKenna (Sharks).
Tries: Fittler (5, 74), Rogers (9, 78), McKenna (21), Sailor (29), Tallis (44), Girdler (54), Timmins (69). **Goals:** Rogers 8

NEW ZEALAND: 1 Richie Barnett (C) (Sydney Roosters), 2 Nigel Vagana (Auckland Warriors), 3 Richie Blackmore (Leeds Rhinos), 4 Henry Paul (Bradford Bulls), 5 Lesley Vainikolo (Canberra Raiders), 6 Robbie Paul (Bradford Bulls), 7 Stacey Jones (Auckland Warriors), 8 Joe Vagana (Auckland Warriors), 9 Richard Swain (Melbourne Storm), 10 Craig Smith (St George Illawarra Dragons), 11 Matt Rua (Melbourne Storm), 12 Stephen Kearney (Melbourne Storm), 13 Tyran Smith (Wests Tigers). *Subs:* 14 Tony Puletua (Penrith Panthers), 15 Jason Lowrie (Wests Tigers), 16 David Kidwell (Parramatta Eels), 17 Tasesa Lavea (Melbourne Storm).

Referee: Bill Harrigan (Australia), **Video referee:** Chris Ward (Australia), **Half-time:** 22-0, **Attendance:** 26,023 *at Stadium Australia on April 27*
League Express Men of the Match:
Australia: Brett Kimmorley, **New Zealand:** Stephen Kearney

Andrew Johns (Newcastle Knights) was chosen for Australia but withdrew through injury and was replaced by Hetherington. Jarrod McCracken (Wests Tigers), Willie Talau (Bulldogs) and Quentin Pongia (Sydney Roosters) were in the original Kiwi squad but withdrew through injury. Ali Lauitiiti (Auckland Warriors) was in the final squad of 18 but not used.

AUSTRALIA 82 ....**PAPUA NEW GUINEA 0**

AUSTRALIA: 1 Darren Lockyer (Brisbane Broncos), 2 Mat Rogers (Sharks), 3 Ryan Girdler (Penrith Panthers), 4 Matthew Gidley (Newcastle Knights), 5 Wendell Sailor (Brisbane Broncos), 6 Brad Fittler (Sydney Roosters) (c), 7 Brett Kimmorley (Melbourne Storm), 8 Shane Webcke (Brisbane Broncos), 9 Andrew Johns (Newcastle Knights), 10 Robbie Kearns (Melbourne Storm), 11 Gorden Tallis (Brisbane Broncos), 12 Bryan Fletcher (Sydney Roosters), 13 Scott Hill (Melbourne Storm). *Subs:* 14 Adam MacDougall (Newcastle Knights), 15 Jason Croker (Canberra Raiders), 16 Darren Britt (Bulldogs), 17 Jason Stevens (Sharks)
Tries: Tallis (3, 22, 66, 68), Girdler (18), MacDougall (28), Fletcher (33), Sailor (40, 72, 76), Lockyer (42, 55), Fittler (47), Kimmorley (68), **Goals:** Rogers 13

PAPUA NEW GUINEA: 17 David Buko (Wagga Wagga), 2 John Wilshere (Brisbane Easts) , 3 Alfred Songoro (Mackay Souths) , 4 Chris Purkulil (Rabaul Island Gurias), 5 Marcus Bai (Melbourne Storm), 6 Mark Mom (Brisbane Easts), 7 Adrian Lam (Sydney Roosters) (c), 8 Bruce Mamando (North Qld Cowboys), 9 Elias Paiyo (Kellyville Bushrangers), 10 Makaili Aizure (Goroka Lahinis), 11 Michael Mondo (Yanco), 12 Raymond Karl (Enga Mioks), 13 Tom O'Reilly (Oldham). *Subs:* 1 Augustine Justine (Mt Hagen Eagles), 14 Duncan Naawi (Brisbane Redcliffe), 15 Alex Krewanty (Sydney Bulls), 16 Andrew Norman (Burdekin Roosters)

Half-time: 34-0, **Referee:** Tim Mander,
Attendance: 21,000 *at Dairy Farmers Stadium, Townsville on October 7*
League Express Men of the Match:
Australia: Gorden Tallis, **PNG:** Bruce Mamando

David Westley (Parramatta Eels) was in the original PNG squad but withdrew through injury.

New Zealand's Lesley Vainikolo on the charge against Australia

INTERNATIONAL FRIENDLIES

AUSTRALIA 108 ....**NZ RESIDENTS 0**
Australia: T - MacDougall 5, Kennedy 2, Barrett 2, Croker 2, Sailor 2, Hill 2, Tallis 2, Rogers, Gower, Fletcher; G - Rogers 13, Johns
AUSTRALIA: Darren Lockyer, Mat Rogers, Jason Croker, Adam MacDougall, Wendell Sailor, Trent Barrett, Andrew Johns, Michael Vella, Craig Gower, Darren Britt, Ben Kennedy, Nathan Hindmarsh, Bryan Fletcher. Subs: Scott Hill, Robbie Kearns, Jason Stevens, Gorden Tallis
NZ RESIDENTS: Luis Sione, Scott Woodgate, Paul Ah Kuoi, Gafa Tuiloma, Alan Lio, Shane Edwards, Johnny Limmer, Shaun Norton, Tyson Marjoriebanks, Phillip Leululai, Anthony Seu Seu, Shane Beyers. Subs: Maurice Emslie, Chris Faifua, Enoka Mamoe, Sinave Faitala.

Referee: Bill Shrimpton (New Zealand)
Attendance: 16,211 *at NorthPower Stadium, Gosford on Oct 14, 2000.*

SOUTH SYDNEY RABBITOAHS 82 ....**USA TOMAHAWKS 12**
Rabbitohs: T - C Caruana 3, B Grogan 2, T Slattery 2, N Merritt 2, P Clarke, N Wood, W Patten, B Moore, J Loomans, K McGuinness; G - K McGuinness 8, B Moore 2, C Caruana
Tomahawks: T- G Smith, C Waters; G - D Niu, M O'Donaghue
Referee: Paul McBlane
Attendance: 20,535 *at Redfern Oval on August 19, 2000*

SOUTH SYDNEY RABBITOHS 42 ....**LEBANON CEDARS 24**
Rabbitohs: T - N Merritt 2, T Slattery, N Wood, J Schloss, G Topham, W Patten; G - W Patten 3, B Moore 2, D Kennedy 2
Cedars: T - H El Masri, M Chahal, B Najjarn, J Stanton; G - F Elchab 4
Referee: Paul McBlane
Attendance: 7,000 *at Redfern Oval on October 26, 2000.*

JUNIOR INTERNATIONAL

JUNIOR KANGAROOS 48 ....**JUNIOR KIWIS 10**
Kangaroos: T - T Clayton 3, L Branighan 2, B Martin, B Finch, J Perry, C Newton; G - A Gorrell 6
Kiwis: T - P Borrell, M Tony; G - M Turner
Referee: Bill Harrigan (Australia)
At NorthPower Stadium on October 14, 2000

6
STATISTICAL REVIEW

BRADFORD BULLS

DATE	FIXTURE	RESULT	SCORERS	LGE	ATT
12/2/00	Hudds-Sheff (h) (CCR4)	W32-4	t:Pryce(2),McAvoy,Withers,Naylor g:H Paul(6)	N/A	6,467
27/2/00	Wakefield (a) (CCR5)	W0-46	t:Withers(3),McAvoy(2),Anderson,Mackay,Naylor,Smith g:H Paul(5)	N/A	8,005
3/3/00	St Helens (a)	W10-32	t:Lowes(2),Withers,McAvoy,R Paul g:H Paul(6)	N/A	10,128
12/3/00	Halifax (a) (CCQF)	W18-28	t:R Paul,Withers,Forshaw,Fielden g:H Paul(6)	N/A	9,827
19/3/00	Warrington (h)	W58-4	t:Brooker(2),R Paul(2),Forshaw,Spruce,Lowes,McAvoy,Mackay,H Paul,Anderson g:H Paul(7)	1st	17,127
25/3/00	Warrington (CCSF)	W44-20	t:Naylor,R Paul,Spruce,Withers,Brooker,H Paul,Peacock g:H Paul(8)	N/A	11,894
2/4/00	Hudds-Sheff (a)	W2-60	t:McAvoy(2),Brooker(2),Mackay,Vaikona,R Paul,Boyle,Anderson,Fielden g:H Paul(10)	1st	7,083
9/4/00	Castleford (h)	W44-12	t:Lowes(2),H Paul,Withers,McAvoy,Spruce,Fielden g:H Paul(7) fg:H Paul,Lowes	1st	15,237
16/4/00	Salford (a)	W1-52	t:Withers(2),Boyle,Mackay,McAvoy,Naylor,H Paul,Spruce,McDermott g:Deacon(8)	1st	6,468
21/4/00	London (h)	W32-12	t:Naylor(2),Lowes,Spruce,Anderson g:Deacon(6)	1st	13,239
29/4/00	Leeds (CCF)	W24-18	t:Withers(2),McAvoy,Fielden g:H Paul(4)	N/A	67,247
3/5/00	Hull (a)	D8-8	t:Pryce g:Deacon(2)	3rd	7,886
7/5/00	Wakefield (h)	W44-16	t:Lowes,Brooker,Mackay,Deacon,Spruce,Naylor,Smith,R Paul g:H Paul(6)	3rd	15,276
12/5/00	Halifax (h)	W62-2	t:Brooker(3),Spruce(2),Naylor(2),Forshaw,H Paul,Anderson,Fielden g:H Paul(9)	3rd	14,082
19/5/00	Leeds (a)	W2-44	t:Spruce(2),McAvoy,Mackay,R Paul,Pryce,Lowes g:H Paul(8)	3rd	18,769
28/5/00	Warrington (a)	L42-32	t:Anderson(2),Pryce,Naylor,R Paul g:H Paul(6)	3rd	8,302
2/6/00	St Helens (h)	W17-16	t:Fielden(2),Boyle g:H Paul(2) fg:Deacon	2nd	13,237
7/6/00	Wigan (a)	D12-12	t:Deacon g:H Paul(2)	1st	17,365
11/6/00	Hudds-Sheff (h)	W48-20	t:Vaikona(3),Sykes(2),Peacock,Deacon,McDermott,Boyle g:H Paul(6)	1st	11,565
16/6/00	Castleford (a)	W10-39	t:Anderson(2),Naylor,Deacon,R Paul,Lowes g:H Paul(7) fg:Boyle	1st	10,015
25/6/00	Salford (h)	W96-16	t:R Paul(4),Peacock(3),Brooker(2),Radford,Naylor,Deacon,Parker,H Paul,McDermott,Mackay,Wilkinson g:H Paul(14)	1st	11,596
30/6/00	Wigan (h)	L18-30	t:Brooker,Deacon,Mackay g:H Paul(3)	2nd	18,815
9/7/00	London (a)	W16-24	t:Vaikona,H Paul,Peacock,R Paul g:H Paul(4)	1st	4,063
14/7/00	Hull (h)	W56-6	t:Spruce(2),McAvoy(2),Fielden(2),R Paul,Naylor,Peacock,Pryce g:H Paul(8)	1st	10,778
23/7/00	Wakefield (a)	W20-30	t:Spruce(2),Fielden,McAvoy,Peacock g:H Paul(5)	1st	6,532
30/7/00	Leeds (h)	L26-28	t:R Paul(2),Naylor,Lowes g:Deacon(4),H Paul	3rd	21,237
6/8/00	Halifax (a)	D20-20	t:Naylor(2) g:H Paul(6)	3rd	7,106
11/8/00	Castleford (h)	W28-8	t:Deacon,Mackay,Spruce,Vaikona,Withers g:H Paul(4)	3rd	11,302
18/8/00	Hudds-Sheff (h)	W52-20	t:H Paul(2),McDermott(2),Spruce,Withers,Deacon,Vaikona,Peacock g:H Paul(8)	3rd	10,164
27/8/00	Wigan (a)	L20-19	t:Pryce,Lowes,Naylor g:H Paul(3) fg:Deacon	3rd	17,737
3/9/00	Halifax (a)	W18-25	t:Withers,Deacon,Lowes,H Paul g:H Paul(4) fg:Deacon	3rd	8,243
8/9/00	Leeds (h)	W14-12	t:Smith,Vaikona g:H Paul(3)	3rd	19,623
17/9/00	Hull (a)	L25-12	t:McAvoy,Stanley g:Deacon(2)	3rd	6,160
22/9/00	St Helens (a) (QPO)	L16-11	t:Peacock,Pryce g:H Paul fg:H Paul	N/A	8,864
30/9/00	Leeds (h) (ESF)	W46-12	t:Pryce(3),Anderson,Fielden,H Paul,Boyle,R Paul g:H Paul(6),Deacon	N/A	15,077
7/10/00	Wigan (a) (FE)	L40-12	t:Naylor,Anderson g:H Paul(2)	N/A	14,620

	APP		TRIES		GOALS		FG		PTS	
	ALL	SL	ALL	SL	ALL	SL	ALL	SL	ALL	SL
Paul Anderson	22(10)	18(9)	11	10	0	0	0	0	44	40
Chris Birchall	(1)	(1)	0	0	0	0	0	0	0	0
David Boyle	13(13)	12(10)	5	5	0	0	1	1	21	21
Justin Brooker	17(5)	17(4)	12	11	0	0	0	0	48	44
Paul Deacon	17(10)	17(10)	9	9	23	23	3	3	85	85
Bernard Dwyer	2(5)	2(2)	0	0	0	0	0	0	0	0
Stuart Fielden	21(12)	20(8)	11	9	0	0	0	0	44	36
Mike Forshaw	31(1)	26(1)	3	2	0	0	0	0	12	8
Gareth Handford	1(1)	1(1)	0	0	0	0	0	0	0	0
Neil Harmon	1	1	0	0	0	0	0	0	0	0
James Lowes	35	30	12	12	0	0	1	1	49	49
Brad Mackay	29(2)	24(2)	9	8	0	0	0	0	36	32
Nathan McAvoy	21(6)	16(6)	15	11	0	0	0	0	60	44
Brian McDermott	29(4)	24(4)	5	5	0	0	0	0	20	20
Craig McDowell	(1)	(1)	0	0	0	0	0	0	0	0
Scott Naylor	32	27	18	15	0	0	0	0	72	60
Robert Parker	(4)	(4)	1	1	0	0	0	0	4	4
Henry Paul	32(1)	27(1)	11	10	179	150	2	2	404	342
Robbie Paul	27(2)	22(2)	19	17	0	0	0	0	76	68
Jamie Peacock	23(12)	21(9)	9	8	0	0	0	0	36	32
Leon Pryce	28(5)	24(4)	12	10	0	0	0	0	48	40
Lee Radford	2(19)	2(16)	1	1	0	0	0	0	4	4
Hudson Smith	11(23)	8(22)	3	2	0	0	0	0	12	8
Stuart Spruce	26	22	16	15	0	0	0	0	64	60
Gareth Stanley	1	1	1	1	0	0	0	0	4	4
Paul Sykes	1(1)	1(1)	2	2	0	0	0	0	8	8
Tevita Vaikona	23(2)	22(2)	8	8	0	0	0	0	32	32
Alex Wilkinson	2(2)	2(2)	1	1	0	0	0	0	4	4
Michael Withers	21	16	15	7	0	0	0	0	60	28

LEAGUE RECORD
P28-W20-D3-L5
(3rd, SL/Final Eliminator)
F1004, A408, Diff+596
43 points.

CHALLENGE CUP
Winners

ATTENDANCES
Best - v Leeds (SL - 21,237)
Worst - v Hudds-Sheff (CC - 6,467)
Total (SL, inc play-offs) - 230,249
Average (SL, inc play-offs) - 15,350
(Up by 1,952 on 1999)

TOP TACKLER
James Lowes

TOP GROUND GAINER
Stuart Fielden

TOP CLEAN BREAKS
Robbie Paul

TOP OFFLOADER
Hudson Smith

CASTLEFORD TIGERS

DATE	FIXTURE	RESULT	SCORERS	LGE	ATT
13/2/00	Oldham SA (h) (CCR4)	W64-8	t:Sampson(3),Eagar(2),Campbell(2),Raper(2),Purcell,Wells,Davis g:Benn(8)	N/A	3,833
27/2/00	Halifax (h) (CCR5)	L10-11	t:Campbell g:Benn(3)	N/A	5,516
5/3/00	Wigan (h)	L24-30	t:Rogers(2),Sampson,Eagar g:Benn(2)	N/A	8,812
19/3/00	Salford (a)	W16-22	t:Campbell,Raper,Vowles,Davis g:Benn(2),Davis	5th	5,534
2/4/00	London (h)	W16-10	t:Orr,Rogers g:Benn(4)	4th	6,372
9/4/00	Bradford (a)	L44-12	t:Harland,Wells g:Benn(2)	8th	15,237
15/4/00	Hull (h)	W22-12	t:Eagar(2),Davis(2) g:Orr(3)	4th	8,358
20/4/00	Wakefield (a)	W12-22	t:Rogers,Orr,Eagar,Wells g:Orr(3)	4th	6,138
24/4/00	Wigan (a)	L30-16	t:Davis,Sampson,Flowers g:Orr(2)	4th	10,098
2/5/00	Halifax (a)	W14-20	t:Smith,Orr,Lynch,Harland g:Orr,Benn	4th	5,160
7/5/00	St Helens (h)	L22-32	t:Rogers(2),Shaw,Purcell g:Orr(3)	5th	7,564
14/5/00	Hudds-Sheff (h)	W26-6	t:Rogers(2),Tonks,Purcell,Lynch g:Orr(3)	4th	7,506
21/5/00	Warrington (a)	W26-37	t:Campbell(2),Mather,Eagar,Sykes,Orr g:Orr(6) fg:Orr	4th	5,915
26/5/00	Salford (h)	W30-4	t:Mather,Orr,Vowles,Flowers,Benn g:Orr(5)	4th	6,303
31/5/00	Leeds (h)	L18-20	t:Davis,Tonks,Sampson g:Orr(3)	4th	11,702
11/6/00	London (a)	W20-26	t:Eagar(2),Sykes,Mather,Tonks g:Orr(3)	4th	8,067
16/6/00	Bradford (h)	L10-39	t:Davis,Sampson g:Orr	4th	10,015
25/6/00	Hull (a)	W4-18	t:Rogers,Eagar,Orr g:Orr(3)	4th	6,501
1/7/00	Leeds (a)	L20-12	t:Orr,Fritz g:Orr(2)	4th	14,492
8/7/00	Wakefield (h)	W16-12	t:Wells(2),Eagar g:Orr(2)	5th	8,043
16/7/00	Halifax (h)	W26-12	t:Wells,Orr,Mather,Rogers,Harland g:Orr(3)	5th	6,823
21/7/00	St Helens (a)	L42-18	t:Orr,Purcell,Mather g:Orr(3)	5th	6,979
28/7/00	Warrington (h)	L18-32	t:Davis,Gay,Lynch g:Orr(3)	5th	7,058
6/8/00	Hudds-Sheff (a)	W16-32	t:Rogers(3),Vowles,Mather,Gay g:Orr(4)	5th	2,102
11/8/00	Bradford (a)	L28-8	t:Rogers,Eagar	5th	11,302
18/8/00	Leeds (h)	W20-16	t:Wells(2),Davis,Rogers g:Orr,Eaton	5th	9,819
27/8/00	Halifax (a)	L36-16	t:Davis,Mather,Wells g:Eaton,Tonks	5th	6,293
3/9/00	London (h)	W30-16	t:Rogers(2),Eagar(2),Flowers,Vowles g:Tonks(2),Eaton	5th	6,387
10/9/00	Hudds-Sheff (a)	W14-28	t:Rogers(2),Wells(2),Pryce g:Orr(4)	5th	2,903
16/9/00	Wakefield (h)	W20-8	t:Wells(2),Orr,Gay g:Orr(2)	5th	6,892
23/9/00	Leeds (a) (EPO)	L22-14	t:Davis,Wells,Mather g:Orr	N/A	13,685

	APP		TRIES		GOALS		FG		PTS	
	ALL	SL	ALL	SL	ALL	SL	ALL	SL	ALL	SL
Danny Arnold	(4)	(4)	0	0	0	0	0	0	0	0
Jamie Benn	5(5)	3(5)	1	1	22	11	0	0	48	26
Logan Campbell	16(2)	14(2)	6	3	0	0	0	0	24	12
Brad Davis	27	25	11	10	1	1	0	0	46	42
Gareth Dobson	(3)	(3)	0	0	0	0	0	0	0	0
Michael Eagar	31	29	14	12	0	0	0	0	56	48
Barry Eaton	1(4)	1(4)	0	0	3	3	0	0	6	6
Dean Ellis	(1)	0	0	0	0	0	0	0	0	0
Jason Flowers	19(4)	19(4)	3	3	0	0	0	0	12	12
Dale Fritz	20	18	1	1	0	0	0	0	4	4
Richard Gay	7(2)	7(2)	3	3	0	0	0	0	12	12
Jonathan Goddard	(1)	(1)	0	0	0	0	0	0	0	0
Lee Harland	24(3)	22(3)	3	3	0	0	0	0	12	12
Andy Lynch	5(15)	5(14)	3	3	0	0	0	0	12	12
Barrie-Jon Mather	16(1)	16(1)	8	8	0	0	0	0	32	32
Danny Orr	27(1)	26(1)	10	10	61	61	1	1	163	163
Waine Pryce	1(4)	1(4)	1	1	0	0	0	0	4	4
Andrew Purcell	16(6)	15(5)	4	3	0	0	0	0	16	12
Aaron Raper	16(3)	14(3)	3	1	0	0	0	0	12	4
Darren Rogers	29	27	20	20	0	0	0	0	80	80
Dean Sampson	21(3)	19(3)	7	4	0	0	0	0	28	16
Darren Shaw	26(5)	26(3)	1	1	0	0	0	0	4	4
Paul Smith	4(15)	4(14)	1	1	0	0	0	0	4	4
Nathan Sykes	17(9)	15(9)	2	2	0	0	0	0	8	8
Ian Tonks	14(15)	14(14)	3	3	3	3	0	0	18	18
Adrian Vowles	31	29	4	4	0	0	0	0	16	16
Jon Wells	29	27	14	13	0	0	0	0	56	52
Craig Wright	1(9)	1(9)	0	0	0	0	0	0	0	0

LEAGUE RECORD
P28-W17-D0-L11
(5th, SL/Elimination Play-Off)
F585, A571, Diff+14
34 points.

CHALLENGE CUP
Round Five

ATTENDANCES
Best - v Leeds (SL - 11,702)
Worst - v Halifax (CC - 5,516)
Total (SL only) - 111,654
Average (SL only) - 7,975
(Up by 1,098 on 1999)

TOP TACKLER
Nathan Sykes

TOP GROUND GAINER
Michael Eagar

TOP CLEAN BREAKS
Michael Eagar

TOP OFFLOADER
Danny Orr

HALIFAX BLUE SOX

DATE	FIXTURE	RESULT	SCORERS	LGE	ATT
13/2/00	Hull KR (h) (CCR4)	W36-8	t:Hassan(3),Gannon,Cardiss,Florimo,Golden g:Pearson(2),Bloem(2)	N/A	4,295
27/2/00	Castleford (a) (CCR5)	W10-11	t:Bloem(2) g:Pearson fg:Dunemann	N/A	5,516
3/3/00	Hull (h)	W30-27	t:Florimo(2),Dunemann,Gibson,Marns,Pearson g:Pearson(3)	N/A	6,124
12/3/00	Bradford (h) (CCQF)	L18-28	t:Mercer,Pearson,Rowley g:Pearson(3)	N/A	9,827
19/3/00	Wakefield (a)	W24-40	t:Marns,Cardiss,Rowley,Dunemann,Pearson,Moana g:Pearson(8)	3rd	4,678
31/3/00	Leeds (h)	W24-16	t:Pearson,Cardiss,Naylor g:Pearson(5),Bloem	3rd	6,817
9/4/00	Wigan (a)	L20-8	t:Goldspink g:Pearson,Bloem	4th	10,825
16/4/00	St Helens (a)	L52-20	t:Cardiss(2),Pearson(2) g:Pearson(2)	5th	8,571
21/4/00	Warrington (h)	L20-30	t:Rowley,Mercer,Tallec,Florimo g:Pearson(2)	7th	6,123
25/4/00	Hudds-Sheff (a)	W24-30	t:Cardiss,Moana,Bloem,Dunemann,Gibson g:Pearson(5)	5th	2,982
2/5/00	Castleford (h)	L14-20	t:Tallec,Marns g:Pearson(3)	5th	5,160
7/5/00	Salford (a)	W20-38	t:Marns,Golden,Rowley,Gannon,Pearson,Gibson g:Pearson(5),Bloem(2)	4th	3,703
12/5/00	Bradford (a)	L62-2	g:Pearson	5th	14,082
19/5/00	London (h)	W22-16	t:Moana,Pearson,Florimo g:Pearson(4),Bloem	5th	3,751
29/5/00	Wakefield (h)	W36-10	t:Golden(2),Mercer,Moana,Rowley,Tallec,Florimo g:Pearson(4)	5th	4,471
4/6/00	Hull (a)	L36-18	t:Pearson(2),Gannon g:Pearson(3)	5th	5,667
9/6/00	Leeds (a)	L36-22	t:Bloem,Hassan,Moana,Marns g:Bloem(2),Pearson	7th	12,963
16/6/00	Wigan (h)	L12-26	t:Moana,Marns g:Pearson,Bloem	7th	6,333
23/6/00	St Helens (h)	L24-28	t:Moana(2),Bloem,Marns g:Pearson(4)	7th	5,476
30/6/00	Hudds-Sheff (h)	W66-2	t:Moana(3),Dunemann(2),Rowley,Pearson,Naylor,Hassan,Marns,Cardiss g:Pearson(11)	7th	4,608
7/7/00	Warrington (a)	L34-12	t:Moana,Dunemann g:Bloem(2)	7th	6,243
16/7/00	Castleford (a)	L26-12	t:Gibson,Rowley g:Bloem(2)	7th	6,823
23/7/00	Salford (a)	L27-26	t:Cardiss,Rowley,Bloem,Dunemann,Marns g:Bloem(3)	7th	3,320
30/7/00	London (h)	L25-20	t:Marns(2),Golden g:Bloem(4)	7th	2,543
6/8/00	Bradford (h)	D20-20	t:Gannon(2),Golden,Gibson g:Bloem,Cardiss	8th	7,106
13/8/00	Wigan (a)	L20-12	t:Moana,Rowley g:Bloem(2)	8th	8,268
20/8/00	Hull (a)	W14-16	t:Gibson,Dunemann,Rowley g:Bloem(2)	8th	4,677
27/8/00	Castleford (h)	W36-16	t:Greenwood(2),Gibson(2),Tickle,Cardiss,Halliwell g:Tickle(4)	8th	6,293
3/9/00	Bradford (h)	L18-25	t:Hobson,Halliwell,Gibson g:Tickle(3)	8th	8,243
10/9/00	Salford (h)	L12-29	t:Gannon,Marns g:Rowley,Bloem	8th	4,646
17/9/00	Hudds-Sheff (h)	W54-18	t:Moana(3),Greenwood(2),Florimo,Dunemann,Mercer,Gannon,Gibson g:Florimo(4),Cardiss(3)	8th	4,843

	APP		TRIES		GOALS		FG		PTS	
	ALL	SL	ALL	SL	ALL	SL	ALL	SL	ALL	SL
Jamie Bloem	29	26	6	4	27	25	0	0	78	66
Daryl Cardiss	23(2)	21(1)	9	8	4	4	0	0	44	40
Ryan Clayton	(1)	(1)	0	0	0	0	0	0	0	0
Andrew Dunemann	30	27	9	9	0	0	1	0	37	36
Danny Ellison	1	0	0	0	0	0	0	0	0	0
Danny Fearon	(2)	(1)	0	0	0	0	0	0	0	0
Matt Firth	4(1)	4(1)	0	0	0	0	0	0	0	0
Greg Florimo	29	26	7	6	4	4	0	0	36	32
David Foster	4(8)	4(8)	0	0	0	0	0	0	0	0
Jim Gannon	29	26	7	6	0	0	0	0	28	24
Damian Gibson	28	25	10	10	0	0	0	0	40	40
Marvin Golden	22(2)	20(2)	6	5	0	0	0	0	24	20
Brett Goldspink	22(3)	19(3)	1	1	0	0	0	0	4	4
Lee Greenwood	4(2)	4(2)	4	4	0	0	0	0	16	16
Danny Halliwell	2(2)	2(2)	2	2	0	0	0	0	8	8
Phil Hassan	15(2)	14(1)	5	2	0	0	0	0	20	8
Andy Hobson	12(17)	12(14)	1	1	0	0	0	0	4	4
Stephen Holgate	3(10)	1(10)	0	0	0	0	0	0	0	0
Simon Knox	(1)	0	0	0	0	0	0	0	0	0
Oliver Marns	18(5)	17(5)	12	12	0	0	0	0	48	48
Casey Mayberry	1(1)	1(1)	0	0	0	0	0	0	0	0
Gary Mercer	30(1)	27(1)	4	3	0	0	0	0	16	12
Martin Moana	29(2)	26(2)	16	16	0	0	0	0	64	64
Jim Naylor	7(6)	7(6)	2	2	0	0	0	0	8	8
Martin Pearson	20(1)	17(1)	11	10	69	63	0	0	182	166
Sean Penkywicz	1	1	0	0	0	0	0	0	0	0
Mike Peters	1	1	0	0	0	0	0	0	0	0
Robert Roberts	(3)	(3)	0	0	0	0	0	0	0	0
Paul Rowley	26	23	10	9	1	1	0	0	42	38
Lokeni Savelio	2(12)	2(11)	0	0	0	0	0	0	0	0
Jonathan Scales	1	1	0	0	0	0	0	0	0	0
Gael Tallec	5(22)	5(19)	3	3	0	0	0	0	12	12
Jamie Thackray	1(5)	1(5)	0	0	0	0	0	0	0	0
Danny Tickle	4(4)	4(4)	1	1	7	7	0	0	18	18

LEAGUE RECORD
P28-W11-D1-L16
(8th, SL)
F664, A703, Diff-39
23 points.

CHALLENGE CUP
Quarter Finalists

ATTENDANCES
Best - v Bradford (CC - 9,827)
Worst - v London (SL - 3,751)
Total (SL only) - 79,994
Average (SL only) - 5,714
(Up by 1,231 on 1999)

TOP TACKLER
Gary Mercer

TOP GROUND GAINER
Gary Mercer

TOP CLEAN BREAKS
Martin Moana

TOP OFFLOADER
Andrew Dunemann

HUDDS-SHEFF GIANTS

DATE	FIXTURE	RESULT	SCORERS	LGE	ATT
12/2/00	Bradford (a) (CCR4)	L32-4	g:Crowther(2)	N/A	6,467
5/3/00	Salford (h)	L10-18	t:Ngamu,Lovell g:Crowther	N/A	3,480
19/3/00	London (a)	L34-18	t:Sovatabua,Lovell,Gleeson g:Crowther(3)	12th	2,856
2/4/00	Bradford (h)	L2-60	g:Crowther	12th	7,083
9/4/00	Hull (a)	L40-24	t:Sovatabua(2),Clinch,Thorman g:Crowther(4)	12th	5,553
16/4/00	Wakefield (h)	W35-34	t:Clinch(2),Hardy,Sovatabua,Lovell,Gleeson g:Crowther(5) fg:Clinch	11th	3,276
21/4/00	Leeds (a)	L20-10	t:Hardy g:Crowther(3)	12th	10,705
25/4/00	Halifax (h)	L24-30	t:Houles,Lovell,Ngamu g:Ngamu(6)	12th	2,982
1/5/00	St Helens (a)	L50-30	t:Sovatabua(2),Lawless,Cardoza,Ngamu g:Ngamu(5)	12th	8,518
7/5/00	Warrington (h)	L28-38	t:Ngamu,Rice,Lovell,Crowther,Cardoza g:Ngamu(4)	12th	3,049
14/5/00	Castleford (a)	L26-6	t:Ngamu g:Ngamu	12th	7,506
21/5/00	Wigan (h)	L8-56	t:Dekkiche g:Ngamu(2)	12th	3,421
26/5/00	London (h)	L16-20	t:Turner(2),Cooper g:Ngamu(2)	12th	2,458
4/6/00	Salford (a)	L18-8	t:Turner g:Ngamu(2)	12th	3,149
11/6/00	Bradford (a)	L48-20	t:Reilly,Laughton,Lomax g:Ngamu(4)	12th	11,565
18/6/00	Hull (h)	L26-34	t:Arnold(3),Gleeson,Bradbury g:Ngamu(3)	12th	3,184
25/6/00	Wakefield (a)	W20-27	t:Thorman(2),Dekkiche,Hardy,Gleeson g:Ngamu(3) fg:Hardy	12th	3,613
30/6/00	Halifax (a)	L66-2	g:Ngamu	12th	4,608
9/7/00	Leeds (h)	L20-48	t:Hardy,Thorman,Russell g:Ngamu(4)	12th	3,226
16/7/00	St Helens (h)	L24-40	t:Sovatabua,Arnold,Dekkiche,Hardy g:Ngamu(2),Thorman(2)	12th	3,317
23/7/00	Warrington (a)	W24-44	t:Cardoza(2),Lawless(2),Clinch(2),Hardy,Laughton g:Ngamu(6)	12th	4,572
30/7/00	Wigan (a)	L68-6	t:Arnold g:Ngamu	12th	7,165
6/8/00	Castleford (h)	L16-32	t:Arnold,Laughton,Ngamu g:Ngamu(2)	12th	2,102
13/8/00	Leeds (h)	L12-20	t:Sovatabua,Arnold g:Ngamu(2)	12th	5,019
18/8/00	Bradford (a)	L52-20	t:Thorman,Rivett,Cardoza,Crowther g:Crowther,Ngamu	12th	10,164
27/8/00	Hull (a)	L34-18	t:Crowther,Russell,Molloy g:Ngamu(3)	12th	4,080
3/9/00	Wakefield (h)	W16-14	t:Ngamu,Thorman g:Ngamu(4)	12th	2,409
10/9/00	Castleford (h)	L14-28	t:Turner,Crowther g:Ngamu(2),Crowther	12th	2,903
17/9/00	Halifax (a)	L54-18	t:Arnold(2),Crowther g:Crowther(3)	12th	4,843

	APP		TRIES		GOALS		FG		PTS	
	ALL	SL	ALL	SL	ALL	SL	ALL	SL	ALL	SL
Danny Arnold	15(2)	15(2)	9	9	0	0	0	0	36	36
David Bradbury	21(2)	21(2)	1	1	0	0	0	0	4	4
Dale Cardoza	5(6)	5(6)	5	5	0	0	0	0	20	20
Gavin Clinch	19(2)	18(2)	5	5	0	0	1	1	21	21
Ben Cooper	9(1)	9(1)	1	1	0	0	0	0	4	4
Matt Crowther	11(4)	10(4)	5	5	24	22	0	0	68	64
Yacine Dekkiche	11(3)	11(3)	3	3	0	0	0	0	12	12
Jamie Fielden	2(5)	2(5)	0	0	0	0	0	0	0	0
Nick Fozzard	1(2)	1(1)	0	0	0	0	0	0	0	0
Martin Gleeson	13(4)	13(3)	4	4	0	0	0	0	16	16
Jeff Hardy	21(5)	20(5)	6	6	0	0	1	1	25	25
Adam Hayes	2(1)	2(1)	0	0	0	0	0	0	0	0
Sylvain Houles	5(2)	5(2)	1	1	0	0	0	0	4	4
Chris Langley	4	4	0	0	0	0	0	0	0	0
Dale Laughton	25	24	3	3	0	0	0	0	12	12
Johnny Lawless	20(6)	19(6)	3	3	0	0	0	0	12	12
David Lomax	24(3)	23(3)	1	1	0	0	0	0	4	4
Karl Lovell	15	14	5	5	0	0	0	0	20	20
Richard Marshall	16(7)	15(7)	0	0	0	0	0	0	0	0
Steve Molloy	15(7)	14(7)	1	1	0	0	0	0	4	4
Chris Molyneux	(6)	(6)	0	0	0	0	0	0	0	0
Mark Moxon	5(1)	5(1)	0	0	0	0	0	0	0	0
Gene Ngamu	25(2)	24(2)	7	7	60	60	0	0	148	148
Paul Reilly	14(3)	13(3)	1	1	0	0	0	0	4	4
Andy Rice	1(8)	1(8)	1	1	0	0	0	0	4	4
Andy Richardson	(2)	(2)	0	0	0	0	0	0	0	0
Leroy Rivett	5(1)	5(1)	1	1	0	0	0	0	4	4
Danny Russell	9(13)	9(13)	2	2	0	0	0	0	8	8
Waisale Sovatabua	24(1)	23(1)	8	8	0	0	0	0	32	32
Chris Thorman	24(3)	23(3)	6	6	2	2	0	0	28	28
Darren Turner	15(3)	15(3)	4	4	0	0	0	0	16	16
Oliver Wilkes	1(5)	1(5)	0	0	0	0	0	0	0	0

LEAGUE RECORD
P28-W4-D0-L24
(12th, SL)
F502, A1026, Diff-524
8 points.

CHALLENGE CUP
Round Four

ATTENDANCES
Best - v Bradford (SL - 7,083)
Worst - v Castleford (SL - 2,102)
Total (SL only) - 47,909
Average (SL only) - 3,422
(Down by 305 on 1999 -
Huddersfield;
Down by 168 on 1999 - Sheffield)

TOP TACKLER
Chris Thorman

TOP GROUND GAINER
Waisale Sovatabua

TOP CLEAN BREAKS
Waisale Sovatabua

TOP OFFLOADER
David Lomax

HULL F.C.

HULL F.C.

DATE	FIXTURE	RESULT	SCORERS	LGE	ATT
13/2/00	Lancashire (h) (CCR4)	W86-0	t:Simon(3),Maiden(2),Gene(2),Bird(2),Horne(2),McDonald,Jenkins, Herron,Daylight,Carney g:Herron(11)	N/A	3,442
27/2/00	Rochdale (h) (CCR5)	W82-10	t:McDonald(3),Hick(2),Bird(2),Simon(2),Gene,Maher,Robinson, Felsch,Collins,Daylight g:Herron(6),Sammut(5)	N/A	3,992
3/3/00	Halifax (a)	L30-27	t:Carney(3),McDonald g:Sammut(5) fg:Wilson	N/A	6,124
11/3/00	Wigan (h) (CCQF)	W14-4	t:Maiden,McDonald g:Sammut(3)	N/A	7,378
17/3/00	St Helens (h)	L20-28	t:Jenkins,Collins,Carney g:Sammut(4)	10th	7,160
26/3/00	Leeds (CCSF)	L22-28	t:Daylight(3),McDonald g:Sammut(3)	N/A	18,068
2/4/00	Warrington (a)	W16-32	t:Sammut(2),Collins,Maher,Grimaldi,McDonald g:Sammut(4)	6th	5,956
9/4/00	Hudds-Sheff (h)	W40-24	t:Simon(2),Maiden,Robinson,Carney,Wilson,Collins g:Sammut(6)	5th	5,553
15/4/00	Castleford (a)	L22-12	t:Daylight,Simon g:Sammut(2)	6th	8,358
21/4/00	Salford (h)	W26-22	t:Horne(2),Robinson,Collins,Bird g:Sammut(3)	5th	5,862
24/4/00	London (a)	L13-8	t:Simon g:Herron(2)	5th	2,588
3/5/00	Bradford (h)	D8-8	t:Bird,Collins	6th	7,886
7/5/00	Wigan (a)	L50-18	t:Collins,Horne,Maher g:Sammut(3)	7th	8,077
14/5/00	Leeds (h)	W26-22	t:Horne,Collins,Felsch,Hick g:Sammut(3),Horne(2)	6th	8,143
21/5/00	Wakefield (a)	W6-34	t:Bird(2),Sammut,McDonald,Poucher g:Sammut(7)	6th	6,750
28/5/00	St Helens (a)	L27-14	t:Carney,McDonald g:Sammut(3)	6th	8,146
4/6/00	Halifax (h)	W36-18	t:Simon,Maher,Maiden,Collins,Horne,Daylight g:Sammut(6)	6th	5,667
9/6/00	Warrington (h)	W26-12	t:Horne,Gene,Simon,Collins g:Sammut(5)	5th	5,650
18/6/00	Hudds-Sheff (a)	W26-34	t:Collins(3),Maher,Maiden,Felsch g:Sammut(5)	5th	3,184
25/6/00	Castleford (h)	L4-18	t:Maher	6th	6,501
2/7/00	London (h)	W40-18	t:Horne(2),Daylight(2),Sammut,Maher,Gene g:Sammut(6)	6th	5,260
9/7/00	Salford (a)	L30-22	t:Maiden,Collins,Horne,Bird g:Sammut(3)	6th	3,494
14/7/00	Bradford (a)	L56-6	t:Felsch g:Sammut	6th	10,778
23/7/00	Wigan (h)	L12-21	t:Horne,Daylight g:Sammut,Cooke	6th	5,168
30/7/00	Wakefield (h)	W56-6	t:Maher(2),Gene(2),Collins,Horne,Jenkins,Simon,Parker,Herron g:Horne(7),Cooke	6th	5,440
4/8/00	Leeds (a)	L34-18	t:Poucher,Broadbent,Maher g:Horne(3)	6th	12,479
13/8/00	Warrington (a)	L41-10	t:Felsch,Gene g:Herron	6th	5,042
20/8/00	Halifax (h)	L14-16	t:Grimaldi,Collins g:Herron(3)	6th	4,677
27/8/00	Hudds-Sheff (h)	W34-18	t:Collins,Robinson,Fletcher,Horne,Carney g:Herron(7)	6th	4,080
3/9/00	Salford (a)	L33-24	t:Collins,Cooke,Maher,Robinson g:Herron(4)	6th	3,526
10/9/00	Wigan (a)	L54-4	t:Daylight	7th	8,409
17/9/00	Bradford (h)	W25-12	t:Simon,King,Daylight,Parker g:Cooke(4) fg:Cooke	7th	6,160

	APP		TRIES		GOALS		FG		PTS	
	ALL	SL	ALL	SL	ALL	SL	ALL	SL	ALL	SL
Deon Bird	17(5)	13(5)	9	5	0	0	0	0	36	20
Paul Broadbent	24(5)	20(5)	1	1	0	0	0	0	4	4
Brian Carney	15(4)	13(3)	8	7	0	0	0	0	32	28
Steve Collins	32	28	18	17	0	0	0	0	72	68
Paul Cooke	11(7)	10(7)	1	1	6	6	1	1	17	17
Steve Craven	1(11)	1(11)	0	0	0	0	0	0	0	0
Matt Daylight	21(1)	17(1)	12	7	0	0	0	0	48	28
Michael Docherty	(2)	(2)	0	0	0	0	0	0	0	0
Craig Farrell	(3)	(3)	0	0	0	0	0	0	0	0
Luke Felsch	29(3)	25(3)	5	4	0	0	0	0	20	16
Richard Fletcher	3(7)	3(6)	1	1	0	0	0	0	4	4
Stanley Gene	7(15)	5(13)	8	5	0	0	0	0	32	20
Tony Grimaldi	27(3)	26(1)	2	2	0	0	0	0	8	8
Ian Herron	11	9	2	1	34	17	0	0	76	38
Andrew Hick	10(10)	9(9)	3	1	0	0	0	0	12	4
Richard Horne	26(1)	25	14	12	12	12	0	0	80	72
Mick Jenkins	27	24	3	2	0	0	0	0	12	8
Paul King	10(14)	8(12)	1	1	0	0	0	0	4	4
Andy Last	1(2)	1(2)	0	0	0	0	0	0	0	0
Adam Maher	25(2)	23(2)	11	10	0	0	0	0	44	40
David Maiden	21(2)	17(2)	7	4	0	0	0	0	28	16
Wayne McDonald	6(11)	5(8)	10	4	0	0	0	0	40	16
Paul Parker	3	3	2	2	0	0	0	0	8	8
Craig Poucher	11(1)	10(1)	2	2	0	0	0	0	8	8
Scott Rhodes	2	2	0	0	0	0	0	0	0	0
Will Robinson	25	22	5	4	0	0	0	0	20	16
Ben Sammut	23	20	4	4	78	67	0	0	172	150
Craig Simon	24(5)	23(2)	13	8	0	0	0	0	52	32
Craig Wilson	4(18)	2(16)	1	1	0	0	1	1	5	5

LEAGUE RECORD
P28-W12-D1-L15
(7th, SL)
F630, A681, Diff-51
25 points.

CHALLENGE CUP
Semi Finalists

ATTENDANCES
Best - v Leeds (SL - 8,143)
Worst - v Lancashire (CC - 3,442)
Total (SL only) - 83,207
Average (SL only) - 5,943
(Up by 1,597 on 1999 - Hull;
Up by 2,048 on 1999 - Gateshead)

TOP TACKLER
Tony Grimaldi

TOP GROUND GAINER
Luke Felsch

TOP CLEAN BREAKS
Richard Horne

TOP OFFLOADER
Tony Grimaldi

LEEDS RHINOS

DATE	FIXTURE	RESULT	SCORERS	LGE	ATT
13/2/00	Featherstone (a) (CCR4)	W12-48	t:Sheridan(3),Sinfield(2),Powell,Barnhill,Harris g:Harris(8)	N/A	4,001
26/2/00	St Helens (h) (CCR5)	W26-20	t:Morley(2),Fleary,Sheridan g:Harris(5)	N/A	12,532
3/3/00	Wakefield (h)	L18-22	t:Hay,Mathiou,Cummins g:Cummins(3)	N/A	13,842
10/3/00	Dewsbury (h) (CCQF)	W42-10	t:Blackmore(2),Harris(2),Sheridan,Barnhill,Mathiou,Morley g:Harris(4),Cummins	N/A	10,533
19/3/00	Wigan (a)	L20-6	t:Harris g:Harris	11th	11,200
26/3/00	Hull (CCSF)	W22-28	t:Blackmore,Sheridan,Cummins,Farrell g:Harris(6)	N/A	18,068
31/3/00	Halifax (a)	L24-16	t:Powell(2),Senior g:Harris,Cummins	11th	6,817
7/4/00	St Helens (h)	L14-42	t:Barnhill,Sheridan g:Cummins(3)	11th	12,651
16/4/00	Warrington (a)	L44-10	t:Hay,Sinfield g:Cummins	12th	6,948
21/4/00	Hudds-Sheff (h)	W20-10	t:Sheridan(2),Morley g:Harris(4)	10th	10,705
29/4/00	Bradford (CCF)	L24-18	t:Hay,St Hilaire g:Harris(5)	N/A	67,247
2/5/00	Salford (h)	W42-16	t:Pratt(2),Senior,Barnhill,Sheridan,Harris,Mackay,McDermott g:Harris(5)	10th	10,008
5/5/00	London (a)	W6-38	t:Sheridan(2),Senior,Cummins,Jackson,Morley g:Harris(7)	8th	2,749
14/5/00	Hull (a)	L26-22	t:Morley,Blackmore,Hay,Pratt g:Harris(3)	8th	8,143
19/5/00	Bradford (h)	L2-44	g:Harris	8th	18,769
26/5/00	Wigan (h)	W26-19	t:Blackmore(2),Barnhill,Cummins g:Harris(5)	8th	11,881
31/5/00	Castleford (a)	W18-20	t:Sterling,Senior,Mackay,Sheridan g:Harris(2)	8th	11,702
4/6/00	Wakefield (a)	W24-30	t:Pratt(3),Sterling(2),Morley g:Harris(3)	8th	6,276
9/6/00	Halifax (h)	W36-22	t:Senior(4),Pratt,Sterling g:Harris(6)	6th	12,963
18/6/00	St Helens (a)	W20-42	t:Harris(2),Pratt(2),Senior,Hay,Cummins g:Harris(7)	6th	8,443
23/6/00	Warrington (h)	W28-24	t:Walker(3),Senior,Cummins g:Harris(4)	5th	11,432
1/7/00	Castleford (h)	W20-12	t:Senior,Sinfield,Barnhill,Mackay g:Harris(2)	5th	14,492
9/7/00	Hudds-Sheff (a)	W20-48	t:Harris(2),Mackay(2),Cummins(2),Hay,Pratt g:Harris(8)	4th	3,226
16/7/00	Salford (a)	W26-34	t:Cummins(2),Jackson,Harris,Sinfield,Hay g:Harris(5)	4th	5,057
21/7/00	London (h)	W42-22	t:Mackay(2),Blackmore,Hay,Sheridan,Cummins,Harris,Senior g:Harris(5)	4th	11,717
30/7/00	Bradford (a)	W26-28	t:Senior(2),Morley,Cummins g:Harris(6)	4th	21,237
4/8/00	Hull (h)	W34-18	t:Sheridan(2),Cummins,Pratt,Mackay,Blackmore g:Harris(5)	4th	12,479
13/8/00	Hudds-Sheff (a)	W12-20	t:Blackmore,Barnhill,Senior,Mackay g:Mackay(2)	4th	5,019
18/8/00	Castleford (a)	L20-16	t:Harris,Sterling g:Harris(4)	4th	9,819
25/8/00	Wakefield (h)	W42-22	t:Harris(2),Senior,Sterling,Mackay,Sheridan,Pratt g:Harris(7)	4th	13,075
1/9/00	St Helens (h)	L20-35	t:Jackson,Walker g:Harris(6)	4th	14,447
8/9/00	Bradford (a)	L14-12	t:Cummins g:Harris(4)	4th	19,623
15/9/00	London (h)	L6-18	t:Sinfield g:Cummins	4th	8,954
23/9/00	Castleford (h) (EPO)	W22-14	t:Sterling,Sinfield,Sheridan,Senior g:Harris(3)	N/A	13,685
30/9/00	Bradford (a) (ESF)	L46-12	t:Hay,Sterling g:Harris(2)	N/A	15,077

	APP		TRIES		GOALS		FG		PTS	
	ALL	SL	ALL	SL	ALL	SL	ALL	SL	ALL	SL
David Barnhill	24(9)	20(8)	7	5	0	0	0	0	28	20
Paul Bell	4	1	0	0	0	0	0	0	0	0
Richie Blackmore	25	20	9	6	0	0	0	0	36	24
Garreth Carvell	(3)	(3)	0	0	0	0	0	0	0	0
Francis Cummins	35	30	14	13	10	9	0	0	76	70
Anthony Farrell	12(16)	9(14)	1	0	0	0	0	0	4	0
Darren Fleary	32(2)	28(1)	1	0	0	0	0	0	4	0
Iestyn Harris	30	25	14	11	134	106	0	0	324	256
Andy Hay	29(5)	27(2)	9	8	0	0	0	0	36	32
Lee Jackson	26(8)	24(5)	3	3	0	0	0	0	12	12
Jamie Jones-Buchanan	(1)	(1)	0	0	0	0	0	0	0	0
Dean Lawford	6(5)	5(5)	0	0	0	0	0	0	0	0
Graham Mackay	12(8)	12(8)	10	10	2	2	0	0	44	44
Jamie Mathiou	6(24)	5(20)	2	1	0	0	0	0	8	4
Barrie McDermott	29	24	1	1	0	0	0	0	4	4
Adrian Morley	26(3)	22(3)	8	5	0	0	0	0	32	20
Daryl Powell	13(19)	8(19)	3	2	0	0	0	0	12	8
Karl Pratt	25(3)	25(2)	12	12	0	0	0	0	48	48
Gareth Raynor	(3)	(3)	0	0	0	0	0	0	0	0
Leroy Rivett	3(4)	1(4)	0	0	0	0	0	0	0	0
Keith Senior	35	30	17	17	0	0	0	0	68	68
Ryan Sheridan	35	30	18	12	0	0	0	0	72	48
Kevin Sinfield	19(7)	16(6)	7	5	0	0	0	0	28	20
Andy Speak	1	0	0	0	0	0	0	0	0	0
Paul Sterling	11(5)	11(5)	8	8	0	0	0	0	32	32
Marcus St Hilaire	5(5)	5(2)	1	0	0	0	0	0	4	0
Chev Walker	10(3)	10(3)	4	4	0	0	0	0	16	16
Danny Ward	2(3)	2(3)	0	0	0	0	0	0	0	0
David Wrench	(1)	(1)	0	0	0	0	0	0	0	0

LEAGUE RECORD
P28-W17-D0-L11
(4th, SL/Elimination Semi)
F692, A626, Diff+66
34 points.

CHALLENGE CUP
Runners Up

ATTENDANCES
Best - v Bradford (SL - 18,769)
Worst - v London (SL - 8,954)
Total (SL, inc play-offs) - 191,100
Average (SL, inc play-offs) - 12,740
(Down by 963 on 1999)

TOP TACKLER
Lee Jackson

TOP GROUND GAINER
Keith Senior

TOP CLEAN BREAKS
Keith Senior

TOP OFFLOADER
Barrie McDermott

LONDON BRONCOS

DATE	FIXTURE	RESULT	SCORERS	LGE	ATT
13/2/00	Wath Brow (h) (CCR4)	W44-18	t:Callaway,Wynyard,Edwards,Moore,Retchless,Tollett,Hammond, Toshack g:Tollett(4),Warton(2)	N/A	1,511
27/2/00	Salford (h) (CCR5)	L21-22	t:Johnson,Callaway,Tollett,Fleming g:Tollett(2) fg:Hammond	N/A	1,577
5/3/00	Warrington (a)	L48-18	t:Tollett,Callaway,Retchless g:Tollett(3)	N/A	8,718
19/3/00	Hudds-Sheff (h)	W34-18	t:Tollett,Magnus,Warton,Toshack,Johnson,Fleming g:Warton(5)	7th	2,856
2/4/00	Castleford (a)	L16-10	t:Fleming(2) g:Warton	8th	6,372
9/4/00	Salford (h)	L24-33	t:Fleming(2),Tollett,Johnson g:Warton(4)	9th	2,549
14/4/00	Wigan (a)	L48-6	t:Tollett g:Tollett	10th	6,697
21/4/00	Bradford (a)	L32-12	t:Wynyard,Davidson g:Tollett(2)	11th	13,239
24/4/00	Hull (h)	W13-8	t:Tollett,Davidson g:Tollett(2) fg:Hammond	10th	2,588
1/5/00	Wakefield (a)	W10-14	t:Peters,Callaway g:Tollett(3)	9th	4,695
5/5/00	Leeds (h)	L6-38	t:Peters g:Tollett	10th	2,749
12/5/00	St Helens (h)	L20-26	t:Tollett,Air,Cram g:Warton(4)	11th	3,063
19/5/00	Halifax (a)	L22-16	t:Napoli,Warton,Air g:Warton(2)	10th	3,751
26/5/00	Hudds-Sheff (a)	W16-20	t:Warton,Hammond,Air,Seibold g:Warton(2)	9th	2,458
4/6/00	Warrington (h)	L18-28	t:Toshack,Hughes,Davidson g:Warton(3)	9th	4,174
11/6/00	Castleford (h)	L20-26	t:Johnson,Hammond,Retchless,Tollett g:Warton(2)	9th	8,067
18/6/00	Salford (a)	L42-26	t:Hammond,Fleming,Warton,Lupton g:Warton(5)	11th	3,011
25/6/00	Wigan (h)	L12-16	t:Millard,Air g:Warton(2)	11th	4,351
2/7/00	Hull (a)	L40-18	t:Warton(2),Hammond g:Warton(3)	11th	5,260
9/7/00	Bradford (h)	L16-24	t:Fleming,Hammond,Tollett g:Warton(2)	11th	4,063
16/7/00	Wakefield (h)	L22-27	t:Fleming,Hammond,Warton,Tollett g:Warton(3)	11th	2,619
21/7/00	Leeds (a)	L42-22	t:Johnson,Hammond,Tollett,Callaway g:Warton(3)	11th	11,717
30/7/00	Halifax (h)	W25-20	t:Fleming,Warton,Johnson,Napoli g:Warton(4) fg:Hammond	11th	2,543
6/8/00	St Helens (a)	L46-12	t:Peters,Millard g:Warton(2)	11th	6,912
13/8/00	Salford (h)	L10-16	t:Johnson,Seibold g:Warton	11th	2,040
20/8/00	Wakefield (a)	L22-0	No Scorers	11th	2,370
25/8/00	Warrington (h)	L16-32	t:Clarke,Truelove,Crouthers g:Warton(2)	11th	2,054
3/9/00	Castleford (a)	L30-16	t:Timu,Johnson,Davidson g:Lupton(2)	11th	6,387
9/9/00	St Helens (h)	L12-38	t:Air,Lupton g:Warton(2)	11th	4,156
15/9/00	Leeds (a)	W6-18	t:Warton,Peters,Callaway g:Warton(3)	11th	8,954

	APP		TRIES		GOALS		FG		PTS	
	ALL	SL	ALL	SL	ALL	SL	ALL	SL	ALL	SL
Glen Air	13(3)	13(3)	5	5	0	0	0	0	20	20
Steve Barrow	2	2	0	0	0	0	0	0	0	0
Darren Bradstreet	(5)	(3)	0	0	0	0	0	0	0	0
Dean Callaway	11(15)	9(15)	6	4	0	0	0	0	24	16
Jon Clarke	18(5)	18(5)	1	1	0	0	0	0	4	4
Scott Cram	17(7)	15(7)	1	1	0	0	0	0	4	4
Kevin Crouthers	6(4)	6(4)	1	1	0	0	0	0	4	4
Paul Davidson	6(10)	6(10)	4	4	0	0	0	0	16	16
Justin Dooley	26(3)	26(1)	0	0	0	0	0	0	0	0
Shaun Edwards	4	2	1	0	0	0	0	0	4	0
Greg Fleming	19	18	10	9	0	0	0	0	40	36
Karle Hammond	21	19	8	7	0	0	3	2	35	30
Stefan Hughes	(2)	(2)	1	1	0	0	0	0	4	4
Olu Iwenofu	1(1)	1(1)	0	0	0	0	0	0	0	0
Andy Johnson	19(9)	18(8)	8	7	0	0	0	0	32	28
Peter Lupton	7(9)	7(9)	2	2	2	2	0	0	12	12
Brendan Magnus	3	3	1	1	0	0	0	0	4	4
Shane Millard	20(7)	18(7)	2	2	0	0	0	0	8	8
Danny Moore	9	7	1	0	0	0	0	0	4	0
Frank Napoli	16(6)	14(6)	2	2	0	0	0	0	8	8
Dominic Peters	19(2)	19(2)	4	4	0	0	0	0	16	16
Steele Retchless	27(3)	25(3)	3	2	0	0	0	0	12	8
Jonathan Roper	4	4	0	0	0	0	0	0	0	0
Anthony Seibold	13(16)	11(16)	2	2	0	0	0	0	8	8
Rob Smyth	3(1)	3(1)	0	0	0	0	0	0	0	0
Yusef Sozi	(1)	(1)	0	0	0	0	0	0	0	0
John Timu	16(2)	14(2)	1	1	0	0	0	0	4	4
Tulsen Tollett	22(2)	22	12	10	18	12	0	0	84	64
Matt Toshack	20(1)	19(1)	3	2	0	0	0	0	12	8
George Truelove	5	5	1	1	0	0	0	0	4	4
Brett Warton	25(1)	23(1)	9	9	57	55	0	0	150	146
Andrew Wynyard	19(3)	18(2)	2	1	0	0	0	0	8	4

LEAGUE RECORD
P28-W6-D0-L22
(11th, SL)
F456, A770, Diff-314
12 points.

CHALLENGE CUP
Round Five

ATTENDANCES
Best - v Castleford (SL - 8,067)
Worst - v Wath Brow (CC - 1,511)
Total (SL only) - 47,872
Average (SL only) - 3,419
(Up by 484 on 1999)

TOP TACKLER
Steele Retchless

TOP GROUND GAINER
Justin Dooley

TOP CLEAN BREAKS
Greg Fleming

TOP OFFLOADER
Justin Dooley

SALFORD CITY REDS

DATE	FIXTURE	RESULT	SCORERS	LGE	ATT
13/2/00	Barrow (a) (CCR4)	W18-34	t:Pinkney(2),Alker,Littler,Southern,Offiah g:Brown(5)	N/A	3,630
27/2/00	London (a) (CCR5)	W21-22	t:Pinkney,Highton,Offiah,Webber g:Southern(2),Brown	N/A	1,577
5/3/00	Hudds-Sheff (a)	W10-18	t:Svabic(2),Webber g:Svabic(3)	N/A	3,480
12/3/00	Warrington (h) (CCQF)	L20-22	t:Tassell,Offiah,Smith,Brown g:Svabic(2)	N/A	6,700
19/3/00	Castleford (h)	L16-22	t:Offiah,Tassell,Webber g:Svabic(2)	4th	5,534
2/4/00	Wigan (h)	L0-32	No Scorers	9th	6,663
9/4/00	London (a)	W24-33	t:Brown(2),Smith,Crompton,Offiah g:Brown(6) fg:Crompton	7th	2,549
16/4/00	Bradford (h)	L1-52	fg:Offiah	9th	6,468
21/4/00	Hull (a)	L26-22	t:Webber(2),Tassell,Offiah,Crompton g:Southern	9th	5,862
24/4/00	Wakefield (h)	L14-22	t:Makin,Tassell g:Southern(2),Duffy	9th	4,224
2/5/00	Leeds (a)	L42-16	t:Offiah,Faimalo,Broadbent g:Svabic(2)	11th	10,008
7/5/00	Halifax (h)	L20-38	t:Alker(2),Pinkney g:Blakeley(4)	11th	3,703
14/5/00	Warrington (h)	W31-12	t:Nicol(2),Pinkney,Smith,Littler g:Blakeley(5) fg:Duffy	10th	4,005
21/5/00	St Helens (a)	L46-22	t:Webber,Smith,Alker,Broadbent g:Blakeley(3)	11th	7,862
26/5/00	Castleford (a)	L30-4	t:Brown	11th	6,303
4/6/00	Hudds-Sheff (h)	W18-8	t:Wainwright,Southern,Broadbent g:Blakeley(3)	10th	3,149
11/6/00	Wigan (a)	L52-20	t:Brown,Smith,Pinkney,Blakeley g:Blakeley(2)	10th	7,748
18/6/00	London (h)	W42-26	t:Webber(2),Holroyd(2),Wainwright,Pinkney,Broadbent g:Blakeley(7)	9th	3,011
25/6/00	Bradford (a)	L96-16	t:Nicol,Pinkney,Napolitano g:Blakeley(2)	9th	11,596
2/7/00	Wakefield (a)	L36-10	t:Offiah,Littler g:Blakeley	10th	3,345
9/7/00	Hull (h)	W30-22	t:Pinkney(2),Webber,Smith,Tassell g:Blakeley(5)	9th	3,494
16/7/00	Leeds (a)	L26-34	t:Alker(2),Offiah,Baynes g:Blakeley(5)	10th	5,057
23/7/00	Halifax (h)	W27-26	t:Pinkney,Alker,Offiah,Nicol g:Blakeley(5) fg:Offiah	9th	3,320
30/7/00	St Helens (h)	L4-58	t:Webber	9th	5,409
6/8/00	Warrington (a)	L32-18	t:Pinkney,Johnson,Webber g:Blakeley(3)	9th	5,609
13/8/00	London (a)	W10-16	t:Broadbent,Offiah g:Blakeley(4)	9th	2,040
20/8/00	Wigan (h)	L18-30	t:Broadbent,Nicol g:Roper(3)	10th	4,704
27/8/00	St Helens (a)	L50-28	t:Offiah(2),Alker,Southern,Broadbent g:Blakeley(4)	10th	6,694
3/9/00	Hull (h)	W33-24	t:Offiah(2),Alker,Tassell,Pinkney,Roper g:Blakeley(3),Holroyd fg:Holroyd	9th	3,526
10/9/00	Halifax (a)	W12-29	t:Holroyd,Smith,Tassell g:Blakeley(7),Holroyd fg:Holroyd	9th	4,646
17/9/00	Warrington (a)	L38-10	t:Tassell,Offiah g:Holroyd	9th	6,969

	APP		TRIES		GOALS		FG		PTS		
	ALL	SL	ALL	SL	ALL	SL	ALL	SL	ALL	SL	
Malcolm Alker	30(1)	27(1)	9	8	0	0	0	0	36	32	
Warren Ayres	(1)	0	0	0	0	0	0	0	0	0	
Neil Baynes	20(6)	20(3)	1	1	0	0	0	0	4	4	
Steve Blakeley	19	19	1	1	63	63	0	0	130	130	
Gary Broadbent	30	27	8	8	0	0	0	0	32	32	
Darren Brown	24	21	5	4	12	6	0	0	44	28	
Martin Crompton	9	6	2	2	0	0	1	1	9	9	
John Duffy	3(11)	3(11)	0	0	1	1	1	1	3	3	
Joe Faimalo	5(15)	5(14)	1	1	0	0	0	0	4	4	
Brad Hepi	3(5)	3(5)	0	0	0	0	0	0	0	0	
Paul Highton	12(16)	9(16)	1	0	0	0	0	0	4	0	
Graham Holroyd	14(1)	14(1)	3	3	3	3	2	2	20	20	
Mark Johnson	1(11)	1(8)	1	1	0	0	0	0	4	4	
Mark Lee	4(3)	4(3)	0	0	0	0	0	0	0	0	
Matthew Leigh	1(7)	(6)	0	0	0	0	0	0	0	0	
Stuart Littler	5(9)	4(8)	3	2	0	0	0	0	12	8	
Craig Makin	6(9)	3(9)	1	1	0	0	0	0	4	4	
Craig Murdock	(2)	(2)	0	0	0	0	0	0	0	0	
Carlo Napolitano	(3)	(3)	1	1	0	0	0	0	4	4	
Jason Nicol	22	22	5	5	0	0	0	0	20	20	
Martin Offiah	25	22	16	13	0	0	2	2	66	54	
Nick Pinkney	31	28	13	10	0	0	0	0	52	40	
Jonathan Roper	1(4)	1(4)	1	1	3	3	0	0	10	10	
James Smith	25(3)	23(3)	7	6	0	0	0	0	28	24	
Paul Southern	25(5)	22(5)	3	2	5	3	0	0	22	14	
Simon Svabic	4(1)	3(1)	2	2	9	7	0	0	26	22	
Kris Tassell	24(4)	22(4)	8	7	0	0	0	0	32	28	
Mike Wainwright	26(3)	24(2)	2	2	0	0	0	0	8	8	
Jason Webber	28(1)	25(1)	11	10	0	0	0	0	44	40	

LEAGUE RECORD
P28-W10-D0-L18
(9th, SL)
F542, A910, Diff-368
20 points.

CHALLENGE CUP
Quarter Finalists

ATTENDANCES
Best - v Warrington (CC - 6,700)
Worst - v London (SL - 3,011)
Total (SL only) - 62,267
Average (SL only) - 4,448
(Down by 57 on 1999)

TOP TACKLER
Malcolm Alker

TOP GROUND GAINER
Neil Baynes

TOP CLEAN BREAKS
Nick Pinkney

TOP OFFLOADER
Mike Wainwright

ST HELENS

DATE	FIXTURE	RESULT	SCORERS	LGE	ATT
13/2/00	Swinton (a) (CCR4)	W22-36	t:Iro(3),Newlove,Sculthorpe,Long,Hoppe g:Long(4)	N/A	3,169
26/2/00	Leeds (a) (CCR5)	L26-20	t:Sculthorpe,Long g:Long(6)	N/A	12,532
3/3/00	Bradford (h)	L10-32	t:Joynt,Cunningham g:Long	N/A	10,128
17/3/00	Hull (a)	W20-28	t:Wellens(2),Long,Joynt,Sculthorpe g:Long(4)	8th	7,160
2/4/00	Wakefield (h)	W29-22	t:Cunningham(2),Newlove,Long,Martyn g:Long(4) fg:Martyn	5th	7,569
7/4/00	Leeds (a)	W14-42	t:Sullivan(3),Martyn,Long,Iro,Smith,Perelini g:Long(5)	3rd	12,651
16/4/00	Halifax (h)	W52-20	t:Martyn(2),Cunningham(2),Long,Iro,Wellens,Perelini,Hall g:Long(8)	3rd	8,571
21/4/00	Wigan (h)	W38-14	t:Iro(3),Martyn(2),O'Neill g:Long(7)	3rd	13,307
24/4/00	Warrington (a)	W34-47	t:Long(2),Hoppe,Iro,Perelini,Tuilagi,Nickle g:Long(9) fg:Martyn	3rd	9,086
1/5/00	Hudds-Sheff (h)	W50-30	t:Iro(5),Perelini(2),Hoppe,Stankevitch g:Long(3),Martyn(2)	2nd	8,518
7/5/00	Castleford (a)	W22-32	t:Sullivan(2),Iro,Joynt,Stankevitch,Martyn g:Martyn(4)	2nd	7,564
12/5/00	London (a)	W20-26	t:Long(2),Joynt,Newlove g:Martyn(5)	2nd	3,063
21/5/00	Salford (h)	W46-22	t:Iro(2),Sullivan(2),Long(2),Martyn,Newlove g:Long(7)	2nd	7,862
28/5/00	Hull (h)	W27-14	t:Joynt,Henare,Stewart,Atcheson g:Long(5) fg:Sculthorpe	1st	8,146
2/6/00	Bradford (a)	L17-16	t:Joynt(2),Long g:Long(2)	1st	13,237
11/6/00	Wakefield (a)	W22-30	t:Sullivan(2),Newlove,Wellens,Long,Smith g:Long(2),Martyn	2nd	5,104
18/6/00	Leeds (h)	L20-42	t:Stewart,Newlove,Hall g:Long(4)	3rd	8,443
23/6/00	Halifax (a)	W24-28	t:Wellens(2),Martyn,Stewart,Sullivan g:Long(4)	3rd	5,476
30/6/00	Warrington (h)	W50-20	t:Wellens(2),Cunningham(2),Martyn,West,Joynt,Barrow,Sullivan g:Long(7)	3rd	7,296
9/7/00	Wigan (a)	W28-30	t:Martyn(3),Hoppe,Sullivan g:Long(5)	2nd	17,428
16/7/00	Hudds-Sheff (a)	W24-40	t:Long(2),Tuilagi(2),Cunningham,Hall,Wellens g:Long(6)	2nd	3,317
21/7/00	Castleford (h)	W42-18	t:Cunningham(2),Long(2),Sculthorpe,Joynt,Wellens g:Long(7)	2nd	6,979
30/7/00	Salford (a)	W4-58	t:Iro(2),Sculthorpe(2),Martyn(2),Tuilagi,Long,Joynt,Hoppe g:Long(9)	1st	5,409
6/8/00	London (h)	W46-12	t:Martyn(2),Long(2),Matautia,Joynt,Tuilagi,West g:Long(7)	1st	6,912
13/8/00	Wakefield (a)	L32-16	t:Tuilagi(2),Sullivan g:Long(2)	2nd	3,642
20/8/00	Warrington (h)	W58-18	t:Martyn(3),Sullivan,Wellens,Iro,Cunningham,West,Stankevitch,Sculthorpe g:Long(9)	2nd	7,139
27/8/00	Salford (h)	W50-28	t:Cunningham(2),Perelini,Hall,Long,Sculthorpe,Joynt,Stewart,Stankevitch g:Long(7)	2nd	6,694
1/9/00	Leeds (a)	W20-35	t:Cunningham(2),Newlove(2),Wellens,Nickle g:Long(5) fg:Sculthorpe	2nd	14,447
9/9/00	London (a)	W12-38	t:Tuilagi(2),Sullivan,Wellens,Stankevitch,Joynt g:Long(7)	2nd	4,156
15/9/00	Wigan (h)	L4-42	t:Joynt	2nd	16,030
22/9/00	Bradford (h) (QPO)	W16-11	t:Hoppe,Martyn,Joynt g:Long(2)	N/A	8,864
29/9/00	Wigan (a) (QSF)	W16-54	t:Iro(2),Long(2),Hall,Cunningham,Sullivan,Martyn,Hoppe g:Long(9)	N/A	19,186
14/10/00	Wigan (GF)	W29-16	t:Joynt(2),Hoppe,Tuilagi,Jonkers g:Long(4) fg:Sculthorpe	N/A	58,132

	APP		TRIES		GOALS		FG		PTS	
	ALL	SL	ALL	SL	ALL	SL	ALL	SL	ALL	SL
Paul Atcheson	5(3)	3(3)	1	1	0	0	0	0	4	4
Scott Barrow	4(4)	4(4)	1	1	0	0	0	0	4	4
Mike Bennett	(7)	(7)	0	0	0	0	0	0	0	0
Keiron Cunningham	27(1)	25(1)	16	16	0	0	0	0	64	64
Mark Edmondson	(1)	(1)	0	0	0	0	0	0	0	0
Steve Hall	14(9)	14(9)	5	5	0	0	0	0	20	20
Bryan Henare	5(12)	4(11)	1	1	0	0	0	0	4	4
Sean Hoppe	25(2)	23(2)	8	7	0	0	0	0	32	28
Kevin Iro	27	25	22	19	0	0	0	0	88	76
Tim Jonkers	4(13)	4(13)	1	1	0	0	0	0	4	4
Chris Joynt	33	31	18	18	0	0	0	0	72	72
Sean Long	29	27	24	22	161	151	0	0	418	390
Tommy Martyn	27	27	22	22	12	12	2	2	114	114
Vila Matautia	2(10)	2(10)	1	1	0	0	0	0	4	4
Paul Newlove	16	14	8	7	0	0	0	0	32	28
Sonny Nickle	18(10)	16(10)	2	2	0	0	0	0	8	8
Julian O'Neill	26(6)	25(5)	1	1	0	0	0	0	4	4
Apollo Perelini	28(5)	27(4)	6	6	0	0	0	0	24	24
Paul Sculthorpe	27	25	8	6	0	0	3	3	35	27
Chris Smith	14(2)	12(2)	2	2	0	0	0	0	8	8
John Stankevitch	7(18)	7(18)	5	5	0	0	0	0	20	20
Anthony Stewart	4(7)	4(6)	4	4	0	0	0	0	16	16
Anthony Sullivan	30(1)	30	16	16	0	0	0	0	64	64
Darrell Trindall	2		0	0	0	0	0	0	0	0
Fereti Tuilagi	22(5)	21(4)	10	10	0	0	0	0	40	40
Paul Wellens	28(1)	28	13	13	0	0	0	0	52	52
Dwayne West	3(8)	3(8)	3	3	0	0	0	0	12	12

LEAGUE RECORD
P28-W23-D0-L5
(2nd, SL/Grand Final Winners, Champions)
F988, A627, Diff+361
46 points.

CHALLENGE CUP
Round Five

ATTENDANCES
Best - v Wigan (SL - 16,030)
Worst - v Salford (SL - 6,694)
Total (SL, inc play-offs) - 132,458
Average (SL, inc play-offs) - 8,830
(Up by 370 on 1999)

TOP TACKLER
Chris Joynt

TOP GROUND GAINER
Sean Long

TOP CLEAN BREAKS
Sean Long

TOP OFFLOADER
Keiron Cunningham

WAKEFIELD T WILDCATS

DATE	FIXTURE	RESULT	SCORERS	LGE	ATT
13/2/00	Leigh (a) (CCR4)	W28-40	t:Hughes(2),Stephenson,Hudson,Maloney,N Law g:McNamara(8)	N/A	3,810
27/2/00	Bradford (h) (CCR5)	L0-46	No Scorers	N/A	8,005
3/3/00	Leeds (a)	W18-22	t:Stephenson,Hughes,Sampson,McNamara g:McNamara(3)	N/A	13,842
19/3/00	Halifax (h)	L24-40	t:Jowitt,Price,Hughes g:McNamara(6)	6th	4,678
2/4/00	St Helens (a)	L29-22	t:Stephenson,Jowitt,N Law,P March g:McNamara(2),Maloney	7th	7,569
9/4/00	Warrington (h)	W28-24	t:Poching(2),Goulding,Price,Maloney g:McNamara(4)	6th	4,634
16/4/00	Hudds-Sheff (a)	L35-34	t:N Law(2),Sampson,Hughes,Poching,Price g:McNamara(4),Goulding	8th	3,276
20/4/00	Castleford (h)	L12-22	t:Prescott g:McNamara(4)	8th	6,138
24/4/00	Salford (a)	W14-22	t:P March(2),Hughes,Sampson g:McNamara(3)	7th	4,224
1/5/00	London (h)	L10-14	t:Tomlinson g:McNamara(3)	7th	4,695
7/5/00	Bradford (a)	L44-16	t:Sampson,Westwood,McNamara g:McNamara(2)	9th	15,276
14/5/00	Wigan (a)	L48-30	t:Hughes(2),Stephenson,N Law,Sampson g:G Law(5)	9th	8,214
21/5/00	Hull (h)	L6-34	t:Tomlinson g:G Law	9th	6,750
29/5/00	Halifax (a)	L36-10	t:Watene,Sodje g:G Law	10th	4,471
4/6/00	Leeds (h)	L24-30	t:Tomlinson,Stephenson,Hudson,Price g:Prescott(4)	11th	6,276
11/6/00	St Helens (h)	L22-30	t:Jowitt,Poching,Masella g:Prescott(5)	11th	5,104
18/6/00	Warrington (a)	W16-32	t:Goulding(2),Critchley,Speak,Masella g:Goulding(5) fg:Goulding(2)	10th	6,225
25/6/00	Hudds-Sheff (h)	L20-27	t:Critchley,Price,Jackson g:Goulding(3),Prescott	10th	3,613
2/7/00	Salford (h)	W36-10	t:Sodje(2),Jowitt(2),Speak,Price g:Goulding(6)	9th	3,345
8/7/00	Castleford (a)	L16-12	t:Field,Jowitt g:Goulding(2)	10th	8,043
16/7/00	London (a)	W22-27	t:Sampson,Sodje,Prescott g:Goulding(5) fg:Goulding	9th	2,619
23/7/00	Bradford (h)	L20-30	t:Tatupu(2),Critchley,Sampson g:Goulding(2)	10th	6,532
30/7/00	Hull (a)	L56-6	t:Critchley g:McNamara	10th	5,440
6/8/00	Wigan (h)	L6-56	t:Prescott g:McNamara	10th	3,650
13/8/00	St Helens (h)	W32-16	t:Watene,Jowitt,P March,Westwood,N Law,Holland g:G Law(4)	10th	3,642
20/8/00	London (h)	W22-0	t:N Law(2),Masella,Fisher g:Prescott(3)	9th	2,370
25/8/00	Leeds (a)	L42-22	t:Tomlinson,Masella,N Law,Jowitt g:P March(3)	9th	13,075
3/9/00	Hudds-Sheff (a)	L16-14	t:D March,N Law,P March g:P March	10th	2,409
10/9/00	Warrington (h)	L18-26	t:P March,Poching,Hudson g:G Law(3)	10th	3,187
16/9/00	Castleford (a)	L20-8	t:Handforth g:G Law(2)	10th	6,892

	APP		TRIES		GOALS		FG		PTS	
	ALL	SL	ALL	SL	ALL	SL	ALL	SL	ALL	SL
Jason Critchley	7(1)	7(1)	4	4	0	0	0	0	16	16
Dane Dorahy	2	2	0	0	0	0	0	0	0	0
Gareth Ellis	2(8)	2(8)	0	0	0	0	0	0	0	0
Jamie Field	12(13)	12(13)	1	1	0	0	0	0	4	4
Andy Fisher	10(8)	10(8)	1	1	0	0	0	0	4	4
Bobbie Goulding	13	12	3	3	25	25	3	3	65	65
Paul Handforth	(2)	(2)	1	1	0	0	0	0	4	4
Martyn Holland	2	2	1	1	0	0	0	0	4	4
Ryan Hudson	19(8)	17(8)	3	2	0	0	0	0	12	8
Adam Hughes	20(1)	19	8	6	0	0	0	0	32	24
Paul Jackson	14(10)	14(8)	1	1	0	0	0	0	4	4
Warren Jowitt	21(3)	19(3)	8	8	0	0	0	0	32	32
Tony Kemp	1(1)	(1)	0	0	0	0	0	0	0	0
Graham Law	9(2)	9(1)	0	0	16	16	0	0	32	32
Neil Law	22	20	10	9	0	0	0	0	40	36
Francis Maloney	13	11	2	1	1	1	0	0	10	6
David March	7(1)	7(1)	1	1	0	0	0	0	4	4
Paul March	10(11)	10(10)	6	6	4	4	0	0	32	32
Martin Masella	16(8)	14(8)	4	4	0	0	0	0	16	16
Keith Mason	(2)	(2)	0	0	0	0	0	0	0	0
Steve McNamara	17(2)	15(2)	2	2	40	32	0	0	88	72
Willie Poching	21(2)	19(2)	5	5	0	0	0	0	20	20
Steve Prescott	24(1)	22(1)	3	3	13	13	0	0	38	38
Gary Price	18(7)	18(5)	6	6	0	0	0	0	24	24
Paul Sampson	18	17	8	8	0	0	0	0	32	32
Bright Sodje	16	15	4	4	0	0	0	0	16	16
Andy Speak	6(5)	6(5)	2	2	0	0	0	0	8	8
Francis Stephenson	22(1)	20(1)	5	4	0	0	0	0	20	16
Tony Tatupu	20	18	2	2	0	0	0	0	8	8
Glen Tomlinson	17(3)	16(2)	4	4	0	0	0	0	16	16
Frank Watene	2(15)	2(15)	2	2	0	0	0	0	8	8
Ben Westwood	8(3)	8(3)	2	2	0	0	0	0	8	8
David White	(1)	(1)	0	0	0	0	0	0	0	0

LEAGUE RECORD
P28-W8-D0-L20
(10th, SL)
F557, A771, Diff-214
16 points.

CHALLENGE CUP
Round Five

ATTENDANCES
Best - v Bradford (CC - 8,005)
Worst - v London (SL - 2,370)
Total (SL only) - 64,614
Average (SL only) - 4,615
(Up by 380 on 1999)

TOP TACKLER
Ryan Hudson

TOP GROUND GAINER
Warren Jowitt

TOP CLEAN BREAKS
Paul Sampson

TOP OFFLOADER
Willie Poching

WARRINGTON WOLVES

DATE	FIXTURE	RESULT	SCORERS	LGE	ATT
13/2/00	Hunslet (a) (CCR4)	W4-46	t:Farrar(2),Parsley,Knott,McCurrie,Forster,Penny,Nikau g:Briers(7)	N/A	2,249
27/2/00	York (h) (CCR5)	W84-1	t:Briers(3),Kohe-Love(2),Hunte(2),Chambers(2),Knott,Langer, McCurrie,Farrar,Guisset g:Briers(14)	N/A	4,770
5/3/00	London (h)	W48-18	t:Hunte(2),Nikau,McCurrie,Briers,Langer,Guisset,Forster g:Briers(8)	N/A	8,718
12/3/00	Salford (a) (CCQF)	W20-22	t:Briers(2),Penny,Hunte g:Briers(3)	N/A	6,700
19/3/00	Bradford (a)	L58-4	t:Penny	9th	17,127
25/3/00	Bradford (CCSF)	L44-20	t:McCurrie(2),Knott g:Briers(4)	N/A	11,894
2/4/00	Hull (h)	L16-32	t:Sibbit,Hunte g:Briers(4)	10th	5,956
9/4/00	Wakefield (a)	L28-24	t:Forster,Hunte,Nutley,Langer,McCurrie g:Blakeley(2)	10th	4,634
16/4/00	Leeds (h)	W44-10	t:Sibbit(2),Hunte(2),Forster,Gee,Penny,Guisset g:Briers(6)	7th	6,948
21/4/00	Halifax (a)	W20-30	t:Kohe-Love(2),Farrar,Hunte,Briers g:Blakeley(3),Briers(2)	6th	6,123
24/4/00	St Helens (h)	L34-47	t:Penny(2),Gee,Nikau,Blakeley,Langer g:Blakeley(4),Briers	6th	9,086
1/5/00	Wigan (h)	L16-42	t:Knott,Roper,Briers g:Briers(2)	8th	7,983
7/5/00	Hudds-Sheff (a)	W28-38	t:Sibbit(3),Langer(2),Kohe-Love,Briers,McCurrie g:Briers(3)	6th	3,049
14/5/00	Salford (a)	L31-12	t:Penny,Kohe-Love g:Briers(2)	7th	4,005
21/5/00	Castleford (h)	L26-37	t:Guisset(2),Hunte,Roper,Farrar g:Roper(2),Briers	7th	5,915
28/5/00	Bradford (h)	W42-32	t:Langer(2),Busby,Roper,Knott,Penny,McCurrie g:Roper(7)	7th	8,302
4/6/00	London (a)	W18-28	t:Penny,Farrar,Briers,Hunte,Knott g:Briers(3),Roper	7th	4,174
9/6/00	Hull (a)	L26-12	t:Roper,Guisset,Kohe-Love	8th	5,650
18/6/00	Wakefield (h)	L16-32	t:Knott,Roper,Penny g:Roper,Briers	8th	6,225
23/6/00	Leeds (h)	L28-24	t:Penny(4) g:Roper(4)	8th	11,432
30/6/00	St Helens (a)	L50-20	t:Briers,Roper,McCurrie,Campbell g:Roper(2)	8th	7,296
7/7/00	Halifax (h)	W34-12	t:McCurrie(2),Hunte,Langer,Briers,Cowell g:Briers(5)	8th	6,243
16/7/00	Wigan (a)	L26-4	t:Peters	8th	8,225
23/7/00	Hudds-Sheff (h)	L24-44	t:Smyth(4),Campbell g:Briers(2)	8th	4,572
28/7/00	Castleford (a)	W18-32	t:Kohe-Love(2),Briers(2),Farrar,McCurrie g:Briers(4)	8th	7,058
6/8/00	Salford (h)	W32-18	t:McCurrie(2),Noone,Gee,Kohe-Love,Penny g:Briers(4)	7th	5,609
13/8/00	Hull (h)	W41-10	t:Kohe-Love(3),Smyth,McCurrie,Briers,Knott,Noone g:Briers(4) fg:Briers	7th	5,042
20/8/00	St Helens (a)	L58-18	t:Langer,Hunte,Busby g:Briers(3)	7th	7,139
25/8/00	London (a)	W16-32	t:Stenhouse(2),Kohe-Love(2),Gee,Knott g:Briers(4)	7th	2,054
3/9/00	Wigan (h)	L20-50	t:Langer(2),Briers,Hunte g:Briers(2)	7th	8,643
10/9/00	Wakefield (a)	W18-26	t:Hunte(2),Stenhouse,Penny,Forster g:Briers(3)	6th	3,187
17/9/00	Salford (h)	W38-10	t:McCurrie(2),Hunte(2),Briers,Kohe-Love,Guisset g:Langer(4),Briers	6th	6,969

	APP		TRIES		GOALS		FG		PTS	
	ALL	SL	ALL	SL	ALL	SL	ALL	SL	ALL	SL
David Alstead	(3)	(3)	0	0	0	0	0	0	0	0
Steve Blakeley	4(7)	4(3)	1	1	9	9	0	0	22	22
Lee Briers	23(9)	19(9)	17	12	93	65	1	1	255	179
Dean Busby	6(14)	6(12)	2	2	0	0	0	0	8	8
Chris Campbell	7(1)	7(1)	2	2	0	0	0	0	8	8
Gary Chambers	(13)	(11)	2	0	0	0	0	0	8	0
Will Cowell	5(2)	5(2)	1	1	0	0	0	0	4	4
Danny Farrar	31	27	7	4	0	0	0	0	28	16
Mark Forster	14	10	5	4	0	0	0	0	20	16
Andrew Gee	31	27	4	4	0	0	0	0	16	16
Mark Gleeson	(1)	(1)	0	0	0	0	0	0	0	0
Jerome Guisset	12(19)	11(16)	7	6	0	0	0	0	28	24
David Highton	(9)	(9)	0	0	0	0	0	0	0	0
Mark Hilton	6(16)	6(15)	0	0	0	0	0	0	0	0
Alan Hunte	31	28	19	16	0	0	0	0	76	64
Ian Knott	24(7)	21(6)	9	6	0	0	0	0	36	24
Toa Kohe-Love	26	22	16	14	0	0	0	0	64	56
Allan Langer	32	28	12	11	4	4	0	0	56	52
Steve McCurrie	30(1)	26(1)	17	13	0	0	0	0	68	52
Tawera Nikau	31	27	3	2	0	0	0	0	12	8
Paul Noone	8(5)	8(5)	2	2	0	0	0	0	8	8
Danny Nutley	27	23	1	1	0	0	0	0	4	4
Neil Parsley	1	0	1	0	0	0	0	0	4	0
Lee Penny	30	26	16	14	0	0	0	0	64	56
Mike Peters	2(12)	2(12)	1	1	0	0	0	0	4	4
Jonathan Roper	18(1)	14(1)	6	6	17	17	0	0	58	58
Ian Sibbit	10(4)	10(1)	6	6	0	0	0	0	24	24
Rob Smyth	4	4	5	5	0	0	0	0	20	20
Jamie Stenhouse	3	3	3	3	0	0	0	0	12	12
Paul Wood	(2)	(2)	0	0	0	0	0	0	0	0

LEAGUE RECORD
P28-W13-D0-L15
(6th, SL)
F735, A817, Diff-82
26 points.

CHALLENGE CUP
Semi Finalists

ATTENDANCES
Best - v St Helens (SL - 9,086)
Worst - v Hudds-Sheff (SL - 4,572)
Total (SL only) - 96,211
Average (SL only) - 6,872
(Up by 1,762 on 1999)

TOP TACKLER
Danny Farrar

TOP GROUND GAINER
Lee Penny

TOP CLEAN BREAKS
Toa Kohe-Love

TOP OFFLOADER
Tawera Nikau

WIGAN WARRIORS

DATE	FIXTURE	RESULT	SCORERS	LGE	ATT
13/2/00	Whitehaven (h) (CCR4)	W98-4	t:Robinson(3),Renouf(2),Radlinski(2),T Smith(2),Newton,Jones, Farrell,Dallas,Mestrov,Gilmour,Cassidy,Davies g:Farrell(15)	N/A	6,532
27/2/00	Doncaster (h) (CCR5)	W38-2	t:Farrell,Connolly,Peters,Newton,Dallas,Renouf,Radlinski g:Farrell(5)	N/A	6,225
5/3/00	Castleford (a)	W24-30	t:T Smith(2),Peters,Radlinski,Dallas g:Farrell(5)	N/A	8,812
11/3/00	Hull (a) (CCQF)	L14-4	g:Farrell(2)	N/A	7,378
19/3/00	Leeds (h)	W20-6	t:Farrell,Dallas,Betts g:Farrell(3),Peters	2nd	11,200
2/4/00	Salford (a)	W0-32	t:Renouf(2),T Smith,Peters,Johnson g:Farrell(6)	2nd	6,663
9/4/00	Halifax (h)	W20-8	t:Gilmour,Cassidy,Dallas g:Farrell(4)	2nd	10,825
14/4/00	London (h)	W48-6	t:Dallas(2),Cowie,Renouf,Radlinski,Robinson,Peters,Johnson g:Farrell(8)	2nd	6,697
21/4/00	St Helens (a)	L38-14	t:Johnson,Radlinski g:Farrell(3)	2nd	13,307
24/4/00	Castleford (h)	W30-16	t:Farrell,Dallas,Newton,Peters,Hodgson g:Farrell(5)	2nd	10,098
1/5/00	Warrington (a)	W16-42	t:Renouf(2),Radlinski,Robinson,O'Connor,Haughton,Betts g:Farrell(7)	1st	7,983
7/5/00	Hull (h)	W50-18	t:Robinson(2),Cassidy,Haughton,Radlinski,Dallas,Newton,Renouf g:Farrell(9)	1st	8,077
14/5/00	Wakefield (h)	W48-30	t:Peters(2),Robinson(2),Newton,Dallas,M Smith,Radlinski g:Farrell(8)	1st	8,214
21/5/00	Hudds-Sheff (a)	W8-56	t:Renouf(2),Robinson(2),Connolly,Dallas,Radlinski,Gilmour,Cassidy g:Farrell(10)	1st	3,421
26/5/00	Leeds (a)	L26-19	t:Radlinski,Dallas,Peters g:Farrell(3) fg:Peters	2nd	11,881
7/6/00	Bradford (h)	D12-12	t:Newton,Connolly g:Farrell fg:Peters,Farrell	3rd	17,365
11/6/00	Salford (h)	W52-20	t:Dallas(3),Robinson(2),Renouf,Chester,Malam,Peters g:Farrell(6),Peters(2)	3rd	7,748
16/6/00	Halifax (a)	W12-26	t:Connolly(2),Peters,Dallas,Chester g:Peters(2),Jones	2nd	6,333
25/6/00	London (a)	W12-16	t:Farrell,Newton,Dallas g:Farrell(2)	2nd	4,351
30/6/00	Bradford (a)	W18-30	t:Newton(2),Robinson,Betts,Gilmour g:Farrell(4) fg:Peters,Cowie	1st	18,815
9/7/00	St Helens (h)	L28-30	t:Renouf(2),Hodgson,Chester g:Farrell(5) fg:Peters(2)	3rd	17,428
16/7/00	Warrington (h)	W26-4	t:Cassidy,Haughton,Connolly,Robinson,Renouf g:Farrell(3)	3rd	8,225
23/7/00	Hull (a)	W12-21	t:Peters,Renouf,Betts g:Farrell(4) fg:Peters	3rd	5,168
30/7/00	Hudds-Sheff (h)	W68-6	t:Farrell(3),Renouf(2),Gilmour,Betts,Peters,Robinson,Mestrov, Radlinski,Connolly g:Farrell(10)	2nd	7,165
6/8/00	Wakefield (a)	W6-56	t:Betts(2),Gilmour(2),M Smith(2),Radlinski(2),Robinson,Cassidy g:Farrell(8)	2nd	3,650
13/8/00	Halifax (h)	W20-12	t:Radlinski(2),Newton g:Farrell(4)	1st	8,268
20/8/00	Salford (a)	W18-30	t:Radlinski(2),T Smith,Cassidy,Farrell g:Farrell(5)	1st	4,704
27/8/00	Bradford (h)	W20-19	t:Newton,Betts,Radlinski g:Farrell(4)	1st	17,737
3/9/00	Warrington (a)	W20-50	t:Newton(3),Renouf(2),Farrell,Connolly,Radlinski g:Farrell(9)	1st	8,643
10/9/00	Hull (h)	W54-4	t:Hodgson(3),Robinson(3),Davies,Peters,Betts,Connolly g:Farrell(7)	1st	8,409
15/9/00	St Helens (a)	W4-42	t:Peters(2),Cowie,Dallas,Renouf,Robinson,Connolly g:Farrell(7)	1st	16,030
29/9/00	St Helens (h) (QSF)	L16-54	t:Renouf(2),T Smith g:Farrell(2)	N/A	19,186
7/10/00	Bradford (h) (FE)	W40-12	t:Dallas(3),Robinson(2),Peters,Connolly g:Farrell(6)	N/A	14,620
14/10/00	St Helens (GF)	L29-16	t:Farrell,Hodgson,T Smith g:Farrell(2)	N/A	58,132

	APP		TRIES		GOALS		FG		PTS		
	ALL	SL	ALL	SL	ALL	SL	ALL	SL	ALL	SL	
Rob Ball	(1)	(1)	0	0	0	0	0	0	0	0	**LEAGUE RECORD** P28-W24-D1-L3
Denis Betts	32(2)	30(1)	9	9	0	0	0	0	36	36	(1st, SL/Grand Final Runners Up)
Mick Cassidy	32(2)	29(2)	7	6	0	0	0	0	28	24	F960, A405, Diff+555
Chris Chester	11(9)	11(9)	3	3	0	0	0	0	12	12	49 points.
Gary Connolly	27(2)	24(2)	11	10	0	0	0	0	44	40	
Neil Cowie	33	31	2	2	0	0	1	1	9	9	**CHALLENGE CUP**
Brett Dallas	24	21	21	19	0	0	0	0	84	76	Quarter Finalists
Wes Davies	6(13)	6(12)	2	1	0	0	0	0	8	4	
Andy Farrell	33	30	11	9	182	160	1	1	409	357	**ATTENDANCES**
Lee Gilmour	14(18)	14(15)	7	6	0	0	0	0	28	24	Best - v St Helens (QSF - 19,186)
Simon Haughton	8(8)	7(6)	2	2	0	0	0	0	8	8	Worst - v Doncaster (CC - 6,225)
David Hodgson	8(6)	8(6)	7	7	0	0	0	0	28	28	Total (SL, inc play-offs) - 181,262
Paul Johnson	2(4)	2(3)	3	3	0	0	0	0	12	12	Average (SL, inc play-offs) - 11,329
Phil Jones	2(2)	1(1)	1	0	1	1	0	0	6	2	(Up by 1,863 on 1999)
Brady Malam	7(21)	5(20)	1	1	0	0	0	0	4	4	
Tony Mestrov	(27)	(25)	2	1	0	0	0	0	8	4	**TOP TACKLER**
Terry Newton	29(2)	26(2)	14	12	0	0	0	0	56	48	Mick Cassidy
Terry O'Connor	28(5)	26(5)	1	1	0	0	0	0	4	4	
Willie Peters	31	29	16	15	5	5	6	6	80	76	**TOP GROUND GAINER**
Kris Radlinski	33	30	20	17	0	0	0	0	80	68	Terry O'Connor
Mark Reber	(3)	(3)	0	0	0	0	0	0	0	0	
Steve Renouf	32	29	23	20	0	0	0	0	92	80	**TOP CLEAN BREAKS**
Jason Robinson	34	31	23	20	0	0	0	0	92	80	Jason Robinson
Mark Smith	5(4)	5(4)	3	3	0	0	0	0	12	12	
Tony Smith	11(5)	8(5)	8	6	0	0	0	0	32	24	**TOP OFFLOADER** Andy Farrell

BARROW BORDER RAIDERS

DATE	FIXTURE	RESULT	SCORERS	LGE	ATT
26/12/99	Whitehaven (h)	W31-4	t:Atkinson(2),Smith,Whitehead,Hutton,Marshall g:Holt(3) fg:Holt	N/A	1,637
3/1/00	Featherstone (a)	L35-14	t:Manihera,Rawlinson g:Holt(3)	10th	1,908
9/1/00	Workington (a)	W18-35	t:Atkinson(2),Magorian,Rawlinson,Hutton,Charlton g:Holt(5) fg:Holt	7th	992
16/1/00	Oldham (h)	W19-16	t:Atkinson(2),Smith g:Holt(3) fg:Holt	4th	1,618
23/1/00	Leigh (a)	L48-22	t:Rhodes,Rawlinson,Salmon,Charlton g:Holt(3)	9th	2,070
30/1/00	F'stone L (h) (CCR3)	W42-12	t:Magorian(2),Manihera,Massey,Smith,Hutton,Salmon,Clark g:Holt(5)	N/A	719
6/2/00	Lancashire (h)	W40-6	t:Magorian(4),Hutton,Holt,Smith g:Holt(6)	6th	871
13/2/00	Salford (h) (CCR4)	L18-34	t:Holt(2),Rhodes g:Holt(3)	N/A	3,630
20/2/00	Widnes (a)	L17-10	t:Holt g:Holt(2),Carter	9th	3,058
5/3/00	Rochdale (h)	W32-14	t:Hutton(2),Rhodes(2),Holt,Clark g:Holt(4)	8th	1,169
12/3/00	Swinton (a)	L35-22	t:Charlton,Rhodes,Clark,Carter g:Holt(3)	10th	808
19/3/00	Sheffield (h)	W34-16	t:Clark(2),Carter(2),Hutton,Luxon g:Holt(5)	8th	1,172
26/3/00	Hunslet (h)	W36-18	t:Rhodes(2),Massey(2),Hutton,Maybon g:Holt(6)	8th	1,116
2/4/00	York (a)	L20-18	t:Clark,Okul g:Holt(5)	8th	388
9/4/00	Batley (h)	W28-25	t:Maybon(2),Magorian,Luxon,Okul g:Holt(4)	8th	1,530
16/4/00	Keighley (a)	L66-6	t:Whitehead g:Holt	9th	2,142
21/4/00	Whitehaven (a)	L30-0	No Scorers	10th	808
24/4/00	Featherstone (h)	W38-10	t:Rhodes(2),Maybon,Carter,Hutton,Holt g:Holt(7)	9th	1,363
1/5/00	Hull KR (h)	W42-12	t:Atkinson(2),Hutton(2),Charlton,Luxon,Magorian g:Holt(7)	9th	1,763
7/5/00	Doncaster (a)	L68-12	t:Hutton,Holt g:Holt(2)	9th	1,286
10/5/00	Dewsbury (h)	L10-36	t:Wilson,Magorian g:Holt	9th	1,421
14/5/00	Workington (h)	L22-24	t:Okul(2),Kavanagh g:Holt(5)	9th	1,416
21/5/00	Oldham (a)	L30-16	t:Charlton,Atkinson,Hutton g:Holt(2)	10th	1,604
26/5/00	Leigh (a)	W20-12	t:Wilson,Hutton,King g:Holt(3) fg:Holt,Kavanagh	9th	1,170
29/5/00	Lancashire (a)	W14-50	t:Hutton(2),Maybon,Magorian,Luxon,Massey,Whitter,Marshall g:Holt(9)	9th	223
4/6/00	Widnes (h)	W20-17	t:Luxon(2),Magorian g:Holt(4)	9th	1,829
11/6/00	Dewsbury (a)	L42-20	t:Clark(2),Holt,Hutton g:Holt(2)	10th	1,000
18/6/00	Swinton (h)	W34-22	t:Maybon(2),Clark,Manihera,Rhodes,Whitter g:Holt(4),Atkinson	9th	1,114
25/6/00	Sheffield (a)	L30-2	g:Holt	10th	1,188
2/7/00	Hull KR (a)	L26-14	t:Atkinson,Maybon g:Holt(3)	10th	2,379

	APP		TRIES		GOALS		FG		PTS	
	ALL	NFP	ALL	NFP	ALL	NFP	ALL	NFP	ALL	NFP
Phil Atkinson	19(1)	19(1)	10	10	1	1	0	0	42	42
William Burns	7(3)	7(3)	0	0	0	0	0	0	0	0
Darren Carter	13(5)	12(4)	4	4	1	1	0	0	18	18
Gary Charlton	17(4)	15(4)	5	5	0	0	0	0	20	20
Dave Clark	19(2)	17(2)	9	8	0	0	0	0	36	32
Adrian Gardner	1	1	0	0	0	0	0	0	0	0
Paul Gardner	(1)	(1)	0	0	0	0	0	0	0	0
Darren Holt	30	28	8	6	111	103	4	4	258	234
Glen Hutton	27(1)	25(1)	17	16	0	0	0	0	68	64
Shane Irabor	(1)	(1)	0	0	0	0	0	0	0	0
Steve Jackson	11(16)	10(15)	0	0	0	0	0	0	0	0
Mike Kavanagh	10(3)	10(3)	1	1	0	0	1	1	5	5
Dave King	4(7)	4(7)	1	1	0	0	0	0	4	4
Geoff Luxon	26(1)	25(1)	6	6	0	0	0	0	24	24
Stuart Magorian	27(2)	25(2)	12	10	0	0	0	0	48	40
Tane Manihera	29	27	3	2	0	0	0	0	12	8
Jamie Marshall	5(6)	5(6)	2	2	0	0	0	0	8	8
Chris Massey	2(13)	1(13)	4	3	0	0	0	0	16	12
Rod Maybon	21	21	8	8	0	0	0	0	32	32
Ian McAllister	(2)	(2)	0	0	0	0	0	0	0	0
John Okul	6(6)	6(6)	4	4	0	0	0	0	16	16
Gareth Pratt	9(1)	8	0	0	0	0	0	0	0	0
Ian Rawlinson	1(10)	(9)	3	3	0	0	0	0	12	12
Stuart Rhodes	27	25	10	9	0	0	0	0	40	36
Andy Rigby	(2)	(2)	0	0	0	0	0	0	0	0
Paul Salmon	9	7	2	1	0	0	0	0	8	4
Jamie Smith	22(3)	20(3)	4	3	0	0	0	0	16	12
Jason Thurlow	(1)	(1)	0	0	0	0	0	0	0	0
Mike Whitehead	16(5)	15(4)	2	2	0	0	0	0	8	8
Chris Whiteley	6(2)	5(1)	0	0	0	0	0	0	0	0
Damien Whitter	17(7)	17(6)	2	2	0	0	0	0	8	8
Darren Wilson	9(1)	9(1)	2	2	0	0	0	0	8	8

Rod Maybon

LEAGUE RECORD
P28-W14-D0-L14
(10th, NFP)
F647, A711, Diff-64
28 points.

CHALLENGE CUP
Round Four

ATTENDANCES
Best - v Salford (CC - 3,630)
Worst - v F'stone L (CC - 719)
Total (NFP only) - 19,189
Average (NFP only) - 1,371
(Up by 240 on 1999)

BATLEY BULLDOGS

DATE	FIXTURE	RESULT	SCORERS	LGE	ATT
26/12/99	Dewsbury (h)	L8-18	t:Gleadhill g:Price(2)	N/A	2,381
2/1/00	Doncaster (a)	L42-8	t:R Simpson g:Price(2)	15th	1,768
9/1/00	Keighley (h)	L18-28	t:Middleton(2),Flynn g:Price(2) fg:Price,G Barnett	16th	1,260
16/1/00	Sheffield (a)	W12-22	t:Clarke,Cass,G Barnett,Moxon g:Price(3)	15th	1,612
23/1/00	Hunslet (h)	L18-27	t:Gleadhill,Lingard,Moxon g:Price(3)	15th	748
30/1/00	Oldham SA (h) (CCR3)	L0-10	No Scorers	N/A	601
6/2/00	York (a)	W8-10	t:Jackson g:Price(2) fg:Price,Jackson	15th	701
20/2/00	Swinton (a)	W16-32	t:Jackson(2),Price,Lingard,N Simpson,Flynn g:Price(4)	12th	885
5/3/00	Hull KR (h)	L14-32	t:Kimmel,Lingard,Gleadhill g:Price	12th	1,027
12/3/00	Featherstone (a)	L38-16	t:Flynn,Gleadhill,Jackson g:Jackson(2)	13th	1,684
19/3/00	Rochdale (h)	W24-12	t:Flynn,N Simpson,Gleadhill,Price g:Price(4)	12th	464
26/3/00	Widnes (a)	L30-10	t:Gleadhill,Lingard g:Price	12th	3,001
2/4/00	Lancashire (h)	W34-16	t:Lingard(2),Gleadhill(2),N Simpson,S Barnett g:Price(5)	11th	324
9/4/00	Barrow (a)	L28-25	t:Lingard,Cass,R Simpson g:Price(6) fg:G Barnett	11th	1,530
16/4/00	Oldham (h)	L16-28	t:R Simpson,G Barnett,Gleadhill g:Price(2)	11th	805
21/4/00	Dewsbury (a)	L45-10	t:Lingard(2) g:Jackson	13th	1,900
24/4/00	Doncaster (h)	L20-28	t:Lingard(2),Gleadhill,Stevens g:Jackson,Stevens	15th	948
1/5/00	Workington (h)	L10-30	t:R Simpson(2) g:Price	15th	398
7/5/00	Leigh (a)	L44-40	t:R Simpson,Beevers,Price,McWilliam,Gleadhill g:Price(6)	16th	1,550
14/5/00	Keighley (a)	L40-12	t:Lingard,G Barnett g:Price(2)	16th	1,790
21/5/00	Sheffield (h)	L14-21	t:Lingard,Flynn g:Price(3)	16th	513
26/5/00	Hunslet (a)	W10-17	t:Gleadhill(2),Bargate g:Price(2) fg:Price	16th	523
29/5/00	York (h)	L10-33	t:G Barnett,Gleadhill g:Price	16th	451
4/6/00	Swinton (h)	L24-28	t:Lingard,R Simpson,Cass,S Barnett g:Price(4)	16th	360
11/6/00	Hull KR (a)	L30-10	t:Beevers g:Price(3)	16th	1,879
14/6/00	Whitehaven (a)	L20-14	t:Jackson,R Simpson,Gleadhill g:Gleadhill	16th	520
18/6/00	Featherstone (h)	L18-38	t:Lingard,Price g:Price(5)	16th	838
25/6/00	Rochdale (a)	L33-20	t:Lingard(3),Gleadhill g:Price(2)	16th	908
2/7/00	Widnes (h)	L8-24	t:Lingard g:Price(2)	16th	685

	APP		TRIES		GOALS		FG		PTS	
	ALL	NFP	ALL	NFP	ALL	NFP	ALL	NFP	ALL	NFP
Lee Bargate	12	12	1	1	0	0	0	0	4	4
Craig Barker	(1)	(1)	0	0	0	0	0	0	0	0
Gary Barnett	20	20	4	4	0	0	2	2	18	18
Steve Barnett	13(7)	13(7)	2	2	0	0	0	0	8	8
Chris Beevers	3(5)	3(5)	2	2	0	0	0	0	8	8
Will Cartledge	(3)	(3)	0	0	0	0	0	0	0	0
Mark Cass	5(21)	4(21)	3	3	0	0	0	0	12	12
John Clarke	24	23	1	1	0	0	0	0	4	4
Gareth Duckett	(1)	(1)	0	0	0	0	0	0	0	0
Jeremy Dyson	(3)	(3)	0	0	0	0	0	0	0	0
Wayne Flynn	27	26	5	5	0	0	0	0	20	20
Paul Gleadhill	28	27	16	16	1	1	0	0	66	66
Phil Hardwick	3(3)	3(3)	0	0	0	0	0	0	0	0
Paul Hicks	24(4)	24(3)	0	0	0	0	0	0	0	0
Simon Jackson	18(4)	17(4)	5	5	4	4	1	1	29	29
David Kimmel	10(1)	9(1)	1	1	0	0	0	0	4	4
Craig Lingard	25(2)	24(2)	19	19	0	0	0	0	76	76
David Luckwell	25(1)	24(1)	0	0	0	0	0	0	0	0
Chris McWilliam	15(1)	14(1)	1	1	0	0	0	0	4	4
Graham Middleton	15(1)	15(1)	2	2	0	0	0	0	8	8
Grant Miers	15(7)	14(7)	0	0	0	0	0	0	0	0
Darren Moxon	11(2)	10(2)	2	2	0	0	0	0	8	8
Rob Padgett	6(15)	6(14)	0	0	0	0	0	0	0	0
Ian Popplewell	2(2)	2(2)	0	0	0	0	0	0	0	0
Richard Price	25	24	4	4	68	68	3	3	155	155
David Rourke	(2)	(2)	0	0	0	0	0	0	0	0
Nick Simpson	20(3)	19(3)	3	3	0	0	0	0	12	12
Roger Simpson	24	24	10	10	0	0	0	0	40	40
Craig Stevens	1(6)	1(5)	1	1	1	1	0	0	6	6
Tony Walton	(9)	(9)	0	0	0	0	0	0	0	0
Andy Wray	6(10)	6(9)	0	0	0	0	0	0	0	0

Graham Middleton

LEAGUE RECORD
P28-W6-D0-L22
(16th, NFP)
F482, A759, Diff-277
12 points.

CHALLENGE CUP
Round Three

ATTENDANCES
Best - v Dewsbury (NFP - 2,381)
Worst - v Lancashire (NFP - 324)
Total (NFP only) - 11,202
Average (NFP only) - 800
(Up by 14 on 1999)

DEWSBURY RAMS

DATE	FIXTURE	RESULT	SCORERS	LGE	ATT
26/12/99	Batley (a)	W8-18	t:Graham,Godfrey g:Eaton(4),Agar	N/A	2,381
2/1/00	Hull KR (h)	W14-2	t:Potter,Flynn g:Eaton(3)	4th	2,119
9/1/00	Featherstone (a)	W2-38	t:Ball(2),Eaton,Godfrey,Flynn,Agar,Graham g:Eaton(5)	1st	2,589
16/1/00	Workington (h)	W36-6	t:Flynn(2),Ball,O'Meara,Richardson,Graham g:Eaton(5),Agar	1st	1,558
23/1/00	Doncaster (h)	W20-16	t:Ball,Godfrey,Richardson g:Eaton(3) fg:Agar,Talbot	1st	3,180
30/1/00	Stanley (h) (CCR3)	W66-0	t:Mycoe(2),Wood(2),Flynn(2),Potter(2),Long,A Spink,Baker,Talbot g:Eaton(9)	N/A	1,579
4/2/00	Keighley (a)	L22-6	t:Graham g:Eaton	1st	2,440
13/2/00	Widnes (h) (CCR4)	W29-16	t:Talbot(2),Richardson,Flynn,Ball g:Eaton(4) fg:Eaton	N/A	2,445
20/2/00	Sheffield (h)	W33-18	t:Godfrey(2),Potter,Talbot,Graham,Flynn g:Eaton(4) fg:Talbot	1st	1,459
27/2/00	Villeneuve (h) (CCR5)	W35-10	t:O'Meara,Talbot,Eaton,Jowitt,Mycoe,Potter g:Eaton(5) fg:Eaton	N/A	1,326
5/3/00	Hunslet (a)	W10-22	t:Graham,Potter,Talbot,Flynn g:Eaton(3)	2nd	1,112
10/3/00	Leeds (a) (CCQF)	L42-10	t:Wood,Potter g:Eaton	N/A	10,533
15/3/00	York (h)	W26-19	t:Kershaw(3),Graham g:Eaton(5)	2nd	1,010
19/3/00	Oldham (a)	W12-14	t:Baker,Richardson,Flynn g:Eaton	2nd	2,115
26/3/00	Leigh (h)	L18-22	t:Richardson(2),A Spink g:Eaton(3)	4th	3,027
2/4/00	Whitehaven (a)	W10-36	t:Talbot,Ball,Eaton,O'Meara,Long,Graham,Flynn g:Eaton(4)	3rd	596
9/4/00	Swinton (a)	D14-14	t:Ball,Potter g:Eaton(3)	4th	1,041
12/4/00	Leigh (h) (TPCF)	W10-8	t:Graham,Godfrey g:Eaton	N/A	2,465
16/4/00	Widnes (h)	W42-24	t:Potter(2),Graham(2),Godfrey,Long,Ball g:Eaton(7)	3rd	2,097
21/4/00	Batley (h)	W45-10	t:Flynn(2),Potter,Godfrey,Eaton,Kershaw,Richardson g:Eaton(8) fg:Eaton	1st	1,900
24/4/00	Hull KR (a)	L20-12	t:Graham,Eaton g:Eaton(2)	3rd	2,303
1/5/00	Rochdale (h)	W26-2	t:Eaton,O'Meara,Frame g:Eaton(7)	2nd	1,009
7/5/00	Lancashire (h)	W72-13	t:Graham(3),Kershaw(2),Baker(2),Godfrey(2),Richardson(2), K Spink,Wood g:Eaton(10)	2nd	932
10/5/00	Barrow (a)	W10-36	t:Eaton,Frame,Graham,Richardson,Baker g:Eaton(8)	1st	1,421
14/5/00	Featherstone (h)	W46-26	t:Potter(2),Frame,Ball(2),Richardson,O'Meara g:Eaton(7)	1st	1,670
21/5/00	Workington (a)	W6-58	t:Flynn(4),Eaton(2),Frame,Potter,Mycoe,Williams g:Eaton(9)	1st	1,088
26/5/00	Doncaster (a)	L33-10	t:A Spink(2) g:Eaton	2nd	1,765
29/5/00	Hunslet (h)	W46-0	t:Godfrey(2),Wood(2),Frame,Richardson,A Spink,Long g:Eaton(7)	1st	1,211
4/6/00	Sheffield (a)	W8-30	t:Baker(2),Frame,Ball,Richardson,Godfrey g:Eaton(3)	1st	1,478
11/6/00	Barrow (h)	W42-20	t:Godfrey(2),Eaton(2),Wood,Mycoe,O'Meara,Baker g:Eaton(5)	1st	1,000
18/6/00	York (a)	W17-56	t:Ball(2),A Spink(2),Godfrey(2),Potter(2),Eaton,Wood g:Eaton(8)	1st	744
25/6/00	Oldham (h)	W16-12	t:Graham(2),Baker g:Eaton(2)	1st	1,456
2/7/00	Leigh (a)	L38-16	t:Potter,Eaton,Godfrey g:Eaton(2)	1st	2,320
9/7/00	Leigh (h) (PSF)	L12-29	t:Baker,Ball g:Eaton(2)	N/A	2,500
16/7/00	Featherstone (h) (MiSF)	W25-18	t:O'Meara,Ball,Long,Richardson g:Eaton(4) fg:Eaton	N/A	2,226
23/7/00	Keighley (h) (MaSF)	W38-12	t:Graham,Potter,Eaton,Baker,Flynn g:Eaton(7)	N/A	3,363
29/7/00	Leigh (GF)	W13-12	t:Eaton,Long g:Eaton(2) fg:Agar	N/A	8,487

	APP		TRIES		GOALS		FG		PTS	
	ALL	NFP	ALL	NFP	ALL	NFP	ALL	NFP	ALL	NFP
Richard Agar	15(2)	15(2)	1	1	2	2	2	2	10	10
Richard Baker	25(6)	21(6)	11	10	0	0	0	0	44	40
Damian Ball	34(1)	30(1)	15	14	0	0	0	0	60	56
Mark Cain	3(4)	3(4)	0	0	0	0	0	0	0	0
Gareth Cochrane	1(3)	(3)	0	0	0	0	0	0	0	0
Paul Delaney	2(11)	2(10)	0	0	0	0	0	0	0	0
Scott Dyson	7(1)	7(1)	0	0	0	0	0	0	0	0
Barry Eaton	37	32	15	14	165	145	4	2	394	348
Adrian Flynn	28	23	18	15	0	0	0	0	72	60
Daniel Frame	14(1)	14(1)	7	7	0	0	0	0	28	28
Alex Godfrey	20(7)	19(4)	18	17	0	0	0	0	72	68
Nathan Graham	36	31	20	19	0	0	0	0	80	76
Mark Haigh	22(2)	21(2)	0	0	0	0	0	0	0	0
Simon Hicks	5(13)	4(10)	0	0	0	0	0	0	0	0
Robin Jowitt	8(6)	6(4)	1	0	0	0	0	0	4	0
Billy Kershaw	17(9)	13(9)	6	6	0	0	0	0	24	24
Matthew Long	25(5)	20(5)	6	5	0	0	0	0	24	20
Ryan McDonald	8(21)	8(19)	0	0	0	0	0	0	0	0
David Mycoe	32(4)	27(4)	5	2	0	0	0	0	20	8
Brendan O'Meara	31(2)	27(2)	7	6	0	0	0	0	28	24
Dan Potter	32(2)	28(2)	18	14	0	0	0	0	72	56
Sean Richardson	32(5)	28(4)	14	13	0	0	0	0	56	52
Andrew Spink	12(11)	10(9)	7	6	0	0	0	0	28	24
Kevin Spink	(2)	(1)	1	1	0	0	0	0	4	4
Ian Talbot	12(6)	7(6)	7	3	0	0	2	2	30	14
Shayne Williams	10(9)	9(8)	1	1	0	0	0	0	4	4
Gavin Wood	13(13)	11(10)	8	5	0	0	0	0	32	20

Damian Ball

LEAGUE RECORD
P28-W22-D1-L5
(1st, NFP/Grand Final Winners, Champions)
F848, A400, Diff+448
45 points.

CHALLENGE CUP
Quarter Finalists

ATTENDANCES
Best - v Keighley (MaSF - 3,363)
Worst - v Lancashire (NFP - 932)
Total (NFP, inc play-offs) - 31,717
Average (NFP, inc play-offs) - 1,866
(Up by 610 on 1999)

DONCASTER DRAGONS

DATE	FIXTURE	RESULT	SCORERS	LGE	ATT
26/12/99	York (a)	W1-36	t:Tawhai(2),Weston(2),Sini,Hall,Berry g:Stott(2),Weston(2)	N/A	1,554
2/1/00	Batley (h)	W42-8	t:Parker(2),Miller,Sini,Hall,Weston,Berry,Coult g:Stott(4),Weston	1st	1,768
9/1/00	Hull KR (a)	L8-4	t:Hall	4th	2,804
16/1/00	Featherstone (h)	W32-14	t:Hall(2),Tawhai,Weston,Sini,Gillespie,Amone g:Stott(2)	2nd	2,071
23/1/00	Dewsbury (a)	L20-16	t:Weston,Sini,Adams g:Stott(2)	4th	3,180
30/1/00	St Gaudens (h) (CCR3)	W40-10	t:Tawhai(2),Carter(2),Moore(2),Bunyan,Sini g:Stott(4)	N/A	1,593
6/2/00	Oldham (h)	W26-16	t:Weston(2),Sini(2),Wilson g:Stott(3)	3rd	2,130
13/2/00	Workington (h) (CCR4)	W54-6	t:Weston(3),Sini(2),Bunyan(2),Edwards(2),Hall,Stott g:Stott(5)	N/A	1,466
20/2/00	Keighley (h)	W19-12	t:Sini,Carter,Hall,Tawhai g:Stott fg:Stott	4th	1,883
27/2/00	Wigan (a) (CCR5)	L38-2	g:Weston	N/A	6,225
5/3/00	Sheffield (a)	W10-16	t:Stott,Bunyan,Weston,Hall	5th	2,732
12/3/00	Hunslet (h)	W52-12	t:Stott(3),Weston(2),Hall,Miller,Sini,Gillespie,Tawhai g:Weston(5),Stott	4th	1,572
19/3/00	Leigh (a)	L22-6	t:Stott g:Weston	5th	2,767
26/3/00	Whitehaven (a)	W14-24	t:Hall(2),Tawhai,Weston g:Weston(4)	5th	804
2/4/00	Swinton (h)	W28-14	t:Weston(2),Booth,Stott,Carter g:Weston(3) fg:Weston(2)	5th	1,076
9/4/00	Rochdale (a)	W18-20	t:Hall(2),Coult,Weston g:Weston(2)	5th	1,179
16/4/00	Lancashire (h)	W82-4	t:Tawhai(2),Hall(2),Gillespie(2),Wilson,Carter,Stott,Amone,Weston,Sini,Morgan,Edwards g:Weston(11)	4th	1,195
21/4/00	York (h)	W70-8	t:Booth(2),Weston(2),Stott(2),Coult(2),Tawhai,Hall,Sini,Edwards g:Weston(9)	2nd	1,379
24/4/00	Batley (a)	W20-28	t:Coult(2),Sini,Booth,Bunyan g:Weston(4)	1st	948
30/4/00	Widnes (a)	L19-18	t:Weston,Miller,Bennett,Booth g:Weston	4th	3,171
7/5/00	Barrow (h)	W68-12	t:Bennett(4),Weston(3),Hall,Miller,Edwards,Bunyan,Stott,Sini g:Booth(8)	4th	1,286
10/5/00	Workington (a)	L23-18	t:Edwards,Booth,Tawhai g:Booth(3)	4th	778
14/5/00	Hull KR (h)	W50-12	t:Booth(3),Bunyan(3),Stott(2),Walker,Conway g:Booth(5)	4th	1,738
21/5/00	Featherstone (a)	L16-10	t:Booth,Stott g:Booth	4th	2,365
26/5/00	Dewsbury (h)	W33-10	t:Booth(2),Stott,Amone,Hall g:Booth(6) fg:Tawhai	4th	1,765
29/5/00	Oldham (a)	L25-6	t:Weston g:Booth	5th	2,043
4/6/00	Keighley (a)	W27-30	t:Bennett(3),Wilson,Booth g:Booth(5)	5th	2,112
11/6/00	Sheffield (h)	W29-8	t:Booth(2),Sini,Stott g:Booth(6) fg:Parker	5th	1,553
18/6/00	Hunslet (a)	W10-24	t:Wilson,Parker,Hall,Bennett g:Weston(3),Booth	5th	1,046
25/6/00	Leigh (h)	W29-18	t:Stott,Bennett,Hall,Berry g:Weston(4) fg:Parker(4),Booth	4th	1,841
2/7/00	Whitehaven (h)	W64-16	t:Bennett(2),Stott(2),Sini,Booth,Bunyan,Hall,Wilson,Parker,Leighton,Weston g:Weston(8)	3rd	1,284
9/7/00	Keighley (a) (PSF)	L44-22	t:Berry,Bunyan,Booth,Hall g:Weston(3)	N/A	2,594
16/7/00	Oldham (h) (MiSF)	L17-24 *(aet)*	t:Bennett(2),Hall,Stott fg:Booth	N/A	2,599

	APP		TRIES		GOALS		FG		PTS	
	ALL	NFP	ALL	NFP	ALL	NFP	ALL	NFP	ALL	NFP
Guy Adams	(5)	(3)	1	1	0	0	0	0	4	4
Neil Alexander	2(3)	2(3)	0	0	0	0	0	0	0	0
Kieran Allen	(1)	(1)	0	0	0	0	0	0	0	0
Asa Amone	29(4)	26(4)	3	3	0	0	0	0	12	12
Neil Bennett	11(1)	11(1)	14	14	0	0	0	0	56	56
Joe Berry	19(6)	18(6)	4	4	0	0	0	0	16	16
Steve Booth	19	19	19	19	36	36	2	2	150	150
James Bunyan	28	26	11	8	0	0	0	0	44	32
Colin Carter	12(5)	9(5)	5	3	0	0	0	0	20	12
Billy Conway	(10)	(8)	1	1	0	0	0	0	4	4
Mick Coult	6(21)	5(19)	6	6	0	0	0	0	24	24
Peter Edwards	33	30	6	4	0	0	0	0	24	16
Lafaele Filipo	1(4)	1(4)	0	0	0	0	0	0	0	0
Carl Gillespie	15(5)	14(4)	4	4	0	0	0	0	16	16
Carl Hall	30(1)	27(1)	21	20	0	0	0	0	84	80
Jamie Leighton	9(1)	9(1)	1	1	0	0	0	0	4	4
Paul Lister	3(13)	1(12)	0	0	0	0	0	0	0	0
Tony Miller	29(2)	26(2)	4	4	0	0	0	0	16	16
Craig Moore	3(1)	1(1)	2	0	0	0	0	0	8	0
Gavin Morgan	1(11)	1(10)	1	1	0	0	0	0	4	4
Wayne Parker	17(10)	16(10)	4	4	0	0	5	5	21	21
Basil Richards	14(11)	14(10)	0	0	0	0	0	0	0	0
Fata Sini	27(3)	25(3)	17	14	0	0	0	0	68	56
Lynton Stott	30	27	20	19	24	15	1	1	129	107
Latham Tawhai	26	23	14	12	0	0	1	1	57	49
James Walker	3(6)	3(4)	1	1	0	0	0	0	4	4
Craig Weston	32(1)	29(1)	26	23	62	61	2	2	230	216
Rob Wilson	30	27	5	5	0	0	0	0	20	20

Craig Weston

LEAGUE RECORD
P28-W21-D0-L7
(3rd, NFP/Minor Semi Finalists)
F880, A397, Diff+483
42 points.

CHALLENGE CUP
Round Five

ATTENDANCES
Best - v Oldham (MiSF - 2,599)
Worst - v Swinton (NFP - 1,076)
Total (NFP, inc play-offs) - 25,140
Average (NFP, inc play-offs) - 1,676
(Up by 996 on 1999)

FEATHERSTONE ROVERS

DATE	FIXTURE	RESULT	SCORERS	LGE	ATT
27/12/99	Hull KR (a)	D2-2	g:Rooney	N/A	3,402
3/1/00	Barrow (h)	W35-14	t:Bramald(2),Langley,Stokes,Lowe g:Rooney(7) fg:Rooney	6th	1,908
9/1/00	Dewsbury (h)	L2-38	g:Rooney	10th	2,589
16/1/00	Doncaster (a)	L32-14	t:Helliwell,Lambert g:Rooney(3)	11th	2,071
23/1/00	Keighley (h)	W34-20	t:Bramald,Clarkson,Dickens,Chapman,Rooney,Stokes g:Rooney(5)	10th	1,987
30/1/00	Wigan St P (h) (CCR3)	W64-6	t:Chapman(4),Rooney(3),Thompson,Clarkson,Dooler,Lambert, Rhodes g:Rooney(8)	N/A	940
6/2/00	Sheffield (h)	W45-13	t:Bramald(2),Rhodes(2),Clarkson,Dooler,Evans,Stokes g:Rooney(6) fg:Rooney	9th	1,867
13/2/00	Leeds (h) (CCR4)	L12-48	t:Langley,Hepi g:Rooney(2)	N/A	4,001
20/2/00	Hunslet (h)	W36-4	t:Rhodes,Langley,Hepi,Stokes,Lowe g:Rooney(8)	5th	1,868
27/2/00	Lancashire (a)	W6-34	t:Slatter(2),Rhodes,Rooney,Dickens,Stokes g:Rooney(5)	3rd	332
5/3/00	York (a)	W12-25	t:Bramald,Rooney,Coventry,Stokes g:Rooney(4) fg:Rooney	3rd	1,013
12/3/00	Batley (h)	W38-16	t:Dickens,Rhodes,Thompson,Coventry,Stokes,Chapman g:Rooney(6),Heptinstall	2nd	1,684
19/3/00	Workington (a)	W25-42	t:Thompson(2),Rooney(2),Stokes,Lowe,Dooler,Coventry g:Rooney(4) fg:Rooney(2)	3rd	829
26/3/00	Oldham (h)	W61-26	t:Stokes(2),Chapman(2),Rooney(2),Bastow,Law,Lambert, Thompson,Lowe g:Rooney(8) fg:Rooney	2nd	2,071
2/4/00	Leigh (a)	L18-8	t:Bastow,Bramald	4th	3,010
9/4/00	Whitehaven (h)	W44-20	t:Lowe(2),Stokes(2),Rooney,Chapman,Law,Bramald g:Rooney(6)	3rd	1,474
16/4/00	Rochdale (a)	L31-16	t:Coventry,Bramald g:Rooney(4)	5th	1,273
21/4/00	Hull KR (h)	W28-8	t:Stokes,Bastow,Dooler,Thompson g:Rooney(5) fg:Rooney(2)	4th	2,409
24/4/00	Barrow (a)	L38-10	t:Chapman,Lowe g:Rooney	6th	1,363
1/5/00	Swinton (h)	W28-14	t:Evans(2),Rooney,Lambert,Stokes g:Rooney(4)	5th	1,691
7/5/00	Widnes (h)	W28-22	t:Law,Rhodes,Chapman,Dooler g:Rooney(6)	5th	2,033
14/5/00	Dewsbury (a)	L46-26	t:Evans(3),Lowe,Law g:Rooney(3)	5th	1,670
21/5/00	Doncaster (h)	W16-10	t:Rooney,Bramald g:Rooney(4)	5th	2,365
26/5/00	Whitehaven (a)	W14-29	t:Heptinstall(2),Bastow,Law,Stokes g:Rooney(4) fg:Rooney	5th	569
29/5/00	Sheffield (a)	W14-29	t:Stokes(2),Chapman(2),Bramald g:Rooney(4) fg:Rooney	4th	1,359
4/6/00	Hunslet (a)	W12-13	t:Lowe,Coventry g:Rooney,Dickens fg:Heptinstall	4th	1,115
11/6/00	York (h)	W56-12	t:Bastow(2),Evans(2),Chapman,Thompson,Dickens,Rhodes, Spurr,Stokes g:Dickens(5),Booth(3)	4th	1,550
18/6/00	Batley (a)	W18-38	t:Rhodes(2),Lambert,Lowe,Dickens,Stokes g:Rooney(7)	4th	838
25/6/00	Workington (h)	W58-6	t:Rooney(2),Bramald,Coventry,Chapman,Dickens,Stokes,Spurr, Bastow,Law g:Rooney(5),Booth(2)	3rd	1,480
2/7/00	Oldham (a)	L32-0	No Scorers	5th	2,132
9/7/00	Widnes (h) (ESF)	W43-24	t:Stokes(2),Dooler(2),Lowe,Bramald,Dickens g:Rooney(7) fg:Rooney	N/A	1,922
16/7/00	Dewsbury (a) (MiSF)	L25-18	t:Bramald(3),Stokes g:Rooney	N/A	2,226

	APP		TRIES		GOALS		FG		PTS	
	ALL	NFP	ALL	NFP	ALL	NFP	ALL	NFP	ALL	NFP
Andy Bastow	25(1)	23(1)	7	7	0	0	0	0	28	28
Craig Booth	6(9)	6(9)	0	0	5	5	0	0	10	10
Matt Bramald	28(4)	26(4)	17	17	0	0	0	0	68	68
Shane Byrne	1		0	0	0	0	0	0	0	0
Richard Chapman	17(14)	17(12)	15	11	0	0	0	0	60	44
Micky Clarkson	6(3)	4(3)	3	2	0	0	0	0	12	8
Jamie Coventry	17(4)	16(4)	6	6	0	0	0	0	24	24
Maea David	22(3)	20(3)	0	0	0	0	0	0	0	0
Stuart Dickens	26(6)	26(4)	7	7	6	6	0	0	40	40
Steve Dooler	19(8)	19(6)	7	6	0	0	0	0	28	24
Danny Evans	24(6)	22(6)	8	8	0	0	0	0	32	32
Richard Gibson	4(8)	4(7)	0	0	0	0	0	0	0	0
Paddy Handley	3(14)	3(14)	0	0	0	0	0	0	0	0
Ricky Helliwell	3(4)	3(4)	1	1	0	0	0	0	4	4
Brad Hepi	7	5	2	1	0	0	0	0	8	4
Andy Heptinstall	17(13)	15(13)	2	2	1	1	1	1	11	11
Rhys Jones-Orris	3	3	0	0	0	0	0	0	0	0
Matt Lambert	23(8)	21(8)	5	4	0	0	0	0	20	16
Chris Langley	5(1)	4(1)	3	2	0	0	0	0	12	8
Martin Law	26(2)	25(2)	6	6	0	0	0	0	24	24
Neil Lowe	21(8)	21(8)	11	11	0	0	0	0	44	44
Michael Rhodes	28	26	10	9	0	0	0	0	40	36
Jamie Rooney	30(1)	28(1)	15	12	130	120	11	11	331	299
Anthony Slatter	2	2	2	2	0	0	0	0	8	8
Ben Smallman	(1)	(1)	0	0	0	0	0	0	0	0
Chris Spurr	2(2)	2(2)	2	2	0	0	0	0	8	8
Jamie Stokes	31	30	23	23	0	0	0	0	92	92
Ian Thompson	20(1)	18(1)	7	6	0	0	0	0	28	24
Matt Turner	1	1	0	0	0	0	0	0	0	0
Mark Webster	(2)	(2)	0	0	0	0	0	0	0	0

Jamie Rooney

LEAGUE RECORD
P28-W20-D1-L7
(5th, NFP/Minor Semi Finalists)
F795, A523, Diff+272
41 points.

CHALLENGE CUP
Round Four

ATTENDANCES
Best - v Leeds (CC - 4,001)
Worst - v Wigan St Pats (CC - 940)
Total (NFP, inc play-offs) - 28,898
Average (NFP, inc play-offs) - 1,926
(Up by 148 on 1999)

HULL KINGSTON ROVERS

DATE	FIXTURE	RESULT	SCORERS	LGE	ATT
27/12/99	Featherstone (h)	D2-2	g:Hewitt	N/A	3,402
2/1/00	Dewsbury (a)	L14-2	g:Hewitt	12th	2,119
9/1/00	Doncaster (h)	W8-4	t:Dixon g:Hewitt(2)	9th	2,804
16/1/00	Keighley (a)	W10-24	t:Dixon(2),Aston,Taewa g:Hewitt(4)	7th	2,809
23/1/00	Sheffield (h)	W6-4	t:Taewa g:Hewitt	3rd	2,244
30/1/00	Ideal Isberg (h) (CCR3)	W32-4	t:Bovill(2),Nolan,Taewa,Wray,Aston g:Hewitt(4)	N/A	2,528
6/2/00	Hunslet (a)	W14-21	t:Wray(2),Dixon,Bovill g:Hewitt(2) fg:Joe	2nd	1,373
13/2/00	Halifax (a) (CCR4)	L36-8	t:Chambers g:Hewitt(2)	N/A	4,295
20/2/00	York (h)	W30-10	t:Wray(2),Everitt,Hardy,Molloy g:Hewitt(4),Charles	2nd	2,007
27/2/00	Leigh (h)	L14-18	t:Nolan,Joe g:Hewitt(3)	4th	2,207
5/3/00	Batley (a)	W14-32	t:Wray(2),Andrews,Taewa,Joe,Nolan g:Hewitt(4)	4th	1,027
12/3/00	Whitehaven (h)	W22-14	t:Andrews(2),Nolan g:Hewitt(5)	3rd	1,823
19/3/00	Swinton (h)	W54-16	t:Everitt(2),Nolan(2),Taewa(2),Fletcher,Hewitt,Bovill g:Hewitt(9)	4th	2,073
26/3/00	Rochdale (a)	W26-38	t:Taewa(2),Wray,Nolan,Dixon,Fletcher g:Hewitt(7)	3rd	1,253
2/4/00	Widnes (h)	W24-10	t:Joe,Nolan,Dixon,Wray g:Hewitt(4)	2nd	2,155
9/4/00	Lancashire (a)	W6-60	t:Nolan(2),Taewa(2),Wray(2),Everitt,Joe,Hewitt,Dixon g:Hewitt(10)	1st	378
16/4/00	Workington (a)	L20-10	t:Kirke g:Hewitt(3)	2nd	873
21/4/00	Featherstone (a)	L28-8	t:Andrews g:Hewitt(2)	5th	2,409
24/4/00	Dewsbury (h)	W20-12	t:Joe(2),Nolan g:Hewitt(4)	4th	2,303
1/5/00	Barrow (a)	L42-12	t:Dixon,Taewa g:Hewitt(2)	6th	1,763
7/5/00	Oldham (h)	L12-32	t:Andrews g:Hewitt(4)	7th	2,005
14/5/00	Doncaster (a)	L50-12	t:Fletcher,Taewa g:Hewitt(2)	7th	1,738
21/5/00	Keighley (h)	L8-30	t:Kennedy g:Hewitt,Charles	8th	2,507
26/5/00	Sheffield (a)	L10-8	t:Bovill,Molloy	8th	1,021
29/5/00	Workington (h)	W48-7	t:Taewa(2),Joe(2),Molloy(2),Bovill,Hewitt g:Hewitt(7),Charles	8th	1,305
4/6/00	York (a)	W6-24	t:Taewa,Molloy,Charles,Nolan g:Hewitt(4)	8th	1,195
11/6/00	Batley (h)	W30-10	t:Fletcher(2),Taewa(2),Joe g:Hewitt(5)	8th	1,879
18/6/00	Whitehaven (a)	L44-12	t:Molloy,Leatham g:Hewitt(2)	8th	590
25/6/00	Widnes (a)	W14-16	t:Taewa,Leatham g:Hewitt(4)	7th	3,455
2/7/00	Barrow (h)	W26-14	t:Charles(2),Wray,Taewa g:Hewitt(5)	7th	2,379
9/7/00	Oldham (a) (ESF)	L22-14	t:Wray,Taewa,Hewitt g:Charles	N/A	2,584

	APP		TRIES		GOALS		FG		PTS	
	ALL	NFP	ALL	NFP	ALL	NFP	ALL	NFP	ALL	NFP
Dean Andrews	24(1)	22(1)	5	5	0	0	0	0	20	20
Jon Aston	6(2)	5(2)	2	1	0	0	0	0	8	4
Scott Bennett	(1)	(1)	0	0	0	0	0	0	0	0
Mark Blanchard	5(7)	5(7)	0	0	0	0	0	0	0	0
Simon Booth	1(7)	(7)	0	0	0	0	0	0	0	0
Jamie Bovill	7(13)	6(12)	6	4	0	0	0	0	24	16
Anthony Chambers	3(4)	3(2)	1	0	0	0	0	0	4	0
Chris Charles	28	27	3	3	4	4	0	0	20	20
Steven Cochrane	4	4	0	0	0	0	0	0	0	0
Mick Crane	8(11)	7(10)	0	0	0	0	0	0	0	0
Mike Dixon	26(3)	24(3)	8	8	0	0	0	0	32	32
Mark Dooley	(1)	(1)	0	0	0	0	0	0	0	0
Allan Dunham	3(12)	3(11)	0	0	0	0	0	0	0	0
Bob Everitt	15	14	4	4	0	0	0	0	16	16
Paul Fletcher	26(5)	24(5)	5	5	0	0	0	0	20	20
Mike Hall	1	1	0	0	0	0	0	0	0	0
Craig Hardy	21(8)	20(8)	1	1	0	0	0	0	4	4
Mark Hewitt	29(1)	27(1)	4	4	108	102	0	0	232	220
Leroy Joe	29(1)	27(1)	9	9	0	0	1	1	37	37
Phil Kennedy	3(1)	3(1)	1	1	0	0	0	0	4	4
Ian Kirke	4(14)	4(12)	1	1	0	0	0	0	4	4
Jim Leatham	9	9	2	2	0	0	0	0	8	8
Gavin Molloy	10(7)	10(6)	6	6	0	0	0	0	24	24
Rob Nolan	30	28	12	11	0	0	0	0	48	44
Richard Slater	19	18	0	0	0	0	0	0	0	0
Andy Smith	18(2)	16(2)	0	0	0	0	0	0	0	0
Whetu Taewa	31	29	20	19	0	0	0	0	80	76
Andrew Taylor	4(1)	4(1)	0	0	0	0	0	0	0	0
Jon Wilkins	(7)	(7)	0	0	0	0	0	0	0	0
Richard Wilson	9(2)	9(2)	0	0	0	0	0	0	0	0
Ryan Woods	(4)	(4)	0	0	0	0	0	0	0	0
Jon Wray	30	28	13	12	0	0	0	0	52	48
Scott Yeaman	(2)	(2)	0	0	0	0	0	0	0	0

Rob Nolan

LEAGUE RECORD
P28-W17-D1-L10
(7th, NFP/Elimination Semi Finalists)
F583, A481, Diff+102
35 points.

CHALLENGE CUP
Round Four

ATTENDANCES
Best - v Featherstone (NFP - 3,402)
Worst - v Workington (NFP - 1,305)
Total (NFP only) - 31,093
Average (NFP only) - 2,221
(Up by 71 on 1999)

HUNSLET HAWKS

DATE	FIXTURE	RESULT	SCORERS	LGE	ATT
27/12/99	Keighley (h)	L12-21	t:Ross(2) g:Ross(2)	N/A	2,054
9/1/00	Widnes (a)	L30-21	t:Walker,Hanger,Kennedy g:Fletcher(4) fg:Fletcher	15th	3,758
16/1/00	York (h)	W30-6	t:Windley(2),Hanger,Hughes,A Campbell g:Ross(5)	12th	997
23/1/00	Batley (a)	W18-27	t:Leatham(2),Pachniuk,Coyle,Hughes g:Ross(3) fg:Ross	12th	748
25/1/00	Sheffield (a)	L17-12	t:Hughes,A Campbell g:Ross(2)	12th	1,278
6/2/00	Hull KR (h)	L14-21	t:Irwin(2),Pachniuk g:Ross	12th	1,373
13/2/00	Warrington (h) (CCR4)	L4-46	t:D King	N/A	2,249
20/2/00	Featherstone (a)	L36-4	g:Ross(2)	14th	1,868
5/3/00	Dewsbury (h)	L10-22	t:Coyle,Briggs g:Ross	13th	1,112
12/3/00	Doncaster (a)	L52-12	t:Leatham,Hughes g:Ross(2)	14th	1,572
19/3/00	Lancashire (h)	W24-16	t:Plange,Hughes,Windley,Irwin g:Ross(4)	13th	666
26/3/00	Barrow (h)	L36-18	t:Pachniuk,North,Ross g:Ross(3)	14th	1,116
2/4/00	Workington (h)	W22-8	t:Ross,Hughes,Swann,Irwin g:Ross(3)	13th	645
9/4/00	Oldham (a)	L44-18	t:Ross(2),Pachniuk g:Ross(3)	13th	1,544
16/4/00	Whitehaven (h)	W24-2	t:Coyle,Irwin,C Moore,Ross g:Ross(4)	12th	615
21/4/00	Keighley (a)	L24-23	t:Hughes(2),Coyle,Pachniuk g:Ross(3) fg:Swann	11th	2,098
24/4/00	Sheffield (h)	L6-27	t:Thackray g:Ross	13th	863
1/5/00	Leigh (h)	L10-24	t:Swann g:Ross(3)	14th	1,062
7/5/00	Swinton (a)	W24-31	t:Dobson(3),Naylor(2), g:Ross(5) fg:Coyle	13th	849
10/5/00	Rochdale (a)	L24-16	t:Swann,Lord g:Embling(3),Ross	13th	921
14/5/00	Widnes (h)	L10-34	t:Dobson,C Moore g:Embling	14th	846
21/5/00	York (a)	W18-22	t:Swann,Ross,Hughes g:Ross(5)	14th	581
26/5/00	Batley (h)	L10-17	t:Hughes,Ross g:Ross	15th	523
29/5/00	Dewsbury (a)	L46-0	No Scorers	15th	1,211
4/6/00	Featherstone (h)	L12-13	t:Ross,North g:Ross(2)	15th	1,115
11/6/00	Leigh (a)	L44-4	t:Plange	15th	1,675
18/6/00	Doncaster (h)	L10-24	t:Plange g:Ross(3)	15th	1,046
25/6/00	Lancashire (a)	W6-66	t:Swann(6),Fella(2),Dobson(2),Plange,Ross g:Ross(9)	15th	222
2/7/00	Rochdale (h)	L19-24	t:Ross,Pryce,McHugh g:Ross(3) fg:Coyle	15th	633

Steve Pryce

	APP		TRIES		GOALS		FG		PTS	
	ALL	NFP	ALL	NFP	ALL	NFP	ALL	NFP	ALL	NFP
Andy Atha	2(7)	2(7)	0	0	0	0	0	0	0	0
Steve Booth	(2)	(2)	0	0	0	0	0	0	0	0
Neil Bradbrook	(2)	(2)	0	0	0	0	0	0	0	0
Carl Briggs	5(1)	5(1)	1	1	0	0	0	0	4	4
Aaron Campbell	19(2)	18(2)	2	2	0	0	0	0	8	8
Steve Campbell	6(1)	6(1)	0	0	0	0	0	0	0	0
Paul Cook	1	1	0	0	0	0	0	0	0	0
Mick Coyle	26(2)	25(2)	4	4	0	0	2	2	18	18
Shelton Davis	3(2)	3(2)	0	0	0	0	0	0	0	0
Nicky Dobson	11(4)	10(4)	6	6	0	0	0	0	24	24
Steve Embling	1(1)	1(1)	0	0	4	4	0	0	8	8
Tony Fella	10(1)	10(1)	2	2	0	0	0	0	8	8
Mike Fletcher	1	1	0	0	4	4	1	1	9	9
Graeme Hallas	6(1)	5(1)	0	0	0	0	0	0	0	0
Dean Hanger	3	3	2	2	0	0	0	0	8	8
Anthony Henderson	(3)	(2)	0	0	0	0	0	0	0	0
Darren Hughes	28	27	10	10	0	0	0	0	40	40
Craig Ibbotson	(6)	(6)	0	0	0	0	0	0	0	0
Shaun Irwin	22	22	5	5	0	0	0	0	20	20
Dave Jessey	(12)	(12)	0	0	0	0	0	0	0	0
Alan Julian	1(4)	1(3)	0	0	0	0	0	0	0	0
Phil Kennedy	6(6)	6(6)	1	1	0	0	0	0	4	4
Dave King	5(3)	5(2)	1	0	0	0	0	0	4	0
Gareth King	7	7	0	0	0	0	0	0	0	0
Jim Leatham	14(1)	13(1)	3	3	0	0	0	0	12	12
Jamie Leighton	15	14	0	0	0	0	0	0	0	0
Gary Lord	13(1)	13(1)	1	1	0	0	0	0	4	4
Wayne McHugh	2	2	1	1	0	0	0	0	4	4
Adam Moore	(1)	(1)	0	0	0	0	0	0	0	0
Craig Moore	6(3)	6(3)	2	2	0	0	0	0	8	8
Hamish Munton	4(4)	4(4)	0	0	0	0	0	0	0	0
Gareth Naylor	10(1)	10(1)	2	2	0	0	0	0	8	8
Chris North	15(6)	14(6)	2	2	0	0	0	0	8	8
Richard Pachniuk	17	16	5	5	0	0	0	0	20	20
Steve Parnell	1	1	0	0	0	0	0	0	0	0
David Plange	6(2)	6(2)	4	4	0	0	0	0	16	16
Steve Pryce	21(7)	20(7)	1	1	0	0	0	0	4	4
Craig Richards	(3)	(3)	0	0	0	0	0	0	0	0
Chris Ross	28	27	12	12	71	71	1	1	191	191
Darren Simpson	4(1)	4(1)	0	0	0	0	0	0	0	0
Ben Skerrett	5(15)	5(14)	0	0	0	0	0	0	0	0
Willie Swann	21	21	10	10	0	0	1	1	41	41
Jamie Thackray	15(4)	14(4)	1	1	0	0	0	0	4	4
James Walker	3	3	1	1	0	0	0	0	4	4
Johan Windley	14	13	3	3	0	0	0	0	12	12

LEAGUE RECORD
P28-W8-D0-L20
(15th, NFP)
F487, A678, Diff-191
16 points.

CHALLENGE CUP
Round Four

ATTENDANCES
Best - v Warrington (CC - 2,249)
Worst - v Batley (NFP - 523)
Total (NFP only) - 13,550
Average (NFP only) - 968
(Down by 586 on 1999)

KEIGHLEY COUGARS

DATE	FIXTURE	RESULT	SCORERS	LGE	ATT
27/12/99	Hunslet (a)	W12-21	t:Robinson(2),Rushforth,Lee g:Robinson(2) fg:Wood	N/A	2,054
2/1/00	York (h)	W32-13	t:Owen,Foster,Wood,Antonik,Pickles,Hughes g:Wood(3),Robinson	3rd	2,450
9/1/00	Batley (a)	W18-28	t:Horne,Harrison,Pickles,Owen,Hughes g:Wood(4)	2nd	1,260
16/1/00	Hull KR (h)	L10-24	t:Horne,Rushforth g:Wood	5th	2,809
23/1/00	Featherstone (a)	L34-20	t:K Smith,Ramshaw,Owen,Antonik g:Wood(2)	8th	1,987
30/1/00	Cardiff (h) (CCR3)	W90-0	t:Lee(4),Antonik(3),Tomlinson(2),Wood(2),Pickles,Ramshaw, Hughes,K Smith,Harrison,Owen g:Wood(11)	N/A	1,192
4/2/00	Dewsbury (h)	W22-6	t:Lee,Antonik,Rushforth,Pickles,R Smith g:Wood	7th	2,440
13/2/00	Villeneuve (h) (CCR4)	L14-16	t:R Smith,Stephenson g:Lee(3)	N/A	1,956
20/2/00	Doncaster (a)	L19-12	t:Hughes,Rushforth g:Lee(2)	10th	1,883
5/3/00	Leigh (h)	L28-36	t:Harrison(2),Lee,R Smith,Pickles g:Wood(4)	11th	2,422
12/3/00	Sheffield (h)	W36-2	t:Owen(3),Wood,Seal,Hanger,Lee g:Wood(4)	9th	1,596
19/3/00	Whitehaven (a)	W10-56	t:Lee(5),Hughes(2),Pickles,Walker g:Wood(10)	7th	905
26/3/00	Swinton (a)	W12-34	t:Horne,Hughes,Lee,Antonik,Wood,Thompson g:Wood(5)	7th	1,250
2/4/00	Rochdale (h)	W26-14	t:Antonik(2),R Smith,Owen g:Wood(5)	6th	1,450
9/4/00	Widnes (a)	W18-30	t:Wood(2),Seal,Antonik,Hughes g:Wood(5)	6th	3,308
16/4/00	Barrow (h)	W66-6	t:Hughes(2),Pickles(2),Owen(2),Wood,Hanger,Lee,Seal,Antonik, Hallas g:Wood(9)	6th	2,142
21/4/00	Hunslet (h)	W24-23	t:Wood,Owen,Hallas,Antonik,Hanger g:Wood(2)	6th	2,098
24/4/00	York (a)	W2-26	t:Hallas,Tomlinson,Hanger,Ramshaw g:Wood(3),Antonik(2)	5th	1,048
1/5/00	Lancashire (a)	W4-98	t:Seal(4),Harrison(2),Antonik(2),Ramshaw(2),Lee(2),Pickles, R Smith,Wood,Stephenson,Hanger g:Wood(15)	3rd	707
7/5/00	Workington (h)	W54-8	t:Wood(3),Hallas,Lee,R Smith,Antonik,Seal,Tomlinson g:Wood(7),Lee(2)	3rd	1,912
10/5/00	Oldham (a)	W14-24	t:Ramshaw,Stephenson,Wood,Lee g:Wood(4)	2nd	2,528
14/5/00	Batley (h)	W40-12	t:Hanger,Pickles,Walker,Wood,Ramshaw,Antonik g:Wood(8)	2nd	1,790
21/5/00	Hull KR (a)	W8-30	t:Tomlinson(2),Lee,Hanger,Harrison,Slicker g:Wood(3)	2nd	2,507
26/5/00	Lancashire (h)	W68-0	t:Hughes(2),Antonik(2),Seal(2),Hallas,Ramshaw,Wood,Rushforth, Lee,Calvert g:Wood(7),Lee(3)	1st	1,699
29/5/00	Leigh (a)	L26-16	t:Hanger,Seal,Ramshaw g:Wood(2)	2nd	3,066
4/6/00	Doncaster (h)	L27-30	t:Antonik(2),Lee,Rushforth g:Wood(5) fg:Ramshaw	2nd	2,112
11/6/00	Rochdale (a)	W10-30	t:Hanger(2),Lee,Horne,Walker g:Wood(3)	2nd	1,349
18/6/00	Sheffield (a)	W16-28	t:Harrison,Rushforth,Lee,Antonik,Hallas g:Wood(4)	2nd	1,424
25/6/00	Whitehaven (h)	W50-12	t:Ramshaw(2),Rushforth,Wood,Seal,Lord,Hughes,Hallas,Lee g:Wood(7)	2nd	1,603
2/7/00	Swinton (h)	W66-12	t:Seal(3),Pickles(3),Ramshaw(2),Antonik,Lee,Hughes,Hallas g:Wood(9)	2nd	1,665
9/7/00	Doncaster (h) (PSF)	W44-22	t:Lee(2),Seal,Wood,Ramshaw,Stephenson,Rushforth g:Wood(8)	N/A	2,594
23/7/00	Dewsbury (a) (MaSF)	L38-12	t:Antonik,Seal g:Wood(2)	N/A	3,363

	APP		TRIES		GOALS		FG		PTS	
	ALL	NFP	ALL	NFP	ALL	NFP	ALL	NFP	ALL	NFP
Nathan Antonik	31	29	23	20	2	2	0	0	96	84
Alan Boothroyd	23(2)	21(2)	0	0	0	0	0	0	0	0
Stuart Calvert	2(1)	2(1)	1	1	0	0	0	0	4	4
Matthew Foster	3	2	1	1	0	0	0	0	4	4
Steve Hall	19(3)	19(1)	0	0	0	0	0	0	0	0
Graeme Hallas	17	17	8	8	0	0	0	0	32	32
Dean Hanger	17(2)	17(2)	10	10	0	0	0	0	40	40
Chris Hannah	(4)	(4)	0	0	0	0	0	0	0	0
Paul Harrison	29	27	8	7	0	0	0	0	32	28
Craig Horne	19	18	4	4	0	0	0	0	16	16
Ian Hughes	30(1)	28(1)	14	13	0	0	0	0	56	52
Kris Kirk	1	1	0	0	0	0	0	0	0	0
Jason Lee	32	30	28	24	10	7	0	0	132	110
Gary Lord	2(3)	2(3)	1	1	0	0	0	0	4	4
Paul Owen	8(19)	6(19)	11	10	0	0	0	0	44	40
Steve Pickles	19(12)	17(12)	13	12	0	0	0	0	52	48
Jason Ramshaw	19(1)	17(1)	14	13	0	0	1	1	57	53
Craig Robinson	4(3)	4(2)	2	2	3	3	0	0	14	14
James Rushforth	14(3)	12(3)	9	9	0	0	0	0	36	36
Carlos Sanchez	(1)	(1)	0	0	0	0	0	0	0	0
Danny Seal	22(1)	22(1)	17	17	0	0	0	0	68	68
Michael Slicker	13(11)	11(11)	1	1	0	0	0	0	4	4
Karl Smith	22(1)	21(1)	2	1	0	0	0	0	8	4
Richard Smith	16(1)	15	6	5	0	0	0	0	24	20
Phil Stephenson	7(21)	7(19)	4	3	0	0	0	0	16	12
Ben Thompson	1(11)	1(9)	1	1	0	0	0	0	4	4
Max Tomlinson	10(1)	9(1)	6	4	0	0	0	0	24	16
Matt Walker	5(23)	5(23)	3	3	0	0	0	0	12	12
Martin Wood	31	30	19	17	153	142	1	1	383	353

Martin Wood

LEAGUE RECORD
P28-W22-D0-L6
(2nd, NFP/Major Semi Finalists)
F1002, A401, Diff+601
44 points.

CHALLENGE CUP
Round Four

ATTENDANCES
Best - v Hull KR (NFP - 2,809)
Worst - v Cardiff (CC - 1,192)
Total (NFP, inc play-offs) - 30,782
Average (NFP, inc play-offs) - 2,052
(Up by 184 on 1999)

LANCASHIRE LYNX

DATE	FIXTURE	RESULT	SCORERS	LGE	ATT
28/12/99	Sheffield (h)	L20-33	t:Rostance,Demetriou,Smith,O'Loughlin g:Roberts(2)	N/A	888
2/1/00	Widnes (a)	L64-8	t:Smith g:Roberts(2)	18th	3,837
9/1/00	Rochdale (h)	L22-38	t:Demetriou(2),O'Loughlin g:Roberts(5)	18th	435
16/1/00	Swinton (a)	L54-6	t:Roberts g:Roberts	18th	942
23/1/00	Whitehaven (h)	W22-12	t:Roberts,Houghton,J Doherty,Alexander g:Alexander(2) fg:Hilton,Demetriou	17th	223
30/1/00	Walney (h) (CCR3)	W18-6	t:P Farrell,J Doherty,Rostance,Kay g:Alexander	N/A	530
6/2/00	Barrow (a)	L40-6	t:Hilton g:Roberts	17th	871
13/2/00	Hull (a) (CCR4)	L86-0	No Scorers	N/A	3,442
20/2/00	Workington (h)	L12-34	t:O'Loughlin,N Roden g:Roberts(2)	18th	254
27/2/00	Featherstone (h)	L6-34	t:Butler g:Roberts	18th	332
5/3/00	Oldham (a)	L50-8	t:Alexander,Demetriou	18th	1,522
12/3/00	Leigh (h)	L6-68	t:Roberts g:Roberts	18th	1,232
19/3/00	Hunslet (a)	L24-16	t:J Doherty(2) g:Roberts(3) fg:J Doherty(2)	18th	666
26/3/00	York (h)	L18-26	t:Alexander,Houghton g:Roberts(4),Alexander	18th	214
2/4/00	Batley (a)	L34-16	t:Garcia,Alexander,Butler g:Alexander(2)	18th	324
9/4/00	Hull KR (h)	L6-60	t:Ramsdale g:J Doherty	18th	378
16/4/00	Doncaster (a)	L82-4	t:Cayzer	18th	1,195
21/4/00	Sheffield (a)	L56-12	t:Roberts,Norton g:Roberts(2)	18th	1,177
24/4/00	Widnes (h)	L14-30	t:Alexander(2) g:Roberts(3)	18th	701
1/5/00	Keighley (h)	L4-98	t:Jones	18th	707
7/5/00	Dewsbury (a)	L72-13	t:Norton,Jones g:Roberts(2) fg:Alexander	18th	932
14/5/00	Rochdale (a)	L50-8	t:Vincent g:Roberts(2)	18th	895
21/5/00	Swinton (h)	L6-68	t:Pekepo g:Roberts	18th	212
26/5/00	Keighley (a)	L68-0	No Scorers	18th	1,699
29/5/00	Barrow (h)	L14-50	t:Norton,P Birdsall g:Roberts(2),Probert	18th	223
4/6/00	Workington (a)	L38-8	t:D Birdsall,Pekepo	18th	562
11/6/00	Oldham (h)	L14-48	t:Tickle,Vincent,Hunt g:Wolford	18th	616
18/6/00	Leigh (a)	L50-14	t:G Doherty,Wolford g:Pickles(3)	18th	1,424
25/6/00	Hunslet (h)	L6-66	t:Vincent g:Pickles	18th	222
30/6/00	York (a)	L14-12	t:Lowe,Tickle g:Pickles(2)	18th	351

	APP		TRIES		GOALS		FG		PTS	
	ALL	NFP	ALL	NFP	ALL	NFP	ALL	NFP	ALL	NFP
Neil Alexander	17(1)	15(1)	6	6	6	5	1	1	37	35
Barry Ashall	(1)	(1)	0	0	0	0	0	0	0	0
Craig Barker	5	5	0	0	0	0	0	0	0	0
Brendan Barr	(2)	(2)	0	0	0	0	0	0	0	0
Dave Birdsall	5(1)	5(1)	1	1	0	0	0	0	4	4
Paul Birdsall	6(1)	6(1)	1	1	0	0	0	0	4	4
Dean Blankley	3	3	0	0	0	0	0	0	0	0
Sean Boylan	4(1)	4(1)	0	0	0	0	0	0	0	0
Carl Briscoe	(1)	(1)	0	0	0	0	0	0	0	0
Danny Butler	10(4)	10(4)	2	2	0	0	0	0	8	8
David Cayzer	(4)	(4)	1	1	0	0	0	0	4	4
Steve Charnley	(3)	(3)	0	0	0	0	0	0	0	0
Dale Christy	1(4)	1(4)	0	0	0	0	0	0	0	0
Paul Crook	(2)	(2)	0	0	0	0	0	0	0	0
Chris Davey	(1)	(1)	0	0	0	0	0	0	0	0
Joe Davies	1(4)	1(4)	0	0	0	0	0	0	0	0
Jason Demetriou	10	8	4	4	0	0	1	1	17	17
Gary Doherty	14	14	1	1	0	0	0	0	4	4
Jon-Paul Doherty	16	14	4	3	1	1	2	2	20	16
Mick Farrell	2	2	0	0	0	0	0	0	0	0
Phil Farrell	4	2	1	0	0	0	0	0	4	0
Andy Fisher	1(1)	1(1)	0	0	0	0	0	0	0	0
Anton Garcia	25	24	1	1	0	0	0	0	4	4
Darren Geritas	(3)	(3)	0	0	0	0	0	0	0	0
Shaun Geritas	2(2)	2(2)	0	0	0	0	0	0	0	0
Gavin Gordon	2	2	0	0	0	0	0	0	0	0
Gary Hall	1(4)	1(4)	0	0	0	0	0	0	0	0
Steve Hampson	(1)	(1)	0	0	0	0	0	0	0	0
Sheldon Hannan	7(1)	6	0	0	0	0	0	0	0	0
Neil Hicks	1(1)	1(1)	0	0	0	0	0	0	0	0
Shaun Hilton	3(3)	2(2)	1	1	0	0	1	1	5	5
Tommy Hodgkinson	4	4	0	0	0	0	0	0	0	0
Danny Houghton	3(10)	3(8)	2	2	0	0	0	0	8	8
Martin Hunt	6	6	1	1	0	0	0	0	4	4
Matt Jeffries	1	1	0	0	0	0	0	0	0	0
David Jones	23	21	2	2	0	0	0	0	8	8
Mark Kay	14	12	1	0	0	0	0	0	4	0
Phil Knowles	3(1)	2(1)	0	0	0	0	0	0	0	0
Dave Lewis	1(6)	1(6)	0	0	0	0	0	0	0	0
Gordon Long	4	4	0	0	0	0	0	0	0	0
Gary Lowe	3	3	1	1	0	0	0	0	4	4
Adrian Meade	4	4	0	0	0	0	0	0	0	0
Craig Millard	8	8	0	0	0	0	0	0	0	0
Doc Murray	1	1	0	0	0	0	0	0	0	0
Paul Norton	27(1)	25(1)	3	3	0	0	0	0	12	12

	APP		TRIES		GOALS		FG		PTS	
	ALL	NFP	ALL	NFP	ALL	NFP	ALL	NFP	ALL	NFP
Scott O'Kelly	(1)	(1)	0	0	0	0	0	0	0	0
Kevin O'Loughlin	14(3)	14(2)	3	3	0	0	0	0	12	12
Carl Parker	3(1)	3(1)	0	0	0	0	0	0	0	0
Jayson Pekepo	14(1)	14(1)	2	2	0	0	0	0	8	8
Damieon Pickles	3	3	0	0	6	6	0	0	12	12
Gareth Potter	4(4)	4(4)	0	0	0	0	0	0	0	0
Mike Prescott	12(4)	10(4)	0	0	0	0	0	0	0	0
Neil Prescott	(3)	(3)	0	0	0	0	0	0	0	0
Dave Probert	1	1	0	0	1	1	0	0	2	2
Chris Ramsdale	8(9)	8(8)	1	1	0	0	0	0	4	4
Paul Roberts	23	22	4	4	34	34	0	0	84	84
Alan Robinson	(2)	(2)	0	0	0	0	0	0	0	0
James Roden	1(1)	1(1)	0	0	0	0	0	0	0	0
Martin Roden	6	6	0	0	0	0	0	0	0	0
Neil Roden	4(1)	2(1)	1	1	0	0	0	0	4	4
Paul Rostance	4(1)	3(1)	2	1	0	0	0	0	8	4
Dave Smith	16	14	2	2	0	0	0	0	8	8
Craig Stanley	(1)	(1)	0	0	0	0	0	0	0	0
Peter Steels	1(2)	1(2)	0	0	0	0	0	0	0	0
Martin Taylor	3	3	0	0	0	0	0	0	0	0
Chris Thair	1(1)	1(1)	0	0	0	0	0	0	0	0
Simon Tickle	3(1)	3(1)	2	2	0	0	0	0	8	8
Luke Vincent	15(10)	15(8)	3	3	0	0	0	0	12	12
Des Waerea	3	3	0	0	0	0	0	0	0	0
Darren Williams	1(2)	1(2)	0	0	0	0	0	0	0	0
Dave Wolford	6(1)	6(1)	1	1	1	1	0	0	6	6
Charles Yeoman	1(1)	1(1)	0	0	0	0	0	0	0	0

LEAGUE RECORD
P28-W1-D0-L27
(18th, NFP)
F301, A1361, Diff-1060
2 points.

CHALLENGE CUP
Round Four

ATTENDANCES
Best - v Leigh (NFP - 1,232)
Worst - v Swinton (NFP - 212)
Total (NFP only) - 5,930
Average (NFP only) - 424
(Up by 31 on 1999)

LEIGH CENTURIONS

DATE	FIXTURE	RESULT	SCORERS	LGE	ATT
26/12/99	Widnes (h)	W24-16	t:Donlan,Purtill,Baldwin,Ingram,Cross g:Close(2)	N/A	4,468
2/1/00	Rochdale (a)	W14-42	t:Higham(2),Ingram(2),Dean,Anderson,Fairclough g:Close(6),Wingfield	2nd	2,112
9/1/00	Swinton (h)	L20-22	t:Dean,Murray,Donlan g:Close(2),Wingfield(2)	6th	2,681
16/1/00	Whitehaven (a)	L24-6	t:Cross g:Wingfield	10th	1,400
23/1/00	Barrow (h)	W48-22	t:Cross(3),Bristow(2),Whittle,Higham,Ingram,Fairclough g:Wingfield(6)	7th	2,070
30/1/00	Siddal (h) (CCR3)	W34-12	t:Donlan(2),Higham(2),Kendrick,Fairclough g:Wingfield(5)	N/A	1,643
6/2/00	Workington (a)	W6-46	t:Kendrick(3),Fairclough(2),Anderson,Bowker,Wingfield g:Wingfield(7)	4th	620
13/2/00	Wakefield (h) (CCR4)	L28-40	t:Higham,Cross,Kendrick,Hadcroft,Cruckshank g:Wingfield(4)	N/A	3,810
20/2/00	Oldham (h)	W28-10	t:Purtill(2),Donlan,Bristow,Cross g:Wingfield(3),Baldwin	3rd	2,780
27/2/00	Hull KR (a)	W14-18	t:Fairclough,Murray,Cross g:Wingfield(3)	1st	2,207
5/3/00	Keighley (a)	W28-36	t:Wingfield(2),Bristow,Hadcroft,Bowker,Fairclough,Murray g:Wingfield(4)	1st	2,422
12/3/00	Lancashire (a)	W6-68	t:Bowker(3),Cross(3),Higham(2),Wingfield,Anderson,Fairclough,Donlan g:Wingfield(10)	1st	1,232
19/3/00	Doncaster (h)	W22-6	t:Cross,Higham,Dean,Baldwin g:Wingfield(3)	1st	2,767
26/3/00	Dewsbury (a)	W18-22	t:Baldwin,Bristow,Norman,Donlan,Higham g:Wingfield	1st	3,027
2/4/00	Featherstone (h)	W18-8	t:Donlan,Fairclough,Anderson g:Wingfield(3)	1st	3,010
9/4/00	Sheffield (a)	L24-26	t:Wingfield,Dean,Higham,Street g:Wingfield(4)	2nd	2,250
12/4/00	Dewsbury (a) (TPCF)	L10-8	t:Murray g:Wingfield(2)	N/A	2,465
16/4/00	York (h)	W22-28	t:Anderson(2),Purtill(2),Donlan g:Wingfield(4)	1st	814
21/4/00	Widnes (a)	L28-16	t:Anderson,Bristow g:Wingfield(4)	3rd	4,237
24/4/00	Rochdale (h)	W42-10	t:Higham(2),Anderson,Fairclough,Wingfield,Ingram,Cross,Bowker g:Wingfield(5)	2nd	1,832
1/5/00	Hunslet (a)	W10-24	t:Whittle,Anderson,Wingfield,Kendrick g:Wingfield(4)	1st	1,062
7/5/00	Batley (h)	W44-40	t:Higham(2),Ingram,Anderson,Whittle,Bristow,Purtill,Cross g:Wingfield(6)	1st	1,550
14/5/00	Swinton (a)	W12-46	t:Leathem,Anderson,Higham,Donlan,Bristow,Wingfield,Baldwin g:Wingfield(9)	3rd	1,348
21/5/00	Whitehaven (h)	W34-8	t:Bristow(2),Anderson,Purtill,Street g:Wingfield(7)	3rd	1,879
26/5/00	Barrow (a)	L20-12	t:Fairclough,Donlan g:Wingfield,Dean	3rd	1,170
29/5/00	Keighley (h)	W26-16	t:Baldwin,Street,Higham,Fairclough,Ingram g:Dean(3)	3rd	3,066
4/6/00	Oldham (a)	L27-10	t:Arkwright g:Anderson(3)	3rd	2,823
11/6/00	Hunslet (h)	W44-4	t:Donlan(2),Cross,Fairclough,Kendrick,Anderson,Cruckshank,Higham g:Anderson(6)	3rd	1,675
18/6/00	Lancashire (h)	W50-14	t:Higham(2),Bretherton,Donlan,Arkwright,Cross,Dean,Ingram,Street g:Anderson(5),Bretherton(2)	3rd	1,424
25/6/00	Doncaster (a)	L29-18	t:Fairclough,Cross,Ingram g:Anderson(3)	5th	1,841
2/7/00	Dewsbury (h)	W38-16	t:Donlan(2),Anderson,Purtill,Kendrick,Bowker,Bretherton g:Bretherton(5)	4th	2,320
9/7/00	Dewsbury (a) (PSF)	W12-29	t:Cross(2),Kendrick,Donlan,Bretherton g:Bretherton(4) fg:Bretherton	N/A	2,500
23/7/00	Oldham (h) (MaSF)	W18-10	t:Anderson(2),Bristow g:Bretherton(3)	N/A	5,836
29/7/00	Dewsbury (GF)	L13-12	t:Higham(2) g:Bretherton(2)	N/A	8,487

	APP		TRIES		GOALS		FG		PTS	
	ALL	NFP	ALL	NFP	ALL	NFP	ALL	NFP	ALL	NFP
Paul Anderson	34	31	16	16	17	17	0	0	98	98
James Arkwright	4(7)	4(7)	2	2	0	0	0	0	8	8
Simon Baldwin	29(1)	27(1)	5	5	1	1	0	0	22	22
Radney Bowker	10(15)	9(13)	7	7	0	0	0	0	28	28
Liam Bretherton	5	5	3	3	16	16	1	1	45	45
Adam Bristow	33(1)	30(1)	11	11	0	0	0	0	44	44
Jim Cassidy	(2)	(2)	0	0	0	0	0	0	0	0
Chris Causey	1(11)	1(10)	0	0	0	0	0	0	0	0
Graeme Close	3(3)	3(3)	0	0	10	10	0	0	20	20
Dean Conway	(1)	0	0	0	0	0	0	0	0	0
Alan Cross	31(1)	28(1)	19	18	0	0	0	0	76	72
Heath Cruckshank	24(2)	22(2)	2	1	0	0	0	0	8	4
Craig Dean	15	15	5	5	4	4	0	0	28	28
Stuart Donlan	32	29	17	15	0	0	0	0	68	60
Andy Fairclough	32	29	14	13	0	0	0	0	56	52
Alan Hadcroft	13(2)	11(1)	2	1	0	0	0	0	8	4
Chris Halliwell	(1)	0	0	0	0	0	0	0	0	0
Mick Higham	29(3)	27(3)	22	19	0	0	0	0	88	76
David Ingram	15(7)	15(7)	9	9	0	0	0	0	36	36
Phil Kendrick	11(7)	9(7)	9	7	0	0	0	0	36	28
Andy Leathem	5(7)	5(7)	1	1	0	0	0	0	4	4
Anthony Murray	4(14)	3(12)	4	3	0	0	0	0	16	12
Paul Norman	4(23)	3(21)	1	1	0	0	0	0	4	4
Safraz Patel	1(2)	1(1)	0	0	0	0	0	0	0	0
Kieron Purtill	29(1)	26(1)	8	8	0	0	0	0	32	32
Tim Street	29(5)	27(4)	4	4	0	0	0	0	16	16
Graham Taberner	1(1)	1(1)	0	0	0	0	0	0	0	0
Richard Varkulis	(2)	(2)	0	0	0	0	0	0	0	0
Simon Warhurst	(1)	(1)	0	0	0	0	0	0	0	0
David Whittle	26(8)	23(8)	3	3	0	0	0	0	12	12
Paul Wingfield	22(3)	19(3)	8	8	99	88	0	0	230	208

Mick Higham

LEAGUE RECORD
P28-W21-D0-L7
(4th, NFP/Grand Final Runners Up)
F854, A476, Diff+378
42 points.

CHALLENGE CUP
Round Four

ATTENDANCES
Best - v Oldham (MaSF - 5,836)
Worst - v Lancashire (NFP - 1,424)
Total (NFP, inc play-offs) - 39,608
Average (NFP, inc play-offs) - 2,640
(Up by 765 on 1999)

OLDHAM

DATE	FIXTURE	RESULT	SCORERS	LGE	ATT
27/12/99	Rochdale (h)	W23-20	t:Rogers,Campbell,Hough g:Sibson(5) fg:A Gibbons	N/A	3,562
2/1/00	Swinton (a)	W18-23	t:Sibson(2),Campbell,A Gibbons g:Sibson(3) fg:Brennan	5th	2,567
9/1/00	Whitehaven (h)	W26-22	t:Hayes(2),A Gibbons,Rich,Mannion g:Sibson(3)	3rd	2,446
16/1/00	Barrow (a)	L19-16	t:Sibson,O'Reilly,Casey g:Sibson(2)	6th	1,618
23/1/00	Workington (h)	W30-17	t:A Gibbons(2),Brennan,D Gibbons,Hough g:Rich(5)	2nd	2,222
6/2/00	Doncaster (a)	L26-16	t:Hayes,Rich,Moseley g:Rich(2)	8th	2,130
8/2/00	Wigan St J (h) (CCR3)	W44-0	t:Sibson(4),Hough(2),Hayes,Ferris g:Rich(6)	N/A	1,376
13/2/00	Rochdale (a) (CCR4)	L30-14	t:Guest g:Rich(5)	N/A	2,168
20/2/00	Leigh (a)	L28-10	t:Ford,Barrow g:Rich	11th	2,780
5/3/00	Lancashire (h)	W50-8	t:Hough(2),Hayes(2),D Gibbons,Barrow,Guest,Sibson,A Gibbons,Ford g:Rich(5)	9th	1,522
12/3/00	Widnes (a)	W20-31	t:Sibson(2),Rich,Hough g:Rich(7) fg:Ford	8th	3,300
19/3/00	Dewsbury (h)	L12-14	t:D Gibbons,Hayes g:Rich(2)	9th	2,115
26/3/00	Featherstone (a)	L61-26	t:Sibson(2),Hayes,D Gibbons,A Gibbons g:Rich(3)	9th	2,071
2/4/00	Sheffield (a)	W6-28	t:McMenemy,Ford,Farrell,D Gibbons,Rich g:Rich(4)	9th	1,220
9/4/00	Hunslet (h)	W44-18	t:Hayes(2),Hough(2),Campbell,Rich,A Gibbons,Sibson g:Rich(6)	9th	1,544
16/4/00	Batley (a)	W16-28	t:A Gibbons(2),Rich,Roden g:Rich(6)	7th	805
21/4/00	Rochdale (a)	W12-13	t:Hough,Barrow g:Rich(2) fg:McMenemy	7th	2,288
24/4/00	Swinton (h)	W34-28	t:Barrow,Hough,Campbell,Roden,Hayes,Rich g:Rich(5)	7th	1,908
1/5/00	York (h)	W40-18	t:A Gibbons(2),Hayes(2),Sibson(2),Campbell,Farrell g:Rich(4)	7th	1,852
7/5/00	Hull KR (a)	W12-32	t:Farrell,Hough,Barrow,Hayes,Mannion,D Gibbons g:Rich(4)	6th	2,005
10/5/00	Keighley (h)	L14-24	t:Barrow,D Gibbons,Sibson g:Rich	6th	2,528
14/5/00	Whitehaven (a)	L26-18	t:Sibson(2),McMenemy g:McMenemy(3)	6th	808
21/5/00	Barrow (h)	W30-16	t:A Gibbons(2),Sibson,Hough,Procter g:Rich(5)	6th	1,604
26/5/00	Workington (a)	D12-12	t:Hayes,Barrow g:Rich(2)	6th	595
29/5/00	Doncaster (h)	W25-6	t:Ford(2),Hough,Sibson,Rich g:Rich(2) fg:Ford	6th	2,043
4/6/00	Leigh (h)	W27-10	t:Hough(2),Barrow,Rich,Farrell g:Rich(3) fg:Roden	6th	2,823
11/6/00	Lancashire (a)	W14-48	t:Sibson(3),Roden(2),Rich,Barrow,Hough,A Gibbons g:Rich(6)	6th	616
18/6/00	Widnes (h)	W34-26	t:Molloy,Barrow,A Gibbons,D Gibbons,Hayes,Guest g:Rich(5)	6th	2,073
25/6/00	Dewsbury (a)	L16-12	t:Hayes,Mannion g:Rich(2)	6th	1,456
2/7/00	Featherstone (h)	W32-0	t:Cross(2),Barrow,McMenemy,Roden g:Rich(6)	6th	2,132
9/7/00	Hull KR (h) (ESF)	W22-14	t:Cross,Farrell,D Gibbons,A Gibbons g:Rich(2) fg:Ford,Roden	N/A	2,584
16/7/00	Doncaster (a) (MiSF)	W17-24 *(aet)*	t:Cross,Roden,Ford g:Rich(6)	N/A	2,599
23/7/00	Leigh (a) (MaSF)	L18-10	t:Barrow,D Gibbons g:Rich	N/A	5,836

	APP		TRIES		GOALS		FG		PTS	
	ALL	NFP	ALL	NFP	ALL	NFP	ALL	NFP	ALL	NFP
Warren Barrow	22(1)	22(1)	12	12	0	0	0	0	48	48
Keith Brennan	1(4)	1(3)	1	1	0	0	1	1	5	5
Mark Campbell	22(5)	20(5)	5	5	0	0	0	0	20	20
Leo Casey	17(7)	17(6)	1	1	0	0	0	0	4	4
Jason Clegg	20(9)	18(9)	0	0	0	0	0	0	0	0
Dean Cross	3(1)	3(1)	4	4	0	0	0	0	16	16
Gavin Dodd	(1)	(1)	0	0	0	0	0	0	0	0
Lee Doran	(5)	(5)	0	0	0	0	0	0	0	0
Phil Farrell	20(1)	20(1)	5	5	0	0	0	0	20	20
Peter Ferris	5	3	1	1	0	0	0	0	4	4
Kevin Fitzpatrick	(1)	0	0	0	0	0	0	0	0	0
Mike Ford	18(4)	18(4)	6	6	0	0	3	3	27	27
Anthony Gibbons	30	28	16	16	0	0	1	1	65	65
David Gibbons	32	31	10	10	0	0	0	0	40	40
Danny Guest	1(19)	1(17)	3	2	0	0	0	0	12	8
Joey Hayes	30	28	17	16	0	0	0	0	68	64
Chris Holland	4(14)	4(12)	0	0	0	0	0	0	0	0
John Hough	33	31	17	15	0	0	0	0	68	60
Kevin Mannion	23(3)	21(3)	3	3	0	0	0	0	12	12
Shayne McMenemy	20(2)	20(2)	3	3	3	3	1	1	19	19
Joe McNicholas	9(2)	8(2)	0	0	0	0	0	0	0	0
Steve Molloy	6	6	1	1	0	0	0	0	4	4
Tate Moseley	2(1)	(1)	1	1	0	0	0	0	4	4
Chris Naylor	(1)	(1)	0	0	0	0	0	0	0	0
Tom O'Reilly	9	7	1	1	0	0	0	0	4	4
Andy Procter	21(5)	19(5)	1	1	0	0	0	0	4	4
Pat Rich	31	29	10	10	108	97	0	0	256	234
Neil Roden	14(5)	14(5)	6	6	0	0	2	2	26	26
Wes Rogers	2(8)	2(7)	1	1	0	0	0	0	4	4
Graeme Shaw	(2)	(2)	0	0	0	0	0	0	0	0
Mark Sibson	33	31	23	19	13	13	0	0	118	102
Ian Sinfield	1(19)	1(19)	0	0	0	0	0	0	0	0

Shayne McMenemy

LEAGUE RECORD
P28-W19-D1-L8
(6th, NFP/Major Semi Finalists)
F734, A513, Diff+221
39 points.

CHALLENGE CUP
Round Four

ATTENDANCES
Best - v Rochdale (NFP - 3,562)
Worst - v Wigan St J (CC - 1,376)
Total (NFP, inc play-offs) - 32,958
Average (NFP, inc play-offs) - 2,197
(Up by 1,014 on 1999)

ROCHDALE HORNETS

DATE	FIXTURE	RESULT	SCORERS	LGE	ATT
27/12/99	Oldham (a)	L23-20	t:Robinson,Hudson,Newall,Martin g:Dorahy(2)	N/A	3,562
2/1/00	Leigh (h)	L14-42	t:Martin,Hudson,Cooper g:Dorahy	14th	2,112
9/1/00	Lancashire (a)	W22-38	t:Dorahy(2),Wood,Swinson,Cooper,Best g:Dorahy(7)	13th	435
23/1/00	York (h)	W24-14	t:Martin(2),Bunce,Newall,Wood g:Dorahy(2)	13th	823
30/1/00	The Army (h) (CCR3)	W66-6	t:Wood(3),Hilton(2),Swinson,Miller,Dorahy,McMenemy,Martin,Maher, McKinney g:Dorahy(9)	N/A	700
6/2/00	Swinton (a)	L34-16	t:Price-Jones(3) g:Wood(2)	13th	1,112
13/2/00	Oldham (h) (CCR4)	W30-14	t:Hilton(2),Newall,Dorahy,Wood,Bunce,Swinson g:Wood	N/A	2,168
20/2/00	Whitehaven (h)	L20-22	t:McMenemy,Newall,Cooper g:Wood(4)	13th	784
27/2/00	Hull (a) (CCR5)	L82-10	t:Wilde,Wood g:Wood	N/A	3,992
1/3/00	Widnes (h)	L8-34	t:Cooper g:Wood(2)	15th	807
5/3/00	Barrow (a)	L32-14	t:Robinson,Wilde g:Wood(3)	15th	1,169
12/3/00	Workington (h)	W32-28	t:Dorahy,Wood,Robinson,Cooper g:Wood(6)	12th	794
19/3/00	Batley (a)	L24-12	t:Cooper,Demetriou g:Wood(2)	14th	464
26/3/00	Hull KR (h)	L26-38	t:Robinson,Dorahy,Martin,Demetriou g:Wood(5)	13th	1,253
2/4/00	Keighley (a)	L26-14	t:Robinson,Wood,Wilde g:Wood	14th	1,450
9/4/00	Doncaster (h)	L18-20	t:Cooper(2),Robinson g:Wood(3)	15th	1,179
16/4/00	Featherstone (h)	W31-16	t:Robinson,Price-Jones,Swinson,Hudson,Martindale g:Wood(5) fg:Demetriou	14th	1,273
21/4/00	Oldham (h)	L12-13	t:Robinson,Wood g:Wood(2)	15th	2,288
24/4/00	Leigh (a)	L42-10	t:Swinson,Ireland g:Wood	16th	1,832
1/5/00	Dewsbury (a)	L26-2	g:Wood	16th	1,009
7/5/00	Sheffield (a)	W19-22	t:Martin,Miller,Waring,Demetriou g:Wood(3)	15th	1,055
10/5/00	Hunslet (h)	W24-16	t:Demetriou,Dorahy,Robinson,D Sculthorpe g:Wood(4)	14th	921
14/5/00	Lancashire (h)	W50-8	t:Martindale(2),Robinson(2),Demetriou,Murray,Miller,Green,Cooper g:Wood(5),Dorahy(2)	13th	895
21/5/00	Widnes (a)	L38-10	t:Wood,Miller g:Wood	13th	3,170
26/5/00	York (a)	W22-42	t:Martin(3),Miller(2),Wood(2),Murray g:Wood(5)	13th	331
29/5/00	Swinton (h)	L21-32	t:Newall,Hudson,Ireland g:Dorahy(4) fg:Dorahy	13th	1,061
4/6/00	Whitehaven (a)	L14-8	t:Cooper g:Dorahy(2)	13th	510
11/6/00	Keighley (h)	L10-30	t:Derose,Cooper g:Dorahy	13th	1,349
18/6/00	Workington (a)	L22-8	t:Miller g:Wood(2)	13th	491
25/6/00	Batley (h)	W33-20	t:Robinson(3),Martin(2),Price-Jones g:Dorahy(4) fg:Dorahy	13th	908
2/7/00	Hunslet (a)	W19-24	t:Robinson,Cooper,Dorahy,Maher g:Robinson(4)	13th	633

	APP		TRIES		GOALS		FG		PTS	
	ALL	NFP	ALL	NFP	ALL	NFP	ALL	NFP	ALL	NFP
Paul Ashton	3(3)	2(3)	0	0	0	0	0	0	0	0
David Best	(2)	(2)	1	1	0	0	0	0	4	4
Martin Bunce	14(14)	13(12)	2	1	0	0	0	0	8	4
Steve Cameron	(6)	(6)	0	0	0	0	0	0	0	0
Sean Cooper	26(3)	26(2)	12	12	0	0	0	0	48	48
Jason Demetriou	20	20	5	5	0	0	1	1	21	21
Darrell Derose	11(4)	10(4)	1	1	0	0	0	0	4	4
Dane Dorahy	23	21	9	7	34	25	2	2	106	80
Mickey Edwards	5	5	0	0	0	0	0	0	0	0
Paul Forber	(2)	(2)	0	0	0	0	0	0	0	0
Peter Green	3(4)	3(4)	1	1	0	0	0	0	4	4
Rob Hall	(1)	(1)	0	0	0	0	0	0	0	0
Phil Harrison	(5)	(4)	0	0	0	0	0	0	0	0
Chris Hilton	10	7	4	0	0	0	0	0	16	0
Gareth Hooson	2	2	0	0	0	0	0	0	0	0
Chris Hough	(1)	(1)	0	0	0	0	0	0	0	0
Lee Hudson	12(1)	11(1)	4	4	0	0	0	0	16	16
Andy Ireland	17	17	2	2	0	0	0	0	8	8
Lee Maher	20	17	2	1	0	0	0	0	8	4
Scott Martin	24(5)	21(5)	12	11	0	0	0	0	48	44
Mick Martindale	7(7)	7(7)	3	3	0	0	0	0	12	12
Chris McKinney	26	23	1	0	0	0	0	0	4	0
Shayne McMenemy	7	5	2	1	0	0	0	0	8	4
Marlon Miller	17(1)	15(1)	7	6	0	0	0	0	28	24
Adrian Moore	2(1)	2(1)	0	0	0	0	0	0	0	0
Anthony Murray	6	6	2	2	0	0	0	0	8	8
Chris Newall	14(4)	12(3)	5	4	0	0	0	0	20	16
Mark Powell	3	3	0	0	0	0	0	0	0	0
Lee Prest	1(6)	1(6)	0	0	0	0	0	0	0	0
Gavin Price-Jones	22(3)	20(2)	5	5	0	0	0	0	20	20
Andy Pucill	(3)	(2)	0	0	0	0	0	0	0	0
Darren Robinson	21(7)	21(4)	15	15	4	4	0	0	68	68
Danny Sculthorpe	22	19	1	1	0	0	0	0	4	4
Lee Sculthorpe	(6)	(6)	0	0	0	0	0	0	0	0
James Simeonovich	2(1)	2(1)	0	0	0	0	0	0	0	0
Ben Simpson	1(3)	1(3)	0	0	0	0	0	0	0	0
David Stephenson	(5)	(5)	0	0	0	0	0	0	0	0
Gavin Swinson	7(6)	4(6)	5	3	0	0	0	0	20	12
Phil Waring	17(11)	14(11)	1	1	0	0	0	0	4	4
Steve Wilde	13	12	3	2	0	0	0	0	12	8
Danny Wood	25(1)	22(1)	13	8	59	57	0	0	170	146

Danny Wood

LEAGUE RECORD
P28-W10-D0-L18
(13th, NFP)
F563, A696, Diff-133
20 points.

CHALLENGE CUP
Round Five

ATTENDANCES
Best - v Oldham (NFP - 2,288)
Worst - v The Army (CC - 700)
Total (NFP only) - 16,447
Average (NFP only) - 1,175
(Up by 217 on 1999)

225

SHEFFIELD EAGLES

DATE	FIXTURE	RESULT	SCORERS	LGE	ATT
28/12/99	Lancashire (a)	W20-33	t:Bruce,I Brown,Strange,G Brown,Robinson,Johnson g:G Brown(3),Aston fg:G Brown	N/A	888
9/1/00	York (a)	L16-15	t:Bruce,Strange,Williamson g:G Brown fg:Strange	11th	971
16/1/00	Batley (h)	L12-22	t:Johnson,Walker g:Robinson(2)	13th	1,612
23/1/00	Hull KR (a)	L6-4	t:I Brown	14th	2,244
25/1/00	Hunslet (h)	W17-12	t:Larder,Crouthers g:Aston(4) fg:Vassilakopoulos	13th	1,278
30/1/00	Thornhill (h) (CCR3)	L14-16	t:Wright,Bruce g:Goddard(3)	N/A	1,100
6/2/00	Featherstone (h)	L45-13	t:Morley,Walker g:Goddard(2) fg:Aston	14th	1,867
20/2/00	Dewsbury (a)	L33-18	t:Williamson,Wright,I Brown g:Goddard(3)	15th	1,459
27/2/00	Widnes (a)	L3-0	No Scorers	15th	2,871
5/3/00	Doncaster (h)	L10-16	t:I Brown g:Goddard(3)	14th	2,732
12/3/00	Keighley (a)	L36-2	g:Goddard	15th	1,596
19/3/00	Barrow (a)	L34-16	t:Johnson,Kite,Morley g:Goddard(2)	15th	1,172
26/3/00	Workington (h)	L18-20	t:Goddard(2),G Brown g:Goddard(3)	16th	1,177
2/4/00	Oldham (h)	L6-28	t:Strange g:Aston	17th	1,220
9/4/00	Leigh (a)	W24-26	t:Morley,G Freeman,Robinson,Williamson g:G Brown(5)	16th	2,250
16/4/00	Swinton (a)	L38-30	t:Kite(2),Williamson,Robinson,Strange g:Robinson(3),G Brown(2)	16th	962
21/4/00	Lancashire (h)	W56-12	t:Kite(3),W Freeman,Brent,G Freeman,Wray,Robinson,Hanlan g:G Brown(7),Goddard	16th	1,177
24/4/00	Hunslet (a)	W6-27	t:Morley,Vassilakopoulos,G Brown,Hanlan g:G Brown(4),Robinson fg:G Brown	12th	863
1/5/00	Whitehaven (h)	L19-22	t:Walker,Robinson,Larder g:G Brown(3) fg:G Brown	13th	1,098
7/5/00	Rochdale (h)	L19-22	t:W Freeman,Goddard g:G Brown(5) fg:Robinson	14th	1,055
14/5/00	York (h)	D12-12	t:Kite g:G Brown(3),Goddard	15th	1,038
21/5/00	Batley (a)	W14-21	t:G Brown(2),Goddard,Wright g:G Brown(2) fg:Robinson	15th	513
26/5/00	Hull KR (h)	W10-8	t:Kite g:G Brown(3)	14th	1,021
29/5/00	Featherstone (h)	L14-29	t:I Brown,Walker g:G Brown(3)	14th	1,359
4/6/00	Dewsbury (h)	L8-30	t:Briggs g:G Brown(2)	14th	1,478
11/6/00	Doncaster (a)	L29-8	t:Strange g:G Brown,Goddard	14th	1,553
18/6/00	Keighley (h)	L16-28	t:Strange,Wray,I Brown g:Goddard,G Brown	14th	1,424
25/6/00	Barrow (h)	W30-2	t:I Brown(2),Bruce,Kite,Wittenberg g:Goddard(5)	14th	1,188
2/7/00	Workington (a)	W18-19	t:Goddard,Vassilakopoulos,Johnson g:Goddard(2),G Brown fg:Vassilakopoulos	14th	659

	APP		TRIES		GOALS		FG		PTS	
	ALL	NFP	ALL	NFP	ALL	NFP	ALL	NFP	ALL	NFP
Mark Aston	8(3)	8(3)	0	0	6	6	1	1	13	13
Lee Bettinson	4(6)	3(6)	0	0	0	0	0	0	0	0
Andrew Brent	8(12)	8(11)	1	1	0	0	0	0	4	4
Carl Briggs	5(3)	5(3)	1	1	0	0	0	0	4	4
Gavin Brown	19(1)	19(1)	5	5	46	46	3	3	115	115
Ian Brown	9(10)	8(10)	8	8	0	0	0	0	32	32
John Bruce	14(15)	14(14)	4	3	0	0	0	0	16	12
Kevin Crouthers	9	8	1	1	0	0	0	0	4	4
Glen Freeman	8(13)	8(13)	2	2	0	0	0	0	8	8
Wayne Freeman	26(2)	25(2)	3	3	0	0	0	0	12	12
Marc Gibson	4(1)	3(1)	0	0	0	0	0	0	0	0
Richard Goddard	18(4)	17(4)	5	5	28	25	0	0	76	70
Lee Hanlan	(5)	(5)	2	2	0	0	0	0	8	8
Michael Jackson	5(2)	5(2)	0	0	0	0	0	0	0	0
Mickey Johnson	10(5)	9(5)	4	4	0	0	0	0	16	16
Mark Kear	(3)	(3)	0	0	0	0	0	0	0	0
Michael Kent	2	2	0	0	0	0	0	0	0	0
Neil Kite	18	18	9	9	0	0	0	0	36	36
David Larder	21(1)	20(1)	2	2	0	0	0	0	8	8
Chris Morley	20(1)	20	4	4	0	0	0	0	16	16
Chris Robinson	21(1)	21(1)	5	5	6	6	2	2	34	34
John Strange	18(4)	18(3)	6	6	0	0	1	1	25	25
Darren Summerill	(3)	(3)	0	0	0	0	0	0	0	0
Alex Thompson	9(4)	8(4)	0	0	0	0	0	0	0	0
Marcus Vassilakopoulos	24	23	2	2	0	0	2	2	10	10
Steve Walker	22(1)	22(1)	4	4	0	0	0	0	16	16
Leon Williamson	17	16	4	4	0	0	0	0	16	16
Jeff Wittenberg	16(3)	16(3)	1	1	0	0	0	0	4	4
Simon Wray	28	27	2	2	0	0	0	0	8	8
Ricky Wright	14(10)	13(10)	3	2	0	0	0	0	12	8

Chris Morley

LEAGUE RECORD
P28-W9-D1-L18
(14th, NFP)
F479, A585, Diff-106
19 points.

CHALLENGE CUP
Round Three

ATTENDANCES
Best - v Doncaster (NFP - 2,732)
Worst - v Hull KR (NFP - 1,021)
Total (NFP only) - 16,460
Average (NFP only) - 1,176

SWINTON LIONS

DATE	FIXTURE	RESULT	SCORERS	LGE	ATT
26/12/99	Workington (a)	W10-21	t:Billy,Loughlin,Bateman,Roach g:Watson(2) fg:Casey	N/A	1,111
2/1/00	Oldham (h)	L18-23	t:Smith,Coussons,Bateman g:Watson(3)	11th	2,567
9/1/00	Leigh (a)	W20-22	t:Smith(2),Coussons,Coley g:Watson(3)	8th	2,681
16/1/00	Lancashire (h)	W54-6	t:Loughlin(3),Coley(2),Pickavance(2),Craig,Watson,Billy g:Watson(7)	3rd	942
23/1/00	Widnes (a)	L22-14	t:Coley(2),Craig g:Watson	6th	3,695
1/2/00	Waterhead (h) (CCR3)	W74-1	t:Coussons(2),Craig(2),P Barrow(2),Henare(2),Casey,Highton,Smith, English,T Barrow,Coley,Bateman,Roach g:Watson(5)	N/A	588
6/2/00	Rochdale (h)	W34-16	t:Coussons,P Barrow,Craig,Roach g:Watson(9)	5th	1,112
13/2/00	St Helens (h) (CCR4)	L22-36	t:Coley,Casey,Bateman,Coussons g:Watson(2),Loughlin	N/A	3,169
20/2/00	Batley (h)	L16-32	t:Craig,Smith,Nanyn g:Watson(2)	7th	885
5/3/00	Whitehaven (a)	W16-20	t:Craig,Coussons,Smith,Roach g:Nanyn(2)	7th	927
12/3/00	Barrow (h)	W35-22	t:Billy(3),Casey,Roach,Smith,Coussons g:Nanyn(3) fg:Casey	7th	808
19/3/00	Hull KR (a)	L54-16	t:Smith,Randall,Bateman g:Nanyn(2)	10th	2,073
26/3/00	Keighley (h)	L12-34	t:Craig,Watson g:Watson(2)	10th	1,250
2/4/00	Doncaster (a)	L28-14	t:Smith,Henare g:Watson(2),Nanyn	10th	1,076
9/4/00	Dewsbury (h)	D14-14	t:Coussons,Craig g:Nanyn,Watson fg:Watson(2)	10th	1,041
16/4/00	Sheffield (h)	W38-30	t:Henare(2),English,Coussons,Watson,Roach,Nanyn g:Watson(5)	10th	962
21/4/00	Workington (h)	W38-34	t:English,Billy,Henare,Coussons,Furey,Roach,Pickavance g:Watson(3),Nanyn(2)	9th	936
24/4/00	Oldham (a)	L34-28	t:Roach(2),Smith,Watson,Billy g:Watson(4)	10th	1,908
1/5/00	Featherstone (a)	L28-14	t:Loughlin,Coussons,Henare g:Watson	10th	1,691
7/5/00	Hunslet (h)	L24-31	t:Roach(2),English,Coussons,Smith g:Watson(2)	10th	849
10/5/00	York (a)	W14-30	t:Coussons(2),Cushion,Loughlin,Henare g:Watson(5)	10th	377
14/5/00	Leigh (h)	L12-46	t:Roach,Coussons g:Watson(2)	10th	1,348
21/5/00	Lancashire (a)	W6-68	t:S Barrow(2),Craig(2),Nanyn(2),Knowles,Roach,Furey,Coussons, Smith,Billy,Henare g:Watson(8)	9th	212
26/5/00	Widnes (h)	L12-28	t:Watson,Roach g:Watson(2)	10th	1,336
29/5/00	Rochdale (a)	W21-32	t:Smith(2),Randall,Nanyn,Billy,Knowles g:Watson(2),Nanyn(2)	10th	1,061
4/6/00	Batley (a)	W24-28	t:Craig(2),Nanyn(2),Billy,Roach g:Watson(2)	10th	360
9/6/00	Whitehaven (h)	D28-28	t:Randall(2),Smith,Craig,Casey g:Nanyn(4)	9th	672
18/6/00	Barrow (a)	L34-22	t:Randall,Craig,Bateman,Nanyn g:Craig(2),Nanyn	10th	1,114
25/6/00	York (h)	W50-12	t:Henare,Casey,Billy,Craig,Coussons,Roach,English,Loughlin, Cushion g:Watson(7)	9th	757
2/7/00	Keighley (a)	L66-12	t:Henare,Smith g:Watson(2)	9th	1,665

	APP		TRIES		GOALS		FG		PTS	
	ALL	NFP	ALL	NFP	ALL	NFP	ALL	NFP	ALL	NFP
Paul Barrow	7(11)	7(9)	3	1	0	0	0	0	12	4
Steve Barrow	3	3	2	2	0	0	0	0	8	8
Tony Barrow	8(19)	7(18)	1	0	0	0	0	0	4	0
Matt Bateman	14(2)	12(2)	6	4	0	0	0	0	24	16
Marlon Billy	25(3)	23(3)	11	11	0	0	0	0	44	44
Sean Casey	17	15	5	3	0	0	2	2	22	14
Andy Coley	7(1)	5(1)	7	5	0	0	0	0	28	20
Phil Coussons	28	26	18	15	0	0	0	0	72	60
Andy Craig	25(1)	23(1)	16	14	2	2	0	0	68	60
Phil Cushion	6(12)	6(12)	2	2	0	0	0	0	8	8
Wayne English	12(3)	11(3)	5	4	0	0	0	0	20	16
Jim Evans	6(13)	6(12)	0	0	0	0	0	0	0	0
Sean Furey	13(2)	13(2)	2	2	0	0	0	0	8	8
Steve Gartland	2(2)	2(2)	0	0	0	0	0	0	0	0
Richard Henare	9(8)	9(7)	11	9	0	0	0	0	44	36
Chris Highton	20(1)	18(1)	1	0	0	0	0	0	4	0
Matt Knowles	16(7)	15(6)	2	2	0	0	0	0	8	8
Paul Loughlin	14(5)	13(5)	7	7	1	0	0	0	30	28
Mick Nanyn	12(7)	12(7)	8	8	18	18	0	0	68	68
Jonathan Neill	24(2)	23(1)	0	0	0	0	0	0	0	0
Ian Pickavance	23(3)	22(2)	3	3	0	0	0	0	12	12
Craig Randall	13(3)	13(3)	5	5	0	0	0	0	20	20
Jason Roach	25(3)	23(3)	16	15	0	0	0	0	64	60
Paul Smith	29	27	16	15	0	0	0	0	64	60
Ryan Stazicker	3(6)	3(6)	0	0	0	0	0	0	0	0
Ian Watson	28	26	5	5	84	77	2	2	190	176
Mark Welsby	1(2)	1(2)	0	0	0	0	0	0	0	0

Andy Craig

LEAGUE RECORD
P28-W13-D2-L13
(9th, NFP)
F726, A733, Diff-7
28 points.

CHALLENGE CUP
Round Four

ATTENDANCES
Best - v ST Helens (CC - 3,169)
Worst - v Waterhead (CC - 588)
Total (NFP only) - 15,463
Average (NFP only) - 1,104
(Up by 58 on 1999)

WHITEHAVEN WARRIORS

DATE	FIXTURE	RESULT	SCORERS	LGE	ATT
26/12/99	Barrow (a)	L31-4	t:Frazer	N/A	1,637
2/1/00	Workington (h)	W42-0	t:Nelson(2),Seeds(2),Lester,Morton,Frazer,G Purdham g:Kitchin(5)	8th	1,548
9/1/00	Oldham (a)	L26-22	t:Frazer(2),Ruddy,Kitchin,Lester g:Kitchin	12th	2,446
16/1/00	Leigh (h)	W24-6	t:Frazer,Nelson,Seeds,Lester,Lynch g:Hetherington(2)	9th	1,400
23/1/00	Lancashire (a)	L22-12	t:Lester,Hetherington g:R Purdham,Hetherington	11th	223
30/1/00	Shaw Cross (h) (CCR3)	W42-0	t:Frazer(2),Keenan(2),Armstrong,Lester,Seeds g:Hetherington(7)	N/A	503
6/2/00	Widnes (h)	W13-6	t:Kiddie,Frazer g:Hetherington(2) fg:Hetherington	11th	1,384
13/2/00	Wigan (a) (CCR4)	L98-4	t:Kiddie	N/A	6,532
20/2/00	Rochdale (a)	W20-22	t:Nelson,Keenan,Walsh,Hetherington g:Hetherington(3)	8th	784
5/3/00	Swinton (h)	L16-20	t:Walsh,Morton g:Hetherington(4)	10th	927
12/3/00	Hull KR (a)	L22-14	t:Keenan,Walsh g:Kitchin(2),Hetherington	11th	1,823
19/3/00	Keighley (h)	L10-56	t:Morton,Walsh g:Kitchin	11th	905
26/3/00	Doncaster (h)	L14-24	t:Kiddie,Hill,Wilson g:Hetherington	11th	804
2/4/00	Dewsbury (h)	L10-36	t:Hill,Seeds g:Stoddart	12th	596
9/4/00	Featherstone (a)	L44-20	t:Seeds,Hill,R Purdham,Walsh g:Stoddart(2)	12th	1,474
16/4/00	Hunslet (a)	L24-2	g:R Purdham	15th	615
21/4/00	Barrow (h)	W30-0	t:Frazer(2),Seeds(2),Kitchin,Hetherington g:Hetherington(2), R Purdham	12th	808
24/4/00	Workington (a)	L27-18	t:Kiddie,Bone,Kitchin g:Hetherington(3)	14th	1,886
1/5/00	Sheffield (a)	W19-22	t:Frazer(2),Hill g:Hetherington(5)	12th	1,098
7/5/00	York (h)	W44-12	t:Walsh(3),Lester,Kiddie,Seeds,Hill,Smith g:Hetherington(6)	11th	592
14/5/00	Oldham (h)	W26-18	t:G Purdham,Hill,Seeds,Currie g:Hetherington(5)	12th	808
21/5/00	Leigh (a)	L34-8	t:G Purdham g:Hetherington(2)	12th	1,879
26/5/00	Featherstone (h)	L14-29	t:Lester,Kiddie g:Hetherington(3)	12th	569
29/5/00	Widnes (a)	L22-12	t:Stoddart,Hill g:Hetherington(2)	12th	3,186
4/6/00	Rochdale (h)	W14-8	t:Bone,Chambers,R Purdham g:Hetherington	12th	510
9/6/00	Swinton (a)	D28-28	t:Chambers,Walsh,Morton,Kiddie,Seeds g:Hetherington(4)	12th	672
14/6/00	Batley (h)	W20-14	t:Kitchin,Kiddie,Wilson g:R Purdham(4)	12th	520
18/6/00	Hull KR (h)	W44-12	t:Seeds(2),Walsh(2),Lester,Morton,Kitchin,G Purdham g:Hetherington(6)	11th	590
25/6/00	Keighley (a)	L50-12	t:R Purdham,Wilson g:Hetherington,Stoddart	11th	1,603
2/7/00	Doncaster (a)	L64-16	t:Hetherington(2),Campbell,Seeds	11th	1,284

	APP		TRIES		GOALS		FG		PTS	
	ALL	NFP	ALL	NFP	ALL	NFP	ALL	NFP	ALL	NFP
Colin Armstrong	11(4)	9(4)	1	0	0	0	0	0	4	0
Alan Bone	22(5)	20(5)	2	2	0	0	0	0	8	8
Ryan Campbell	2(2)	2(2)	1	1	0	0	0	0	4	4
Craig Chambers	12(4)	12(4)	2	2	0	0	0	0	8	8
Graeme Colley	(1)	(1)	0	0	0	0	0	0	0	0
Mark Cox	6(2)	4(2)	0	0	0	0	0	0	0	0
David Currie	(5)	(5)	1	1	0	0	0	0	4	4
David Fatialofa	22(5)	22(4)	0	0	0	0	0	0	0	0
Neil Frazer	25(1)	23(1)	12	10	0	0	0	0	48	40
Kevin Hetherington	24(3)	22(3)	5	5	61	54	1	1	143	129
Howard Hill	24	22	7	7	0	0	0	0	28	28
Mark Keenan	9(3)	7(3)	4	2	0	0	0	0	16	8
Lee Kiddie	25	23	8	7	0	0	0	0	32	28
Wayne Kitchin	20(7)	18(7)	5	5	9	9	0	0	38	38
Aaron Lester	20(1)	18(1)	8	7	0	0	0	0	32	28
Matt Lynch	(9)	(7)	1	1	0	0	0	0	4	4
Stephen McCourt	1(4)	1(4)	0	0	0	0	0	0	0	0
Spencer Miller	(14)	(14)	0	0	0	0	0	0	0	0
Graeme Morton	18(7)	18(7)	5	5	0	0	0	0	20	20
Andrew Nelson	13(1)	11(1)	4	4	0	0	0	0	16	16
Paul O'Neill	1(1)	1(1)	0	0	0	0	0	0	0	0
Garry Purdham	26(3)	24(3)	4	4	0	0	0	0	16	16
Robert Purdham	21(1)	21(1)	3	3	7	7	0	0	26	26
Gary Ruddy	3	3	1	1	0	0	0	0	4	4
Paul Seagar	(1)	(1)	0	0	0	0	0	0	0	0
David Seeds	26(1)	24(1)	14	13	0	0	0	0	56	52
Gary Smith	(7)	(7)	1	1	0	0	0	0	4	4
Stephen Stoddart	4(2)	4(2)	1	1	4	4	0	0	12	12
George Suafoa	(8)	(7)	0	0	0	0	0	0	0	0
Chris Thompson	(2)	(2)	0	0	0	0	0	0	0	0
Dean Vaughan	21(5)	21(3)	0	0	0	0	0	0	0	0
Craig Walsh	20(3)	20(1)	11	11	0	0	0	0	44	44
Wesley Wilson	14(1)	14(1)	3	3	0	0	0	0	12	12

Neil Frazer

LEAGUE RECORD
P28-W11-D1-L16
(11th, NFP)
F533, A674, Diff-141
23 points.

CHALLENGE CUP
Round Four

ATTENDANCES
Best - v Workington (NFP - 1,548)
Worst - v Shaw Cross (CC - 503)
Total (NFP only) - 11,961
Average (NFP only) - 854
(Down by 1 on 1999)

WIDNES VIKINGS

DATE	FIXTURE	RESULT	SCORERS	LGE	ATT
26/12/99	Leigh (a)	L24-16	t:Munro,Verbickas,Gee,Mansson	N/A	4,468
2/1/00	Lancashire (h)	W64-8	t:Munro(3),Eccles(2),Briers(2),Donohue(2),Verbickas,Cantillon g:Verbickas(10)	7th	3,837
9/1/00	Hunslet (h)	W30-21	t:Cheetham,Donohue,Verbickas,Hulme,Hansen g:Verbickas(5)	5th	3,758
23/1/00	Swinton (h)	W22-14	t:Cantillon(2),Munro g:Verbickas(5)	5th	3,695
30/1/00	West Hull (h) (CCR3)	W76-8	t:Cantillon(4),Munro(2),Percival(2),D Smith(2),Hulme,Verbickas, Hansen,Cheetham g:Verbickas(10)	N/A	2,301
6/2/00	Whitehaven (a)	L13-6	t:Mansson g:Verbickas	10th	1,384
13/2/00	Dewsbury (a) (CCR4)	L29-16	t:Eccles,Cheetham,Gee g:Verbickas(2)	N/A	2,445
20/2/00	Barrow (h)	W17-10	t:Gee(2),Cantillon g:Verbickas(2) fg:Fitzpatrick	6th	3,058
27/2/00	Sheffield (h)	W3-0	g:Verbickas fg:Fitzpatrick	6th	2,871
1/3/00	Rochdale (a)	W8-34	t:Verbickas(3),D Smith,Eccles,Gee g:Verbickas(5)	2nd	807
5/3/00	Workington (a)	L16-10	t:Eccles,Mansson g:Verbickas	6th	882
12/3/00	Oldham (h)	L20-31	t:Gee,Cantillon,Mansson g:Verbickas(4)	6th	3,300
19/3/00	York (a)	W18-50	t:Cheetham(3),Percival(2),Gee,Cantillon,Mansson,Fitzpatrick,Hulme g:Verbickas(5)	6th	757
26/3/00	Batley (h)	W30-10	t:Mansson(2),Cheetham,Cantillon,Eccles g:Jones(5)	6th	3,001
2/4/00	Hull KR (a)	L24-10	t:Munro,Leuila g:Jones	7th	2,155
9/4/00	Keighley (h)	L18-30	t:Jones(2),Munro,Cheetham g:Jones	7th	3,308
16/4/00	Dewsbury (a)	L42-24	t:Cantillon(2),Gee(2) g:Jones(4)	8th	2,097
21/4/00	Leigh (h)	W28-16	t:Mansson,Cheetham,Cantillon,Munro g:Jones(6)	8th	4,237
24/4/00	Lancashire (a)	W14-30	t:Mansson(2),Jones,Murphy,Munro,Gee g:Jones(3)	8th	701
30/4/00	Doncaster (h)	W19-18	t:Jones(2),Leuila g:Jones(3) fg:Mansson	8th	3,171
7/5/00	Featherstone (a)	L28-22	t:Munro(2),P Smith,Cantillon g:Jones(3)	8th	2,033
14/5/00	Hunslet (a)	W10-34	t:Cantillon(3),P Smith,Munro,Mansson,Leuila g:Jones(2),Birdseye	8th	846
21/5/00	Rochdale (h)	W38-10	t:Cantillon(5),Kilgannon,Munro g:Jones(5)	7th	3,170
26/5/00	Swinton (h)	W12-28	t:Argent,Fitzpatrick,Knox,Percival g:Jones(6)	7th	1,336
29/5/00	Whitehaven (h)	W22-12	t:Cantillon,Mansson,Hodgkinson,Jones g:Jones(3)	7th	3,186
4/6/00	Barrow (a)	L20-17	t:Mansson,Percival,Gee g:Jones(2) fg:Cheetham	7th	1,829
11/6/00	Workington (h)	W42-16	t:Cantillon(3),Leuila,Gee,Percival,Argent,Knox g:Jones(4),Birdseye	7th	3,162
18/6/00	Oldham (a)	L34-26	t:Gee(2),Cantillon,Murphy,Fitzpatrick g:Briers,Birdseye,Jones	7th	2,073
25/6/00	Hull KR (h)	L14-16	t:Percival,Cantillon,Munro g:Birdseye	8th	3,455
2/7/00	Batley (a)	W8-24	t:Birdseye,Cantillon,Briers,Munro g:Birdseye(3),Jones	8th	685
9/7/00	Featherstone (a) (ESF)	L43-24	t:Percival(2),Briers,Argent,Murphy g:Jones(2)	N/A	1,922

	APP		TRIES		GOALS		FG		PTS	
	ALL	NFP	ALL	NFP	ALL	NFP	ALL	NFP	ALL	NFP
Gareth Adams	3(5)	2(4)	0	0	0	0	0	0	0	0
Steve Argent	17(3)	17(3)	3	3	0	0	0	0	12	12
Lee Birdseye	12(1)	12(1)	1	1	7	7	0	0	18	18
James Briers	9(2)	8(2)	4	4	1	1	0	0	18	18
Phil Cantillon	31	29	30	26	0	0	0	0	120	104
Andy Cheetham	20(2)	19(1)	9	7	0	0	1	1	37	29
Jason Donohue	7(5)	6(5)	3	3	0	0	0	0	12	12
Cliff Eccles	14	12	6	5	0	0	0	0	24	20
Esene Faimalo	2(3)	2(3)	0	0	0	0	0	0	0	0
Karl Fitzpatrick	10(7)	10(6)	3	3	0	0	2	2	14	14
Steve Gee	22(5)	21(4)	14	13	0	0	0	0	56	52
Paul George	(1)	(1)	0	0	0	0	0	0	0	0
Lee Hansen	17(14)	15(14)	2	1	0	0	0	0	8	4
Mike Hill	16(10)	16(8)	0	0	0	0	0	0	0	0
Tommy Hodgkinson	14(2)	14(2)	1	1	0	0	0	0	4	4
Adam Hughes	1	1	0	0	0	0	0	0	0	0
David Hulme	15(2)	13(2)	3	2	0	0	0	0	12	8
Liam Jones	18	18	6	6	52	52	0	0	128	128
Eddie Kilgannon	12	12	1	1	0	0	0	0	4	4
Simon Knox	12(3)	12(3)	2	2	0	0	0	0	8	8
Afi Leuila	18(8)	16(8)	4	4	0	0	0	0	16	16
Karl Long	8(8)	8(8)	0	0	0	0	0	0	0	0
George Mann	7(8)	5(8)	0	0	0	0	0	0	0	0
Paul Mansson	28	26	13	13	0	0	1	1	53	53
Damian Munro	27(2)	25(2)	17	15	0	0	0	0	68	60
Chris Murphy	4(8)	4(8)	3	3	0	0	0	0	12	12
Danny Myler	7(2)	7(2)	0	0	0	0	0	0	0	0
Andrew O'Neill	(3)	(3)	0	0	0	0	0	0	0	0
Chris Percival	22(1)	20(1)	10	8	0	0	0	0	40	32
David Smith	13(8)	12(7)	3	1	0	0	0	0	12	4
Peter Smith	3(1)	3(1)	2	2	0	0	0	0	8	8
Simon Verbickas	14(1)	12(1)	7	6	51	39	0	0	130	102

Phil Cantillon

LEAGUE RECORD
P28-W17-D0-L11
(8th, NFP/Elimination Semi Finalists)
F698, A483, Diff+215
34 points.

CHALLENGE CUP
Round Four

ATTENDANCES
Best - v Leigh (NFP - 4,237)
Worst - v West Hull (CC - 2,301)
Total (NFP only) - 47,209
Average (NFP only) - 3,372
(Up by 204 on 1999)

WORKINGTON TOWN

DATE	FIXTURE	RESULT	SCORERS	LGE	ATT
26/12/99	Swinton (h)	L10-21	t:Liku g:Nixon(3)	N/A	1,111
2/1/00	Whitehaven (a)	L42-0	No Scorers	16th	1,548
9/1/00	Barrow (h)	L18-35	t:Smith(3) g:Cook(3)	17th	992
16/1/00	Dewsbury (a)	L36-6	t:Hoyles g:Cook	17th	1,558
23/1/00	Oldham (a)	L30-17	t:Dempsey,Lewthwaite,Charters g:Cook(2) fg:Cook	18th	2,222
30/1/00	Skirlaugh (h) (CCR3)	W12-2	t:Lewthwaite,Smith g:Cook(2)	N/A	599
6/2/00	Leigh (h)	L6-46	t:Watson g:Cook	18th	620
13/2/00	Doncaster (a) (CCR4)	L54-6	t:Beaumont g:Cook	N/A	1,466
20/2/00	Lancashire (a)	W12-34	t:Watson,Smith,Lewthwaite,M Stalker,Watson,Samuel g:Cook(5)	17th	254
5/3/00	Widnes (h)	W16-10	t:Samuel,Lewthwaite g:Cook(4)	16th	882
12/3/00	Rochdale (a)	L32-28	t:Charters,Beaumont,Smith,McGrady,Watson g:Cook(4)	16th	794
19/3/00	Featherstone (h)	L25-42	t:McGrady,Sice,Sturm,Samuel g:Cook(3) fg:Cook(3)	16th	829
26/3/00	Sheffield (a)	W18-20	t:Dempsey,Smith g:Cook(6)	15th	1,177
2/4/00	Hunslet (a)	L22-8	t:Williamson g:Cook(2)	16th	645
9/4/00	York (h)	W23-7	t:Smith(2),Hoyles,Lewthwaite g:Cook(3) fg:Cook	14th	658
16/4/00	Hull KR (h)	W20-10	t:Watson,Beaumont,Blackburn g:Cook(3) fg:Cook(2)	13th	873
21/4/00	Swinton (a)	L38-34	t:Sturm(2),Watson,McGrady,Samuel,Smith g:Cook(5)	14th	936
24/4/00	Whitehaven (h)	W27-18	t:Horner,Lewthwaite,Samuel,Watson g:Cook(5) fg:Cook	11th	1,886
1/5/00	Batley (a)	W10-30	t:Lewthwaite(3),Smith g:Cook(7)	11th	398
7/5/00	Keighley (a)	L54-8	t:Hoyles,Blackburn	12th	1,912
10/5/00	Doncaster (h)	W23-18	t:Watson(2),Williamson g:Cook(5) fg:Cook	11th	778
14/5/00	Barrow (a)	W22-24	t:Smith,Fisher,Horner g:Cook(5) fg:Cook(2)	11th	1,416
21/5/00	Dewsbury (h)	L6-58	t:Smith g:Cook	11th	1,088
26/5/00	Oldham (h)	D12-12	t:Cook,Samuel g:Cook(2)	11th	595
29/5/00	Hull KR (a)	L48-7	t:McGrady g:Cook fg:Cook	11th	1,305
4/6/00	Lancashire (h)	W38-8	t:Smith,McGrady,Blackburn,Beaumont,Cook,Hoyles,Barker g:Cook(5)	11th	562
11/6/00	Widnes (a)	L42-16	t:Dempsey,Blackburn,Beaumont g:Cook(2)	11th	3,162
18/6/00	Rochdale (h)	W22-8	t:Watson,Smith,Beaumont,Lewthwaite g:Cook(3)	12th	491
25/6/00	Featherstone (a)	L58-6	t:Beaumont g:Fisher	12th	1,480
2/7/00	Sheffield (h)	L18-19	t:Smith,Sice,J Allen g:McGee(3)	12th	659

	APP		TRIES		GOALS		FG		PTS	
	ALL	NFP	ALL	NFP	ALL	NFP	ALL	NFP	ALL	NFP
John Addison	1(5)	1(5)	0	0	0	0	0	0	0	0
John Allen	8(7)	6(7)	1	1	0	0	0	0	4	4
Lee Allen	6	5	0	0	0	0	0	0	0	0
Craig Armstrong	(1)	(1)	0	0	0	0	0	0	0	0
Craig Barker	2(11)	2(11)	1	1	0	0	0	0	4	4
Jamie Beaumont	18(11)	18(9)	7	6	0	0	0	0	28	24
Mike Bethwaite	4(3)	2(3)	0	0	0	0	0	0	0	0
William Blackburn	3(7)	3(7)	4	4	0	0	0	0	16	16
Ryan Charters	12(2)	10(2)	2	2	0	0	0	0	8	8
Lee Chilton	2	2	0	0	0	0	0	0	0	0
Scott Chilton	7	7	0	0	0	0	0	0	0	0
Paul Cook	27	25	2	2	81	78	12	12	182	176
Nicky Crellin	1(2)	1(2)	0	0	0	0	0	0	0	0
Michael Dempsey	12(1)	11(1)	3	3	0	0	0	0	12	12
Tony Dymtrowski	1	1	0	0	0	0	0	0	0	0
Craig Fisher	7(3)	7(3)	1	1	1	1	0	0	6	6
Jonathan Heaney	6(5)	4(5)	0	0	0	0	0	0	0	0
Stephen Holgate	3	3	0	0	0	0	0	0	0	0
Mick Horner	11	11	2	2	0	0	0	0	8	8
Stuart Hoyles	22(4)	20(4)	4	4	0	0	0	0	16	16
Anthony Huddart	7(2)	7(2)	0	0	0	0	0	0	0	0
Dave King	4	4	0	0	0	0	0	0	0	0
Graeme Lewthwaite	28	26	10	9	0	0	0	0	40	36
Tau Liku	17(9)	17(7)	1	1	0	0	0	0	4	4
Paul McGee	1(3)	1(3)	0	0	3	3	0	0	6	6
Steve McGrady	23(2)	23	5	5	0	0	0	0	20	20
Gary Murdock	6	6	0	0	0	0	0	0	0	0
Joe Naidole	6(2)	4(2)	0	0	0	0	0	0	0	0
Jamie Nixon	2(2)	2(2)	0	0	3	3	0	0	6	6
Anthony Samuel	28	26	6	6	0	0	0	0	24	24
Carl Sice	6(12)	6(12)	2	2	0	0	0	0	8	8
Leigh Smith	28	26	16	15	0	0	0	0	64	60
Craig Stalker	7(2)	7(2)	0	0	0	0	0	0	0	0
Martin Stalker	7	7	1	1	0	0	0	0	4	4
Matt Sturm	27	25	3	3	0	0	0	0	12	12
Matt Tunstall	2(3)	2(3)	0	0	0	0	0	0	0	0
Dave Watson	22(1)	20(1)	10	10	0	0	0	0	40	40
Owen Williamson	15(3)	15(2)	2	2	0	0	0	0	8	8

Matt Sturm

LEAGUE RECORD
P28-W11-D1-L16
(12th, NFP)
F502, A776, Diff-274
23 points.

CHALLENGE CUP
Round Four

ATTENDANCES
Best - v Whitehaven (NFP - 1,886)
Worst - v Rochdale (NFP - 491)
Total (NFP only) - 12,024
Average (NFP only) - 859
(Down by 192 on 1999)

YORK WASPS

DATE	FIXTURE	RESULT	SCORERS	LGE	ATT
26/12/99	Doncaster (h)	L1-36	fg:Callaghan	N/A	1,554
2/1/00	Keighley (a)	L32-13	t:Woodcock,McKenzie g:Gray(2) fg:Callaghan	17th	2,450
9/1/00	Sheffield (h)	W16-15	t:Judge,Austerfield g:Paterson(3) fg:Cain,Precious	14th	971
16/1/00	Hunslet (a)	L30-6	t:Booth g:Gray	16th	997
23/1/00	Rochdale (a)	L24-14	t:Austerfield,Cain g:Booth(3)	16th	823
30/1/00	Dudley Hill (h) (CCR3)	W56-10	t:Booth(4),Preston(2),Austerfield,McTigue,McKenzie,Hargrave, Woodcock g:Booth(6)	N/A	577
6/2/00	Batley (h)	L8-10	t:Lee g:Booth(2)	16th	701
13/2/00	Thornhill (h) (CCR4)	W56-2	t:Cain(3),Atkins,Dobson,McKenzie,A Hill,S Hill,Callaghan g:Booth(7),Cain(3)	N/A	803
20/2/00	Hull KR (a)	L30-10	t:Austerfield,McTigue g:Gray	16th	2,007
27/2/00	Warrington (a) (CCR5)	L84-1	fg:Cain	N/A	4,770
5/3/00	Featherstone (h)	L12-25	t:Booth(2) g:Booth(2)	17th	1,013
15/3/00	Dewsbury (a)	L26-19	t:Lee,Dobson,Cain g:Booth(3) fg:Cain	17th	1,010
19/3/00	Widnes (h)	L18-50	t:Booth(2),Hargrave g:Booth(3)	17th	757
26/3/00	Lancashire (a)	W18-26	t:Lee(2),Ryce(2),Hargrave g:Cain(3)	17th	214
2/4/00	Barrow (h)	W20-18	t:Cain(2),Ryce g:Gray(4)	15th	388
9/4/00	Workington (a)	L23-7	t:Callaghan g:Gray fg:Cain	17th	658
16/4/00	Leigh (h)	L22-28	t:Woodcock,A Hill,Lambert,Preston g:Precious(3)	17th	814
21/4/00	Doncaster (a)	L70-8	t:Gray g:Precious(2)	17th	1,379
24/4/00	Keighley (h)	L2-26	fg:Cain(2)	17th	1,048
1/5/00	Oldham (a)	L40-18	t:McCracken(2),Ryce,Gray g:Cain	17th	1,852
7/5/00	Whitehaven (h)	L44-12	t:Callaghan,Dobson g:Gray(2)	17th	592
10/5/00	Swinton (h)	L14-30	t:Thomas,Irving,Cain g:Irving	17th	377
14/5/00	Sheffield (a)	D12-12	t:Woodcock,Pallister g:Irving(2)	17th	1,038
21/5/00	Hunslet (h)	L18-22	t:Cain,A Hill,Smith g:Irving(3)	17th	581
26/5/00	Rochdale (h)	L22-42	t:Lambert(2),Smith,Hargrave g:Irving(3)	17th	331
29/5/00	Batley (a)	W10-33	t:A Hill,Callaghan,Darley,Lambert,Judge g:Irving(6) fg:Cain	17th	451
4/6/00	Hull KR (h)	L6-24	t:Hargrave g:Gray	17th	1,195
11/6/00	Featherstone (a)	L56-12	t:A Hill,Forsyth g:Callaghan(2)	17th	1,550
18/6/00	Dewsbury (h)	L17-56	t:Hargrave,A Hill,Lloyd g:Callaghan(2) fg:Callaghan	17th	744
25/6/00	Swinton (a)	L50-12	t:Lambert g:Callaghan(2)	17th	757
30/6/00	Lancashire (h)	W14-12	t:Hammerton,Smith g:Callaghan(3)	17th	351

	APP		TRIES		GOALS		FG		PTS	
	ALL	NFP	ALL	NFP	ALL	NFP	ALL	NFP	ALL	NFP
Gary Atkins	6	5	1	0	0	0	0	0	4	0
Shaun Austerfield	7(3)	6(2)	4	3	0	0	0	0	16	12
Craig Booth	8(2)	6(2)	9	5	26	13	0	0	88	46
Dan Briggs	(1)	(1)	0	0	0	0	0	0	0	0
Mark Cain	23	20	9	6	7	4	7	6	57	38
Darren Callaghan	20(3)	18(2)	4	3	9	9	3	3	37	33
Paul Darley	10(8)	9(6)	1	1	0	0	0	0	4	4
Gareth Dobson	16(3)	13(3)	3	2	0	0	0	0	12	8
Craig Forsyth	9(7)	9(7)	1	1	0	0	0	0	4	4
Kevin Gray	14(6)	13(6)	2	2	12	12	0	0	32	32
Mick Hagan	6(14)	6(11)	0	0	0	0	0	0	0	0
Chris Hammerton	4(1)	4(1)	1	1	0	0	0	0	4	4
Spencer Hargrave	22(3)	19(3)	6	5	0	0	0	0	24	20
Richard Hayes	20	19	0	0	0	0	0	0	0	0
Andy Hill	23(2)	20(2)	6	5	0	0	0	0	24	20
Steve Hill	27(3)	24(3)	1	0	0	0	0	0	4	0
Simon Irving	9	9	1	1	15	15	0	0	34	34
Chris Judge	19(4)	19(4)	2	2	0	0	0	0	8	8
Andrew Lambert	20	19	6	6	0	0	0	0	24	24
Rob Lee	9(1)	7(1)	4	4	0	0	0	0	16	16
Gareth Lloyd	5(1)	5(1)	1	1	0	0	0	0	4	4
John McCracken	5(7)	5(6)	2	2	0	0	0	0	8	8
Leroy McKenzie	14(2)	11(2)	3	1	0	0	0	0	12	4
Lee McTigue	4(7)	2(6)	2	1	0	0	0	0	8	4
Matthew Mulholland	1(2)	1(2)	0	0	0	0	0	0	0	0
Alan Pallister	21(5)	21(3)	1	1	0	0	0	0	4	4
Carl Paterson	2(1)	2(1)	0	0	3	3	0	0	6	6
Andy Precious	3(5)	3(5)	0	0	5	5	1	1	11	11
Andy Preston	22	19	3	1	0	0	0	0	12	4
Mick Ramsden	7(3)	7(3)	0	0	0	0	0	0	0	0
Craig Robinson	5(4)	5(4)	0	0	0	0	0	0	0	0
Max Ryce	8(6)	8(6)	4	4	0	0	0	0	16	16
Michael Smith	2(5)	2(5)	3	3	0	0	0	0	12	12
Dean Thomas	3(2)	3(2)	1	1	0	0	0	0	4	4
Lea Tichener	4(8)	2(8)	0	0	0	0	0	0	0	0
Matthew Woodcock	25(2)	23(1)	4	3	0	0	0	0	16	12

Rob Lee

LEAGUE RECORD
P28-W5-D1-L22
(17th, NFP)
F392, A859, Diff-467
11 points.

CHALLENGE CUP
Round Five

ATTENDANCES
Best - v Doncaster (NFP - 1,554)
Worst - v Rochdale (NFP - 331)
Total (NFP only) - 10,825
Average (NFP only) - 773
(Down by 187 on 1999)

SILK CUT CHALLENGE CUP

ROUND FOUR

SWINTON LIONS 22 ST HELENS 36
LIONS: 1 Jason Roach, 2 Matt Bateman, 3 Phil Coussons, 4 Paul Loughlin, 5 Marlon Billy, 6 Andy Craig, 7 Ian Watson, 8 Jon Neill, 9 Chris Highton, 10 Ian Pickavance, 11 Andy Coley, 12 Paul Smith, 13 Sean Casey. Subs: 14 Jim Evans for Loughlin (30), 15 Tony Barrow for Pickavance (27), 16 Matt Knowles for Neill (24), 17 Paul Barrow for Coley (34), Pickavance for Casey (48), Neill for T Barrow (66)
Tries: Coley (17), Casey (21), Bateman (25), Coussons (69), **Goals:** Watson 2, Loughlin
Sin bin: Watson (14) - fighting
SAINTS: 1 Paul Atcheson, 2 Chris Smith, 3 Kevin Iro, 4 Paul Newlove, 15 Sean Hoppe, 7 Sean Long, 6 Darrell Trindall (D), 8 Apollo Perelini, 9 Keiron Cunningham, 12 Sonny Nickle, 11 Chris Joynt, 14 Fereti Tuilagi, 13 Paul Sculthorpe . Subs: 10 Julian O'Neill for Perelini (23), 17 Paul Wellens for Trindall (55), 18 Bryan Henare for Tuilagi (50), 19 Anthony Stewart for Iro (53), Perelini for Nickle (34), Nickle for Perelini (40), Trindall for Wellens (63), Wellens for Long (64)
Tries: Newlove (3), Iro (28,52,54), Sculthorpe (44), Long (46), Hoppe (58), **Goals:** Long 4
Sin bin: Trindall (14) - fighting
League Express Men of the Match:
Lions: Andy Craig, **Saints**: Keiron Cunningham
Penalty count: 6-8
Half-time: 16-10, **Referee:** Nick Oddy (Halifax), **Att** 3,169

BARROW BORDER RAIDERS 18 SALFORD CITY REDS 34
BORDER RAIDERS: 1 Jamie Smith, 2 Glen Hutton, 3 Stuart Magorian, 4 Darren Carter, 5 Paul Salmon, 6 Tane Manihera, 7 Darren Holt, 8 Mike Whitehead, 9 Dave Clark, 10 Chris Whiteley, 11 Stewart Rhodes, 12 Gareth Pratt, 13 Gary Charlton. Subs: 14 Chris Massey not used, 15 Steve Jackson for Whiteley (22), 16 Ian Rawlinson for Pratt (18), 17 Damien Whitter for Whitehead (47), Whiteley for Jackson (57)
Tries: Rhodes (32), Holt (39, 74), **Goals:** Holt 3
CITY REDS: 1 Gary Broadbent, 2 Nick Pinkney (D), 18 Stuart Littler, 4 Jason Webber (D), 5 Martin Offiah (D), 12 Darren Brown, 7 Martin Crompton, 8 Paul Southern, 9 Malcolm Alker, 10 Craig Makin, 16 Paul Highton, 20 Matthew Leigh (D), 23 Mike Wainwright (D). Subs: 17 Mark Johnson for Littler (45), 21 Warren Ayres for Pinkney (74), 14 Joe Faimalo for Makin (18), 15 Neil Baynes for Leigh (24), Leigh for Wainwright (52), Littler for Offiah (60), Makin for Baynes (72)
Tries: Alker (3), Pinkney (18, 55), Littler (22), Southern (44), Offiah (53), **Goals:** Brown 5
Sin bin: Faimalo (30) - persistent offside
League Express Men of the Match:
Border Raiders: Darren Holt, **City Reds:** Gary Broadbent
Penalty count: 12-14
Half-time: 12-18, **Referee:** Steve Nicholson (Whitehaven), **Att** 3,630

ROCHDALE HORNETS 30 OLDHAM 14
HORNETS: 1 Lee Maher, 2 Marlon Miller, 3 Scott Martin, 4 Danny Wood, 5 Chris Hilton, 6 Phil Waring, 7 Dane Dorahy, 8 Danny Sculthorpe, 9 Gavin Swinson, 10 Shane McMenemy, 11 Chris McKinney, 12 Gavin Price-Jones, 13 Chris Newall. Subs: 14 Darren Robinson for Swinson (69), 15 Martin Bunce for McKinney (22BB, rev 40) , 16 Sean Cooper for Waring (41), 17 Andy Pucill for Sculthorpe (24BB, rev 35) , Bunce for McKinney (47), Pucill for Sculthorpe (60), Waring for Maher (51BB. rev 61), Waring for Dorahy (68), Sculthorpe for McMenemy (71)
Tries: Newall (3), Dorahy (13), Wood (21), Bunce (27), Swinson (52), Hilton (55, 72) , **Goal:** Wood
Sin bin: Sculthorpe (80) - professional foul
ROUGHYEDS: 1 Mark Sibson, 2 Joey Hayes, 3 Peter Ferris, 4 Pat Rich, 5 Joe McNicholas, 6 Tom O'Reilly, 7 Anthony Gibbons, 8 Jason Clegg, 9 John Hough, 10 Andy Procter, 11 Mark Campbell, 12 Tate Moseley, 13 Kevin Mannion. Subs: 14 Keith Brennan for Ferris (28), 15 Chris Holland for Mannion (4BB, rev 24) , 16 Leo Casey for Moseley (28), 17 Danny Guest for Moseley (67), Moseley for Clegg (47), Ferris for Brennan (53), Clegg for Procter (68)
Try: Guest (74), **Goals:** Rich 5
Dismissal: Leo Casey (51) - high tackle
League Express Men of the Match:
Hornets: Danny Sculthorpe, **Roughyeds:** Mark Sibson
Penalty count: 9-13
Half-time: 16-6, **Referee:** Alan Bates (Workington), **Att** 2,168

DONCASTER DRAGONS 54 WORKINGTON TOWN 6
DRAGONS: 1 Lynton Stott, 2 Carl Hall, 3 Craig Weston, 4 James Bunyan, 5 Fata Sini, 6 Wayne Parker, 7 Latham Tawhai, 8 Asa Amone, 9 Peter Edwards, 10 Paul Lister, 11 Rob Wilson, 12 Tony Miller, 13 Colin Carter. Subs: 14 Mick Coult for Rob Wilson (40), 15 Basil Richards for Paul Lister (21), 16 Guy Adams for Colin Carter (40), 17 Carl Gillespie for Sini (40), Lister for Asa Amone (58), Sini for Lynton Stott (61), Guy Adams off - no sub (62)
Tries: Hall (6), Weston (9,19,47), Sini (22, 40), Bunyan (31,52), Edwards (35, 43), Stott (49) , Goals: Stott 5
TOWN,: 1 Dave Watson, 2 Leigh Smith, 3 Jonathan Heaney, 4 John Allen, 5 Graeme Lewthwaite, 6 Paul Cook, 7 Lee Allen, 8 Joe Naidole, 9 Michael Bethwaite, 10 Ryan Charters, 11 Matt Sturm, 12 Anthony Samuel, 13 Stuart Hoyles. Subs: 14 Steven McGrady for Heaney (45), 15 Tau Liku for Charters (28), 16 Owen Williamson not used, 17 Jamie Beaumont for Matt Sturm (12)
Try: Beaumont (16), **Goal:** Cook
League Express Men of the Match:
Dragons: Stott, **Town:** Lee Allen
Penalty count: 4-2
Half-time: 36-6, **Referee:** Peter Taberner (Wigan), **Att** 1,466

HULL FC 86 LANCASHIRE LYNX 0
HULL FC: 1 Craig Poucher, 2 Matt Daylight, 3 Steve Collins, 4 Deon Bird, 5 Ian Herron, 6 Craig Simon, 7 Stanley Gene (D), 8 Paul Broadbent (D), 9 Mick Jenkins, 10 Wayne McDonald (D), 11 Adam Maher, 12 Luke Felsch, 13 David Maiden. Subs: 14 Brian Carney for Maiden (58), 15 Richard Horne for Gene (40BB), 16 Craig Wilson for Maher (30), 17 Paul King for Felsch (30), Gene for Horne (54BB), Horne for Simon (56), Maher for Broadbent (60)
Tries: McDonald (2) Simon (10, 28, 44) Maiden (21, 56) Gene (38, 59) Jenkins (41), Bird (48, 70) Horne (46, 52) Herron (63) Daylight (67) Carney (73) , **Goals:** Herron 11
LYNX: 1 Paul Roberts, 2 Mark Kay, 3 Neil Roden, 4 Anton Garcia, 5 David Jones, 6 Jason Demetriou, 7 Neil Alexander, 8 Mike Prescott, 9 Shaun Hilton, 10 Paul Norton, 11 Philip Farrell, 12 David Smith, 13 John-Paul Doherty. Subs: 14 Sheldon Hannan for Hilton (65), 15 Kevin O'Loughlin for Smith (32), 16 Daniel Houghton for Doherty (54), 17 Luke Vincent for Prescott (32), Smith for Houghton (58)
League Express Men of the Match:
Hull FC: David Maiden, **Lynx:** Jason Demetriou
Penalty count: 9-6
Half-time: 24-0, **Referee:** Karl Kirkpatrick (Warrington), **Att** 3,442

KEIGHLEY COUGARS 14 VILLENEUVE 16
COUGARS: 1 Matthew Foster, 2 Craig Horne, 3 James Rushforth, 4 Richard Smith, 5 Jason Lee, 6 Paul Owen, 7 Nathan Antonik, 8 Michael Slicker, 9 Jason Ramshaw, 10 Alan Boothroyd, 11 Paul Harrison, 12 Ian Hughes, 13 Steve Pickles. Subs: 14 Craig Robinson for Foster (68), 15 Steve Hall for Ramshaw (16), 16 Phil Stephenson for Slicker (33), 17 Ben Thompson for Harrison (50), Slicker for Hall (73), Hall for Stephenson (77)
Tries: Smith (25), Stephenson (56), **Goals:** Lee 3
VILLENEUVE: 1 Frederic Banquet, 2 Ludovic Perolari, 3 Gilles Cornut, 4 Regis Brioux, 5 Richard Doste, 6 Laurent Frayssinous, 7 David Despin, 8 David Collado, 9 Vincent Wulf, 10 Romaine Gagliazzo, 11 Grant Doorey, 12 Pierre Sabatié, 13 Laurent Carrasco. Subs: 14 Vea Bloomfield for Gagliazzo (33), 15 Artie Shead for Sabatie (26), 16 Julien Rinaldi for Brioux (48), 17 Christophe Canal for Rinaldi (52), Sabatié for Carrasco (57), Gagliazzo for Bloomfield (77)
Tries: Cornut (4), Perolari (12), Sabatie (21), Doorey (69)
League Express Men of the Match:
Cougars: Steve Hall, **Villeneuve:** Vincent Wulf
Penalty count: 13-2
Half-time: 8-12, **Referee:** Graeme Shaw (Wigan), Att **1,956**

HUNSLET HAWKS 4 WARRINGTON WOLVES 46
HAWKS: 1 Chris Ross, 2 Chris North, 3 Graeme Hallas, 4 Darren Hughes, 5 Aaron Campbell, 6 Nicky Dobson, 7 Johan Windley, 8 Steve Pryce, 9 Richard Pachniuk, 10 Jim Leatham, 11 Jamie Leighton, 12 Jamie Thackray, 13 Mick Coyle. Subs: 14 Alan Julian for Henderson (34), 15 Dave King for Pryce (29), 16 Ben Skerrett for Leighton (64), 17 Anthony Henderson for Dobson (24), Dobson for Ross (34), Pryce for Leatham (51)
Try: King (71)
WOLVES: 1 Lee Penny, 15 Neil Parsley (D), 4 Toa Kohe-Love, 2 Jon Roper, 5 Mark Forster, 6 Lee Briers, 7 Allan Langer (D), 8 Andrew Gee (D), 9 Danny Farrar (C), 10 Danny Nutley, 12 Ian Knott, 14 Steve McCurrie, 13 Tawera Nikau (D). Subs: 11 Dean Busby for McCurrie (59), 16 Gary Chambers for Gee (50), 17 Steve Blakeley (D) for Briers (60), 21 Jerome Guisset (D) for Nutley (50)
Tries: Parsley (11), Knott (23), McCurrie (32), Farrar (34, 37), Forster (42), Penny (45), Nikau (53),
Goals: Briers 7
League Express Men of the Match:
Hawks: Richard Pachniuk, **Wolves:** Danny Farrar
Penalty count: 10-3
Half-time: 0-30, **Referee:** Ian Smith (Oldham), **Att** 2,446

LONDON BRONCOS 44 WATH BROW HORNETS 18
BRONCOS: 5 Brett Warton, 16 Frank Napoli (D), 3 Danny Moore (D), 22 John Timu, 13 Mat Toshack, 6 Karle Hammond (C), 7 Shaun Edwards, 10 Scott Cram, 9 Dean Callaway, 17 Anthony Seibold, 12 Steele Retchless, 14 Andrew Wynyard, 11 Shane Millard. Subs: 11 Justin Dooley (D) for Cram (26), 15 Andy Johnson (D) for Wynyard (30), 1 Tulsen Tollett for Warton (24), 8 Darren Bradstreet for Millard (40), Cram for Seibold (63), Wynyard for Dooley (69)
Tries: Callaway (6), Wynyard (14), Edwards (25), Moore (33), Retchless (38), Tollett (41), Hammond (47), Toshack (76), **Goals:** Warton 2 Tollett 4
Sin bin: Moore (66) - holding down
HORNETS: 1 Gary Elliott, 2 David Charlton, 3 Ian Rooney (C), 4 Andrew Stables, 5 Lee Power, 6 Craig Johnstone, 7 Andrew Hocking, 8 Neil Gregg, 9 Marc Jackson, 10 Paul Davidson, 11 Paul McCarron, 12 Neil Stewart, 13 Scott Anderson. Subs: 14 Neil McCartney not used, 15 Gavin Curwen for Johnstone (67), 16 Michael McAllister for McCarron (23), 17 Mark Troughtman for Davidson (27), McAllen for Gregg (50)
Tries: Elliott (1), Hocking (55), **Goals:** Jackson 5
League Express Men of the Match:
Broncos: Scott Cram, **Hornets:** Marc Jackson
Penalty count: 7-8
Half-time: 30-8, **Referee:** Richard Silverwood (Mirfield), **Att** 1,511

OLDHAM ST ANNES 8 CASTLEFORD TIGERS 64
ST ANNES: 1 Chris Wright, 2 Adrian Belle, 3 Matt Calland, 4 Rob Rose, 5 Lee Charlesworth, 6 Richard Badby, 7 Paul Kay, 8 Martin Taylor, 9 Steven Crowther, 10 Michael Deakin, 11 Jon Brierley, 12 Martin Kay, 13 Patrick Mitchell. Subs: 14 Graeme Sykes for Charlesworth (53), 15 Keiran Deakin for Taylor (17), 16 Phil Russell for M Deakin (50), 17 Jason Akeroyd for Wright (60), K Taylor for Deakin (70)
Try: Taylor (71), **Goals:** Rose 2
TIGERS: 20 Jamie Benn, 5 Darren Rogers, 3 Michael Eagar, 4 Logan Campbell (D), 16 Jon Wells, 22 Andrew Purcell (D), 7 Brad Davis, 8 Nathan Sykes, 9 Aaron Raper (D), 10 Dean Sampson, 11 Lee Harland, 12 Dale Fritz, 13 Adrian Vowles. Subs: 16 Darren Shaw (D) for Sykes (25), 18 Paul Smith for Fritz (60), 19 Andy Lynch for Shaw (79), 24 Dean Ellis (D) for Rogers (6BB, rev 24), Ellis for Rogers (35BB, rev 53), Sykes for Harland (57), Fritz for Raper (75)
Tries: Eagar (10, 78), Purcell (15), Campbell (21, 80), Wells (24), Sampson (32, 40, 60), Davis (42), Raper (64,67), **Goals:** Benn 8
League Express Men of the Match:
St Annes: Patrick Mitchell, **Tigers:** Dean Sampson
Penalty count: 6-8
Half-time: 0-34, **Referee:** Colin Morris (Huddersfield), **Att** 3,833

DEWSBURY RAMS 29 WIDNES VIKINGS 16
RAMS: 1 Nathan Graham (C), 2 Richard Baker, 3 Brendan O'Meara, 4 Gavin Wood, 5 Adrian Flynn, 6 David Mycoe, 7 Barry Eaton, 8 Matthew Long, 9 Ian Talbot, 10 Simon Hicks, 11 Sean Richardson, 12 Billy Kershaw, 13 Damian Ball. Subs: 14 Alex Godfrey for O'Meara (16), 15 Andrew Spink for Hicks (30), 16 Shayne Williams for Kershaw (55), 17 Robin Jowitt for Long (26), Long for Jowitt (61), Hicks for Spink (71)
Tries: Talbot (8,29), Richardson (60), Flynn (63), Ball (70), **Goals:** Eaton 4, Field goal: Eaton
Sin bin: Eaton (40) - dissent
VIKINGS: 1 Damian Munro, 2 Andy Cheetham , 3 Chris Percival, 4 Afi Leuila, 5 Simon Verbickas, 6 Paul Mansson, 7 David Hulme, 8 Lee Hansen, 9 Phil Cantillon, 10 Cliff Eccles, 11 George Mann (C), 12 Gareth Adams, 13 David Smith. Subs: 14 Danny Myler not used, 15 Mike Hill for Hansen (28), 16 Karl Fitzpatrick for Smith (32), 17 Steve Gee for Adams (30), Hansen for Eccles (57), Adams for Hill (64)
Tries: Eccles (2), Cheetham (45), Gee (54), **Goals**: Verbickas 2
Sin bin: Mann (50) - dissent
League Express Men of the Match:
Rams: Nathan Graham, **Vikings:** Phil Cantillon
Penalty count: 14-7
Half-time: 12-8, **Referee:** John Connolly (Wigan), **Att** 2,445

LEIGH CENTURIONS 28 WAKEFIELD TRINITY WILDCATS 40
CENTURIONS: 1 Stuart Donlan, 5 Paul Wingfield, 4 Paul Anderson, 2 Phil Kendrick, 3 Alan Cross, 6 Andy Fairclough, 7 Kieron Purtill (C), 8 Tim Street, 9 Mick Higham, 10 Dave Whittle, 11 Simon Baldwin, 12 Heath Cruckshank, 13 Adam Bristow. Subs: 14 Anthony Murray for Higham (60), 15 Paul Norman for Street (35), 16 Alan Hadcroft for Kendrick (46), 17 Radney Bowker for Whittle (58), Street for Cruckshank (67), Whittle for Norman (75)
Tries: Higham (4), Cross (24), Kendrick (38), Hadcroft (62), Cruckshank (66), **Goals:** Wingfield 4
Sin bin: Bristow (7) holding down
WILDCATS: 1 Steve Prescott (D), 5 Bright Sodje (D), 3 Francis Maloney (D), 4 Tony Tatupu (D), 2 Neil Law, 6 Tony Kemp, 25 Bobbie Goulding (D), 8 Francis Stephenson, 21 Ryan Hudson (D), 10 Martin Masella (D), 11 Warren Jowitt (D), 12 Willie Poching, 13 Steve McNamara (D) (C). Subs: 7 Glen Tomlinson for Hudson (68), 15 Gary Price for Poching (41), 20 Adam Hughes for Kemp (28), 18 Paul Jackson for Masella (23), Masella for Stephenson (67), Poching for Jowitt (78)
Tries: Stephenson (9), Hudson (16), Hughes (29, 77), Maloney (49), Law (56), **Goals:** McNamara 8
Half-time: 20-20, **Referee:** Stuart Cummings (Widnes), **Att** 3,810
Penalty count: 9-8
League Express Men of the Match:
Centurions: Kieron Purtill, **Wildcats:** Steve McNamara

HALIFAX BLUE SOX 36 HULL KR 8
BLUE SOX: 3 Damian Gibson, 5 Phil Hassan (D), 14 Martin Pearson, 12 Jamie Bloem, 4 Marvin Golden (D), 6 Greg Florimo (C) (D), 7 Andrew Dunemann, 23 Brett Goldspink, 9 Paul Rowley, 10 Jim Gannon, 11 Gary Mercer, 20 Stephen Holgate (D), 13 Martin Moana. Subs: 24 Danny Fearon for Mercer (55), 8 Andy Hobson for Goldspink (27), 1 Daryl Cardiss for Pearson (40), 17 Gael Tallec (D) for Holgate (63), Goldspink for Gannon (58), Pearson for Bloem (70)
Tries: Hassan (5,14,27), Gannon (43), Cardiss (51), Florimo (53), Golden (78), **Goals:** Pearson 2, Bloem 2
ROVERS: 1 Mick Crane, 2 Dean Andrews, 3 Rob Nolan, 4 Whetu Taewa, 5 Jon Wray, 6 Leroy Joe, 7 Mark Hewitt, 8 Paul Fletcher, 9 Mike Dixon, 10 Jamie Bovill, 11 Andy Smith, 12 Chris Charles, 13 Richard Slater. Subs: 14 Anthony Chambers for Kirke (55), 15 Gavin Molloy for Crane (54), 16 Alan Dunham for Dixon (58), 17 Ian Kirke for Bovill (27), Bovill for Charles (60)
Try: Chambers, **Goals:** Hewitt 2
Penalty count: 6-13
Half-time: 14-2, **Referee:** Russell Smith (Castleford), **Att** 4,295

YORK WASPS 56 THORNHILL TROJANS 2
WASPS: 1 Andy Preston, 2 Leroy McKenzie, 3 Spencer Hargrave, 4 Rob Lee, 5 Matt Woodcock, 6 Mark Cain, 7 Garry Atkins, 8 Lea Tichener, 9 Gareth Dobson, 10 Steve Hill, 11 Andy Hill, 12 Lee McTigue, 13 Craig Booth. Subs: 14 Darren Callaghan for Preston (59), 15 Mick

Hagan for Tichener (30), 16 Alan Pallister for Dobson (59), 17 Paul Darley for Booth (26), Tichener for Hagan (39), Booth for McTigue (62)
Tries: Atkins (15), Dobson (21), McKenzie (24), Andy Hill (52), Steve Hill (61), Callaghan (72), Cain (74, 77, 80) , **Goals:** Booth 7, Cain 3
TROJANS: 1 Andrew Smith, 2 Barry Drummond, 3 Jimmy Gittings, 4 Sean Senior, 5 Andrew Field, 6 Jason Firth, 7 Ian Bates, 8 Steve Naylor, 9 Rob Simpson, 10 Rob Hoyle, 11 James Folan, 12 Chris Woodcock, 13 Anthony Broadhead. Subs: 14 Richard Sedgwick for Broadhead (56), 15 Sean Day for Senior (60), 16 Abe Phillips for Hoyle (25), 17 Craig Wood for Folan (40), Hoyle for Naylor (36), Bradshaw for Woodcock (76)
Goal: Woodcock
Dismissal: Gittings (66) - high tackle
Sin bin: Hoyle (47) - dissent; Woodcock (51) - laying on
League Express Men of the Match:
York: Steve Hill, **Trojans:** Ian Bates
Penalty count: 8-13
Half-time: 20-2, **Referee:** Ronnie Laughton (Barnsley), **Att** 803

FEATHERSTONE ROVERS 48 LEEDS RHINOS 12,
ROVERS: 1 Michael Rhodes, 2 Jamie Stokes, 3 Chris Langley, 4 Matt Bramald, 5 Ian Thompson, 6 Andy Bastow, 7 Jamie Rooney, 8 Mickey Clarkson, 9 Andy Heptinstall, 10 Maea David, 11 Danny Evans, 12 Brad Hepi (D), 13 Matt Lambert. Subs: 14 Richard Gibson for Bastow (68), 15 Steve Dooler for Lambert (50), 16 Richard Chapman for Heptinstall (31), 17 Stuart Dickens for Clarkson (34), Clarkson for Evans (74), Heptinstall for Dooler (79)
Tries: Langley (29), Hepi (76), **Goals:** Rooney 2
Sin bin: Evans (35) - persistent offside
RHINOS: 1 Iestyn Harris, 5 Francis Cummins, 3 Richie Blackmore, 15 Paul Bell (D), 4 Keith Senior, 6 Daryl Powell, 7 Ryan Sheridan, 8 Darren Fleary, 9 Lee Jackson, 10 Barrie McDermott, 11 Adrian Morley, 12 David Barnhill (D), 13 Kevin Sinfield. Subs: 16 Andy Hay for Morley (35), 17 Anthony Farrell for McDermott (38, rev 50), 20 Jamie Mathiou for Fleary (25), 21 Karl Pratt for Jackson (65), Fleary for Barnhill (60), Morley for McDermott (76)
Tries: Sinfield (8, 42), Sheridan (13, 44, 66), Powell (34), Barnhill (40), Harris (80) **Goals:** Harris 8
Sin bin: Barnhill (46) - persistent offside
League Express Men of the Match:
Rovers: Jamie Rooney, **Rhinos:** Ryan Sheridan
Penalty count: 7-9
Att 4,001, **Referee:** Robert Connolly (Wigan), **Half-time:** 6-26

WIGAN WARRIORS 98 WHITEHAVEN WARRIORS 4
WARRIORS: 1 Kris Radlinski, 2 Brett Dallas (D), 3 Steve Renouf (D), 4 Gary Connolly, 5 Jason Robinson, 6 Tony Smith, 20 Phil Jones, 8 Terry O'Connor, 9 Terry Newton (D), 23 Brady Malam (D), 11 Mick Cassidy, 12 Denis Betts, 13 Andrew Farrell. Subs: 14 Lee Gilmour for Newton (40), 16 Simon Haughton for O'Connor (31), 17 Tony Mestrov for Malam (31), 18 Wes Davies for Radlinski (50), O'Connor for Haughton (41, BB), Newton for Cassidy (60), Malam for O'Connor (63), Cassidy for Betts (73)
Tries: Renouf (2,51), Newton (13), Radlinski (18,30), Jones (24), Smith (28,37), Robinson (32,67,80), Farrell (34), Dallas (40), Mestrov (44), Gilmour (56), Cassidy (59), Davies (62), **Goals:** Farrell 15
WARRIORS: 1 David Seeds, 2 Neil Frazer, 3 Andrew Nelson, 4 Kevin Hetherington, 5 Mark Keenan, 6 Lee Kiddie, 7 Wayne Kitchin, 8 Colin Armstrong, 9 Aaron Lester, 10 Mark Cox, 11 Howard Hill, 12 Alan Bone, 13 Gary Purdham. Subs: 14 Craig Walsh for Keenan (40), 15 Matt Lynch for Bone (54), 16 Dean Vaughan for Cox (54), 17 David Fatialofa for Armstrong (30)
Try: Kiddie (21)
League Express Men of the Match:
Wigan: Andrew Farrell, **Whitehaven:** Gary Purdham
Penalty count: 8-6
Half-time: 58-4, **Referee:** Steve Ganson (St Helens), **Att** 6,532

BRADFORD BULLS 32
HUDDERSFIELD-SHEFFIELD GIANTS 4
BULLS: 5 Michael Withers, 4 Nathan McAvoy, 11 David Boyle, 20 Scott Naylor, 3 Leon Pryce, 6 Henry Paul, 1 Robbie Paul (C), 29 Stuart Fielden, 9 James Lowes, 22 Brian McDermott, 15 Hudson Smith (D), 12 Mike Forshaw, 13 Brad Mackay. Subs: 18 Lee Radford for Mackay (45), 19 Jamie Peacock for Dwyer (60), 23 Bernard Dwyer for Smith (27), 10 Paul Anderson for Fielden (0), Fielden for Anderson (23), Anderson for McDermott (69)
Tries: Pryce (7,36), McAvoy (56), Withers (68), Naylor (78), **Goals:** H Paul 6
Sin bin: Pryce (64) - interference at play the ball
GIANTS: 14 Paul Reilly, 19 Chris Thorman, 3 Karl Lovell, 1 Waisale Sovatabua, 5 Matt Crowther, 6 Gene Ngamu, 7 Gavin Clinch (D), 8 Steve Molloy (C), 9 Johnny Lawless, 10 Dale Laughton, 11 David Lomax (D), 12 Richard Marshall (D), 13 Jeff Hardy. Subs: 16 Nick Fozzard for Molloy (27), Molloy for Fozzard (63), Fozzard for Molloy (71), 17 Martin Gleeson for Marshall (15 - bb - rev 36), Gleeson for Lomax (39), Lomax for Laughton (51), Laughton for Marshall (68), 24 Mark Moxon not used, 28 Andy Rice not used
Goals: Crowther 2
League Express Men of the Match:
Bulls: Scott Naylor, Giants: Paul Reilly
Penalty count: 11-16
Half-time: 16-2, **Referee:** Steve Presley (Castleford), **Att** 6,467

ROUND FIVE

CASTLEFORD TIGERS 10 HALIFAX BLUE SOX 11
TIGERS: 10 Jamie Benn, 16 Jon Wells, 4 Logan Campbell, 3 Michael Eagar, 5 Darren Rogers, 6 Danny Orr, 7 Brad Davis, 10 Dean Sampson, 9 Aaron Raper, 8 Nathan Sykes, 11 Lee Harland, 12 Dale Fritz, 13 Adrian Vowles (C). Subs: 15 Darren Shaw for Sykes (25), 22 Andrew Purcell for Orr (51), 17 Ian Tonks for Harland (56), 18 Paul Smith not used, Harland for Fritz (73)
Try: Campbell (66), **Goals:** Benn 3
Sin bin: Dean Sampson (4) - fighting, **On Report:** Jamie Benn (58) - high tackle
BLUE SOX: 1 Daryl Cardiss, 3 Damian Gibson, 12 Jamie Bloem, 6 Greg Florimo (C), 4 Marvin Golden, 14 Martin Pearson, 7 Andrew Dunemann, 23 Brett Goldspink, 9 Paul Rowley, 10 James Gannon, 11 Gary Mercer, 20 Stephen Holgate, 13 Martin Moana. Subs: 5 Phil Hassan for Holgate (53), 8 Andy Hobson for Goldspink (24), 21 Gael Tallec for Cardiss (58), 24 Danny Fearon not used, Holgate for Tallec (73), Goldspink for Hobson (52,60,73BB)
Tries: Bloem (7, 15), **Goals:** Pearson
Sin bin: James Gannon (4) - fighting; Jamie Bloem (22) - holding down
League Express Men of the Match:
Tigers: Aaron Raper, **Blue Sox:** Andrew Dunemann
Penalty count: 11-9
Half-time: 0-10, **Referee:** Steve Ganson (St Helens), **Att** 5,516

HULL FC 82 ROCHDALE HORNETS 10
HULL: 1 Ben Sammut, 2 Matt Daylight, 3 Deon Bird, 4 Steve Collins, 5 Ian Herron, 6 Stanley Gene, 7 Will Robinson (C), 8 Paul Broadbent, 9 Mick Jenkins, 10 Andrew Hick, 11 Adam Maher, 12 Luke Felsch, 13 David Maiden. Subs: 14 Craig Simon for Herron (39), 16 Craig Wilson for Bird (68), 17 Paul King for Jenkins (31), 18 Wayne McDonald for Broadbent (27), Jenkins for Felsch (41), Broadbent for Hick (58)
Tries: Gene (4), Hicks (12, 34), Maher (15), Robinson (19), Bird (30, 57), McDonald (38, 41, 74), Felsch (40), Simon (60, 71), Collins (63), Daylight (80) ,
Goals: Herron 6, Sammut 5
HORNETS: 1 Lee Maher, 2 Lee Hudson, 3 Steve Wilde, 4 Danny Wood, 5 Chris Hilton, 6 Phil Waring, 7 Paul Ashton, 8 Danny Sculthorpe, 9 Gavin Swinson, 10 Martin Bunce, 11 Chris McKinney, 12 Gavin Price-Jones, 13 Scott Martin. Subs: 14 Darren Robinson for Swinson (31), 15 Chris Newall for Bunce (55), 16 Sean Cooper not used, 17 Phil Harrison for Sculthorpe (51), Bunce for Hilton (61), Swinson for McKinney (72)
Sin bin: McKinney (54) - holding down
Tries: Wilde (25), Wood (47), **Goal:** Wood
League Express Men of the Match:
Hull: David Maiden, **Hornets:** Danny Sculthorpe
Half-time: 44-6
Penalty count: 14-5, **Referee:** Nick Oddy (Halifax), **Att** 3,992

LONDON BRONCOS 21 SALFORD REDS 22
BRONCOS: 4 Greg Fleming, 5 Brett Warton, 22 John Timu, 3 Danny Moore, 16 Frank Napoli, 6 Karle Hammond (C), 7 Shaun Edwards, 10 Scott Cram, 9 Dean Callaway, 17 Anthony Seibold, 11 Shane Millard, 12 Steele Retchless, 15 Andy Johnson. Subs: 1 Tulsen Tollett for Warton (14), 8 Darren Bradstreet for Johnson (50), 14 Andrew Wynyard for Seibold (50), 18 Justin Dooley for Cram (25), Cram for Dooley (63)
Tries: Johnson (7), Callaway (15), Tollett (42), Fleming (51), **Goals:** Tollett 2, Field goal: Hammond
REDS: 1 Gary Broadbent, 2 Nick Pinkney, 3 Kris Tassell (D), 4 Jason Webber, 5 Martin Offiah, 12 Darren Brown (C), 7 Martin Crompton, 8 Paul Southern, 9 Malcolm Alker, 10 Craig Makin, 11 James Smith (D), 16 Paul Highton, 23 Mike Wainwright. Subs: 15 Neil Baynes for Makin (22), 17 Mark Johnson for Wainwright (66), 18 Stuart Littler for Leigh (71), 20 Matthew Leigh for Smith (29), Smith for Southern (57)
Tries: Pinkney (2), Highton (46), Offiah (71), Webber (74), **Goals:** Southern 2, Brown
League Express Men of the Match:
Broncos: Karle Hammond, **Reds:** Gary Broadbent
Penalty count: 7-9
Half-time: 10-8, **Referee:** Karl Kirkpatrick, **Att** 1,577

WAKEFIELD TRINITY WILDCATS 0 BRADFORD BULLS 46
WILDCATS: 1 Steve Prescott, 24 Paul Sampson (D), 4 Tony Tatupu, 20 Adam Hughes, 2 Neil Law, 3 Francis Maloney, 7 Glen Tomlinson, 8 Francis Stephenson, 21 Ryan Hudson, 10 Martin Masella, 11 Warren Jowitt, 12 Willie Poching, 13 Steve McNamara. Subs: 14 Paul March for Tomlinson (40), 15 Gary Price for Jowitt (40), 18 Paul Jackson for Masella (22), 22 Graham Law for Poching (40), Jowitt for Jackson (68), Masella for Stephenson (68)
BULLS: 28 Stuart Spruce, 3 Leon Pryce, 5 Michael Withers, 20 Scott Naylor, 4 Nathan McAvoy, 6 Henry Paul, 1 Robbie Paul, 10 Paul Anderson, 9 James Lowes, 22 Bran McDermott, 12 Mike Forshaw, 15 Hudson Smith, 1 Brad Mackay. Subs: 29 Stuart Fielden for Anderson (9BB, rev 21), 11 David Boyle for Withers (21BB), 19 Jamie Peacock for Spruce (46), 18 Lee Radford for Mackay (50), Fielden for Anderson (29BB), Boyle for Smith (29), Anderson for McDermott (55), Smith for Forshaw (66)
Tries: Withers (3, 14, 50), McAvoy (39, 79), Anderson (21), Mackay (46), Naylor (62), Smith (70),
Goals: H Paul 5
League Express Men of the Match:
Wildcats: Paul Sampson, **Bulls:** Michael Withers
Penalty count: 8-4
Half-time: 0-20, **Referee:** Robert Connolly (Wigan), **Att** 8,005

LEEDS RHINOS 26 ST HELENS 20
RHINOS: 1 Iestyn Harris (C), 5 Francis Cummins, 3 Richie Blackmore, 15 Paul Bell, 4 Keith Senior, 6 Daryl Powell, 7 Ryan Sheridan, 8 Darren Fleary, 17 Anthony Farrell, 10 Barrie McDermott, 11 Adrian Morley, 12 David Barnhill, 13 Kevin Sinfield. Subs: 9 Lee Jackson for Farrell (29), 20 Jamie Mathiou for McDermott (29), 16 Andy Hay for Sinfield (40), 14 Marcus St Hilaire for Powell (47), McDermott for Fleary (57), Farrell for Mathiou (49)
Tries: Fleary (48), Morley (51, 84), Sheridan (62),
Goals: Harris 5
Sin bin: Mathiou (38) - fighting
SAINTS: 1 Paul Atcheson, 2 Chris Smith, 3 Kevin Iro, 4 Paul Newlove, 15 Sean Hoppe, 7 Sean Long, 6 Darrell Trindall, 12 Sonny Nickle, 9 Keiron Cunningham, 10 Julian O'Neill, 11 Chris Joynt, 18 Bryan Henare, 13 Paul Sculthorpe. Subs: 8 Apollo Perelini for O'Neill (18), 14 Fereti Tuilagi for Henare (25), 5 Anthony Sullivan for Hoppe (52), 17 Paul Wellens not used, Henare for Perelini (55), Hoppe for Newlove (75)
Tries: Sculthorpe (36), Long (78), **Goals:** Long 6
Sin bin: Nickle (38) - fighting
League Express Men of the Match:
Rhinos: Ryan Sheridan, **Saints:** Keiron Cunningham
Penalty count: 10-11
Half-time: 2-12, **Referee:** Russell Smith (Castleford), **Att** 12,532

DEWSBURY RAMS 35 VILLENEUVE LEOPARDS 10
RAMS: 1 Nathan Graham, 2 Richard Baker, 3 Brendan O'Meara, 4 Dan Potter, 5 Adrian Flynn, 6 David Mycoe, 7 Barry Eaton, 8 Matthew Long, 9 Ian Talbot, 10 Shayne Williams, 11 Sean Richardson, 12 Billy Kershaw, 13 Damian Ball. Subs: 14 Alex Godfrey for Kershaw (65), 15 Gavin Wood for Graham (10), 16 Simon Hicks for Williams (20), 17 Robin Jowitt for Long (28), Graham for Talbot (18), Long for Flynn (72), Williams for Hicks (73)
Tries: O'Meara (4), Talbot (11), Eaton (38), Jowitt (56), Mycoe (67), Potter (78) , **Goals:** Eaton 5,
Field goals: Eaton
LEOPARDS: 1 Freddie Banquet, 2 Michael Van Snick, 3 Gilles Cornut, 4 Ludovic Perolari, 5 Richard Doste, 6 Laurent Frayssinous, 7 David Despin, 8 David Collado, 9 Vincent Wulf, 10 Romain Gagliazzo, 11 Grant Doorey, 12 Pierre Sabatié, 13 Laurent Carrasco. Subs: 14 Vea Bloomfield for Gagliazzo (26), 15 Artie Shead for Sabatié (35), 16 Christophe Canal for Wulf (64), 17 Olivier Charles for Doste (73), Gagliazzo for Bloomfield (54), Sabatié for Doorey (61)
Tries: Cornut (31), Wulf (45), **Goal:** Banquet
On report: Collado
League Express Men of the Match:
Rams: Barry Eaton, **Villeneuve:** Freddie Banquet
Penalty count: 9-7
Half-time: 16-4, **Referee:** Ian Smith (Oldham), **Att** 1,326

WARRINGTON WOLVES 84 YORK WASPS 1
WOLVES: 1 Lee Penny , 2 Jon Roper , 3 Alan Hunte , 4 Toa Kohe-Love , 5 Mark Forster , 6 Lee Briers , 7 Allan Langer , 8 Andrew Gee , 9 Danny Farrar , 10 Danny Nutley , 12 Ian Knott, 14 Steve McCurrie, 13 Tawera Nikau . Subs: 17 Steve Blakeley for Roper (15), 16 Gary Chambers for Knott (50) , 21 Jerome Guisset for Penny (25), 20 Ian Sibbit for Nutley (50)
Tries: Knott (5), Kohe-Love (10,17), Briers (20,42, 77), Langer (30), McCurrie (35), Farrar (37), Hunte (39, 49), Guisset (53), Chambers (60, 76), **Goals:** Briers 14
WASPS: 1 Andy Preston, 2 Leroy McKenzie , 3 Rob Lee, 4 Andrew Lambert, 5 Matt Woodcock , 6 Mark Cain , 7 Darren Callaghan, 8 Lea Tichener , 9 Gareth Dobson , 10 Steve Hill , 11 Andy Hill , 12 Lee McTigue , 13 Spencer Hargrave . Subs: 14 Shaun Austerfield for Lee (33), 15 Mick Hagan for Tichener (20), 16 Alan Pallister for McTigue (61), 17 Paul Darley for A Hill (52)
Field goal: Cain
League Express Men of the Match:
Wolves: Lee Briers , **Wasps:** Mark Cain
Penalty count: 8-8
Referee: Steve Nicholson (Whitehaven),
Half-time: 48-1, **Att** 4,770

WIGAN WARRIORS 38 DONCASTER DRAGONS 2
WARRIORS: 1 Kris Radlinski, 2 Brett Dallas, 3 Steve Renouf, 4 Gary Connolly, 5 Jason Robinson, 6 Tony Smith, 7 Willie Peters (D), 8 Terry O'Connor, 9 Terry Newton, 10 Neil Cowie, 11 Mick Cassidy, 16 Simon Haughton, 13 Andrew Farrell. Subs: 12 Denis Betts for O'Connor (34), 14 Lee Gilmour for Cassidy (48), 20 Phil Jones for Smith (59), 23 Brady Malam for Neil Cowie (34), Cowie for Malam (67), O'Connor for Betts (67)
Tries: Farrell (35), Connolly (39), Peters (46), Newton (55), Dallas (58), Renouf (66), Radlinski (69),
Goals: Farrell 5
DRAGONS: 1 Lynton Stott, 2 Craig Moore, 3 Craig Weston, 4 Carl Hall, 5 Mick Coult, 6 Colin Carter, 7 Latham Tawhai, 8 Asa Amone, 9 Peter Edwards, 10 Joe Berry, 11 Rob Wilson, 12 Tony Miller, 13 Carl Gillespie. Subs: 14 James Walker for Moore (67), 15 Paul Lister for Amone (56), 16 Billy Conway for Edwards (67), 17 Gavin Morgan for Berry (56), Edwards for Gillespie (72BB)
Goal: Weston
League Express Men of the Match:
Warriors: Terry Newton, **Dragons:** Latham Tawhai
Penalty count: 12-12
Half-time: 12-2, **Referee:** Steve Presley (Castleford), **Att** 6,225

QUARTER-FINALS

SALFORD REDS 20 WARRINGTON WOLVES 22
REDS: 1 Gary Broadbent, 2 Nick Pinkney, 3 Kris Tassell,

4 Jason Webber, 5 Martin Offiah, 19 Simon Svabic, 7 Martin Crompton, 8 Paul Southern, 9 Malcolm Alker, 10 Craig Makin, 11 James Smith, 12 Darren Brown (C), 16 Paul Highton. Subs: 23 Mike Wainwright for Broadbent (40), 15 Neil Baynes for Makin (22), 17 Mark Johnson for Smith (63), Makin for Baynes (63), Smith for Wainwright (65), 18 Stuart Littler not used
Tries: Tassell (19), Offiah (37), Smith (54), Brown (65) , **Goals:** Svabic 2
WOLVES: 1 Lee Penny, 3 Alan Hunte, 4 Toa Kohe-Love, 2 Jon Roper, 5 Mark Forster, 6 Lee Briers, 7 Allan Langer (C), 8 Andrew Gee, 9 Danny Farrar, 10 Danny Nutley, 14 Steve McCurrie, 12 Ian Knott, 13 Tawera Nikau. Subs: 21 Jerome Guisset for McCurrie (29), 11 Dean Busby for Guisset (54), Guisset for Busby (67), 20 Ian Sibbit for Guisset (77), 17 Steve Blakeley not used
Tries: Penny (12), Briers (48, 70), Hunte (80) , **Goals:** Briers 3
Penalty count: 8-4
Half-time: 10-6, **Referee:** Steve Ganson (St Helens), **Att** 6,700
League Express Men of the Match:
Wolves: Danny Nutley, **Reds:** Darren Brown

LEEDS RHINOS 42 DEWSBURY RAMS 10
RHINOS: 1 Iestyn Harris (C), 2 Francis Cummins, 3 Richie Blackmore, 15 Paul Bell, 4 Keith Senior, 6 Daryl Powell, 7 Ryan Sheridan, 20 Jamie Mathiou, 9 Lee Jackson, 10 Barrie McDermott, 11 Adrian Morley, 12 David Barnhill, 16 Andy Hay. Subs: 6 Darren Fleary for Mathiou (20), 21 Karl Pratt for Sheridan (20BB, rev 34) , 17 Anthony Farrell for Barnhill (25), Pratt for Bell (39), 18 Kevin Sinfield for Powell (47BB), Barnhill for Hay (59), Mathiou for McDermott (65), Powell for Harris (68)
Tries: Blackmore (26, 50), Harris (33, 53), Sheridan (35), Barnhill (68), Mathiou (67), Morley (79), **Goals:** Harris 4, Cummins
RAMS: 1 Nathan Graham (C), 2 Richard Baker, 3 Gavin Wood, 4 Dan Potter, 5 Adrian Flynn, 6 David Mycoe, 7 Barry Eaton, 8 Matthew Long, 9 Ian Talbot, 10 Robin Jowitt, 11 Sean Richardson, 12 Billy Kershaw, 13 Damian Ball. Subs: 16 Simon Hicks for Long (18), 15 Andy Spink for Jowitt (28), 14 Alex Godfrey for Wood (51), 17 Kevin Spink (D) for Kershaw (68), Long for A. Spink (56), Jowitt for Hicks (59)
Tries: Wood (7), Potter (47), Goals: Eaton
League Express Men of the Match:
Rhinos: Barrie McDermott, **Rams:** Nathan Graham
Penalty count: 6-3
Half-time: 14-6, **Referee:** Stuart Cummings (Widnes), **Att** 10,533

HULL FC 14 WIGAN WARRIORS 4
HULL: 1 Ben Sammut, 17 Brian Carney, 3 Deon Bird, 14 Steve Collins, 2 Matt Daylight, 7 Will Robinson (C), 20 Richard Horne, 8 Paul Broadbent, 9 Mick Jenkins, 19 Paul King, 11 Craig Wilson, 12 Luke Felsch, 15 David Maiden. Subs: 4 Craig Simon for Bird (5BB, rev 29), 25 Richard Fletcher for Wilson (10), 18 Wayne McDonald for King (31), King for Felsch (47), 6 Stanley Gene for Jenkins (60), Simon for Fletcher (60)
Tries: Maiden (14), McDonald (65), **Goals:** Sammut 3
Sin bin: Brian Carney (33) - deliberate offside
WARRIORS,: 1 Kris Radlinski, 2 Brett Dallas, 4 Gary Connolly, 3 Steve Renouf, 5 Jason Robinson, 6 Tony Smith, 7 Willie Peters, 23 Brady Malam, 9 Terry Newton, 10 Neil Cowie, 11 Mick Cassidy, 12 Denis Betts, 13 Andrew Farrell (C). Subs: 16 Simon Haughton for Smith (29BB, rev 40bb), 14 Lee Gilmour for Malam (31), 17 Tony Mestrov for Cowie (31), Haughton for Cassidy (47), Cowie for Gilmour (60), Malam for Mestrov (70), 15 Paul Johnson for Renouf (76)
Goals: Farrell 2
On report: Tony Smith - high tackle (12)
League Express Men of the Match:
Hull: Will Robinson, **Wigan:** Andrew Farrell
Penalty count: 9-6
Half-time: 8-2 , **Referee:** Russell Smith (Castleford), **Att** 7,378

HALIFAX BLUE SOX 18, BRADFORD BULLS 28
BLUE SOX: 1 Daryl Cardiss, 17 Oliver Marns, 6 Greg Florimo (C), 3 Damian Gibson, 2 Danny Ellison, 14 Martin Pearson, 7 Andrew Dunemann, 23 Brett Goldspink, 9 Paul Rowley, 10 Jim Gannon, 11 Gary Mercer, 12 Jamie Bloem, 13 Martin Moana. Subs: 21 Gael Tallec for Florimo (3BB, rev 5), 16 Simon Knox for Moana (20), Tallec for Ellison (22), 8 Andy Hobson for Goldspink (27), Goldspink for Knox (44), 15 Lokeni Savelio (D) for Goldspink (63)
Tries: Mercer (42), Pearson (55), Rowley (73), **Goals:** Pearson 3
Sin bin: Cardiss (30) - holding down; Dunemann (73) - fighting.
BULLS: 28 Stuart Spruce, 4 Nathan McAvoy, 20 Scott Naylor, 5 Michael Withers, 3 Leon Pryce, 6 Henry Paul, 1 Robbie Paul, 29 Stuart Fielden, 9 James Lowes, 22 Brian McDermott, 15 Hudson Smith, 12 Mike Forshaw, 13 Brad Mackay. Subs: 11 David Boyle for Smith (22), 10 Paul Anderson for McDermott (24), 18 Lee Radford for Mackay (45), 19 Jamie Peacock for Boyle (58), Smith for Peacock (73), McDermott for Anderson (77)
Tries: R Paul (19), Withers (35), Forshaw (50), Fielden (70), **Goals:** H Paul 6
Sin bin: Lowes (32) - interference at penalty; Fielden (73) - fighting
Penalty count: 8-4
Half-time: 0-16, **Referee:** Robert Connolly (Wigan), **Att** 9,827
League Express Men of the Match:
Blue Sox: Gary Mercer, **Bulls:** Robbie Paul

SEMI-FINALS

HULL FC 22 LEEDS RHINOS 28
HULL FC: 1 Ben Sammut, 2 Matt Daylight, 3 Deon Bird, 14 Steve Collins, 17 Brian Carney, 26 Paul Cooke, 7 Will Robinson, 8 Paul Broadbent, 19 Paul King, 12 Luke Felsch, 11 Craig Wilson, 13 Tony Grimaldi (C), 15 David Maiden. Subs: 6 Stanley Gene for King (29), 18 Wayne McDonald for Broadbent (29), 10 Andrew Hick for Wilson (32), Broadbent for Felsch (65), 4 Craig Simon for Cooke (72)
Tries: Daylight (19, 28, 48), McDonald (79), **Goals:** Sammut 3
RHINOS: 1 Iestyn Harris (C), 18 Leroy Rivett, 3 Richie Blackmore, 4 Keith Senior, 5 Francis Cummins, 6 Daryl Powell, 7 Ryan Sheridan, 8 Darren Fleary, 25 Andy Speak, 10 Barrie McDermott, 12 David Barnhill, 17 Anthony Farrell, 13 Kevin Sinfield. Subs: 20 Jamie Mathiou for McDermott (28), 9 Lee Jackson for Speak (32), 14 Marcus St Hilaire for Powell (40), 16 Andy Hay for Farrell (49), McDermott for Fleary (63), Farrell for Mathiou (71)
Tries: Blackmore (5), Sheridan (23), Cummins (52), Farrell (74), **Goals:** Harris 6
League Express Men of the Match:
Hull FC: Matt Daylight, **Rhinos:** Iestyn Harris
Penalty count: 7-7
Half-time: 10-14, **Referee:** Stuart Cummings (Widnes), **Att** 18,068

BRADFORD BULLS 44 WARRINGTON WOLVES 20
BULLS: 28 Stuart Spruce, 3 Leon Pryce, 5 Michael Withers, 20 Scott Naylor, 4 Nathan McAvoy, 6 Henry Paul, 1 Robbie Paul (C), 22 Brian McDermott, 9 James Lowes, 10 Paul Anderson, 19 Jamie Peacock, 12 Mike Forshaw, 13 Brad Mackay. Subs: 14 Justin Brooker (D) for R Paul (13, bb, rev 26), 15 Hudson Smith for Peacock (23, bb, rev 53), 29 Stuart Fielden for Anderson (25), Brooker for R Paul (47, bb, rev 51), Anderson for McDermott (53), Brooker for Spruce (56), 23 Bernard Dwyer for Mackay (57), McDermott for Dwyer (77)
Tries: Naylor (13), R Paul (32), Spruce (40), Withers (58), Brooker (63), H Paul (69), Peacock (76), **Goals:** H Paul 8
WOLVES: 1 Lee Penny, 3 Alan Hunte, 4 Toa Kohe-Love, 2 Jon Roper, 5 Mark Forster, 6 Lee Briers, 7 Allan Langer (C), 8 Andrew Gee, 9 Danny Farrar, 10 Danny Nutley, 21 Jerome Guisset, 14 Steve McCurrie, 13 Tawera Nikau. Subs: 12 Ian Knott for Guisset (47), 18 Mark Hilton for Gee (52), Gee for Nutley (65), 20 Ian Sibbit for McCurrie (74), Nutley for Gee (79), 17 Steve Blakeley for Penny (79)
Tries: McCurrie (19, 29), Knott (66), **Goals:** Briers 4
Sin bin: Nikau (25) - laying on, **On report:** Kohe Love (74) - alleged high tackle
Penalty count: 14-10
Referee: Russell Smith (Castleford), **Half time:** 18-14, **Att** 11,894
League Express Men of the Match:
Bulls: Henry Paul, **Wolves:** Steve McCurrie

CHALLENGE CUP FINAL

BRADFORD BULLS 24 LEEDS RHINOS 18
BULLS: 28 Stuart Spruce, 4 Nathan McAvoy, 20 Scott Naylor, 5 Michael Withers, 2 Tevita Vaikona, 6 Henry Paul, 1 Robbie Paul (C), 22 Brian McDermott, 9 James Lowes, 10 Paul Anderson, 19 Jamie Peacock, 12 Mike Forshaw, 13 Brad Mackay. Subs: 29 Stuart Fielden for Anderson (20), 11 David Boyle for Peacock (26), 3 Leon Pryce for McAvoy (31), 23 Bernard Dwyer for Mackay (70), Anderson for McDermott (71), McDermott for Fielden (75)
Tries: Withers (9,16), McAvoy (28), Fielden (48), **Goals:** Paul 4
RHINOS: 1 Iestyn Harris (C), 18 Leroy Rivett, 3 Richie Blackmore, 4 Keith Senior, 5 Francis Cummins, 6 Daryl Powell, 7 Ryan Sheridan, 8 Darren Fleary, 19 Dean Lawford, 10 Barrie McDermott, 11 Adrian Morley, 17 Anthony Farrell, 16 Andy Hay . Subs: 20 Jamie Mathiou for McDermott (22), 9 Lee Jackson for Lawford (28), 12 David Barnhill for Farrell (ht), 14 Marcus St Hilaire for Powell (50), McDermott for Fleary (54), Farrell for Morley (60BB, rev 65), Fleary for Mathiou (69), Farrell for Morley (70BB, rev 75)
Tries: Hay (53), St Hilaire (74), **Goals:** Harris 5
League Express Men of the Match:
Bulls: Michael Withers, **Rhinos:** Adrian Morley
Penalty count: Bulls 7-6, **Half-time:** Bulls 14-2, **Referee:** Steve Presley (Castleford), **Att** 67,247

SUPER LEAGUE V

ROUND ONE

WARRINGTON WOLVES 48 LONDON BRONCOS 18
WOLVES: 1 Lee Penny, 3 Alan Hunte, 20 Ian Sibbit, 4 Toa Kohe-Love, 5 Mark Forster, 6 Lee Briers, 7 Allan Langer (C), 8 Andrew Gee, 9 Danny Farrar, 10 Danny Nutley, 12 Ian Knott, 14 Steve McCurrie, 13 Tawera Nikau. Subs: 21 Jerome Guisset for Knott (48), 16 Gary Chambers for Gee (68), 17 Steve Blakeley for Briers (73), Briers for Blakeley (77), 19 David Highton not used.
Tries: Nikau (13), Hunte (23, 44), McCurrie (53), Briers (59), Langer (68), Guisset (71), Forster (80). **Goals:** Briers 8
BRONCOS: 4 Greg Fleming, 16 Frank Napoli, 3 Danny Moore, 13 Matt Toshack, 1 Tulsen Tollett, 6 Karle Hammond (C), 7 Shaun Edwards, 10 Scott Cram, 9 Dean Callaway, 18 Justin Dooley, 11 Shane Millard, 12 Steele Retchless, 14 Andrew Wynyard. Subs: 27 Paul Davidson (D) for Dooley (24), 17 Anthony Seibold for Cram (30), 8 Darren Bradstreet for Callaway (40), 15 Andy Johnson for Davidson (58), Cram for Seibold (65), Dooley for Wynyard (65)
Tries: Tollett (10), Callaway (38), Retchless (49). **Goals:** Tollett 3
League Express Men of the Match:
Wolves: Allan Langer, **Broncos:** Steele Retchless
Half-time: 16-14. **Penalty count:** 7-6. **Referee:** Robert Connolly (Wigan), **Att** 8,718

CASTLEFORD TIGERS 24 WIGAN WARRIORS 30
TIGERS: 20 Jamie Benn, 16 Jon Wells, 4 Logan Campbell, 3 Michael Eagar, 5 Darren Rogers, 22 Andrew Purcell, 7 Brad Davis, 10 Dean Sampson, 9 Aaron Raper, 15 Darren Shaw, 11 Lee Harland, 12 Dale Fritz, 13 Adrian Vowles (C). Subs: 8 Nathan Sykes for Shaw (20), 18 Paul Smith for Harland (32), 23 Craig Wright (D) for Fritz (65), 19 Andy Lynch (not used), Shaw for Sampson (30), Sampson for Smith (51), Harland for Sampson (57 BB, rev 65)
Tries: Rogers (14, 69, 80) Sampson (72) Eagar (77). **Goals:** Benn 2
WARRIORS: 1 Kris Radlinski, 2 Brett Dallas, 4 Gary Connolly, 3 Steve Renouf, 5 Jason Robinson, 6 Tony Smith, 7 Willie Peters, 8 Terry O'Connor, 9 Terry Newton, 10 Neil Cowie, 11 Mick Cassidy, 12 Denis Betts, 13 Andy Farrell (C). Subs: 20 Phil Jones for Peters (67), 17 Tony Mestrov for Cowie (30), 16 Simon Haughton for O' Connor (30), 14 Lee Gilmour for Cassidy (46), O' Connor for Haughton (52)
Tries: Peters (24) Smith (31, 50) Radlinski (55) Dallas (64). **Goals:** Farrell (5)
League Express Men of the Match:
Tigers: Darren Rogers, **Warriors:** Tony Smith
Penalty count: 6-3. **Half-time:** 4-12. **Referee:** Stuart Cummings (Widnes). **Att** 8,812

ST HELENS 10 BRADFORD BULLS 32
SAINTS: 1 Paul Atcheson, 2 Chris Smith, 3 Kevin Iro, 15 Sean Hoppe, 5 Anthony Sullivan, 17 Paul Wellens, 6 Sean Long, 12 Sonny Nickle, 9 Keiron Cunningham, 10 Julian O'Neill, 11 Chris Joynt, 18 Bryan Henare, 13 Paul Sculthorpe. Subs: 8 Apollo Perelini for Nickle (23), 14 Fereti Tuilagi for O'Neill (31), Nickle for Atcheson (33), 19 Tony Stewart for Henare (61), 26 John Stankevitch for Tuilagi (64), O'Neill for Nickle (74)
Tries: Joynt (11), Cunningham (68), **Goal:** Long,
BULLS: 28 Stuart Spruce, 4 Nathan McAvoy, 20 Scott Naylor, 5 Michael Withers, 3 Leon Pryce, 6 Henry Paul, 1 Robbie Paul, 23 Bernard Dwyer, 9 James Lowes, 22 Brian McDermott, 12 Mike Forshaw, 15 Hudson Smith, 13 Brad Mackay. Subs: 29 Stuart Fielden for Dwyer (15), 11 David Boyle for Hudson Smith (22), 18 Lee Radford for Mackay (54), 19 Jamie Peacock for Withers (58), Dwyer for McDermott (66)
Tries: Lowes (25, 32), Withers (48), McAvoy (55), R Paul (61). **Goals:** H Paul 6
League Express Men of the Match:
Saints: Keiron Cunningham, **Bulls:** Brian McDermott
Penalty count: 9-8. **Half-time:** 6-12. **Referee:** Steve Presley (Castleford), **Att** 10,128

HUDDERSFIELD GIANTS 10 SALFORD CITY REDS 18
GIANTS: 14 Paul Reilly, 1 Waisale Sovatabua, 17 Martin Gleeson, 3 Karl Lovell, 5 Matt Crowther, 6 Gene Ngamu, 7 Gavin Clinch, 8 Steve Molloy (C), 9 Johnny Lawless, 10 Dale Laughton, 11 David Lomax, 12 Richard Marshall, 13 Jeff Hardy. Subs: 28 Andy Rice (D) for Marshall (16), 16 Nick Fozzard for Molloy (33), 18 Danny Russell for Lawless (46), Molloy for Laughton (54), 2 Danny Arnold for Gleeson (65), Laughton for Molloy (72)
Tries: Ngamu (27), Lovell (70), **Goal:** Crowther
CITY REDS: 1 Gary Broadbent, 2 Nick Pinkney, 3 Kris Tassell, 4 Jason Webber, 5 Martin Offiah, 19 Simon Svabic, 7 Martin Crompton, 8 Paul Southern, 9 Malcolm Alker, 10 Craig Makin, 11 James Smith, 12 Darren Brown (C), 16 Paul Highton. Subs: 15 Neil Baynes for Southern (18), 23 Mike Wainwright for Makin (28), 18 Stuart Littler for Smith (67), Makin for Baynes (73), 17 Mark Johnson for Wainwright (77)
Tries: Svabic (32, 46) Webber (14). **Goals:** Svabic 3
League Express Men of the Match:
Giants: David Lomax, **Reds:** Simon Svabic
Penalty count: 9-10. **Half-time:** 4-10. **Referee:** Russell Smith (Castleford), **Att:** 3,480

HALIFAX BLUE SOX 30 HULL FC 27
BLUE SOX: 3 Damian Gibson, 12 Jamie Bloem, 6 Greg Florimo (C), 5 Phil Hassan, 4 Marvin Golden, 14 Martin Pearson, 7 Andrew Dunemann, 23 Brett Goldspink, 9 Paul Rowley, 10 Jim Gannon, 11 Gary Mercer, 21 Gael Tallec, 13 Martin Moana. Subs: 17 Olly Marns for Golden (42), 8 Andy Hobson for Goldspink (48), 24 Danny Fearon for Pearson (60), 15 Lokeni Savelio for Fearon (78)
Tries: Dunemann (34), Gibson (37), Marns (46), Florimo (50, 79), Pearson (53). **Goals:** Pearson 3
HULL: 1 Ben Sammut, 2 Matt Daylight, 3 Deon Bird, 14 Steve Collins, 17 Brian Carney, 4 Craig Simon, 7 Will Robinson, 8 Paul Broadbent, 9 Mick Jenkins, 10 Andrew Hick, 16 Adam Maher, 12 Luke Felsch, 15 David Maiden. Subs: 11 Craig Wilson for Maher (30), 18 Wayne McDonald for Hick (30), 6 Stanley Gene for Bird (48), 19 Paul King for Jenkins (58), Hick for Broadbent (70), Jenkins for King (75)
Tries: Carney (16, 60, 63), McDonald (71). **Goals:** Sammut 5, **Field goal:** Wilson
League Express Men of the Match:
Blue Sox: Andrew Dunemann, **Hull:** Brian Carney
Penalty count: 7-11. **Half-time:** 12-8. **Referee:** Karl Kirkpatrick (Warrington), **Att:** 6,124

LEEDS RHINOS 18 WAKEFIELD TRINITY WILDCATS 22
RHINOS: 14 Marcus St Hilaire, 5 Francis Cummins, 3 Richie Blackmore, 15 Paul Bell, 4 Keith Senior, 6 Daryl Powell (C), 7 Ryan Sheridan, 8 Darren Fleary, 17 Anthony Farrell, 10 Barrie McDermott, 11 Adrian Morley, 12 David Barnhill, 16 Andy Hay. Subs: 9 Lee Jackson for McDermott (22), 21 Karl Pratt for St Hilaire (24), 20 Jamie Mathiou for Fleary (ht), 13 Kevin Sinfield for Barnhill (58), McDermott for Farrell (65), Farrell for McDermott (70)
Tries: Hay (56), Mathiou (63), Cummins (70). **Goals:** Cummins 3
WILDCATS: 1 Steve Prescott, 24 Paul Sampson, 4 Tony Tatupu, 20 Adam Hughes, 2 Neil Law, 3 Francis Maloney, 7 Glen Tomlinson, 8 Francis Stephenson, 21 Ryan Hudson, 16 Andy Fisher, 11 Warren Jowitt, 12 Willie Poching, 13 Steve McNamara. Subs: 10 Martin Masella for Stephenson (15), 19 Jamie Field for Fisher (28), Stephenson for Masella (33), 15 Gary Price for Poching (51), Masella for Stephenson (59), Fisher for Field (68), Stephenson for Masella (70), 14 Paul March for Tomlinson (76)
Tries: Stephenson (2), Hughes (25), Sampson (46), McNamara (80). **Goals:** McNamara 3
League Express Men of the Match:
Rhinos: Jamie Mathiou, **Wildcats:** Steve McNamara
Penalty count: 6-2. **Half-time:** 0-12. **Referee:** Steve Ganson (St Helens), **Att:** 13,842

ROUND 2

WAKEFIELD TRINITY WILDCATS 24 HALIFAX BLUE SOX 40
WILDCATS: 1 Steve Prescott, 24 Paul Sampson, 4 Tony Tatupu, 20 Adam Hughes, 2 Neil Law, 3 Francis Maloney, 7 Glen Tomlinson, 8 Francis Stephenson, 21 Ryan Hudson, 16 Andy Fisher, 11 Warren Jowitt, 15 Gary Price, 13 Steve McNamara (C). Subs: 14 Paul March for Tomlinson (22), 10 Martin Masella for Stephenson (16), 19 Jamie Field for Fisher (22), 27 Ben Westwood for Price (76), Stephenson for Masella (60), Fisher for Field (76)
Tries: Jowitt (27), Price (29), Hughes (39). **Goals:** McNamara 6
BLUE SOX: 1 Daryl Cardiss, 18 Mike Peters (D), 3 Damian Gibson, 6 Greg Florimo (C), 17 Oliver Marns, 14 Martin Pearson, 7 Andrew Dunemann, 23 Brett Goldspink, 9 Paul Rowley, 10 Jamie Gannon, 11 Gary Mercer, 12 Jamie Bloem, 13 Martin Moana. Subs: 8 Andy Hobson for Goldspink (30), 15 Luke Savelio for Hobson (75), David Foster not used, 21 Gael Tallec for Gibson (37), Goldspink for Moana (45), Moana for Marns (62)
Tries: Marns (8), Cardiss (10), Rowley (15), Dunemann (21), Pearson (78), Moana (80). **Goals:** Pearson 8
League Express Men of the Match:
Wildcats: Steve McNamara **Blue Sox** Martin Pearson
Penalty count: 8-8. **Half-time:** 22-24. **Referee:** Russell Smith (Castleford), **Att:** 4,678

WIGAN WARRIORS 20 LEEDS RHINOS 6
WARRIORS: 1 Kris Radlinski, 2 Brett Dallas, 4 Gary Connolly, 3 Steve Renouf, 5 Jason Robinson, 13 Andrew Farrell (C), 7 Willie Peters, 8 Terry O'Connor, 9 Terry Newton, 10 Neil Cowie, 11 Mick Cassidy, 16 Simon Haughton, 12 Denis Betts. Subs: 17 Tony Mestrov for O'Connor (26), 15 Paul Johnson for Cassidy (60BB), 18 Wes Davies for Renouf (76), 14 Lee Gilmour for Cassidy (35), O'Connor for Cowie (47), Cassidy for Gilmour (56), Cowie for Mestrov (60)
Tries: Farrell (3), Dallas (6), Betts (23). **Goals:** Farrell 3, Peters
Sin bin: Cowie (17) - fighting; Farrell (28) - interference at the play-the-ball.
RHINOS: 5 Francis Cummins, 18 Leroy Rivett, 3 Richie Blackmore, 4 Keith Senior, 21 Karl Pratt, 1 Iestyn Harris (C), 7 Ryan Sheridan, 8 Darren Fleary, 9 Lee Jackson, 10 Barrie McDermott, 11 Adrian Morley, 17 Anthony Farrell, 16 Andy Hay. Subs: 13 Kevin Sinfield for Hay (30), 12 David Barnhill for Farrell (27), 19 Dean Lawford for Sheridan (75), 6 Daryl Powell for Harris (49), Farrell for McDermott (48), Harris for Jackson (61), McDermott for Fleary (68)
Tries: Harris (9). **Goals:** Harris
League Express Men of the Match:
Warriors: Andy Farrell, **Rhinos:** Adrian Morley
Penalty count: 9-8. **Half-time:** 20-6. **Referee:** Steve Presley (Castleford), **Att:** 11,200

BRADFORD BULLS 58 WARRINGTON WOLVES 4
BULLS: 28 Stuart Spruce, 4 Nathan McAvoy, 20 Scott Naylor, 3 Leon Pryce, 14 Justin Brooker, 6 Henry Paul, 1 Robbie Paul (C), 22 Brian McDermott, 9 James Lowes, 10 Paul Anderson, 19 Jamie Peacock, 12 Mike Forshaw, 13 Brad Mackay. Subs: 15 Hudson Smith for McDermott (42), 2 Tevita Vaikona for R Paul (40), 23 Bernard Dwyer for Anderson (40), 11 David Boyle for Forshaw (22), Anderson for Peacock (62)
Tries: Brooker (2, 22), R Paul (6, 27), Forshaw (12), Spruce (18), Lowes (20), McAvoy (38), Mackay (53), H Paul (56), Anderson (74). **Goals:** H Paul 7, **Sin bin:** Dwyer (49) – fighting
WOLVES: 1 Lee Penny, 3 Alan Hunte, 4 Toa Kohe-Love, 2 Jon Roper, 5 Mark Forster, 6 Lee Briers, 7 Allan Langer, 8 Andrew Gee, 9 Danny Farrar, 10 Danny Nutley, 12 Ian Knott, 14 Steve McCurrie, 13 Tawera Nikau. Subs: 21 Jerome Guisset for McCurrie (18), 18 Mark Hilton for Nutley (30), 20 Ian Sibbit for Knott (18), 17 Steve Blakeley for Briers (14), McCurrie for Guisset (55), Knott for Sibbit (61), **Try:** Penny (67), **Sin bin:** Gee (49) – fighting
League Express Men of the Match:
Bulls: Jamie Peacock. **Wolves:** Danny Farrar
Penalty count: 6-7. **Half-time:** 42-0. **Referee:** John Connolly (Wigan), **Att:** 17, 127

LONDON BRONCOS 34 HUDDERSFIELD-SHEFFIELD GIANTS 18
BRONCOS: 4 Greg Fleming, 1 Tulsen Tollett, 3 Danny Moore, 13 Mat Toshack, 5 Brett Warton, 25 Brendan Magnus (D), 7 Shaun Edwards, 18 Justin Dooley, 9 Dean Callaway, 17 Anthony Seibold, 11 Shane Millard, 12 Steele Retchless, 6 Karle Hammond (C). Subs: 10 Scott Cram for Seibold (40), 14 Andrew Wynyard for Retchless (51), 15 Andy Johnson for Edwards (31), 16 Frank Napoli for Tollett (68), Retchless for Callaway (75)
Tries: Tollett (16), Magnus (28), Warton (58), Toshack (62), Johnson (69), Fleming (77). **Goals:** Warton 5
GIANTS: 14 Paul Reilly, 1 Waisale Sovatabua, 3 Karl Lovell, 17 Martin Gleeson, 5 Matt Crowther, 6 Gene Ngamu, 7 Gavin Clinch, 8 Steve Molloy (C), 18 Danny Russell, 10 Dale Laughton, 11 David Lomax, 16 Nick Fozzard, 13 Jeff Hardy. Subs: 9 Johnny Lawless for Russell (35), 28 Andy Rice for Lomax (53), 19 Chris Thorman for Reilly (46), 21 Chris Molyneux for Laughton (42 bb), Laughton for Molyneux (58 BB rev 59), Lomax for Molloy (60)
Tries: Sovatabua (7), Lovell (23), Gleeson (48). **Goals:** Crowther 3.
League Express Men of the Match:
Broncos: Brendan Magnus, **Giants:** Nick Fozzard
Half-time: 12-12. **Referee:** Steve Ganson (St Helens), **Att:** 2,856. **Penalty count:** 12-8

SALFORD CITY REDS 16 CASTLEFORD TIGERS 22
CITY REDS: 1 Gary Broadbent, 2 Nick Pinkney, 3 Kris Tassell, 4 Jason Webber, 5 Martin Offiah, 19 Simon Svabic, 7 Martin Crompton, 8 Paul Southern, 9 Malcolm Alker, 10 Craig Makin, 11 James Smith, 12 Darren Brown (C), 16 Paul Highton. Subs: 16 Neil Baynes for Makin (15), 17 Mark Johnson for Faimalo (72), 14 Joe Faimalo for Smith (54), 29 Brad Hepi (D) for Highton (16), Highton for Southern (58)
Tries: Offiah (21), Tassell (48), Webber (79). **Goals:** Svabic 2
TIGERS: 3 Michael Eagar, 16 Jon Wells, 13 Adrian Vowles (C), 4 Logan Campbell, 5 Darren Rogers, 6 Danny Orr, 7 Brad Davis, 10 Dean Sampson, 9 Aaron Raper, 15 Darren Shaw, 11 Lee Harland, 12 Dale Fritz, 22 Andrew Purcell. Subs: 20 Jamie Benn for Fritz (65), 8 Nathan Sykes for Sampson (24), 17 Ian Tonks for Purcell (58), 18 Paul Smith for Sykes (75), Sampson for Shaw (53)
Tries: Campbell (3), Raper (9), Vowles (61), Davis (73). **Goals:** Davis, Benn 2. **Penalty count:** 8-6
League Express Men of the Match:
Reds: Gary Broadbent. **Tigers:** Aaron Raper
Half-time: 6-10. **Referee:** Karl Kirkpatrick (Warrington). **Att:** 5, 534

HULL FC 20 ST HELENS 28
HULL FC: 1 Ben Sammut, 17 Brian Carney, 14 Steve Collins, 3 Deon Bird, 2 Matt Daylight, 7 Will Robinson (C), 20 Richard Horne, 8 Paul Broadbent, 9 Mick Jenkins, 10 Andrew Hick, 12 Luke Felsch, 12 Adam Maher, 15 David Maiden. Subs: 18 Wayne McDonald for Hick (23), 6 Stanley Gene for Jenkins (27), 4 Craig Simon for Horne (48), 13 Tony Grimaldi for Maher (51), Hick for Broadbent (61), Maher for Felsch (73)
Tries: Jenkins (25), Collins (35), Carney (78). **Goals:** Sammut 4, **Sin bin:** Bird (46) - fighting
SAINTS: 17 Paul Wellens, 2 Chris Smith, 3 Kevin Iro, 4 Paul Newlove, 5 Anthony Sullivan, 20 Tommy Martyn, 7 Sean Long, 12 Sonny Nickle, 9 Keiron Cunningham, 10 Julian O'Neill, 11 Chris Joynt (C), 14 Fereti Tuilagi, 13 Paul Sculthorpe. Subs: 16 Vila Matautia for O'Neill (26), 8 Apollo Perelini for Tuilagi (28), Tuilagi for Nickle (54), 15 Sean Hoppe for Martyn (58), O'Neill for Matautia (64), Nickle for Tuilagi (67BB, rev 71), 26 John Stankevitch for Perelini (72)
Tries: Wellens (2, 16), Long (61), Joynt (66), Sculthorpe (75). **Goals:** Long 4, **Sin bin:** Matautia (46) – fighting
League Express Men of the Match:
Hull: Will Robinson, **Saints:** Sean Long
Penalty count: 7-2. **Half-time:** 14-12. **Referee:** Stuart Cummings (Widnes), **Att:** 7,160

ROUND 3

SALFORD CITY REDS 0 WIGAN WARRIORS 32
CITY REDS: 1 Gary Broadbent, 2 Nick Pinkney, 3 Kris Tassell, 30 Jason Nicol, 5 Martin Offiah, 4 Jason Webber, 7 Martin Crompton, 8 Paul Southern, 9 Malcolm Alker, 15 Neil Baynes, 23 Mike Wainwright, 12 Darren Brown (C), 16 Paul Highton. Subs: 14 Joe Faimalo for Highton (31), 10 Craig Makin for Baynes (49), 20 Matty Leigh for Tassell (65), 17 Mark Johnson for Wainwright (71), Baynes for Southern (71)
WARRIORS: 1 Kris Radlinski, 2 Brett Dallas, 3 Steve Renouf, 4 Gary Connolly, 5 Jason Robinson, 6 Tony Smith, 7 Willie Peters, 8 Terry O'Connor, 9 Terry Newton, 10 Neil Cowie, 14 Lee Gilmour, 16 Simon Haughton, 13 Andy Farrell. Subs: 17 Tony Mestrov for O'Connor (28), 11 Mick Cassidy for Newton (34), 12 Denis Betts for Cowie (36), 15 Paul Johnson for Mestrov (51), Cowie for Haughton (68), Mestrov for Gilmour (68)
Tries: Smith (21), Renouf (30, 42), Peters (65), Johnson (72). **Goals:** Farrell 6
League Express Men of the Match:
City Reds: Martin Crompton, **Warriors:** Andy Farrell.
Penalty count: 10-6. **Half-time:** 0-14. **Referee:** Russell Smith (Castleford). **Att:** 6,663

ST HELENS 29 WAKEFIELD TRINITY WILDCATS 22
SAINTS: 17 Paul Wellens, 2 Chris Smith, 3 Kevin Iro, 4 Paul Newlove, 5 Anthony Sullivan, 20 Tommy Martyn, 7 Sean Long, 12 Sonny Nickle, 9 Keiron Cunningham, 10 Julian O'Neill, 11 Chris Joynt (C), 14 Fereti Tuilagi, 13 Paul Sculthorpe. Subs: 18 Bryan Henare for Nickle (57), 8 Apollo Perelini for O'Neill (31), 15 Sean Hoppe for Newlove (76), 26 John Stankevitch for Tuilagi (38), Tuilagi for Stankevitch (70), Nickle for Perelini (72)
Tries: Newlove (2), Long (7), Cunningham (40, 61), Martyn (67). **Goals:** Long 4, **Field goal:** Martyn
WILDCATS: 1 Steve Prescott, 24 Paul Sampson, 4 Tony Tatupu, 20 Adam Hughes, 2 Neil Law, 3 Francis Maloney, 14 Paul March, 8 Francis Stephenson, 21 Ryan Hudson, 10 Martin Masella, 11 Warren Jowitt, 12 Willie Poching, 13 Steve McNamara (C). Subs: 15 Gary Price for McNamara (40), 19 Jamie Field for Masella (53), 16 Andy Fisher for Stephenson (56), McNamara for Poching (65), 23 Martyn Holland not used
Tries: Stephenson (23), Jowitt (30), Law (32), March (44). **Goals:** McNamara 2, Maloney
League Express Men of the Match:
Saints: Tommy Martyn, **Wildcats:** Steve McNamara.
Penalty count: 8-8. **Half-time:** 18-16. **Referee:** Robert Connolly (Wigan), **Att:** 7,569,

HALIFAX BLUE SOX 24 LEEDS RHINOS 16
BLUE SOX: 1 Daryl Cardiss, 12 Jamie Bloem, 6 Greg Florimo (C), 4 Marvin Golden, 5 Phil Hassan, 14 Martin Pearson, 7 Andrew Dunemann, 23 Brett Goldspink, 9 Paul Rowley, 10 Jamie Gannon, 11 Gary Mercer, 19 David Foster, 13 Martin Moana. Subs: 8 Andy Hobson for Foster (35), 21 Gael Tallec for Moana (35), 15 Lokeni Savelio for Goldspink (39), Goldspink for Savelio (56), 27 Jim Naylor (D) for Hobson (64)
Tries: Pearson (3), Cardiss (24), Naylor (74). **Goals:** Bloem, Pearson 5, **Sin bin:** Pearson (9) - fighting; Gannon (27) - dissent
RHINOS: 1 Iestyn Harris (C), 21 Karl Pratt, 3 Richie Blackmore, 4 Keith Senior, 5 Francis Cummins, 6 Daryl Powell, 7 Ryan Sheridan, 8 Darren Fleary, 19 Dean Lawford, 10 Barrie McDermott, 12 David Barnhill, 17 Anthony Farrell, 13 Kevin Sinfield. Subs: 23 Danny Ward for McDermott (19BB, rev 30), 18 Leroy Rivett for Harris (26), 9 Lee Jackson for Lawford (38), Ward for Fleary (50), 16 Andy Hay for McDermott (60), McDermott for Farrell (70)
Tries: Senior (30), Powell (34, 47). **Goals:** Harris, Cummins, **Sin bin:** Cummins (9) - fighting, **On report:** Cummins (9) - stamping; McDermott (60) - high tackle
League Express Men of the Match:
Blue Sox: Gary Mercer, **Rhinos:** Daryl Powell
Penalty count: 6-8. **Half-time:** 14-10. **Referee:** Steve Ganson (St Helens), **Att:** 6,817

HUDDERSFIELD-SHEFFIELD GIANTS 2 BRADFORD BULLS 60
GIANTS: 14 Paul Reilly, 1 Waisale Sovatabua, 17 Martin Gleeson, 3 Karl Lovell, 5 Matt Crowther, 6 Gene Ngamu, 7 Gavin Clinch, 8 Steve Molloy (C), 18 Danny Russell, 10 Dale Laughton, 11 David Lomax, 22 David Bradbury (D), 13 Jeff Hardy. Subs: 30 Sylvain Houles (D) for Lovell (60), 9 Johnny Lawless for Russell (54), 21 Chris Molyneux for Lomax (48), 29 Jamie Fielden for Laughton (30), Laughton for Molloy (60), Molloy for Fielden (77), **Goal:** Crowther, **On Report:** Reilly (36) - high tackle
BULLS: 5 Michael Withers, 2 Tevita Vaikona, 20 Scott Naylor, 14 Justin Brooker, 4 Nathan McAvoy, 6 Henry Paul, 1 Robbie Paul (C), 22 Brian McDermott, 9 James Lowes, 10 Paul Anderson, 19 Jamie Peacock, 11 David Boyle, 13 Brad Mackay. Subs: 29 Stuart Fielden for Anderson (25), 15 Hudson Smith for Peacock (48), 18 Lee Radford for Mackay (48), 3 Leon Pryce for Naylor (40), Anderson for Boyle (60), Mackay for Pryce (67), Naylor for Withers (62bb, rev 72)
Tries: McAvoy (23, 78), Mackay (30), Vaikona (33), R Paul (41), Boyle (48), Brooker (57, 59), Anderson (63), Fielden (71). **Goals:** H Paul 10
League Express Men of the Match:
Giants: David Lomax, **Bulls:** Henry Paul
Penalty count: 7-14. **Half-time:** 2-20. **Referee:** Karl Kirkpatrick (Warrington), **Att:** 7,083

WARRINGTON WOLVES 16 HULL FC 32
WOLVES: 3 Alan Hunte, 2 Jon Roper, 4 Toa Kohe-Love, 20 Ian Sibbit, 5 Mark Forster, 6 Lee Briers, 7 Allan Langer (C), 8 Andrew Gee, 9 Danny Farrar, 10 Danny Nutley, 21 Jerome Guisset, 14 Steve McCurrie, 13 Tawera Nikau. Subs: 12 Ian Knott for Roper (41), 18 Mark Hilton for Gee (55), 11 Dean Busby for Guisset (55), 16 Gary Chambers for Nutley (58), Gee for Hilton (71)
Tries: Sibbit (22), Hunte (26). **Goals:** Briers 4
HULL FC: 1 Ben Sammut, 17 Brian Carney, 14 Steve Collins, 4 Craig Simon, 2 Matt Daylight, 26 Paul Cooke, 7 Will Robinson, 10 Andrew Hick, 9 Mick Jenkins, 12 Luke Felsch, 16 Adam Maher, 13 Tony Grimaldi (C), 15 David Maiden. Subs: 8 Paul Broadbent for Hick (31), Hick for Broadbent (41), 18 Wayne McDonald for Grimaldi (49), Broadbent for Maher (55 BB), 19 Paul King for Hick (69), 3 Deon Bird for Carney (62)
Tries: Collins (7), Maher (10), Sammut (38, 63), Grimaldi (43), McDonald (74). **Goals:** Sammut 4
League Express Men of Match:
Wolves: Lee Briers, **Hull FC:** Luke Felsch.
Penalty count: 7-8. **Half-time:** 16-16. **Referee:** Steve Presley (Castleford), **Att:** 5,956

CASTLEFORD TIGERS 16 LONDON BRONCOS 10
TIGERS: 20 Jamie Benn, 5 Darren Rogers, 3 Michael Eagar, 4 Logan Campbell, 16 Jon Wells, 6 Danny Orr, 7 Brad Davis, 10 Dean Sampson, 22 Andrew Purcell, 15 Darren Shaw, 11 Lee Harland, 12 Dale Fritz, 13 Adrian Vowles (C). Subs: 8 Nathan Sykes for Sampson (34), 17 Ian Tonks for Orr (20), 18 Paul Smith for Eagar (54), 23 Craig Wright for Tonks (70), Sampson for Shaw (75)
Tries: Orr (10), Rogers (28). **Goals:** Benn 4

BRONCOS: 4 Greg Fleming, 1 Tulsen Tollett, 3 Danny Moore, 13 Mat Toshack, 5 Brett Warton, 6 Karle Hammond (C), 25 Brendan Magnus, 17 Anthony Seibold, 9 Dean Callaway, 10 Scott Cram, 11 Shane Millard, 12 Steele Retchless, 14 Andrew Wynyard. Subs: 15 Andy Johnson for Retchless (23), 16 Frank Napoli for Wynyard (65), 21 Jon Clarke (D) for Callaway (53), 27 Paul Davidson for Cram (23), Retchless for Seibold (56)
Tries: Fleming (14, 60), **Goal:** Warton
League Express Men of the Match:
Tigers: Dale Fritz, **Broncos:** Greg Fleming.
Penalty count: 6-5. **Half-time:** 10-6. **Referee:** Stuart Cummings (Widnes), **Att:** 6,372

ROUND 4

HULL FC 40 HUDDERSFIELD SHEFFIELD GIANTS 24
HULL: 1 Ben Sammut, 2 Matt Daylight, 4 Craig Simon, 14 Steve Collins, 17 Brian Carney, 7 Will Robinson, 20 Richard Horne, 8 Paul Broadbent, 9 Mick Jenkins, 12 Luke Felsch, 16 Adam Maher, 13 Tony Grimaldi (C), 15 David Maiden. Subs: 3 Deon Bird for Robinson (60), 11 Craig Wilson for Maiden (47), 18 Wayne McDonald for Broadbent (30), 10 Andrew Hick for Felsch (25), Broadbent for Hick (74), Robinson for Collins (74)
Tries: Maiden (11), Robinson (16), Carney (24), Simon (46, 73), Wilson (55), Collins (65). **Goals:** Sammut 6, **Dismissal:** Adam Maher (14) - punching
GIANTS: 14 Paul Reilly, 1 Waisale Sovatabua, 17 Martin Gleeson, 3 Karl Lovell, 5 Matt Crowther, 6 Gene Ngamu, 7 Gavin Clinch, 8 Steve Molloy (C), 18 Danny Russell, 10 Dale Laughton, 11 David Lomax, 22 David Bradbury, 13 Jeff Hardy. Subs: 19 Chris Thorman for Ngamu (42), 9 John Lawless for Russell (47), 30 Sylvain Houles for Laughton (34), 15 Darren Turner for Molloy (25), Laughton for Gleeson (62), Molloy for Turner (74)
Tries: Sovatabua (35, 68), Clinch (52), Thorman (77). **Goals**: Crowther 4, **Dismissal:** Lomax (14) - high tackle, **On report:** Sovatabua (58) - high tackle
League Express Men of the Match:
Hull: Richard Horne, **Giants:** David Bradbury.
Penalty count: 11-9. **Half-time:** 18-6. **Referee:** Steve Ganson (St Helens), **Att:** 5,553

WIGAN WARRIORS 20 HALIFAX BLUE SOX 8
WARRIORS: 1 Kris Radlinski, 5 Jason Robinson, 3 Steve Renouf, 4 Gary Connolly, 2 Brett Dallas, 13 Andy Farrell, 7 Willie Peters, 8 Terry O'Connor, 9 Terry Newton, 10 Neil Cowie, 12 Denis Betts, 16 Simon Haughton, 14 Lee Gilmour. Subs: 17 Tony Mestrov for O'Connor (28), 11 Mick Cassidy for Haughton (40), 15 Paul Johnson for Renouf (60), 22 Mark Reber for Newton (60), Newton for Reber (69BB), Cowie for Mestrov (71)
Tries: Gilmour (9), Cassidy (43), Dallas (59). **Goals:** Farrell 4
BLUE SOX: 1 Daryl Cardiss, 12 Jamie Bloem, 6 Greg Florimo (C), 4 Marvin Golden, 5 Phil Hassan, 14 Martin Pearson, 7 Andrew Dunemann, 23 Brett Goldspink, 9 Paul Rowley, 10 Jim Gannon, 11 Gary Mercer, 19 David Foster, 13 Marty Moana. Subs: 8 Andy Hobson for Goldspink (32), 21 Gael Tallec for Foster (24), 15 Lokeni Savelio for Gannon (64), 27 Jim Naylor for Mercer (52), Goldspink for Hobson (57), Foster for Pearson (69)
Tries: Goldspink (75). **Goals:** Pearson, Bloem
League Express Men of the Match:
Warriors: Andy Farrell, **Blue Sox**: Jamie Bloem.
Penalty count: 8-7. **Half-time:** 8-2. **Referee:** Steve Presley (Castleford), **Att:** 10,825

LEEDS RHINOS 14 ST HELENS 42
RHINOS: 5 Francis Cummins, 22 Chev Walker, 3 Richie Blackmore, 4 Keith Senior, 14 Marcus St Hilaire, 6 Daryl Powell (C), 7 Ryan Sheridan, 8 Darren Fleary, 9 Lee Jackson, 23 Danny Ward, 16 Andy Hay, 12 David Barnhill, 13 Kevin Sinfield. Subs: 17 Anthony Farrell for Fleary (21), 19 Dean Lawford for Powell (27), 28 Jamie Jones-Buchanan for Fleary (46BB, rev 61), 18 Leroy Rivett for Sinfield (68), Fleary for Ward (40), Jones-Buchanan for Barnhill (42), Sinfield for Walker (73)
Tries: Barnhill (29), Sheridan (76). **Goals:** Cummins 3
SAINTS: 17 Paul Wellens, 2 Chris Smith, 3 Kevin Iro, 15 Sean Hoppe, 5 Anthony Sullivan, 20 Tommy Martyn, 7 Sean Long, 8 Apollo Perelini, 9 Keiron Cunningham, 10 Julian O'Neill, 11 Chris Joynt (C), 14 Fereti Tuilagi, 13 Paul Sculthorpe. Subs: 16 Vila Matautia for Perelini (17BB, rev 26), 18 Bryan Henare for Perelini (34BB, rev 40), 26 John Stankevitch for Tuilagi (37), 24 Steve Hall for Iro (72), Matautia for O'Neill (30), O'Neill for Matautia (55), Henare for Stankevitch (56), Tuilagi for Joynt (67)
Tries: Martyn (5), Long (45), Iro (47), Sullivan (55, 62, 80), Smith (69), Perelini (72). **Goals:** Long 5, **Sin bin:** Perelini (60) - professional foul
League Express Men of the Match:
Rhinos: Francis Cummins, **Saints:** Sean Long.
Penalty count: 10-4. **Half-time:** 8-8. **Referee:** Stuart Cummings (Widnes), **Att:** 12,651,

WAKEFIELD TRINITY WILDCATS 28
WARRINGTON WOLVES 24
WILDCATS: 1 Steve Prescott, 24 Paul Sampson, 3 Francis Maloney, 2 Neil Law, 14 Paul March, 25 Bobbie Goulding, 8 Francis Stephenson, 21 Ryan Hudson, 10 Martin Masella, 11 Warren Jowitt, 12 Willie Poching, 13 Steve McNamara (C). Subs: 15 Gary Price for Poching (34), 16 Andy Fisher for Masella (31), 19 Jamie Field for Stephenson (29BB, rev 61), 27 Ben Westwood for Hudson (75), Masella for Fisher (64), Poching for Jowitt (69)
Tries: Poching (24, 79), Goulding (39), Price (42), Maloney (72). **Goals:** McNamara 4, **On report:** Steve McNamara (3) – kneeing
WOLVES: 1 Lee Penny, 3 Alan Hunte, 4 Toa Kohe-Love, 20 Ian Sibbit, 5 Mark Forster, 17 Steve Blakeley, 7 Allan Langer (C), 8 Andrew Gee, 9 Danny Farrar, 10 Danny Nutley, 14 Steve McCurrie, 12 Ian Knott, 13 Tawera Nikau. Subs: 6 Lee Briers for Penny (55), 11 Dean Busby for Knott (45), 16 Gary Chambers for Hilton (73), 18 Mark Hilton for Nutley (59), Penny for McCurrie (63)
Tries: Forster (30), Hunte (33), Nutley (46), Langer (50), McCurrie (60). **Goals:** Blakeley 2, **Sin bin:** Allan Langer (70) - holding down
League Express Men of the Match:
Wildcats: Willie Poching, **Wolves:** Danny Farrar.
Penalty count: 8-9. **Half-time:** 12-8. **Referee:** Russell Smith (Castleford), **Att:** 4,634

BRADFORD BULLS 44 CASTLEFORD TIGERS 12
BULLS: 28 Stuart Spruce, 4 Nathan McAvoy, 20 Scott Naylor, 5 Michael Withers, 14 Justin Brooker, 6 Henry Paul, 1 Robbie Paul (C), 22 Brian McDermott, 9 James Lowes, 10 Paul Anderson, 19 Jamie Peacock, 12 Mike Forshaw, 13 Brad Mackay. Subs: 29 Stuart Fielden for Anderson (21), 2 Tevita Vaikona for Naylor (52), 18 Lee Radford for Forshaw (58), 11 David Boyle for Peacock (45), Anderson for Fielden (48), Fielden for McDermott (52)
Tries: H Paul (17), Withers (46), McAvoy (52), Lowes (64, 79), Spruce (69), Fielden (75). **Goals:** H Paul 7, Field goals: H Paul, Lowes, **On report:** Fielden (27) - late tackle, **Sin bin:** Fielden (27) - late tackle
TIGERS: 20 Jamie Benn, 5 Darren Rogers, 3 Michael Eagar, 4 Logan Campbell, 16 Jon Wells, 6 Danny Orr, 7 Brad Davis, 10 Dean Sampson, 22 Andrew Purcell, 15 Darren Shaw, 11 Lee Harland, 12 Dale Fritz, 13 Adrian Vowles (C). Subs: 8 Nathan Sykes for Sampson (33), 18 Paul Smith not used, 25 Danny Arnold (D) for Benn (68), 17 Ian Tonks for Shaw (52), Sampson for Harland (52)
Tries: Harland (6), Wells (59). **Goals:** Benn 2, **Dismissal:** Sampson (74) - use of elbow
League Express Men of the Match:
Bulls: Paul Anderson, **Tigers:** Andrew Purcell
Penalty count: 8-3, **Half time:** 9-6. **Referee:** Robert Connolly (Wigan), **Att:** 15,237

LONDON BRONCOS 24 SALFORD CITY REDS 33
BRONCOS: 4 Greg Fleming, 1 Tulsen Tollett, 3 Danny Moore, 13 Mat Toshack, 5 Brett Warton, 6 Karle Hammond (C), 25 Brendan Magnus, 18 Justin Dooley, 9 Dean Callaway, 23 Steve Barrow (D), 11 Shane Millard, 12 Steele Retchless, 14 Andrew Wynyard. Subs: 2 Rob Smyth for Magnus (61), 15 Andy Johnson for Wynyard (25), 17 Anthony Seibold for Barrow (25), 21 Jon Clarke for Callaway (44), Wynyard for Dooley (66), Barrow for Seibold (71)
Tries: Tollett (2), Fleming (34, 44), Johnson (79). **Goals:** Warton 4, **Sin bin:** Hammond (68) - dissent, **Dismissal:** Hammond (68) - abusing referee
CITY REDS: 1 Gary Broadbent, 2 Nick Pinkney, 3 Kris Tassell, 30 Jason Nicol (D), 5 Martin Offiah, 12 Darren Brown (C), 7 Martin Crompton, 8 Paul Southern, 9 Malcolm Alker, 15 Neil Baynes, 23 Mike Wainwright, 11 James Smith, 29 Brad Hepi. Subs: 10 Craig Makin for Southern (29), 14 Joe Faimalo for Baynes (53), 4 Jason Webber for Tassell (11), 28 John Duffy (D) for Hepi (63), Baynes for Makin (70), Hepi for Faimalo (74), Makin for Wainwright (75BB)
Tries: Smith (26), Crompton (26), Brown (39, 47), Offiah (75). **Goals:** Brown 6, **Field goal:** Crompton
League Express Men of the Match:
Broncos: Greg Fleming, **City Reds:** Darren Brown.
Penalty count: 6-7. **Half-time:** 14-18. **Referee:** Karl Kirkpatrick (Warrington), **Att:** 2,549

ROUND 5

WARRINGTON WOLVES 44 LEEDS RHINOS 10
WOLVES: 1 Lee Penny, 3 Alan Hunte, 4 Toa Kohe-Love, 20 Ian Sibbit, 5 Mark Forster, 17 Steve Blakeley, 7 Allan Langer (C), 8 Andrew Gee, 9 Danny Farrar, 10 Danny Nutley, 21 Jerome Guisset, 12 Ian Knott, 13 Tawera Nikau. Subs: 6 Lee Briers for Blakeley (15), 16 Gary Chambers for Nutley (58), 2 Jon Roper for Forster (40), 11 Dean Busby for Knott (70), Nutley for Gee (74)
Tries: Forster (8), Sibbit (31, 79), Gee (39), Hunte (60, 64), Penny (69), Guisset (74). **Goals:** Briers (6), **Sin bin:** Gee (20) - fighting
RHINOS: 5 Francis Cummins, 22 Chev Walker, 3 Richie Blackmore, 4 Keith Senior, 14 Marcus St Hilaire, 6 Daryl Powell (C), 7 Ryan Sheridan, 8 Darren Fleary, 9 Lee Jackson, 17 Anthony Farrell, 11 Adrian Morley, 12 David Barnhill, 16 Andy Hay. Subs: 13 Kevin Sinfield for Farrell (32), 19 Dean Lawford for Jackson (40), 18 Leroy Rivett for Blackmore (63), 20 Jamie Mathiou for Fleary (25), Farrell for Powell (57), Powell for Mathiou (70)
Tries: Hay (23), Sinfield (49). **Goals:** Cummins,
League Express Men of the Match:
Wolves: Tawera Nikau, **Rhinos:** Adrian Morley.
Penalty count: 5-5. **Half-time:** 16-4. **Referee:** Robert Connolly (Wigan), **Att:** 6,948,

WIGAN WARRIORS 48 LONDON BRONCOS 6
WIGAN: 1 Kris Radlinski, 2 Brett Dallas, 3 Steve Renouf, 15 Paul Johnson, 5 Jason Robinson, 13 Andy Farrell (c), 7 Willie Peters, 8 Terry O'Connor, 9 Terry Newton, 10 Neil Cowie, 11 Mick Cassidy, 12 Denis Betts, 14 Lee Gilmour. Subs: 17 Tony Mestrov for O'Connor (29), 16 Simon Haughton for Gilmour (40), 22 Mark Reber for Newton (59), 4 Gary Connolly for Cassidy (63), O'Connor for Cowie (40), Cowie for Mestrov (67)
Tries: Cowie (9), Dallas (32, 44), Renouf (39), Radlinski (54), Robinson (61), Peters (66), Johnson (71). **Goals:** Farrell 8, **Sin bin:** Farrell (13) - holding down
BRONCOS: 4 Greg Fleming, 2 Rob Smyth, 3 Danny Moore (c), 13 Mat Toshack, 5 Brett Warton, 15 Andy Johnson, 1 Tulsen Tollett, 18 Justin Dooley, 21 Jon Clarke, 23 Steve Barrow, 11 Shane Millard, 12 Steele Retchless, 14 Andrew Wynyard. Subs: 19 Dom Peters for Millard (8 - bb - rev - 18), Peters for Warton (63), 17 Anthony Seibold for Barrow (20), 10 Scott Cram for Dooley (30), Dooley for
League Express, Men of the Match:
Wigan: Brett Dallas, **Broncos:** Shane Millard
Penalty count: 6-9, **Halftime:** 20-0, **Crowd:** 6,697.
Referee: Steve Ganson (St Helens)

HUDDERSFIELD-SHEFFIELD GIANTS 35
WAKEFIELD TRINITY WILDCATS 34
GIANTS: 14 Paul Reilly, 30 Sylvain Houles, 3 Karl Lovell, 5 Matt Crowther, 1 Waisale Sovatabua, 19 Chris Thorman, 7 Gavin Clinch, 29 Jamie Fielden, 9 Johnny Lawless, 10 Dale Laughton, 15 Darren Turner, 22 David Bradbury, 13 Jeff Hardy (C). Subs: 17 Martin Gleeson for Laughton (43), 6 Gene Ngamu not used, 18 Danny Russell for Lawless (53), 8 Steve Molloy for Fielden (23), Laughton for Bradbury (51), Turner for Laughton (70BB)
Tries: Hardy (4), Clinch (29, 72), Sovatabua (35), Lovell (51), Gleeson (59). **Goals:** Crowther 5, **Field goal:** Clinch, **On report:** Darren Turner (55) - kneeing
WILDCATS: 1 Steve Prescott, 24 Paul Sampson, 4 Tony Tatupu, 20 Adam Hughes, 2 Neil Law, 3 Francis Maloney, 25 Bobbie Goulding, 8 Francis Stephenson, 21 Ryan Hudson, 19 Jamie Field, 11 Warren Jowitt, 12 Willie Poching, 13 Steve McNamara (C). Subs: 14 Paul March for Maloney (40), 15 Gary Price for Jowitt (24), 10 Martin Masella for Field (36), 18 Paul Jackson for Stephenson (52), Maloney for Hudson (7BB)
Tries: Sampson (6), Hughes (11), Poching (21), Price (25), Law (47, 67). **Goals:** McNamara 4, Goulding
League Express Men of the Match:
Giants: Gavin Clinch, **Wildcats:** Willie Poching.
Penalty count: 7-8. **Half-time:** 16-22. **Referee:** Steve Presley (Castleford), **Att:** 3,276

SALFORD CITY REDS 1 BRADFORD BULLS 52
CITY REDS: 1 Gary Broadbent, 2 Nick Pinkney, 30 Jason Nicol, 4 Jason Webber, 5 Martin Offiah, 12 Darren Brown (C), 28 John Duffy, 8 Paul Southern, 9 Malcolm Alker, 15 Neil Baynes, 11 James Smith, 29 Brad Hepi, 23 Mike Wainwright. Subs: 10 Craig Makin for Southern (28), 3 Kris Tassell for Webber (35), 13 Craig Murdock (D) for Hepi (44), 14 Joe Faimalo for Baynes (28), Baynes for Makin (66), Webber for Murdock (76), **Field goal:** Offiah,
BULLS: 28 Stuart Spruce, 4 Nathan McAvoy, 20 Scott Naylor, 5 Michael Withers, 2 Tevita Vaikona, 1 Robbie Paul (C), 7 Paul Deacon, 22 Brian McDermott, 9 James Lowes, 29 Stuart Fielden, 11 David Boyle, 12 Mike Forshaw, 13 Brad Mackay. Subs: 6 Henry Paul for R Paul (41), 15 Hudson Smith for McDermott (26), 18 Lee Radford for Forshaw (43), 19 Jamie Peacock for Lowes (50), McDermott for Boyle (66)
Tries: Boyle (20), Mackay (28), McAvoy (32), Naylor (40), H Paul (48), Spruce (58), Withers (61, 63), McDermott (68). **Goals:** Deacon 8, **Sin bin:** Boyle (37) - holding down, **On report:** McDermott (76) - alleged late challenge
League Express Men of the Match:
City Reds: Malcolm Alker, **Bulls:** Brad Mackay.
Penalty count: 11-5. **Referee:** Stuart Cummings (Widnes). **Half-time:** 1-22, **Att:** 6,468

ST HELENS 52 HALIFAX BLUE SOX 20
SAINTS: 17 Paul Wellens, 2 Chris Smith, 3 Kevin Iro, 15 Sean Hoppe, 5 Anthony Sullivan, 20 Tommy Martyn, 7 Sean Long, 8 Apollo Perelini, 9 Keiron Cunningham, 10 Julian O'Neill, 11 Chris Joynt (C), 12 Fereti Tuilagi, 13 Paul Sculthorpe. Subs: 18 Bryan Henare for O'Neill (56), 24 Steve Hall for Sculthorpe (60), 26 John Stankevitch for Tuilagi (34), 16 Vila Matautia for O'Neill (16), O'Neill for Matautia (40), Tuilagi for Martyn (46)
Tries: Long (3), Iro (7), Martyn (21, 44), Cunningham (33, 59), Wellens (37), Perelini (41), Hall (79).. **Goals:** Long 8, **Sin bin:** Stankevitch (54) ball-stealing.
BLUE SOX: 1 Daryl Cardiss, 12 Jamie Bloem, 6 Greg Florimo (C), 4 Marvin Golden, 5 Phil Hassan, 14 Martin Pearson, 7 Andrew Dunemann, 23 Brett Goldspink, 9 Paul Rowley, 10 Jim Gannon, 11 Gary Mercer, 19 David Foster, 13 Martin Moana. Subs: 8 Andy Hobson for Goldspink (26) (bb), 21 Gael Tallec for Moana (45), 15 Lokeni Savelio for Gannon (68), 27 Jim Naylor for Foster (45), Goldspink for Hobson (28) (bb), Hobson for Goldspink (58), Foster for Bloem (77)
Tries: Cardiss (12, 55), Pearson (14, 72).. **Goals:** Pearson 2, **Sin bin:** Gannon (58) - off the ball tackle
League Express Men of the Match:
St Helens: Keiron Cunningham, **Blue Sox:** Daryl Cardiss.
Half-time: 30-10, **Penalty count:** 9-5. **Referee:** Karl Kirkpatrick (Warrington), **Att:** 8,571

CASTLEFORD TIGERS 22 HULL FC 12
TIGERS: 1 Jason Flowers, 16 Jon Wells, 4 Logan Campbell, 3 Michael Eagar, 5 Darren Rogers, 6 Danny Orr, 7 Brad Davis, 15 Darren Shaw, 9 Aaron Raper (c), 17 Ian Tonks, 12 Dale Fritz, 11 Lee Harland, 13 Adrian Vowles. Subs: 8 Nathan Sykes for Fritz (25), Fritz for Harland (65), 22 Andrew Purcell for Tonks (25), Tonks for Shaw (58), 18 Paul Smith for Sykes (72), 25 Danny Arnold - not used
Tries: Eagar (16, 60), Davis (21, 72). **Goals:** Orr 3
HULL: 1 Ben Sammut, 17 Brian Carney, 14 Steve Collins, 4 Craig Simon, 2 Matt Daylight, 7 Will Robinson, 20 Richard Horne, 8 Paul Broadbent, 9 Mick Jenkins, 10 Andrew Hick, 11 Craig Wilson, 13 Tony Grimaldi (c), 15 David Maiden. Subs: 3 Deon Bird for Simon (50), Simon for Daylight (51), 19 Paul King for Jenkins (12 - bb - rev 19), 12 Luke Felsch for Broadbent (26), Broadbent for

Felsch (64), 18 Wayne McDonald for Hick (26)
Tries: Daylight (43), Simon (47). Goals: Sammut 2
League Express Men of the Match: Tigers: Aaron Raper, Hull: Wayne McDonald. Penalty count: 6-7. Half-time: 10-0. Referee: John Connolly (Wigan), Att: 8,358

ROUND 6

ST HELENS 38 WIGAN WARRIORS 14
SAINTS: 17 Paul Wellens, 2 Chris Smith, 3 Kevin Iro, 15 Sean Hoppe, 5 Anthony Sullivan, 20 Tommy Martyn, 7 Sean Long, 8 Apollo Perelini, 9 Keiron Cunningham, 10 Julian O'Neill, 14 Fereti Tuilagi, 26 John Stankevitch, 11 Chris Joynt (C). Subs: 12 Sonny Nickle for O'Neill (21), 24 Steve Hall for Hoppe (22BB, rev 36), O'Neill for Perelini (48), 18 Bryan Henare for Tuilagi (49), Tuilagi for Stankevitch (68), Perelini for O'Neill (70), Hall for Smith (72), 30 Mike Bennett (D) for Nickle (79)
Tries: O'Neill (13), Iro (16, 67, 74), Martyn (32, 77). **Goals**: Long 7
WARRIORS: 1 Kris Radlinski, 2 Brett Dallas, 15 Paul Johnson, 3 Steve Renouf, 5 Jason Robinson, 6 Tony Smith, 7 Willie Peters, 8 Terry O'Connor, 9 Terry Newton, 10 Neil Cowie, 11 Mick Cassidy, 12 Denis Betts, 13 Andy Farrell. Subs: 4 Gary Connolly for Renouf (10), 17 Tony Mestrov for O'Connor (29), 16 Simon Haughton for Cassidy (40), 14 Lee Gilmour for Connolly (45BB, rev 59), Gilmour for Robinson (59BB, rev 66), Gilmour for Connolly (69), O'Connor for Mestrov (69)
Tries: Johnson (4), Radlinski (52). **Goals:** Farrell 3
League Express Men of the Match: Saints: Paul Wellens, **Warriors:** Denis Betts.. **Penalty count:** 7-6. **Half-time**: 20-8. **Referee:** Stuart Cummings (Widnes), **Att:** 13,307

BRADFORD BULLS 32 LONDON BRONCOS 12
BULLS: 28 Stuart Spruce, 2 Tevita Vaikona, 20 Scott Naylor, 5 Michael Withers, 14 Justin Brooker, 3 Leon Pryce, 7 Paul Deacon, 22 Brian McDermott, 9 James Lowes (C), 10 Paul Anderson, 19 Jamie Peacock, 12 Mike Forshaw, 13 Brad Mackay. Subs: 23 Bernard Dwyer for Peacock (23), 15 Hudson Smith for Anderson (28), 18 Lee Radford for Naylor (45), 14 Nathan McAvoy for Withers (51), Peacock for Radford (55), Withers for Vaikona (67BB), Anderson for Smith (71)
Tries: Lowes (5), Naylor (11, 37), Spruce (17), Anderson (80). **Goals:** Deacon 6
BRONCOS: 4 Greg Fleming, 16 Frank Napoli, 3 Danny Moore, 13 Mat Toshack, 19 Dominic Peters, 15 Andy Johnson, 1 Tulsen Tollett, 18 Justin Dooley, 21 Jon Clarke, 17 Anthony Seibold, 27 Paul Davidson, 12 Steele Retchless, 14 Andrew Wynyard. Subs: 9 Dean Callaway for Clarke (26), 11 Shane Millard for Retchless (49), 10 Scott Cram for Seibold (40), 28 Kevin Crouthers (D) for Dooley (62), Clarke for Callaway (69)
Tries: Wynyard (32), Davidson (49). **Goals:** Tollett 2.
League Express Men of the Match:
Bulls: Brian McDermott. **Broncos:** Dominic Peters
Penalty count: 6-5. **Half-time:** 24-6.
Referee: Karl Kirkpatrick (Warrington), **Att**: 13, 239

LEEDS RHINOS 20
HUDDERSFIELD-SHEFFIELD GIANTS 10
RHINOS: 1 Iestyn Harris (C), 14 Marcus St Hilaire, 5 Francis Cummins, 4 Keith Senior, 22 Chev Walker, 13 Kevin Sinfield, 7 Ryan Sheridan, 8 Darren Fleary, 19 Dean Lawford, 10 Barrie McDermott, 11 Adrian Morley, 16 Andy Hay, 6 Daryl Powell. Subs: 18 Leroy Rivett for Cummins (5BB, rev 50), 20 Jamie Mathiou for McDermott (31), 12 David Barnhill for Sinfield (34), Rivett for Powell (51), McDermott for Fleary (55), 17 Anthony Farrell for Morley (61), Sinfield for Hay (71)
Tries: Morley (2), Sheridan (28, 60). **Goals:** Harris 4, **Sin bin:** Senior (19) - obstruction; St Hilaire (77) - obstruction.
GIANTS: 14 Paul Reilly, 30 Sylvain Houles, 3 Karl Lovell, 5 Matt Crowther, 1 Waisale Sovatabua, 19 Chris Thorman, 7 Gavin Clinch, 8 Steve Molloy, 9 Johnny Lawless, 10 Dale Laughton, 15 Darren Turner, 12 Richard Marshall, 13 Jeff Hardy (C). Subs: 21 Chris Molyneux for Laughton (10), 17 Martin Gleeson for Molloy (31), Laughton for Marshall (35), 6 Gene Ngamu for Reilly (53), Marshall for Turner (68), Molloy for Laughton (78), 18 Danny Russell not used
Try: Hardy (77). **Goals:** Crowther 3
League Express Men of the Match: Rhinos: Leroy Rivett, **Giants:** Jeff Hardy. **Penalty count:** 11-7. **Half-time:** 10-2. **Referee:** John Connolly (Wigan), **Att:** 10,705

HULL FC 26 SALFORD CITY REDS 22
HULL: 1 Ben Sammut, 17 Brian Carney, 14 Steve Collins, 15 David Maiden, 5 Ian Herron, 7 Will Robinson, 20 Richard Horne, 10 Andrew Hick, 9 Mick Jenkins, 12 Luke Felsch, 16 Adam Maher, 18 Wayne McDonald, 13 Tony Grimaldi (C). Subs: 8 Paul Broadbent for McDonald (30), 11 Craig Wilson for Hick (30), 3 Dean Bird for Carney (ht), 4 Craig Simon for Maher (56), McDonald for Felsch (62), Hick for Broadbent (68BB), Felsch for Wilson (74)
Tries: Robinson (2), Horne (4, 58), Collins (43), Bird (71). **Goals:** Sammut 3
CITY REDS: 1 Gary Broadbent, 2 Nick Pinkney, 3 Kris Tassell, 4 Jason Webber, 5 Martin Offiah, 12 Darren Brown (C), 7 Martin Crompton, 8 Paul Southern, 9 Malcolm Alker, 15 Neil Baynes, 11 James Smith, 14 Joe Faimalo, 23 Mike Wainwright. Subs: 17 Mark Johnson for Tassell (20BB), 10 Craig Makin for Baynes (33), 16 Paul Highton for Faimalo (31), Faimalo for Southern (62), Southern for Makin (71), 28 John Duffy not used
Tries: Tassell (13), Offiah (19), Webber (28, 48), Crompton (56). **Goals:** Southern
League Express Men of the Match: Hull: Richard Horne, **City Reds:** Martin Crompton. **Penalty count:** 4-5. **Half-time:** 12-14. **Referee:** Robert Connolly (Wigan), **Att:** 5,862

HALIFAX BLUE SOX 20 WARRINGTON WOLVES 30
BLUE SOX: 1 Daryl Cardiss, 17 Oliver Marns, 6 Greg Florimo (C), 4 Marvin Golden, 3 Damian Gibson, 7 Andrew Dunemann, 14 Martin Pearson, 23 Brett Goldspink, 9 Paul Rowley, 15 Lokeni Savelio, 11 Gary Mercer, 21 Gael Tallec, 12 Jamie Bloem. Subs: 8 Andy Hobson for Savelio (27), 13 Martin Moana for Goldspink (32), 27 Jim Naylor for Cardiss (35), Goldspink for Tallec (52), Savelio for Hobson (68), 18 Mike Peters not used
Tries: Rowley (10), Mercer (14), Tallec (17), Florimo (63). **Goals:** Pearson 2
WOLVES: 1 Lee Penny, 2 Jon Roper, 20 Ian Sibbit, 4 Toa Kohe-Love, 3 Alan Hunte, 17 Steve Blakeley, 7 Allan Langer (C), 8 Andrew Gee, 9 Danny Farrar, 10 Danny Nutley, 21 Jerome Guisset, 12 Ian Knott, 13 Tawera Nikau. Subs: 14 Steve McCurrie for Guisset (26), 7 Lee Briers for Blakeley (59), 16 Gary Chambers for Gee (67), 11 Dean Busby for McCurrie (75), McCurrie for Nutley (79)
Tries: Farrar (5), Kohe-Love (30, 51), Hunte (33), Briers (77). **Goals:** Blakeley 3, Briers 2
League Express Men of the Match: Blue Sox: Greg Florimo (C). **Wolves:** Ian Knott
Half time: 16-16. **Referee:** Steve Presley (Castleford), **Att:** 6,123. **Penalty count:** 4-7

WAKEFIELD TRINITY WILDCATS 12
CASTLEFORD TIGERS 22
WILDCATS: 1 Steve Prescott, 24 Paul Sampson, 4 Tony Tatupu, 20 Adam Hughes, 2 Neil Law, 14 Paul March, 25 Bobbie Goulding, 8 Francis Stephenson, 21 Ryan Hudson, 19 Jamie Field, 15 Gary Price, 12 Willie Poching, 13 Steve McNamara (C). Subs: 10 Martin Masella for Stephenson (25), 16 Andy Fisher for Field (30), 6 Tony Kemp for Hudson (40), 18 Paul Jackson for Price (50BB, rev 60), Jackson for Poching (64), Stephenson for Masella (66), Hudson for Kemp (72)
Tries: Prescott (28). **Goals:** McNamara 4
TIGERS: 1 Jason Flowers, 16 Jon Wells, 3 Michael Eagar, 4 Logan Campbell, 5 Darren Rogers, 6 Danny Orr, 7 Brad Davis, 10 Dean Sampson, 9 Aaron Raper, 15 Darren Shaw, 11 Lee Harland, 12 Dale Fritz, 13 Adrian Vowles (C). Subs: 17 Ian Tonks for Shaw (23), 22 Andrew Purcell for Harland (50), 8 Nathan Sykes for Sampson (54), Harland for Fritz (65), 25 Danny Arnold for Wells (73), Sampson for Tonks (73)
Tries: Rogers (7), Orr (33), Eagar (68), Wells (71). **Goals:** Orr 3
League Express Men of the Match: Wildcats: Steve McNamara. **Tigers:** Michael Eagar. **Penalty count:** 10-10. **Half-time:** 10-10. **Referee:** Steve Ganson (St Helens). **Att:** 6,138

ROUND 7

WARRINGTON WOLVES 34 ST HELENS 47
WOLVES: 1 Lee Penny, 3 Alan Hunte, 4 Toa Kohe-Love, 20 Ian Sibbit, 2 Jon Roper, 17 Steve Blakeley, 7 Allan Langer (C), 8 Andrew Gee, 9 Danny Farrar, 10 Danny Nutley, 14 Steve McCurrie, 12 Ian Knott, 13 Tawera Nikau, Subs, 18 Mark Hilton for Gee (50), 6 Lee Briers for Blakeley (62), 21 Jerome Guisset for McCurrie (65), 16 Gary Chambers for Nutley (67), McCurrie for Guisset (72)
Tries: Penny (10, 77), Gee (13), Nikau (36), Blakeley (39), Langer (55), **Goals:** Blakeley 4, Briers , **On report:** Kohe-Love (1) - alleged high tackle, Sin bin: Penny (63) - professional foul
SAINTS: 17 Paul Wellens, 2 Chris Smith, 3 Kevin Iro, 15 Sean Hoppe, 5 Anthony Sullivan, 20 Tommy Martyn, 7 Sean Long, 8 Apollo Perelini, 9 Keiron Cunningham, 10 Julian O'Neill, 14 Fereti Tuilagi, 26 John Stankevich, 11 Chris Joynt (C), Subs, 18 Bryan Henare for Stankevich (46), 24 Steve Hall for Hoppe (75), 12 Sonny Nickle for O'Neill (20), 30 Mike Bennett for Joynt (75), O'Neill for Perelini (50), Perelini for Tuilagi (65), Stankevich for Perelini (74)
Tries: Long (3, 73), Hoppe (27), Iro (31), Perelini (51), Tuilagi (59), Nickle (79), **Goals:** Long 9, **Field goal:** Martyn, **On report:** O'Neill (18) - alleged high tackle, **Sin bin:** Joynt (19) – dissent
Penalty count: 6-9, **Half-time:** 22-16, **Referee:** Russell Smith (Castleford), **Att** 9,086
League Express Men of the Match: Saints: Sean Long, **Wolves:** Allan Langer

WIGAN WARRIORS 30 CASTLEFORD TIGERS 16
(from Round 13)
WARRIORS: 18 Wes Davies, 2 Brett Dallas, 1 Kris Radlinski, 14 Lee Gilmour, 5 Jason Robinson, 6 Tony Smith, 7 Willie Peters, 23 Brady Malam, 9 Terry Newton, 10 Neil Cowie, 11 Mick Cassidy, 12 Denis Betts, 13 Andy Farrell (C), Subs, 26 David Hodgson (D) for Dallas (44BB), 8 Terry O'Connor for Cowie (51), 16 Simon Haughton for Malam (51), 22 Mark Reber for Newton (59), Malam for Cassidy (69), Newton for Reber (72),
Tries: Farrell (5), Dallas (31), Newton (55), Peters (58), Hodgson (71), **Goals:** Farrell 5
TIGERS: 1 Jason Flowers, 16 Jon Wells, 3 Michael Eager, 4 Logan Campbell, 5 Darren Rogers, 6 Danny Orr, 7 Brad Davis, 10 Dean Sampson, 9 Aaron Raper, 15 Darren Shaw, 11 Lee Harland, 12 Dale Fritz, 13 Adrian Vowles (C), Subs, 22 Andrew Purcell for Davis (23), 25 Danny Arnold for Wells (24), 8 Nathan Sykes for Shaw (32), 17 Ian Tonks for Fritz (56), Fritz for Sampson (70), Shaw for Fritz (72), **Tries:** Davis (8), Sampson (46), Flowers (66), **Goals:** Orr 2
League Express Men of the Match:
Warriors: Andy Farrell , **Tigers:** Danny Orr
Penalty count: 6-8, **Half-time:** 12-6, **Referee:** Stuart Cummings (Widnes), Att 10,098

SALFORD CITY REDS 14
WAKEFIELD TRINITY WILDCATS 22
REDS: 1 Gary Broadbent, 2 Nick Pinkney, 3 Kris Tassell, 30 Jason Nicol, 5 Martin Offiah, 28 John Duffy, 7 Martin Crompton, 8 Paul Southern, 9 Malcolm Alker, 10 Craig Makin, 29 Brad Hepi, 11 Jim Smith, 23 Mike Wainwright, Subs, 14 Joe Faimalo for Southern (19), 16 Paul Highton for Hepi (19), 17 Mark Johnson not used, 13 Craig Murdock for Duffy (59), Southern for Faimalo (62), Duffy for Crompton (68)
Tries: Makin (23), Tassell (63), **Goals**: Duffy, Southern 2
Sin bin : Broadbent (14) - holding down
WILDCATS: 1 Steve Prescott, 24 Paul Sampson, 20 Adam Hughes, 4 Tony Tatupu, 2 Neil Law, 25 Bobbie Goulding, 7 Glen Tomlinson, 8 Francis Stephenson, 21 Ryan Hudson, 18 Paul Jackson, 15 Gary Price, 12 Willie Poching, 13 Steve McNamara, Subs, 14 Paul March for Law (30), 17 Steve Watene for Stephenson (40), 19 Jamie Field for Watene (52), 16 Andy Fisher for Price (49), Price for Goulding (59), Goulding for Hughes (74)
Tries: Hughes (2), Sampson (17), March (37, 70),
Goals: McNamara 3, **Penalty count:** 7-4,
League Express Men of the Match:
Reds: Jason Nicol **Wildcats:** Glen Tomlinson
Half-time: 6-18, **Referee:** John Connolly (Wigan)
Att 4, 224

LONDON BRONCOS 13 HULL FC 8
BRONCOS: 4 Greg Fleming, 16 Frank Napoli, 3 Danny Moore, 13 Mat Toshack, 19 Dom Peters, 6 Karle Hammond (C), 1 Tulsen Tollett, 18 Justin Dooley, 21 Jon Clarke, 10 Scott Cram, 27 Paul Davidson, 11 Shane Millard, 14 Andrew Wynyard. Subs: 9 Dean Callaway for Clarke (31BB, rev 68), 12 Steele Retchless for Cram (12), 15 Andy Johnson for Millard (62), 28 Kevin Crouthers for Moore (31), Cram for Dooley (62), Dooley for Retchless (68)
Tries: Tollett (4), Davidson (33), **Goals:** Tollett 2 , **Field goal:** Hammond
Sin bin : Dooley (19) - holding down.
On report: Davidson - alleged bite on Robinson
HULL FC: 1 Ben Sammut, 17 Brian Carney, 14 Steve Collins, 4 Craig Simon, 5 Ian Herron, 7 Will Robinson, 20 Richard Horne, 8 Paul Broadbent, 19 Paul King, 12 Luke Felsch, 18 Wayne McDonald, 13 Tony Grimaldi (C), 15 David Maiden, Subs, 10 Andrew Hick for Broadbent (26), 16 Adam Maher for McDonald (27), 3 Dean Bird for Herron (50), 11 Craig Wilson for King (51BB), McDonald for Carney (51), Broadbent for Felsch (62BB, rev 67)
Try: Simon (59), **Goals:** Herron 2
Penalty count: 8-13, **Half-time:** 12-4,
Referee: Steve Ganson (St Helens), **Att** 2,588
League Express Men of the Match:
Broncos: Paul Davidson, **Hull FC:** Craig Simon

HUDDERSFIELD-SHEFFIELD GIANTS 24
HALIFAX BLUE SOX 30
GIANTS: 6 Gene Ngamu, 14 Paul Reilly, 3 Karl Lovell, 17 Martin Gleeson, 30 Sylvain Houles, 19 Chris Thorman, 7 Gavin Clinch, 11 David Lomax, 18 Danny Russell, 10 Dale Laughton, 15 Darren Turner, 12 Richard Marshall, 13 Jeff Hardy (C). Subs: 8 Steve Molloy for Laughton (22), 1 Waisale Sovatabua for Lomax (45), 9 Johnny Lawless for Hardy (48), 31 Yacine Dekkiche for Molloy (63), Lomax for Marshall (65), Molloy for Houles (75),
Tries: Houles (23), Lovell (49), Ngamu (69), **Goals:** Ngamu 6
BLUE SOX: 1 Daryl Cardiss, 17 Oliver Marns, 6 Greg Florimo (C), 4 Marvin Golden, 3 Damian Gibson, 7 Andrew Dunemann, 14 Martin Pearson, 23 Brett Goldspink, 9 Paul Rowley, 15 Lokeni Savelio, 11 Gary Mercer, 12 Jamie Bloem, 13 Martin Moana. Subs: 8 Andy Hobson for Savelio (24), 21 Gael Tallec for Goldspink (56), Goldspink for Hobson (64), 19 David Foster for Bloem (66), 18 Mike Peters not used
Tries: Cardiss (11), Moana (14), Bloem (36), Dunemann (66), Gibson (75), **Goals:** Pearson 5, **On report:** Marns (33) - contact with knees in tackle
League Express Men of the Match: Giants: Gene Ngamu, **Blue Sox:** Andrew Dunemann
Penalty count: 7-6, **Half-time:** 12-18, **Referee:** Bob Connolly (Wigan), **Att** 2,982

ROUND 8

HALIFAX BLUE SOX 14 CASTLEFORD TIGERS 20
BLUE SOX: 1 Daryl Cardiss, 27 Jim Naylor, 3 Damian Gibson, 4 Marvin Golden, 17 Oliver Marns, 7 Andrew Dunemann, 14 Martin Pearson, 23 Brett Goldspink, 9 Paul Rowley, 10 Jim Gannon, 11 Gary Mercer, 12 Jamie Bloem, 13 Martin Moana. Subs: 8 Andy Hobson for Goldspink (24), 21 Gael Tallec for Bloem (33), Goldspink for Hobson (61), 19 David Foster not used, 5 Phil Hassan not used, **Tries:** Tallec (49), Marns (57), **Goals:** Pearson 3, **On report:** Moana (77) - hight tackle
TIGERS: 1 Jason Flowers, 16 Jon Wells, 4 Logan Campbell, 3 Michael Eagar, 5 Darren Rogers, 6 Danny Orr, 9 Aaron Raper , 10 Dean Sampson, 17 Ian Tonks, 15 Darren Shaw, 11 Lee Harland, 18 Paul Smith, 13 Adrian Vowles (C). Subs: 8 Nathan Sykes for Shaw (23), Shaw for Smith (31BB, rev 51), 19 Andy Lynch for Sampson (44), 20 Jamie Benn for Tonks (64), Shaw for Smith (66), Tonks for Lynch (73BB, rev 77), 25 Danny Arnold not used, **Tries:** Smith (31), Orr (33), Lynch (45), Harland (70), **Goals:** Orr, Benn
League Express Men of the Match:
Blue Sox: Daryl Cardiss, **Tigers:** Lee Harland
Half-time: 2-10, **Referee:** John Connolly (Wigan), **Att** 5,160, **Penalty count**: 5-6

HULL FC 8 BRADFORD BULLS 8
HULL FC: 1 Ben Sammut, 21 Craig Poucher, 14 Steve Collins, 15 David Maiden, 3 Deon Bird, 20 Richard Horne, 7 Will Robinson, 10 Andrew Hick, 9 Mick Jenkins, 12 Luke Felsch, 16 Adam Maher, 18 Wayne McDonald, 13 Tony Grimaldi. Subs: 8 Paul Broadbent for Hick (29), 6 Stanley Gene for Jenkins (33), Jenkins for Sammut (45), Wilson for Gene (53BB, rev 63), 11 Craig Wilson for Maher (69), Hick for Felsch (71), 24 Matt Schultz not used, **Tries:** Bird (33), Collins (75)
BULLS: 26 Paul Sykes, 2 Tevita Vaikona, 20 Scott Naylor, 11 David Boyle, 3 Leon Pryce, 1 Robbie Paul, 7 Paul Deacon, 29 Stuart Fielden, 9 James Lowes, 8 Neil Harmon, 15 Hudson Smith, 23 Bernard Dwyer, 18 Lee Radford. Subs: 10 Paul Anderson for Harmon (20), 19 Jamie Peacock for Smith (30), 12 Mike Forshaw for Fielden (40), 13 Brad Mackay for Radford (50), Smith for Anderson (59), Harmon for Dwyer (63BB, rev 74), Anderson for Harmon (79), **Tries:** Pryce (20), **Goals:** Deacon 2
League Express Men of the Match:
Hull: Deon Bird, **Bulls:** David Boyle
Penalty count: 8-6, **Half-time:** 4-8, **Referee:** Stuart Cummings (Widnes), **Att** 7,886

LEEDS RHINOS 42 SALFORD CITY REDS 16
RHINOS: 14 Marcus St Hilaire, 21 Karl Pratt, 22 Chev Walker, 4 Keith Senior, 5 Francis Cummins, 1 Iestyn Harris, 7 Ryan Sheridan, 23 Danny Ward, 19 Dean Lawford, 10 Barrie McDermott, 11 Adrian Morley, 12 David Barnhill, 13 Kevin Sinfield, Subs:, 20 Jamie Mathiou for McDermott (26), 9 Lee Jackson form Lawford (29), 16 Andy Hay for Morley (40), 33 Graham Mackay (D) for Senior (58), McDermott for Ward (49), Lawford for Sheridan (73), **Tries:** Pratt (18,49) Senior (22), Barnhill (21), Sheridan (51), Harris (62), Mackay (64), McDermott (75). **Goals:** Harris 5
CITY REDS: 1 Gary Broadbent, 2 Nick Pinkney, 30 Jason Nicol, 4 Jason Webber, 5 Marin Offiah, 19 Simon Svabic, 22 Mark Lee, 8 Paul Southern, 9 Malcom Alker, 15 Neil Baynes, 11 James Smith, 16 Paul Highton, 28 Mike Wainwright, Subs:, 14 Joe Faimalo for Smith (31), 3 Kris Tassell for Offiah (36), 29 Brad Hepi for Faimalo (50), 19 John Duffy for Svabic (66), Smith for Baynes (51), Faimalo for Highton (69), **Tries:** Offiah (11), Faimalo (39), Broadbent (42). **Goals:** Svabic 2
League Express Men of the Match:
Leeds: Iestyn Harris, **Salford:** Mark Lee
Penalty Count: 9-4, **Half time:** 16-10, **Referee:** Karl Kirkpatrick , **Att:** 10,008

ST HELENS 50 HUDDERSFIELD-SHEFFIELD GIANTS 30
SAINTS: 17 Paul Wellens, 2 Chris Smith, 3 Kevin Iro, 15 Sean Hoppe, 5 Anthony Sullivan, 20 Tommy Martyn, 7 Sean Long, 8 Apollo Perelini, 9 Keiron Cunningham, 12 Sonny Nickle, 14 Fereti Tuilagi, 26 John Stankevitch, 11 Chris Joynt (C). Subs: 10 Julian O'Neill for Perelini (35), 24 Steve Hall for Long (28), 18 Bryan Henare for Nickle (40), 30 Mike Bennett for Tuilagi (65), Perelini for Wellens (55), Tuilagi for Stankevitch (69)
Tries: Hoppe (1), Iro (11, 18, 37, 55, 72), Perelini (20, 62), Stankevitch (23), Joynt (46).
Goals: Long 3, Martyn 2
GIANTS: 6 Gene Ngamu, 30 Sylvain Houles, 3 Karl Lovell, 1 Waisale Sovatabua, 31 Yacine Dekkiche, 19 Chris Thorman, 7 Gavin Clinch, 8 Steve Molloy (C), 9 Johnny Lawless, 11 David Lomax, 22 David Bradbury, 12 Richard Marshall, 15 Darren Turner. Subs: 23 Dale Cardoza for Bradbury (40), 21 Chris Molyneux for Lomax (40), 14 Paul Reilly for Sovatabua (69), 18 Danny Russell for Molloy (26), Lomax for Turner (55), Molloy for Marshall (60)
Tries: Sovatabua (4, 50), Lawless (34), Cardoza (69), Ngamu (75). **Goals:** Ngamu 5
League Express Men of the Match:
Saints: Kevin Iro, **Giants**: Gene Ngamu.
Half-time: 34-12. **Referee:** Robert Connolly (Wigan), **Att:** 8, 518. **Penalty count:** 7-9

WARRINGTON WOLVES 16 WIGAN WARRIORS 42
WOLVES: 1 Lee Penny, 3 Alan Hunte, 4 Toa Kohe-Love, 20 Ian Sibbit, 2 Jon Roper, 6 Lee Briers, 7 Allan Langer (C), 8 Andrew Gee, 9 Danny Farrar, 10 Danny Nutley, 14 Steve McCurrie, 12 Ian Knott, 13 Tawera Nikau. Subs: 18 Mark Hilton for Gee (29BB, rev 40), 21 Jerome Guisset for McCurrie (49), Hilton for Nutley (51), McCurrie for Knott (61), 16 Gary Chambers for Gee (66), 17 Steve Blakeley for Briers (72)
Tries: Knott (33), Roper (37), Briers (40).
Goals: Briers 2,
WARRIORS: 1 Kris Radlinski, 2 Brett Dallas, 14 Lee Gilmour, 3 Steve Renouf, 5 Jason Robinson, 13 Andy Farrell (C), 7 Willie Peters, 23 Brady Malam, 9 Terry Newton, 10 Neil Cowie, 11 Mick Cassidy, 16 Simon Haughton, 12 Dennis Betts. Subs: 8 Terry O'Connor for Cowie (27), 19 Chris Chester for Cassidy (49), Cowie for Malam (49), 26 David Hodgson for Peters (66), 18 Wes Davies for Radlinski (68), Cassidy for Newton (75)
Tries: Radlinski (15), Renouf (18, 48), Robinson (52), O'Connor (58), Haughton (64), Betts (76).
Goals: Farrell 7
League Express Men of the Match:
Wolves: Lee Briers, **Warriors:** Terry Newton
Penalty count: 7-6. **Half-time:** 16-12. **Referee:** Russell Smith (Castleford), **Att:** 7, 983

WAKEFIELD TRINITY WILDCATS 10
LONDON BRONCOS 14
WILDCATS: 1 Steve Prescott, 24 Paul Sampson, 20 Adam Hughes, 4 Tony Tatupu, 5 Bright Sodje, 25 Bobbie Goulding, 7 Glen Tomlinson, 8 Francis Stephenson, 21 Ryan Hudson, 18 Paul Jackson, 15 Gary Price, 12 Willie Poching, 13 Steve McNamara (C). Subs: 14 Paul March for Hudson (54), 17 Frank Watene for Jackson (29), 19 Jamie Field for Stephenson (32), 16 Andy Fisher for Tatupu (53), Stephenson for Watene (60), Jackson for Field (71)
Try: Tomlinson (77), **Goal:** McNamara 3
BRONCOS: 4 Greg Fleming, 16 Frank Napoli, 22 John Timu, 13 Mat Toshack, 19 Dominic Peters, 6 Karle Hammond (C), 1 Tulsen Tollett, 18 Justin Dooley, 21 Jon Clarke, 10 Scott Cram, 11 Shane Millard, 15 Andy Johnson, 14 Andrew Wynyard. Subs: 9 Dean Callaway for Clarke (22), 12 Steele Retchless for Cram (29), 17 Anthony Seibold for Millard (56), 28 Kevin Crouthers for Timu (58), Clarke for Callaway (67), Cram for Dooley (67),
Tries: Peters (28) Callaway (45). **Goals:** Tollett 3
League Express Men of the Match:
Wildcats: Willie Poching. **Broncos:** Karle Hammond.
Penalty count: 12-7. **Half-time:** 4-6. **Referee:** Steve Ganson (St Helens), **Att:** 4,695

ROUND 9

CASTLEFORD TIGERS 22 ST HELENS 32
TIGERS: 1 Jason Flowers, 16 Jon Wells, 4 Logan Campbell, 3 Michael Eagar, 5 Darren Rogers, 6 Danny Orr, 22 Andrew Purcell, 10 Dean Sampson, 17 Ian Tonks, 15 Darren Shaw, 11 Lee Harland, 18 Paul Smith, 13 Adrian Vowles (C). Subs: 19 Andy Lynch for Tonks (65), 8 Nathan Sykes for Smith (41), 23 Craig Wright for Shaw (55), 25 Danny Arnold for Harland (17), Smith for Flowers (59)
Tries: Shaw (17), Purcell (51), Rogers (70, 73). **Goals**: Orr 3
SAINTS: 1 Paul Atcheson, 15 Sean Hoppe, 3 Kevin Iro, 4 Paul Newlove, 5 Anthony Sullivan, 13 Paul Sculthorpe, 20 Tommy Martyn, 8 Apollo Perelini, 9 Keiron Cunningham, 10 Julian O'Neill, 12 Sonny Nickle, 14 Fereti Tuilagi, 11 Chris Joynt (C). Subs: 2 Chris Smith for Nickle (26), 26 John Stankevitch for Cunningham (26), 18 Bryan Henare for O'Neill (30BB, rev 41), 30 Mike Bennett for Atcheson (38BB, rev 41), Henare for O'Neill (55), Bennett for Tuilagi (61), O'Neill for Perelini (64), Perelini for Newlove (68)
Tries: Sullivan (9, 54), Iro (14), Joynt (26), Stankevitch (32), Martyn (58). **Goals:** Martyn 4
League Express Men of the Match:
Tigers: Dean Sampson, **Saints:** Tommy Martyn.
Penalty count: 7-2. **Half-time:** 4-22. **Referee:** Stuart Cummings (Widnes), **Att:** 7,564

LONDON BRONCOS 6 LEEDS RHINOS 38
BRONCOS: 4 Greg Fleming, 16 Frank Napoli, 22 John Timu, 13 Mat Toshack, 19 Dom Peters, 6 Karle Hammond (C), 1 Tulsen Tollett, 18 Justin Dooley, 21 Jon Clarke, 10 Scott Cram, 15 Andy Johnson, 11 Shane Millard, 14 Andrew Wynyard. Subs: 9 Dean Callaway for Clarke (22), 12 Steele Retchless for Cram (24), 17 Anthony Seibold for Johnson (22BB, rev 37), 29 Glen Air for Fleming (43), Cram for Dooley (62), Clarke for Timu (66BB), Dooley for Retchless (70)
Try: Peters (64), **Goal:** Tollett, **Dismissal:** Seibold (70) - high tackle on Harris, **On report:** Dooley - high tackle on Jackson
RHINOS: 1 Iestyn Harris (C), 21 Karl Pratt, 3 Richie Blackmore, 4 Keith Senior, 5 Francis Cummins, 6 Daryl Powell, 7 Ryan Sheridan, 8 Darren Fleary, 19 Dean Lawford, 10 Barrie McDermott, 12 David Barnhill, 17 Anthony Farrell, 16 Andy Hay. Subs: 20 Jamie Mathiou for Fleary (17BB, rev 22), Mathiou for McDermott (23), 9 Lee Jackson for Lawford (27), Lawford for Jackson (38BB, rev ht), 11 Adrian Morley for Barnhill (49), 14 Marcus St Hilaire for Hay (49), McDermott for Fleary (54BB, rev 67), Lawford for Harris (72)
Tries: Senior (44), Sheridan (54, 58), Cummins (60), Jackson (68), Morley (77). **Goals:** Harris 7
League Express Men of the Match:
Broncos: Shane Millard, **Rhinos:** Darren Fleary.
Penalty count: 6-8. Half-time: 2-4. **Referee:** Steve Presley (Castleford), **Att:** 2,749

BRADFORD BULLS 44
WAKEFIELD TRINITY WILDCATS 16
BULLS: 28 Stuart Spruce, 2 Tevita Vaikona, 20 Scott Naylor, 14 Justin Brooker, 3 Leon Pryce, 6 Henry Paul, 7 Paul Deacon, 22 Brian McDermott, 9 James Lowes (C), 29 Stuart Fielden, 15 Hudson Smith, 12 Mike Forshaw, 13 Brad Mackay. Subs: 19 Jamie Peacock for Smith (53), 10 Paul Anderson for Fielden (30), 18 Lee Radford for Forshaw (2BB, rev 13), 1 Robbie Paul for Deacon (53), Radford for Forshaw (48BB), Fielden for McDermott (60), Forshaw for Mackay (63), Mackay for Vaikona (77)
Tries: Lowes (3), Brooker (7), Mackay (10), Deacon (33), Spruce (39), Naylor (47), Smith (50), R Paul (77).
Goals: H Paul 6
WILDCATS: 1 Steve Prescott, 24 Paul Sampson, 20 Adam Hughes, 27 Ben Westwood, 5 Bright Sodje, 22 Graham Law, 7 Glen Tomlinson, 8 Francis Stephenson, 21 Ryan Hudson, 18 Paul Jackson, 15 Gary Price, 16 Andy Fisher, 13 Steve McNamara (C). Subs: 14 Paul March for Jowitt (51), 17 Frank Watene for Stephenson (25), 19 Jamie Field for Fisher (55), 11 Warren Jowitt for Jackson (25), Stephenson for Price (62), Fisher for Hudson (73)
Tries: Sampson (28), Westwood (43), McNamara (70).
Goals: McNamara 2, **On report:** Paul March (65) - kicking out in tackle
League Express Men of the Match:
Bulls: Stuart Spruce. **Wildcats:** Glen Tomlinson
Penalty count: 6-4. **Half-time:** 28-4. **Referee:** Robert Connolly (Wigan), **Att:** 15,276

HUDDERSFIELD-SHEFFIELD GIANTS 28
WARRINGTON WOLVES 38
GIANTS: 6 Gene Ngamu, 30 Sylvain Houles, 23 Dale Cardoza, 1 Waisale Sovatabua, 31 Yacine Dekkiche, 19 Chris Thorman, 7 Gavin Clinch, 12 Richard Marshall, 9 John Lawless, 8 Steve Molloy (C), 11 David Lomax, 3 Karl Lovell, 22 David Bradbury. Subs: 14 Paul Reilly for Houles (14), 5 Matt Crowther for Sovatabua (22), 21 Chris Molyneux for Molloy (28), 28 Andy Rice for Marshall (37), Molloy for Lomax (61BB, rev 74), Marshall for Molyneux (62)
Tries: Ngamu (42), Rice (44), Lovell (48), Crowther (76), Cardoza (67). **Goals:** Ngamu 4
WOLVES: 1 Lee Penny, 3 Alan Hunte, 20 Ian Sibbit, 4 Toa Kohe-Love, 2 Jon Roper, 6 Lee Briers, 7 Allan Langer (C), 18 Mark Hilton, 9 Danny Farrar, 10 Danny Nutley, 12 Ian Knott, 14 Steve McCurrie, 13 Tawera Nikau. Subs: 21 Jerome Guisset for Farrar (73), 11 Dean Busby for Knott (27), 16 Gary Chambers for Hilton (61), 23 Chris Campbell (D) for Penny (59)
Tries: Sibbit (21, 36, 38), Kohe-Love (7), Langer (29, 55), Briers (60), McCurrie (73). **Goals:** Briers 3
League Express Men of the Match:
Giants: Gene Ngamu. **Wolves:** Allan Langer.
Penalty count: 7-10. **Half-time:** 0-24. **Referee:** John Connolly (Wigan), **Att:** 3,049

SALFORD CITY REDS 20 HALIFAX BLUE SOX 38
CITY REDS: 1 Gary Broadbent, 2 Nick Pinkney, 4 Jason Webber, 30 Jason Nicol, 3 Kris Tassell, 31 Steve Blakeley, 22 Mark Lee (C), 15 Neil Baynes, 9 Malcolm Alker, 8 Paul Southern, 11 James Smith, 14 Joe Faimalo, 23 Mike Wainwright. Subs: 20 Matty Leigh for Smith (70), 17 Mark Johnson for Nicol (31), 29 Brad Hepi for Faimalo (24), 28 John Duffy for Leigh (30), Nicol for Johnson (50), Lee for Duffy (59), Faimalo for Baynes (64), Johnson for Webber (66)
Tries: Alker (1, 53), Pinkney (23). **Goals:** Blakeley 4, **Sin bin:** Broadbent (48) - fighting, **Dismissal:** Hepi (60) - high tackle, **On report:** Pinkney (54) - incident in tackle
BLUE SOX: 1 Daryl Cardiss, 4 Marvin Golden, 6 Greg Florimo (C), 3 Damian Gibson, 17 Olly Marns, 14 Martin Pearson, 7 Andrew Dunemann, 23 Brett Goldspink, 9 Paul Rowley, 10 James Gannon, 11 Gary Mercer, 12 Jamie Bloem, 13 Martin Moana. Subs: 21 Gael Tallec for Moana (27), 19 David Foster for Tallec (70), 27 Jim Naylor for Cardiss (74), 8 Andy Hobson for Goldspink (28), Moana for Mercer (62), Goldspink for Hobson (65)
Tries: Marns (18), Golden (31), Rowley (48), Gannon (57), Pearson (70), Gibson (77). **Goals:** Pearson 5, Bloem 2, **Sin bin:** Pearson (48) - fighting
League Express Men of the Match:
City Reds: Neil Baynes, **Blue Sox:** Martin Pearson.
Penalty count: 9-7, **Half-time:** 14-14. **Referee:** Steve Ganson (St Helens), **Att:** 3,703

WIGAN WARRIORS 50 HULL FC 18
WARRIORS: 1 Kris Radlinski, 2 Brett Dallas, 14 Lee Gilmour, 3 Steve Renouf, 5 Jason Robinson, 13 Andy Farrell (C), 7 Willie Peters, 23 Brady Malam, 9 Terry Newton, 10 Neil Cowie, 11 Mick Cassidy, 16 Simon Haughton, 12 Denis Betts. Subs: 19 Chris Chester for Betts (17BB, rev 25), 8 Terry O'Connor for Cowie (28), Cowie for Malam (51), 26 David Hodgson for Newton (54), Chester for Gilmour (60), 18 Wes Davies for Radlinski (67)
Tries: Cassidy (15), Robinson (27, 69), Houghton (32), Radlinski (35), Dallas (45), Newton (53), Renouf (62).
Goals: Farrell 9
HULL FC: 1 Ben Sammut, 17 Brian Carney, 14 Steve Collins, 4 Craig Simon, 3 Deon Bird, 20 Richard Horne, 7 Will Robinson, 10 Andrew Hick, 9 Mick Jenkins, 8 Paul Broadbent, 16 Adam Maher, 18 Wayne McDonald, 13 Tony Grimaldi (C). Subs: 11 Craig Wilson for Maher (20BB, rev 28), 15 David Maiden for Grimaldi (20BB, rev 28), 12 Luke Felsch for Hick (21BB, rev 34), Felsch for Broadbent (37), Maiden for Collins (50BB, rev 54), Wilson for McDonald (41), McDonald for Grimaldi (54BB), 6 Stanley Gene for Wilson (57BB), Broadbent for Hick (65), Maiden for Jenkins (76)
Tries: Collins (18), Horne (57), Maher (64).
Goals: Sammut 3
League Express Men of the Match:
Warriors: Andy Farrell, **Hull FC:** Will Robinson
Penalty count: 7-10, **Half time:** 26-6. **Referee:** Russell Smith (Castleford), **Att:** 8,077

ROUND 10

HULL FC 26 LEEDS RHINOS 22
HULL FC: 1 Ben Sammut, 17 Brian Carney, 14 Steve Collins, 4 Craig Simon, 3 Deon Bird, 20 Richard Horne, 7 Will Robinson, 8 Paul Broadbent, 9 Mick Jenkins, 12 Luke Felsch, 16 Adam Maher, 13 Tony Grimaldi (C), 15 David Maiden. Subs: 6 Stanley Gene for Grimaldi (53), 10 Andrew Hick for Felsch (31), 11 Craig Wilson for Felsch (65BB), 18 Wayne McDonald for Broadbent (31), Felsch for Sammut (62), Broadbent for Hick (77)
Tries: Horne (42), Collins (50), Felsch (64), Hick (76).
Goals: Sammut 3, Horne 2
RHINOS: 1 Iestyn Harris (C), 21 Karl Pratt, 3 Richie Blackmore, 4 Keith Senior, 5 Francis Cummins, 6 Daryl Powell, 7 Ryan Sheridan, 8 Darren Fleary, 19 Dean Lawford, 10 Barrie McDermott, 11 Adrian Morley, 12 David Barnhill, 16 Andy Hay. Subs: 9 Lee Jackson for Lawford (25), 17 Anthony Farrell for Barnhill (25), 14 Marcus St Hilaire for Powell (48), 20 Jamie Mathiou for Fleary (21BB), Barnhill for Morley (38BB), Morley for Barnhill (46)
Tries: Morley (12), Blackmore (23), Hay (37), Pratt (68).
Goals: Harris 3
League Express Men of the Match:
Hull FC: Steve Collins, **Rhinos:** Iestyn Harris.
Penalty count: 9-2. **Half-time:** 4-1. **Referee:** Stuart Cummings (Widnes), **Att:** 8,143

SALFORD CITY REDS 31 WARRINGTON WOLVES 12
CITY REDS: 1 Gary Broadbent, 2 Nick Pinkney, 4 Jason Webber, 3 Kris Tassell, 18 Stuart Littler, 31 Steve Blakeley, 22 Mark Lee (C), 15 Neil Baynes, 9 Malcolm Alker, 8 Paul Southern, 11 James Smith, 30 Jason Nicol, 23 Mike Wainwright. Subs: 16 Paul Highton for Southern (29), 17 Mark Johnson for Tassell (56), 14 Joe Faimalo for Baynes (26), 28 John Duffy for Lee (47BB, rev 63), Baynes for Nicol (60), Duffy for Lee (75BB, rev 77), Nicol for Faimalo (74), Duffy for Lee (78BB)
Tries: Pinkney (7), Nicol (16, 76), Smith (31), Littler (63). **Goals:** Blakeley 35, **Field goal:** Duffy
WOLVES: 1 Lee Penny, 3 Alan Hunte, 20 Ian Sibbit, 4 Toa Kohe-Love, 2 Jon Roper, 6 Lee Briers, 7 Allan Langer (C), 8 Andrew Gee, 9 Danny Farrar, 10 Danny Nutley, 11 Dean Busby, 14 Steve McCurrie, 13 Tawera Nikau. Subs: 21 Jerome Guisset for Busby (63), 12 Ian Knott for Sibbit (12), 16 Gary Chambers for Gee (69), 18 Mark Hilton for Nutley (57), Busby for Knott (74)
Tries: Penny (10), Kohe-Love (36). **Goals**: Briers 2, **On report:** Kohe Love (54) - high tackle
League Express Men of the Match:
Reds: Gary Broadbent. **Wolves:** Tawera Nikau.
Penalty count: 4-3. **Half-time:** 18-12. **Referee:** Bob Connolly (Wigan), **Att:** 4,005

WIGAN WARRIORS 48
WAKEFIELD TRINITY WILDCATS 30
WARRIORS: 1 Kris Radlinski, 2 Brett Dallas, 3 Steve Renouf, 14 Lee Gilmour, 5 Jason Robinson, 13 Andrew Farrell (C), 7 Willie Peters, 23 Brady Malam, 9 Terry Newton, 10 Neil Cowie, 11 Mick Cassidy, 19 Chris Chester, 12 Denis Betts. Subs: 26 David Hodgson for Gilmour (29), 8 Terry O'Connor for Cowie (29), 18 Wes Davies for Radlinski (70), 21 Mark Smith for Newton (ht), Cowie for Malam (ht), Malam for Cowie (74)
Tries: Newton (2), Peters (9, 38), Dallas (29), Smith (50), Radlinski (53), Robinson (65, 68). **Goals:** Farrell 8
WILDCATS: 1 Steve Prescott, 24 Paul Sampson, 27 Ben Westwood, 20 Adam Hughes, 2 Neil Law, 22 Graham Law, 7 Glen Tomlinson, 8 Francis Stephenson, 21 Ryan Hudson, 10 Martin Masella, 15 Gary Price, 16 Andy Fisher, 12 Willie Poching. Subs: 11 Warren Jowitt for Fisher (51), 14 Paul March for Price (60), 17 Frank Watene for Stephenson (23), 18 Paul Jackson for Masella (29 & 55BB), Stephenson for Watene (58), Price for Poching (75)
Tries: Stephenson (19), Hughes (34, 78), N Law (40), Sampson (74), **Goal:** G Law 5
League Express Men of the Match:
Warriors: Willie Peters, **Wildcats:** Willie Poching .
Penalty count: 5-5, **Half-time:** 22-20. **Referee:** Karl Kirkpatrick (Warrington), **Att:** 8,214

LONDON BRONCOS 20 ST HELENS 26
BRONCOS: 5 Brett Warton, 19 Dom Peters, 28 Kevin Crouthers, 13 Mat Toshack, 1 Tulsen Tollett, 6 Karle Hammond (C), 29 Glen Air, 18 Justin Dooley, 21 Jon Clarke, 10 Scott Cram, 15 Andy Johnson, 12 Steele Retchless, 14 Andrew Wynyard. Subs: 8 Darren Bradstreet for Johnson (67), 9 Dean Callaway for Clarke (63), 16 Frank Napoli for Tollett (72), 17 Anthony Seibold for Cram (68)
Tries: Tollett (26), Air (36), Cram (38). **Goals:** Warton 4
SAINTS: 1 Paul Atcheson, 15 Sean Hoppe, 3 Kevin Iro, 4 Paul Newlove, 5 Anthony Sullivan, 20 Tommy Martyn, 7 Sean Long, 8 Apollo Perelini, 18 Bryan Henare, 10 Julian O'Neill, 26 John Stankevitch, 14 Fereti Tuilagi, 11 Chris Joynt (C). Subs: 2 Chris Smith for Stankevitch (63), 12 Sonny Nickle for Perelini (27), 23 Scott Barrow not used, 24 Steve Hall for Henare (30), Perelini for O'Neill (46), Henare for Hoppe (79)
Tries: Long (7, 62), Joynt (48), Newlove (76).
Goals: Martyn 5.
League Express Men of the Match:
Broncos: Justin Dooley, **Saints:** Sean Long
Referee: Russell Smith (Castleford). **Half-time:** 18-8, **Att:** 3,063. **Penalty count:** 9-6

CASTLEFORD TIGERS 26
HUDDERSFIELD-SHEFFIELD GIANTS 6
TIGERS: 1 Jason Flowers, 16 Jon Wells, 4 Logan Campbell, 3 Michael Eagar, 5 Darren Rogers, 6 Danny Orr, 22 Andrew Purcell, 8 Nathan Sykes, 17 Ian Tonks, 15 Darren Shaw, 18 Paul Smith, 12 Dale Fritz, 13 Adrian Vowles (C). Subs: 19 Andy Lynch for Shaw (31), 23 Craig Wright for Smith (27), 20 Jamie Benn for Fritz (57), 24 Gareth Dobson for Sykes (64), Shaw for Tonks (67), Smith for Wright (73)
Tries: Rogers (42, 47), Tonks (3), Purcell (61), Lynch (76). **Goals:** Orr 3,
GIANTS: 6 Gene Ngamu, 14 Paul Reilly, 3 Karl Lovell, 1 Waisale Sovatabua, 25 Ben Cooper (D), 19 Chris Thorman, 7 Gavin Clinch, 11 David Lomax, 9 John Lawless, 10 Dale Laughton, 15 Darren Turner, 22 David Bradbury, 13 Jeff Hardy (C). Subs: 23 Dale Cardoza for Reilly (29), 24 Mark Moxon for Clinch (58), 8 Steve Molloy for Laughton (15-27BB, 40-47BB, 61BB), 12 Richard Marshall for Lomax (24), Lomax for Turner (46), Turner for Bradbury (67)
Try: Ngamu, **Goal:** Ngamu
League Express Men of the Match:
Tigers: Ian Tonks, **Giants:** John Lawless
Penalty count: 10-5. **Half-time:** 4-6. **Referee:** Steve Ganson (St Helens), **Att:** 7,506

BRADFORD BULLS 62 HALIFAX BLUE SOX 2
BULLS: 28 Stuart Spruce, 14 Justin Brooker, 20 Scott Naylor, 11 David Boyle, 3 Leon Pryce, 6 Henry Paul, 1 Robbie Paul, 22 Brian McDermott, 9 James Lowes (C), 29 Stuart Fielden, 15 Hudson Smith, 12 Mike Forshaw, 13 Brad Mackay. Subs: 19 Jamie Peacock for Smith (48), 10 Paul Anderson for McDermott (24), 18 Lee Radford for Mackay (53), 7 Paul Deacon for Lowes (48), Mackay for Spruce (60), Smith for Forshaw (71)
Tries: Brooker (38, 44, 58), Spruce (15, 48), Forshaw (53), Naylor (71, 80), H Paul (7), Anderson (27), Fielden (62). **Goals:** H Paul 9, Sin bin: Smith (26) - fighting, **On report:** Spruce - (39) - foul in tackle
BLUE SOX: 1 Daryl Cardiss, 4 Marvin Golden, 6 Greg Florimo (C), 27 Jim Naylor, 3 Damian Gibson, 14 Martin Pearson, 7 Andrew Dunemann, 23 Brett Goldspink, 9 Paul Rowley, 10 James Gannon, 11 Gary Mercer, 21 Gael Tallec, 12 Jamie Bloem. Subs: 13 Martin Moana for Bloem (50), 17 Oliver Marns for Cardiss (20), 19 David Foster for Mercer (55), 8 Andy Hobson for Goldspink (32), Goldspink for Gannon (61), Mercer for Hobson (74)
Goal: Pearson, **Sin bin:** Gannon (26) - fighting, Bloem (39) - dissent
League Express Men of the Match:
Bulls: Justin Brooker, **Blue Sox:** Jim Naylor
Penalty count: 12-6. **Half-time:** 24-2. **Referee:** Steve Presley (Castleford), **Att:** 14,082,

ROUND 11

HUDDERSFIELD-SHEFFIELD GIANTS 8
WIGAN WARRIORS 56
GIANTS: 6 Gene Ngamu, 14 Paul Reilly, 1 Waisale Sovatabua, 3 Karl Lovell, 25 Ben Cooper, 19 Chris Thorman, 7 Gavin Clinch, 8 Steve Molloy (C), 9 John Lawless, 10 Dale Laughton, 15 Darren Turner, 22 David Bradbury, 13 Jeff Hardy. Subs: 2 Danny Arnold for Reilly (26), 31 Yacine Dekkiche for Turner (38BB), 11 David Lomax for Molloy (21BB), 12 Richard Marshall for Laughton (30BB), Molloy for Lomax (52), Laughton for Marshall (53), Lomax for Lawless (58), Lawless for Lovell (64BB), Marshall for Molloy (65), Molloy for Laughton (73), Lovell for Hardy (73)
Try: Dekkiche (72). **Goals:** Ngamu 2
Sin bin: Ngamu (25) - holding down, **Dismissal:** Bradbury (37) - alleged high tackle
WARRIORS: 1 Kris Radlinski, 2 Brett Dallas, 3 Steve Renouf, 4 Gary Connolly, 5 Jason Robinson, 13 Andrew Farrell (C), 7 Willie Peters, 8 Terry O'Connor, 21 Mark Smith, 10 Neil Cowie, 11 Mick Cassidy, 19 Chris Chester, 12 Denis Betts. Subs: 16 Simon Haughton for Betts (51), 18 Wes Davies for Radlinski (58), 23 Brady Malam for O'Connor (31), O'Connor for Malam (36BB, rev 41), 14 Lee Gilmour for Renouf (50), O'Connor for Cowie (50)
Tries: Renouf (17, 44), Connolly (23), Dallas (40), Robinson (47, 56), Radlinski (52), Gilmour (52), Cassidy (77). **Goals:** Farrell 10
League Express Men of the Match:
Giants: Dale Laughton, **Warriors:** Andy Farrell
Penalty count: 8-9. **Half-time:** 2-22. **Referee:** Steve Ganson (St Helens), **Att:** 3,421

ST HELENS 46 SALFORD CITY REDS 22
SAINTS: 17 Paul Wellens, 2 Chris Smith, 3 Kevin Iro, 4 Paul Newlove, 5 Anthony Sullivan, 20 Tommy Martyn, 7 Sean Long, 8 Apollo Perelini, 23 Scott Barrow, 12 Sonny Nickle, 11 Chris Joynt (C), 14 Fereti Tuilagi, 13 Paul Sculthorpe. Subs: 18 Bryan Henare for Tuilagi (52), 10 Julian O'Neill for Perelini (33), 1 Paul Atcheson for Martyn (67), 30 Mike Bennett for Joynt (60), Perelini for Nickle (57)
Tries: Iro (23, 73), Martyn (31), Sullivan (43, 60), Newlove (46), Long (50, 57). **Goals:** Long 7
CITY REDS: 1 Gary Broadbent, 2 Nick Pinkney, 4 Jason Webber, 3 Kris Tassell, 18 Stuart Littler, 31 Steve Blakeley, 22 Mark Lee (C), 14 Joe Faimalo, 9 Malcolm Alker, 8 Paul Southern, 11 James Smith, 16 Paul Highton, 23 Mike Wainwright. Subs: 10 Craig Makin for Southern (32), 17 Mark Johnson for Makin (68), 28 John Duffy for Lee (68), 27 Carlo Napolitano (D) for Smith (60), Southern for Faimalo (58), Faimalo for Wainwright (73)
Tries: Webber (17), Smith (34), Alker (66), Broadbent (70). **Goals:** Blakeley 3
League Express Men of the Match:
Saints: Sean Long, **City Reds:** Malcolm Alker.
Penalty count: 7-4, **Half time:** 12-10. **Referee:** Karl Kirkpatrick (Warrington), **Att:** 7,862

WAKEFIELD TRINITY WILDCATS 6 HULL FC 34
WILDCATS: 1 Steve Prescott, 24 Paul Sampson, 15 Gary Price, 20 Adam Hughes, 2 Neil Law, 22 Graham Law, 7 Glen Tomlinson (C), 8 Francis Stephenson, 21 Ryan Hudson, 10 Martin Masella, 11 Warren Jowitt, 16 Andy Fisher, 12 Willie Poching. Subs: 9 David March for Hudson (HT), 17 Frank Watene for Masella (27), 19 Jamie Field for Price (21BB, rev28), 18 Paul Jackson for Masella (69), Field for Stephenson (33), Masella for Watene (47), Stephenson for Field (55)
Tries: Tomlinson (79). **Goals:** G. Law, **Sin bin:** Andy Fisher (39) - fighting,
HULL: 1 Ben Sammut, 21 Craig Poucher, 4 Craig Simon, 14 Steve Collins, 3 Deon Bird, 26 Paul Cooke, 20 Richard Horne, 10 Andrew Hick, 9 Mick Jenkins, 12 Luke Felsch, 18 Wayne McDonald, 16 Adam Maher, 13 Tony Grimaldi (C). Subs: 6 Stanley Gene for Jenkins (59), 8 Paul Broadbent for Felsch (25), 11 Craig Wilson for Maher (58), 15 David Maiden for McDonald (35BB, rev 51), Maiden for Grimaldi (67)
Tries: Sammut (14), Bird (20, 54), McDonald (68), Poucher (73). **Goals:** Sammut 7, **Sin bin:** Paul Broadbent (39) - fighting
League Express Men of the Match:
Wildcats: Glen Tomlinson, **Hull:** Richard Horne.
Penalty count: 6-14. **Half-time:** 0-14. **Referee:** Steve Presley (Castleford), **Att:** 6,750

LEEDS RHINOS 2 BRADFORD BULLS 44
RHINOS: 1 Iestyn Harris (C), 21 Karl Pratt, 3 Richie Blackmore, 4 Keith Senior, 5 Francis Cummins, 6 Daryl Powell, 7 Ryan Sheridan, 8 Darren Fleary, 9 Lee Jackson, 10 Barrie McDermott, 11 Adrian Morley, 17 Anthony Farrell, 16 Andy Hay. Subs: 12 David Barnhill for Farrell (20), 20 Jamie Mathiou for McDermott (23), 33 Graham Mackay for Powell (40), McDermott for Fleary (44bb, rev 67), Farrell for Hay (52), 13 Sinfield for Mathiou (63), Hay for Morley (68bb), **Goal:** Harris,
BULLS: 28 Stuart Spruce, 4 Nathan McAvoy, 20 Scott Naylor, 14 Justin Brooker, 3 Leon Pryce, 6 Henry Paul, 1 Robbie Paul (C), 22 Brian McDermott, 9 James Lowes, 29 Stuart Fielden, 15 Hudson Smith, 12 Mike Forshaw, 13 Brad Mackay. Subs: 11 David Boyle for Smith (15), 10 Paul Anderson for McDermott (28), McDermott for Fielden (54), 19 Jamie Peacock for Forshaw (60), Fielden for Anderson (68), 7 Paul Deacon for Spruce (69)
Tries: McAvoy (4), Mackay (20), Spruce (37, 66), R Paul (61), Pryce (72), Lowes (77). **Goals:** H Paul 8, **Sin bin:** Mackay (49) - Interference at the play-the-ball
League Express Men of the Match:
Rhinos: Lee Jackson, **Bulls:** Stuart Fielden.
Penalty count: 10-4. **Half-time:** 2-20. **Referee:** Russell Smith (Castleford), **Att:** 18,769

HALIFAX BLUE SOX 22 LONDON BRONCOS 16
BLUE SOX: 3 Damian Gibson, 28 Casey Mayberry (D), 4 Marvin Golden, 27 Jim Naylor, 5 Phil Hassan, 6 Greg Florimo (C), 7 Andrew Dunemann, 23 Brett Goldspink, 9 Paul Rowley, 10 Jim Gannon, 11 Gary Mercer, 12 Jamie Bloem, 13 Marty Moana. Subs: 8 Andy Hobson for Goldspink (30), 14 Martin Pearson for Mayberry (34), Goldspink for Hobson (56), 21 Gael Tallec for Bloem (59), Hobson for Gannon (62), 19 David Foster for Goldspink (71)
Tries: Moana (42), Pearson (55), Florimo (70). Goals: Bloem, Pearson 4
BRONCOS: 5 Brett Warton, 16 Frank Napoli, 28 Kevin Crouthers, 13 Mat Toshack, 19 Dom Peters, 6 Karle Hammond (C), 29 Glen Air, 18 Justin Dooley, 21 Jon Clarke, 10 Scott Cram, 15 Andy Johnson, 12 Steele Retchless, 13 Andrew Wynyard. Subs: 17 Anthony Seibold for Cram (28), 11 Shane Millard for Wynyard (37), 9 Dean Callaway for Clarke (56), 22 John Timu for Dooley (56), Dooley for Millard (63BB, rev 70), Dooley for Retchless (73), Clarke for Crouthers (79)
Tries: Napoli (27), Warton (47), Air (76).
Goals: Warton 2.
League Express Men of the Match:
Blue Sox: Martin Pearson, **Broncos:** Karle Hammond.
Half-time: 2-8. **Referee:** Robert Connolly (Wigan). **Att:** 3,751. **Penalty count:** 8-6

WARRINGTON WOLVES 26 CASTLEFORD TIGERS 37
WOLVES: 1 Lee Penny, 23 Chris Campbell, 12 Ian Knott, 2 Jon Roper, 3 Alan Hunte, 6 Lee Briers, 7 Allan Langer (C), 8 Andrew Gee, 9 Danny Farrar, 10 Danny Nutley, 21 Jerome Guisset, 14 Steve McCurrie, 13 Tawera Nikau. Subs: 11 Dean Busby for McCurrie (57), 25 Paul Noone (D) for Guisset (69), 18 Mark Hilton for Gee (26BB, rev 40), 19 David Highton for Briers (45), Hilton for Nutley (55), Nutley for Gee (67), Gee for Hilton (76)
Tries: Guisset (12, 19), Hunte (26), Roper (60), Farrar (74). **Goals:** Briers, Roper 2. **Sin bin:** Farrar (47) - tripping
TIGERS: 1 Jason Flowers, 16 Jon Wells, 4 Logan Campbell, 3 Michael Eager, 5 Darren Rogers, 6 Danny Orr, 22 Andrew Purcell, 8 Nathan Sykes, 17 Ian Tonks, 15 Darren Shaw, 18 Paul Smith, 23 Craig Wright, 13 Adrian Vowles (C). Subs: 19 Andy Lynch for Smith (29), 9 Aaron Raper for Purcell (30BB), 20 Jamie Benn for Wells (45), 14 Barrie-Jon Mather (D) for Wright (27), Smith for Lynch (57), Wright for Rogers (64BB), Lynch for Shaw (67), Shaw for Tonks (73)
Tries: Mather (36), Eager (38), Sykes (44), Campbell (49, 56), Orr (52). **Goals:** Orr (6), **Field goal:** Orr
League Express Men of the Match:
Wolves: Jerome Guisset, **Tigers:** Aaron Raper.
Penalty count: 5-6. **Half-time:** 14-12. **Referee:** Stuart Cummings (Widnes), **Att:** 5,915

ROUND 12

HUDDERSFIELD-SHEFFIELD GIANTS 16
LONDON BRONCOS 20
GIANTS: 6 Gene Ngamu, 25 Ben Cooper, 1 Waisale Sovatabua, 3 Karl Lovell, 31 Yacine Dekkiche, 19 Chris Thorman, 7 Gavin Clinch, 8 Steve Molloy (C), 9 John Lawless, 10 Dale Laughton, 11 David Lomax, 15 Darren Turner, 13 Jeff Hardy. Subs: 12 Richard Marshall for Molly (27BB, rev 59), 22 David Bradbury for Lomax (26BB, rev 41), 2 Danny Arnold not used, 17 Martin Gleeson for Dekkiche (54), Bradbury for Laughton (51BB), Laughton for Lawless (69), Lawless for Hardy (78)
Tries: Turner (3, 44), Cooper (72). **Goals:** Ngamu 2
BRONCOS: 5 Brett Warton, 16 Frank Napoli, 22 John Timu, 13 Mat Toshack, 19 Dom Peters, 6 Karle Hammond (C), 29 Glen Air, 18 Justin Dooley, 21 Jon Clarke, 12 Steele Retchless, 11 Shane Millard, 27 Paul Davidson, 15 Andy Johnson. Subs: 9 Dean Callaway for Clarke (28), 17 Anthony Seibold for Davidson (26), 26 Peter Lupton not used, 28 Kevin Crouthers for Air (52), Davidson for Millard (55BB, rev 65), Clarke for Callaway (62), Davidson for Dooley (72), Dooley for Seibold (78)
Tries: Warton (10), Hammond (27), Air (35), Seibold (67). **Goals:** Warton 2
League Express Men of the Match:
Giants: Darren Turner. **Broncos:** Shane Millard
Penalty count: 8-5. **Half-time:** 4-16. **Referee:** Ian Smith (Oldham), **Att:** 2,458

ST HELENS 27 HULL FC 14
SAINTS: 17 Paul Wellens, 2 Chris Smith, 3 Kevin Iro, 4 Paul Newlove, 5 Anthony Sullivan, 13 Paul Sculthorpe, 7 Sean Long, 10 Julian O'Neill, 23 Scott Barrow, 12 Sonny Nickle, 8 Apollo Perelini, 14 Fereti Tuilagi, 11 Chris Joynt (C). Subs: 18 Bryan Henare for O'Neill (35), 19 Tony Stewart for Nickle (66), 1 Paul Atcheson for Barrow (20), 26 John Stankevitch for Tuilagi (28), O'Neill for Henare (76)
Tries: Joynt (24), Henare (63), Stewart (70), Atcheson (78). **Goals:** Long 5, **Field goal:** Sculthorpe
HULL FC: 1 Ben Sammut, 17 Brian Carney, 14 Steve Collins, 4 Craig Simon, 3 Deon Bird, 26 Paul Cooke, 20 Richard Horne, 8 Paul Broadbent, 9 Mick Jenkins, 12 Luke Felsch, 16 Adam Maher, 13 Tony Grimaldi (C), 15 David Maiden. Subs: 6 Stanley Gene for Jenkins (70), 11 Craig Wilson for Maher (57), 18 Wayne McDonald for Carney (22BB), 19 Paul King for Broadbent (53), Broadbent for Felsch (69)
Tries: Carney (1), McDonald (56). **Goals:** Sammut 3, **On report:** Maiden (15) - alleged offence in the tackle on Joynt
League Express Men of the Match:
Saints: Chris Joynt, **Hull FC:** Ben Sammut
Half-time: 6-8, **Att:** 8,146. **Referee:** Russell Smith (Castleford). **Penalty count:** 11-9

LEEDS RHINOS 26 WIGAN WARRIORS 19
RHINOS: 5 Francis Cummins, 2 Paul Sterling, 3 Richie Blackmore, 4 Keith Senior, 21 Karl Pratt, 1 Iestyn Harris (C), 7 Ryan Sheridan, 8 Darren Fleary, 9 Lee Jackson, 10 Barrie McDermott, 11 Adrian Morley, 12 David Barnhill, 16 Andy Hay. Subs: 17 Anthony Farrell for Barnhill (16BB, rev 28), 20 Jamie Mathiou for McDermott (24), 33 Graham Mackay for Senior (26BB, rev 52), 6 Daryl Powell for Jackson (33BB, rev 40), Farrell for Barnhill (40), McDermott for Fleary (49), Barnhill for Hay (56), Powell for Farrell (70), Fleary for McDermott (78)
Tries: Blackmore (32, 55), Barnhill (58), Cummins (78). **Goals:** Harris 5
WARRIORS: 1 Kris Radlinski, 2 Brett Dallas, 3 Steve Renouf, 4 Gary Connolly, 5 Jason Robinson, 18 Andy Farrell (C), 7 Willie Peters, 28 Brady Malam, 9 Terry Newton, 10 Neil Cowie, 11 Mick Cassidy, 19 Chris Chester, 12 Denis Betts. Subs: 8 Terry O'Connor for Malam (13BB, rev 34), 16 Simon Haughton for Cassidy (28), 14 Lee Gilmour for Dallas (40BB, rev 43), O'Connor for Cowie (44), 21 Mark Smith for Newton (49), Cowie for Malam (60), Cassidy for Chester (68), Gilmour for Betts (72)
Tries: Radlinski (17), Dallas (36), Peters (49). **Goals:** Farrell 3, Field goal: Peters, **Sin bin:** Farrell (77) – dissent
League Express Men of the Match:
Rhinos: Richie Blackmore, **Warriors:** Willie Peters
Penalty count: 8-4. **Half-time:** 6-13. **Referee:** Stuart Cummings (Widnes), **Att:** 11,881

CASTLEFORD TIGERS 30 SALFORD CITY REDS 4
TIGERS: 1 Jason Flowers, 14 Barrie-Jon Mather, 4 Logan Campbell, 3 Michael Eagar, 5 Darren Rogers, 6 Danny Orr, 7 Brad Davis, 8 Nathan Sykes, 9 Aaron Raper, 10 Dean Sampson, 15 Darren Shaw, 12 Ian Tonks, 13 Adrian Vowles (C). Subs: 19 Andy Lynch for Sampson (26), 23 Craig Wright for Shaw (60), 20 Jamie Benn for Rogers (36), 24 Gareth Dobson for Raper (63), Sampson for Sykes (56), Sykes for Orr (75)
Tries: Mather (33), Orr (39), Vowles (59), Flowers (64), Benn (72). **Goals:** Orr 5
CITY REDS: 1 Gary Broadbent, 2 Nick Pinkney, 18 Stuart Littler, 3 Kris Tassell, 5 Martin Offiah, 12 Darren Brown (C), 31 Steve Blakeley, 8 Paul Southern, 9 Malcolm Alker, 15 Neil Baynes, 11 James Smith, 16 Paul Highton, 23 Michael Wainwright. Subs: 14 Joe Faimalo for Southern (54), 10 Craig Makin for Blakeley (65), 17 Mark Johnson for Offiah (40), 22 Mark Lee for Broadbent (51), Southern for Baynes (68)
Try: Brown, **Sin bin:** Neil Baynes (24) – deliberate offside
League Express Men of the Match:
Tigers: Danny Orr, **Reds:** Darren Brown. **Penalty count:** 6-3. **Half-time:** 12-0. **Referee:** John Connolly (Wigan), **Att:** 6,303

WARRINGTON WOLVES 42 BRADFORD BULLS 32
WOLVES: 1 Lee Penny, 3 Alan Hunte, 12 Ian Knott, 2 Jon Roper, 23 Chris Campbell, 13 Tawera Nikau, 7 Allan Langer (C), 8 Andrew Gee, 9 Danny Farrar, 10 Danny Nutley, 21 Jerome Guisset, 14 Steve McCurrie, 11 Dean Busby. Subs: 18 Mark Hilton for Nutley (33), 25 Paul Noone for McCurrie (60), 6 Lee Briers for Busby (46), 19 David Highton for Farrar (67), Nutley for Hilton (55), McCurrie for Noone (76)
Tries: Busby (3), Langer (15, 57), Roper (45), Knott (51), Penny (71), McCurrie (78). **Goals:** Roper 7, **Sin bin:** Gee (27) - fighting, On report: 27th minute brawl,
BULLS: 28 Stuart Spruce, 4 Nathan McAvoy, 20 Scott Naylor, 3 Leon Pryce, 14 Justin Brooker, 6 Henry Paul, 1 Robbie Paul (C), 22 Brian McDermott, 9 James Lowes, 10 Paul Anderson, 12 Mike Forshaw, 11 David Boyle, 13 Brad Mackay. Subs: 15 Hudson Smith for Mackay (48), 7 Paul Deacon for McAvoy (4BB, rev 18), 19 Jamie Peacock for Boyle (53), 29 Stuart Fielden for Anderson (22), Anderson for McDermott (24BB, rev 46), Mackay for Peacock (65), Peacock for Forshaw (72), Anderson for Smith (74)
Tries: Pryce (12), Naylor (18), R Paul (23), Anderson (34, 38). **Goals:** H. Paul 6, **Sin bin:** Fielden (27) - fighting, **Dismissal:** McDermott (55) - high tackle, **On report:** 27th minute brawl and Spruce (61) - alleged biting
League Express Men of the Match:
Wolves: Allan Langer, **Bulls:** Paul Anderson, .
Penalty count: 7-8. **Half-time:** 12-30. **Referee:** Steve Ganson (St Helens), **Att:** 8,302

HALIFAX BLUE SOX 36
WAKEFIELD TRINITY WILDCATS 10
BLUE SOX: 1 Daryl Cardiss, 4 Marvin Golden, 6 Greg Florimo (C), 3 Damian Gibson, 5 Phil Hassan, 14 Martin Pearson, 7 Andrew Dunemann, 23 Brett Goldspink, 9 Paul Rowley, 10 Jim Gannon, 11 Gary Mercer, 12 Jamie Bloem, 13 Marty Moana. Subs, 27 Jim Naylor for Cardiss (65), 8 Andy Hobson for Gannon (33), 21 Gael Tallec for Hobson (52), 19 David Foster for Mercer (64), Gannon for Goldspink (52), Hobson for Bloem (71)
Tries: Golden (5, 59), Mercer (34), Moana (51), Rowley (54), Tallec (67), Florimo (70), **Goals:** Pearson 4
WILDCATS: 1 Steve Prescott, 24 Paul Sampson, 2 Neil Law, 20 Adam Hughes, 5 Bright Sodje, 22 Graham Law, 7 Glen Tomlinson, 8 Francis Stephenson, 9 David March, 17 Frank Watene, 15 Gary Price (C), 11 Warren Jowitt, 12 Willie Poching. Subs: 14 Paul March for Hughes (60), 19 Jamie Field for Stephenson (32BB), 18 Paul Jackson for Jowitt (68), 10 Martin Masella for Watene (29), Watene for Masella (60), Stephenson for Field (60), , **Tries:** Watene (11), Sodje (78), **Goal:** Law
League Express Men of the Match:
Blue Sox: Andrew Dunemann, **Wildcats:** Willie Poching
Penalty count: 7-5, , **Half-time:** 10-6, **Referee:** Karl Kirkpatrick (Warrington), **Att** 4,471

CASTLEFORD TIGERS 18 LEEDS RHINOS 20
(from round 7)
TIGERS: 1 Jason Flowers, 16 Jon Wells, 4 Logan Campbell, 3 Michael Eagar, 14 Barrie-Jon Mather, 6 Danny Orr, 7 Brad Davis, 8 Nathan Sykes, 9 Aaron Raper, 10 Dean Sampson, 17 Ian Tonks, 15 Darren Shaw, 13 Adrian Vowles (C), Subs, 19 Andy Lynch for Sykes (56), 11 Lee Harland for Shaw (32), 23 Craig Wright for Tonks (67), 20 Jamie Benn not used, Shaw for Sampson (71), Sykes for Lynch (75), Sampson for Wright (78), , **Tries:** Davis (3), Tonks (17), Sampson (34), **Goals:** Orr 3
RHINOS: 5 Francis Cummins, 2 Paul Sterling, 3 Richie Blackmore, 4 Keith Senior, 21 Karl Pratt, 1 Iestyn Harris (C), 7 Ryan Sheridan, 8 Darren Fleary, 9 Lee Jackson, 10 Barrie McDermott, 11 Adrian Morley, 12 David Barnhill, 16 Andy Hay, Subs, 17 Anthony Farrell for Barnhill (28), 6 Daryl Powell for Jackson (46), 33 Graham Mackay for Pratt (63), 20 Jamie Mathiou for McDermott (28), McDermott for Fleary (55), Barnhill for Hay (67), Jackson for Powell (78)
Tries: Sterling (24), Senior (55), Mackay (67), Sheridan (80), **Goals:** Harris 2
League Express Men of the Match:
Tigers: Aaron Raper, **Rhinos:** Iestyn Harris
Half-time: 18-6, **Att** 11,702, **Penalty count:** 5-6, **Referee:** Robert Connolly (Wigan)

ROUND 13

HULL FC 36 HALIFAX BLUE SOX 18
HULL FC: 1 Ben Sammut, 17 Brian Carney, 14 Steve Collins, 4 Craig Simon, 3 Deon Bird, 20 Richard Horne, 7 Will Robinson, 8 Paul Broadbent, 9 Mick Jenkins, 12 Luke Felsch, 16 Adam Maher, 13 Tony Grimaldi (C), 15 David Maiden. Subs: 11 Craig Wilson for Felsch (53), 6 Stanley Gene for Jenkins (33), 2 Matt Daylight for Robinson (64), 19 Paul King for Broadbent (28bb, rev 59), Jenkins for Gene (61), Felsch for Wilson (72), Wilson for Grimaldi (75BB)
Tries: Simon (7), Maher (15), Maiden (17), Collins (41), Horne (54), Daylight (79). **Goals:** Sammut 6
BLUE SOX: 3 Damian Gibson, 4 Marvin Golden, 6 Greg Florimo (C), 27 Jim Naylor, 5 Phil Hassan, 14 Martin Pearson, 7 Andrew Dunemann, 23 Brett Goldspink, 19 David Foster, 10 James Gannon, 11 Gary Mercer (C), 12 Jamie Bloem, 13 Martin Moana. Subs: 8 Andy Hobson for Goldspink (22), 21 Gael Tallec for Foster (30), 15 Lokeni Savelio for Tallec (61), 17 Olly Marns for Hassan (69), Foster for Bloem (70)
Tries: Pearson (31, 66), Gannon (70). **Goals:** Pearson 3, **Sin bin:** Florimo (17) - dissent; Mercer (60) - late tackle
League Express Men of the Match:
Hull: Tony Grimaldi, **Blue Sox:** Martin Pearson.
Penalty count: 9-8. **Half-time:** 18-6. **Referee:** Steve Presley (Castleford), **Att:** 5,667

LONDON BRONCOS 18 WARRINGTON WOLVES 28
BRONCOS: 5 Brett Warton, 16 Frank Napoli, 27 Paul Davidson, 13 Mat Toshack, 28 Kevin Crouthers, 6 Karle Hammond (C), 26 Peter Lupton (D), 18 Justin Dooley, 21 Jon Clarke, 12 Steele Retchless, 14 Andrew Wynyard, 11 Shane Millard, 15 Andy Johnson. Subs: 9 Dean Callaway for Clarke (48), 20 Steffan Hughes for Millward (38BB, rev 72), 17 Anthony Seibold for Wynyard (31), 19 Dom Peters for Dooley (50), Wynyard for Retchless (59 BB), Dooley for Davidson (59), Davidson for Millard (72)
Tries: Toshack (19), Hughes (41), Davidson (73). **Goals:** Warton 3
WOLVES: 1 Lee Penny, 2 Jon Roper, 4 Toa Kohe-Love, 12 Ian Knott, 3 Alan Hunte, 13 Tawera Nikau, 7 Allan Langer (C), 8 Andrew Gee, 9 Danny Farrar, 10 Danny Nutley, 14 Steve McCurrie, 21 Jerome Guisset, 11 Dean Busby. Subs: 6 Lee Briers for Roper (25), 18 Mark Hilton for Nutley (14), 19 David Highton for Farrar (36BB, rev 58), 26 Michael Peters (D) for Busby (58), Highton for McCurrie (64), McCurrie for Hilton (75)
Tries: Penny (9), Farrar (27), Briers (46), Hunte (57), Knott (79). **Goals:** Roper, Briers 3
League Express Men of the Match:
Broncos: Karle Hammond, **Wolves:** Allan Langer.
Half-time: 6-12. **Referee:** Robert Connolly (Wigan), **Att:** 4,174. **Penalty count:** 6-3

BRADFORD BULLS 17 ST HELENS 16
BULLS: 14 Justin Brooker, 4 Nathan McAvoy, 20 Scott Naylor, 11 David Boyle, 3 Leon Pryce, 6 Henry Paul, 1 Robbie Paul (C), 29 Stuart Fielden, 9 James Lowes, 10 Paul Anderson, 19 Jamie Peacock, 12 Mike Forshaw, 13 Brad Mackay. Subs: 18 Lee Radford for Naylor (30), 27 Robert Parker (D) for Paul Anderson (76BB), 15 Hudson Smith for Anderson (27), 7 Paul Deacon for Brooker (22), Anderson for Smith (54), Smith for Peacock (66)
Tries: Fielden (14, 44), Boyle (36). **Goals:** H. Paul 2, **Field goal:** Deacon
SAINTS: 17 Paul Wellens, 2 Chris Smith, 3 Kevin Iro, 4 Paul Newlove, 5 Anthony Sullivan, 13 Paul Sculthorpe, 7 Sean Long, 10 Julian O'Neill, 23 Scott Barrow, 12 Sonny Nickle, 8 Apollo Perelini, 21 Tony Stewart, 11 Chris Joynt (C). Subs: 18 Bryan Henare for Perelini (15BB, rev 32), 1 Paul Atcheson for Barrow (37), 19 Tim Jonkers for Smith (70), 26 John Stankevitch for O'Neill (50), Henare for Nickle (58), Barrow for Atcheson (71)
Tries: Joynt (28, 55), Long (73). **Goals:** Long 2
League Express Men of the Match:
Bulls: Stuart Fielden, **Saints:** Chris Joynt.
Penalty count: 5-8. **Half-time:** 12-4. **Referee:** John Connolly (Wigan), **Att:** 13,237

SALFORD CITY REDS 18
HUDDERSFIELD-SHEFFIELD GIANTS 8
CITY REDS: 1 Gary Broadbent, 2 Nick Pinkney, 4 Jason Webber, 30 Jason Nicol, 3 Kris Tassell, 31 Steve Blakeley, 6 Graham Holroyd (D), 8 Paul Southern, 9 Malcolm Alker, 14 Joe Faimalo, 11 James Smith, 12 Darren Brown (C), 23 Mike Wainwright. Subs: 16 Paul Highton for Smith (35), 18 Stuart Littler for Webber (24BB, rev 69), 27 Carlo Napolitano for Southern (59), 28 John Duffy for Alker (68), Smith for Faimalo (53), Faimalo for Brown (75), Littler for Faimalo (78)
Tries: Wainwright (3), Southern (54), Broadbent (71). **Goals:** Blakeley 3, **Sin bin:** Pinkney (17) - professional foul
GIANTS: 14 Paul Reilly, 1 Waisale Sovatabua, 17 Martin Gleeson, 3 Karl Lovell, 25 Ben Cooper, 6 Gene Ngamu, 7 Gavin Clinch, 11 David Lomax, 9 Johnny Lawless, 10 Dale Laughton, 22 David Bradbury, 15 Darren Turner, 13 Jeff Hardy (C). Subs: 12 Richard Marshall for Lomax (25), 8 Steve Molloy for Laughton (43), 19 Chris Thorman for Ngamu (59), 18 Danny Russell for Lawless (52), Lomax for Turner (45), Laughton for Molloy (52BB, rev 61)
Try: Turner (17). **Goals:** Ngamu 2
League Express Men of the Match:
City Reds: Joe Faimalo, **Giants:** Jeff Hardy
Penalty count: 2-4. **Half-time:** 6-8. **Referee:** Stuart Cummings (Widnes), **Att:** 3,149

WAKEFIELD TRINITY WILDCATS 24 LEEDS RHINOS 30
WILDCATS: 1 Steve Prescott, 24 Paul Sampson, 2 Neil Law, 20 Adam Hughes, 27 Ben Westwood, 14 Paul March, 7 Glen Tomlinson, 8 Francis Stephenson, 12 Willie Poching, 17 Frank Watene, 19 Jamie Field, 11 Warren Jowitt, 15 Gary Price (C). Subs: 10 Martin Masella for Watene (28), 18 Paul Jackson for Stephenson (53BB, rev 59), 21 Ryan Hudson for March (25), 28 David White (D) for Westwood (4), Jackson for Masella (59), Masella for Jackson (63)
Tries: Tomlinson (10), Stephenson (35), Hudson (44), Price (75). **Goals:** Prescott 4
RHINOS: 5 Francis Cummins, 2 Paul Sterling, 3 Richie Blackmore, 4 Keith Senior, 21 Karl Pratt, 1 Iestyn Harris (C), 7 Ryan Sheridan, 8 Darren Fleary, 9 Lee Jackson, 10 Barrie McDermott, 11 Adrian Morley, 12 David Barnhill, 16 Andy Hay. Subs: 17 Anthony Farrell for Barnhill (28), 6 Daryl Powell for Jackson (56), 33 Graham Mackay for Hay (65), 20 Jamie Mathiou for McDermott (25), McDermott for Fleary (50), Barnhill for Mathiou (50)
Tries: Sterling (3, 24), Morley (6), Pratt (15, 21, 64). **Goals:** Harris 3
League Express Men of the Match:
Wildcats: Willie Poching, **Rhinos:** Karl Pratt . **Half-time:** 12-26. **Referee:** Steve Ganson (St Helens), **Att:** 6,276. **Penalty count:** 10-5

WIGAN WARRIORS 12 BRADFORD BULLS 12
(from round 7)
WARRIORS: 1 Kris Radlinski, 2 Brett Dallas, 4 Gary Connolly, 3 Steve Renouf, 5 Jason Robinson, 13 Andy Farrell (C), 7 Willie Peters, 8 Terry O'Connor, 9 Terry Newton, 10 Neil Cowie, 11 Mick Cassidy, 16 Simon Haughton, 12 Denis Betts, Subs, 17 Tony Mestrov for O'Connor (33), 23 Brady Malam for Cowie (33), 14 Lee Gilmour for Radlinski (18), 19 Chris Chester for Haughton (31BB, rev 58), O'Connor for Malam (60), Cowie for Mestrov (60), Chester for Haughton (77BB)
Tries: Newton (7), Connolly (49), **Goal:** Farrell, **Field goals:** Peters, **Sin bin:** Farrell (26) - head-butting
BULLS: 5 Michael Withers, 4 Nathan McAvoy, 6 Henry Paul, 11 David Boyle, 3 Leon Pryce, 1 Robbie Paul (C), 7 Paul Deacon, 22 Brian McDermott, 9 James Lowes, 10 Paul Anderson, 19 Jamie Peacock, 12 Mike Forshaw, 13 Brad Mackay, Subs, 16 Alex Wilkinson not used, 18 Lee Radford for Mackay (41), 15 Hudson Smith for Peacock (35), 29 Stuart Fielden for Anderson (18), Anderson for McDermott (61), Peacock for Smith (62), Smith for Forshaw (70), , **Tries:** Deacon (37), **Goals:** H Paul 4
Sin bin: Fielden (26) - late tackle on Farrell that sparked the brawl
Half-time: 4-10, **Att** 17,365, **Penalty count:** 7-7, **Referee:** Russell Smith (Castleford)
League Express Men of the Match:
Warriors: Jason Robinson, **Bulls:** Paul Deacon

ROUND 14

WIGAN WARRIORS 52 SALFORD CITY REDS 20
WARRIORS: 18 Wes Davies, 2 Brett Dallas, 3 Steve Renouf, 4 Gary Connolly, 5 Jason Robinson, 13 Andrew Farrell (C), 7 Willie Peters, 8 Terry O'Connor, 9 Terry Newton, 10 Neil Cowie, 11 Mick Cassidy, 16 Simon Haughton, 12 Denis Betts. Subs: 23 Brady Malam for Cowie (30), 17 Tony Mestrov for O'Connor (30), 14 Lee Gilmour for Farrell (49), 19 Chris Chester for Haughton (15), O'Connor for Malam (50), Malam for Mestrov (60)
Tries: Dallas (4, 11, 48), Robinson (9, 29), Renouf (14), Chester (20), Malam (70), Peters (74). **Goals:** Farrell 6, Peters 2
CITY REDS: 1 Gary Broadbent, 2 Nick Pinkney, 30 Jason Nicol, 4 Jason Webber, 3 Kris Tassell, 31 Steve Blakeley, 6 Graham Holroyd, 8 Paul Southern, 9 Malcolm Alker, 14 Joe Faimalo, 12 Darren Brown (C), 11 James Smith, 23 Michael Wainwright. Subs: 28 John Duffy for Alker (35), 10 Craig Makin for Smith (56), 16 Paul Highton for Faimalo (32), 18 Stuart Littler for Broadbent (64), Faimalo for Southern (70)
Tries: Brown (23), Smith (52), Pinkney (65), Blakeley (77). **Goals:** Blakeley 2
League Express Men of the Match:
Warriors: Brett Dallas, **City Reds:** Darren Brown .
Penalty count: 5-6. **Half-time:** 34-6. **Referee:** Karl Kirkpatrick (Warrington). **Att:** 7,748

WAKEFIELD TRINITY WILDCATS 22 ST HELENS 30
WILDCATS: 1 Steve Prescott, 24 Paul Sampson, 26 Gareth Ellis, 20 Adam Hughes, 2 Neil Law, 12 Willie Poching, 7 Glen Tomlinson, 8 Francis Stephenson, 21 Ryan Hudson, 10 Martin Masella, 19 Jamie Field, 11 Warren Jowitt, 15 Gary Price (C). Subs: 17 Frank Watene for Stephenson (37), 18 Paul Jackson for Masella (29), 30 Jason Critchley (D) for Sampson (47), 29 Andy Speak (D) for Hudson (58), Masella for Watene (58), Stephenson for Field (71)
Tries: Jowitt (8), Poching (17), Masella (67). **Goals:** Prescott 5, **Sin bin:** Gary Price (39) - fighting
SAINTS: 17 Paul Wellens, 2 Chris Smith, 3 Kevin Iro, 4 Paul Newlove, 5 Anthony Sullivan, 20 Tommy Martyn, 7 Sean Long, 10 Julian O'Neill, 23 Scott Barrow, 8 Apollo Perelini, 26 John Stankevitch, 11 Chris Joynt (C), 13 Paul Sculthorpe. Subs: 12 Sonny Nickle for O'Neill (29), 18 Bryan Henare for Perelini (58), 19 Tony Stewart for Iro (23), 22 Tim Jonkers for Barrow (71), O'Neill for Stankevitch (61)
Tries: Sullivan (46, 50), Newlove (15), Wellens (22), Long (70), Smith (77). **Goals:** Long 2, Martyn, **Sin bin:** Paul Sculthorpe (39) - fighting; (64) - holding down, **On report:** Paul Newlove (73) - high tackle
League Express Men of the Match:
Wildcats: Willie Poching, **Saints:** Paul Newlove.
Penalty count: 14-11. **Half-time:** 14-12. **Referee:** Russell Smith (Castleford), **Att:** 5,104

LONDON BRONCOS 20 CASTLEFORD TIGERS 26
BRONCOS: 5 Brett Warton, 16 Frank Napoli, 28 Kevin Crouthers, 13 Mat Toshack, 19 Dom Peters, 26 Peter Lupton, 1 Tulsen Tollett, 18 Justin Dooley, 21 Jon Clarke, 12 Steele Retchless, 14 Andrew Wynyard, 15 Andy Johnson, 6 Karle Hammond. Subs: 9 Dean Callaway for Clarke (50), 29 Glen Air for Crouthers (60), 17 Anthony Seibold for Dooley (50), 27 Paul Davidson for Wynyard (26), Dooley for Davidson (60), Davidson for Johnson (72)
Tries: Johnson (29), Hammond (57), Retchless (66), Tollett (88). **Goals:** Warton 2
TIGERS: 1 Jason Flowers, 16 Jon Wells, 3 Michael Eagar, 4 Logan Campbell, 14 Barrie-Jon Mather, 6 Danny Orr, 7 Brad Davis, 8 Nathan Sykes, 9 Aaron Raper, 10 Dean Sampson, 11 Lee Harland, 12 Dale Fritz, 13 Adrian Vowles (C). Subs: 17 Ian Tonks for Fritz (31), 15 Darren Shaw for Sampson (51), 19 Andy Lynch for Fritz (77), 21 Andy McNally not used, Fritz for Harland (62), Harland for Tonks (74), Sampson for Sykes (62)
Tries: Sykes (7), Eagar (10, 23), Mather (69), Tonks (74). **Goals:** Orr 3
League Express Men of the Match:
Broncos: Brett Warton **Tigers:** Danny Orr.
Penalty count: 6-4. **Half-time:** 6-16. **Referee:** Steve Ganson (St Helens), **Att:** 8,067

HULL FC 26 WARRINGTON WOLVES 12
HULL: 1 Ben Sammut, 3 Deon Bird, 14 Steve Collins, 4 Craig Simon, 2 Matt Daylight, 20 Richard Horne, 7 Will Robinson, 8 Paul Broadbent, 9 Mick Jenkins, 12 Luke Felsch, 16 Adam Maher, 13 Tony Grimaldi (C), 15 David Maiden. Subs: 6 Stanley Gene for Jenkins (28), 10 Andrew Hick for Felsch (21), 11 Craig Wilson for Maher (63), 18 Wayne McDonald for Collins (16BB, rev 26), McDonald for Broadbent (49), Felsch for Hick (63), Broadbent for Wilson (69)
Tries: Horne (35), Gene (54), Simon (57), Collins (75).
Goals: Sammut 5
WOLVES: 1 Lee Penny, 2 Jon Roper, 12 Ian Knott, 4 Toa Kohe-Love, 3 Alan Hunte, 13 Tawera Nikau, 7 Allan Langer (C), 8 Andrew Gee, 9 Danny Farrar, 10 Danny Nutley, 14 Steve McCurrie, 21 Jerome Guisset, 11 Dean Busby. Subs: 6 Lee Briers for Busby (32), 18 Mark Hilton for Nutley (58), 19 Dave Highton for Farrar (36), 26 Mike Peters for McCurrie (66), Farrar for Highton (58), Nutley for Gee (76)
Tries: Roper (4), Guisset (39), Love (42), **Sin bin:** Nikau (51) - obstruction, On report: Nikau (51) – obstruction
League Express Men of the Match:
Hull: Stanley Gene. Wolves: Allan Langer. **Penalty count:** 11-5. **Half-time:** 8-8. **Referee:** Robert Connolly (Wigan), Att: 5,650

BRADFORD BULLS 48
HUDDERSFIELD-SHEFFIELD GIANTS 20
BULLS: 5 Michael Withers, 2 Tevita Vaikona, 3 Leon Pryce, 11 David Boyle, 16 Alex Wilkinson (D), 1 Robbie Paul (C), 7 Paul Deacon, 29 Stuart Fielden, 9 James Lowes, 10 Paul Anderson, 19 Jamie Peacock, 18 Lee Radford, 6 Henry Paul. Subs: 26 Paul Sykes for Withers (57), 27 Robert Parker for Peacock (54), 15 Hudson Smith for Radford (31), 22 Brian McDermott for Anderson (24), Anderson for Fielden (64), Fielden for Boyle (74)
Tries: Peacock (5), Vaikona (9, 56, 73), Deacon (43), McDermott (45), Boyle (53), Sykes (69, 79). **Goals:** H Paul 6, **Sin bin:** H Paul (15) - kicking the ball away
GIANTS: 14 Paul Reilly, 2 Danny Arnold, 1 Waisale Sovatabua, 17 Martin Gleeson, 25 Ben Cooper, 6 Gene Ngamu, 19 Chris Thorman, 11 David Lomax, 9 Johnny Lawless, 10 Dale Laughton, 22 David Bradbury, 12 Richard Marshall, 13 Jeff Hardy (C). Subs: 31 Yacine Dekkiche for Gleeson (57), 8 Steve Molloy for Laughton (32), 28 Andy Rice for Lomax (32BB), 18 Danny Russell for Lawless (51), Laughton for Marshall (62), Marshall for Molloy (67, BB), Gleeson for Cooper (75), Molloy for Laughton (78)
Tries: Reilly (24), Laughton (63), Lomax (66).
Goals: Ngamu 4
League Express Men of the Match:
Bulls: Henry Paul, **Giants:** Chris Thorman.
Penalty count: 8-8. **Half-time:** 12-8. **Referee:** Steve Presley (Castleford), **Att:** 11,565

LEEDS RHINOS 36 HALIFAX BLUE SOX 22
RHINOS: 5 Francis Cummins, 2 Paul Sterling, 22 Chev Walker, 4 Keith Senior, 21 Karl Pratt, 1 Iestyn Harris (C), 7 Ryan Sheridan, 8 Darren Fleary, 9 Lee Jackson, 10 Barrie McDermott, 11 Adrian Morley, 12 David Barnhill, 16 Andy Hay. Subs: 6 Daryl Powell for Morley (17), 17 Anthony Farrell for Barnhill (17), 20 Jamie Mathiou for McDermott (31), 33 Graham Mackay for McDermott (66), McDermott for Fleary (51), Barnhill for Hay (60)
Tries: Senior (18, 33, 35, 45), Pratt (21), Sterling (69).
Goals: Harris 6
BLUE SOX: 3 Damian Gibson, 17 Olly Marns, 6 Greg Florimo (C), 27 Jim Naylor, 5 Phil Hassan, 14 Martin Pearson, 7 Andrew Dunemann, 8 Andy Hobson, 30 Matt Firth (D), 10 James Gannon, 11 Gary Mercer, 12 Jamie Bloem, 13 Martin Moana. Subs: 1 Daryl Cardiss for Naylor (22), 21 Gael Tallec for Moana (36), 15 Lokeni Savelio for Hobson (36), 31 Danny Tickle (D) for Tallec (61), Moana for Dunemann (49BB, rev 55), Moana for Pearson (58), Hobson for Moana (70)
Tries: Bloem (18), Hassan (59), Moana (66), Marns (73). **Goals:** Pearson, Bloem 2, **Dismissal:** Gannon (23) – striking
League Express Men of the Match:
Rhinos: Keith Senior, **Blue Sox:** Greg Florimo (C).
Half-time: 24-6. **Referee:** John Connolly, **Att** 12,963.
Penalty count: 8-8

ROUND 15

HALIFAX BLUE SOX 12 WIGAN WARRIORS 26
BLUE SOX: 3 Damian Gibson, 17 Oliver Marns, 6 Greg Florimo (C) (C), 27 Jim Naylor, 5 Phil Hassan, 14 Martin Pearson, 7 Andrew Dunemann, 8 Andy Hobson, 32 Matty Firth, 10 Jim Gannon, 11 Gary Mercer, 12 Jamie Bloem, 13 Marty Moana. Subs: 19 David Foster for Bloem (66), 14 Marvin Golden for Pearson (29), 15 Lokeni Savelio for Hobson (32), 31 Danny Tickle for Hobson (76), Hobson for Gannon (52), Gannon for Savelio (63),
Tries: Moana (42), Marns (79).
Goals: Pearson 1, Bloem 1,
WARRIORS: 1 Kris Radlinski, 2 Brett Dallas, 4 Gary Connolly, 3 Steve Renouf, 5 Jason Robinson, 20 Phil Jones, 7 Willie Peters, 8 Terry O'Connor, 9 Terry Newton, 10 Neil Cowie, 11 Mick Cassidy, 12 Denis Betts (C), 19 Chris Chester. Subs: 18 Wes Davies for Radlinski (74), 17 Tony Mestrov for O'Connor (27), 23 Brady Malam for Cowie (41), 26 David Hodgson for Jones (60), O'Connor for Mestrov (65),
Tries: Peters (15), Dallas (20), Connolly (59, 75), Chester (67). **Goals:** Jones, Peters 2
League Express Men of the Match:, Blue Sox: Greg Florimo (C), **Warriors:** Gary Connolly.
Half-time: 2-10. **Referee:** Karl Kirkpatrick (Warrington), **Att:** 6,333. **Penalty count:** 5-6

WARRINGTON WOLVES 16
WAKEFIELD TRINITY WILDCATS 32
WOLVES: 1 Lee Penny, 3 Alan Hunte, 4 Toa Kohe-Love, 12 Ian Knott, 2 Jon Roper, 13 Tawera Nikau, 7 Allan Langer (C), 8 Andrew Gee, 9 Danny Farrar, 10 Danny Nutley, 21 Jerome Guisset, 14 Steve McCurrie, 11 Dean Busby. Subs: 6 Lee Briers for Busby (28), 18 Mark Hilton for Nutley (25), 19 David Highton for Farrar (68), 26 Mike Peters for Roper (60), Busby for McCurrie (66), Nutley for Gee (71)
Tries: Knott (42), Roper (53), Penny (62). **Goals:** Roper, Briers, **On Report:** Gee (48) - fighting
WILDCATS: 1 Steve Prescott, 5 Bright Sodje, 4 Tony Tatupu, 20 Adam Hughes, 30 Jason Critchley, 7 Glen Tomlinson, 25 Bobbie Goulding (C), 18 Paul Jackson, 29 Andy Speak, 10 Martin Masella, 15 Gary Price, 11 Warren Jowitt, 12 Willie Poching. Subs: 17 Frank Watene for Masella (22), 19 Jamie Field for Poching (16), 26 Gareth Ellis for Tomlinson (54), 21 Ryan Hudson for Speak (46), Masella for Jackson (50), Jackson for Watene (74)
Tries: Critchley (6), Speak (26), Goulding (37, 67), Masella (70). **Goals:** Goulding 5, **Field goal:** Goulding 2
On report: Watene (48) – fighting
League Express Men of the Match:
Wolves: Lee Penny, **Wildcats:** Bobbie Goulding
Penalty count: 5-4. **Half-time:** 0-18. **Referee:** Ian Smith, **Att:** 6,225

SALFORD CITY 42 CITY REDS LONDON BRONCOS 26
CITY REDS: 1 Gary Broadbent, 2 Nick Pinkney, 30 Jason Nicol, 4 Jason Webber, 5 Martin Offiah, 31 Steve Blakeley, 6 Graham Holroyd, 8 Paul Southern, 9 Malcolm Alker, 15 Neil Baynes, 11 James Smith, 12 Darren Brown (C), 23 Mike Wainwright. Subs: 28 John Duffy for Broadbent (69), 3 Kris Tassell for Brown (59), 16 Paul Highton for Baynes (23), 14 Joe Faimalo for Smith (57), Baynes for Southern (51), Southern for Alker (73), Broadbent for Offiah (73)
Tries: Wainwright (5), Webber (10, 50), Holroyd (19, 72), Pinkney (42), Broadbent (61). **Goals:** Blakeley 7
BRONCOS: 5 Brett Warton, 16 Frank Napoli, 4 Greg Fleming, 13 Mat Toshack, 19 Dom Peters, 1 Tulsen Tollett, 29 Glen Air, 18 Justin Dooley, 21 Jon Clarke, 17 Anthony Seibold, 12 Steele Retchless, 11 Shane Millard, 6 Karle Hammond (C). Subs: 9 Dean Callaway for Clarke (51), 8 Darren Bradstreet for Dooley (51), 20 Steffan Hughes for Millard (67), 26 Peter Lupton for Air (48), Air for Toshack (63), Dooley for Seibold (70)
Tries: Hammond (15), Fleming (24), Warton (30), Lupton (75). **Goals:** Warton 5
League Express Men of the Match:
City Reds: Graham Holroyd, **Broncos:** Brett Warton.
Half-time: 18-20. **Referee:** Russell Smith (Castleford), **Att:** 3,011. **Penalty count:** 4-4

CASTLEFORD TIGERS 10 BRADFORD BULLS 39
TIGERS: 1 Jason Flowers, 16 Jon Wells, 14 Barrie-Jon Mather, 3 Michael Eagar, 5 Darren Rogers, 6 Danny Orr, 7 Brad Davis, 10 Dean Sampson, 9 Aaron Raper, 8 Nathan Sykes, 17 Ian Tonks, 12 Dale Fritz, 13 Adrian Vowles (C). Subs: 15 Darren Shaw for Sampson (25), 4 Logan Campbell for Fritz (65), 40 Lee Harland for Sykes (40), 22 Andrew Purcell for Raper (46), Sampson for Tonks (54), Tonks for Shaw (73)
Tries: Davis (24), Sampson (61), **Goal:** Orr, **On report:** Adrian Vowles (77) - high tackle
BULLS: 6 Henry Paul, 4 Nathan McAvoy, 20 Scott Naylor, 3 Leon Pryce, 2 Tevita Vaikona, 1 Robbie Paul (C), 7 Paul Deacon, 29 Stuart Fielden, 9 James Lowes, 22 Brian McDermott, 11 David Boyle, 19 Jamie Peacock, 13 Brad Mackay. Subs: 10 Paul Anderson for McDermott (33), 15 Hudson Smith for Boyle (8), 50 Alex Wilkinson for McAvoy (50), 18 Lee Radford for Mackay (70), McDermott for Smith (62)
Tries: Anderson (45, 72), Naylor (19), Deacon (21), R. Paul (67), Lowes (78). **Goals:** H. Paul 7,
Field goal: Boyle
League Express Men of the Match:
Tigers: Danny Orr, **Bulls:** Henry Paul
Penalty count: 6-6. **Half-time:** 6-15. **Referee:** Stuart Cummings (Widnes), **Att:** 10,015

ST HELENS 20 LEEDS RHINOS 42
SAINTS: 17 Paul Wellens, 24 Steve Hall, 19 Anthony Stewart, 4 Paul Newlove, 5 Anthony Sullivan, 20 Tommy Martyn, 7 Sean Long, 8 Apollo Perelini, 9 Keiron Cunningham, 12 Sonny Nickle, 18 Bryan Henare, 11 Chris Joynt (C), 13 Paul Sculthorpe. Subs: 10 Julian O'Neill for Nickle (25), 23 Scott Barrow for Cunningham (75), 25 Mark Edmondson for Henare (52), 22 Tim Jonkers for Edmondson (72), Nickle for Perelini (52), Perelini for Nickle (67)
Tries: Stewart (25), Newlove (29), Hall (58).
Goals: Long 4, **Sin bin:** Long (80) - scuffling with Sheridan, **On report:** Perelini (44) - alleged high tackle on Sterling
RHINOS: 5 Francis Cummins, 2 Paul Sterling, 22 Chev Walker, 4 Keith Senior, 21 Karl Pratt, 1 Iestyn Harris (C), 7 Ryan Sheridan, 8 Darren Fleary, 9 Lee Jackson, 10 Barrie McDermott, 11 Adrian Morley, 13 Kevin Sinfield, 16 Andy Hay. Subs: 6 Daryl Powell for Sinfield (30), 17 Anthony Farrell for Fleary (57), 20 Jamie Mathiou for McDermott (19), 33 Graham Mackay for Sterling (46BB, rev 63), Mackay for Mathiou (70), Sinfield for Hay (75)
Tries: Senior (9), Harris (32), Pratt (35, 66), Hay (60), Cummins (70), Harris (65). **Goals:** Harris 7
Sin bin: Morley (50) - obstruction; Sheridan (80) - scuffling with Long
League Express Men of the Match:
Saints: Keiron Cunningham, **Rhinos:** Iestyn Harris
Penalty count: 7-5. **Half-time:** 12-18. **Referee:** Steve Presley (Castleford), **Att:** 8,443

HUDDERSFIELD-SHEFFIELD GIANTS 26 HULL FC 34
GIANTS: 14 Paul Reilly, 1 Waisale Sovatabua, 31 Yacine Dekkiche, 17 Martin Gleeson, 2 Danny Arnold, 6 Gene Ngamu, 19 Chris Thorman, 11 David Lomax, 9 John Lawless, 10 Dale Laughton, 12 Richard Marshall, 22 David Bradbury, 13 Jeff Hardy (C). Subs: 15 Darren Turner for Lomax (28), 32 Andy Richardson (D) for Laughton (37), 7 Gavin Clinch for Reilly (52), 18 Danny Russell for Lawless (37), Laughton for Richardson (62)
Tries: Arnold (8, 15, 45), Gleeson (79), Bradbury (50).
Goals: Ngamu 3
HULL: 1 Ben Sammut, 2 Matt Daylight, 4 Craig Simon, 14 Steve Collins, 3 Deon Bird, 26 Paul Cooke, 20 Richard Horne, 8 Paul Broadbent, 9 Mick Jenkins, 12 Luke Felsch, 16 Adam Maher, 13 Tony Grimaldi (C), 15 David Maiden. Subs: 6 Stanley Gene for Collins (26BB, rev 34), 25 Richard Fletcher for Broadbent (63), 10 Andrew Hick for Daylight (21), 19 Paul King for Hick (47), Gene for Jenkins (51), Broadbent for King (73)
Tries: Collins (5, 39, 79), Maher (75), Maiden (30), Felsch (36). **Goals:** Sammut 5
League Express Men of the Match:
Giants: Danny Arnold, **Hull:** Mick Jenkins
Penalty count: 7-4. **Half-time:** 10-28. **Referee:** Robert Connolly (Wigan), **Att:** 3,184

ROUND 16

WAKEFIELD TRINITY WILDCATS 20 HUDDERSFIELD-SHEFFIELD GIANTS 27
WILDCATS: 1 Steve Prescott, 5 Bright Sodje, 4 Tony Tatupu, 20 Adam Hughes, 30 Jason Critchley, 7 Glen Tomlinson, 25 Bobbie Goulding, 8 Francis Stephenson, 29 Andy Speak, 10 Martin Masella, 15 Gary Price (C), 11 Warren Jowitt, 12 Willie Poching. Subs: 17 Frank Watene for Masella (51BB, rev 67), 18 Paul Jackson for Masella (27), 26 Gareth Ellis for Hughes (11), 21 Ryan Hudson for Speak (27), Masella for Goulding (40), Speak for Poching (56), Goulding for Stephenson (56), Stephenson for Jowitt (77)
Tries: Critchley (10), Price (34), Jackson (39).
Goals: Goulding 3, Prescott
GIANTS: 1 Waisale Sovatabua, 25 Ben Cooper, 31 Yacine Dekkiche, 17 Martin Gleeson, 2 Danny Arnold, 6 Gene Ngamu, 19 Chris Thorman, 11 David Lomax, 9 John Lawless, 10 Dale Laughton, 22 David Bradbury, 15 Darren Turner, 13 Jeff Hardy (C). Subs: 7 Gavin Clinch for Gleeson (40), 28 Andy Rice for Turner (44), 12 Richard Marshall for Turner (16BB, rev 24), 32 Andy Richardson for Laughton (33), Marshall for Lomax (31), Lomax for Richardson (48), Laughton for Lomax (51BB, rev 61), Laughton for Marshall (68)
Tries: Thorman (15, 79), Dekkiche (4), Hardy (23), Gleeson (26). **Goals:** Ngamu 3, **Field goal:** Hardy
League Express Men of the Match:
Wildcats: Gary Price, **Giants:** Chris Thorman
Penalty count: 6-7. **Half-time:** 18-20. **Referee:** Ian Smith (Oldham), **Att:** 3,613

BRADFORD BULLS 96 SALFORD CITY REDS 16
BULLS: 6 Henry Paul, 14 Justin Brooker, 20 Scott Naylor, 3 Leon Pryce, 2 Tevita Vaikona, 1 Robbie Paul (C), 7 Paul Deacon, 29 Stuart Fielden, 9 James Lowes, 22 Brian McDermott, 19 Jamie Peacock, 12 Mike Forshaw, 13 Brad Mackay. Subs: 16 Alex Wilkinson for Naylor (46), 27 Robert Parker for Peacock (50), 15 Hudson Smith for Forshaw (35), 18 Lee Radford for Mackay (20), Mackay for Radford (43BB, rev 49), Mackay for Deacon (58), Peacock for McDermott (70),
Tries: R Paul (19, 31, 33, 47), Peacock (2, 17, 73), Brooker (23, 38), Radford (29), Naylor (42), Deacon (49), Parker (52), H Paul (62), McDermott (66), Mackay (68), Wilkinson (79). **Goals:** H Paul 14
CITY REDS: 4 Jason Webber, 2 Nick Pinkney, 30 Jason Nicol, 3 Kris Tassell, 5 Martin Offiah, 6 Graham Holroyd, 31 Steve Blakeley, 15 Neil Baynes, 9 Malcolm Alker (C), 10 Craig Makin, 16 Paul Highton, 14 Joe Faimalo, 23 Mike Wainwright. Subs: 28 John Duffy for Alker (47), 18 Stuart Littler for Webber (2), 20 Matthew Leigh for Faimalo (17), 27 Carlo Napolitano for Baynes (50), Baynes for Wainwright (65)
Tries: Nicol (30), Pinkney (57), Napolitano (63).
Goals: Blakeley 2
League Express Men of the Match:
Bulls: Jamie Peacock, **City Reds:** Nick Pinkney
Penalty count: 3-2. **Half-time:** 44-6. **Referee:** Robert Connolly (Wigan), **Att:** 11,596

HALIFAX BLUE SOX 24 ST HELENS 28
BLUE SOX: 1 Daryl Cardiss, 4 Marvin Golden, 6 Greg Florimo (C), 3 Damian Gibson, 5 Phil Hassan, 14 Martin Pearson, 7 Andrew Dunemann, 8 Andy Hobson, 32 Matty Firth, 10 Jim Gannon, 11 Gary Mercer, 12 Jamie Bloem, 13 Marty Moana. Subs: 17 Oliver Marns for Florimo (25), 23 Brett Goldspink for Hobson (26), 21 Gael Tallec for Gibson (55), Gibson for Cardiss (62), Hobson for Golden (65), 15 Lokeni Savelio for Goldspink (73)
Tries: Moana (45, 57), Bloem (51), Marns (65).
Goals: Pearson 4
SAINTS: 17 Paul Wellens, 24 Steve Hall, 19 Anthony Stewart, 4 Paul Newlove, 5 Anthony Sullivan, 20 Tommy Martyn, 7 Sean Long, 8 Apollo Perelini, 9 Keiron Cunningham, 10 Julian O'Neill, 11 Chris Joynt (C), 12 Sonny Nickle, 26 John Stankevitch. Subs: 18 Bryan Henare for Perelini (26), 22 Tim Jonkers for Stankevitch (27bb, rev 30), 21 Dwayne West (D) for Newlove (39), Perelini for O'Neill (47), O'Neill for Stankevitch (58), Jonkers for Stewart (74), 30 Mike Bennett not used
Tries: Martyn (5), Stewart (9), Sullivan (29), Wellens (72, 78). **Goals:** Long 4, **Sin bin:** Nickle (68) - obstructing Dunemann after he kicked through.
League Express Men of the Match:
Blue Sox: Jamie Bloem, **Saints:** Paul Wellens.
Half-time: 2-16. **Penalty count:** 6-3, Att: 5,476. **Referee:** John Connolly (Wigan)

LEEDS RHINOS 28 WARRINGTON WOLVES 24
RHINOS: 5 Francis Cummins, 33 Graham Mackay, 22 Chev Walker, 4 Keith Senior, 21 Karl Pratt, 1 Iestyn Harris (C), 7 Ryan Sheridan, 8 Darren Fleary, 9 Lee Jackson, 20 Jamie Mathiou, 11 Adrian Morley, 13 Kevin Sinfield, 16 Andy Hay. Subs:, 23 Danny Ward for Mathiou (25), 6 Daryl Powell for Sinfield (30), 12 David Barnhill for Fleary (46), Sinfield for Hay (53bb, reversed 70), Mathiou for Morley (66), 34 Gareth Raynor for Senior (72), Fleary for Mathiou (78)
Tries: Walker (4, 14, 55), Senior (11), Cummins (71).
Goals: Harris 4
WOLVES: 1 Lee Penny, 3 Alan Hunte, 4 Toa Kohe-Love, 20 Ian Sibbit, 2 Jon Roper, 13 Tawera Nikau, 7 Allan Langer (C), 8 Andrew Gee, 9 Danny Farrar, 10 Danny Nutley, 14 Steve McCurrie, 21 Jerome Guisset, 11 Dean Busby. Subs:, 12 Ian Knott for Sibbit (8), 6 Lee Briers for Busby (26), 19 David Highton for Penny (39bb, reversed 40), 18 Mark Hilton for Nutley (56), Busby for McCurrie (63), Highton for Farrar (71), McCurrie for Guisset (79)
Tries: Penny (29, 41, 46, 68). **Goals:** Roper 4, **Sin bin:** Gee (59 - professional foul)
League Express Men of the Match: Rhinos: Graham Mackay. **Wolves:** Lee Penny.
Half-time: 18-6, **Penalty count:** 11-5. **Referee:** Russell Smith (Castleford), **Att:** 11,432

HULL FC 4 CASTLEFORD TIGERS 18
HULL FC: 1 Ben Sammut, 17 Brian Carney, 14 Steve Collins, 4 Craig Simon, 2 Matt Daylight, 26 Paul Cooke, 20 Richard Horne, 8 Paul Broadbent, 9 Mick Jenkins, 10 Andrew Hick, 16 Adam Maher, 13 Tony Grimaldi (C), 15 David Maiden. Subs: 6 Stanley Gene for Jenkins (50), 25 Richard Fletcher for Felsch (68), 12 Luke Felsch for Broadbent (20), 19 Paul King for Hick (35)
Try: Maher (5)
TIGERS: 1 Jason Flowers, 16 Jon Wells, 14 Barrie-Jon Mather, 3 Michael Eagar, 5 Darren Rogers, 6 Danny Orr, 7 Brad Davis, 15 Darren Shaw, 22 Andrew Purcell, 17 Ian Tonks, 11 Lee Harland, 12 Dale Fritz, 13 Adrian Vowles (C). Subs: 10 Dean Sampson for Fritz (10BB, rev 18), 19 Andy Lynch for Fritz (70), 18 Paul Smith for Mather (72), 2 Richard Gay for Harland (59), Sampson for Tonks (26), Tonks for Shaw (52), Harland for Wells (66), Shaw for Tonks (75)
Tries: Rogers (37), Eagar (63), Orr (70). **Goals:** Orr 3
On report: Harland (20) - alleged high tackle on Broadbent
League Express Men of the Match:
Hull FC: Matt Daylight, **Tigers:** Michael Eagar
Penalty count: 7-5. **Half-time:** 4-6. **Referee:** Steve Ganson (St Helens), **Att:** 6,501

LONDON BRONCOS 12 WIGAN WARRIORS 16
BRONCOS: 5 Brett Warton, 16 Frank Napoli, 4 Greg Fleming, 22 John Timu, 19 Dom Peters, 1 Tulsen Tollett, 29 Glen Air, 17 Anthony Seibold, 21 Jon Clarke, 18 Justin Dooley, 11 Shane Millard, 12 Steele Retchless, 6 Karle Hammond (C). Subs: 9 Dean Callaway for Clarke (51), 15 Andy Johnson for Millard (24bb, rev 67), 27 Paul Davidson for Seibold (27), 26 Peter Lupton for Napoli (34), Seibold for Dooley (55), Dooley for Davidson (69)
Tries: Millard (4), Air (12). **Goals:** Warton 2
WARRIORS: 1 Kris Radlinski, 2 Brett Dallas, 3 Steve Renouf, 4 Gary Connolly, 5 Jason Robinson, 13 Andy Farrell (C), 7 Willie Peters, 8 Terry O'Connor, 9 Terry Newton, 10 Neil Cowie, 11 Mick Cassidy, 12 Denis Betts, 19 Chris Chester. Subs: 14 Lee Gilmour for Chester (52), 17 Tony Mestrov for O'Connor (26), 18 Wes Davies not used, 23 Brady Malam for Cowie (29BB, rev 40), Malam for Cowie (54), O'Connor for Mestrov (59), Cowie for Malam (75BB)
Tries: Farrell (8), Newton (30), Dallas (46). **Goals:** Farrell 2. **Penalty count:** 5-9. **Half-time:** 12-12. **Referee:** Stuart Cummings (Widnes), **Att:** 4,351
League Express Men of the Match:
Broncos: Dom Peters, **Warriors:** Andy Farrell

ROUND 17

HALIFAX BLUE SOX 66 HUDDERSFIELD-SHEFFIELD GIANTS 2
BLUE SOX: 1 Daryl Cardiss, 17 Oliver Marns, 27 Jim Naylor, 3 Damian Gibson, 5 Phil Hassan, 14 Martin Pearson, 7 Andrew Dunemann (C), 8 Andy Hobson, 9 Paul Rowley, 10 Jim Gannon, 11 Gary Mercer, 12 Jamie Bloem, 13 Marty Moana. Subs: 20 Stephen Holgate for Mercer (41), 21 Gael Tallec for Bloem (61), 15 Lokeni Savelio for Gannon (52), 23 Brett Goldspink for Hobson (31), Hobson for Goldspink (71)
Tries: Dunemann (18, 25), Rowley (22), Pearson (31), Naylor (37), Hassan (40), Marns (56), Cardiss (58), Moana (61, 67, 80). **Goals:** Pearson 11
GIANTS: 1 Waisale Sovatabua, 25 Ben Cooper, 17 Martin Gleeson, 31 Yacine Dekkiche, 2 Danny Arnold, 6 Gene Ngamu, 19 Chris Thorman, 11 David Lomax, 9 Johnny Lawless, 10 Dale Laughton, 15 Darren Turner, 22 David Bradbury, 13 Jeff Hardy (C). Subs: 18 Danny Russell for Lawless (51), 12 Richard Marshall for Lomax (31), 28 Andy Rice for Laughton (34), 23 Dale Cardoza for Gleeson (62), Lomax for Bradbury (57), Laughton for Rice (62)
Goal: Ngamu
League Express Men of the Match:
Blue Sox: Martin Pearson, **Giants:** David Bradbury
Penalty count: 8-8. **Half-time:** 36-2. **Referee:** Steve Ganson (St Helens), **Att:** 4,608

LEEDS RHINOS 20 CASTLEFORD TIGERS 12
RHINOS: 5 Francis Cummins, 33 Graham Mackay, 22 Chev Walker, 4 Keith Senior, 2 Karl Pratt, 1 Iestyn Harris (C), 7 Ryan Sheridan, 8 Darren Fleary, 9 Lee Jackson, 20 Jamie Mathiou, 11 Adrian Morley, 13 Kevin Sinfield, 16 Andy Hay. Subs: 17 Anthony Farrell for Mathiou (20), 6 Daryl Powell for Sinfield (29), 12 David Barnhill for Morley (39), 34 Gareth Raynor for Fleary (62), Sinfield for Jackson (44), Jackson for Powell (58), Mathiou for Cummins (74BB, rev 78)
Tries: Senior (20), Sinfield (29), Barnhill (68), Mackay (78). **Goals:** Harris 2
TIGERS: 1 Jason Flowers, 16 Jon Wells, 14 Barrie-Jon Mather, 3 Michael Eagar, 5 Darren Rogers, 6 Danny Orr, 7 Brad Davis, 15 Darren Shaw, 20 Andrew Purcell, 8 Nathan Sykes, 11 Lee Harland, 12 Dale Fritz, 13 Adrian Vowles (C). Subs: 17 Ian Tonks for Harland (12), 12 Dean Sampson for Shaw (21), 2 Richard Gay for Vowles (33), 18 Paul Smith for Sampson (63), Shaw for Sykes (62), Vowles for Tonks (72)
Tries: Orr (23), Fritz (33). **Goals:** Orr 2
League Express Men of the Match:
Rhinos: Kevin Sinfield. **Tigers:** Nathan Sykes. **Penalty count:** 3-5. **Half-time:** 8-12. **Referee:** Stuart Cummings (Widnes), **Att:** 14,492

ST HELENS 50 WARRINGTON WOLVES 20
SAINTS: 17 Paul Wellens, 24 Steve Hall, 15 Sean Hoppe, 21 Dwayne West, 5 Anthony Sullivan, 20 Tommy Martyn, 7 Sean Long, 12 Sonny Nickle, 9 Keiron Cunningham, 10 Julian O' Neill, 26 John Stankevitch, 8 Apollo Perelini, 11 Chris Joynt (C). Subs: 16 Vila Matautia for O' Neill (34), 22 Tim Jonkers for Stankevitch (18), 23 Scott Barrow for Perelini (68), 30 Mike Bennett for West (54), O' Neill for Matautia (63), Matautia for Nickle (72)
Tries: Martyn (5), West (35), Wellens (39, 62), Joynt (48), Cunningham (55, 66), Barrow (71), Sullivan (73).
Goals: Long 7
WOLVES: 1 Lee Penny, 2 Jon Roper, 4 Toa Kohe-Love, 3 Alan Hunte, 23 Chris Campbell, 6 Lee Briers, 7 Allan Langer (C), 8 Andrew Gee, 9 Danny Farrar, 10 Danny Nutley, 14 Steve McCurrie, 21 Jerome Guisset, 13 Tawera Nikau. Subs: 12 Ian Knott for Roper (32), 25 Paul Noone for Guisset (68), 19 Dave Highton for Farrar (63), 18 Mark Hilton for Nutley (59), Nutley for Kohe-Love (72)
Tries: Briers (7), Roper (11), McCurrie (16), Campbell (44). **Goals:** Roper 2
League Express Men of the Match:
Saints: Tommy Martyn. **Wolves:** Lee Briers.
Penalty count: 4-3. **Half-time:** 20-16. **Referee:** Robert Connolly (Wigan), **Att:** 7,296

BRADFORD BULLS 18 WIGAN WARRIORS 30
BULLS: 6 Henry Paul, 14 Justin Brooker, 20 Scott Naylor, 3 Leon Pryce, 2 Tevita Vaikona, 1 Robbie Paul (C), 7 Paul Deacon, 29 Stuart Fielden, 9 James Lowes, 22 Brian McDermott, 19 Jamie Peacock, 12 Mike Forshaw, 13 Brad Mackay. Subs: 4 Nathan McAvoy for Pryce (40), 10 Paul Anderson for McDermott (23), 18 Lee Radford for Smith (58), 15 Hudson Smith for Mackay (46), McDermott for Anderson (63), Anderson for Peacock (73)
Tries: Brooker (17), Deacon (25), Mackay (27).
Goals: H. Paul 3
WARRIORS: 1 Kris Radlinski, 2 Brett Dallas, 4 Gary Connolly, 3 Steve Renouf, 5 Jason Robinson, 13 Andy Farrell (C), 7 Willie Peters, 8 Terry O'Connor, 9 Terry Newton, 10 Neil Cowie, 11 Mick Cassidy, 12 Denis Betts, 19 Chris Chester. Subs: 14 Lee Gilmour for Betts (44BB, rev 53), 17 Tony Mestrov for Cowie (26), 18 Wes Davies for Dallas (9BB), 23 Brady Malam for O'Connor (40), Cowie for Mestrov (60), Gilmour for Chester (67), O'Connor for Malam (69)
Tries: Newton (10,65), Robinson (37), Betts (57), Gilmour (79). **Goals:** Farrell 4, **Field goals:** Peters, Cowie. **Penalty count:** 4-6. **Half-time:** 18-14. **Referee:** Russell Smith (Castleford), **Att:** 18,815
League Express Men of the Match:
Bulls: Justin Brooker, **Warriors:** Terry Newton

HULL FC 40 LONDON BRONCOS 18
HULL FC: 1 Ben Sammut, 3 Deon Bird, 14 Steve Collins, 4 Craig Simon, 2 Matt Daylight, 20 Richard Horne, 7 Will Robinson, 19 Paul King, 9 Mick Jenkins, 12 Luke Felsch, 16 Adam Maher, 13 Tony Grimaldi (C), 15 David Maiden. Subs: 6 Stanley Gene for Maiden (50), 22 Steve Craven for King (14BB, rev 29), 25 Richard Fletcher for Craven (66), 26 Paul Cooke for Robinson (59), Craven for Felsch (36), Felsch for King (57), Maiden for Simon (67)
Tries: Horne (17, 52), Daylight (28, 58), Sammut (44), Maher (73), Gene (80). **Goals:** Sammut 6
BRONCOS: 5 Brett Warton, 1 Tulsen Tollett, 4 Greg Fleming, 22 John Timu, 19 Dom Peters, 26 Peter Lupton, 29 Glen Air, 18 Justin Dooley, 21 Jon Clarke, 17 Anthony Seibold, 11 Shane Millard, 12 Steele Retchless, 6 Karle Hammond (C). Subs: 9 Dean Callaway for Clarke (45), 10 Scott Cram for Air (32), 16 Frank Napoli for Tollett (21), 27 Paul Davidson for Millard (13BB, rev 45), Davidson for Dooley (53), Dooley for Seibold (65), Clarke for Davidson (65)
Tries: Hammond (37), Warton (47, 68).
Goals: Warton 3.
League Express Men of the Match:
Hull FC: Richard Horne, **Broncos:** Brett Warton
Penalty count: 7-2. **Half-time:** 10-6. **Referee:** John Connolly (Wigan), **Att:** 5,260

WAKEFIELD TRINITY WILDCATS 36 SALFORD CITY REDS 10
WILDCATS: 1 Steve Prescott, 5 Bright Sodje, 4 Tony Tatupu, 30 Jason Critchley, 2 Neil Law, 13 Steve McNamara, 25 Bobbie Goulding, 18 Paul Jackson, 21 Ryan Hudson, 10 Martin Masella, 19 Jamie Field, 11 Warren Jowitt, 15 Gary Price (C). Subs: 14 Paul March for Masella (67), 29 Andy Speak for Hudson (32), 26 Gareth Ellis for Price (17-40bb), 8 Francis Stephenson for Masella (18), Masella for Stephenson (52), Hudson for Field (75)
Tries: Sodje (5,79), Jowitt (20,72), Speak (46), Price (53). **Goals:** Goulding 6
CITY REDS: 1 Gary Broadbent, 2 Nick Pinkney, 4 Jason Webber, 3 Kris Tassell, 5 Martin Offiah, 6 Graham Holroyd, 31 Steve Blakeley, 15 Neil Baynes, 9 Malcolm Alker (C), 8 Paul Southern, 11 James Smith, 30 Jason Nicol, 16 Paul Highton. Subs: 28 John Duffy for Highton (65), 18 Stuart Littler for Pinkney (68), 20 Matthew Leigh for Smith (60), 10 Craig Makin for Baynes (25), Baynes for Southern (60), Smith for Nicol (68)
Tries: Offiah (38), Littler (69). **Goals:** Blakeley
League Express, Men of the Match:
Wildcats: Warren Jowitt, **City Reds:** Steve Blakeley.
Half-time: 12-6. **Penalty count:** 6-7, **Att:** 3,345. **Referee:** Karl Kirkpatrick (Warrington)

ROUND 18

SALFORD CITY REDS 30 HULL FC 22
CITY REDS: 1 Gary Broadbent, 2 Nick Pinkney, 4 Jason Webber, 3 Kris Tassell, 5 Martin Offiah, 31 Steve Blakeley, 6 Graham Holroyd, 15 Neil Baynes, 9 Malcolm Alker, 11 Jim Smith, 30 Jason Nicol, 12 Darren Brown (C), 23 Mike Wainwright. Subs: 8 Paul Southern for Baynes (25), 16 Paul Highton for Smith (35), 18 Stuart Littler for Tassell (76), 28 John Duffy not used, Smith for Highton (54), Baynes for Southern (62), Highton for Wainwright (71)
Tries: Pinkney (19, 62), Webber (24), Smith (31), Tassell (37). Goals: Blakeley 5
Sin bin: Gary Broadbent (48) - professional foul
HULL FC: 1 Ben Sammut, 2 Matt Daylight, 3 Deon Bird, 14 Steve Collins, 17 Brian Carney, 20 Richard Horne, 7 Will Robinson, 12 Luke Felsch, 9 Mick Jenkins, 19 Paul King, 16 Adam Maher, 13 Tony Grimaldi (C), 15 David Maiden. Subs: 6 Stanley Gene for Jenkins (25), 25 Richard Fletcher for Maher (48), 26 Paul Cooke for Craven (64), 22 Steve Craven for King (25), Jenkins for Carney (70)
Tries: Maiden (13), Collins (48), Horne (54), Bird (73).
Goals: Sammut 3
League Express Men of the Match:
City Reds: Nick Pinkney, **Hull FC:** Tony Grimaldi.
Penalty count: 9-7. **Half-time**: 24-6. **Referee**: Graeme Shaw (Wigan), **Att:** 3,494

CASTLEFORD TIGERS 16
WAKEFIELD TRINITY WILDCATS 12
TIGERS: 2 Richard Gay, 16 Jon Wells, 14 Barrie-Jon Mather, 3 Michael Eagar, 5 Darren Rogers, 6 Danny Orr, 7 Brad Davis, 15 Darren Shaw, 22 Andrew Purcell, 8 Nathan Sykes, 17 Ian Tonks, 1 Jason Flowers, 13 Adrian Vowles (C). Subs: 10 Dean Sampson for Shaw (29), 9 Aaron Raper for Tonks (58), 23 Craig Wright for Flowers (54), 19 Andy Lynch for Purcell (78), Shaw for Sykes (66)
Tries: Wells (28,47), Eagar (19). **Goals:** Orr 2.
Dismissal: Dean Sampson (58) - punch
WILDCATS: 1 Steve Prescott, 5 Bright Sodje, 3 Francis Maloney, 30 Jason Critchley, 2 Neil Law, 13 Steve McNamara, 25 Bobbie Goulding, 18 Paul Jackson, 21 Ryan Hudson, 10 Martin Masella, 19 Jamie Field, 11 Warren Jowitt, 15 Gary Price (C). Subs: 14 Frank Watene for Poching (58), 29 Andy Speak for Hudson (58), 26 Gareth Ellis for Law (53), 12 Willie Poching for Masella (23), Masella for Jackson (45bb), Hudson for Jowitt (69), Jackson for McNamara (69)
Tries: Field (26), Jowitt (65). **Goals:** Goulding 2. **On report:** Willie Poching (58) – late tackle.
League Express Men of the Match:
Tigers: Richard Gay. **Wildcats:** Francis Maloney
Penalty count: 4-5. **Half-time:** 10-6. **Referee:** Robert Connolly (Wigan), **Att:** 8,043

HUDDERSFIELD-SHEFFIELD GIANTS 20
LEEDS RHINOS 48
GIANTS: 1 Waisale Sovatabua, 25 Ben Cooper, 17 Martin Gleeson, 31 Yacine Dekkiche, 2 Danny Arnold, 6 Gene Ngamu, 19 Chris Thorman, 12 Richard Marshall, 9 Johnny Lawless, 10 Dale Laughton, 22 David Bradbury, 15 Darren Turner, 13 Jeff Hardy (C). Subs: 11 David Lomax for Laughton (29), 18 Danny Russell for Lawless (47), 23 Dale Cardoza for Cooper (50), 28 Andy Rice for Lomax (56), Lomax for Hardy (73)
Tries: Hardy (5), Thorman (69), Russell (80).
Goals: Ngamu 4
Sin bin: Sovatabua (54) - professional foul
RHINOS: 5 Francis Cummins, 33 Graham Mackay, 22 Chev Walker, 4 Keith Senior, 21 Karl Pratt, 1 Iestyn Harris (C), 7 Ryan Sheridan, 8 Darren Fleary, 9 Lee Jackson, 20 Jamie Mathiou, 12 David Barnhill, 13 Kevin Sinfield, 16 Andy Hay. Subs: 23 Danny Ward for Fleary (27), 24 Dave Wrench for Hay (52), 19 Dean Lawford for Sheridan (65), 34 Gareth Raynor for Cummins (67), Fleary for Mathiou (51), Mathiou for Fleary (76)
Tries: Harris (14, 77), Hay (19), Mackay (31, 64), Cummins (45, 57), Pratt (75). **Goals:** Harris 8
Sin bin: Barnhill (72) - professional foul
League Express Men of the Match:
Giants: Chris Thorman, **Rhinos:** Lee Jackson
Penalty count: 4-6. **Half-time**: 8-18. **Referee:** Steve Ganson (St Helens), **Att:** 3,226

WARRINGTON WOLVES 34 HALIFAX BLUE SOX 12
WOLVES: 1 Lee Penny, 23 Chris Campbell, 3 Alan Hunte, 12 Ian Knott, 22 Will Cowell, 6 Lee Briers, 7 Allan Langer (C), 8 Andrew Gee, 9 Danny Farrar, 10 Danny Nutley, 14 Steve McCurrie, 25 Paul Noone, 13 Tawera Nikau. Subs:, 21 Jerome Guisset for Noone (33), 18 Mark Hilton for Nutley (36), Noone for Gee (57), 26 Mike Peters for McCurrie (70), 19 David Highton for Farrar (70)
Tries: McCurrie (7, 29), Hunte (24), Langer (44), Briers (59), Cowell (71). **Goals:** Briers (5)
BLUE SOX: 1 Daryl Cardiss, 17 Olly Marns, 6 Greg Florimo (C), 3 Damian Gibson, 5 Phil Hassan, 14 Martin Pearson, 7 Andrew Dunemann, 8 Andy Hobson, 9 Paul Rowley, 10 Jim Gannon, 11 Gary Mercer, 12 Jamie Bloem, 13 Marty Moana. Subs:, 23 Brett Goldspink for Hobson (25), 4 Marvin Golden for Hassan (40), 20 Stephen Holgate for Pearson (55), 21 Gael Tallec for Holgate (60), Hobson for Gannon (60), Gannon for Florimo (72)
Tries: Moana (62), Dunemann (77). **Goals:** Bloem 2. **Sin bin:** Gibson (68) - professional foul
League Express Men of the Match:
Wolves: Allan Langer, **Blue Sox:** Paul Rowley
Referee: John Connolly (Wigan), **Att:** 6,243, **Half time:** 18-0. **Penalty count:** 10-6

WIGAN WARRIORS 28 ST HELENS 30
WARRIORS: 1 Kris Radlinski, 26 David Hodgson, 4 Gary Connolly, 3 Steve Renouf, 5 Jason Robinson, 13 Andrew Farrell (C), 7 Willie Peters, 8 Terry O'Connor, 9 Terry Newton, 10 Neil Cowie, 11 Mick Cassidy, 12 Denis Betts, 19 Chris Chester. Subs: 14 Lee Gilmour for Chester (41), 17 Tony Mestrov for Cowie (35), 18 Wes Davies for Connolly (68), 23 Brady Malam for O'Connor (41), O'Connor for Mestrov (66)
Tries: Renouf (4, 59), Hodgson (8), Chester (11).
Goals: Farrell 5, Field goals: Peters 2
SAINTS: 17 Paul Wellens, 24 Steve Hall, 3 Kevin Iro, 15 Sean Hoppe, 5 Anthony Sullivan, 20 Tommy Martyn, 7 Sean Long, 12 Sonny Nickle, 9 Keiron Cunningham, 10 Julian O'Neill, 11 Chris Joynt (C), 8 Apollo Perelini, 13 Paul Sculthorpe. Subs: 16 Vila Matautia for Nickle (28), 22 Tim Jonkers for Iro (41), 23 Scott Barrow not used, 30 Mike Bennett not used, Nickle for O'Neill (52), O'Neill for Matautia (69)
Tries: Hoppe (23), Martyn (28, 51, 77), Sullivan (66).
Goals: Long 5, **On report:** Matautia (41) - leading with forearm
League Express Men of the Match:
Warriors: Willie Peters, **Saints:** Tommy Martyn.
Half-time: 18-14, Att: 17,428. **Referee:** Stuart Cummings (Widnes). **Penalty count:** 9-2

LONDON BRONCOS 16 BRADFORD BULLS 24
BRONCOS: 4 Greg Fleming, 16 Frank Napoli, 1 Tulsen Tollett, 22 John Timu, 19 Dom Peters, 6 Karle Hammond (C), 5 Brett Warton, 18 Justin Dooley, 9 Dean Callaway, 17 Anthony Seibold, 27 Paul Davidson, 12 Steele Retchless, 21 Jon Clarke. Subs: 15 Andy Johnson for Timu (23), 10 Scott Cram for Seibold (21), 11 Shane Millard for Retchless (33), 26 Peter Lupton for Clarke (63), Retchless for Johnson (56BB, rev 68), Clarke for Callaway (72), Retchless for Dooley (72), Seibold for Millard (74BB)
Tries: Fleming (47), Hammond (68), Tollett (77).
Goals: Warton 2
BULLS: 28 Stuart Spruce, 2 Tevita Vaikona, 14 Justin Brooker, 20 Scott Naylor, 4 Nathan McAvoy, 6 Henry Paul, 1 Robbie Paul (C), 22 Brian McDermott, 9 James Lowes, 10 Paul Anderson, 19 Jamie Peacock, 29 Stuart Fielden, 12 Mike Forshaw. Subs: 30 Gareth Handford (D) for Forshaw (71), 7 Paul Deacon for Anderson (24), 15 Hudson Smith for Peacock (55), 3 Leon Pryce for Spruce (60), Anderson for McDermott (48), McDermott for Anderson (79)
Tries: Vaikona (13), Henry Paul (34), Peacock (35), Robbie Paul (50). **Goals:** Henry Paul 4
League Express Men of the Match:
Broncos: Dean Callaway, **Bulls:** Jamie Peacock.
Half-time: 0-18. **Referee:** Peter Taberner (Wigan), **Att:** 4,063. **Penalty count:** 6-7

ROUND 19

LONDON BRONCOS 22
WAKEFIELD TRINITY WILDCATS 27
BRONCOS: 4 Greg Fleming, 5 Brett Warton, 1 Tulsen Tollett, 30 Jon Roper (D), 16 Frank Napoli, 6 Karle Hammond (C), 29 Glen Air, 18 Justin Dooley, 9 Dean Callaway, 10 Scott Cram, 27 Paul Davidson, 12 Steele Retchless, 21 Jon Clarke. Subs: 11 Shane Millard for Davidson (24), 15 Andy Johnson for Retchless (24), 17 Anthony Seibold for Cram (51), 26 Peter Lupton for Clarke (48), Retchless for Millard (45 bb), Cram for Dooley (67), Davidson for Seibold (71)
Tries: Fleming (26), Hammond (51), Warton (59), Tollett (62) **Goals:** Warton 3. **Dismissal:** Davidson (75) - kicking
WILDCATS: 1 Steve Prescott, 5 Bright Sodje, 3 Francis Maloney, 4 Tony Tatupu, 24 Paul Sampson, 13 Steve McNamara (C), 25 Bobbie Goulding, 18 Paul Jackson, 21 Ryan Hudson, 10 Martin Masella, 19 Jamie Field, 11 Warren Jowitt, 15 Gary Price. Subs: 17 Frank Watene for Masella (24), 29 Andy Speak for Tatupu (54), 26 Gareth Ellis for Watene (50), 14 Paul March for Hudson (64), Masella for Jackson (61)
Tries: Sodje (12), Sampson (18, 65), Prescott (68).
Goals: Goulding 5, **Field goal:** Goulding
League Express Men of the Match:
Broncos: Karle Hammond, **Wildcats:** Bobbie Goulding
Penalty count: 6-6. **Half-time:** 6-12. **Referee:** Ian Smith (Oldham), **Att:** 2,619

SALFORD CITY REDS 26 LEEDS RHINOS 34
CITY REDS: 1 Gary Broadbent, 2 Nick Pinkney, 4 Jason Webber, 3 Kris Tassell, 5 Martin Offiah, 31 Steve Blakeley, 6 Graham Holroyd, 15 Neil Baynes, 9 Malcolm Alker, 11 Jim Smith, 30 Jason Nicol, 12 Darren Brown (C), 23 Mike Wainwright. Subs: 8 Paul Southern for Baynes (20), 16 Paul Highton for Nicol (36), 18 Stuart Littler not used, 28 John Duffy for Blakeley (74), Baynes for Southern (60)
Tries: Alker (5, 14), Offiah (35), Baynes (65).
Goals: Blakeley 5
RHINOS: 5 Francis Cummins, 13 Graham Mackay, 22 Chev Walker, 4 Keith Senior, 21 Karl Pratt, 1 Iestyn Harris (C), 7 Ryan Sheridan, 8 Darren Fleary, 9 Lee Jackson, 10 Barrie McDermott, 13 Kevin Sinfield, 12 Dave Barnhill, 16 Andy Hay. Subs: 6 Daryl Powell for Barnhill (31), 20 Jamie Mathiou for McDermott (30), 11 Adrian Morley for Hay (49), 34 Gareth Raynor not used, McDermott for Fleary (58), Hay for Powell (70)
Tries: Jackson (17), Cummins (30, 54), Harris (49), Sinfield (68), Hay (79). **Goals:** Harris 5
League Express Men of the Match:
Reds: Graham Holroyd, **Rhinos:** Ryan Sheridan
Penalty count: 5-5. **Half-time:** 18-14. **Referee:** Karl Kirkpatrick (Warrington), **Att:** 5,057

HUDDERSFIELD-SHEFFIELD GIANTS 24 ST HELENS 40
GIANTS: 6 Gene Ngamu, 2 Danny Arnold, 3 Yacine Dekkiche, 17 Martin Gleeson, 1 Waisale Sovatabua, 19 Chris Thorman, 24 Mark Moxon, 29 Jamie Fielden, 9 Johnny Lawless, 10 Dale Laughton, 11 David Lomax, 28 Andy Rice, 13 Jeff Hardy (C). Subs: 25 Ben Cooper for Ngamu (31), 27 Oliver Wilkes for Fielden (26), 23 Dale Cardoza for Gleeson (54), 18 Danny Russell for Laughton (44), Fielden for Lomax (60), Laughton for Rice (75)
Tries: Sovatabua (14), Arnold (19), Dekkiche (63), Hardy (76). **Goals:** Ngamu 2, Thorman 2
SAINTS: 17 Paul Wellens, 24 Steve Hall, 14 Fereti Tuilagi, 4 Sean Hoppe, 5 Anthony Sullivan, 20 Tommy Martyn, 7 Sean Long, 10 Julian O'Neill, 9 Keiron Cunningham, 12 Sonny Nickle, 22 Tim Jonkers, 11 Chris Joynt (C), 13 Paul Sculthorpe. Subs: 8 Apollo Perelini for O'Neill (40), 16 Vila Matautia for Nickle (23), 23 Scott Barrow for Martyn (53), 30 Mike Bennett for Joynt (66), O'Neill for Matautia (59)
Tries: Cunningham (3), Long (22, 69), Hall (29), Tuilagi (44, 61), Wellens (65). **Goals:** Long 6
League Express Men of the Match:
Giants: Waisale Sovatabua, **Saints:** Sean Long
Penalty count: 4-11. **Half-time:** 14-18. **Referee:** Graeme Shaw (Wigan), **Att:** 3,317

BRADFORD BULLS 56 HULL FC 6
BULLS: 28 Stuart Spruce, 4 Nathan McAvoy, 20 Scott Naylor, 14 Justin Brooker, 2 Tevita Vaikona, 1 Robbie Paul (C), 6 Henry Paul, 22 Brian McDermott, 9 James Lowes, 10 Paul Anderson, 19 Jamie Peacock, 29 Stuart Fielden, 12 Mike Forshaw. Subs: 7 Paul Deacon for Anderson (30), 3 Leon Pryce for Brooker (49), 15 Hudson Smith for Peacock (55), Anderson for McDermott (61), 18 Lee Radford for Forshaw (67), McDermott for R Paul (71)
Tries: R. Paul (16), Naylor (24), Peacock (35), Spruce (37, 66), Pryce (60), McAvoy (62, 74), Fielden (69, 79).
Goals: H. Paul 8
HULL: 1 Ben Sammut, 21 Craig Poucher, 15 David Maiden, 14 Steve Collins, 3 Deon Bird, 20 Richard Horne, 7 Will Robinson, 22 Steve Craven, 9 Mick Jenkins, 19 Paul King, 12 Luke Felsch, 13 Tony Grimaldi (c), 6 Stanley Gene. Subs: 25 Richard Fletcher for King (52), 28 Craig Farrell for Maiden (57), 27 Andy Last for Craven (58), 26 Paul Cooke for Robinson (64), King for Jenkins (70), Robinson for Bird (73)
Try: Felsch (42), **Goal:** Sammut, **Sin bin:** Tony Grimaldi (34) – holding down
League Express, Men of the Match:
Bulls: Robbie Paul, **Hull FC:** Luke Felsch
Referee: John Connolly (Wigan). **Penalty count:** 10-7.
Half-time: 26-0, **Att:** 10,778

WIGAN WARRIORS 26 WARRINGTON WOLVES 4
WARRIORS: 1 Kris Radlinski, 26 David Hodgson, 4 Gary Connolly, 3 Steve Renouf, 5 Jason Robinson, 13 Andrew Farrell (C), 7 Willie Peters, 8 Terry O'Connor, 9 Terry Newton, 10 Neil Cowie, 11 Mick Cassidy, 12 Denis Betts, 14 Lee Gilmour. Subs: 21 Mark Smith for Newton (17BB, rev 27), 17 Tony Mestrov for O'Connor (16BB, rev 25), 18 Wes Davies for Hodgson (56), 23 Brady Malam for Cowie (31), Mestrov for O'Connor (47BB, rev 66), Smith for Newton (56), Cowie for Malam (66)
Tries: Cassidy (19), Hodgson (36), Connolly (38), Robinson (41), Renouf (46). **Goals:** Farrell 3
Sin bin: Cassidy (63) - fighting
WOLVES: 1 Lee Penny, 22 Will Cowell, 12 Ian Knott, 3 Alan Hunte, 23 Chris Campbell, 6 Lee Briers, 7 Allan Langer (C), 8 Andrew Gee, 9 Danny Farrar, 18 Mark Hilton, 14 Steve McCurrie, 25 Paul Noone, 13 Tawera Nikau. Subs: 21 Jerome Guisset for Hilton (23), 16 Gary Chambers for Guisset (67), 26 Mike Peters for McCurrie (43), 19 David Highton for Farrar (29BB, rev 32), McCurrie for Farrar (76)
Try: Peters (57), **Sin bin:** Gee (63) – fighting
League Express Men of the Match:
Warriors: Denis Betts, **Wolves:** Allan Langer
Penalty count: 5-5. **Half-time:** 16-0. **Referee:** Steve Presley (Castleford), **Att:** 8,225

CASTLEFORD TIGERS 26 HALIFAX BLUE SOX 12
TIGERS: 2 Richard Gay, 16 Jon Wells, 14 Barrie-Jon Mather, 3 Michael Eagar, 5 Darren Rogers, 6 Danny Orr, 7 Brad Davis, 15 Darren Shaw, 9 Aaron Raper, 8 Nathan Sykes, 22 Andrew Purcell, 12 Dale Fritz, 13 Adrian Vowles (C). Subs: 1 Jason Flowers for Fritz (46), 17 Ian Tonks for Shaw (33), 11 Lee Harland for Purcell (40), 4 Logan Campbell not used, Purcell for Raper (47), Shaw for Sykes (64), Sykes for Vowles (72)
Tries: Wells (9), Orr (13), Mather (35), Rogers (65), Harland (74). **Goals:** Orr 3
BLUE SOX: 1 Daryl Cardiss, 25 Jon Scales (D), 5 Phil Hassan, 3 Damian Gibson, 4 Marvin Golden, 6 Greg Florimo (C), 7 Andrew Dunemann, 23 Brett Goldspink, 9 Paul Rowley, 10 James Gannon, 11 Gary Mercer, 12 Jamie Bloem, 13 Martin Moana. Subs: 8 Andy Hobson for Goldspink (33), 17 Oliver Marns for Scales (49), 21 Gael Tallec for Cardiss (75), 20 Stephen Holgate for Gannon (36), Goldspink for Holgate (51), Gannon for Hobson (70)
Tries: Gibson (27), Rowley (78). **Goals:** Bloem 2
League Express Men of the Match: Tigers: Barrie-Jon Mather, Blue Sox: Martin Moana
Half-time: 16-6 . **Penalty count:** 7-6, **Att:** 6,823.
Referee: Stuart Cummings (Widnes)

ROUND 20

LEEDS RHINOS 42 LONDON BRONCOS 22
RHINOS: 5 Francis Cummins, 35 Graham Mackay, 3 Richie Blackmore, 4 Keith Senior, 21 Karl Pratt, 1 Iestyn Harris (C), 7 Ryan Sheridan, 8 Darren Fleary, 9 Lee

Jackson, 10 Barrie McDermott, 11 Adrian Morley, 13 Kevin Sinfield, 16 Andy Hay. Subs: 10 Jamie Mathiou for McDermott (26), 12 David Barnhill for Hay (33), 6 Daryl Powell for Morley (49), 2 Paul Sterling for Pratt (57), McDermott for Fleary (52), Hay for Sinfield (71)
Tries: Blackmore (6), Mackay (11, 35), Hay (14), Sheridan (52), Cummins (54), Harris (61), Senior (70).
Goals: Harris 5
BRONCOS: 4 Greg Fleming, 35 George Truelove (D), 1 Tulsen Tollett, 30 Jon Roper, 19 Dom Peters, 26 Peter Lupton, 5 Brett Warton, 18 Justin Dooley, 9 Dean Callaway, 17 Anthony Seibold, 12 Steele Retchless, 18 Andy Johnson, 6 Karle Hammond (C). Subs: 10 Scott Cram for Seibold (25), 11 Shane Millard for Retchless (30), 23 John Timu for Roper (47), 14 Andrew Wynyard for Dooley (63), Retchless for Millard (53), Seibold for Johnson (67)
Tries: Johnson (39), Hammond (41), Tollett (60), Callaway (78). **Goals:** Warton 3
League Express Men of the Match:
Rhinos: Darren Fleary, **Broncos:** Brett Warton
Penalty count: 6-4. **Half-time:** 20-4. **Referee:** John Connolly (Wigan), **Att:** 11,717

SALFORD CITY REDS 27 HALIFAX BLUE SOX 26
CITY REDS: 1 Gary Broadbent, 2 Nick Pinkney, 4 Jason Webber, 3 Kris Tassell, 5 Martin Offiah, 31 Steve Blakeley, 6 Graham Holroyd, 15 Neil Baynes, 9 Malcolm Alker, 11 James Smith, 12 Darren Brown (C), 30 Jason Nicol, 23 Mike Wainwright. Subs: 18 Stuart Littler for Tassell (9), 8 Paul Southern for Baynes (27), Baynes for Smith (44), 16 Paul Highton for Wainwright (55), Wainwright for Baynes (64), Smith for Southern (64), 10 Craig Makin not used.
Tries: Pinkney (6), Alker (22), Offiah (40), Nicol (65),
Goals: Blakeley 5, **Field goal:** Offiah
Sin bin: Alker (31) - fighting
BLUE SOX: 3 Damian Gibson, 4 Marvin Golden, 6 Greg Florimo (C), 12 Jamie Bloem, 17 Oliver Marns, 1 Daryl Cardiss, 7 Andrew Dunemann, 8 Andy Hobson, 9 Paul Rowley, 23 Brett Goldspink, 11 Gary Mercer, 10 Jim Gannon, 13 Martin Moana. Subs: 20 Stephen Holgate for Goldspink (39BB, rev 41), Holgate for Goldspink (51), 15 Lokeni Savelio for Hobson (57), Goldspink for Gannon (60), Gannon for Holgate (65), Hobson for Savelio (73), 5 Phil Hassan not used, 19 David Foster not used
Tries: Cardiss (11), Rowley (14), Bloem (25), Dunemann (34), Marns (73). **Goals:** Bloem 3
Sin bin: Rowley (31) – fighting
Half-time: 18-20. **Referee:** Steve Nicholson (Whitehaven), **Att:** 3,320

WARRINGTON WOLVES 24 HUDDERSFIELD SHEFFIELD GIANTS 44
WOLVES: 1 Lee Penny, 27 Rob Smyth (D), 12 Ian Knott, 3 Alan Hunte, 23 Chris Campbell, 6 Lee Briers, 7 Allan Langer (C), 8 Andrew Gee, 9 Danny Farrar, 18 Mark Hilton, 26 Mike Peters, 25 Paul Noone, 14 Steve McCurrie. Subs: 11 Dean Busby for Chambers (52), 16 Gary Chambers for Hilton (30), 21 Jerome Guisset for Peters (45), 22 Will Cowell for Penny (30BB, rev 40), Peters for McCurrie (64)
Tries: Smyth (6, 14, 20, 24), Campbell (39).
Goals: Briers 2
GIANTS: 6 Gene Ngamu, 2 Danny Arnold, 31 Yacine Dekkiche, 17 Martin Gleeson, 1 Waisale Sovatabua, 19 Chris Thorman, 7 Gavin Clinch, 11 David Lomax, 9 Johnny Lawless, 10 Dale Laughton, 12 Richard Marshall, 22 David Bradbury, 13 Jeff Hardy (C). Subs: 33 Adam Hayes for Bradbury (76), 27 Oliver Wilkes for Laughton (37), 23 Dale Cardoza for Dekkiche (23), 18 Danny Russell for Lomax (45), Laughton for Lawless (60), Lomax for Hardy (76)
Tries: Cardoza (27, 72), Lawless (45, 56), Hardy (51), Clinch (69, 75), Laughton (79). **Goals:** Ngamu 6
League Express Men of the Match:
Wolves: Rob Smyth, **Giants:** Dale Cardoza
Penalty count: 5-5. **Half-time:** 24-6, **Att:** 4,572. **Referee:** Ian Smith (Oldham)

ST HELENS 42 CASTLEFORD TIGERS 18
SAINTS: 17 Paul Wellens, 24 Steve Hall, 3 Kevin Iro, 15 Sean Hoppe, 5 Anthony Sullivan, 20 Tommy Martyn, 7 Sean Long, 8 Apollo Perelini, 9 Keiron Cunningham, 12 Sonny Nickle, 11 Chris Joynt (C), 14 Fereti Tuilagi, 13 Paul Sculthorpe. Subs: 16 Vila Matautia for Perelini (32), 10 Julian O'Neill for Nickle (33), Perelini for Tuilagi (53), Nickle for Matautia (62), 22 Tim Jonkers for O'Neill (67), 21 Dwayne West for Iro (70),
Tries: Cunningham (17, 49), Sculthorpe (33), Joynt (39), Wellens (69), Long (44, 71). **Goals:** Long 7,
TIGERS: 2 Richard Gay, 16 Jon Wells, 14 Barrie-Jon Mather, 3 Michael Eagar, 5 Darren Rogers, 6 Danny Orr, 7 Brad Davis, 8 Nathan Sykes, 22 Andrew Purcell, 15 Darren Shaw, 11 Lee Harland, 12 Dale Fritz, 13 Adrian Vowles (C). Subs: 1 Jason Flowers for Harland (34), 17 Ian Tonks for Shaw (34), 19 Andy Lynch for Davis (41), Shaw for Tonks (58), Tonks for Sykes (63), Harland for Fritz (74), 4 Logan Campbell not used,
Tries: Orr (12), Purcell (53), Mather (62). **Goals**: Orr 3
League Express Men of the Match:
Saints: Sean Long, **Tigers:** Michael Eagar
Half-time: 18-8. **Referee:** Stuart Cummings (Widnes), **Att:** 6,979. **Penalty count:** 4-9,

HULL FC 12 WIGAN WARRIORS 21
HULL FC: 1 Ben Sammut, 2 Matt Daylight, 4 Craig Simon, 21 Craig Poucher, 6 Stanley Gene, 7 Will Robinson, 19 Paul King, 9 Mick Jenkins, 11 Craig Wilson, 12 Luke Felsch, 13 Tony Grimaldi (C), 14 Steve Collins, 20 Richard Horne. Subs: 26 Paul Cooke for Sammut (41), 8 Paul Broadbent for Felsch (61), 14 Adam Maher for Wilson (62), 22 Steve Craven for Jenkins (74)
Tries: Horne (6), Daylight (63). **Goals:** Sammut, Cooke
WARRIORS: 1 Kris Radlinski, 26 David Hodgson, 3 Steve Renouf, 4 Gary Connolly, 5 Jason Robinson, 13 Andy Farrell (C), 7 Willie Peters, 8 Terry O'Connor, 21 Mark Smith, 10 Neil Cowie, 12 Denis Betts, 11 Mick Cassidy, 14 Lee Gilmour. Subs: 17 Tony Mestrov for O'Connor (32), 18 Wes Davies for Radlinski (32BB, rev 41), 23 Brady Malam for Cowie (48), 25 Rob Ball for Betts (12BB, rev 23), O'Connor for Mestrov (58), Davies for Gilmour (70), Cowie for O'Connor (73)
Tries: Peters (26), Renouf (53), Betts (76).
Goals: Farrell 4, **Field goal:** Peters
League Express Men of the Match:
Hull: Will Robinson, **Wigan:** Willie Peters
Half-time: 6-8. **Referee:** Karl Kirkpatrick (Warrington), **Att:** 5,168

WAKEFIELD TRINITY WILDCATS 20 BRADFORD BULLS 30
WILDCATS: 1 Steve Prescott, 5 Bright Sodje, 3 Francis Maloney, 30 Jason Critchley, 24 Paul Sampson, 13 Steve McNamara, 25 Bobbie Goulding, 18 Paul Jackson, 29 Andy Speak, 10 Martin Masella, 19 Jamie Field, 15 Gary Price (C), 4 Tony Tatupu. Subs: 17 Frank Watene for Fisher (52), 21 Ryan Hudson for Field (62), 26 Gareth Ellis for Maloney (38), 16 Andy Fisher for Masella (25), Masella for Watene (69)
Tries: Tatupu (32,41), Critchley (39), Sampson (56).
Goals: Goulding 2
BULLS: 28 Stuart Spruce, 4 Nathan McAvoy, 20 Scott Naylor, 14 Justin Brooker, 2 Tevita Vaikona, 6 Henry Paul, 7 Paul Deacon, 22 Brian McDermott, 9 James Lowes (C), 29 Stuart Fielden, 15 Hudson Smith, 12 Mike Forshaw, 13 Brad Mackay. Subs: 3 Leon Pryce for Brooker (53), 1 Robbie Paul not used, 10 Paul Anderson for Mackay (27), 19 Jamie Peacock for Smith (26), Mackay for Fielden (45), Fielden for Anderson (72), Smith for McDermott (77)
Tries: Spruce (5,15), Fielden (13), McAvoy (37), Pryce (62). **Goals:** H. Paul 5
League Express Men of the Match:
Wildcats: Tony Tatupu, **Bulls:** Mike Forshaw
Penalty count: 7-6. **Referee:** Russell Smith (Bradford), **Att:** 6,532. **Half-time:** 12-24

ROUND 21

HULL FC 56 WAKEFIELD TRINITY WILDCATS 6
HULL FC: 21 Craig Poucher, 29 Paul Parker, 14 Steve Collins, 4 Craig Simon, 5 Ian Herron, 7 Will Robinson, 20 Richard Horne, 8 Paul Broadbent, 9 Mick Jenkins, 12 Luke Felsch, 16 Adam Maher, 6 Stanley Gene, 13 Tony Grimaldi (C). Subs: 26 Paul Cooke for Robinson (30BB, rev 50), 22 Steve Craven for Broadbent (34), 11 Craig Wilson for Grimaldi (53), 19 Paul King for Felsch (61), Broadbent for Jenkins (71)
Tries: Maher (5, 52), Collins (17), Horne (24), Jenkins (39), Gene (60, 75), Simon (63), Parker (66), Herron (70). **Goals:** Horne 7, Cooke
WILDCATS: 1 Steve Prescott, 30 Jason Critchley, 3 Francis Maloney, 4 Tony Tatupu, 5 Bright Sodje, 13 Steve McNamara (C), 31 Dane Dorahy (D), 10 Martin Masella, 29 Andy Speak, 18 Paul Jackson, 11 Warren Jowitt, 19 Jamie Field, 15 Gary Price. Subs: 16 Andy Fisher for Masella (20), 21 Ryan Hudson for Speak (32), 7 Glen Tomlinson for Dorahy (35), 26 Gareth Ellis for Fisher (ht), Dorahy for Jackson (58), Masella for Field (64)
Try: Critchley (54), **Goal:** McNamara
League Express Men of the Match:
Hull: Richard Horne, **Wildcats:** Steve Prescott
Penalty count: 10-6. **Half-time:** 22-2. **Referee:** Steve Presley (Castleford), **Att:** 5,440

CASTLEFORD TIGERS 18 WARRINGTON WOLVES 32
TIGERS: 2 Richard Gay, 16 Jon Wells, 14 Barrie-Jon Mather, 3 Michael Eagar, 5 Darren Rogers, 22 Andrew Purcell, 7 Brad Davis, 15 Darren Shaw, 17 Ian Tonks, 8 Nathan Sykes, 11 Lee Harland, 12 Dale Fritz, 13 Adrian Vowles (C). Subs: 6 Danny Orr for Purcell (19), 1 Jason Flowers for Tonks (44), 4 Logan Campbell for Wells (49), 19 Andy Lynch for Shaw (30), Purcell for Harland (58), Shaw for Sykes (74)
Tries: Davis (40), Gay (76), Lynch (79). Goals: Orr 3
WOLVES: 1 Lee Penny, 27 Rob Smyth, 4 Toa Kohe-Love, 3 Alan Hunte, 23 Chris Campbell, 6 Lee Briers, 7 Allan Langer (C), 8 Andrew Gee, 9 Danny Farrar, 10 Danny Nutley, 25 Paul Noone, 14 Steve McCurrie, 13 Tawera Nikau. Subs: 22 Will Cowell not used, 26 Mike Peters for Hilton (71), 18 Mark Hilton for Nutley (8), 21 Jerome Guisset for McCurrie (21), McCurrie for Farrar (77)
Tries: Kohe-Love (23,29), Briers (43,62), Farrar (1), McCurrie (55). **Goals:** Briers 4
League Express Men of the Match:
Tigers: Richard Gay, **Wolves:** Lee Briers
Penalty count: 11-3. **Half-time:** 6-14. **Referee:** Ian Smith (Oldham), **Att:** 7,058

WIGAN WARRIORS 68 HUDDERSFIELD-SHEFFIELD GIANTS 6
WARRIORS: 1 Kris Radlinski, 26 Dave Hodgson, 3 Steve Renouf, 4 Gary Connolly, 2 Jason Robinson, 13 Andy Farrell (C), 7 Willie Peters, 8 Terry O'Connor, 21 Mark Smith, 10 Neil Cowie, 11 Mick Cassidy, 12 Denis Betts, 14 Lee Gilmour. Subs: 17 Tony Mestrov for Cowie (31), 23 Brady Malam for O'Connor (31), 18 Wes Davies for Peters (50), O'Connor for Malam (62), Cowie for Mestrov (62), 19 Chris Chester for Betts (66)
Tries: Farrell (14, 57, 75), Gilmour (19), Betts (37), Peters (39), Robinson (43), Mestrov (47), Renouf (53, 69), Radlinski (60), Connolly (77). Goals: Farrell 10
GIANTS: Gene Ngamu, 2 Danny Arnold, 31 Yacine Dekkiche, 23 Dale Cardoza, 1 Waisale Sovatabua, 19 Chris Thorman, 7 Gavin Clinch, 11 Dave Lomax, 9 Johnny Lawless, 10 Dale Laughton, 12 Richard Marshall, 22 Dave Bradbury, 13 Jeff Hardy (C). Subs: 16 Darren Turner for Lomax (16), 27 Oliver Wilkes for Laughton (37), 18 Danny Russell for Marshall (47), Lomax for Turner (55), Marshall for Bradbury (68), 5 Matt Crowther for Clinch (74)
Try: Arnold (26). **Goals:** Ngamu
Sin bin: Johnny Lawless (30) - professional foul
League Express Men of the Match:
Wigan: Andy Farrell, **Giants:** Gene Ngamu
Penalty count: 10-2. **Half-time:** 26-6. **Referee:** Karl Kirkpatrick (Warrington), **Att:** 7,165

SALFORD CITY REDS 4 ST HELENS 58
CITY REDS: 1 Gary Broadbent, 2 Nick Pinkney, 4 Jason Webber, 30 Jason Nicol, 5 Martin Offiah, 28 John Duffy, 6 Graham Holroyd, 15 Neil Baynes, 9 Malcolm Alker, 11 James Smith, 12 Darren Brown (C), 16 Paul Highton, 23 Mike Wainwright. Subs: 8 Paul Southern for Baynes (28), 18 Stuart Littler for Smith (35), 22 Mark Lee for Duffy (48), Smith for Wainwright (57), Baynes for Highton (57), 20 Matthew Leigh for Holroyd (63).
Try: Webber (65)
SAINTS: 17 Paul Wellens, 5 Anthony Sullivan, 3 Kevin Iro, 15 Sean Hoppe, 24 Steve Hall, 20 Tommy Martyn, 7 Sean Long, 12 Sonny Nickle, 9 Keiron Cunningham, 8 Apollo Perelini, 11 Chris Joynt (C), 14 Fereti Tuilagi, 13 Paul Sculthorpe. Subs: 10 Julian O'Neill for Perelini (21), Perelini for O'Neill (28), O'Neill for Nickle (30), 16 Vila Matautia for Perelini (60), Nickle for O'Neill (60), 21 Dwayne West for Iro (68), 22 Tim Jonkers for Joynt (70)
Tries: Iro (8, 50), Tuilagi (35), Sculthorpe (40, 69), Long (52), Joynt (56), Hoppe (59), Martyn (61, 76).
Goals: Long 9
League Express Men of the Match:
City Reds: Neil Baynes, **Saints:** Tommy Martyn
Penalty count: 4-5. **Half-time:** 0-18. **Referee:** Russell Smith (Castleford), **Att:** 5,409

LONDON BRONCOS 25 HALIFAX BLUE SOX 20
BRONCOS: 4 Greg Fleming, 16 Frank Napoli, 22 John Timu, 30 Jon Roper, 19 Dom Peters, 1 Tulsen Tollett, 5 Brett Warton, 18 Justin Dooley, 9 Dean Callaway, 10 Scott Cram, 12 Steele Retchless, 15 Andy Johnson, 6 Karle Hammond (C). Subs: 11 Shane Millard for Cam (33), 32 Yusef Sozi not used, 17 Anthony Seibold for Millard (54), 26 Peter Lupton for Tollett (22), Cram for Dooley (52), Dooley for Seibold (67)
Tries: Fleming (19), Warton (47), Johnson (62), Napoli (72). **Goals:** Warton 4, **Field goal:** Hammond
BLUE SOX: 3 Damian Gibson, 17 Oliver Marns, 6 Greg Florimo (C), 12 Jamie Bloem, 4 Marvin Golden, 1 Daryl Cardiss, 7 Andrew Dunemann, 23 Brett Goldspink, 9 Paul Rowley, 8 Andy Hobson, 21 Gael Tallec, 10 James Gannon, 13 Martin Moana. Subs: 33 Lee Greenwood (D) for Hobson (50), 26 Rob Roberts (D) for Holgate (55), 20 Stephen Holgate for Goldspink (26BB, rev 41), 11 Gary Mercer for Gibson (25), Holgate for Tallec (41), Hobson for Bloem (65), Gibson for Roberts (79)
Tries: Golden (11), Marns (13,55). **Goals:** Bloem 4
League Express Men of the Match:
Broncos: Justin Dooley, **Blue Sox:** Paul Rowley
Penalty count: 10-5. **Half-time:** 6-14. **Referee:** John Connolly (Wigan), **Att:** 2,543

BRADFORD BULLS 26 LEEDS RHINOS 28
BULLS: 28 Stuart Spruce, 4 Nathan McAvoy, 20 Scott Naylor, 3 Leon Pryce, 2 Tevita Vaikona, 6 Henry Paul, 1 Robbie Paul (C), 10 Paul Anderson, 9 James Lowes, 29 Stuart Fielden, 19 Jamie Peacock, 12 Mike Forshaw, 13 Brad Mackay. Subs: 7 Paul Deacon for H Paul (19), 15 Hudson Smith for Mackay (54), 14 Justin Brooker for McAvoy (30), 22 Brian McDermott for Anderson (24), Mackay for Spruce (59), Anderson for Peacock (68)
Tries: Naylor (35), R Paul (58, 78), Lowes (61).
Goals: H Paul, Deacon 4
RHINOS: 5 Francis Cummins, 35 Graham Mackay, 3 Richie Blackmore, 4 Keith Senior, 21 Karl Pratt, 1 Iestyn Harris (C), 7 Ryan Sheridan, 8 Darren Fleary, 9 Lee Jackson, 10 Barrie McDermott, 11 Adrian Morley, 12 David Barnhill, 16 Andy Hay. Subs: 10 Jamie Mathiou for Fleary (24BB, rev 29), 26 Garreth Carvell for Mathiou (77), 6 Daryl Powell for Barnhill (30), 2 Paul Sterling for Mackay (50), Mathiou for McDermott (30), Barnhill for Hay (67)
Tries: Morley (26), Senior (38, 53), Cummins (76).
Goals: Harris 6
League Express Men of the Match:
Bulls: Mike Forshaw, **Rhinos:** Iestyn Harris
Half-time: 8-12. **Referee:** Stuart Cummings (Widnes), **Att:** 21,247. **Penalty count:** 12-6

ROUND 22

WARRINGTON WOLVES 32 SALFORD CITY REDS 18
WOLVES: 1 Lee Penny, 27 Rob Smyth, 4 Toa Kohe-Love, 3 Alan Hunte, 22 Will Cowell, 6 Lee Briers, 7 Allan Langer (C), 8 Andrew Gee, 9 Danny Farrar, 18 Mark Hilton, 14 Steve McCurrie, 25 Paul Noone, 13 Tawera Nikau. Subs: 12 Ian Knott for Noone (21), 26 Mike Peters for Smyth (60), 11 Dean Busby for McCurrie (71), 21 Jerome Guisset for Hilton (31BB, rev 55)
Tries: Noone (13), McCurrie (24, 64), Gee (43), Love (61), Penny (78). **Goals:** Briers 4
CITY REDS: 1 Gary Broadbent, 2 Nick Pinkney, 4 Jason Webber, 18 Stuart Littler, 17 Mark Johnson, 31 Steve Blakeley, 12 Darren Brown (C), 15 Neil Baynes, 9 Malcolm Alker, 10 Paul Southern, 11 James Smith, 16 Paul Highton, 23 Mike Wainwright. Subs: 26 Robert Russell not used, 19 Simon Svabic for Blakeley (77), 22

Mark Lee for Leigh (65), 20 Matthew Leigh for Baynes (30), Baynes for Highton (57), Highton for Smith (65), Leigh for Southern (70)
Tries: Pinkney (3), Johnson (20), Webber (34).
Goals: Blakeley 3
League Express Men of the Match:
Wolves: Steve McCurrie, **Reds:** Malcolm Alker
Half time: 10-18. **Referee:** Robert Connolly (Wigan), **Att:** 5,609. **Penalty count:** 4-6

WAKEFIELD TRINITY WILDCATS 6 WIGAN WARRIORS 56

WILDCATS: 1 Steve Prescott, 24 Paul Sampson, 3 Francis Maloney, 4 Tony Tatupu, 30 Jason Critchley, 31 Dane Dorahy, 25 Bobbie Goulding, 10 Martin Masella, 29 Andy Speak, 8 Francis Stephenson, 11 Warren Jowitt, 19 Jamie Field, 13 Steve McNamara (C). Subs: 12 Willie Poching for Dorahy (2), 21 Ryan Hudson for Speak (27), 7 Glen Tomlinson for Field (50), 17 Frank Watene for Masella (21), Field for Prescott (69)
Try: Prescott (55), **Goal:** Goulding, **Sin bin:** Jowitt (79) - fighting
WARRIORS: 1 Kris Radlinski, 26 Dave Hodgson, 3 Steve Renouf, 4 Gary Connolly, 5 Jason Robinson, 13 Andy Farrell (C), 7 Willie Peters, 8 Terry O'Connor, 21 Mark Smith, 10 Neil Cowie, 11 Mick Cassidy, 12 Denis Betts, 14 Lee Gilmour. Subs: 17 Tony Mestrov for Cowie (40), 23 Brady Malam for O'Connor (40), 9 Terry Newton for Gilmour (50), 18 Wes Davies for Peters (18)
Tries: Betts (8, 38), Gilmour (11, 17), Robinson (27), Cassidy (32), Smith (41, 63), Radlinski (50, 65). **Goals:** Farrell 8, **Sin bin:** Mestrov (79) - fighting.
League Express Men of the Match: Wildcats: Frank Watene, **Warriors:** Andy Farrell
Half-time: 32-0. **Referee:** Stuart Cummings (Widnes), **Att:** 3,650

ST HELENS 46 LONDON BRONCOS 12

SAINTS: 17 Paul Wellens, 24 Steve Hall, 15 Sean Hoppe, 3 Kevin Iro, 5 Anthony Sullivan, 20 Tommy Martyn, 7 Sean Long, 16 Vila Matautia, 9 Keiron Cunningham, 8 Apollo Perelini, 11 Chris Joynt (C), 14 Fereti Tuilagi, 13 Paul Sculthorpe. Subs: 26 John Stankevitch for Joynt (33BB), 12 Sonny Nickle for Matautia (25), 21 Dwayne West for Wellens (66), 22 Tim Jonkers for Martyn (54), Joynt for Perelini (ht), Matautia for Tuilagi (58), Wellens for Cunningham (76)
Tries: Martyn (5, 24), Matautia (17), Joynt (20), Long (37, 44), Tuilagi (53), West (77). **Goals:** Long 7
BRONCOS: 4 Greg Fleming (C), 35 George Truelove, 22 John Timu, 30 Jon Roper, 19 Dom Peters, 1 Tulsen Tollett, 5 Brett Warton, 18 Justin Dooley, 9 Dean Callaway, 10 Scott Cram, 12 Steele Retchless, 14 Andrew Wynyard, 15 Andy Johnson. Subs: 11 Shane Millard for Cram (25), 25 Glen Air for Tollett (54), 17 Anthony Seibold for Wynyard (25), 26 Peter Lupton for Peters (65), Wynyard for Millard (27BB, rev 31), Cram for Dooley (34), Wynyard for Callaway (58), Callaway for Millard (60BB, rev 63)
Tries: Peters (30), Millard (64). **Goals:** Warton 2
League Express Men of the Match:
Saints: Keiron Cunningham, **Broncos:** Andy Johnson
Penalty count: 5-8. **Half-time:** 30-6. **Referee:** Karl Kirkpatrick (Warrington), **Att:** 6,912

LEEDS RHINOS 34 HULL FC 18

RHINOS: 5 Francis Cummins, 33 Graham Mackay, 3 Richie Blackmore, 4 Keith Senior, 21 Karl Pratt, 1 Iestyn Harris (C), 7 Ryan Sheridan, 8 Darren Fleary, 9 Lee Jackson, 10 Barrie McDermott, 11 Adrian Morley, 12 David Barnhill, 16 Andy Hay. Subs: 6 Daryl Powell for Morley (21), 20 Jamie Mathiou for McDermott (25), 2 Paul Sterling for Senior (31BB, rev 49), 26 Gareth Carvell for Pratt (56BB, rev 79), Sterling for Barnhill (44), McDermott for Fleary (58), Barnhill for Hay (68), Carvell for Senior (76)
Tries: Sheridan (2, 31) Cummins (43), Pratt (49), Mackay (57), Blackmore (62). **Goals:** Harris 5
HULL FC: 21 Craig Poucher, 5 Ian Herron, 14 Steve Collins, 4 Craig Simon, 29 Paul Parker, 4 Will Robinson, 20 Richard Horne, 8 Paul Broadbent, 9 Mick Jenkins, 12 Luke Felsch, 16 Adam Maher, 6 Stanley Gene, 13 Tony Grimaldi (C). Subs: 19 Paul King for Jenkins (21BB, rev 31), 22 Steve Craven for Broadbent (29), 11 Craig Wilson for Felsch (51), 26 Paul Cooke for Robinson (56), King for Jenkins (43), Broadbent for King (60), King for Craven (73)
Tries: Poucher (15), Broadbent (68), Maher (76).
Goals: Horne 3
League Express Men of the Match:
Rhinos: Francis Cummins, **Hull:** Adam Maher
Penalty count: 4-6. **Half-time:** 12-8. **Referee:** Russell Smith, **Att:** 12,479

HALIFAX BLUE SOX 20 BRADFORD BULLS 20

BLUE SOX: 1 Daryl Cardiss, 17 Olly Marns, 6 Greg Florimo (C), 2 Damian Gibson, 4 Marvin Golden, 13 Marty Moana, 7 Andrew Dunemann, 23 Brett Goldspink, 9 Paul Rowley, 8 Andy Hobson, 11 Gary Mercer, 10 Jim Gannon, 12 Jamie Bloem. Subs: 20 Stephen Holgate for Goldspink (47), 26 Robert Roberts for Gannon (53), 29 Jamie Thackray was not used, 31 Danny Tickle for Mercer (53), Mercer for Bloem (58), Gannon for Roberts (70), Holgate for Goldspink (70)
Tries: Gannon (32, 59), Golden (26), Gibson (35), Goal: Bloem, Cardiss
Sin bins: Dunemann (7) - obstruction; Rowley (45) - dissent, **Dismissal:** Hobson (22) - use of knees
BULLS: 28 Stuart Spruce, 3 Tevita Vaikona, 20 Scott Naylor, 14 Justin Brooker, 1 Michael Withers, 2 Henry Paul, 1 Robbie Paul (C), 22 Brian McDermott, 9 James Lowes, 10 Paul Anderson, 15 Hudson Smith, 12 Mike Forshaw, 13 Brad Mackay. Subs: 1 Paul Deacon for R Paul (19), 11 David Boyle for Lowes (56), 19 Jamie Peacock for Smith (46), 29 Stuart Fielden for Anderson (33), Anderson for McDermott (63), Lowes for Mackay (73), Peacock for Mackay (19BB, rev 26), Boyle for Spruce (19BB, rev 24)
Tries: Naylor (13, 66). **Goals:** H Paul 6
League Express Men of the Match:
Blue Sox: Gary Mercer, **Bulls:** Scott Naylor.
Half-time: 12-12. **Referee:** Steve Presley (Castleford), **Att:** 7,106. **Penalty count:** 7-9

HUDDS-SHEFFIELD GIANTS 16 CASTLEFORD TIGERS 32

GIANTS: 6 Gene Ngamu, 2 Danny Arnold, 31 Yacine Dekkiche, 23 Dale Cardoza, 1 Waisale Sovatabua, 19 Chris Thorman, 7 Gavin Clinch, 11 Dave Lomax, 9 Johnny Lawless, 10 Dale Laughton, 12 Richard Marshall, 22 Dave Bradbury, 13 Jeff Hardy (C). Subs: 8 Steve Molloy for Lomax (19), 27 Oliver Wilkes for Marshall (49), 18 Danny Russell for Lawless (25), 34 Leroy Rivett (D) for Dekkiche (46), Lomax for Laughton (66), Dekkiche for Thorman (70)
Tries: Arnold (51), Laughton (57), Ngamu (73).
Goals: Ngamu 2
TIGERS: 1 Jason Flowers, 2 Richard Gay, 14 Barrie-Jon Mather, 3 Michael Eagar, 5 Darren Rogers, 6 Danny Orr, 7 Brad Davis, 19 Andy Lynch, 12 Dale Fritz, 8 Nathan Sykes, 11 Lee Harland, 15 Darren Shaw, 13 Adrian Vowles (C). Subs: 17 Ian Tonks for Lynch (25), 23 Craig Wright for Tonks (58), 18 Paul Smith for Mather, 20 Barry Eaton (D) for Shaw (52), Lynch for Harland (58), Shaw for Sykes (65)
Tries: Rogers (2, 11, 18), Vowles (34), Mather (65), Gay (79). **Goals:** Orr 4
League Express Men of the Match:
Giants: Dale Laughton, **Tigers:** Adrian Vowles
Penalty count: 3-3. **Half-time:** 0-20. **Referee:** John Connolly (Wigan), **Att:** 2,102

ROUND 23

WIGAN WARRIORS 20 HALIFAX BLUE SOX 12

WARRIORS: 1 Kris Radlinski, 18 Wes Davies, 4 Gary Connolly, 3 Steve Renouf, 5 Jason Robinson, 13 Andrew Farrell (C), 6 Tony Smith, 8 Terry O'Connor, 21 Mark Smith, 10 Neil Cowie, 11 Mick Cassidy, 12 Denis Betts, 14 Lee Gilmour. Subs: 17 Tony Mestrov for O'Connor (28), 23 Brady Malam for Cowie (41), 9 Terry Newton for M Smith (59), 26 David Hodgson for Connolly (41), O'Connor for Mestrov (69)
Tries: Radlinski (64, 70), Newton (72). **Goals:** Farrell 4
Sin bin: T Smith (37) - retaliation
BLUE SOX: 1 Daryl Cardiss, 4 Marvin Golden, 3 Damian Gibson, 6 Greg Florimo (C), 17 Olly Marns, 13 Marty Moana, 7 Andrew Dunemann, 23 Brett Goldspink, 9 Paul Rowley, 10 Jim Gannon, 11 Gary Mercer, 31 Danny Tickle, 12 Jamie Bloem. Subs: 20 Stephen Holgate for Goldspink (23), 26 Robert Roberts for Holgate (63), 5 Phil Hassan for Cardiss (19), 21 Gael Tallec for Tickle (37BB, rev 50), Goldspink for Gannon (52), Gannon for Goldspink (68), Cardiss for Marns (68), Tallec for Tickle (75BB)
Tries: Moana (11), Rowley (79). **Goals:** Bloem 2
Sin bin: Gibson (37) - offence in the tackle on Tony Smith
League Express Men of the Match:
Warriors: Kris Radlinski, **Blue Sox:** Paul Rowley
Penalty count: 7-6. **Half-time:** 4-8, **Att:** 8,268. **Referee:** Russell Smith (Castleford)

LONDON BRONCOS 10 SALFORD CITY REDS 16

BRONCOS: 4 Greg Fleming, 19 Dom Peters, 1 Tulsen Tollett, 22 John Timu, 33 George Truelove, 5 Brett Warton, 29 Glen Air, 18 Justin Dooley, 11 Shane Millard, 10 Scott Cram, 12 Steele Retchless, 14 Andrew Wynyard, 15 Andy Johnson. Subs: 13 Mat Toshack for Fleming (26), 21 Jon Clarke for Wynyard (24), 26 Peter Lupton for Air (64), 17 Anthony Seibold for Cram (24), Cram for Dooley (54), Wynyard for Millard (62BB), Dooley for Seibold (69), Air for Peters (74BB)
Tries: Johnson (33), Seibold (37), **Goal:** Warton
CITY REDS: 1 Gary Broadbent, 2 Nick Pinkney, 3 Kris Tassell, 4 Jason Webber, 5 Martin Offiah, 31 Steve Blakeley, 6 Graham Holroyd, 11 James Smith, 9 Malcolm Alker, 15 Neil Baynes, 30 Jason Nicol, 12 Darren Brown, 23 Michael Wainwright. Subs: 16 Paul Highton for Smith (25), 8 Paul Southern for Baynes (17), 18 Stuart Littler not used, 29 Brad Hepi not used, Smith for Highton (53), Baynes for Nicol (59), Nicol for Holroyd (66)
Tries: Broadbent (47), Offiah (67). **Goals:** Blakeley 4
League Express Men of the Match:
Broncos: Shane Millard, **City Reds:** Steve Blakeley
Penalty count: 8-11. **Half-time:** 10-2. **Referee:** Steve Ganson (St Helens), **Att:** 2,040

HUDDERSFIELD-SHEFFIELD GIANTS 12 LEEDS RHINOS 20

GIANTS: 6 Gene Ngamu, 2 Danny Arnold, 1 Waisale Sovatabua, 23 Dale Cardoza, 34 Leroy Rivett, 19 Chris Thorman, 7 Gavin Clinch, 11 David Lomax, 19 Danny Russell, 10 Dale Laughton (C), 12 Richard Marshall, 22 David Bradbury, 33 Adam Hayes. Subs: 8 Steve Molloy for Lomax (28), 27 Oliver Wilkes for Laughton (31BB, rev 56), 9 John Lawless for Russell (48), 5 Matt Crowther for Cardoza (63), Lomax for Molloy (66), Wilkes for Bradbury (73), Russell for Hayes (78)
Tries: Sovatabua (10), Arnold (79). **Goals:** Ngamu 2
RHINOS: 5 Francis Cummins, 2 Paul Sterling, 3 Richie Blackmore, 4 Keith Senior, 33 Graham Mackay, 13 Kevin Sinfield, 7 Ryan Sheridan (C), 8 Darren Fleary, 9 Lee Jackson, 10 Barrie McDermott, 17 Anthony Farrell, 12 David Barnhill, 16 Andy Hay. Subs: 20 Jamie Mathiou for McDermott (26), 6 Daryl Powell for Farrell (30), 21 Karl Pratt for Sterling (62), 19 Dean Lawford for Barnhill (69), Farrell for Fleary (55), McDermott for Hay (63)
Tries: Blackmore (16), Barnhill (19), Senior (38), Mackay (64). **Goals:** Mackay 2
League Express Men of the Match: G iants: Chris Thorman, **Rhinos:** Ryan Sheridan
Penalty count: 10-7. **Half-time:** 6-14. **Referee:** Ian Smith (Oldham), **Att:** 5,019

BRADFORD BULLS 28 CASTLEFORD TIGERS 8

BULLS: 28 Stuart Spruce, 3 Leon Pryce, 20 Scott Naylor, 5 Michael Withers, 2 Tevita Vaikona, 6 Henry Paul, 7 Paul Deacon, 22 Brian McDermott, 9 James Lowes (C), 29 Stuart Fielden, 19 Jamie Peacock, 12 Mike Forshaw, 13 Brad Mackay. Subs: 11 David Boyle for Naylor (38), 18 Lee Radford for Spruce (63), 15 Hudson Smith for Forshaw (53), 10 Paul Anderson for Fielden (31), Fielden for McDermott (53BB, rev 66), Fielden for Anderson (66), Forshaw for Peacock (71)
Tries: Deacon (10), Mackay (15), Spruce (37), Vaikona (39), Withers (47). **Goals:** Paul 4
Sin bin: Brian McDermott (77) – obstruction.
TIGERS: 1 Jason Flowers, 16 Jon Wells, 13 Adrian Vowles (C), 3 Michael Eagar, 5 Darren Rogers, 6 Danny Orr, 7 Brad Davis, 10 Dean Sampson, 12 Dale Fritz, 8 Nathan Sykes, 15 Darren Shaw, 17 Ian Tonks, 11 Lee Harland. Subs: 19 Andy Lynch for Sykes (55), 23 Wright for Tonks (31), 67 Paul Smith for Harland (67), 20 Barry Eaton for Shaw (52), Tonks for Sampson (65)
Tries: Rogers (26), Eagar (79)
League Express Men of the Match:
Bulls: James Lowes, **Tigers:** Darren Rogers
Half-time: 24-4. **Penalty count:** 9-7, **Att:** 11,302.
Referee: John Connolly (Wigan)

WARRINGTON WOLVES 41 HULL FC 10

WOLVES: 1 Lee Penny, 27 Rob Smyth, 4 Toa Kohe-Love, 3 Alan Hunte, 22 Will Cowell, 6 Lee Briers, 7 Allan Langer (C), 8 Andrew Gee, 9 Danny Farrar, 18 Mark Hilton, 14 Steve McCurrie, 12 Ian Knott, 13 Tawera Nikau. Subs: 11 Dean Busby for Guisset (30), 25 Paul Noone for McCurrie (53), 26 Mike Peters for Busby (71), 21 Jerome Guisset for Hilton (5), McCurrie for Gee (72)
Tries: Smyth (17), Love (25, 40, 75), McCurrie (35), Briers (63), Knott (67), Noone (80). **Goals:** Briers 4,
Field goal: Briers. **On report:** Love (61) - high tackle on Wilson
HULL: 27 Craig Poucher, 2 Matt Daylight, 14 Steve Collins, 4 Craig Simon, 5 Ian Herron, 20 Richard Horne, 7 Will Robinson, 8 Paul Broadbent, 9 Mick Jenkins, 12 Luke Felsch, 16 Adam Maher, 6 Stanley Gene, 13 Tony Grimaldi (C). Subs: 19 Paul King for Broadbent (55), 22 Steve Craven for Gene (49), 11 Craig Wilson for Maher (27), 26 Paul Cooke for Horne (65), Broadbent for Felsch (71)
Tries: Felsch (7), Gene (43). **Goals:** Herron
League Express Men of the Match:
Wolves: Allan Langer, **Hull:** Luke Felsch
Half time: 21-4. **Referee:** Stuart Cummings (Widnes), **Att:** 5,042. **Penalty count:** 5-5

WAKEFIELD TRINITY WILDCATS 32 ST HELENS 16

WILDCATS: 23 Martyn Holland, 2 Neil Law, 20 Adam Hughes, 4 Tony Tatupu, 5 Bright Sodje, 14 Paul March, 7 Glen Tomlinson, 18 Paul Jackson, 9 David March, 8 Francis Stephenson, 16 Andy Fisher, 22 Graham Law, 12 Willie Poching (C). Subs: 27 Ben Westwood for Hughes (7), 21 Ryan Hudson for P March (70), 11 Warren Jowitt for Fisher (22), 17 Frank Watene for Stephenson (21BB, rev 36), Fisher for Stephenson (70)
Tries: Watene (32), Jowitt (39), P March (44), Westwood (51), N. Law (57), Holland (76).
Goals: G Law 4
SAINTS: 19 Tony Stewart, 24 Steve Hall, 15 Sean Hoppe, 3 Kevin Iro, 5 Anthony Sullivan, 20 Tommy Martyn, 7 Sean Long, 10 Julian O'Neill, 16 Vila Matautia, 8 Apollo Perelini, 11 Chris Joynt (C), 14 Fereti Tuilagi, 13 Paul Sculthorpe. Subs: 26 John Stankevitch for O'Neill (24), 9 Keiron Cunningham for Stankevitch (54), 21 Dwayne West for Stewart (56), 22 Tim Jonkers for Perelini (73), O'Neill for Matautia (40), Matautia for O'Neill (70)
Tries: Tuilagi (8,36), Sullivan (67). **Goals:** Long 2
League Express Men of the Match:
Wildcats: Willie Poching, **Saints:** Freddie Tuilagi
Penalty count: 7-4. **Half-time:** 12-12. **Referee:** Robert Connolly (Wigan), **Att:** 3,642

ROUND 24

BRADFORD BULLS 52 HUDDERSFIELD-SHEFFIELD GIANTS 20

BULLS: 28 Stuart Spruce, 2 Tevita Vaikona, 4 Nathan McAvoy, 5 Michael Withers, 3 Leon Pryce, 6 Henry Paul, 7 Paul Deacon, 22 Brian McDermott, 9 James Lowes (C), 29 Stuart Fielden, 19 Jamie Peacock, 12 Mike Forshaw, 11 David Boyle. Subs: 14 Justin Brooker for McAvoy (46), 13 Brad Mackay for Forshaw (49), 15 Hudson Smith for Peacock (46), 10 Paul Anderson for Fielden (26), Fielden for Anderson (65), Peacock for McDermott (69),
Tries: Paul (3, 48), McDermott (18, 62), Spruce (14), Withers (22), Deacon (35), Vaikona (55), Peacock (74).
Goals: Paul 8,
GIANTS: 1 Waisale Sovatabua, 2 Danny Arnold, 23 Dale Cardoza, 5 Matt Crowther, 34 Leroy Rivett, 19 Chris Thorman, 24 Martin Moxon, 11 David Lomax, 18 Danny Russell, 8 Steve Molloy, 22 David Bradbury, 27 Oliver Wilkes, 33 Adam Hayes. Subs: 6 Gene Ngamu for Sovatabua (59), 13 Jeff Hardy for Hayes (48), 9 Johnny Lawless for Russell (48), 29 Jamie Fielden for Lomax (20), Lomax for Fielden (59), Hayes for Wilkes (66),
Tries: Thorman (25), Rivett (52), Cardoza (61), Crowther (78). **Goals:** Crowther, Ngamu

League Express Men of the Match:
Bulls: Henry Paul, **Giants:** Steve Molloy
Half-time: 28-6. **Referee:** Graeme Shaw (Wigan), **Att:** 10,164. **Penalty count:** 7-4

CASTLEFORD TIGERS 20 LEEDS RHINOS 16
TIGERS: 1 Jason Flowers, 16 Jon Wells, 14 Barrie-Jon Mather, 3 Michael Eagar, 5 Darren Rogers, 6 Danny Orr, 7 Brad Davis, 10 Dean Sampson, 12 Dale Fritz, 8 Nathan Sykes, 15 Darren Shaw, 11 Lee Harland, 13 Adrian Vowles (C). Subs: 19 Andy Lynch for Sampson (28), 17 Ian Tonks for Shaw (52), 67 Paul Smith for Sykes (65), 20 Barry Eaton for Orr (50), Sykes for Lynch (72)
Tries: Wells (5, 68), Davis (1), Rogers (57).
Goals: Orr, Eaton
RHINOS: 5 Cummins, 33 Graham Mackay, 3 Richie Blackmore, 4 Keith Senior, 21 Karl Pratt, 1 Iestyn Harris (C), 7 Ryan Sheridan, 8 Darren Fleary, 9 Lee Jackson, 10 Barrie McDermott, 12 David Barnhill, 17 Anthony Farrell, 16 Andy Hay. Subs: 11 Adrian Morley for Barnhill (28), 13 Kevin Sinfield for Hay (53), 2 Paul Sterling for Farrell (23), 20 Jamie Mathiou for McDermott (33), Farrell for Fleary (58), McDermott for Mathiou (63)
Tries: Harris (28), Sterling (48). **Goals:** Harris 4.
Dismissal: Richie Blackmore (12) - illegal use of elbow, **Sin bin:** Lee Jackson (74) - late tackle, **On report:** Lee Jackson (74) - late tackle
League Express Men of the Match:
Tigers: Brad Davis, **Rhinos:** Iestyn Harris
Penalty count: 5-8. **Half-time:** 10-8. **Referee:** Steve Ganson (St Helens), **Att:** 9,819

WAKEFIELD TRINITY WILDCATS 22 LONDON BRONCOS 0
WILDCATS: 23 Martyn Holland, 2 Neil Law, 27 Ben Westwood, 4 Tony Tatupu, 5 Bright Sodje, 14 Paul March, 7 Glen Tomlinson, 18 Paul Jackson, 9 David March, 8 Francis Stephenson, 11 Warren Jowitt, 22 Graham Law, 12 Willie Poching (C). Subs: 1 Steve Prescott for G Law (36), 10 Martin Masella for Stephenson (22), 16 Andy Fisher for Jackson (62), 19 Jamie Field for Tatupu (51), Stephenson for Masella (55), G Law for P March (71)
Tries: N Law (35,58), Masella (46), Fisher (70).
Goals: Prescott 3. **Sin bin:** Andy Fisher (75) - fighting
BRONCOS: 5 Brett Warton, 2 Rob Smyth, 13 Mat Toshack, 22 John Timu, 33 George Truelove, 1 Tulsen Tollett, 29 Glen Air, 18 Justin Dooley, 11 Shane Millard, 10 Scott Cram, 12 Steel Retchless (C), 14 Andrew Wynyard, 15 Andy Johnson. Subs: 27 Paul Davidson for Toshack (32), 21 Jon Clarke for Wynyard (23), 26 Peter Lupton for Millard (51), 17 Anthony Seibold for Dooley (29), Dooley for Cram (61), Wynyard for Davidson (64)
Sin bin: Justin Dooley (75) - fighting
League Express Men of the Match:
Wildcats: Willie Poching, **Broncos:** Brett Warton
Att: 2,370. **Penalty count:** 6-7. **Half-time:** 4-0. **Referee:** Steve Presley (Castleford)

SALFORD CITY REDS 18 WIGAN WARRIORS 30
CITY REDS: 1 Gary Broadbent, 2 Nick Pinkney, 4 Jason Webber, 3 Kris Tassell, 5 Martin Offiah, 31 Steve Blakeley, 6 Graham Holroyd, 15 Neil Baynes, 9 Malcolm Alker, 8 Paul Southern, 30 Jason Nicol, 12 Darren Brown (C), 23 Mike Wainwright. Subs: 11 Jim Smith for Baynes (9), 16 Paul Highton for Smith (46), 32 Jon Roper (D) for Holroyd (21), 29 Brad Hepi for Nicol (49), Nicol for Highton (63BB), Smith for Hepi (71), Highton for Smith (76)
Tries: Broadbent (37, 57), Nicol (70). **Goals:** Roper 3
WARRIORS: 1 Kris Radlinski, 26 David Hodgson, 4 Gary Connolly, 3 Steve Renouf, 5 Jason Robinson, 13 Andrew Farrell (C), 6 Tony Smith, 8 Terry O'Connor, 9 Terry Newton, 10 Neil Cowie, 11 Mick Cassidy, 12 Denis Betts, 14 Lee Gilmour. Subs: 23 Brady Malam for Cowie (38), 17 Tony Mestrov for O'Connor (30), 19 Chris Chester for Connolly (56BB, rev 62), 21 Mark Smith for Newton (69), Chester for Gilmour (67), O'Connor for Mestrov (67)
Tries: T Smith (4), Cassidy (15), Radlinski (42, 49), Farrell (78). **Goals:** Farrell 5
League Express Men of the Match:
City Reds: Gary Broadbent, **Warriors:** Kris Radlinski
Half-time: 6-12. **Referee:** Ian Smith (Oldham), **Att:** 4,704. **Penalty count:** 6-4

HULL FC 14 HALIFAX BLUE SOX 16
HULL FC: 21 Craig Poucher, 2 Matt Daylight, 14 Steve Collins, 4 Craig Simon, 5 Ian Herron, 20 Richard Horne, 7 Will Robinson, 8 Paul Broadbent, 9 Mick Jenkins, 12 Luke Felsch, 16 Adam Maher, 13 Tony Grimaldi (C), 26 Paul Cooke. Subs: 25 Richard Fletcher for Craven (71), 19 Paul King for Jenkins (14), 11 Craig Wilson for Collins (40BB), 22 Steve Craven for Broadbent (30), Collins for Wilson (47), Jenkins for King (65), Wilson for Grimaldi (70BB)
Tries: Grimaldi (19), Collins (54). **Goals:** Herron 3
Sin bin: Craven (49) - fighting
BLUE SOX: 3 Damian Gibson, 17 Oliver Marns, 6 Greg Florimo (C), 5 Phil Hassan, 4 Marvin Golden, 13 Martin Moana, 7 Andrew Dunemann, 10 James Gannon, 9 Paul Rowley, 20 Stephen Holgate, 11 Gary Mercer, 31 Danny Tickle, 12 Jamie Bloem. Subs: 21 Gael Tallec for Holgate (25), 33 Lee Greenwood for Marns (58), 19 Dave Foster for Hassan (52), 29 Jamie Thackray for Gannon (33), Gannon for Tickle (40), Holgate for Tallec (76)
Tries: Gibson (64), Dunemann (69), Rowley (74). **Goals:** Bloem 2. **Sin bin:** Gannon (49) - fighting
League Express Men of the Match:
Hull FC: Tony Grimaldi, **Blue Sox:** Andrew Dunemann
Penalty count: 9-7. **Half-time:** 8-2. **Referee:** Karl Kirkpatrick (Warrington), **Att:** 4,677

ST HELENS 58 WARRINGTON WOLVES 18
SAINTS: 17 Paul Wellens, 24 Steve Hall, 3 Kevin Iro, 15 Sean Hoppe, 5 Anthony Sullivan, 20 Tommy Martyn, 7 Sean Long, 8 Apollo Perelini, 9 Keiron Cunningham, 10 Julian O'Neill, 11 Chris Joynt (C), 14 Fereti Tuilagi, 13 Paul Sculthorpe. Subs: 16 Vila Matautia for O'Neill (22), 19 Tony Stewart for Iro (60), 21 Dwayne West for Hoppe (60), 26 John Stankevitch for O'Neill (63), O'Neill for Perelini (33), Hoppe for Tuilagi (65)
Tries: Martyn (3, 21, 49), Sullivan (34), Wellens (52), Iro (54), Cunningham (57), West (64), Stankevitch (76), Sculthorpe (79). **Goals:** Long 9. **Sin bin:** O'Neill (43) - interference at play-the-ball.
WOLVES: 1 Lee Penny, 22 Will Cowell, 4 Toa Kohe-Love, 3 Alan Hunte, 5 Mark Forster, 6 Lee Briers, 7 Allan Langer (C), 8 Andrew Gee, 9 Danny Farrar, 18 Mark Hilton, 14 Steve McCurrie, 12 Ian Knott, 13 Tawera Nikau. Subs: 11 Dean Busby for Knott (54), 25 Paul Noone for Farrar (14BB, rev 23), 21 Jerome Guisset for Hilton (23), 26 Mike Peters for McCurrie (68), Noone for Farrar (57), McCurrie for Busby (70)
Tries: Langer (11), Hunte (46), Busby (68).
Goals: Briers 3. **Sin bins:** Hunte (31), Gee (56) and Nikau (76) - all for interference at the play the ball. **On report:** Penny (75) - late challenge on Joynt
League Express Men of the Match:
Saints: Tommy Martyn, **Wolves:** Allan Langer
Half-time: 16-6, **Att:** 7,139. **Penalty count:** 12-7. **Referee:** John Connolly (Wigan)

ROUND 25

LONDON BRONCOS 16 WARRINGTON WOLVES 32
BRONCOS: 5 Brett Warton, 2 Rob Smyth, 22 John Timu, 28 Kevin Crouthers, 33 George Truelove, 1 Tulsen Tollett, 29 Glen Air, 18 Justin Dooley, 11 Shane Millard, 10 Scott Cram, 14 Andrew Wynyard, 12 Steele Retchless (C), 15 Andy Johnson. Subs: 17 Anthony Seibold for Cram (49), 21 Jon Clarke for Millard (35), 26 Peter Lupton for Tollett (4), 27 Paul Davidson for Wynyard (19), Wynyard for Davidson (36BB, rev 37), Millard for Clarke (68), Clarke for Dooley (73), Cram for Millard (76BB)
Tries: Clarke (55), Truelove (58), Crouthers (73).
Goals: Warton 2
WOLVES: 1 Lee Penny, 30 Jamie Stenhouse (D), 3 Alan Hunte, 4 Toa Kohe-Love, 5 Mark Forster, 6 Lee Briers, 7 Allan Langer (C), 8 Andrew Gee, 25 Paul Noone, 10 Danny Nutley, 14 Steve McCurrie, 12 Ian Knott, 13 Tawera Nikau. Subs: 11 Dean Busby for McCurrie (30), 21 Jerome Guisset for Gee (65), 31 Mark Gleeson (D) for Noone (42), 26 Mike Peters for Penny (24BB, rev 30), Peters for Knott (57), Guisset for McCurrie (74)
Tries: Stenhouse (6,21), Kohe-Love (10,65), Gee (14), Knott (30). **Goals:** Briers 4
League Express Men of the Match:
Broncos: Paul Davidson, **Wolves:** Lee Penny
Half-time: 0-28. **Referee:** Steve Ganson (St Helens), **Att:** 2,054. **Penalty count:** 6-8

HALIFAX BLUE SOX 36 CASTLEFORD TIGERS 16
BLUE SOX: 1 Daryl Cardiss, 33 Lee Greenwood, 6 Greg Florimo (C), 3 Damian Gibson, 4 Marvin Golden, 13 Martin Moana, 7 Andrew Dunemann, 8 Andy Hobson, 9 Paul Rowley, 10 James Gannon, 11 Gary Mercer, 12 Jamie Bloem, 31 Danny Tickle. Subs: 21 Gael Tallec for Bloem (11), 20 Stephen Holgate for Gannon (60), 34 Danny Halliwell (D) for Moana (17BB, rev 21), 29 Jamie Thackray for Hobson (27), Hobson for Tallec (43), Halliwell for Moana (63), Gannon for Mercer (67), Moana for Florimo (73BB), Tallec for Thackray (75)
Tries: Greenwood (20,39), Gibson (10,57), Tickle (6), Cardiss (13), Halliwell (68). **Goals:** Tickle 4
TIGERS: 1 Jason Flowers, 16 Jon Wells, 14 Barrie Jon Mather, 3 Michael Eagar, 5 Darren Rogers, 20 Barry Eaton, 7 Brad Davis, 10 Dean Sampson, 15 Darren Shaw, 8 Nathan Sykes, 17 Ian Tonks, 11 Lee Harland, 13 Adrian Vowles (C). Subs: 19 Andy Lynch for Sykes (31), 9 Aaron Raper for Eaton (45BB, rev 55), 67 Paul Smith for Tonks (14BB, rev 27), 25 Waine Pryce (D) for Wells (58), Smith for Harland (58), Harland for Davis (69)
Tries: Davis (32), Mather (43), Wells (51).
Goals: Eaton, Tonks
League Express Men of the Match:
Blue Sox: Andrew Dunemann, **Tigers:** Brad Davis
Penalty count: 7-4. **Half-time:** 24-6. **Referee:** Ian Smith (Oldham), **Att:** 6,293

LEEDS RHINOS 42 WAKEFIELD TRINITY WILDCATS 22
RHINOS: 5 Francis Cummins, 2 Paul Sterling, 33 Graham Mackay, 4 Keith Senior, 21 Karl Pratt, 1 Iestyn Harris (C), 7 Ryan Sheridan, 8 Darren Fleary, 9 Lee Jackson, 10 Barrie McDermott, 11 Adrian Morley, 12 David Barnhill, 13 Kevin Sinfield. Subs: 17 Anthony Farrell for Barnhill (29), 20 Jamie Mathiou for McDermott (30), 6 Daryl Powell for Fleary (50), 22 Chev Walker for Mackay (61), Barnhill for Morley (65), McDermott for Sinfield (65)
Tries: Senior (9), Harris (30, 49), Sterling (36), Mackay (58), Sheridan (63), Pratt (70). **Goals:** Harris 7
WILDCATS:2 Neil Law, 27 Ben Westwood, 3 Francis Maloney, 4 Tony Tatupu, 5 Bright Sodje, 14 Paul March, 7 Glen Tomlinson, 8 Francis Stephenson, 9 David March, 18 Paul Jackson, 11 Warren Jowitt, 16 Andy Fisher, 12 Willie Poching (C). Subs: 10 Martin Masella for Jackson (11), 19 Jamie Field for Stephenson (25), 13 Steve McNamara for D March (59), 22 Graham Law for Tatupu (70), Stephenson for Masella (48), D March for Poching (73)
Tries: Tomlinson (22), Masella (42), N Law (66), Jowitt (79). **Goals:** P March 3
League Express Men of the Match:
Rhinos: Lee Jackson, **Wildcats:** Neil Law
Penalty count: 6-7. **Half-time:** 18-6. **Referee:** Stuart Cummings (Widnes), **Att:** 13,075

WIGAN WARRIORS 20 BRADFORD BULLS 19
WARRIORS: 1 Kris Radlinski, 18 Wes Davies, 4 Gary Connolly, 3 Steve Renouf, 5 Jason Robinson, 13 Andrew Farrell (C), 7 Willie Peters, 8 Terry O'Connor, 9 Terry Newton, 10 Neil Cowie, 11 Mick Cassidy, 12 Denis Betts, 14 Lee Gilmour. Subs: 23 Brady Malam for O'Connor (41), 17 Tony Mestrov for Cowie (31BB), 19 Chris Chester for Gilmour (28), 6 Tony Smith for Newton (60), Cowie For Malam (65), O'Connor for Mestrov (65)
Tries: Newton (52), Betts (70), Radlinski (80).
Goals: Farrell 4. **Sin bin:** Mestrov (32) - retaliation
BULLS: 28 Stuart Spruce, 2 Tevita Vaikona, 20 Scott Naylor, 14 Justin Brooker, 3 Leon Pryce, 6 Henry Paul, 7 Paul Deacon, 22 Brian McDermott, 9 James Lowes (C), 10 Paul Anderson, 19 Jamie Peacock, 12 Mike Forshaw, 13 Brad Mackay. Subs: 29 Stuart Fielden for Anderson (21), 11 David Boyle for Peacock (28BB), 4 Nathan McAvoy for Pryce (23BB, rev 31), 15 Hudson Smith for McDermott (47), Peacock for Boyle (65), Anderson for Mackay (67), Mackay for Smith (71)
Tries: Pryce (2), Lowes (5), Naylor (48). **Goals:** Paul 3, **Field goal:** Deacon. **Sin bin:** Lowes (32) - obstruction, Naylor (75) - obstruction off the ball, Spruce (76) – interference
League Express Men of the Match:
Warriors: Andrew Farrell, **Bulls:** Henry Paul
Half-time: 2-13. **Referee:** Russell Smith (Castleford), **Att:** 17,737. **Penalty count:** 12-4

ST HELENS 50 SALFORD CITY REDS 28
SAINTS: 17 Paul Wellens, 24 Steve Hall, 21 Dwayne West, 15 Sean Hoppe, 5 Anthony Sullivan, 20 Tommy Martyn, 7 Sean Long, 8 Apollo Perelini, 9 Keiron Cunningham, 10 Julian O'Neill, 11 Chris Joynt (C), 14 Fereti Tuilagi, 13 Paul Sculthorpe. Subs: 22 Tim Jonkers for Martyn (49), 19 Tony Stewart for West (37), 12 Sonny Nickle for Perelini (29), 26 John Stankevitch for O'Neill (47), O'Neill for Joynt (73), Perelini for Tuilagi (74)
Tries: Perelini (6), Cunningham (10, 42), Hall (21), Long (25), Sculthorpe (28), Joynt (54), Stewart (59), Stankevitch (64). **Goals:** Long 7
CITY REDS: 1 Gary Broadbent, 2 Nick Pinkney, 4 Jason Webber, 3 Kris Tassell, 5 Martin Offiah, 31 Steve Blakeley, 6 Graham Holroyd, 8 Paul Southern, 9 Malcolm Alker, 11 Jim Smith, 30 Jason Nicol, 12 Darren Brown (C), 23 Mike Wainwright. Subs: 14 Joe Faimalo for Southern (29), 16 Paul Highton for Smith (29), 32 Jon Roper for Nicol (56), 29 Brad Hepi for Alker (62), Smith for Brown (66), Southern for Faimalo (69)
Tries: Alker (2), Southern (18), Offiah (34, 70), Broadbent (38). **Goals:** Blakeley 4
Sin bins: Highton (54) - holding down; Broadbent (54) - dissent., **On report:** Faimalo (51) - high tackle on Joynt
League Express Men of the Match:
Saints: Sean Long, **City Reds:** Mike Wainwright
Half-time: 28-22, **Att:** 6,694. **Referee:** Karl Kirkpatrick (Warrington). **Penalty count:** 9-6

HULL FC 34 HUDDERSFIELD-SHEFFIELD GIANTS 18
HULL: 14 Steve Collins, 2 Matt Daylight, 20 Richard Horne, 4 Craig Simon, 5 Ian Herron, 26 Paul Cooke, 7 Will Robinson, 8 Paul Broadbent, 19 Paul King, 12 Luke Felsch, 25 Richard Fletcher, 16 Adam Maher, 13 Tony Grimaldi (C). Subs: 30 Michael Docherty (D) for Broadbent (36), 21 Craig Poucher for Horne (69), 22 Steve Craven for Felsch (30), 17 Brian Carney for Docherty (54), Broadbent for Fletcher (54)
Tries: Collins (14), Robinson (24), Fletcher (33), Horne (67), Carney (79). **Goals:** Herron 7
GIANTS: 6 Gene Ngamu, 25 Ben Cooper, 5 Matt Crowther, 36 Chris Langley (D), 2 Danny Arnold, 19 Chris Thorman, 7 Gavin Clinch, 8 Steve Molloy (C), 9 Johnny Lawless, 10 Dale Laughton, 12 Richard Marshall, 22 David Bradbury, 15 Darren Turner. Subs: 18 Danny Russell for Lawless (45), 13 Jeff Hardy for Turner (12BB, rev 21), 11 David Lomax for Molloy (38), 29 Jamie Fielden for Laughton (27), Hardy for Clinch (51), Laughton for Fielden (61), Molloy for Marshall (71)
Tries: Crowther (17), Russell (71), Molloy (76).
Goals: Ngamu 3
League Express Men of the Match:
Hull: Steve Collins, **Giants:** Chris Thorman
Penalty count: 7-4. **Half-time:** 22-6. **Referee:** Graeme Shaw (Wigan), **Att:** 4,080

ROUND 26

CASTLEFORD TIGERS 30 LONDON BRONCOS 16
TIGERS: 1 Jason Flowers, 16 Jon Wells, 14 Barrie-Jon Mather, 3 Michael Eagar, 5 Darren Rogers, 6 Danny Orr, 7 Brad Davis, 10 Dean Sampson, 9 Aaron Raper, 19 Andy Lynch, 15 Darren Shaw, 11 Lee Harland, 13 Adrian Vowles (C). Subs: 17 Ian Tonks for Sampson (14BB, rev 22), 20 Barry Eaton for Orr (33), 18 Paul Smith for Shaw (47), 25 Waine Pryce for Flowers (67), Tonks for Lynch (25), Shaw for Harland (64), Lynch for Smith (73)
Tries: Rogers (1,30), Eagar (27,50), Flowers (32), Vowles (57). **Goals:** Tonks 2, Eaton
BRONCOS: 5 Brett Warton, 13 Mat Toshack, 22 John Timu, 28 Kevin Crouthers, 19 Dom Peters, 26 Peter Lupton, 29 Glen Air, 18 Justin Dooley, 21 Jon Clarke, 17 Anthony Seibold, 11 Shane Millard, 12 Steele Retchless (C), 15 Andy Johnson. Subs: 10 Scott Cram for Seibold (27), 9 Dean Callaway for Jon Clarke (56), 16 Frank Napoli for Warton (9), 27 Paul Davidson for Millard (27), Millard for Davidson (58BB), Seibold for Dooley (68), Dooley for Peters (73)
Tries: Timu (19), Johnson (37), Davidson (44).
Goals: Lupton 2
League Express Men of the Match:
Tigers: Michael Eagar, **Broncos:** John Timu
Penalty count: 4-8. **Half-time:** 20-10. **Referee:** Robert Connolly (Wigan), **Att:** 6,387

SALFORD CITY 33 CITY REDS HULL FC 24
CITY REDS: 1 Gary Broadbent, 2 Nick Pinkney, 4 Jason Webber, 3 Kris Tassell, 5 Martin Offiah, 31 Steve Blakeley, 6 Graham Holroyd, 8 Paul Southern, 9 Malcolm Alker, 11 Jim Smith, 30 Jason Nicol, 12 Darren Brown (C), 23 Mike Wainwright. Subs: 15 Neil Baynes for Smith (23), 16 Paul Highton for Nicol (31), 32 Jon Roper for Tassell (48), 14 Joe Faimalo for Southern (57), Nicol for Highton (57)
Tries: Alker (24), Tassell (38), Pinkney (40), Offiah (72, 80), Roper (78). **Goals:** Blakeley 3, Holroyd, **Field goal:** Holroyd. **Sin bin:** Baynes (37) retaliation
HULL FC: 14 Steve Collins, 5 Ian Herron, 20 Richard Horne, 4 Craig Simon, 2 Matt Daylight, 26 Paul Cooke, 7 Will Robinson, 8 Paul Broadbent, 9 Mick Jenkins, 12 Luke Felsch, 16 Adam Maher, 25 Richard Fletcher, 13 Tony Grimaldi (C). Subs: 22 Steve Craven for Broadbent (31), 19 Paul King for Fletcher (22BB, rev 32), 21 Craig Poucher not used, 17 Brian Carney for Fletcher (59), King for Jenkins (49), Broadbent for Craven (59)
Tries: Collins (8), Cooke (16), Maher (47), Robinson (66). **Goals:** Herron 4. **Sin bin:** Felsch (37) - head-butting in scrum
League Express Men of the Match:
City Reds: Malcolm Alker, **Hull FC:** Will Robinson
Penalty count: 3-6. **Half-time:** 14-12. **Referee:** Ian Smith (Oldham), **Att:** 3,526

HALIFAX BLUE SOX 18 BRADFORD BULLS 25
BLUE SOX: 3 Damian Gibson, 33 Lee Greenwood, 6 Greg Florimo (C), 34 Danny Halliwell, 17 Olly Marns, 13 Marty Moana, 32 Matty Firth, 8 Andy Hobson, 9 Paul Rowley, 23 Brett Goldspink, 10 James Gannon, 11 Gary Mercer, 31 Danny Tickle. Subs: 20 Stephen Holgate for Goldspink (26), 21 Gael Tallec for Mercer (34BB, rev 40), 29 Jamie Thackray for Hobson (30), 28 Casey Mayberry for Halliwell (48), Hobson for Thackray (49), Goldspink for Holgate (56)
Tries: Hobson (22), Halliwell (42), Gibson (67).
Goals: Tickle 3. **Sin bin:** Gannon (79) - fighting
BULLS: 28 Stuart Spruce, 2 Tevita Vaikona, 20 Scott Naylor, 5 Michael Withers, 3 Leon Pryce, 6 Henry Paul, 7 Paul Deacon, 29 Stuart Fielden, 9 James Lowes (C), 10 Paul Anderson, 19 Jamie Peacock, 12 Mike Forshaw, 11 David Boyle. Subs: 22 Brian McDermott for Anderson (26), 15 Hudson Smith for Boyle (28), 4 Nathan McAvoy for Brooker (47), 14 Justin Brooker for Naylor (40), Brooker for Vaikona (63), Anderson for Forshaw (72)
Tries: Withers (8), Deacon (15), Lowes (35), Paul (54).
Goals: Paul 4. **Field goal:** Deacon. **Sin bin:** Lowes (3 & 63) - dissent; Fielden (79) - fighting
League Express Men of the Match:
Blue Sox: Paul Rowley, **Bulls:** Jamie Peacock.
Half-time: 6-18. **Referee:** Steve Ganson (St Helens), **Att:** 8, 243. **Penalty count:** 10-5

LEEDS RHINOS 20 ST HELENS 35
RHINOS: 5 Francis Cummins, 2 Paul Sterling, 33 Graham Mackay, 4 Keith Senior, 21 Karl Pratt, 1 Iestyn Harris (C), 7 Ryan Sheridan, 8 Darren Fleary, 9 Lee Jackson, 10 Barrie McDermott, 11 Adrian Morley, 12 David Barnhill, 16 Andy Hay. Subs: 13 Kevin Sinfield for Barnhill (22), 17 Anthony Farrell for McDermott (22), 6 Daryl Powell for Hay (40), 22 Chev Walker for Pratt (44), Hay for Mackay (51BB), McDermott for Fleary (55), Barnhill for Jackson (68)
Tries: Jackson (31), Walker (47). **Goals:** Harris 6
SAINTS: 17 Paul Wellens, 15 Sean Hoppe, 3 Kevin Iro, 4 Paul Newlove, 5 Anthony Sullivan, 13 Paul Sculthorpe, 7 Sean Long, 8 Apollo Perelini, 9 Keiron Cunningham, 10 Julian O'Neill, 12 Sonny Nickle, 14 Fereti Tuilagi, 11 Chris Joynt (C). Subs: 16 Vila Matautia for O'Neill (26), 19 Tony Stewart for Perelini (51), O'Neill for Matautia (55), 24 Steve Hall for Stewart (71), 26 John Stankevitch for Nickle (73)
Tries: Wellens (3), Cunningham (28, 75), Nickle (59), Newlove (62, 64). **Goals:** Long 5, **Field goal:** Sculthorpe
Sin bin: Nickle (38) - holding down, **On report:** Matautia (51) - swinging arm
League Express Men of the Match: Rhinos: Kevin Sinfield, **Saints:** Keiron Cunningham
Penalty count: 9-12. **Half-time:** 12-12. **Referee:** Russell Smith, **Att:** 14,447

HUDDERSFIELD-SHEFFIELD GIANTS 16 WAKEFIELD TRINITY WILDCATS 14
GIANTS: 6 Gene Ngamu, 2 Danny Arnold, 5 Matt Crowther, 36 Chris Langley, 34 Leroy Rivett, 19 Chris Thorman, 24 Mark Moxon, 8 Steve Molloy (C), 18 Danny Russell, 10 Dale Laughton, 11 David Lomax, 12 Richard Marshall, 15 Darren Turner. Subs: 22 David Bradbury for Lomax (29), 29 Jamie Fielden for Laughton (29), 25 Ben Cooper not used, 13 Jeff Hardy for Thorman (48), Laughton for Molloy (56), Lomax for Fielden (60), Molloy for Lomax (73)
Tries: Ngamu (32), Thorman (34). **Goals:** Ngamu 4
WILDCATS:2 Neil Law, 5 Bright Sodje, 20 Adam Hughes, 22 Graham Law, 27 Ben Westwood, 14 Paul March, 7 Glen Tomlinson, 10 Martin Masella, 9 David March, 8 Francis Stephenson, 11 Warren Jowitt, 16 Andy Fisher, 12 Willie Poching (C). Subs: 13 Steve McNamara for Masella (23), 19 Jamie Field for Stephenson (31), 21 Ryan Hudson for D March (65), 32 Keith Mason (D) for Fisher (50), Stephenson for P March (56), Masella for Field (73)
Tries: D March (5), N Law (11) P March (46).
Goals: P March. **Sin bin:** Tomlinson (58) - holding down in tackle
League Express Men of the Match:
Giants: Steve Molloy, **Wildcats:** Warren Jowitt
Penalty count: 8-7. **Half-time:** 14-10. **Referee:** Karl Kirkpatrick (Warrington), **Att:** 2,409

WARRINGTON WOLVES 20 WIGAN WARRIORS 50
WOLVES: 3 Alan Hunte, 26 Mike Peters, 4 Toa Kohe-Love, 12 Ian Knott, 5 Mark Forster, 6 Lee Briers, 7 Allan Langer (C), 8 Andrew Gee, 9 Danny Farrar, 10 Danny Nutley, 14 Steve McCurrie, 25 Paul Noone, 13 Tawera Nikau. Subs: 11 Dean Busby for Farrar (60 BB, rev 67), 21 Jerome Guisset for Nutley (54), 24 David Alstead (D) for Peters (26BB, rev 35), 22 Will Cowell for Knott (1), Nutley for McCurrie (60BB, rev 63), Alstead for Kohe-Love (60), Busby for Noone (67), Nutley for Gee (70)
Tries: Langer (21, 43), Briers (34), Hunte (80).
Goals: Briers 2
WARRIORS: 1 Kris Radlinski, 18 Wes Davies, 4 Gary Connolly, 3 Steve Renouf, 5 Jason Robinson, 13 Andy Farrell (C), 7 Willie Peters, 8 Terry O' Connor, 9 Terry Newton, 10 Neil Cowie, 11 Mick Cassidy, 12 Denis Betts, 19 Chris Chester. Subs: 23 Brady Malam for Cowie (31), 17 Tony Mestrov for O' Connor (31), 26 David Hodgson not used, 6 Tony Smith for Peters (67), Cowie for Malam (62), O' Connor for Mestrov (62)
Tries: Newton (5, 69, 74), Renouf (18, 53), Farrell (51), Connolly (62), Radlinski (72). **Goals:** Farrell 9
League Express Men of the Match:
Wolves: Allan Langer, **Warriors:** Terry Newton
Half-time: 10-14. **Referee:** Stuart Cummings (Widnes), **Att:** 8,643. **Penalty count:** 5-3

ROUND 27

HALIFAX BLUE SOX 12 SALFORD CITY REDS 29
BLUE SOX: 1 Daryl Cardiss, 33 Lee Greenwood, 3 Damian Gibson, 34 Danny Halliwell, 17 Olly Marns, 13 Marty Moana, 7 Andrew Dunemann, 8 Andy Hobson, 9 Paul Rowley, 10 James Gannon, 11 Gary Mercer, 12 Jamie Bloem, 6 Greg Florimo (C). Subs: 20 Stephen Holgate for Thackray (46), 31 Danny Tickle for Bloem (52), 29 Jamie Thackray for Hobson (29), 28 Casey Mayberry not used, Hobson for Gannon (50), Gannon for Florimo (54), Florimo for Moana (67), Bloem for Holgate (69)
Tries: Gannon (34), Marns (57). **Goals:** Rowley, Bloem
Sin bin: Bloem (17) - minor skirmish with Broadbent,
On report: Dunemann (44) - late challenge on Blakeley
CITY REDS: 1 Gary Broadbent, 2 Nick Pinkney, 4 Jason Webber, 3 Kris Tassell, 5 Martin Offiah, 31 Steve Blakeley, 6 Graham Holroyd, 8 Paul Southern, 9 Malcolm Alker, 15 Neil Baynes, 30 Jason Nicol, 12 Darren Brown (C), 23 Mike Wainwright. Subs: 14 Joe Faimalo for Southern (26), 16 Paul Highton for Nicol (54), 32 Jon Roper for Tassell (75), 11 James Smith for Baynes (28), Southern for Faimalo (60), Baynes for Smith (66)
Tries: Holroyd (5), Smith (38), Tassell (71).
Goals: Blakeley 7, Holroyd, **Field goal:** Holroyd
Sin bin: Broadbent (17) - minor skirmish with Bloem
League Express Men of the Match:
Blue Sox: Andrew Dunemann, **City Reds:** Steve Blakeley
Half-time: 8-16, **Att:** 4,646. **Referee:** Russell Smith (Castleford). **Penalty count:** 10-13

HUDDERSFIELD-SHEFFIELD GIANTS 14 CASTLEFORD TIGERS 28
GIANTS: 6 Gene Ngamu, 2 Danny Arnold, 5 Matt Crowther, 36 Chris Langley, 34 Leroy Rivett, 19 Chris Thorman, 24 Mark Moxon, 8 Steve Molloy, 18 Danny Russell, 10 Dale Laughton (C), 22 David Bradbury, 11 David Lomax, 15 Darren Turner. Subs: 12 Richard Marshall for Lomax (24), 29 Jamie Fielden for Laughton (24), 13 Jeff Hardy for Fielden (55), 14 Paul Reilly for Ngamu (44), Laughton for Molloy (53), Lomax for Marshall (72)
Tries: Turner (31), Crowther (79). **Goals:** Ngamu (2), Crowther. **Sin bin:** Dale Laughton (62) - fighting, **On report:** Dale Laughton (62) – fighting
TIGERS: 13 Adrian Vowles (C), 16 Jon Wells, 14 Barrie-Jon Mather, 3 Michael Eagar, 5 Darren Rogers, 6 Danny Orr, 7 Brad Davis, 10 Dean Sampson, 9 Aaron Raper, 19 Andy Lynch, 17 Ian Tonks, 15 Darren Shaw, 11 Lee Harland. Subs: 25 Waine Pryce (D) for Lynch (52), 22 Andrew Purcell for Mather (60BB), 24 Gareth Dobson for Sampson (71), 18 Paul Smith for Sampson (26, rev 35), Smith for Tonks (40)
Tries: Rogers (2,59), Wells (25,43), Pryce (68).
Goals: Orr 4. **Sin bin:** Aaron Raper (62) - fighting, **On report:** Aaron Raper (62) – fighting
League Express, Men of the Match:
Giants: Danny Russell, **Tigers:** Aaron Raper
Half-time: 8-10. **Penalty count:** 9-8, **Att:** 2,903. **Referee:** John Connolly (Wigan)

WAKEFIELD TRINITY WILDCATS 18 WARRINGTON WOLVES 26
WILDCATS: 2 Neil Law, 27 Ben Westwood, 22 Graham Law, 4 Tony Tatupu, 20 Adam Hughes, 21 Ryan Hudson, 14 Paul March, 18 Paul Jackson, 9 David March, 16 Andy Fisher, 19 Jamie Field, 26 Gareth Ellis, 12 Willie Poching (C). Subs: 17 Frank Watene for Jackson (52), 29 Andy Speak for D March (58), 15 Gary Price for Ellis (25), 33 Paul Handforth (D) for Poching (63), Jackson for Fisher (64), Ellis for Watene (72)
Tries: P March (26), Poching (51), Hudson (54).
Goals: G Law 3. **Sin bin:** D March (34) - dissent
WOLVES: 1 Lee Penny, 30 Jamie Stenhouse, 3 Alan Hunte, 12 Ian Knott, 5 Mark Forster, 6 Lee Briers, 7 Allan Langer (C), 8 Andrew Gee, 9 Danny Farrar, 10 Danny Nutley, 14 Steve McCurrie, 25 Paul Noone, 13 Tawera Nikau. Subs: 24 Dave Alstead for Stenhouse (67), 26 Mike Peters for Noone (22), 28 Paul Wood (D) for Nutley (74), 21 Jerome Guisset for Peters (54)
Tries: Stenhouse (8), Penny (12), Forster (34), Hunte (38, 44). **Goals:** Briers 3. **Sin bin:** Farrar (49) - interference.
League Express Men of the Match:
Wildcats: Willie Poching, **Wolves:** Lee Briers
Referee: Robert Connolly (Wigan). **Half-time:** 6-20, **Att:** 3,187. **Penalty count:** 8-6

BRADFORD BULLS 14 LEEDS RHINOS 12
BULLS: 28 Stuart Spruce (C), 2 Tevita Vaikona, 20 Scott Naylor, 5 Michael Withers, 3 Leon Pryce, 6 Henry Paul, 7 Paul Deacon, 22 Brian McDermott, 9 James Lowes, 10 Paul Anderson, 19 Jamie Peacock, 12 Mike Forshaw, 13 Brad Mackay. Subs: 14 Justin Brooker for Withers (56), 11 David Boyle for Mackay (44), 15 Hudson Smith for Anderson (27), 18 Lee Radford for Peacock (74), Anderson for McDermott (59), McDermott for Smith (66BB, rev77), Withers for Naylor (79)
Tries: Smith (29), Vaikona (65). **Goals:** Paul 3
RHINOS: 5 Francis Cummins, 2 Paul Sterling, 3 Richie Blackmore, 4 Keith Senior, 21 Karl Pratt, 1 Iestyn Harris (C), 7 Ryan Sheridan, 8 Darren Fleary, 9 Lee Jackson, 20 Jamie Mathiou, 11 Adrian Morley, 13 Kevin Sinfield, 16 Andy Hay. Subs: 17 Anthony Farrell for Fleary (30), 6 Daryl Powell for Hay (40), 12 David Barnhill for Sinfield (30), 22 Chev Walker not used, Hay for Morley (53), Fleary for Mathiou (59), Sinfield for Barnhill (70)
Try: Cummins (58). **Goals:** Harris 4
League Express Men of the Match:
Bulls: James Lowes, **Rhinos:** Iestyn Harris
Penalty count: 6-7. **Half-time:** 8-6, **Att:** 19,623. **Referee:** Stuart Cummings (Widnes)

LONDON BRONCOS 12 ST HELENS 38
BRONCOS: 5 Brett Warton, 19 Dom Peters, 22 John Timu, 15 Andy Johnson, 13 Mat Toshack, 26 Peter Lupton, 19 Glen Air, 17 Anthony Seibold, 21 Jon Clarke, 10 Scott Cram, 11 Shane Millard, 12 Steele Retchless (C), 14 Andrew Wynyard. Subs: 9 Dean Callaway for Wynyard (48), 18 Justin Dooley for Seibold (21BB, rev 54), 27 Paul Davidson for Millard (1), 31 Olu Iwenofu (D) for Davidson (32), Dooley for Warton (57BB), Davidson for Clarke (67), Wynyard for Dooley (85)
Tries: Air (25), Lupton (49). **Goals:** Warton 2
SAINTS: 17 Paul Wellens, 24 Steve Hall, 21 Dwayne West, 15 Sean Hoppe, 5 Anthony Sullivan, 20 Tommy Martyn, 7 Sean Long, 8 Apollo Perelini, 9 Keiron Cunningham, 10 Julian O'Neill, 11 Chris Joynt (C), 14 Fereti Tuilagi, 13 Paul Sculthorpe. Subs: 12 Sonny Nickle for O'Neill (23), 23 Scott Barrow for Cunningham (17), 22 Tim Jonkers for Joynt (35BB, rev 61), 26 John Stankevitch for Perelini (35), O'Neill for Tuilagi (58), Jonkers for Martyn (61BB), Tuilagi for West (69)
Tries: Tuilagi (1,87), Sullivan (15), Wellens (27), Stankevitch (42), Joynt (62). **Goals:** Long 7
On report: Paul Sculthorpe (54) - suspected spear tackle on Justin Dooley
League Express Men of the Match:
Broncos: Peter Lupton, **Saints:** Paul Sculthorpe
Half-time: 6-20. **Referee:** Karl Kirkpatrick (Warrington), **Att:** 4,156. **Penalty count:** 8-4

WIGAN WARRIORS 54 HULL FC 4
WARRIORS: 18 Wes Davies, 26 Dave Hodgson, 1 Kris Radlinski, 4 Gary Connolly, 5 Jason Robinson, 13 Andy Farrell (C), 7 Willie Peters, 8 Terry O'Connor, 9 Terry Newton, 10 Neil Cowie, 11 Mick Cassidy, 12 Denis Betts, 19 Chris Chester. Subs: 17 Tony Mestrov for Cowie (32), 27 Brady Malam for O'Connor (32), 6 Tony Smith for Newton (15), 14 Lee Gilmour for Cassidy (51), O'Connor for Mestrov (69), Cassidy for Betts (74)
Tries: Hodgson (1, 45, 77), Robinson (7, 21, 26), Davies (39), Peters (41), Betts (60), Connolly (63).
Goals: Farrell 7
HULL: 21 Craig Poucher, 5 Ian Herron, 14 Steve Collins, 4 Craig Simon, 2 Matt Daylight, 26 Paul Cooke, 31 Scott Rhodes (D), 8 Paul Broadbent, 19 Paul King, 12 Luke Felsch, 16 Adam Maher, 25 Richard Fletcher, 13 Tony Grimaldi (C). Subs: 22 Steve Craven for Fletcher (25), 28 Craig Farrell for Herron (65), 27 Andy Last for King (18), 17 Brian Carney for Maher (55), King for Broadbent (51), Fletcher for Felsch (74BB), Broadbent for Last (75)
Try: Daylight (55)
League Express Men of the Match:
Warriors: Jason Robinson, **Hull FC:** Scott Rhodes
Referee: Steve Ganson (St Helens), **Att:** 8,409. Penalty count: 4-7. **Half-time:** 26-0

ROUND 28

CASTLEFORD TIGERS 20 WAKEFIELD TRINITY WILDCATS 8
TIGERS: 2 Richard Gay, 16 Jon Wells, 5 Darren Rogers, 3 Michael Eagar, 25 Waine Pryce, 6 Danny Orr, 7 Brad Davis, 10 Dean Sampson, 9 Aaron Raper, 19 Andy Lynch, 11 Lee Harland, 22 Andrew Purcell, 13 Adrian Vowles (C). Subs: 15 Darren Shaw for Raper (19), 17 Ian Tonks for Lynch (31), 18 Paul Smith for Shaw (40), 26 Jonathan Goddard (D) for Purcell (64), Lynch for Tonks (67), Purcell for Gay (77)
Tries: Wells (6,76), Orr (12), Gay (52). **Goals:** Orr 2
WILDCATS: 2 Neil Law, 20 Adam Hughes, 27 Ben Westwood, 22 Graham Law, 5 Bright Sodje, 14 Paul March, 9 David March, 16 Andy Fisher, 29 Andy Speak, 18 Paul Jackson, 19 Jamie Field, 15 Gary Price (C), 21 Ryan Hudson. Subs: 17 Frank Watene for Fisher (50), 26 Gareth Ellis for Price (54), 32 Keith Mason for Field (55), 33 Paul Handforth for Speak (33), Speak for D March (66)
Tries: Handforth (71). Goals: G Law 2,, **On report:** Andy Fisher (38) – off-the-ball high tackle
League Express Men of the Match:
Tigers: Danny Orr, **Wildcats:** Neil Law
Half-time: 10-4 . **Penalty count:** 9-6, **Att:** 6,892.
Referee: Karl Kirkpatrick (Warrington)

LEEDS RHINOS 6 LONDON BRONCOS 18
RHINOS: 5 Francis Cummins, 2 Paul Sterling, 3 Richie Blackmore, 4 Keith Senior, 21 Karl Pratt, 13 Kevin

Sinfield, 7 Ryan Sheridan (C), 20 Jamie Mathiou, 9 Lee Jackson, 10 Barrie McDermott, 17 Anthony Farrell, 12 David Barnhill, 16 Andy Hay. Subs: 6 Daryl Powell for Hay (27), 20 Chev Walker for Blackmore (47), 8 Darren Fleary for McDermott (48), 26 Garreth Carvell for Farrell (70), Hay for Barnhill (58), McDermott for Mathiou (64)
Try: Sinfield (48), **Goal:** Cummins
BRONCOS: 13 Mat Toshack, 31 Olu Iwenofu, 13 Andy Johnson, 22 John Timu, 19 Dominic Peters, 26 Peter Lupton, 29 Glen Air, 18 Justin Dooley, 21 Jon Clarke, 17 Anthony Seibold, 10 Scott Cram, 12 Steele Retchless (C), 14 Andrew Wynyard. Subs: 32 Yusef Sozi (D) for Seibold (25), 27 Paul Davidson for Dooley (32), 9 Dean Callaway for Clarke (38), 5 Brett Warton for Iwenofu (53), Dooley for Davidson (38), Clarke For Wynyard (56), Davidson for Sozi (70BB), Wynyard for Cram (73BB)
Tries: Warton (69), Peters (75), Callaway (77). **Goals:** Warton 3. **Penalty count:** 2-5. **Half-time:** 0-0. **Referee:** Steve Ganson (St Helens), **Att:** 8,954
League Express Men of the Match:
Rhinos: Kevin Sinfield, **Broncos:** Glen Air

ST HELENS 4 WIGAN WARRIORS 42
SAINTS: 17 Paul Wellens, 15 Sean Hoppe, 3 Kevin Iro, 4 Paul Newlove, 24 Steve Hall, 20 Tommy Martyn, 7 Sean Long, 8 Apollo Perelini, 9 Keiron Cunningham, 10 Julian O'Neill, 11 Chris Joynt (C), 14 Fereti Tuilagi, 13 Paul Sculthorpe. Subs: 12 Sonny Nickle for Perelini (23), Perelini for O'Neill (47), 22 Tim Jonkers for Nickle (58), 21 Dwayne West for Iro (70), 26 John Stankevitch for Tuilagi (58)
Try: Joynt (63). **Sin bin:** Cunningham (32) - fighting
WARRIORS: 1 Kris Radlinski, 2 Brett Dallas, 4 Gary Connolly, 3 Steve Renouf, 5 Jason Robinson, 13 Andrew Farrell (C), 7 Willie Peters, 8 Terry O'Connor, 9 Terry Newton, 10 Neil Cowie, 11 Mick Cassidy, 12 Denis Betts, 19 Chris Chester. Subs: 17 Tony Mestrov for Cowie (31), 14 Lee Gilmour for Chester (44), 23 Brady Malam for O'Connor (47), Cowie for Mestrov (51), 6 Tony Smith for Betts (57), O'Connor for Newton (61bb, rev 62), Mestrov for Cowie (67), O'Connor for Malam (71)
Tries: Cowie (5), Peters (15, 20), Dallas (26), Renouf (45), Robinson (57), Connolly (79). **Goals:** Farrell 7
League Express Men of the Match:
Saints: Chris Joynt, **Warriors:** Willie Peters
Att: 16,030. **Referee:** Russell Smith (Castleford).
Penalty count: 11-9. **Half-time:** 0-24

HALIFAX BLUE SOX 54
HUDDERSFIELD-SHEFFIELD GIANTS 18
BLUE SOX: 1 Daryl Cardiss, 33 Lee Greenwood, 6 Greg Florimo (C), 3 Damian Gibson, 17 Olly Marns, 13 Marty Moana, 7 Andrew Dunemann, 8 Andy Hobson, 35 Sean Penkywicz (D), 10 Jim Gannon, 11 Gary Mercer, 29 Jamie Thackray, 21 Gael Tallec. Subs: 36 Ryan Clayton (D) for Foster (62), 32 Matty Firth for Penkywicz (32), 34 Danny Halliwell for Marns (49), 19 David Foster for Thackray (26), Thackray for Hobson (59), Hobson for Thackray (73)
Tries: Greenwood (14, 18), Florimo (22), Moana (38, 65, 70), Dunemann (52), Mercer (63), Gannon (67), Gibson (76). **Goals:** Cardiss 3, Florimo 4. **Sin bin:** Tallec (58) - fighting
GIANTS: 14 Paul Reilly, 34 Leroy Rivett, 3 Karl Lovell, 36 Chris Langley, 2 Danny Arnold, 19 Chris Thorman, 24 Mark Moxon, 8 Steve Molloy, 18 Danny Russell (C), 11 David Lomax, 12 Richard Marshall, 22 David Bradbury, 15 Darren Turner. Subs: 5 Matt Crowther for Lovell (2), 13 Jeff Hardy for Reilly (8), 21 Chris Molyneux for Lomax (13BB, rev 25), 28 Andy Rice for Bradbury (50BB), Molyneux for Molloy (53), Reilly for Lomax (55), Lomax for Marshall (64), Molloy for Molyneux (70), Marshall for Lomax (73)
Tries: Crowther (28), Arnold (43, 47). **Goals:** Crowther 3
Sin bin: Turner (58) – fighting
League Express Men of the Match:
Blue Sox: Andrew Dunemann, **Giants:** Chris Thorman
Half-time: 22-8, **Att:** 4,843. **Referee:** Robert Connolly (Wigan). **Penalty count:** 8-6

HULL FC 25 BRADFORD BULLS 12
HULL FC: 14 Steve Collins, 2 Matt Daylight, 4 Craig Simon, 29 Paul Parker, 21 Craig Poucher, 20 Richard Horne, 31 Scott Rhodes, 8 Paul Broadbent, 27 Andy Last, 19 Paul King, 12 Luke Felsch, 13 Tony Grimaldi (C), 26 Paul Cooke. Subs: 22 Steve Craven for King (45), 11 Craig Wilson for Grimaldi (26BB), 28 Craig Farrell for Collins (30BB), 30 Michael Docherty for Broadbent (45), Collins for Farrell (ht), Grimaldi for Wilson (50BB), Broadbent for Craven (65), Wilson for Felsch (73)
Tries: Simon (6), King (13), Daylight (18), Parker (58).
Goals: Cooke 4, **Field goal:** Cooke,
BULLS: 14 Justin Brooker, 3 Leon Pryce, 4 Nathan McAvoy, 5 Michael Withers, 16 Alex Wilkinson, 1 Robbie Paul (C), 7 Paul Deacon, 30 Gareth Handford, 24 Gareth Stanley (D), 29 Stuart Fielden, 15 Hudson Smith, 11 David Boyle, 13 Brad Mackay. Subs: 18 Lee Radford for Smith (25), 25 Craig McDowell (D) for Stanley (54), 27 Robert Parker for Boyle (52), 17 Chris Birchall (D) for Handford (26), Smith for Birchall (70)
Tries: McAvoy (26), Stanley (38). **Goals:** Deacon 2
On report: Birchall (50) - foul tackle
League Express Men of the Match:
Hull: Paul Cooke, **Bulls:** Paul Deacon
Penalty count: 12-7. **Half-time:** 18-12. **Referee:** John Connolly (Wigan), **Att:** 6,160

WARRINGTON WOLVES 38 SALFORD CITY REDS 10
WOLVES: 1 Lee Penny, 30 Jamie Stenhouse, 5 Mark Forster, 4 Toa Kohe-Love, 3 Alan Hunte, 6 Lee Briers, 7 Allan Langer (C), 8 Andrew Gee, 9 Danny Farrar, 10 Danny Nutley, 14 Steve McCurrie, 21 Jerome Guisset, 13 Tawera Nikau. Subs: 12 Ian Knott for Briers (31), 26 Mike Peters for Stenhouse (61), 24 Dave Alstead for Penny (27), 28 Paul Wood for Gee (66)
Tries: Briers (16), Kohe-Love (31), Guisset (37), McCurrie (40, 46), Hunte (61, 76).
Goals: Briers, Langer 4
CITY REDS: 1 Gary Broadbent, 2 Nick Pinkney, 4 Jason Webber, 32 Jon Roper, 5 Martin Offiah, 31 Steve Blakeley, 6 Graham Holroyd, 15 Neil Baynes, 9 Malcolm Alker, 8 Paul Southern, 12 Darren Brown (C), 30 Jason Nicol, 23 Michael Wainwright. Subs: 3 Kris Tassell for Nicol (4), 11 James Smith for Roper (ht), 16 Paul Highton for Wainwright 63), 14 Joe Faimalo for Baynes (30), Baynes for Southern (63)
Tries: Tassell (56), Offiah (73), **Goal:** Holroyd
League Express Men of the Match: Wolves: Danny Farrar, **Reds:** Darren Brown
Penalty count: 6-9. **Half-time:** 24-0. **Referee:** Stuart Cummings (Widnes), **Att:** 6,969

FINALS SERIES

QUALIFYING PLAY-OFF

ST HELENS 16 BRADFORD BULLS 11
SAINTS: 17 Paul Wellens, 15 Sean Hoppe, 3 Kevin Iro, 4 Paul Newlove, 5 Anthony Sullivan, 20 Tommy Martyn, 7 Sean Long, 8 Apollo Perelini, 9 Keiron Cunningham, 10 Julian O'Neill, 11 Chris Joynt (C), 22 Tim Jonkers, 13 Paul Sculthorpe. Subs: 14 Fereti Tuilagi for Jonkers (22), 26 John Stankevitch for O'Neill (23), 24 Steve Hall for Tuilagi (75), 21 Dwayne West for Newlove (78BB), O'Neill for Perelini (35), Perelini for O'Neill (52), Jonkers for Stankevitch (73)
Tries: Hoppe (55), Martyn (59), Joynt (80).
Goals: Long 2. **Sin bin:** Chris Joynt (37) - interfering at play the ball
BULLS: 28 Stuart Spruce, 3 Leon Pryce, 5 Michael Withers, 20 Scott Naylor, 2 Tevita Vaikona, 6 Henry Paul, 7 Paul Deacon, 22 Brian McDermott, 9 James Lowes (C), 10 Paul Anderson, 12 Mike Forshaw, 19 Jamie Peacock, 13 Brad Mackay. Subs: 29 Stuart Fielden for Anderson (21), 1 Robbie Paul for Deacon (35), 15 Hudson Smith for McDermott (50), 4 Nathan McAvoy for Withers (55), Anderson for Peacock (69)
Tries: Peacock (24), Pryce (65). **Goals:** H Paul. **Field goals:** H Paul
League Express Men of the Match: Saints: Chris Joynt, Bulls: Henry Paul
Penalty count: 10-9. **Half-time:** 0-4. **Att:** 8,864. **Referee:** Russell Smith (Castleford)

QUALIFYING PLAY-OFF

LEEDS RHINOS 22 CASTLEFORD TIGERS 14
RHINOS: 5 Francis Cummins, 2 Paul Sterling, 3 Richie Blackmore, 4 Keith Senior, 21 Karl Pratt, 1 Iestyn Harris (C), 7 Ryan Sheridan, 8 Darren Fleary, 9 Lee Jackson, 10 Barrie McDermott, 11 Adrian Morley, 13 Kevin Sinfield, 16 Andy Hay . Subs: 35 Graham Mackay for Pratt (40), 17 Anthony Farrell for Hay (60), 20 Jamie Mathiou for Fleary (26), 6 Daryl Powell for Sinfield (35), Fleary for McDermott (49), Pratt for Sterling (67), Sinfield for Morley (76bb)
Tries: Sterling (16), Sinfield (23), Sheridan (55), Senior (64) , **Goals:** Harris 3
TIGERS: 2 Richard Gay, 16 Jon Wells, 14 Barrie-Jon Mather, 3 Michael Eagar, 5 Darren Rogers, 6 Danny Orr, 7 Brad Davis, 10 Dean Sampson, 22 Andrew Purcell , 19 Andy Lynch, 11 Lee Harland, 15 Darren Shaw , 13 Adrian Vowles (C). Subs: 15 Darren Shaw for , 17 Ian Tonks for Lynch (21) , 18 Paul Smith for Shaw (53), 1 Jason Flowers for Gay (32), 25 Waine Pryce for Flowers (67), Lynch for Tonks (49), Tonks for Sampson (53-65bb)
Tries: Davis (4), Wells (31), Mather (48). **Goals:** Orr
League Express Men of the Match:
Rhinos: Iestyn Harris, **Tigers:** Brad Davis
Half-time: 12-10. **Penalty count:** 5-9. **Att:** 13,685.
Referee: Stuart Cummings (Widnes)

QUALIFYING SEMI-FINAL

WIGAN WARRIORS 16 ST HELENS 54
WARRIORS: 1 Kris Radlinski, 2 Brett Dallas, 4 Gary Connolly, 3 Steve Renouf, 5 Jason Robinson, 13 Andrew Farrell (C), 7 Willie Peters, 8 Terry O'Connor, 9 Terry Newton, 10 Neil Cowie, 11 Mick Cassidy, 12 Denis Betts, 19 Chris Chester. Subs: 14 Lee Gilmour for Betts (49), 6 Tony Smith for Newton (49BB), 23 Brady Malam for O'Connor (34), 17 Tony Mestrov for Cowie (28), Newton for Connolly (54BB), Cowie for Mestrov (60), O'Connor for Malam (60)
Tries: Renouf (3, 62), Smith (55). **Goals:** Farrell 2
SAINTS: 17 Paul Wellens, 15 Sean Hoppe, 3 Kevin Iro, 4 Paul Newlove, 5 Anthony Sullivan, 20 Tommy Martyn, 7 Sean Long, 8 Apollo Perelini, 9 Keiron Cunningham, 10 Julian O'Neill, 11 Chris Joynt (C), 22 Tim Jonkers, 13 Paul Sculthorpe. Subs: 14 Fereti Tuilagi for O'Neill (21), 26 John Stankevitch for Nickle (36BB, rev 59), 24 Steve Hall for Newlove (6), 12 Sonny Nickle for Perelini (26), Stankevitch for Martyn (61), Perelini for Joynt (61BB, rev 71), O'Neill for Jonkers (69), Perelini for Cunningham (71)
Tries: Hall (7), Cunningham (26), Sullivan (40), Iro (44, 67), Long (47, 59), Martyn (53), Hoppe (72).
Goals: Long 9
League Express Men of the Match:
Warriors: Terry Newton, **Saints:** Sean Long
Referee: Stuart Cummings (Widnes).
Penalty count: 9-7. **Half-time:** 6-18. **Att:** 19,186

ELIMINATION SEMI-FINAL

BRADFORD BULLS 46 LEEDS RHINOS 12
BULLS: 28 Stuart Spruce, 2 Tevita Vaikona, 5 Michael Withers, 20 Scott Naylor, 3 Leon Pryce, 6 Henry Paul, 7 Robbie Paul (C), 10 Paul Anderson, 9 James Lowes, 29 Stuart Fielden, 12 Mike Forshaw, 19 Jamie Peacock, 13 Brad Mackay. Subs: 7 Paul Deacon for R Paul (34BB, rev 44), 11 David Boyle for Peacock (52), 22 Brian McDermott for Anderson (24), 15 Hudson Smith for Forshaw (54), Deacon for H. Paul (59), Anderson for Mackay (62)
Tries: Pryce (3,47,75), Anderson (20), Fielden (36), H. Paul (53), Boyle (56), R Paul (63). **Goals:** H Paul 6, Deacon
RHINOS: 5 Francis Cummins, 33 Graham Mackay , 3 Richie Blackmore, 4 Keith Senior, 21 Karl Pratt, 1 Iestyn Harris (C), 7 Ryan Sheridan, 8 Darren Fleary, 9 Lee Jackson, 10 Barrie McDermott, 11 Adrian Morley, 13 Kevin Sinfield, 16 Andy Hay . Subs: 2 Paul Sterling for Senior (22), 17 Anthony Farrell for McDermott (21), 12 David Barnhill for Hay (51), 6 Daryl Powell for Jackson (37), McDermott for Fleary (51), Senior for Sinfield (54BB, rev 65), Jackson for Sheridan (58)
Tries: Hay (22), Sterling (79). **Goals:** Harris 2
League Express Men of the Match:
Bulls: Henry Paul, **Rhinos:** Lee Jackson
Half-time: 20-6. **Penalty count:** 9-7. **Att:** 15,077.
Referee: Russell Smith (Castleford)

FINAL ELIMINATOR

WIGAN WARRIORS 40 BRADFORD BULLS 12
WARRIORS: 1 Kris Radlinski, 2 Brett Dallas, 4 Gary Connolly, 3 Steve Renouf, 5 Jason Robinson, 6 Tony Smith, 7 Willie Peters, 8 Terry O'Connor, 9 Terry Newton, 10 Neil Cowie, 11 Mick Cassidy, 12 Denis Betts, 13 Andrew Farrell (C). Subs: 14 Lee Gilmour for Connolly (27), 23 Brady Malam for Cowie (33), 17 Tony Mestrov for O'Connor (45), 19 Chris Chester for Betts (53), Betts for Newton (71), Cowie for Malam (78)
Tries: Peters (7), Robinson (15, 65), Connolly (26), Dallas (28, 33, 44). **Goals:** Farrell 6
On report: Newton (12) - alleged spear tackle on Spruce,
Sin bin: Cassidy (69) - holding down
BULLS: 28 Stuart Spruce, 2 Tevita Vaikona, 20 Scott Naylor, 5 Michael Withers, 3 Leon Pryce, 6 Henry Paul, 1 Robbie Paul (C), 22 Brian McDermott, 9 James Lowes, 10 Paul Anderson, 29 Stuart Fielden, 19 Jamie Peacock, 12 Mike Forshaw. Subs: 15 Hudson Smith for Anderson (20), 11 David Boyle for Peacock (34), 4 Nathan McAvoy for Spruce (34BB), Anderson for Smith (45), 7 Paul Deacon for McAvoy (49), Peacock for McDermott (52), McAvoy for Withers (60), McDermott for Anderson (75)
Tries: Naylor (10), Anderson (69). **Goals:** H Paul 2
League Express Men of the Match:
Warriors: Brett Dallas, **Bulls:** Henry Paul
Half-time: 28-6. **Att:** 14,620. **Referee:** Russell Smith (Castleford). **Penalty count:** 5-10

GRAND FINAL

ST HELENS 29 WIGAN WARRIORS 16
SAINTS: 17 Paul Wellens, 24 Steve Hall, 3 Kevin Iro, 15 Sean Hoppe, 5 Anthony Sullivan, 20 Tommy Martyn, 7 Sean Long, 8 Apollo Perelini, 9 Keiron Cunningfham, 10 Julian O'Neill, 11 Chris Joynt (C), 22 Tim Jonkers, 13 Paul Sculthorpe. Subs: 14 Fereti Tuilagi for O'Neill (20), 12 Sonny Nickle for Perelini (28), 26 John Stankevitch for Jonkers (50), Perelini for Nickle (52), Jonkers for Stankevitch (66), Stankevitch for Perelini (67), O'Neill for Hall (74), 23 Scott Barrow not used
Tries: Hoppe (7), Joynt (28, 50), Tuilagi (69), Jonkers (80). **Goals:** Long 4. **Field goal:** Sculthorpe
WARRIORS: 5 Jason Robinson, 2 Brett Dallas, 1 Kris Radlinski, 3 Steve Renouf, 26 David Hodgson, 6 Tony Smith, 7 Willie Peters, 8 Terry O'Connor, 9 Terry Newton, 10 Neil Cowie, 11 Mick Cassidy, 12 Denis Betts, 13 Andrew Farrell (C). Subs: 23 Brady Malam for Cowie (30), 17 Tony Mestrov for O'Connor (43), 19 Chris Chester for Cassidy (47BB, rev 69), 14 Lee Gilmour for Betts (51), O'Connor for Mestrov (61), Cowie for Malam (67), Chester for Newton (75)
Tries: Farrell (13), Hodgson (58), Smith (61).
Goals: Farrell 2
League Express Men of the Match:
Saints: Chris Joynt, **Warriors:** Andrew Farrell
Half-time: 11-4. **Penalty count:** 10-6. **Referee:** Russell Smith (Castleford). **Att:** 58,132

FIXTURES 2001

ROUND 1
Friday 2 March
Bradford v St Helens
Wigan v Warrington
Saturday 3 March
London v Leeds
Sunday 4 March
Huddersfield v Halifax
Hull v Salford
Wakefield v Castleford

ROUND 2
Friday 16 March
Salford v Bradford
Leeds v Wakefield
St Helens v Huddersfield
Saturday 17 March
Castleford v Wigan
Sunday 18 March
Warrington v Hull
Halifax London

ROUND 3
Friday 23 March
Wigan v Leeds
Saturday 24 March
London v St Helens
Sunday 25 March
Warrington v Salford
Huddersfield v Bradford
Hull v Castleford
Wakefield v Halifax

ROUND 4
Friday 6 April
Halifax v Wigan
St Helens v Wakefield
Leeds v Hull
Saturday 7 April
Castleford v Warrington
Sunday 8 April
Salford v Huddersfield
Bradford London

ROUND 5
Thursday 12 April
Warrington v Leeds
Friday 13 April GOOD FRIDAY
Wigan v St Helens
Castleford v Salford
London v Huddersfield
Hull v Halifax
Wakefield Bradford

ROUND 6
Monday 16 April EASTER MONDAY
Bradford v Wigan
Huddersfield v Wakefield
Halifax v Warrington
Salford v London
Leeds v Castleford
St Helens v Hull

ROUND 7
Friday 20 April
Warrington v St Helens
Wigan v Huddersfield
Saturday 21 April
Hull v Bradford
Sunday 22 April
Castleford v Halifax
Salford v Leeds
Wakefield v London

ROUND 8
Monday 30 April
Halifax v Leeds
Huddersfield v Hull
London v Wigan
St Helens v Castleford
Wakefield v Salford
Bradford v Warrington

ROUND 9
Friday 4 May
Leeds v St Helens
Wigan v Wakefield
Saturday 5 May
Castleford v Bradford
Sunday 6 May
Warrington v Huddersfield
Halifax v Salford
Hull v London

ROUND 10
Friday 11 May
St Helens v Halifax
Saturday 12 May
Leeds v Bradford
Sunday 13 May
Huddersfield v Castleford
Salford v Wigan
London v Warrington
Wakefield v Hull

ROUND 11
Friday 18 May
Bradford v Halifax
St Helens v Salford
Leeds v Huddersfield
Saturday 19 May
Hull v Wigan
Sunday 20 May
Warrington v Wakefield
Castleford v London

ROUND 12
Friday 25 May
Huddersfield v St Helens
Wigan v Castleford
Saturday 26 May
Wakefield v Leeds
Sunday 27 May
London v Halifax
Hull v Warrington
Bradford v Salford

ROUND 13
Friday 1 June
Warrington v Wigan
Leeds v London
Saturday 2 June
St Helens v Bradford
Castleford v Wakefield
Sunday 3 June
Halifax v Huddersfield
Salford v Hull

ROUND 14
Friday 8 June
Salford v Warrington
St Helens v London
Saturday 9 June
Leeds v Wigan
Sunday 10 June
Castleford v Hull
Halifax v Wakefield
Bradford v Huddersfield

ROUND 15
Friday 15 June
Wigan v Halifax
Sunday 17 June
Warrington v Castleford
Huddersfield v Salford
London v Bradford
Hull v Leeds
Wakefield v St Helens

ROUND 16
Friday 22 June
Leeds v Warrington
St Helens v Wigan
Sunday 24 June
Halifax v Hull
Huddersfield v London
Salford v Castleford
Bradford v Wakefield

ROUND 17
Friday 29 June
Wigan v Bradford
Castleford v Leeds
Sunday 30 June
Warrington v Halifax
London v Salford
Hull v St Helens
Wakefield v Huddersfield

ROUND 18
Friday 6 July
Leeds v Salford
St Helens v Warrington
Bradford v Hull
Sunday 8 July
Halifax v Castleford
Huddersfield v Wigan
London v Wakefield

ROUND 19
Friday 13 July
St Helens v Leeds
Sunday 15 July
Salford v Halifax
Huddersfield v Warrington
London v Hull
Wakefield v Wigan
Bradford v Castleford

ROUND 20
Friday 20 July
Wigan v Salford
Sunday 22 July
Warrington v London
Castleford v Huddersfield
Halifax v St Helens
Bradford v Leeds
Hull v Wakefield

ROUND 21
Friday 27 July
Wigan v Hull
Sunday 29 July
Huddersfield v Leeds
Salford v St Helens
London v Castleford
Wakefield v Warrington
Halifax v Bradford

ROUND 22
Friday 3 August
Leeds v Halifax
Wigan v London
Sunday 5 August
Warrington v Bradford
Castleford v St Helens
Salford v Wakefield
Hull v Huddersfield

ROUND 23
Friday 10 August
Leeds v Bradford
St Helens Wigan
Sunday 12 August
Hull Halifax
Huddersfield v Salford
London v Wakefield
Warrington v Castleford

ROUND 24
Friday 17 August
Bradford v St Helens
Wigan v Warrington
Saturday 18 August
Castleford v Leeds
Sunday 19 August
Halifax v Huddersfield
Hull v London
Wakefield v Salford

ROUND 25
Friday 24 August
Leeds v Wigan
Sunday 26 August
Bradford v Castleford
Wakefield v Hull
London v Huddersfield
Salford v Halifax
Warrington v St Helens

ROUND 26
Friday 31 August
Leeds v Warrington
St Helens v Castleford
Wigan v Bradford
Sunday 2 September
Halifax v Wakefield
Huddersfield v Hull
Salford v London

ROUND 27
Friday 7 September
St Helens v Leeds
Sunday 9 September
Castleford v Wigan
Hull v Salford
London v Halifax
Wakefield v Huddersfield
Warrington v Bradford

ROUND 28
Friday 14 September
Bradford v Leeds
Wigan v St Helens
Sunday 16 September
Castleford v Warrington
Halifax v Hull
Salford v Wakefield
Huddersfield v London

**GRAND FINAL AND
PLAY-OFF SERIES**

Friday 21 September
Qualifying Play-off

Saturday 22 September
Elimination Play-off

Friday 28 September
Qualifying Semi

Saturday 29 September
Elimination Semi

Saturday 6 October
Final Eliminator

Saturday 13 October
Grand Final

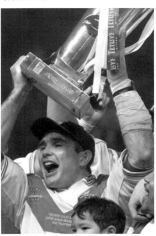

FIXTURES 2001

SUNDAY 3rd DECEMBER 2000
Barrow v Oldham
Chorley v Swinton
Dewsbury v Featherstone
Gateshead v Hull KR
Hunslet v Keighley
Sheffield v Batley
Widnes v Whitehaven
Workington v Rochdale
York v Doncaster
Bye: Leigh

SUNDAY 10th DECEMBER 2000
Batley v Gateshead
Doncaster v Hunslet
Featherstone v Sheffield
Hull KR v York
Keighley v Dewsbury
Leigh v Barrow
Oldham v Chorley
Rochdale v Widnes
Whitehaven v Swinton
Bye: Workington

SUNDAY 17th DECEMBER 2000
Batley v Doncaster
Dewsbury v Hull KR
Featherstone v Gateshead
Hunslet v Sheffield
Rochdale v Chorley
Swinton v Barrow
Whitehaven v Leigh
Workington v Oldham
York v Keighley
Bye: Widnes

SUNDAY 24th DECEMBER 2000
Gateshead v Keighley
Rochdale v Oldham

TUESDAY 26th DECEMBER 2000
Chorley v Barrow
Dewsbury v Batley
Doncaster v Sheffield
Hull KR v Featherstone
Widnes v Leigh
Workington v Whitehaven
York v Hunslet
Bye: Swinton

SUNDAY 31st DECEMBER 2000
Barrow v Workington
Sheffield v Gateshead

MONDAY 1st JANUARY
Batley v York
Featherstone v Doncaster
Hunslet v Dewsbury
Keighley v Hull KR
Leigh v Swinton
Oldham v Widnes
Whitehaven v Chorley
Bye: Rochdale

SUNDAY 7th JANUARY 2001
Barrow v Whitehaven
Batley v Featherstone
Chorley v Leigh
Dewsbury v York
Gateshead v Doncaster
Hull KR v Hunslet
Sheffield v Keighley
Swinton v Rochdale
Widnes v Workington
Bye: Oldham

SUNDAY 14th JANUARY
Gateshead v Dewsbury
Hull KR v Doncaster
Hunslet v Batley
Keighley v Featherstone
Oldham v Leigh
Rochdale v Barrow
Widnes v Swinton
Workington v Chorley
York v Sheffield
Bye: Whitehaven

SUNDAY 21st JANUARY
Batley v Hull KR
Chorley v Widnes
Doncaster v Keighley
Featherstone v Hunslet
Leigh v Workington
Sheffield v Dewsbury
Swinton v Oldham
Whitehaven v Rochdale
York v Gateshead
Bye: Barrow

SUNDAY 4th FEBRUARY
Barrow v Widnes
Doncaster v Dewsbury
Gateshead v Hunslet
Keighley v Batley
Leigh v Rochdale
Oldham v Whitehaven
Sheffield v Hull KR
Swinton v Workington
York v Featherstone
Bye: Chorley

SUNDAY 18th FEBRUARY
Batley v Barrow
Dewsbury v Chorley
Featherstone v Leigh
Hull KR v Whitehaven
Hunslet v Swinton
Oldham v Gateshead
Rochdale v Doncaster
Widnes v York
Workington v Sheffield
Bye: Keighley

SUNDAY 4th MARCH
Chorley v Hull KR
Doncaster v Workington
Gateshead v Widnes
Keighley v Rochdale
Oldham v Hunslet
Sheffield v Barrow
Swinton v Dewsbury
Whitehaven v Featherstone
York v Leigh
Bye: Batley

SUNDAY 11th MARCH
Barrow v Doncaster
Dewsbury v Oldham
Featherstone v Chorley
Gateshead v Whitehaven
Hull KR v Swinton
Hunslet v Rochdale
Leigh v Batley
Sheffield v Widnes
Workington v Keighley
Bye: York Wasps

SUNDAY 18th MARCH
Batley v Whitehaven
Chorley v York
Keighley v Barrow

Leigh v Gateshead
Oldham v Sheffield
Rochdale v Dewsbury
Swinton v Featherstone
Widnes v Doncaster
Workington v Hunslet
Bye: Hull KR

SUNDAY 25th MARCH

Barrow v Hunslet
Chorley v Batley
Doncaster v Leigh
Featherstone v Oldham
Gateshead v Workington
Hull KR v Rochdale
Swinton v York
Whitehaven v Sheffield
Widnes v Keighley
Bye: Dewsbury

SUNDAY 1st APRIL

Dewsbury v Barrow
Doncaster v Whitehaven
Gateshead v Rochdale
Keighley v Leigh
Sheffield v Chorley
Swinton v Batley
Widnes v Hunslet
Workington v Hull KR
York v Oldham
Bye: Featherstone

SUNDAY 8th APRIL

Chorley v Gateshead
Dewsbury v Widnes
Featherstone v Workington
Hull KR v Barrow
Hunslet v Leigh
Oldham v Batley
Rochdale v York
Swinton v Sheffield
Whitehaven v Keighley
Bye: Doncaster

FRIDAY 13th APRIL

Barrow v Chorley
Batley v Dewsbury
Featherstone v Hull KR
Hunslet v York
Keighley v Swinton
Leigh v Widnes
Oldham v Rochdale
Sheffield v Doncaster
Whitehaven v Workington
Bye: Gateshead

MONDAY 16th APRIL

Chorley v Whitehaven
Dewsbury v Gateshead
Doncaster v Featherstone
Hull KR v Keighley
Swinton v Leigh
Widnes v Oldham
Workington v Barrow
York v Batley

TUESDAY 17th APRIL

Rochdale v Sheffield
Bye: Hunslet

SUNDAY 22nd APRIL

Barrow v Gateshead
Batley v Oldham
Featherstone v Rochdale
Keighley v Chorley
Leigh v Dewsbury
Swinton v Doncaster
Whitehaven v Hunslet
Widnes v Hull KR
York v Workington
Bye: Sheffield

SUNDAY 29th APRIL

Batley v Widnes
Dewsbury v Workington
Gateshead v Featherstone
Hull KR v Chorley

Oldham v Keighley
Sheffield v Leigh
York v Whitehaven
Byes: Barrow, Doncaster, Hunslet,
Rochdale; Swinton

SUNDAY 6th MAY

Batley v Sheffield
Doncaster v York
Featherstone v Dewsbury
Keighley v Hunslet
Leigh v Hull KR
Oldham v Barrow
Rochdale v Workington
Swinton v Gateshead
Whitehaven v Widnes
Bye: Chorley

WEDNESDAY 9th MAY

Barrow v Featherstone
Batley v Swinton
Doncaster v Chorley
Keighley v Whitehaven
Leigh v Hunslet
Rochdale v Hull KR
Widnes v Gateshead
Byes: Dewsbury, Oldham, Sheffield,
Workington, York

SUNDAY 13th MAY

Barrow v Leigh
Chorley v Oldham
Dewsbury v Keighley
Doncaster v Swinton
Hunslet v Gateshead
Sheffield v Featherstone
Widnes v Rochdale
Workington v Batley
York v Hull KR
Bye: Whitehaven

SUNDAY 20th MAY

Barrow v Swinton
Chorley v Rochdale
Doncaster v Batley
Gateshead v York
Hull KR v Dewsbury
Leigh v Whitehaven

Oldham v Workington
Sheffield v Hunslet
Widnes v Featherstone
Bye: Keighley

SUNDAY 27th MAY

Gateshead v Batley
Hunslet v Hull KR
Keighley v Sheffield
Leigh v Chorley
Oldham v Doncaster
Rochdale v Swinton
Whitehaven v Barrow
Workington v Widnes
York v Dewsbury
Bye: Featherstone

SUNDAY 3rd JUNE

Batley v Rochdale
Chorley v Workington
Doncaster v Hull KR
Featherstone v Keighley
Gateshead v Oldham
Hunslet v Barrow
Sheffield v York
Swinton v Widnes
Whitehaven v Dewsbury
Bye: Leigh

SUNDAY 10th JUNE

Barrow v York
Dewsbury v Sheffield
Hull KR v Gateshead
Hunslet v Featherstone
Keighley v Doncaster
Oldham v Swinton
Rochdale v Whitehaven
Widnes v Chorley
Workington v Leigh
Bye: Batley

SUNDAY 17th JUNE

Batley v Keighley
Dewsbury v Doncaster
Featherstone v York
Gateshead v Barrow
Hull KR v Sheffield
Hunslet v Chorley
Rochdale v Leigh
Whitehaven v Oldham
Workington v Swinton
Bye: Widnes

SUNDAY 24th JUNE

Barrow v Batley
Chorley v Dewsbury
Doncaster v Rochdale
Keighley v Oldham
Leigh v Featherstone
Sheffield v Workington
Swinton v Hunslet
Whitehaven v Gateshead
York v Widnes
Bye: Hull KR

SUNDAY 1st JULY

Barrow v Sheffield
Chorley v Keighley
Dewsbury v Swinton
Featherstone v Whitehaven
Hull KR v Oldham
Hunslet v Widnes
Leigh v York
Rochdale v Batley
Workington v Doncaster
Bye: Gateshead

SUNDAY 8th JULY
PRELIMINARY SEMI FINALS
ELIMINATION SEMI FINALS

SUNDAY 15th JULY
MINOR SEMI FINALS

SUNDAY 22nd JULY
MAJOR SEMI FINALS

SATURDAY 28th JULY
GRAND FINAL

251

SUPER LEAGUE

(Play-offs in brackets, inc. in totals)

TRIES

1. Sean Long
   St Helens 22 (2)
   Tommy Martyn
   St Helens 22 (2)
3. Darren Rogers
   Castleford 20 (0)
   Steve Renouf
   Wigan 20 (2)
   Jason Robinson
   Wigan 20 (2)
6. Kevin Iro
   St Helens 19 (2)
   Brett Dallas
   Wigan 19 (3)
8. Chris Joynt
   St Helens 18 (3)
9. Robbie Paul
   Bradford 17 (1)
   Steve Collins
   Hull . . . . .17 (-)
   Keith Senior
   Leeds 17 (1)
   Kris Radlinski
   Wigan 17 (0)

GOALS

1. Andy Farrell
   Wigan 160 (10)
2. Sean Long
   St Helens 151 (15)
3. Henry Paul
   Bradford 150 (9)
4. Iestyn Harris
   Leeds 106 (5)
5. Steve Blakeley
   Salford . . . . .72 (-)
   (inc. 9 for Warrington)
6. Ben Sammut
   Hull . . . . .67 (-)
7. Lee Briers
   Warrington . . . . .65 (-)
8. Martin Pearson
   Halifax . . . . .63 (-)
9. Danny Orr
   Castleford 61 (1)
10. Gene Ngamu
    Hudds-Sheff . . . . .60 (-)

POINTS

1. Sean Long
   St Helens 390 (38)
2. Andy Farrell
   Wigan 357 (24)
3. Henry Paul
   Bradford 342 (23)
4. Iestyn Harris
   Leeds 256 (10)
5. Lee Briers
   Warrington . . . . .179 (-)
6. Martin Pearson
   Halifax . . . . .166 (-)
7. Danny Orr
   Castleford 163 (2)
8. Steve Blakeley
   Salford . . . . .152 (-)
   (inc. 22 for Warrington)
9. Ben Sammut
   Hull . . . . .150 (-)
10. Gene Ngamu
    Hudds-Sheff . . . . .148 (-)

PREMIERSHIP

(Play-offs in brackets, inc. in totals)

TRIES

1. Phil Cantillon
   Widnes 26 (0)
2. Jason Lee
   Keighley 24 (2)
3. Craig Weston
   Doncaster 23 (0)
   Jamie Stokes
   Featherstone 23 (3)
5. Carl Hall
   Doncaster 20 (2)
   Nathan Antonik
   Keighley 20 (1)
7. Craig Lingard
   Batley . . . . .19 (-)
   Nathan Graham
   Dewsbury 19 (2)
   Steve Booth
   Doncaster 19 (1)
   Lynton Stott
   Doncaster 19 (1)
   Whetu Taewa
   Hull KR 19 (1)
   Mick Higham
   Leigh 19 (2)
   Mark Sibson
   Oldham 19 (0)

GOALS

1. Barry Eaton
   Dewsbury 145 (15)
2. Martin Wood
   Keighley 142 (10)
3. Jamie Rooney
   Featherstone 120 (8)
4. Darren Holt
   Barrow . . . . .103 (-)
5. Mark Hewitt
   Hull KR 102 (0)
6. Pat Rich
   Oldham 97 (9)
7. Paul Wingfield
   Leigh 88 (0)
8. Paul Cook
   Workington . . . . .78 (-)
9. Ian Watson
   Swinton . . . . .77 (-)
10. Chris Ross
    Hunslet . . . . .71 (-)

POINTS

1. Martin Wood
   Keighley 353 (24)
2. Barry Eaton
   Dewsbury 348 (39)
3. Jamie Rooney
   Featherstone 299 (17)
4. Darren Holt
   Barrow . . . . .234 (-)
   Pat Rich
   Oldham 234 (18)
6. Mark Hewitt
   Hull KR 220 (4)
7. Craig Weston
   Doncaster 216 (6)
8. Paul Wingfield
   Leigh 208 (0)
9. Chris Ross
   Hunslet . . . . .191 (-)
10. Paul Cook
    Workington . . . . .176 (-)
    Ian Watson
    Swinton . . . . .176 (-)

CHALLENGE CUP

TRIES

1. Michael Withers
   Bradford 8
2. Wayne McDonald
   Hull 6
   Ryan Sheridan
   Leeds 6
4. Matt Daylight
   Hull 5
   Craig Simon
   Hull 5
   Danny Wood
   Rochdale 5
   Lee Briers
   Warrington 5

GOALS

1. Henry Paul
   Bradford 29
2. Lee Briers
   Warrington 28
   Iestyn Harris
   Leeds 28
4. Andy Farrell
   Wigan 22
5. Barry Eaton
   Dewsbury 19
6. Ian Herron
   Hull 17
7. Craig Booth
   York 13
8. Simon Verbickas
   Widnes 12
9. Jamie Benn
   Castleford 11
   Pat Rich
   Oldham 11
   Ben Sammut
   Hull 11
   Martin Wood
   Keighley 11

POINTS

1. Lee Briers
   Warrington 76
2. Iestyn Harris
   Leeds 68
3. Henry Paul
   Bradford 62
4. Andy Farrell
   Wigan 52
5. Barry Eaton
   Dewsbury 44
6. Craig Booth
   York 42
7. Ian Herron
   Hull 38
8. Jamie Rooney
   Featherstone 32
   Michael Withers
   Bradford 32
10. Martin Wood
    Keighley 30

Sean Long

Martin Wood

Michael Withers

ALL COMPETITIONS

TRIES

1	Phil Cantillon	
	Widnes	.30
2	Jason Lee	
	Keighley	.28
3	Craig Weston	
	Doncaster	.26
4	Sean Long	
	St Helens	.24
5	Jamie Stokes	
	Featherstone	.23
	Nathan Antonik	
	Keighley	.23
	Mark Sibson	
	Oldham	.23
	Steve Renouf	
	Wigan	.23
	Jason Robinson	
	Wigan	.23
10	Mick Higham	
	Leigh	.22
	Kevin Iro	
	St Helens	.22
	Tommy Martyn	
	St Helens	.22

GOALS

1	Andy Farrell	
	Wigan	.182
2	Henry Paul	
	Bradford	.179
3	Barry Eaton	
	Dewsbury	.165
4	Sean Long	
	St Helens	.161
5	Martin Wood	
	Keighley	.153
6	Iestyn Harris	
	Leeds	.134
7	Jamie Rooney	
	Featherstone	.130
8	Darren Holt	
	Barrow	.111
9	Mark Hewitt	
	Hull KR	.108
	Pat Rich	
	Oldham	.108

POINTS

1	Sean Long	
	St Helens	.418
2	Andy Farrell	
	Wigan	.409
3	Henry Paul	
	Bradford	.404
4	Barry Eaton	
	Dewsbury	.394
5	Martin Wood	
	Keighley	.383
6	Jamie Rooney	
	Featherstone	.331
7	Iestyn Harris	
	Leeds	.324
8	Darren Holt	
	Barrow	.258
9	Pat Rich	
	Oldham	.256
10	Lee Briers	
	Warrington	.255

TABLES & ATTENDANCES

SUPER LEAGUE

	P	W	D	L	F	A	D	PTS
Wigan	28	24	1	3	960	405	555	49
St Helens	28	23	0	5	988	627	361	46
Bradford	28	20	3	5	1004	408	596	43
Leeds	28	17	0	11	692	626	66	34
Castleford	28	17	0	11	585	571	14	34
Warrington	28	13	0	15	735	817	-82	26
Hull	28	12	1	15	630	681	-51	25
Halifax	28	11	1	16	664	703	-39	23
Salford	28	10	0	18	542	910	-368	20
Wakefield	28	8	0	20	557	771	-214	16
London	28	6	0	22	456	770	-314	12
H'dds-Sheff	28	4	0	24	502	1026	-524	8

	2000 Avg	1999 Avg	Diff
Bradford	15,350	13,398	+1,952
Leeds	12,740	13,703	-963
Wigan	11,329	9,466	+1,863
St Helens	8,830	8,460	+370
Castleford	7,975	6,877	+1,098
Warrington	6,872	5,110	+1,762
Hull	5,943	4,346(H)	
		3,895(G)	+1,597(H)
			+2,048(G)
Halifax	5,714	4,483	+1,231
Wakefield	4,615	4,235	+380
Salford	4,448	4,505	-57
Hudds-Sheff	3,422		
		3,727(H)	
		3,590(S)	
			-305(H)
			-168(S)
London	3,419	2,935	+484

'00 Avg 7,555 / **'99 Avg** 6,409 / **Diff** +1,146

BEST CROWDS

58,132	St Helens v Wigan *(GF)*	. . . . .14/10/00
21,237	Bradford v Leeds *(R21)*	. . . . .30/7/00
19,623	Bradford v Leeds *(R27)*	. . . . .8/9/00
19,186	Wigan v St Helens *(QSF)*	. . . . .29/9/00
18,815	Bradford v Wigan *(R17)*	. . . . .30/6/00
18,769	Leeds v Bradford *(R11)*	. . . . .19/5/00
17,737	Wigan v Bradford *(R25)*	. . . . .27/8/00
17,428	Wigan v St Helens *(R18)*	. . . . .9/7/00
17,365	Wigan v Bradford *(R13)*	. . . . .7/6/00
17,127	Bradford v Warrington *(R2)*	. . . . .19/3/00

WORST CROWDS

2,040	London v Salford *(R23)*	. . . . .13/8/00
2,054	London v Warrington *(R25)*	. . . . .25/8/00
2,102	Hudds-Sheff v Castleford *(R22)*	. . . . . .6/8/00
2,370	Wakefield v London *(R24)*	. . . . .20/8/00
2,409	Hudds-Sheff v Wakefield *(R26)*	. . . . . .3/9/00
2,458	Hudds-Sheff v London *(R12)*	. . . . . .26/5/00
2,543	London v Halifax *(R21)*	. . . . .30/7/00
2,549	London v Salford *(R4)*	. . . . .9/4/00
2,588	London v Hull *(R7)*	. . . . .24/4/00
2,619	London v Wakefield *(R19)*	. . . . .16/7/00

CHALLENGE CUP

BEST CROWDS

67,247	Bradford v Leeds *(F)*	. . . . .29/4/00
18,068	Hull v Leeds *(SF)*	. . . . .26/3/00
12,532	Leeds v St Helens *(R5)*	. . . . .26/2/00
11,894	Bradford v Warrington *(SF)*	. . . . .25/3/00
10,533	Leeds v Dewsbury *(QF)*	. . . . .10/3/00
9,827	Halifax v Bradford *(QF)*	. . . . .12/3/00
8,005	Wakefield v Bradford *(R5)*	. . . . .27/2/00
7,378	Hull v Wigan *(QF)*	. . . . .11/3/00
6,700	Salford v Warrington *(QF)*	. . . . .12/3/00
6,532	Wigan v Whitehaven *(R4)*	. . . . .13/2/00

WORST CROWDS

503	Whitehaven v Shaw Cross *(R3)*	. .30/1/00
530	Lancashire v Walney *(R3)*	. . . . .30/1/00
577	York v Dudley Hill *(R3)*	. . . . .30/1/00
588	Swinton v Waterhead *(R3)*	. . . . .1/2/00
599	Workington v Skirlaugh *(R3)*	. . . . . .30/1/00
601	Batley v Oldham St Annes *(R3)*	. .30/1/00
700	Rochdale v The Army *(R3)*	. . . . .30/1/00
719	Barrow v Featherstone L *(R3)*	. . . . . .30/1/00
803	York v Thornhill *(R4)*	. . . . .13/2/00
940	Featherstone v Wigan St Pats *(R3)*	. .30/1/00

PREMIERSHIP

	P	W	D	L	F	A	D	PTS
Dewsbury	28	22	1	5	848	400	448	45
Keighley	28	22	0	6	1002	401	601	44
Doncaster	28	21	0	7	880	397	483	42
Leigh	28	21	0	7	854	476	378	42
F'therstone	28	20	1	7	795	523	272	41
Oldham	28	19	1	8	734	513	221	39
Hull KR	28	17	1	10	583	481	102	35
Widnes	28	17	0	11	698	483	215	34
Swinton	28	13	2	13	726	733	-7	28
Barrow	28	14	0	14	647	711	-64	28
Whitehaven	28	11	1	16	533	674	-141	23
Workington	28	11	1	16	502	776	-274	23
Rochdale	28	10	0	18	563	696	-133	20
Sheffield	28	9	1	18	479	585	-106	19
Hunslet	28	8	0	20	487	678	-191	16
Batley	28	6	0	22	482	759	-277	12
York	28	5	1	22	392	859	-467	11
Lancashire	28	1	0	27	301	1361	-1060	2

	2000 Avg	1999 Avg	Diff
Widnes	3,372	3,168	+204
Leigh	2,640	1,875	+765
Hull KR	2,221	2,150	+71
Oldham	2,197	1,183	+1,014
Keighley	2,052	1,868	+184
Featherstone	1,926	1,778	+148
Dewsbury	1,866	1,256	+610
Doncaster	1,676	680	+996
Barrow	1,371	1,131	+240
Sheffield	1,176	N/A	N/A
Rochdale	1,175	958	+217
Swinton	1,104	1,046	+58
Hunslet	968	1,554	-586
Workington	859	1,051	-192
Whitehaven	854	855	-1
Batley	800	786	+14
York	773	960	-187
Lancashire	424	393	+31

'00 Avg 1,525 / **'99 Avg** 1,291 / **Diff** +234

BEST CROWDS

8,487	Dewsbury v Leigh *(GF)*	. . . . .29/7/00
5,836	Leigh v Oldham *(MaSF)*	. . . . .23/7/00
4,468	Leigh v Widnes *(R1)*	. . . . .26/12/99
4,237	Widnes v Leigh *(R15)*	. . . . .21/4/00
3,837	Widnes v Lancashire *(R2)*	. . . . .2/1/00
3,758	Widnes v Hunslet *(R3)*	. . . . .9/1/00
3,695	Widnes v Swinton *(R5)*	. . . . .23/1/00
3,562	Oldham v Rochdale *(R1)*	. . . . .27/12/99
3,455	Widnes v Hull KR *(R27)*	. . . . .25/6/00
3,402	Hull KR v Featherstone *(R1)*	. . . . . . .27/12/99

WORST CROWDS

212	Lancashire v Swinton *(R21)*	. . . . .21/5/00
214	Lancashire v York *(R11)*	. . . . .26/3/00
222	Lancashire v Hunslet *(R27)*	. . . . .25/6/00
223	Lancashire v Whitehaven *(R5)*	. . . . .23/1/00
223	Lancashire v Barrow *(R23)*	. . . . .29/5/00
254	Lancashire v Workington *(R7)*	. . . . .20/2/00
324	Batley v Lancashire *(R12)*	. . . . .2/4/00
331	York v Rochdale *(R22)*	. . . . .26/5/00
332	Lancashire v Featherstone *(R8)*	. .27/2/00
351	York v Lancashire *(R28)*	. . . . .30/6/00

Phil Cantillon

Andy Farrell